Money Supply, Money Demand, and Macroeconomic Models

John T. Boorman, *University of Maryland*
Thomas M. Havrilesky, *Duke University*

Allyn and Bacon, Inc., Boston

Library of Congress Catalog Card
Number: 79-167998

Second printing . . . August, 1973

CONTENTS

PART 2/ MONEY DEMAND

PART 3/ EFFECTS OF MONEY SUPPLY AND MONEY DEMAND ON MACROECONOMIC MODELS

Preface

In the last decade, one of the most fertile areas of economic controversy has been monetary theory. Relegated to a relatively obscure niche in the mosaic of Keynesian developments of the 40's and early 50's, monetary theory surged into prominence in the 60's. With a vanguard of established economists such as Milton Friedman, James Tobin, Don Patinkin, Karl Brunner, and Allan Meltzer leading a body of enthusiastic younger scholars, and spurred by the failures of stabilization policy, the controversies of monetary theory promise to come into new prominence during the 1970's.

Skirmishes in the continuing struggle between Keynesians and Monetarists are increasingly in the public eye. The issues are numerous and complex: Can the money supply be readily controlled by the Federal Reserve System? Is either the money stock or some other monetary aggregate superior to "the" interest rate as a target for monetary policy? Is fiscal stabilization policy effective? These are only a sampling of the questions facing the policy-maker and his constituency. At the core of much of the controversy there lies a fundamental disagreement among economists about the nature of the supply of and demand for money and their role in macroeconomic theories.

How can the undergraduate economics student taking a course in Money and Banking or Macroeconomic Theory or a beginning graduate student be given a grounding in money supply theory, money demand theory, and their impact on macroeconomic theory sufficient to understand this profound disagreement? Aside from his own teaching skills, the economist-educator has only three tools in his arsenal: the book on money and banking, the book on macroeconomic theory, and the book of readings on monetary economics. When it comes to this task, all of these tools have evident shortcomings.

While steadily improving in theoretical content, books on money and banking traditionally have emphasized historical and institutional material. Macroeconomic theory books usually lack comprehensive study of such vital areas as money supply theory and empirical money demand. One volume books of readings on "monetary economics" often parallel the interesting but broad, descriptive precedent set by the money and banking books. In addition, their treatment of monetary theory, while it occasionally may surpass that of standard money and banking books in interpretive excellence, lacks the unity and comprehensibility of such books.

This book is intended to carry the student of monetary theory from just beyond the principles level to the level of competence expected of well-trained undergraduate economics majors. At Duke University, Rice University, and the University of Maryland, it has been used in manuscript form for specialized study by advanced undergraduates, for review by graduate students, and as a supplement to money and banking and macroeconomic theory books. The chapters are grouped into three subject areas: Part 1 - *Money Supply*, Part 2 - *Money Demand* and Part 3 - *The Effects of Money Supply and Demand on Macroeconomic Models*. Each of the parts of the book is followed by a series of from 4 to 7 readings by outstanding monetary economists. The readings are selected not only because they amplify and extend the basic analysis of the preceding chapters, but also because they carry the student to the threshold of recent theoretical developments. In addition, a few readings provide the seminal insight into contemporary theoretical issues that only a masterwork can offer. Also, one of the authors has prepared his own survey of empirical studies of the demand for money as a reading following Part 2.

In order to benefit from this book, the reader needs only some training in algebra and a one semester course in macroeconomic principles; differential calculus would be helpful, but is by no means necessary. Since the book's main audience consists of students, sets of class-tested questions are appended to each chapter in order to allow the student to check his understanding of the material. For further reading and for research purposes, a selected bibliography follows each chapter.

The book is not specifically addressed to monetary policy issues which lie outside the realm of monetary theory. However, most of these topics, such as Federal Reserve independence and bank merger problems, usually receive adequate treatment in standard books on money and banking, or books of readings on monetary economics.

This book is not intended as a comprehensive study of all monetary theory; rather it is concerned with money supply, money demand, and their respective effects on macroeconomic models. Such important matters as the theory of the term structure of interest rates, the theory of monetary policy (instruments, objectives, lags, etc.), and monetary growth theories fall outside its domain.

We are grateful for the suggestions of Professor Lloyd Atkinson, Professor William Yohe, Professor Edward Kane, and our editor, Sigurd Hermansen, as well as for the reactions of our undergraduate and graduate students at Duke University, Rice University, and the University of Maryland. We should like to thank the authors of the articles used in this book, as well as their publishers, for permission to use copyrighted material.

We are grateful to Paul Holden for his proofreading of the manuscript and we are especially indebted to Susan Havrilesky for her patience and her helpful comments in proofreading, typing, and retyping the manuscript.

John T. Boorman
Thomas M. Havrilesky

Introduction

A major concern of modern man is his "standard of living." There may be several ways of measuring the prosperity man enjoys, but the most popular is the level of per capita income in an economy. The level and growth of an economy's per capita income are closely related to the degree to which that economy utilizes its productive resources and thereby eliminates underemployment. However, the real value of a dollar of income also depends on the general level of prices for goods and services which that income can buy. If the general price level rises more quickly than nominal income, the real value of income declines. Consequently, modern man is concerned with the general level of prices, as well as the level of his nominal income.

Modern economists are often called upon by business and government to evaluate alternative means of maintaining and increasing man's prosperity. To do this, they develop models which explain and predict the level of income, employment, and prices in the economy as a whole. These models focus on the aggregate behavior of economic entities: households, government, and business firms.

Practically all theories about the level of aggregate income, employment, and prices assign an important theoretical role to the supply of and the demand for money. This book proposes to examine theoretical issues about the supply of and the demand for money because they are so intimately related to overall prosperity and well-being in society.

The term "money" appears regularly when economists theorize about how aggregate household, business, and government behavior affects the level of aggregate income, employment, and prices. Why do economists believe that the supply of and demand for money have a more prominent effect on the level of economic activity than the supply of and demand for, say, used cars?

The answer is that economists believe that money, among all goods, performs unique functions, and because of these functions it affects and is affected by the level of income and prices. First, money functions as a *universally acceptable medium of exchange.* As there is usually a lag between the receipt and disbursement of income, money might be held to facilitate transactions. Economists long have maintained that since money is held between its receipt as income and its disbursement in exchange for goods and services, it can affect the volume of goods and services produced, or their price level, or both. For instance, a primitive theory in economics states that, as the quantity of money supplied increases, proportionately more money is exchanged for goods and services and the prices of these goods and services invariably are bid upward. One inference of this theory is that price inflation can be prevented simply if the money supply is allowed to grow at a slower rate relative to the growth of output of goods and services.

Another function of money is that it may serve as a good *store of value.* Some economists have emphasized the advantages of holding money because it can be easily converted to other asset forms with little cost or inconvenience, i.e., you do not have to "cash it in" in order to acquire another asset. Other economists have emphasized the advantages of holding money because its nominal market value is usually more predictable than that of other assets, and by holding it, individuals avoid the risk of a decline in the market value of their wealth.

Both of these approaches view holding money as an alternative to holding other assets. Therefore, the demand for money as a store of value depends on the benefits from holding other assets (for example, their yields). Since a change in the quantity of money can induce individuals to change their demand for these alternative assets, it thereby affects the prices and yields of other assets. Elementary economic theory teaches that a change in the yields of financial assets (the level of interest rates) affects the level of investment spending, and henceforth the level of income, employment, and prices in the economy.

Other less-important functions or characteristics of money have been adduced, but these two reflect its most relevant aspects in modern macroeconomic theory.

Economists differ in the emphasis they place upon the medium-of-exchange and store-of-value characteristics of money. Some eschew these *a priori* distinctions altogether, believing them to be misleading. As we shall see in chapters 3, 4 and 5, relating to the demand for money, these differences in emphasis lead to dissimilar theoretical explanations of the public's desire to hold money, which, in turn, as we discover in chapters 6, 7, and 8, lead to distinct theories about the manner in which money affects the level of income, employment, and prices.

The aggregate money supply is believed to be important in a modern economy because of its influence on the level of economic activity. Chapter 1 examines the theory of the supply of money. It develops a series of simplified models of the real-world behavior of banks and individuals as they affect the quantity of money supplied. The chapter carries the reader to the threshold of modern money-supply theory.

Practically all the money that people receive and spend reaches them through banks—either because it is borrowed from a bank or delivered from a checking account at a bank. Because bank activities are of paramount influence in the determination of the money supply, chapter 2 deals with the portfolio behavior of modern commercial banks.

In elementary microeconomic theory it is learned that supply and demand determine equilibrium prices and quantities in the market. So it is with money: an hypothesis about the determination of the money supply (discussed in Part 1, chapters 1 and 2) must be combined with an hypothesis about the determination of the demand for money in order to understand how certain market variables (for example, the interest rate and the level of income) are affected. Different hypotheses about the demand for money are presented in Part 2 (chapters 3, 4 and 5).

When a specific hypothesis about the determination of the demand for money is combined in a more extensive macroeconomic model with specific hypotheses about the determination of: (1) the supply of money, (2) the level of aggregate expenditures, (3) the supply of and demand for labor, and (4) an assumption about the technical conditions of production, differing policy prescriptions emerge. In Part 3 (chapters 6 through 9), a series of macroeconomic models is developed, showing how different policy implications follow from different demand-for-money hypotheses.

We began this introduction by saying that money is believed to be an important device because it has characteristics that relate it more closely than other specific goods to theories about the determination of the level of aggregate income, employment and prices. Therefore, the nine chapters of this book are addressed primarily to basic theories of the supply of and demand for money and their impact on aggregate economic models.

Yet because theories conflict and have quite different implications for dealing with the problems of inadequate aggregate income, low employment and rapid price inflation, they are continually being challenged, tested, and refined. To capture the quality and direction of the keen intellectual competition among outstanding monetary economists, readings drawn from the professional literature follow Parts 1, 2, and 3. Thus, this book integrates basic monetary theory and closely related readings in one volume.

On the one hand, the theoretical chapters provide the essential knowledge that students of monetary matters must have in order to appreciate fully the contemporary views of those economists presented in the readings. On the other hand, the readings really are the foundation of the book, since the controversies they reflect have influenced the authors to develop in their own chapters those aspects of basic theoretical developments that provide maximum insight into recent theoretical conflict and progress.

MONEY SUPPLY

PART **1**

1

A Framework for the Determination of the Money Supply

INTRODUCTION

It has frequently been assumed in both theoretical and empirical analyses that the money stock (demand deposits plus currency in circulation) is determined unequivocally by the monetary authority. This tradition is currently under attack and is being superseded by an alternative approach that views the money supply as an endogenously determined variable. It is now customary to present the determination of the money stock as a process which results from the complex interaction of the behavior of various economic agents rather than as a process dominated by an external authority.

To understand the work being done in this field, it is necessary to examine both the behavior of the various groups that influence the money supply and the institutional framework within which this behavior occurs. In this chapter, we shall proceed to describe this framework and the role of these behavioral patterns. The analysis begins with the derivation of the Bank Reserve Equation from the Federal Reserve Balance Sheet and the monetary accounts of the Treasury.

THE MONETARY ACCOUNTS

The monetary system of the United States is made up of the nation's 13,500 commercial banks, the twelve Federal Reserve district banks, the Board of Governors of the Federal Reserve System, and the U.S. Treasury. The primary business of commercial banks in this system is to issue deposit liabilities (demand deposits and time and savings deposits) to the public and to acquire income-earning financial assets with the funds created through these deposits. The one characteristic that best distinguishes commercial banks from the other (non-monetary) institutions in our financial system is their ability to issue deposit liabilities which are due on demand; that is, deposit liabilities which may be converted into currency or legal tender money immediately upon request of the depositor or transferred to another person simply by writing a check.* No other institution in our system may issue liabilities with this characteristic. Essentially it is the acceptance by the public of these liabilities as "money" which explains the preeminent role of commercial banks in our economy. In 1971, for example, the average total money supply in the U.S. was approximately 220 billion dollars. Of this amount, 170 billion dollars, or slightly over 75 percent of the total, consisted of demand deposit liabilities of the nation's commercial banks.

As money creating institutions, commercial banks are subject to special regulation and supervision. For example, they are required to hold some of their assets in a legally approved form specified by the Federal Reserve System or by state banking authorities. Specifically, for every dollar of deposit liabilities outstanding, commercial banks must hold some fraction (also set by the monetary authorities) in one of the approved asset forms. For example, commercial banks that are members of the Federal Reserve System are currently permitted to hold their legally required reserves either in the form of deposit balances at a district Federal Reserve bank or as cash in their own vaults. Consequently, the most important restrictions on the volume of member bank deposit liabilities outstanding at any time are the fractional reserve requirements set by the monetary authorities and the stock of legal reserves that are available for these banks to hold.

In this section we shall examine the accounts of the Federal Reserve

---

*Money which has been declared "legal tender" by the government must be accepted as payment for all debts, public and private. In the U.S., Treasury issues and Federal Reserve Notes, which form the bulk of our "paper money," have been declared "legal tender."

banks and the U.S. Treasury to determine how the stock of these reserve funds is created. We begin with a consolidated balance sheet of the twelve Federal Reserve banks.

Consolidated Balance Sheet of the 12 Federal Reserve Banks

Assets	Liabilities and Net Worth
Gold Certificates	Federal Reserve Notes Outstanding
Cash	Member Bank Reserve Deposits
Federal Reserve Credit	Deposits due to:
U.S. Government Securities	The U.S. Treasury
Acceptances	Foreign Depositors
Discounts and Advances	Other
Float	Other (capital and minor items)
Other	

The twelve Federal Reserve District banks, like commercial banks, issue deposit liabilities (claims against themselves held primarily by member commercial banks, the U.S. Treasury, and foreign central banks and institutions) and purchase income-earning assets (primarily U.S. government securities and loans to commercial banks). In addition, they issue Federal Reserve notes (claims against the district banks which serve as the primary form of paper money used in the U.S.) and they hold an asset not at present available to any one else in the country, gold certificates—claims against the gold stock owned by the U.S. Treasury.

A glance at the consolidated balance sheet above shows that if our entire currency stock consisted of Federal Reserve notes, the total amount of funds available to be held as reserves by commercial banks would depend upon the willingness of the Federal Reserve to issue certain liabilities (Federal Reserve notes outstanding and reserve deposits of member banks), and on the distribution of the Federal Reserve notes between the banks and the public. However, the United States Treasury also has the power to issue currency, and these coins and notes perform the same functions as Federal Reserve notes. Therefore, if the Treasury increased the volume of its outstanding currency (by making expenditures with newly printed bills, for example), there would be more funds available to be held by the public or by the commercial banks as vault cash. Since vault cash can be counted as reserves by member banks, the issuance of Treasury currency could increase total bank reserves.

We may account for the influence of Treasury currency on bank reserves by means of the *Bank Reserve Equation*. Basically, the *Bank Reserve Equation* is an accounting statement that lists sources and uses of funds that are potentially available to be used as bank reserves. This statement is derived by modifying the consolidated balance sheet of the Federal Reserve banks to take account of Treasury influences on the monetary system. We present the *Bank Reserve Equation* below:

The Bank Reserve Equation

Sources	Uses

Federal Reserve Credit
  U.S. Government Securities
  Acceptances
  Discounts and Advances
  Float
(b) Gold Stock
(a) Treasury Currency Out-
    standing
	(a) Currency in Circulation Outside
	    the Federal Reserve, the Trea-
	    sury and Commercial Banks
	    (i.e., Currency in Circulation
	    with the Nonbank Public)
	(a)(b) Treasury Cash Holdings
	    Deposit Liabilities of the
	    Federal Reserve due to:
	      The Treasury
	      Foreign Depositors
	      Others
	    Other Accounts (net)
	    Bank Reserves:
	      Member Bank Reserve De-
	      posits plus Vault Cash

A reconciliation between this statement and the consolidated Federal Reserve bank balance sheet is fairly easy to establish. All the accounts listed under Federal Reserve Credit and Deposit Liabilities of the Federal Reserve appear in the *Bank Reserve Equation* exactly as in the Federal Reserve balance sheet. The modifications made in the other accounts are as follows:

(a) Treasury Currency Outstanding. This account includes all current *monetary* liabilities of the U.S. Treasury. It appears as a source of bank reserve funds since any currency issued by the Treasury could find its way into the commercial banking system and, as vault cash in that system, could serve as bank reserves. For example, if an employee of the Federal government were to be paid in newly printed paper money issued by the Treasury, he would be perfectly free to take this currency to a commercial bank and deposit it in either his demand or time deposit account. In either case it would increase both bank deposit liabilities and bank reserves (in the form of vault cash). When the Treasury paid out the newly issued currency, according to the *Bank Reserve Equation*, a source of funds, namely Treasury Currency Outstanding, and a use of funds, namely Currency in Circulation with the Nonbank Public, would both increase. When this currency was deposited with a commercial bank, an alternative use of funds, Currency in Circulation with the Nonbank Public, would decrease, and bank reserves (vault cash) would increase. Hence, the net effect of these transactions would be to increase commercial bank reserves.

There are two other differences between the Federal Reserve Balance Sheet and the *Bank Reserve Equation* that involve Treasury currency. One difference is that *Cash* in the Federal Reserve balance sheet refers simply to Treasury currency in the vaults of the Federal Reserve banks. In the *Bank Reserve Equation*, this item is included under Treasury Currency Outstanding. Thus, Treasury Currency Outstanding in the *Bank Reserve Equation* refers to the total stock of outstanding currency issued by the Treasury, whether held by the nonbank public, commercial banks, or the Federal Reserve. A second difference is that Federal Reserve Notes Outstanding appear as a single, explicit item in the Federal Reserve Balance Sheet, but in the *Bank Reserve Equation* these central bank liabilities are divided among several different accounts. Federal Reserve notes held by the nonbank public are combined with Treasury currency held by the nonbank public under Total Currency in Circulation. Federal Reserve notes held by the Treasury are included under Treasury Cash Holdings. And Federal Reserve notes held by commercial banks appear together with bank holdings of outstanding Treasury currency as Vault Cash under Member Bank Reserves. As a result, the difference between Federal Reserve Notes Outstanding in the Federal Reserve Balance Sheet, and Federal Reserve Notes in Circulation with the Nonbank Public, listed under Currency in Circulation in the *Bank Reserve Equation* is that the latter account excludes notes held by the Treasury and notes held by commercial banks. These modifications provide some insight into currency flows between the public, the banks, and the Treasury, and their effects on commercial bank reserves.

(b) Gold Stock. A further modification made in deriving the *Bank Reserve Equation* involves the treatment of the gold stock. Gold certificates, claims against the gold stock that is held by the Treasury, are issued by the Treasury and held by the Federal Reserve banks. The difference between the volume of gold certificates outstanding (all of which are held by Federal Reserve banks) and the total gold stock is obviously that value of gold against which no certificates have been issued. This is gold held by the Treasury for backing of certain outstanding Treasury currencies and other minor uses. It generally represents a small portion of the total gold stock and is included within the category of Treasury Cash Holdings. Hence, the *Bank Reserve Equation* includes the entire gold stock as a source of bank reserves, and counts under the category of Treasury Cash Holdings (as an alternative use of those funds) that value of the gold stock which does not have gold certificate claims outstanding against it.

Hence, the differences between the Federal Reserve Balance Sheet and the *Bank Reserve Equation* involve only the issuance and holding of currency within the monetary system (specifically, the role of the U.S. Treasury in this process) and the treatment of the gold stock.

The *Bank Reserve Equation* is written to focus attention on total commercial bank reserves (either reserve deposits held at Federal Reserve banks or commercial bank vault cash). A more useful concept that will find frequent application in the following discussion involves the combined measure of total bank reserves and currency in circulation. This quantity, referred to as the *monetary base*, can be easily derived from the bank reserve equation.* This derivation is shown below:

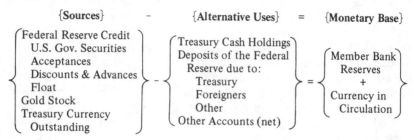

{Sources} − {Alternative Uses} = {Monetary Base}

$$\left\{\begin{array}{l}\text{Federal Reserve Credit}\\ \text{U.S. Gov. Securities}\\ \text{Acceptances}\\ \text{Discounts \& Advances}\\ \text{Float}\\ \text{Gold Stock}\\ \text{Treasury Currency}\\ \text{Outstanding}\end{array}\right\} - \left\{\begin{array}{l}\text{Treasury Cash Holdings}\\ \text{Deposits of the Federal}\\ \text{Reserve due to:}\\ \quad\text{Treasury}\\ \quad\text{Foreigners}\\ \quad\text{Other}\\ \text{Other Accounts (net)}\end{array}\right\} = \left\{\begin{array}{l}\text{Member Bank}\\ \text{Reserves}\\ +\\ \text{Currency in}\\ \text{Circulation}\end{array}\right\}$$

A comparison of the figures in this monetary base equation at two different points in time will illustrate the process by which bank reserves and currency are supplied to the economy. In Table 1 we present figures for December 1962 and December 1968.

During this six year period currency holdings of the nonbank public *increased* by over thirteen and one-half billion dollars, while total bank reserves *increased* by over seven billion dollars. At the same time, the monetary gold stock, a source of funds in the monetary base equation, *decreased* by five and one-half billion dollars as a result of continuing deficits in the U.S. balance of payments. To account for these changes, other sources of funds must have increased, or alternative uses decreased by a net amount of over twenty-six billion dollars.

Examination of Table 1 indicates that the bulk of these funds were supplied through the purchase of government securities by the Federal Reserve. The monetary authorities increased their portfolio of these securities by almost twenty-two billion dollars. Thus, open market purchase of securities was the primary means used by the Federal Reserve both to offset the nation's gold outflow and to bring about the large net increase that occurred in the monetary base from December 1962 to December 1968. Other accounts in the table indicate that another two billion dollars were supplied through increases in Treasury currency issues and Federal Reserve Float. Another 2,153 million dollars became available through the *decrease* in Other Federal Reserve Accounts listed as an

*For an interesting perspective on this equation, *see* Leonall C. Andersen, "Three Approaches to Money Stock Determination," The Federal Reserve Bank of St. Louis *Review* (October, 1967).

TABLE 1

Factors Supplying and Absorbing Reserve Funds
(in millions of dollars)

	Dec. 1962	Dec. 1968	Change
Sources:			
Federal Reserve Credit			
U.S. Government Securities	30,546	52,529	+21,983
Discounts and Advances	305	765	+ 460
Acceptances (and industrial loans)	69	65	– 4
Float	2,298	3,251	+ 953
Gold Stock	15,978	10,367	– 5,611
Treasury Currency Outstanding	5,561	6,810	+ 1,249
Alternative Uses:			
Treasury Cash Holdings	398	756	+ 358
Deposits of the Federal Reserve due to:			
U.S. Treasury	587	360	– 227
Foreigners	222	225	+ 3
Other	290	458	+ 168
Other Federal Reserve Accounts	1,048	–1,105	– 2,153
Monetary Base:			
Member Bank Reserves			
Deposits with Fed. Res. Banks	16,932	22,484	+ 5,552
Currency and Coin	3,107	4,737	+ 1,630
Currency in Circulation	32,173	45,872	13,699
Total Monetary Base:	52,212	73,093	+20,881

Source: *Federal Reserve Bulletin* (May 1969).

alternative use of reserve funds in the monetary base equation. All the other accounts show relatively small changes.

A sense of the pivotal role of the Federal Reserve in our monetary system can be gained from this table. Although the Federal Reserve cannot control all accounts in the monetary base equation, its absolute control over one account, the volume of U.S. Government Securities that it chooses to hold in its portfolio, gives the Federal Reserve an adequate means to offset or to supplement changes which occur in any of the other accounts in the statement. Therefore, control over its own holdings of Government Securities provides the Federal Reserve with the necessary power to determine the size of the monetary base. During the period represented by the data above, for example, the Federal Reserve used open market operations not only to offset a decrease in reserves caused by a five billion dollar gold outflow, but also to bring about a substantial net increase in total bank reserves.

In the next section, we will analyze the link between the monetary base and the nation's money supply, defined as currency plus demand deposits at commercial banks. We then will examine the means by which control over the monetary base allows the Federal Reserve to determine the size of the money stock. In Part 3 of this book we will see how various assumptions about the determination of the money stock may be incorporated into aggregate models of the determination of income, employment, and price level.

THE MECHANISM OF MONEY SUPPLY EXPANSION

INTRODUCTION

The derivation of the monetary base equation represents the first step in the analysis of the monetary system of the United States. The money stock is customarily defined as currency in circulation (i.e., currency outside banks, the Federal Reserve, and the Treasury), and "demand deposits adjusted." Certain minor difficulties are introduced into the analysis by the fact that demand deposits adjusted and total demand deposits at commercial banks are not the same. The differences are caused by the special treatment of the demand deposits of the United States government (the Tax and Loan accounts), interbank deposits, and other minor items such as deposits "in the process of clearing." These differences are relatively minor, will not affect our results in any substantive manner and therefore will be ignored in the remainder of this chapter.

A more important consideration which makes this presentation somewhat unrealistic is the fact that not all commercial banks belong to the Federal Reserve System and that, of those banks that do belong to the System, not all are bound by the same legal reserve requirements. Currently the Federal Reserve System sets different legal reserve requirements for different classes of member banks.*

---

*The Federal Reserve distinguishes two classes of commercial banks, "reserve city banks" and "country banks." The reserve requirement limits established by Congress and the actual requirements set within those limits by the Board of Governors of the Federal Reserve as of January 1970 are shown below:

| | Net Demand Deposits | | | | Time & Savings Deposits | |
| | Reserve City | | Country | | All Banks | |
	Under $5 Million	Over $5 Million	Under $5 Million	Over $5 Million	Under $5 Million	Over $5 Million
Maximum	22%	22%	14%	14%	10%	10%
Minimum	10%	10%	7%	7%	3%	3%
Actual	17%	17½%	12½%	13%	3%	6%

In the presentation which follows we shall abstract from these complications. It will be assumed that the reserve-requirement ratios on demand and time deposits employed refer to weighted average requirements which take account of these special institutional arrangements. These assumptions in no way affect the substance of our results.

This part of the chapter will indicate the way in which the total money supply depends on the size of the monetary base and the allocation of that base between member bank reserves and nonbank currency holdings. The discussion proceeds on the basis of extremely restrictive simplifying assumptions concerning commercial bank operations and the public's asset preferences. These assumptions will be successively relaxed in order to produce more realistic models.

MODEL 1. *A Monetary System with Only Demand Deposits.*

Throughout this chapter, we shall employ static equilibrium models in our analysis and description of the mechanism of money supply expansion (and contraction). More specifically, our models will consist of systems of equations embodying the interdependencies that we assume to exist among the included variables. In the initial formulations of these models, all the equations will be linear in form and will embody either a simplified description of the behavior of some agent important in the determination of the money stock, or an institutional, legal, or definitional relation required to characterize our monetary system. The solution of these systems of equations will yield equilibrium values for the dependent variables. These are values which could be maintained indefinitely in the absence of changes in the behavioral, institutional, or legal characteristics (parameters) of the model. Through the use of these models, we shall be able to answer such questions as: by what amount will the money supply change if legal reserve requirements are raised by one percent? Or, by what amount will the volume of demand deposit liabilities change if the monetary authorities allow the monetary base to increase by one billion dollars?

The analysis begins with a set of very restrictive assumptions. First, we assume that commercial banks issue only demand deposit liabilities (no time or savings deposits) and that these deposits comprise the total money supply (the nonbank public holds no currency). Secondly, we assume that banks automatically create as great a volume of demand deposits liabilities as is legally possible with the reserves at their disposal. In short, commercial banks desire no reserves in excess of legal requirements.

The symbols which shall be employed in our analysis are defined below for the reader's convenience.

Variables

RT	Total commercial bank reserves
RR	Commercial-bank reserves legally required against deposit liabilities; $RR_D + RR_T = RR$
RR_D	Reserves legally required against demand deposit liabilities; $RR_D = r \cdot DD$
RR_T	Reserves legally required against time deposit liabilities; $RR_T = b \cdot TD$
RE	Excess reserve holdings of commercial banks; $RE = RT - RR$
RB	Borrowed reserves
RU	Unborrowed reserves; $RU = RT - RB$
C	Currency holdings of the nonbank public
DD	Demand deposit liabilities of commercial banks
TD	Time deposit liabilities of commercial banks
B	The monetary base; $B = RT + C$
i_T	The interest rate on commercial bank time deposits
i_D	The Federal Reserve discount rate
i_m	A rate of interest on some class of marketable securities
M	The money stock; $M = DD + C$
L	Loans outstanding at commercial banks

Parameters

r	Average legal reserve requirement on commercial bank demand deposit liabilities
b	Average legal reserve requirement on commercial bank time deposit liabilities

Abstracting from all but the most relevant accounts and assuming networth is zero, the balance sheet of an individual bank in this system appears as follows:

A single Commercial Bank in a Multi-Bank System
(millions of dollars)

Assets		Liabilities and Net Worth	
Reserves (Reserve deposits with the Federal Reserve plus vault cash)	20	Demand Deposits	100
Loans & Securities	80		

Under the assumption that the legal reserve requirement on demand deposits is 20% (r = .20), this bank would be required to hold 20 cents in reserves for each dollar of deposit liabilities. Therefore, it is exactly meeting its legal reserve requirements by holding 20 million dollars in reserves against total deposit liabilities of 100 million dollars.

Assume that by means of a sale of securities which it currently holds in its asset portfolio, this bank increases its reserves by 10 million dollars to 30 million dollars. For example, the bank may sell these securities to the Federal Reserve in return for an increase in the bank's reserve deposit account of $10 million. In the bank reserve equation, a source of bank reserves, U.S. government security holdings of the Federal Reserve, has increased by $10 million. Since there is no corresponding decrease in any other source of funds and no increase in any alternative use of funds, this transaction increases total bank reserves by $10 million, the amount of the security purchase by the Federal Reserve.*

Bank A – Balance Sheet
(millions of dollars)

Assets		Liabilities	
Reserves	30	*DD*	100
Loans & Securities	70		

Bank A is now holding $10 million in reserves *in excess of* the amount required against its deposit liabilities.

By what amount can this bank expand its loan and security holdings and its demand deposit liabilities on the basis of these new reserves (i.e., what volume of loans and securities can this bank purchase through the creation of demand deposit liabilities)? Let us assume that we are dealing with a small commercial bank in a large multi-bank system. In such a situation, unless the bank is geographically isolated and has some degree of regional monopoly, it knows that the demand deposit created in the process of making the loan will be spent by the borrower and must worry about the possibility that the person receiving the check will deposit it at a different bank (call it Bank B). When the check is deposited in the recipient's account at Bank B and cleared against the borrower's account at the lending bank (Bank A), the lending bank will lose reserves to Bank B in an amount equal to the value of the check. Since people usually borrow to facilitate expenditures, it is quite reasonable to assume that checks equal to the total value of the loan will soon be drawn against the new account

---

*This transaction is assumed simply as a starting point for our analysis. It should be noted that such a transaction could generally occur only at the initiative of the Federal Reserve, with the cooperation of the bank. In usual circumstances, the Fed buys from government securities dealers. The dealer may or may not be acting as a broker for a commercial bank.

in Bank A, therefore causing Bank A to lose reserves in the amount of the newly created deposits.*

Under these circumstances, the first bank (Bank A) is in a position to lend only an amount equal to the reserves that it can afford to lose without impairing its legal responsibility to maintain 20% of the value of its original deposit liabilities in the form of reserves. In other words, given some original level of deposits, it may lend and hence create new demand deposits in an amount equal to the difference between total reserve holdings, RT, and reserves required against those original deposits, RR, or excess reserves, RE, i.e., $RE = RT - RR$.

The above process is depicted in the following T-accounts:

Bank A—Before Extension of New Loans

Assets		Liabilities	
Reserves	30	DD	100
Loans & Securities	70		

addendum:
$$RT = 30$$
$$RR = 20 \,[(.20)(100)]$$
$$RE = 10$$

Bank A—After Extension of $10 Million in Loans Through the Creation of Demand Deposits

Assets		Liabilities	
Reserves	30	DD	110
Loans & Securities	80		

Now, if as assumed, the borrower spends the amount of the loan and this check is deposited in another bank (Bank B), when the check clears, the lending bank (Bank A) will lose deposits and reserves equal to the amount of the new deposit created by the loan:

Bank A—Balance Sheet†

Assets		Liabilities	
Reserves	20	DD	100
Loans & Securities	80		

*This statement would have to be modified in a situation in which the lending bank requires the borrower to maintain a "compensating balance"—a balance equal to some percentage of the loan—on deposit at the lending bank for the duration of the loan contract. This, in effect, lowers the usable value of the loan to the borrower and raises the effective rate of interest. This modification could affect our analysis of the operation of an individual bank, but it would not change our conclusions about the operation of the commercial banking system as a whole in any substantial way.

†Although this balance sheet appears to be exactly the same as the initial balance sheet assumed for Bank A, one important change must be noted. In moving from

For Bank B, the recipient bank, deposit liabilities and reserves will increase by an equal amount.

Bank B – Changes in Balance Sheet

Assets		Liabilities	
Reserves	+10	*DD*	+10

(Note: Only the *changes* in Bank B's balance sheet are shown as it is assumed that previous to this transaction Bank B was exactly meeting its legal reserve requirements)

There are many mechanisms through which the transfer of a demand deposit may be facilitated. For simplicity, assume that both banks maintain their reserves in the form of deposit balances with their district Federal Reserve bank. In this case the check can clear through the Federal Reserve System. The clearance will take place when the Federal Reserve bank decreases Bank A's reserve balances by $10 million, the amount of the check, and increases Bank B's (the recipient bank's) reserve deposit account by an equal amount. There is no change in total reserves in the system, but the check clearing process has lowered the reserves of the lending bank and increased the reserves of the bank of deposit (the recipient bank).

After this transaction is completed, Bank A again has $20 million in reserves and $100 million in demand deposit liabilities. With a reserve requirement of 20%, it is exactly meeting its legal reserve requirements. If it had loaned out more than $10 million, the amount of its excess reserves, the check clearing process would have reduced its reserves below $20 million and it would have found itself deficient in legal reserves. Likewise, if it had loaned less than $10 million it would have something over $20 million in reserves against its $100 million deposit liabilities, and would still have excess reserves that it did not desire (by assumption) and that could facilitate further expansion. Thus, we may conclude that in a large multi-bank system, in which individual banks are small relative to the system, and in which banks do not desire to hold reserves in excess of the legal minimum, *a single bank will lend an amount exactly equal to its excess reserves and no more.*

But what about Bank B? It was assumed that this bank was exactly meeting its reserve requirements before the inflow of reserves took place. After the $10 million increase in both its demand deposit liabilities and

---

the initial position to this final equilibrium, the bank sold government securities for reserves and then lost the reserves after the expenditure of the deposit which was created in the loan transaction. In effect, government securities have been exchanged for an I.O.U. from a private party, say a corporation. This changes the characteristics of the asset portfolio of Bank A and may have further repercussions on its behavior. These questions will be examined in detail in chapter 2.

its reserve balances (assuming a required reserve ratio of .20 on demand deposits), it must hold an additional $2 million in reserves against these newly acquired deposit liabilities. But since its total reserves have increased by $10 million, it now has $8 million in excess reserves. ($RT - RR = RE$; $10 - $2 = $8). Bank B will expand its loans by $8 million. This will increase its demand deposit liabilities by $8 million. When the borrower spends his newly created demand deposit, in accordance with our previous assumption, these funds will be deposited in another bank, Bank C. The lending bank (Bank B) will lose reserves and deposit liabilities equal to the amount of the expenditure, $8 million.

Bank B—Changes in Balance Sheet
After Loan Expansion and the Check Clearing Process

Assets		Liabilities	
Reserves	+2	*DD*	+10
Loans & Securities	+8		

Bank C will gain an equal volume of both reserves and deposit liabilities.

Bank C—Changes in Balance Sheet

Assets		Liabilities	
Reserves	+8	*DD*	+8

Bank C now has 6.4 million dollars that it can lend out. ($8 × .20 = $1.6 = reserves required against newly acquired deposit liabilities. $8 – $1.6 = $6.4 = RE). This process will continue until all these reserve funds have been absorbed into required reserves at various banks.

The amounts loaned and the deposits created at each stage in this process may be summed to calculate the total loan and deposit expansion for the banking system as a whole. Bank A loaned out an amount (x), equal to its excess reserves (in this example (x) = $10 million). This amount cleared against Bank A and became the reserves of Bank B. But Bank B's demand deposit *liabilities* increased by the same amount (x). Consequently, Bank B could loan out only an amount equal to $[x - (r)x)]$, i.e., the amount of its new total reserves (x) in excess of its new requirements ($(r)x$). This amount cleared against Bank B and became the reserves of Bank C. Bank C, therefore, can loan out an amount equal to its new reserves ($x - (r)x$) in excess of new requirements $[(r)(x - rx)]$, i.e., an amount $[x - (r)x] - [r(x - (r)x)]$. By a continuous process one may add the amounts loaned out at each stage in the expansion process and derive the total expansion of loans, deposits and the money supply. This process is demonstrated in Table 2.

TABLE 2

Banking System Expansion on the Basis of New Reserves
(in millions)

	Deposits Received in Check Clearing Process		Reserves Required Against Received Deposits	Reserves in Excess of Legal Requirements	Demand Deposits Created to Expand Loans		Reserves and Deposits Lost in Check Clearing Process
Bank A	—		—	10		10	10
Bank B	10	$=$ (x)	2	8	$(x - rx) =$	8	8
Bank C	8	$= (x - rx)$	1.6	6.4	$x(1 - r)^2 =$	6.4	6.4
Bank D	6.4	$= x(1 - r)^2$	1.28	5.12	$x(1 - r)^3 =$	5.12	5.12
Bank E	5.12	$= x(1 - r)^3$	1.024	4.096	$x(1 - r)^4 =$	4.096	4.096
Bank F	4.096	$= x(1 - r)^4$	.819	3.277	$x(1 - r)^5 =$	3.277	3.277
Bank G	3.277	$= x(1 - r)^5$	.655	2.622	$x(1 - r)^6 =$	2.622	2.622
Bank H	2.622	$= x(1 - r)^6$					
	.		.		.		.
	.		.				.
	.		.				.
Total	50.0		10.0			50.0	

Since the expansion at each step in this sequence may be represented as the expansion in the previous step times some constant factor $(1 - r)$, the process may be represented by a geometric series and the total expansion of demand deposits and loans may be expressed as follows:

$$\Delta DD = (x) + (x - rx) + [(x - rx) - (r)(x - rx)] + \cdots$$
$$= (x) + (x)(1 - r) + x(1 - r)^2 + \cdots + x(1 - r)^n.$$

Thus, as the sum of a geometric progression, total expansion is equal to

$$\Delta DD = \frac{(x) - (x)(1 - r)^{n+1}}{1 - (1 - r)}. \quad * \tag{1}$$

But as n, the number of stages in the expansion process, becomes large, this expression simplifies greatly; for if $r < 1$, which it always will be,

*Let $k = x + x(1 - r) + x(1 - r)^2 + \cdots x(1 - r)^n$

Then

$$(1 - r)k = x(1 - r) + x(1 - r)^2 + \cdots x(1 - r)^n + x(1 - r)^{n+1}$$

Subtracting:

$$k - (1 - r)k = x - x(1 - r)^{n+1}$$

Factoring the left-hand side and dividing:

$$k = \frac{x - x(1 - r)^{n+1}}{1 - (1 - r)}.$$

$$\lim_{n \to \infty} \frac{(x) - (x)(1 - r)^{n+1}}{1 - (1 - r)} = (1/r) x = (1/r) (\Delta B) \qquad (2)$$

where (r) is the reserve requirement on demand deposits and (x) is the initial injection of excess reserves (the change in the monetary base, ΔB). Thus the total expansion of loans and deposits in the entire multi-bank system in our example will be $(1/.20)(\$10$ million$) = (5)(\$10$ million$) = \$50$ million.

An alternative approach. The multiple expansion of bank loans and demand-deposit liabilities may be demonstrated much more succinctly with the aid of a model that assumes a few simple relationships between the monetary base, bank reserves, and demand deposits. By the assumption of no currency in circulation, the first of these basic relations is:

$$B = RT. \qquad (3)$$

That is, in the absence of currency holdings by the nonbank public, the entire monetary base would consist of bank reserves. Furthermore, by assuming that banks wish to hold no reserves in excess of the legal requirements, total reserves would be employed solely as required reserves against demand-deposit liabilities. This relationship would be implied by a model that assumed that profit maximization was the goal of commercial bankers, and that bank portfolio managers had perfect knowledge (certainty) about the safety, risk and liquidity characteristics of both their assets and liabilities.* Under these conditions, bankers would always prefer interest yielding loans and securities to non-interest yielding reserve balances, and the presence of excess reserves would immediately generate an expansion of deposits as banks attempted to replace reserve balances with earning assets.

Therefore, equilibrium—the absence of any current forces for change— would prevail only when for each individual bank and for the banking system as a whole, total reserves were employed solely as required reserves against demand deposit liabilities:

$$RT = RR_D \qquad (4)$$

$$RR_D = r \cdot DD = RT. \qquad (5)$$

Substitution of equation (5) into (3) yields

$$B = r \cdot DD$$

$$DD = (1/r) \cdot B \qquad (6)$$

*The influence of these factors in the allocation of bank portfolios is discussed in chapter 2.

or, in terms of changes in the levels of the variables

$$\Delta DD = (1/r)(\Delta B). \qquad (7)$$

The term $(1/r)$ is referred to as the demand deposit expansion coefficient since it defines the relation between a given change in the size of the monetary base and the expansion of demand deposits which that change will bring about. This expression is identical to equation (2) derived above. The emphasis in that derivation, however, was on the logic of $(1/r)$ as the outcome of an explicit behavioral process.

The assumptions required to derive the conclusion stated in equation (7) include the following:

(1) banks issue only demand deposit liabilities

(2) there is no currency in the system

(3) banks desire to hold no reserves in excess of legal requirements; i.e., banks are assumed to be profit maximizers in a regime of perfect knowledge

(4) individual banks suffer a loss of reserves in the expenditure and check clearing process equal to the amount of loans they extend.

(Note: the fourth assumption above was made for convenience and is not necessary for the result presented above.)

In the discussion which follows we relax some of our simplifying assumptions. We examine more realistic models of loan and deposit expansion by successively adding currency and time deposit holdings of the public and desired holdings of excess legal reserves and borrowings of commercial banks. In this process only the monetary base equation is considered. We leave it to the reader to examine the manner in which the geometric expansion of demand deposits takes place under these new assumptions through the flow of reserve funds among individual banks.

MODEL 2. A MONETARY SYSTEM WHICH INCLUDES BOTH CURRENCY HOLDINGS AND DEMAND DEPOSITS.

Let us now introduce currency holdings into the system. We continue to assume that there are no time deposits and that banks wish to hold no excess legal reserves. Under these assumptions the monetary base is defined as the sum of total bank reserves plus currency in circulation.

$$B = RT + C. \qquad (8)$$

So long as we continue to assume that banks issue no time deposits and that desired reserves in excess of legal requirements are zero, banks will be in equilibrium (in the sense of desiring no expansion or contraction of loans and deposits) only when all reserves are required against their demand deposit liabilities. Thus:

$$RR_D = r \cdot DD \tag{9}$$
$$RT = RR_D = r \cdot DD \tag{10}$$

Substitution of (9) and (10) into (8) yields

$$B = r \cdot DD + C. \tag{11}$$

Within this model the non-bank public determines the *relative* amounts of currency and demand deposits it holds. Although the size of the total money stock (or the monetary base) may actively be controlled by the monetary authorities, the composition of that stock is determined by the public's own preferences. However, from equation (8) it can be seen that the greater the public's currency holdings, the fewer the funds available out of a given monetary base to serve as reserves against demand deposit liabilities. Therefore, the total level of deposit liabilities and loans outstanding at commercial banks will depend on the public's relative preferences for the different forms in which they may hold their monetary assets.

Rewriting equation (11), we derive the following basic relation:

$$DD = (1/r)(B - C). \tag{12}$$

Writing this relation in a form that expresses the *change in the stock of deposits* with respect to a *change in the base*:

$$\Delta DD = (1/r)(\Delta B - \Delta C). \tag{13}$$

If the monetary base changes, but currency holdings of the public remain constant ($\Delta C = 0$), then $\Delta DD = (1/r)(\Delta B)$, which is identical to equation (2) above. Thus, if we include currency holdings within our model but assume that those holdings remain constant, the expansion mechanism of the commercial banking system is seen to operate exactly as in a model which assumes that no currency is held by the public. However, rather than assuming that currency holdings remain constant, it may be more realistic to assume that the public desires to hold the components of its total monetary wealth ($DD + C$) in fixed proportions.

Assume, for example, that the public wishes to maintain a 4 to 1 ratio between its holdings of demand deposits and currency. That is, for each dollar held in checking accounts, people wish to hold twenty five cents in currency. This may be expressed as follows:

$$C = s \cdot DD = .25(DD) \tag{14}$$

and for changes in the levels of these variables:

$$\Delta C = s \cdot \Delta DD = .25(\Delta DD). \tag{15}$$

Substitute this expression into the bank reserve equation (11) as follows:

$$\Delta B = r \cdot \Delta DD + \Delta C$$
$$= r \cdot \Delta DD + s \cdot \Delta DD$$
$$= \Delta DD(r + s)$$
$$\Delta DD = \frac{1}{r + s}(\Delta B). \tag{16}$$

Assume as above that $r = .20$, $s = .25$, and bank reserves increase by $10 million, $\Delta B = 10 million.

$$\Delta DD = \frac{1}{r + s}(\Delta B) = \frac{1}{(.20) + (.25)}(10 \text{ million}) = \frac{1}{(.45)}(10 \text{ million})$$
$$= (2.22)(10 \text{ million}) = 22.22 \text{ mil.}$$

Thus, an increase in the monetary base of $10 million (which supplies undesired excess reserves to the banking system and thereby disrupts the initial equilibrium and stimulates expansion) will bring about an increase in demand deposits outstanding of $22.22 million.

When we assumed that there were no currency holdings, an increase in the monetary base of $10 million increased demand deposit liabilities by $50 million; but with currency holdings introduced, the same expansion in the base increases deposit liabilities by only $22.22 million. In the first model, every new dollar of funds supplied by the rise in the monetary base was available to serve as reserve backing for newly created demand deposits. *In the second model, for every dollar of demand deposits created, an additional twenty-five cents was withdrawn from the banking system by the public to be held in the form of currency.* Currency drains represent a decrease in the amount of funds remaining within the banking system available to be held as reserves against deposit liabilities. Therefore, with an assumed currency drain, the given increase in the base supports a smaller increase in the volume of deposit liabilities than would occur in the absence of such a drain.

By how much will currency holdings increase in this process? This figure may be derived from the actual change that occurred in demand deposits:

$$\Delta C = s \cdot \Delta DD$$

$$= (.25)(\$22.22 \text{ million}) = \$5.56 \text{ million};$$

or by substitution:

$$\Delta C = s \cdot \Delta DD = s\left[1/(r+s)\right](\Delta B) = \left[s/(r+s)\right]\Delta B \qquad (17)$$

$$\stackrel{.}{=} \frac{.25}{(.20)+(.25)}\ (\$10 \text{ million}) = (5/9)(\$10 \text{ million}) = \$5.56 \text{ million}$$

where $[s/(r+s)]$ is referred to as the currency expansion coefficient. To double check our computations, we can calculate the total amount of funds that flow out of the banks in the form of currency plus the amount which remains in the banks to support the newly created demand deposit liabilities. This total must exhaust the total increase in the monetary base.

$$B = RT + C = RR_D + C$$

$$= (.20)(22.22) + (5.56) = (4.44) + (5.56) = \$10 \text{ million}.$$

Loans outstanding for the banking system as a whole have increased by an amount equal to the total expansion of currency *and* demand deposits. For example, given an injection of $10 million in excess reserves, a single bank will create new deposits and expand its loans by exactly that amount. As the $10 million in newly created demand deposits is spent and the checks which transfer these deposits clear, an amount of currency equal to $2 million will be withdrawn from the banking system and only $8 million will be redeposited. The joint expansion of demand deposits and currency by $8 million and $2 million, respectively, maintains the 4:1 ratio between these two forms of monetary wealth that the nonbank public is assumed to want. In addition, we see that the sum of the new currency holdings of the public and the new deposit liabilities at the second bank is equal to the volume of loans created at the first bank.

The second bank in this process will expand its loans by an amount equal to its inflow of *excess* reserves [$8 million – (.2) ($8 million) = $6.4 million]. Of this amount, $1.28 million will be withdrawn as currency and $5.12 million will be redeposited in the third bank. At each stage of the expansion, the outflow of currency from the system enables the nonbank public to maintain the desired ratio between the components of its monetary wealth, but at the same time reduces the volume of reserves that flow to the next bank in the expansion process. Loans created at each stage of the process equal the outflow of currency at that stage plus the value of demand deposits which flow to the bank at the next stage of the expansion process. The process continues in this fashion throughout the banking system.

Therefore we may calculate the total volume of loan expansion as follows:

$$\Delta L = \Delta DD + \Delta C = \$22.22 \text{ million} + 5.56 \text{ million}$$

$$= \$27.78 \text{ million.} \tag{18}$$

Using the definition of the money supply, we can show that the money stock expansion coefficient equals $(1 + s)/(r + s)$

$$M = DD + C$$

$$\Delta M = \Delta DD + \Delta C. \tag{19}$$

Substituting the relations above for (ΔDD) and (ΔC),

$$\Delta M = \left(\frac{1}{r + s}\right) \Delta B + \left(\frac{s}{r + s}\right) \Delta B = \left(\frac{1 + s}{r + s}\right) \Delta B. \tag{20}$$

In our present example:

$$\Delta M = \frac{(1) + (.25)(\$10 \text{ million})}{(.20) + (.25)} = (2.778)(\$10 \text{ million}) = \$27.78 \text{ million.}$$

(Note: As seen subsequently, the equality between the expansion of the money supply and the expansion of loans outstanding is not a *necessary* result).

MODEL 3. A MONETARY SYSTEM WHICH INCLUDES TIME DEPOSIT LIABILITIES.

We continue to assume that banks want no excess legal reserves and therefore will expand or contract their outstanding loans and securities any time total reserves differ from required reserves. In addition, assume that banks may now issue time and savings deposits as well as demand deposits. Reserve requirements against the time and savings deposit accounts will now absorb some bank reserves. To take account of this, we formulate our third model as follows:

$$B = RT + C$$

$$RT = RR_D + RR_T = r \cdot DD + b \cdot TD \tag{21}$$

where $(b = .10)$ is assumed to be the reserve requirement ratio on time and savings deposits. Substituting (21) into the monetary base equation yields:

$$B = r \cdot DD + b \cdot TD + C \tag{22}$$

or in terms of changes in the levels of the variables

$$\Delta B = r \cdot \Delta DD + b \cdot \Delta TD + \Delta C. \tag{23}$$

By what amount will demand deposits (and currency, time deposits, loans, and the money supply) expand in response to a given increase in the monetary base? As in the case of currency holdings, rather than assume a constant stock of any monetary asset, we assume that the public maintains fixed proportions between time and demand deposits, i.e., $TD = n \cdot DD$. Specifically, we assume that for every dollar of demand deposits, the public wishes to hold fifty cents in time deposits.

$$TD = .50(DD). \tag{24}$$

Continue to assume the desired four to one ratio between currency holdings and demand deposits and substitute equations (14) and (24) into the monetary base equation (22)

$$B = r \cdot DD + b \cdot TD + C$$

or in terms of changes in the levels of the variables,

$$\Delta B = r \cdot \Delta DD + b \cdot \Delta TD + \Delta C$$

$$= r \cdot \Delta DD + b \cdot n \cdot \Delta DD + s \cdot \Delta DD$$

$$= \Delta DD \cdot (r + bn + s)$$

$$\Delta DD = \left(\frac{1}{r + bn + s}\right) \cdot \Delta B. \tag{25}$$

Returning to our example, if the base is increased by $10 million, demand deposits will increase by $20 million:

$$\Delta DD = \frac{1}{.20 + (.10)(.50) + .25}(\$10 \text{ million}) = \frac{1}{.50}(10 \text{ million})$$

$$= (2)(\$10 \text{ million}) = \$20 \text{ million}.$$

In this case the expansion of demand deposits on the basis of the $10 million increase in the monetary base is smaller than in either of the two previous models. The reason for this should be obvious. In the first model, the entire increase in the monetary base was available to serve as reserves required against newly created demand deposits. In the second model the increase in the monetary base ultimately served two functions; increased currency holdings by the public and increased required reserves against demand deposits issued by commercial banks. In the third model however, in addition to the drain into currency holdings, there is an additional drain into reserves required against newly created time deposits. Notice again that it makes no difference how the initial increase in the base comes about nor in what form the banks prefer to expand their liabilities. The final result will be the same since the public, through its asset preferences, decides how the new funds shall be allocated.

In this model, time deposits will expand by:

$$\Delta TD = n \cdot \Delta DD = n \frac{1}{r + bn + s} \cdot \Delta B = \frac{n}{r + bn + s} \cdot \Delta B$$

$$= (.50/.50)(\$10) = \$10 \text{ million}$$

where $n/(r + bn + s)$ is the time deposit expansion coefficient. Currency holdings will increase by

$$\Delta C = s \cdot \Delta DD = s \frac{1}{r + bn + s} \cdot \Delta B = \frac{s}{r + bn + s} \cdot \Delta B$$

$$= (.25/.50)(\$10) = \$5 \text{ million}$$

where $s/(r + bn + s)$ is the currency expansion coefficient.

These increases exhaust the increase in the monetary base:

$$\Delta B = r \cdot \Delta DD + b \cdot \Delta TD + \Delta C$$

$$= (.20)(\$20) + (.10)(\$10) + \$5 = \$10 \text{ million}.$$

The money-supply expansion in this case is:

$$\Delta M = \Delta DD + \Delta C$$

$$= \frac{1}{r + bn + s} \Delta B + \frac{s}{r + bn + s} \Delta B = \frac{1 + s}{r + bn + s} \Delta B = \$25 \text{ million.}$$

Finally, loans outstanding increased by the sum of the expansion of currency, demand deposits and time deposits, i.e.,

$$\Delta L = \Delta C + \Delta DD + \Delta TD = (\$20) + (\$10) + (\$5) = \$35 \text{ million.}$$

(Note that in this case loan expansion is *greater than* the expansion in the money stock. If the reader investigates what would have happened had we defined "money" to include time deposits, he should see why this is so).

MODEL 4. A MODEL WITH DESIRED EXCESS LEGAL RESERVES.

It is quite reasonable (and historically accurate) to assume that commercial banks may not act like the "automatic dispensers of credit" pictured above. On the contrary, they may quite possibly wish to hold reserves in excess of legal requirements, even though these reserves yield no explicit monetary income. That is, commercial banks may choose not to expand loans and deposit liabilities to the full extent permitted by law. For various reasons they may wish to maintain a positive level of excess reserves as a contingency against unusually large adverse clearing balances, unusually large withdrawals of currency, or as a speculative balance. This assumption is completely consistent with our assumed goal of profit maximization by the commercial banks. In the face of uncertainty, an individual bank must weigh the cost of holding reserves in excess of legal requirements with the cost of falling below the required reserve minimum if unexpected cash withdrawals or adverse clearing balances occur at a time when the bank is just meeting its reserve requirements. The former cost may be represented by the income foregone on earning assets which could have been acquired with excess reserves. The latter cost may be represented by the cost of borrowing from the Federal Reserve or in the Federal Funds market to correct a reserve deficient position. When the cost of a reserve deficiency is greater than zero and there is some finite probability attached to the risk of such a deficiency, it is perfectly reasonable for a profit maximizing bank to hold reserves in excess of those required by law.

This extra complication adds little that is new to the analysis. We may assume that banks wish to maintain a fixed proportional relation between their holdings of excess reserves and their demand-deposit liabilities, that is:

$$RE = w \cdot DD$$

The rationale for this assumption is that the larger the demand deposit liabilities, the greater is the risk of a deposit loss of given size, and the greater the demand for excess reserves to protect the bank from this risk. We must modify the monetary base equation to allow for these holdings of excess legal reserves:

$$B = RT + C$$

but

$$RT = RR_D + RR_T + RE$$
$$= r \cdot DD + b \cdot TD + RE.$$

Thus

$$B = r \cdot DD + b \cdot TD + RE + C.$$

Employing the proportionality relations assumed above:

$$C = s \cdot DD \tag{14}$$

$$TD = n \cdot DD \tag{24}$$

$$RE = w \cdot DD \tag{26}$$

and making the appropriate substitutions

$$B = r \cdot DD + b(n \cdot DD) + w \cdot DD + s \cdot DD$$
$$= DD(r + bn + s + w)$$
$$DD = \frac{1}{r + bn + s + w} \cdot B \tag{27}$$

or in terms of changes in the levels of the variables

$$\Delta DD = \frac{1}{r + bn + s + w} \cdot \Delta B \tag{28}$$

Substituting back into (14), (24) and (26) and employing changes in the levels of the variables:

$$\Delta C = s \cdot \Delta DD = \frac{s}{r + bn + s + w} \cdot \Delta B \tag{29}$$

$$\Delta TD = n \cdot \Delta DD = \frac{n}{r + bn + s + w} \cdot \Delta B \tag{30}$$

$$\Delta RE = w \cdot \Delta DD = \frac{w}{r + bn + s + w} \cdot \Delta B. \tag{31}$$

Likewise, since $\Delta M = \Delta DD + \Delta C$

$$\Delta M = \frac{1 + s}{r + bn + s + w} \cdot \Delta B. \tag{32}$$

The coefficients of the change in the base term, ΔB, represent the various asset expansion coefficients. Equations (28) through (32) represent a rather general model for bank expansion and contraction caused by increases or decreases in the monetary base.

Continuing with our example (assuming all parameter values as above, $r = .20, b = .10, n = .50, \Delta B = \$10$ million and $w = .10$)

$$\Delta DD = \frac{1}{(.20) + (.10)(.50) + (.25) + (.10)} (\$10 \text{ million}) = \frac{1}{(.6)} (\$10 \text{ million})$$

$$= \$16.67 \text{ million}$$

$\Delta C = s \cdot \Delta DD = (.25)(\$16.67) = \$4.17$ million

$\Delta TD = n \cdot \Delta DD = (.50)(\$16.67) = \$8.34$ million

$\Delta RE = w \cdot \Delta DD = (.10)(\$16.67) = \$1.67$ million

$\Delta M = \Delta DD + \Delta C = \$4.17 + \$16.67 = \$20.84$ million

$\Delta L = \Delta C + \Delta DD + \Delta TD = \$4.17 + \$16.67 + \$8.34 = \$29.18$ million

Check: $\Delta B = r \cdot \Delta DD + b \cdot \Delta TD + \Delta RE + \Delta C$

$= (.20)(\$16.67) + (.10)(\$8.34) + (\$1.67) + (\$4.17) = \$10$ million.

GENERALIZED MODELS OF MONETARY EXPANSION

RELAXING THE PROPORTIONALITY ASSUMPTIONS

The results obtained in the above models depend directly on specific assumptions made about the asset preferences of the banks and the public. Let us examine what changes occur when alternative assumptions are specified to describe these asset preferences.

We continue to assume that the monetary base is somehow determined outside the commercial banking system by the monetary authorities, and that its size can be taken as given by the commercial banks. In our "general" case (Model 4), in equilibrium, the monetary base would be divided among the following uses:

(1) currency in circulation (C)

(2) reserves required against demand deposits (RR_D)

(3) reserves required against time deposits (RR_T)

(4) excess legal reserves held by commercial banks (RE)

$$B = r \cdot DD + b \cdot TD + RE + C. \tag{33}$$

Assuming that the size of the base B and the reserve requirement ratios (r and b) are determined by the authorities, we have one equation in four unknowns. In deriving a solution for these quantities, simple behavioral equations were specified to represent the asset preferences of banks and the public. These were formulated as proportionality relations within our model:

$$C = s \cdot DD \tag{14}$$

$$TD = n \cdot DD \tag{24}$$

$$RE = w \cdot DD \tag{26}$$

where s, n and w are the factors of proportionality.*

Assuming that the values of these parameters (s, n and w) are known from past experience, and that the ratios they represent remain stable over time,** the system now contains *four* equations in *four* unknowns. Substitution of equations (14), (24) and (26) into equation (33) yields:

$$B = r \cdot DD + bn \cdot DD + s \cdot DD = w \cdot DD$$

$$DD = \frac{1}{r + bn + s + w} \cdot B.$$

Thus, the demand deposit expansion coefficient is derived. All other expansion coefficients can be derived from this equation, equations (14),

---

*If we assume that *DD* may be taken as a proxy variable for either wealth or income, the interpretation given to these relations within the model may be broadened substantially. The importance of wealth in the money (and deposit) demand function is pointed out in Part 2. Financial wealth may also be important in the consumption function. This is discussed in chapter 9.

**In fact, these ratios have not remained constant over time and can be highly volatile even over a short period of time. We shall see below how we may incorporate more complicated behavioral forms into our model.

(24), and (26), and the definition of money, equation (19). Note, however, how the results rely heavily on the forms of the assumed asset preference relations. These very special (and not very realistic) assumptions greatly limit the general applicability and empirical value of these results.

Consider the implications of these assumptions. A way is needed to describe the holdings of time deposits and currency desired by the public and the holdings of excess legal reserves desired by commercial banks which will allow solution of our monetary base equation. This was done above by assuming one of the simplest possible relations (proportionality) between these measures and the level of demand deposits. Let us suppose that empirical tests indicate that the assumption of proportionality does not accurately describe asset preferences in one of these cases. In particular, let us assume that proportionality is found to be a good description of banks' holdings of excess legal reserves and the public's holdings of time deposits, but that currency holdings do not conform to this pattern. It will then be necessary to try a different functional form to describe the relationship between the public's holdings of demand deposits and currency.

Suppose that we chose a *linear but non-proportional form to explain these currency holdings,* $C = a + d \cdot DD$. This change would modify the expansion coefficients derived above. Our model would now appear as follows:

$$B = r \cdot DD + b \cdot TD + RE + C$$
$$TD = n \cdot DD$$
$$RE = w \cdot DD$$
$$C = a + d \cdot DD \tag{34}$$

Substituting the asset preference relations into the monetary base equation:

$$B = r \cdot DD + b(n) \cdot DD + w \cdot DD + a + d \cdot DD$$
$$= DD(r + bn + w + d) + a$$
$$DD = (B - a)/(r + bn + w + d).$$

To derive a currency expansion coefficient, we substitute

$$C = a + d \cdot DD = a + \frac{d(B - a)}{(r + bn + w + d)}.$$

The slight complication in the currency demand function adds a complicating factor to all our results.

This example shows that although the money supply mechanism described above is not completely "general" as it stands, it provides a flexible framework within which an analyst may experiment with various functional forms.

MODELS WITH INTEREST RATES AND OTHER VARIABLES IN THE BEHAVIORAL RELATIONS.

In reality, only quite complicated functions may accurately describe the true relationships that determine the public's asset preferences.* This may involve the introduction of new variables into our model. Let us suppose, for example, that we found a linear currency demand function to be a satisfactory explanation of the "true" relationship between the public's holdings of demand deposits and currency, and we found too, a proportional relationship to be an accurate explanation of actual bank holdings of excess legal reserves. However, what if neither of these functional forms satisfactorily explains the time deposit holdings of the public? We must search for an explanation through other functional forms including the introduction of new variables.

That time deposit balances yield an interest return to their holders while demand balances do not, ought to influence the public's decisions as to how to allocate their monetary assets. For example, the higher the rate of interest on time deposits, *ceteris paribus*, the more costly it would be in terms of foregone income to hold a dollar in the form of demand deposits or currency. Therefore, the level of the interest rate on time deposit balances as well as the size of demand deposit balances (or wealth) may influence desired time deposit holdings. One might postulate, for example, that time deposit holdings are a linear function of both the stock of demand deposit balances and the rate of interest on time deposits, i.e.,

$$TD = e + f \cdot DD + g \cdot i_T. \tag{35}$$

These modifications in the time-deposit demand equation would affect all the expansion coefficients we derived above. Recalling our assumption:

$$B = r \cdot DD + b \cdot TD + RE + C$$

$$RE = w \cdot DD$$

$$C = a + d \cdot DD$$

$$TD = e + f \cdot DD + g \cdot i_T$$

*See Frank de Leeuw, "A Model of the Financial Sector," *The Brookings Quarterly Econometric Model of the United States*, James S. Duesenberry *et al.*, editors (Amsterdam: North Holland Publishing Co., 1965).

Substituting

$$B = r \cdot DD + b[e + f \cdot DD + g \cdot i_T] + w \cdot DD + a + d \cdot DD$$

$$= DD(r + bf + w + d) + b[e + g \cdot i_T] + a$$

$$DD = \frac{B - (a + be) - bg \cdot i_T}{(r + bf + w + d)}.$$

By substituting the behavioral relations representing the public's and the bank's asset preferences into the definition of the monetary base, we have derived a "reduced form" equation* that specifies the equilibrium volume of demand deposits consistent with given values of the monetary base B, the interest rate on time deposits i_T and the legal (r and h) and behavioral (w, a, c, d, f, g) parameters of the monetary system. Since the legal parameters and the monetary base are under the control of the monetary authority, if we could estimate the behavioral parameters of the system (say, by regression techniques), a knowledge of the current level of the interest rate on time deposits would enable us to predict the equilibrium level of demand deposit balances.

As one further example, let us suppose that the asset preferences of the banks and the public are dependent on some market interest rates.** For example, the public may consider very short-term U. S. government securities as an alternative to their holdings of currency and time deposits.*** The greater the rate on these securities, the greater the opportunity cost of holding currency or time deposits. Likewise, commercial banks may be influenced by the rate on these securities when determining their desired level of excess legal reserves.† The greater the market rate, the more costly it is to hold non-earning excess reserves. In this instance the asset-preference functions may be written as linear equations:

*A "reduced form" equation specifies the equilibrium value of an endogenous variable—a variable whose value is determined within the framework of our model, such as demand deposits—as a function of the parameters and exogenous variables that appear in the structural equations (asset preference equations and definitions) of our model.

**Though very many individual interest rates exist on the market at any one moment, let us assume that one of those rates or some composite of those rates is the most important rate in determining the asset preferences specified in our model. This would represent a very formidable problem if we were to try to estimate our model empirically.

***The importance of the role of the interest rate in the determination of the demand for money (whether or not we consider time deposits in our definition of money) is discussed in Part 2.

†For example, the rate on these securities may influence the trade-off between the income foregone and the risk averted when commercial banks hold excess legal reserves.

$$TD = e + f \cdot DD + g \cdot i_m$$
$$C = a + d \cdot DD + c \cdot i_m$$
$$RE = v + w \cdot DD + h \cdot i_m.$$

In each case desired asset holdings depend upon both the volume of bank demand deposit liabilities and the market rate of interest (i_m). The relation between these asset holdings and the market rate will be inverse, i.e., the signs attached to g, c and h will be negative. Therefore, when the interest rate on short-term securities or some other market instruments rises, the public will desire a smaller volume of currency and time deposits and the banks will desire fewer excess legal reserves.

Incorporating these relations into our basic framework,

$$B = r \cdot DD + b \cdot TD + C + RE$$

$$B = r \cdot DD + b \left[e + f \cdot DD + g \cdot i_m \right] + a + d \cdot DD + c \cdot i_m$$
$$+ v + w \cdot DD + h \cdot i_m$$
$$= r \cdot DD + bf \cdot DD + d \cdot DD + w \cdot DD + be + a + v + bg \cdot i_m$$
$$+ c \cdot i_m + h \cdot i_m$$
$$= DD \left[r + bf + d + w \right] + \left[be + a + v \right] + \left[bg + c + h \right] i_m$$

$$DD = \frac{B - \left[be + a + v \right] - \left[bg + c + h \right] i_m}{\left[r + bf + d + w \right]}$$

Let

$$\zeta = \left[be + a + v \right] \qquad \text{and}$$
$$\gamma = \left[bg + c + h \right]$$

Then

$$DD = \frac{B - \zeta - \gamma \cdot i_m}{\left[r + bf + d + w \right]} \tag{36}$$

Equation (36) is a "reduced form" equation. In this form, $\gamma \cdot i_m$ represents the total influence of the short-term market interest rate on the volume of demand deposit liabilities through its effects on the preferred asset holdings of the public and the banks. Since the parameters g, c and h above are negative and b is positive, γ is also negative. Since (negative) γ is preceded by a minus sign in the above expression, as the market rate increases, the equilibrium quantity of demand deposits increases. This relation is depicted graphically in Figure 1.

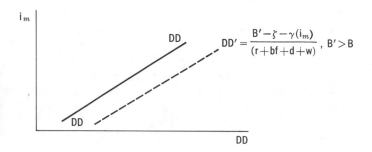

Figure 1. Reduced form DD relation.

An examination of the intercept term

$$\frac{(B - \zeta)}{r + bf + d + w}$$

reveals that an increase in the monetary base, B, will cause the curve to shift to the right increasing the quantity of demand deposits supplied at all levels of the interest rate. Similarly, the curve will shift out to the right if any one of the parameters in the denominator of the intercept term is decreased. For example, a reduction in the reserve-requirement ratio on bank demand deposits will increase the supply of deposits at all interest rates. A relationship similar to this one will be employed in chapter 8 when the money-supply relationship is included as one of the behavioral equations in a model of the determination of national income.

This discussion shows that there could be numerous money multipliers or expansion coefficients and that the money supply could be influenced by several different interest rates. The form of the expansion coefficients and the choice of interest rate variables that affect the money supply as demonstrated above, depend directly on the form of behavioral relations employed to explain the asset preferences of the banks and the public. These equations could be expanded to include additional variables such as income, wealth, expectations, and the many other factors that may be important in the determination of the public's and the banks' asset preferences.* The "best" money supply model will be the one that ex-

*For example, studies by George Kaufman and Phillip Cagan have suggested that the desired currency ratio varies *inversely* with the level of income because, as income increases, proportionately more transactions are handled by check. In addition,

plains the actual data (actual past values of these variables) and predicts future values better than any of the other models tested.

SUMMARY OF THE MONEY EXPANSION PROCESS.

In the section of this chapter entitled "Monetary Accounts," we examined various accounts of the Federal Reserve Banks and the Treasury and presented statements specifying all the major factors affecting the generation or absorption of the monetary base (total commercial bank reserves plus currency in circulation). The section entitled "The Mechanism of Money Supply Expansion" demonstrated how the total money supply (demand deposits plus currency in circulation) and other commercial bank deposit liabilities against which reserves are required, may be supported by this monetary base. That section began with a highly abstract model which assumed that demand deposits were the only liabilities issued by commercial banks and that there was no currency in the system. We then developed progressively more realistic models. In the section labelled "Generalized Models of Monetary Expansion," we demonstrated that the form of the money supply mechanism described in the previous section was the result of the specific behavioral assumptions that underlie the model. Nonetheless, the basic framework was shown to be rather general. Various modifications were made in our behavioral relations in order to examine the effects of these changes on the coefficients in the reduced form equation for demand deposits.

Thus, we have indicated the major factors which supply funds for the base of the monetary system and, given that base, we have shown how the currency and deposit demands of the public and the demand for excess legal reserves by the banks may be included in models describing the determination of the money stock.

THE MONETARY BASE AND MEMBER-BANK BORROWED RESERVES

Quite often it is assumed that the monetary base, B, is exogenously determined by the monetary authorities. Let us investigate this assumption and its implications more closely. All factors which either supply or

---

the desired time deposit ratio may vary *directly* with income, if time deposits are a luxury good. *See* Phillip Cagan, *Determinants and Effects of Changes in the Stock of Money 1875-1960.* (New York, Columbia University Press, 1965) and George G. Kaufman, *The Demand for Currency*, Staff Economic Study, Board of Governors of the Federal Reserve System.

divert to alternative uses funds which are potentially available to serve as currency or bank reserves are listed in the monetary base equation. Therefore, to determine which factors influence the size of the monetary base, B, we must examine the determinants of the items in that statement.

The only item in the statement of the sources and uses of bank reserves over which the monetary authority, the Federal Reserve, has absolute control, is "U.S. government securities" held by the Federal Reserve, listed under Federal Reserve Credit. This account represents the largest single source of funds in the monetary base equation. Other items listed as sources and alternative uses of funds are not under the control of the Federal Reserve. For example, variations in the level of the gold stock are determined primarily by the conditions in the U.S. balance of payments and the world money markets. Foreign deposits at the Federal Reserve and deposits other than those of member banks are varied at the discretion of the holder. "Float,"* a technical item that arises in the check-clearing process, can be affected by strikes, by the weather, and by any other factors that can delay the delivery of checks.

From the point of view of the monetary authorities, however, control over just one item in the monetary base equation, particularly an item as important and flexible as System security holdings, may be as good as control over all accounts. For, if the Federal Reserve can predict the changes that will occur in the items which it does not directly control, it can take appropriate measures to offset the effects of these changes simply by adjusting its holdings of U.S. government securities through open market operations.** Even if the authorities cannot predict these changes before they occur, the Director of the System's Open Market Account can move fairly rapidly to take corrective measures to offset the effects of any change that comes to his attention. For example, suppose there is a decrease in Treasury deposits at the Federal Reserve. As an alternative use of funds in the monetary base equation, this would lead to an increase in bank reserves (assuming other accounts remain constant). However, if the Treasury notifies the Federal Reserve of impending changes in the level of its deposits, the Federal Reserve can sell securities on the open market

---

*Federal Reserve "Float" is the difference between "cash items in process of collection" and "deferred availability cash items" in the consolidated balance sheet of the Federal Reserve Banks. Float results from the practice of crediting a member bank's reserve account for checks deposited in Federal Reserve Banks before the checks are actually collected from another commercial bank. Consequently, strikes and bad weather that interfere with the check collection process can cause an increase in float and, thereby, an increase in total bank reserves.

**See the example given above in the section of this chapter called "Monetary Accounts." For a discussion of some of the problems that arise in trying to achieve this kind of control, see Sherman T. Maisel, "Controlling Monetary Aggregates," ibid.

thereby decreasing the size of their security portfolio and offsetting the effects of the Treasury action on bank reserves. Or suppose there is an outflow of gold to a foreign country. By itself, this movement would decrease the nation's gold stock, a source of member bank reserves. However, the result could easily be negated by a purchase of securities by the Federal Reserve. Thus, it would appear that through defensive (offsetting) open market operations, the monetary authorities can control the level of the monetary base and, therefore, the level of bank reserves.

However, there is an item in the list that is varied primarily at the discretion of commercial banks. This is member bank borrowing from the Federal Reserve, included under "discounts and advances" in the monetary base equation. When a commercial bank finds itself temporarily short of reserves for whatever reason, it has the privilege of borrowing reserves from its district Federal Reserve bank. These funds are borrowed on a very short term basis under conditions set by the Federal Reserve Board to restore its reserves to the level required by law.

By itself, an increase in member bank borrowing from the Federal Reserve increases total member bank reserves. If there is no change in the other accounts in the bank reserve equation, this borrowing causes a net increase in the monetary base and will support a multiple expansion of loans and deposits just as an increase in reserves from any other source would. However, many observers believe that the Federal Reserve generally (though perhaps only partially) offsets changes in commercial bank borrowing through open market operations. For example, when commercial banks borrow, the authorities could sell securities on the open market. The net effect of these two actions would be to maintain total member bank reserves at a constant level determined by the monetary authorities.

Whether the Federal Reserve actually offsets every change in the level of member bank borrowing or simply lets such borrowing change the volume of total reserves as banks desire, is an empirical question (with very important policy implications).* Regardless of their actual policy, we may assume that the authorities find it useful to be able to predict member bank borrowing. Let us view the role of these borrowed reserves within the money supply framework. This modification in our model may be demonstrated rather simply.

We may view the total reserve stock available to commercial banks as composed of two separate elements:

---

*For example, the impact of monetary policy on the level of income is estimated to be relatively weak if unborrowed reserves are used as an (exogenous) measure of monetary policy. *See* Richard Davis, "How Much Does Money Matter? A Look at Some Evidence," *Monthly Review,* Federal Reserve Bank of New York, Vol. 51 (June 1969), pp. 119-133.

(1) all reserve funds supplied to the commercial banks by the Federal Reserve other than through the borrowing mechanism. This component is called unborrowed reserves, RU.

(2) those reserves created through commercial bank borrowing from the Federal Reserve, RB.

Therefore, we write the following definition: $RT = RU + RB$.

If the Federal Reserve does not offset every movement in reserve borrowing by changes in the level of unborrowed reserves (RU) supplied to commercial banks, bank borrowing will affect the total stock of reserves in the system.

How will this new element introduced into the analysis modify the money multipliers and expansion coefficients derived in the section on "Generalized Models of Monetary Expansion"?   Let us assume that the sum of the unborrowed reserve and currency components of the monetary base are determined by the Federal Reserve.   Note that this does not deny the possibility that the authorities could in fact offset member bank borrowing through variations in RU, but it does provide a convenient framework to relate borrowed reserves to our money expansion model.

Recall our two definitions of aggregate bank reserves:

$RT = RR + RE$

$RT = RU + RB$.

By substitution: $RU = RR + RE - RB*$.

Define a new measure: the unborrowed monetary base, $\overline{B}$.

$\overline{B} = B - RB$

$\overline{B} = RT - RB + C = RU + C$.

Therefore,

*We may define another measure called "free reserves," equal to excess reserves less commercial bank borrowing, $RF = RE - RB$. This measure frequently is mentioned as a target variable used by the Federal Reserve in its open market operations and as an "indicator" used by the financial community in interpreting this policy. Some analysts have chosen to focus on this measure as the behavioral variable in studying commercial bank behavior and in relating that behavior to the money supply process. For several very good reasons presented elsewhere, we choose not to focus our attention on this combined measure, but rather to investigate each of the components separately. *See* A.J. Meigs, *Free Reserves and the Money Supply* (Chicago: University of Chicago Press, 1962) and Karl Brunner and Allan H. Meltzer, "The Federal Reserve's Attachment to Free Reserves," Testimony before the Subcommittee on Domestic Finance of the House Committee on Banking and Currency, 88th Congress, 2nd Session, May 7, 1964, pp. 1-27.

$$\overline{B} = RR + RE - RB + C$$

$$= r - DD + b \cdot TD + RE - RB + C.$$

To derive the money multipliers and expansion coefficients we need only proceed, as before, to specify behavioral relations for each of the variables in the equation and to substitute these relations in the equation for the monetary base (now $\overline{B}$) and solve. For example, we may once again assume the familiar proportionality relations for time deposits and currency.

$$TD = n \cdot DD$$

$$C = s \cdot DD.$$

What can we assume about the demand for excess reserves and the demand for borrowed reserves by commercial banks? This question will be taken up in detail in chapter 2. At the present, in anticipation of the results of that discussion, assume that the demand for excess reserves of commercial banks is a linear function of some market interest rate (the alternative cost of holding funds in the form of reserve balances) and the volume of demand deposit liabilities,

$$RE = v + w \cdot DD + h \cdot i_m$$

Assume that bank borrowing depends on the relationship between the discount rate (the explicit monetary costs of borrowed reserves) and a market interest rate (the return to be earned from acquiring earnings assets with the borrowed funds). Assume also that the instability or volatility of commercial bank deposits will influence borrowing behavior. Let this latter factor remain unspecified but be represented by the symbol (λ). Then postulate that the level of commercial bank borrowing is a linear function of the stability factor (λ) and the algebraic difference between the market interest rate (i_m) and the discount rate (i_D)

$$RB = a + d(i_m - i_D) + z(\lambda)$$

Substituting these behavioral relations into the basic relation above yields the reduced form equation for demand deposits:

$$\overline{B} = r \cdot DD + bn \cdot DD + s \cdot DD + v + w \cdot DD + h \cdot i_m - a - d(i_m - i_D)$$

$$- z(\lambda)$$

$$= DD\,[r + bn + s + w] + [v - a] + h \cdot i_m - d(i_m - i_D) - z(\lambda)$$

$$DD = \frac{\overline{B} - h(i_m) + d(i_m - i_D) + z(\lambda) - (v - a)}{[r + bn + s + w]}$$

Since the money supply has been defined as demand deposits plus currency in circulation, we may write:

$$M = DD + C = DD + s \cdot DD = (1 + s) DD$$

$$M = \frac{1 + s}{[r + bn + s + w]} [\overline{B} - h \cdot i_m + d(i_m - i_D) + z(\lambda) - (v - a)]$$

This result represents a reduced form equation relating equilibrium values of the money stock to the legal and behavioral parameters and exogenous variables of our model.* Suppose, for example, that the reserve requirement ratios (b and r), the parameters of the behavioral equations (n, s, v, w, h, a, d, z), λ, and the market interest rate all remain constant, but that the Federal Reserve increases the discount rate. What effect will this action have on the money supply? Since all factors but i_D remain constant and the coefficient d (from the borrowed reserve demand equation) is likely to be positive—a greater positive differential between the market rate and the discount rate stimulating additional borrowing—an increase in i_D will lower ($i_m - i_D$) and thereby lower the money supply.

Estimates of the parameters of the behavioral equations and information on the usefulness of our assumed functional forms can be derived through the use of statistical methods—primarily regression analysis. Some work has been done on this problem over the past several years.** Much of this work has been inspired by the "new view" that the behavior of the public and the commercial banks (as influenced by factors such as the rate of interest, the level of income and other economic conditions) so dominates the money supply determination process, that there is no close predictable relationship between the money supply and the variables controlled by the monetary authority.*** Although no great confidence can yet be attached to the estimates derived through econometric analysis, some guidance can be given to the monetary authorities on questions such as the one posed above.

---

*For a review of several money supply functions which incorporate alternative assumptions concerning portfolio adjustments by the banks and the public, *see* David I. Fand, "Some Issues in Monetary Economics," reprinted at the end of Part 1.

***See* David I. Fand, "Some Implications of Money Supply Analysis," *The American Economic Review*, Vol. 57 (May 1967), pp. 380-400.

***For a discussion of the "new view" of monetary theory, *see* the survey article by David Fand that follows Part 2 in this book.

SUMMARY AND CONCLUSION

In this chapter, we have attempted to describe a framework within which to analyze the process through which the money stock is determined. This task has included the derivation of the *Bank Reserve Equation* from The Federal Reserve Banks' consolidated balance sheet and certain U.S. Treasury accounts, the demonstration of the role and operation of individual banks within a multi-bank system and the influence of the behavior of the banks and the public on the equilibrium money stock. Our objective has not been to present the money-supply process in a completely precise and empirically relevant manner. We have, however, indicated the outlines of a money supply determination model and the role of assumed behavioral relations in such a model.

Note: the following footnote refers to material to be found on page 37, paragraph 3 of this book:

For example, the impact of monetary policy on the level of income is estimated to be relatively weak if unborrowed reserves are used as an (exogenous) measure of monetary policy. *See* Richard Davis, "How Much Does Money Matter? A Look at Some Evidence," *Monthly Review*, Federal Reserve Bank of New York, Vol. 51, June 1969, pp. 119–131.

Questions / *chapter 1*

1. Assume that the public and commercial banks are in "equilibrium," i.e., the public is holding its preferred relative amounts of currency, demand deposits and time deposits and banks are holding their desired level of excess reserves. Given the data below, use the kind of proportionality relations we employed in the early models of this chapter to answer the following questions:

Current required reserve ratio on demand deposits = .15

Current required reserve ratio on time deposits = .10

Currency outstanding = $50 billion

DD liabilities of commercial banks = $200 billion

TD liabilities of commercial banks = $100 billion

Total Reserves held by banks = $50 billion

(a) What is the value of the demand deposit expansion coefficient?

(b) By how much will demand deposits increase if the Fed increases bank reserves by $5 billion (by a direct purchase of government securities from the bank, for example)?

(c) By how much will the injection of reserves in part (b) increase the money supply?

(d) What volume of excess reserves will the banks hold *after* the above deposit expansion has been completed?

2. The currency needs of the public are strongly influenced by "seasonal" factors. For example, the traveling, shopping, and gift giving traditions associated with Christmas greatly increase the public's need for cash. Describe the problems which this seasonal variation in currency demand might cause for the monetary authorities. How would such variations affect their ability to control the money stock?

3. What relationship is generally postulated between a change in the interest rate on time deposits and the quantity of time deposits demanded as a percentage of demand deposits? How does this relationship affect the quantity of money supplied?

4. What relationship is generally hypothesized between the market rate of interest and:

(a) The demand for currency as a percentage of demand deposits.

(b) The demand for time deposits as a percentage of demand deposits.

(c) The demand for excess reserves.

(d) The quantity of money supplied. (Be sure you can explain this one by using (a) (b) and (c) above.)

Bibliography / *chapter 1*

Andersen, Leonall C., "Federal Reserve Open Market Transactions and the Money Supply," *Federal Reserve Bank of St. Louis, Review,* Vol. 47 (April 1965), pp. 10–16.

──── , "Three Approaches to Money Stock Determination," *Federal Reserve Bank of St. Louis, Review,* Vol. 49 (October 1967), pp. 6–13.

Andersen, L. C. and **J. Jordan**, "The Monetary Base: Explanation and Analytical Use," *Federal Reserve Bank of St. Louis, Review,* Vol. 49 (August 1967), pp. 7–11.

Argy, V., "Money Supply Theory and the Money Multiplier," *Australian Economic Papers,* Vol. 4 (June/December 1965), pp. 27–36.

Ascheim, Joseph, "Commercial Banks and Financial Intermediaries: Fallacies and Policy Implications," *Journal of Political Economy,* Vol. 67 (February 1959), pp. 59–71.

Black, Robert P., "The Impact of Member Bank Reserves Upon the Money Supply," *Southern Economic Journal,* Vol. 29 (January 1963), pp. 199–210.

Brunner, Karl, "A Schema for the Supply Theory of Money," *International Economic Review,* Vol. 11 (January 1961), pp. 79–109.

Brunner, Karl and **Allan H. Meltzer**, "Some Further Investigations of Demand and Supply Functions for Money," *Journal of Finance,* Vol. 19 (May 1964), pp. 240–283.

Cagan, Phillip, *Determinants and Effects of Changes in the Stock of Money 1875–1960.* New York: Columbia University Press, 1965.

Canterbery, E. Ray, "A Note on Recent Money Supply Behavior," *Western Journal of Economics*, Vol. 4, 1965, pp. 91–98.

de Leeuw, Frank, "A Model of Financial Behavior," *The Brookings Quarterly Econometric Model of the United States*, James S. Duesenberry *et al.*, editors. Chicago: Rand McNally & Co., 1965, pp. 465–532.

Fand, David I., "Some Implications of Money Supply Analysis," *The American Economic Review*, Vol. 57 (May 1967), pp. 380–400.

_____, "Some Issues in Monetary Economics," *Federal Reserve Bank of St. Louis Review*, Vol. 52 (January 1970), pp. 10–27.

Friedman, Milton and Anna Schwartz, *A Monetary History of the U.S. 1867-1960.* Princeton: The Princeton University Press, 1963, Appendix B.

Goldfeld, Stephen M., *Commercial Bank Behavior and Economic Activity*. Amsterdam: North Holland Publishing Company, 1966.

Gurley, John G. and Edward S. Shaw, *Money in a Theory of Finance.* Washington: The Brookings Institution, 1960.

Guttentag, Jack M., and Robert Lindsay, "The Uniqueness of Commercial Banks," *Journal of Political Economy,* Vol. 67 (October 1968), pp. 991–1014.

Kaufman, George G., "Proposed Experiment in Monetary Policy," *Financial Analysts Journal* (Nov./Dec. 1968).

Maisel, Sherman J., "Controlling Monetary Aggregates," Proceedings of the Boston Federal Reserve Bank Conference: *Controlling Monetary Aggregates* (June 1969).

Meigs, A. J., *Free Reserves and the Money Supply*. Chicago: University of Chicago Press, 1962.

Meltzer, Allan H., "Money Supply Revisited: A Review Article," *Journal of Political Economy*, Vol. 75 (April 1967), pp. 169–182.

Newlyn, W. T., "The Supply of Money and Its Control," *Economic Journal*, Vol. 74 (June 1964), pp. 327–346.

Orr, Daniel and W. G. Mellon, "Stochastic Reserve Losses and Expansion of Bank Credit," *The American Economic Review,* Vol. 51, No. 4 (September 1961), pp. 614–623.

Phillips, C. A., *Bank Credit.* New York: Macmillan, 1926.

Smith, Paul F., "Concepts of Money and Commercial Banks," *Journal of Finance*, Vol. 21(December 1966), pp. 635–648.

Smith, Warren, "Financial Intermediaries and the Effectiveness of Monetary Controls," *Quarterly Journal of Economics,* Vol. 73 (November 1959), pp. 533–553.

Teigen, Ronald, "Demand and Supply Functions for Money in the United States: Some Structural Estimates," *Econometrica*, Vol. 32, No. 4 (October 1964), pp. 476–509.

Tobin, James, "Commercial Banks as Creators of 'Money' " in Deane Carson (editor), *Banking and Monetary Studies.* Homewood, Illinois: Richard D. Irwin, Inc., 1963, pp. 408–419.

2

Bank Reserves and
Portfolio Management

INTRODUCTION

The previous chapter presents a framework for analyzing the determinants of the money stock. The model developed in that discussion demonstrates how the public's demand for currency and time deposits, as well as the commercial banks' demand for excess reserves and borrowings, may be incorporated into an analysis of the money supply determination process. The influence of these demand functions was explicitly summarized in the money supply expansion coefficient in the reduced form money supply equation.

To understand the money supply determination process more completely, we must examine the behavior of the public and of the banks as it influences the values of the parameters in the models of chapter 1. In this chapter, then, we turn to an analysis of the commercial bank's demand for excess reserves and borrowings from the Federal Reserve. This task necessitates an extensive study of bank operations.* The analysis begins with an examination of the major accounts in a commercial bank's balance sheet and the relation between these accounts and a bank's liquidity. The major constraints and priorities of bank portfolio management will be studied in order to isolate some of the primary factors that determine the total liquidity needs of a commercial bank. This model will serve as a guide in the examination of the role of excess reserves and borrowings in providing the desired level of bank liquidity.

THE COMMERCIAL BANK BALANCE SHEET: I/ AN EXPOSITION OF THE MAJOR ACCOUNTS

Our analysis begins with an examination of the major accounts in the commercial bank balance sheet. A consolidated balance sheet of all member banks of the Federal Reserve System is displayed in Table 1.

All commercial banks that belong to the Federal Reserve System** are required by law to hold reserve balances equal to some minimum percentage of their demand and time deposit liabilities. Prior to 1959, these banks could count as legal reserves only balances held on deposit with Federal Reserve District Banks. Since that time, however, member banks have been permitted to count their vault cash as reserves as well. In the consolidated balance sheet presented below, total member bank reserves are $27 billion, of which $5 billion is held in the form of coin and currency in bank vaults, and $22 billion is held on deposit with District Federal Reserve Banks.

If the total volume of reserves held by banks is greater than the amount which they are required to hold against deposit liabilities, these banks are said to be holding *excess reserves* (i.e., excess reserves = total reserves – required reserves). Total Reserve balances serve two primary purposes: they satisfy legal requirements on deposit liabilities (required reserves) and they provide the ultimate in liquidity to the banks (excess reserves). In the preceding balance sheet, for example, if the reserve requirement ratio on demand deposits were 10 percent and the ratio on time and savings deposits were 5 percent, required reserves against demand deposits would be seventeen and one-half billion dollars ($175 × .10 = $17.5) and required

---

*As in the previous chapter, we ignore the difficulties posed by the existence of member and nonmember banks and the distinctions made among the various "classes" of member banks.

**As of 1971, though slightly less than one-half of all commercial banks belonged to the Federal Reserve System, member banks accounted for over 80% of all deposit liabilities, and an even higher percentage of total bank transactions (check clearings, etc.).

TABLE 1

Consolidated Balance Sheet of Member
Banks of the Federal Reserve System

Assets		Liabilities and Net Worth	
(amounts in billions of dollars)			
Total Bank Reserves	27.0	Deposits:	
Vault Cash 5.0		Demand	175.0
Reserve Deposit Balances 22.0		Time & Savings	160.0
Loans	240.0	Borrowed Reserves	0.5
Investments	95.0	Other (including	
Other	48.0	capital accounts)	74.5

The amounts presented in this table closely approximate the actual data for June 30, 1970. Rounding facilitated the preparation of numerical examples which appear below.

reserves against time deposits would be eight billion dollars ($160 × .05 = $8.0). Total required reserves would be 25.5 billion dollars. With total reserves of 27 billion dollars, excess reserves would be 1.5 billion dollars. Since these reserves are in excess of the amount which the banks are required to hold against their current deposit liabilities, they are immediately available to the banks for a variety of purposes: to meet currency withdrawals, to cover reserve losses which occur in the check clearing process, or to serve as loan funds in the case of increased customer loan demand.

In the consolidated commercial bank balance sheet, earning assets are separated into two classes: (1) loans and (2) investments. A loan is generally an individual credit transaction personally negotiated between the borrower and his bank. Loans are frequently of relatively short maturity. Often, there exists no broadly based, well-organized market for the resale of such assets. Included in the loan account are short term (a year or less) commercial loans, bankers' acceptances, brokers' loans, mortgages on residential and business property, consumer installment paper, personal and automobile loans, and loans to other financial businesses.

An investment, on the other hand, generally represents the purchase of an open-market instrument—a security for which there exists some organized trading market.* "Investments" are usually of longer maturity

---

*The existence of a "trading market" does not necessarily imply a specific geographical location, such as the New York Stock Exchange. It denotes only the ability to resell an asset to another party before maturity. Consequently, "marketability" cannot be represented by any unique measure. Clearly, the better organized the market is for a security, the larger the daily volume of trade in that security; and the more broadly based the holdings of that security are, the easier it will be to resell one's holding of such a security. This, of course, influences the price at which the security can be sold and the cost of facilitating that sale. Thus, the "marketability"

than are "loans." The investment portfolios of commercial banks include, among other things, holdings of U.S. Government securities, the securities of Federal Agencies and state and local governments, certain loans to individuals which are guaranteed by Federal Agencies, and the securities of corporations.*

This distinction between "loans" and "investments" is somewhat arbitrary, however, and by no means represents a clearcut delineation of all bank lending activity. For example, a well-organized secondary market exists for trading in F.H.A. and V.A. guaranteed mortgages. Yet these are classed as "loans." Likewise, although often there exists almost no market for the resale of the securities of some small municipalities, these securities are classed as "investments." Listed below in Table 2 are the more important components of "loans" and "investments" and their relative sizes in December 1945 and June 1970.

The other accounts in the consolidated member bank balance sheet (Table 1) should be self-explanatory. "Borrowed reserves" are the reserves borrowed from the Federal Reserve District Banks. This account does not include interbank borrowing in the Federal funds market.** Such operations involve very short-term borrowing by reserve deficient banks from banks holding excess legal reserves or from dealers specializing in these transactions. Federal funds borrowing among banks does not alter the total stock of bank reserves in the system but merely shifts reserves between banks.

The availability of interbank borrowing surely affects the behavior of banks. However, the analysis of this chapter systematically considers only reserves borrowed from the Federal Reserve System through the discount mechanism. This is the sole means by which banks may independently increase the total stock of bank reserves.

---

of an asset has been said to refer to "... the proportion of its present market value that can be realized in cash at different time intervals after the decision to sell." Basil J. Moore, *An Introduction to the Theory of Finance* (New York; The Free Press, 1968), p. 13.

*The term "investments," as employed in this chapter, refers solely to transactions in financial assets. This should not be confused with "Investment" employed in later chapters of this book to refer to purchases of newly produced capital goods—the produced means of production.

**Federal (reserve) funds are deposits in Federal Reserve Banks. As we have seen in chapter 1, the largest of these deposits are those of member commercial banks. Although large non-financial corporations, Government securities dealers and foreign banks all trade in the Federal Funds market at times, most activity in this market (approximately 80–90 percent of the total dollar volume of transactions reported) involves transactions between commercial banks. The typical transaction in this market involves an unsecured overnight loan from one commercial bank with excess legal reserves on deposit with the Federal Reserve to a reserve deficient bank.

TABLE 2

Loans and Investments of Member Banks of the Federal Reserve System

	Percent of Total Loans and Investments	
	Dec. 31, 1945	June 30, 1970
Loans:	21.3	69.4
Commercial and Industrial	8.0	26.3
Agricultural	0.9	2.7
To Brokers and Others for Purchasing or Carrying Securities	6.2	1.8
To Financial Institutions	N.A.	3.9
Real Estate	3.2	17.2
To Consumers and Individuals	1.8	15.7
Other*	1.1	1.7
Investments:	78.7	30.4
U. S. Government Securities		
Bills (initial maturity: less than one year)	18.0 ⎫	
Notes (initial maturity: one to five years)	13.3 ⎬	12.2
Bonds (initial maturity: more than five years)	41.8 ⎭	
State & Local Government Securities	3.0	15.3
Other	2.6	3.0

(Figures may not add to totals because of rounding)

*Loans to Financial Institutions are included under "Other Loans" for Dec. 31, 1945.
Source: *Federal Reserve Bulletins*, Nov. 1969 and Dec. 1970.
N.A.—Not available.

THE COMMERCIAL BANK BALANCE SHEET: II/ AN EXAMINATION OF BANK LIQUIDITY

Liquidity is a concept which applies both to individual classes of assets as well as to the entire balance sheet. In neither sense is liquidity an operationally measurable magnitude. Rather, it depends on certain generally non-quantifiable characteristics either of assets or of the collection of assets and liabilities in a balance sheet.

Most simply, the liquidity of an *asset* reflects the ease, convenience, and cost (in terms of time, specific fees and lost principal value) of converting an asset into money. For an asset held by a bank, the definition may be extended to consider the exchange of that asset for legal reserves.

The liquidity of a *balance sheet* may be defined as a measure of the ability of the individual or firm represented in that statement to meet claims presented to it for payment. For individual commercial banks, the importance of the liquidity of the balance sheet arises primarily from adverse *net* claims against a bank's cash or reserves that result from the check clearing (and currency withdrawal) process. Since a large proportion of a commercial bank's liabilities are payable on demand, balance sheet liquidity is of paramount concern.*

The ability of a bank to provide for its liquidity needs depends on various characteristics of its asset and liability portfolios, and other factors such as its loan commitments, guaranteed lines of credit, and so forth. Let us examine some of the ways in which banks may manage their asset and liability portfolios to satisfy their liquidity needs.

Asset management for liquidity purposes involves the bank in a basic dilemma. Since less liquid assets generally yield a higher interest return, banks must decide on the optimum trade-off between liquidity and profitability.** Part of the provision of bank liquidity may be effected through holding excess legal reserves. However, since these reserves yield no interest return, they are relatively costly. Consequently, the primary means of meeting liquidity needs is through the proper allocation of funds in the loan and investment accounts.

An important objective in this allocation is to insure adequate marketability. Classified as "loans" are such highly *marketable* instruments as F.H.A. and V.A. guaranteed mortgages and other very liquid assets such as callable brokers' loans and "demand" loans to other banks. In the "investment" account appear various types of Government securities (for

---

*The forces that give rise to these adverse clearings, and other sources of liquidity needs, will be examined in detail in the next section of this chapter.

**This is no simple trade-off of alternatives since the bank which is illiquid may temporarily enjoy a high-yield portfolio but is unlikely to be profitable (or in business) in the long run.

which there exist broad trading markets) that may be converted into cash very easily, with little loss in value, and at very low transactions costs.

In addition to marketability, another aspect of the loan and investment accounts affecting overall portfolio liquidity is the timing of the cash inflow from the repayment on maturing loans and securities. Banks may provide for a substantial portion of their liquidity requirements by allocating specific proportions of their loan and investment portfolios to the instruments listed above, and by arranging the inflow from maturing assets in a way that will provide for expected cash needs.

Besides direct asset management, active control of the array of liabilities and net worth is becoming increasingly important as a means of insuring liquidity for individual banks.* Demand deposits are not the only source of bank funds. Other sources of funds may suggest a less liquid configuration of assets and may be subject to more direct control by the issuing bank than deposits which are legally payable on demand.

For years regular savings and time deposit accounts were considered small but stable sources of bank funds. In the 1960's, however, banks, encouraged by the rapid growth of savings and loan associations, began actively bidding for savings and time deposits, especially through the creation of the certificate of deposit. Ironically, when the interest rates paid on these deposits hit their legal ceilings (prescribed for banks by Regulation Q of the Federal Reserve System) and depositors switched to market instruments yielding higher returns, they became as volatile a source of funds as demand deposits. This has further aggravated the liquidity problems of commercial banks and induced them to employ other means of liability management to meet their needs.

Since 1962, with the approval of the Comptroller of the Currency, large commercial banks have been issuing long-term capital notes on the national credit market just like any other business borrower. This mechanism has provided a relatively stable source of long-term funds to those banks.

Finally, as mentioned earlier, larger banks borrow reserves from other banks with excess reserves in the Federal funds market or from their overseas branches (Euro-dollars). Smaller banks borrow from the larger banks with whom they have a correspondent relationship.

These considerations indicate that in order to meet a loss of funds, rather than selling assets, a bank may instead acquire new liabilities. The Federal funds market, the newly developed markets for certificates of

---

* *See* "Bank Liquidity Reexamined," *Business Conditions*, (The Federal Reserve Bank of Chicago, 1966). Reprinted in *Innovations in Bank Management*, ed. by Paul F. Jessup (New York: Holt, Rinehart and Winston, Inc., 1969), p. 9.

deposit, the Euro-dollar market and the issuance of capital notes provide banks with an alternative to asset management in the provision of liquidity.* These innovations have recently been explored in some detail by James Pierce. As he notes, "By varying the rates they pay for Federal funds and for certificates of deposit, banks can—within limits—determine the size of their total liabilities."** We return to the problem of providing liquidity through management of assets and liabilities subsequently when we discuss the role played by excess legal reserves and bank borrowing from the Federal Reserve in portfolio management.

CONSTRAINTS ON BANK PORTFOLIO MANAGEMENT/ THE SOURCES OF COMMERCIAL BANK LIQUIDITY NEEDS

The consolidated member bank balance sheet in Table 1 provides a framework for the study of commercial bank liquidity needs as part of the more general problem of bank portfolio management. We turn now to an examination of the sources of these liquidity needs and a description of the major constraints that impinge upon commercial bank operations. These constraints originate from two primary sources: (1) the legal statutes that restrict the freedom of banks in acquiring assets and (2) the nature of the commercial banking industry.

LEGALLY REQUIRED RESERVES/ THE BASIC CONSTRAINT ON COMMERCIAL BANK EARNINGS

We shall assume that commercial banks are fundamentally profit-making organizations. Their primary business is to create claims against themselves in exchange for claims against others. They attempt to profit from the differential between the rate of return on the claims they hold and the rate they must pay on the claims they issue against themselves (after covering operating expenses).

As indicated in Table 1, demand and time deposits comprise the bulk of claims issued by commercial banks. These deposit liabilities may originate in several different ways and may be characterized as either *primary* or

----

*See "Sources of Commercial Bank Funds: An Example of 'Creative Response'," *Economic Review*, Federal Reserve Bank of Cleveland (November 1965), reprinted in the readings following Part 1.

**James L. Pierce, "Commercial Bank Liquidity," *Federal Reserve Bulletin* (August 1966), p. 1099. Dr. Pierce's article is included in the readings following Part 1.

derivative deposits. For example, through the acceptance of a primary deposit, a deposit of coin or currency, a bank (Bank A) acquires a claim against the government or the Federal Reserve in return for an increase in its deposit liabilities. The depositor exchanges high powered money (the Treasury currency or Federal Reserve Notes) for a deposit claim against the commercial bank. The effect of this transaction may be shown in terms of a T-account.*

Commercial Bank A

Assets	Liabilities
Reserves:	
Vault cash + $100	Deposit Liabilities + $100

A primary deposit then involves a transaction such as an inflow of coin or paper money which increases *both bank deposit liabilities and bank reserves.*

A derivative deposit, on the other hand, has the effect of increasing deposit liabilities but not *aggregate* bank reserves. For example, if a bank (Bank B) purchases a non-monetary earning asset through the creation of a new deposit liability, this represents an exchange of a non-monetary claim against another (a security or an I.O.U.) for a claim against itself. The T-account representing the effect of a purchase of an I.O.U. from a customer in return for a demand deposit liability is shown below:

Commercial Bank B

Assets	Liabilities
Loans + $100	Demand Deposits + $100

The difference between this transaction and the one in the preceding example is that it results in an increase in the bank's earning assets rather than an increase in its reserves. However, since banks are required to hold fractional reserves against *all* deposits, the deposit liability created in this transaction increases the total amount of legal reserves that this bank must hold.

Thus, since primary deposits increase bank reserves, banks are restricted in the expansion of their liabilities only by their ability to attract such deposits.** But since derivative deposits do not increase actual reserves, banks are seriously restricted in the purchase of earning assets through this mechanism. Deposits may be created to purchase earning assets only as

*A T-account reflects the change in a bank's balance sheet that results from a single transaction.

**When a depositor deposits a check drawn on a second bank in his account, this may be viewed as a primary deposit *for his bank*, since both deposit liabilities and his bank's total reserves increase. However, this is not a primary deposit for the banking system. Aggregate bank reserves are simply redistributed; they do not increase.

long as the bank possesses adequate reserves, since reserves will be lost when these deposits are spent and redeposited in other banks.* As a result, the total volume of deposits that may be created depends upon:

(1) the ability of a bank to attract reserves through primary deposits, and

(2) the legal reserve requirements against deposit liabilities.

For the banking system as a whole, the volume of claims that it may issue against itself will be limited by the current stock of bank reserves available and the size of the fractional reserve requirements.

CONSTRAINTS IMPOSED BY THE NATURE OF COMMERCIAL BANK DEPOSIT LIABILITIES.

The acceptance of claims against others in exchange for claims against itself is not a feature unique to the commercial bank. This is done by most other financial institutions, e.g., savings and loan associations, mutual savings banks, insurance companies, etc. For example, in the issuance of time and savings deposit claims (which are not due on demand and generally yield an interest return), the commercial bank is much like these other institutions. The unique characteristic of the commercial bank derives from the special nature of its *demand* deposit claims. Specifically, *demand* deposit claims may be readily transferred from person to person by means of checks. Consequently, these deposits serve as a medium of exchange and have come to constitute the major part of our money supply. This unique characteristic of commercial bank liabilities is a source of operational concern for individual banks. Since these *monetary* deposits are due on demand (immediately convertible into legal tender currency or bank reserves), each bank in the system must be prepared to honor requests by depositors for either the withdrawal of currency of the shift of funds to another bank (via the check clearing process). As a result, the issuance of monetary claims creates serious liquidity problems for the commercial bank. These deposit shifts and currency withdrawals are potentially highly volatile and may lead to a net loss of reserves that the bank must be able to cover.

Among the factors influencing the stock of liquid assets that a bank will hold to protect itself against net reserve losses, will be the expected size

---

*As demonstrated in chapter 1, a single bank in a multi-bank system can only create derivative deposits equal to the value of its excess reserves (assuming the total deposit is lost by the lending bank when the borrowed funds are spent).

and variability of cash and reserve drains. Any factor that increases deposit volatility may increase bank liquidity needs. Thus, fluctuations in the public's relative demand for demand deposits, currency, and other assets, as well as its expenditure and saving patterns, will influence the volume of liquid assets desired by commercial banks.

Since commercial banks issue various types of deposit liabilities each with its own very distinctive characteristics, an individual bank's liquidity needs will be influenced by the relative proportions of these deposits in its portfolio. The larger the proportion of highly active and/or erratic deposits among total bank liabilities, for example, the larger will be these desired holdings.* Inasmuch as demand deposits may be withdrawn at any time without notice, relatively large amounts of these deposits outstanding may induce commercial banks to hold a larger stock of liquid assets to insure their ability to meet potential drains. Time deposits, on the other hand, generally represent a more secure and stable source of funds to the bank, both because of the purposes for which they are employed by depositors, and because legally, the depositor can be required to present 30 days notice of his intention to withdraw funds from passbook savings accounts. Furthermore, some types of time deposits commit funds to the bank for a specified period of time, 30 days or 90 days, for example. Consequently, as a rule, *a bank's desired liquidity increases as the proportion of demand deposits in total liabilities increases*.

There are several considerations that may qualify this rule. First, since the legal reserve requirements on time and savings deposits are significantly lower than the requirements on demand deposits, a one dollar withdrawal of funds from a time or savings account lowers total required reserve balances by less than a similar withdrawal from a demand deposit account. This may induce banks to hold a greater amount of liquidity (other than legally required reserves) against time and savings deposit withdrawals than they would if equal requirements were applied to all accounts. Secondly, in practice, banks do not require time and savings depositors to give prior notice of withdrawal. They usually honor such withdrawal requests on demand. Hence, a greater volume of liquid assets are held against savings deposits than would be maintained if the 30 day notice requirement were enforced. Finally, the issuance of new types of instruments by commercial banks, such as negotiable certificates of deposit (CD's), has changed the traditional character of time deposit accounts. A large percentage of funds in these accounts are not held by the small saver, who rarely moves his funds in response to interest rate movements. Rather, the new claims have attracted large blocks of corporate funds which are highly sensitive to

*This will depend in part on the average size of individual accounts and the distribution of deposit accounts among personal, corporate, and government holders.

market interest rate variations and continually seek the highest rate of return available. As a result, a change in the open market rate (say, on Treasury bills or commercial paper) may cause a massive movement of funds out of commercial bank and other depository-type time deposits into open market instruments. Therefore, the stability once attributed to time deposits may not be characteristic of these new accounts.*

In summary, the exact influence of a bank's liability configuration on desired liquidity holdings is very difficult to predict on *a priori* grounds alone; but generally, our expectation would be that the greater the proportion of time deposit liabilities, the lower the liquidity needs of the commercial bank.

Regardless of the deposit mix of a commercial bank, the liquidity needs of that bank will be strongly influenced by its growth pattern. In general, *the greater the over-all growth (decline) of a bank's total deposit liabilities, ceteris paribus, the less (greater) need there will be to provide liquidity through asset allocation*. For example, if a bank is expanding, either because of success in competition with other banks or because all banks in its area are expanding, it will experience a net inflow of deposits, currency, and reserves. If the bank expects this trend to continue, it will come to rely on this continuous, predictable net inflow as a source of liquidity. This will reduce its need for liquidity from other sources. Conversely, if a bank is located in an area of deposit decline and continually suffers adverse clearing balances (a net loss of reserves in the check clearing process), it must prepare to meet this decline by replenishing its holdings of liquid assets through the sale of earning assets such as loans and investments. These reserve movements throughout the banking system have important implications for both seasonal and secular problems of liquidity and asset management.

Therefore, the unique character of commercial bank deposit liabilities imposes special liquidity requirements on these institutions. The extent of these liquidity requirements for any one bank will be determined by the particular configuration of its deposit liabilities and by its rate of growth or decline.

CONSTRAINTS IMPOSED BY THE NATURE OF COMMERCIAL BANK EARNING ASSETS.

The nature, size, and stability of bank *liabilities* and the pattern of "net" deposit flows are not the only constraints on commercial bank portfolio

*For an analysis of the relative volatility of private demand deposits, savings deposits, CD's, and other time deposits, *see* George R. Morrison and Richard T. Selden, *Time Deposit Growth and the Employment of Bank Funds.* Chicago: Association of Reserve City Bankers, 1965.

management. Further restrictions result from the nature of the *assets* in which these banks tend to specialize. Traditionally, commercial banks have emphasized that their role as lending institutions primarily involves the direct extension of credit to local borrowers who do not have the alternative of direct and/or easy access to the money markets. Most often, these borrowers are also the regular customers of the bank's non-lending services. These borrowers often represent the younger, growing, predominantly local business firms. Their need for bank funds may result from their inability to generate sufficient capital expansion funds internally because of their lower than average profitability levels.*

The concentration of commercial bank assets in this type of loan was temporarily reduced during World War II when the banks were called upon to supply a large share of the wartime credit needs of the Federal government. However, in the postwar era, direct loans to local businesses (and consumers) have again come to dominate bank asset portfolios. This is evidenced by the (almost) continual increase in the (loan)/(loan plus investment) ratio since 1945 (*see* Table 2, page 51). In 1945, when the extraordinarily large government financing operations ended, the average ratio for all banks was .214. By 1970, because of the trend away from market instruments to direct loans, the ratio was .694.

This specialization has provided the commercial banks with a competitive advantage in the business of direct customer loans. Furthermore, a bank's borrowing customers are most often also depositors of the bank. As a consequence, the development of a good loan relationship also represents a source of deposits and a regular inflow of funds for the bank. In order to protect this relationship and, in part, to compensate its customers for holding large demand deposit balances which yield no interest income, banks provide many technical and advisory services to their regular borrowers. Donald Hodgman has emphasized this aspect of the customer relationship. As he notes:

> The customer relationship into which a bank enters with a typical *demand deposit holder*, (original italics) especially a business firm, has many aspects. Foremost among these are: (1) the deposit itself with attendant costs and benefits to the bank, (2) an implied and often explicit obligation by the bank to make loans to the customer on terms and in amounts which vary with particular circumstances, and (3) the provision by the bank of various other financial services such as registrarships and trusteeships, specialized payroll and account collection services, and others.**

*See Roland I. Robinson, *The Management of Bank Funds* (New York: McGraw-Hill Book Company, 1962), chapter 8.

**Donald R. Hodgman, *Commercial Bank Loan And Investment Policy* (Champaign, Illinois: Bureau of Economic and Business Research, 1963), p. 99.

Consequently, as the bank cultivates local lending business, a fairly intimate relationship develops between the banker and his loan customer. The customer eventually comes to expect the banker to supply readily all his legitimate needs for credit. Therefore, if a bank desires to maintain a business firm as a "regular customer," it must generally satisfy that firm's credit requests.* This entails serious liquidity problems for the bank, however. Since the type of business to which the commercial bank makes the bulk of its loans is highly sensitive to changes in the general level of economic activity (both nationally and locally), the total demand for credit by these bank customers is highly volatile and involves wide cyclical and seasonal variations. *This forces the bank to maintain assets in some highly liquid form* (a form which can easily be converted into reserves) *to permit the extension of credit whenever customer loan demand increases.* **

In summary, then, a commercial bank is not completely free to allocate its asset portfolio so as to maximize its profits in some absolute sense. A commercial bank is subject to various restrictions in this aim. It must first satisfy legal requirements and then provide in part, at least, for the unique liquidity needs dictated by the characteristics of its asset and liability accounts.

PRIORITIES IN COMMERCIAL BANK PORTFOLIO MANAGEMENT†

The constraints on bank portfolio management outlined above suggest that commercial banks allocate their asset portfolio according to the following set of priorities: legal reserves, operating cash balances and "protective" liquid assets, customer loans and open market investments. Let us examine the implications of this set of priorities in more detail.

*Often the bank will extend a "line" of credit, whereby a customer (to smooth out his cash needs or to finance the acquisition of inventory) can have an unsecured, short-term (30 to 90 day) loan over a certain period of time up to a certain specified maximum amount.

**Banks are further constrained in their operations by a necessity to take special precautions to maintain the principal value of earning assets. This involves minimizing the probability of default and capital loss in order to insure the value of its liabilities. Thus, while the goal of bank operation is the maximization of long run earnings, commercial banks are constrained in achieving this goal by the need to guarantee the continuous *safety* as well as the *liquidity* of their asset portfolio. This places severe restrictions on the asset mix which banks may acquire. For example, the need for continuous safety to maintain a relatively constant value of the asset portfolio limits the possibilities for commercial banks to hold highly speculative but sometimes high-yielding market instruments.

†This discussion relies heavily on material presented by Roland Robinson in *The Management of Bank Funds, op. cit.* For a discussion of an alternative approach to

LEGAL RESERVES

The first priority in bank asset management is the provision of a sufficient level of reserves to satisfy the legal requirements against its outstanding deposit liabilities. The volume of reserves required is determined by the *level* of bank time and demand deposit liabilities outstanding and the size of the fractional reserve requirements set by the monetary authorities.

OPERATING CASH BALANCES
AND "PROTECTIVE" LIQUID ASSETS

The requirement that commercial banks hold a portion of their assets in a legally approved form of reserves is of little help in satisfying their liquidity needs. In as much as required reserve balances are reduced by only a small fraction of any deposit withdrawal, banks must rely on other (liquid) assets and the issue of new liabilities to meet the major part of these cash drains. (It is commonly held that legal reserve requirements were instituted to provide governmental *control* over deposit volume and the money supply rather than to provide *liquidity* to the banks.) Consequently, after the provision of *legal* reserve balances, banks still face the task of providing for their basic liquidity needs. As indicated above, these liquidity needs may be satisfied in a variety of ways. We are presently interested only in the contribution of bank asset management to that solution.

A bank may hold specific assets strictly for their liquidity characteristics, or it may attempt to arrange the maturity distribution of the total asset portfolio in order to insure a steady inflow of funds from repayment. We shall examine each of these alternatives in turn.

Three rough measures may be used in judging the liquidity characteristics of a particular credit instrument: (1) "marketability," (2) "capital certainty," and (3) date of maturity. *Marketability* refers to the existence and breadth of a regular transactions market for a particular type of investment. This clearly influences the immediate cash value that can be expected from the sale of an asset before maturity. The *capital certainty* of an asset refers to the predictability with which its expected (future) market value is anticipated. Therefore, the more easily marketable the assets held by a bank and the more certain their capital value, the more liquid the loan and investment account of that commercial bank.

The provision of liquidity through manipulation of the maturity spec-

---

the analysis of the role of liquidity in the management of bank portfolios, *see* James L. Pierce, "Commercial Bank Liquidity," *Federal Reserve Bulletin*, Board of Governors of the Federal Reserve System, Washington (August 1966). Prof. Pierce's article is reprinted following Part 1.

trum of the asset portfolio is a more difficult task. In general, the greater the average period to maturity of the earning assets held by banks, the more remote the cash inflow from repayments and the less reliable this source of liquid funds. (This generalization strictly holds only in the case of nonmarketable loans held by the bank.) On the other hand, if the maturity dates of the asset (particularly, the loan) account are rather well distributed relative to the cash needs of the bank, there will be a stream of assets "coming due," providing cash to meet the bank's needs and allowing potentially attractive reinvestment as interest rates change. The funds realized from the payments on these instruments will provide a reliable cash flow to the banks, and will reduce the desired size of the liquid asset portfolio.

Banks have come to favor various specific assets to satisfy the bulk of their liquidity needs. The safest and most "liquid" of all bank assets are the reserves that it holds in excess of its legal requirements. Deposit balances at other commercial banks are another possibility for the individual bank. (These cancel out in the consolidated balance sheet.) Holding excess reserves or bank balances, however, is also the most costly way of satisfying liquidity needs, for these balances yield no interest return. As a result, we find that banks actually hold a large proportion of their funds for "protective" purposes in the form of very short-term, highly liquid, income-earning assets such as short-term U.S. Treasury bills and callable brokers' loans. (These types of assets are generally referred to as secondary reserves.) Treasury bills, for example, yield an interest return, yet are easily saleable at a relatively stable principal value.

CUSTOMER LOANS

In terms of priorities, once the commercial bank has satisfied its legal reserve requirements, it provides for its "safety" through the allocation of sufficient funds to various liquid asset accounts. The extent of its liquidity needs will depend to a great degree on the character of its direct loan operations. These loans represent the most risky and least liquid part of the bank's asset portfolio, yet over the long run, they are also the most profitable, in part because of the deposit balances which the loan relationship attracts.* As argued above, commercial banks are most favorably equipped for direct lending to customers in a relatively narrow geographic market. Within the economy's credit structure, banks have developed a distinct competitive advantage in extending, servicing, and collecting this type of

---

*Banks sometimes *require* "compensating balances" as a condition for making a loan. These are deposits held at a lending bank by a borrower of that bank. These deposits are generally some stable proportion of the outstanding loan.

loan. They have never been well disposed to compete with insurance companies and other institutions much better suited to operate in the open market. Consequently, except in special circumstances generally dictated by the characteristics of the community in which the bank is located, the legitimate needs of the bank's customers are met before the bank resorts to the investment markets to find an outlet for its funds.

OPEN MARKET INSTRUMENTS

Although high rates of interest on open market instruments relative to the rates on direct customer loans may at times tempt commercial banks to forego direct loans in favor of investments, the long-run profitability of the bank will depend on its continuous service to its borrowing customers. The bank that puts too large a stake in open market investments will not only lose its traditional local markets and fail to develop new ones, but also will suffer a highly variable income over the long run as its fortunes rise and fall with the market.

These arguments suggest that commercial banks should invest in open market instruments only as a means of meeting their current and future liquidity needs under the second priority, "Operating Cash Balances," or as an outlet for funds seeking employment after all reasonable customer demands have been met. This prescription, however, must be modified in light of the tax advantages available to banks that invest in open market instruments. "Tax swapping," for example, arises from the fact that banks may write off net capital losses against current income while capital gains are taxed only at about one-half the corporate income tax rate. This makes it highly profitable for banks to sell securities to establish a capital loss as a write-off against income and then repurchase similar securities to recover the loss which will be taxed only as a long-term capital gain. As another example, the combination of the tax-exempt status of state and local securities and the increased banking needs of the municipalities issuing these securities, provide interesting opportunities for profitable operations with these customers (especially in attracting their deposits). The attractiveness of these opportunities is evidenced by the rapid increase in bank holdings of state and local debt in recent years (*see* Table 2).

The existence of state and local securities and of tax swapping opportunities does not invalidate our basic list of priorities. For the degree to which a bank can take advantage of the possibilities suggested above, depends to some extent upon its size, location, and sophistication. The largest banks in the financial centers perhaps conform least to our scheme. However, these institutions represent a small percentage of all banks in the system and might better be described as "financial department stores" rather than strictly "commercial banks."

This list of priorities derives primarily from the special constraints placed on bank operation. But commercial banking is a rapidly changing industry, and exceptions to the statements above will be easy to find. We have given a general description of the operating characteristics of an industry in which over one-half of the members have less than 5 *million* dollars in deposits while a few of the largest members have deposits in excess of 10 *billion* dollars. Generalizations regarding the nature of such a heterogeneous industry hardly can be considered absolute rules.

THE USE OF RESERVES IN LIQUIDITY MANAGEMENT

As indicated in an earlier section, a commercial bank may achieve its desired liquidity position by holding a variety of liquid assets, each with its own maturity characteristics, marketability and capital certainty, by proper design of the maturity distribution of its portfolio of earning assets and by active management of its liabilities. The exact degree of liquidity desired by a bank at any one time will be determined by the subjective weight the banker applies to each of the factors discussed in the previous sections of this chapter. Those factors which influence potential cash or reserve needs include: (1) the nature, size, and stability of total bank deposit liabilities; (2) the rate of growth or decline of the bank as this affects its net "deposit flow" or clearing balances; (3) the variability of its customer loan demand; and (4) the current maturity configuration of its earning asset account.

One further important influence on the desired level of bank liquidity will be the cost of maintaining that level of liquidity. *In general, total portfolio liquidity will vary inversely with the "cost" of that liquidity.* This "cost" will depend primarily on two factors: (1) the alternative cost of liquid assets; and (2) the cost of covering a deficiency in reserves by borrowing reserves or by attracting new liabilities, rather than through the sale of liquid assets. The higher the return on less liquid loans and investments, or the lower the cost of borrowing or issuing new liabilities,* the greater the cost of maintaining the liquid asset account. Therefore, as this cost increases, liquid asset holdings will be managed more closely and the desired level of liquidity will decrease.

In this section we shall focus on bank holdings of excess legal reserves and reserve borrowings. These are the measures that appear in the final money supply model presented in the previous chapter. It was demonstrated in the derivation of the money supply equation that the banks' demand for excess legal reserves and borrowings influence the actual

---

*Total bank liquidity varies *directly* with the cost of borrowing. The greater the cost of borrowing to provide reserves, the more liquidity will be maintained.

money stock. We now see that these demands are closely related to the liquidity needs of the banks. This section investigates the determinants of the commercial banks' demand for both excess legal reserves and reserve borrowing.

THE DETERMINANTS OF BANK HOLDINGS OF EXCESS RESERVES

A bank's demand for excess reserves must be examined within the context of its *total* liquidity needs. This was our motivation in discussing the factors that influence the *size* of the *total* liquid asset portfolio and in examining the priorities assigned to various asset classes by commercial banks. Given the desired *level* of liquidity as determined by these factors, the *allocation* of bank funds to holdings of excess legal reserves will depend primarily upon: (a) the alternative cost of these reserves; (b) the "penalty" rate for a required reserve deficiency; and (c) the rate of change in the level of unborrowed reserves (RU) supplied by the monetary authorities.

The Alternative Cost of Holding Excess Legal Reserves is the income foregone by not transferring these funds to income-earning liquid assets. Evidence seems to indicate that banks consider short-term U.S. Treasury bills to be the closest interest-yielding substitutes for excess reserves. Therefore, the higher the rate of return on these securities (net of transactions costs), the lower the proportion of liquid asset funds that banks may be expected to allocate to holdings of excess legal reserves.

The Cost Incurred by a Banker in Meeting a Reserve Deficiency depends upon his choice among several alternatives: he may liquidate securities, call in loans, or borrow reserves on a short-term basis, either through the Federal Funds market or from the Federal Reserve. Each of these alternatives has a specific cost associated with it. It follows then that a banker must consider the expected penalty costs of meeting reserve deficiencies by each of these means when setting his desired level of excess legal reserves. The higher the expected cost of covering a given reserve deficiency, the greater the banker's desire to avoid that cost by holding excess reserves.

The total cost of covering a deficiency by liquidating securities or calling in loans includes the earnings foregone from the loss of the security, the possible capital loss from the sale of the instrument before maturity, and any transactions costs involved. The cost of covering the deficiency by borrowing in the Federal Funds market or from the Federal Reserve is the explicit interest rate charged on borrowed funds plus any transactions costs.*

In the banking system as a whole, only the discount mechanism (borrowing from the Federal Reserve) can add to the total of system-wide reserve balances. The other alternatives simply shift reserves among banks. Considering only this alternative, the higher the discount rate (relative to the rate on short-term securities), the less willing banks will be to risk a reserve deficiency and the higher will be desired holdings of excess legal reserves.

The Rate at Which the Federal Reserve Changes the Supply of Unborrowed Reserves (or reserve requirements) will influence system-wide holdings of excess legal reserves in one of two possible ways. First, if bankers do not anticipate the changes in the level of unborrowed reserves, *actual* excess reserves will vary *directly* with these changes. It takes time for the commercial banks to adjust to a higher level of reserves, and during that period actual excess reserves will be higher than the level desired by the banks. In this case, the change in the level of unborrowed reserves may be viewed as a short-term disturbance pushing banks away from their equilibrium positions. Secondly, changes in unborrowed reserves may be anticipated by banks. In that case desired excess legal reserves will vary inversely with expected *changes* in the supply of unborrowed reserves. Thus, the effects of this factor on excess reserves are impossible to predict on *a priori* grounds alone. Only empirical information on the behavior patterns involved can supply a unique answer to this question.

Empirical tests indicate that an inverse relationship exists between bank holdings of excess legal reserve and the U.S. Treasury bill rate, and that a direct relationship exists between these reserve holdings and the Federal Reserve discount rate. While much less evidence has been presented on the third factor discussed above, the information available indicates that excess reserves tend to vary directly with changes in unborrowed reserves (adjusted for changes in reserve requirements).

THE DETERMINANTS OF COMMERCIAL BANK BORROWING

As demonstrated in the previous chapter and as emphasized above, borrowed reserves, like excess reserves, have an important influence on the supply of money. Borrowing reserves serves two primary purposes: first, it covers reserve deficiencies, as discussed immediately above; and secondly,

---

*(There may be other implicit, non-monetary costs involved in these actions, but we shall reserve consideration of these costs until the next section of this chapter.)

it may provide liquidity for short-term credit and money supply expansion. The rather high level of borrowed reserves within the banking system and the almost continuous use of this mechanism by some banks, suggests that both motives for borrowing (not necessarily mutually exclusive, of course) may be relevant to modern analysis. Figures on bank borrowing through the discount window are presented below in Table 3. These data are plotted in Figure 1.

TABLE 3

Bank borrowing in millions of dollars*

Year	Q	Value	Year	Q	Value	Year	Q	Value	Year	Q	Value
1952	I	294	1956	III	809	1961	I	85	1965	III	539
	II	503		IV	716		II	72		IV	465
	III	931					III	52			
	IV	1391	1957	I	627		IV	106	1966	I	477
				II	975					II	674
1953	I	1286		III	970	1962	I	76		III	753
	II	844		IV	775		II	77		IV	634
	III	512					III	99			
	IV	428	1958	I	277		IV	163	1967	I	317
				II	130					II	119
1954	I	194		III	279	1963	I	142		III	89
	II	147		IV	490		II	189		IV	166
	III	82					III	324			
	IV	166	1959	I	555		IV	339	1968	I	423
				II	788					II	707
1955	I	377		III	956	1964	I	273		III	535
	II	421		IV	896		II	246		IV	587
	III	714					III	310			
	IV	913	1960	I	785		IV	327	1969	I	813
				II	510					II	1268
1956	I	866		III	302	1965	I	373		III	1169
	II	933		IV	126		II	501		IV	1154

*Quarterly averages of monthly figures, from Federal Reserve Bulletins

Historically, each of the theories put forward to explain bank borrowing has tended to emphasize one possible motive for bank borrowing to the exclusion of all others. The most important theories presented in this discussion fall under two basic categories: (1) the "profit" theory, and (2) the "needs and reluctance" theory.

The profit theory of commercial bank borrowing holds that bankers (consistent with a profit-maximizing assumption) borrow from the Federal Reserve Banks whenever a profit can be made from the borrowed funds. This occurs whenever a positive differential sufficiently large to overcome transactions costs exists between the market loan rate and the discount

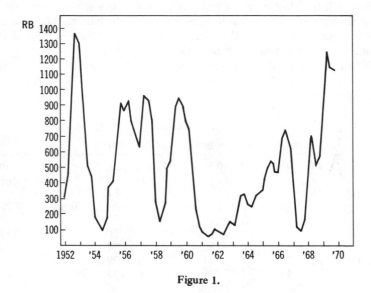

Figure 1.

rate. When such a favorable differential exists, the profit theory postulates that banks capitalize on the potential net returns by increasing loans with borrowed funds.

The "needs and reluctance" theory, on the other hand, holds that bankers are averse to being in debt to the Federal Reserve and borrow funds only when unexpected cash drains force such action. A convincing case for the needs and reluctance theory was presented by W. W. Riefler in the early 1920s.* He claimed that if the profit theory were indeed the true explanation of bank borrowing behavior, this would imply near equality between the discount rate and the market loan rate. If the profit motive were the overriding influence on bank borrowing decisions, whenever the market rate was above the discount rate, an increase in the supply of loans supported by borrowed reserves would lower the market rate until it approached the discount rate and eliminated the profit differential. Since his tests failed to demonstrate this equality, Riefler concluded that the profit theory was an inferior explanation of bank borrowing.

Let us further investigate the implications of these hypotheses. Consider the Federal Reserve's stated position on this matter as reflected in Regulation A of the Board of Governors:**

*W. W. Riefler, *Money Rates and Money Markets in the United States* (New York: Harper and Bros., 1930).

**For a discussion of the suggested revisions in the rules governing the operation of the discount mechanism *see Federal Reserve Bulletin*, July 1968, and Robert C. Holland and George Garvey "The Redesigned Discount Mechanism and The Money Market," Research Paper, Board of Governors of the Federal Reserve System, 1968.

Federal Reserve credit is generally extended on a short term basis to a member bank in order to enable it to adjust its asset position when necessary because of *developments such as a sudden withdrawal of deposits or seasonal requirements for credit beyond those which can reasonably be met by use of the bank's own resources. . . .* (italics added) Under ordinary conditions, the continuous use of Federal Reserve credit by a member bank over a considerable period of time is not regarded as appropriate. . . . It (the district Reserve bank) considers whether the (commercial) bank is borrowing principally for the purpose of obtaining a tax advantage or profiting from rate differentials and whether the bank is extending an undue amount of credit for the speculative carrying of or trading in securities, real estate, or commodities, or otherwise.* (parentheses added)

Obviously the Federal Reserve does not *intend* to be in the business of lending reserves to member banks at a rate of interest below the market rate simply to provide these banks with an opportunity to profit from the differential. Now, as a direct test of the Riefler hypothesis, consider the spread between the market rates and the discount rate. The discount rate, while often above the Treasury bill rate, has almost invariably been below the rate on longer-term instruments, such as long-term government bonds, or the rate on commercial bank loans. The pattern formed by these rates over the period since 1952 is shown in Figure 2. The relations between rates evident in Figure 2 should not be unexpected, however, since the Federal Reserve does not rely solely on the discount rate to control the flow of borrowing. As indicated by Regulation A, and as evident from an examination of the operation of the discount window, at least some reliance is placed upon administrative "moral suasion" and the power of the loan officer to refuse or discourage loans. Therefore, this test is not completely appropriate. In summary, although the monetary authorities personally discourage banks from borrowing strictly for profit purposes, neither their attitude nor the persistence of a variable differential between the discount rate and the market loan rate is sufficient to falsify the hypothesis that banks periodically use the discount mechanism for such purposes. In fact, the very existence of Regulation A suggests that such borrowing is probably attempted.

* This issue remains unresolved when we view borrowing from the commercial bank's side of the discount window. For many depositors, especially larger business and financial depositors, are critical of bank borrowing since, in case of insolvency, creditors' claims take precedence over the claims of depositors.** Thus a bank with large and continuous balances

---

*Board of Governors of the Federal Reserve System, *The Federal Reserve System: Purposes and Functions* (Washington, D.C., 1963), page 43.

**This is particularly important only to depositors with deposits larger than the maximum insured by the F.D.I.C., i.e., $20,000.00. The importance of customer attitudes on certain aspects of bank management is also stressed by Donald Hodgman in his discussion of commercial bank portfolio ratios. (Footnote continued on page 71.)

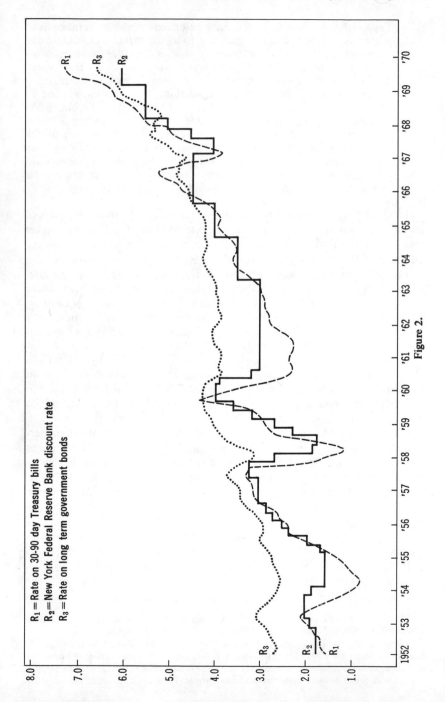

R₁ = Rate on 30-90 day Treasury bills
R₂ = New York Federal Reserve Bank discount rate
R₃ = Rate on long term government bonds

Figure 2.

due to the Federal Reserve runs the risk of alienating some of its more conservative depositors. Furthermore, since the Federal Reserve is in the position of performing certain services for the commercial banks, the rather personal way in which the discount window is administered will insure that banks avoid abuse of the discount privilege so as not to jeopardize the availability of those services. In short, besides the nominal discount rate to be paid on borrowings, there are other real costs to the banker of having large balances outstanding with the Federal Reserve. Hence, even if we know that the discount rate is below the market loan rate, if the "needs and reluctance" theory has any validity at all, the nonmonetary costs incurred by the bank in borrowing reserves makes it impossible to judge whether the *total* real cost of that borrowing is actually above or below the market loan rate. The discount rate by itself, then, is probably best viewed as a measure of the variation in the total cost of borrowing rather than as a complete measure of the entire real cost of such action.

What, then, is the true role of the discount mechanism? Although the evidence fails to discredit the needs and reluctance thesis, there are strong indications that a rational banker will at times use this mechanism, to the extent possible within the framework specified by the attitudes of the Federal Reserve authorities, to increase his profit or decrease his cost. Thus, while somewhat reluctant to use the discount privilege for outright profiteering, for fear of incurring reprisals from the authorities or from his own customers, the commercial banker will borrow when this is the cheapest way of covering a reserve shortage (considering *all real costs* involved). He may even remain in debt for some time rather than repay the advances immediately at the cost of giving up the chance to make a profitable loan. In short, although reluctance may prevent the banker from borrowing from the Federal Reserve every time a profit opportunity presents itself (and thus prevents the equality between the real cost of borrowing and the market loan rate), we cannot conclude that this prevents him from *selective* use of the discount mechanism for profit purposes.*

No bank's management feels comfortable when its key balance sheet ratios get too far out of line with those of other banks regarded as comparable in size and character. Apart from the questions such discrepancies may raise regarding other managements' conflicting assessments of the uncertain future, there are likely to be pressures generated by the inquiries of treasurers of large corporate depositors, investment advisory services, and other individuals whose good opinion is important to the welfare of the individual bank. Bankers do not permit the judgment of such influential outsiders to substitute for their own, but they are forced to concede it some weight or risk adverse comment . . . or even adverse action such as transfer of important deposit accounts to competitors.

Hodgman, *op. cit.*, p. 8.

*Reform and modification of the discount "privilege" has been actively considered by the Federal Reserve for several years. Essentially, the proposed changes would extend to member banks (1) a basic borrowing right, (2) an emergency

If our hypothesis, which includes elements of both traditional theories, is correct, two related sets of factors will influence commercial bank borrowing: first, any forces that affect and modify the bank's basic reluctance to borrow; and secondly, the determinants of the relative cost and profitability of that borrowing. Among the first set of influences, we may list the following factors which could unexpectedly reduce liquid asset accounts below some critical level and thus weaken the reluctance to borrow: (a) adverse changes in total reserve balances or required reserve levels caused by Federal Reserve policy actions; or (b) adverse clearing balances and changes in required reserve levels caused by changes in the public's asset preferences. Since borrowing to cover reserve shortages or to restore liquid asset positions to desired levels after an unexpected change caused by any of the above factors is generally considered a "legitimate" use of the discount mechanism, we would expect that commercial banks, though generally reluctant to borrow, would not hesitate to employ this means to meet such needs.

The extent to which the banks will use the discount mechanism under the above circumstances will depend on the second set of factors: the cost and profit characteristics of the liquid asset alternatives open to the bank. While an unexpected shift of funds from time deposits to demand deposits, for example, would weaken the reluctance to borrow by increasing required reserves, decreasing excess reserves and possibly causing a reserve deficiency, we cannot assign any automaticity to the borrowing decision. The banks will have to consider not simply the direct (real) costs of borrowed funds but also the cost of all alternatives. The possibility of selling securities, for example, introduces the U. S. Treasury bill rate as an alternative cost.

In short, then, we may expect the demand for borrowed reserves by commercial banks to be determined by the following factors: the discount rate and the bill rate, or the relation between the two; Federal Reserve changes in the supply of unborrowed reserves (or reserve requirements); and the stability of the public's asset preferences.*

---

means to deal with large clearing drains, and (3) a seasonal borrowing privilege. For a review of the issues involved in the current debate on the discount mechanism, *see* David M. Jones, "A Review of Recent Academic Literature on the Discount Mechanism," Fundamental Reappraisal of the Discount Mechanism, Project #9, Board of Governors of the Federal Reserve System, February 1968, and "Reappraisal of the Federal Reserve Discount Mechanism," Board of Governors of the Federal Reserve System, *Federal Reserve Bulletin*, July 1968, pp. 545–551.

*Some authors have also emphasized the degree of surveillance of the Federal Reserve over the discount window as a determining factor of commercial bank borrowing. *See* Stephen M. Goldfeld and Edward J. Kane, "The Determinants of Member Bank Borrowing: An Econometric Study," *Journal of Finance*, Vol. 21 (Sept. 1966), pp. 499–514.

CONCLUSION

We have presented an analysis of commercial bank portfolio behavior, focusing on the constraints of bank operation which lead to a specific set of priorities for the management of bank funds. Within this priority listing, we have concentrated on the specific problem of bank liquidity management and the role played by excess legal reserves and borrowed reserves in the solution of this problem. The factors that determine the desired volume of excess legal reserves and borrowed reserves are doubly important because of their subsequent influence on the money supply. The way in which these factors may potentially influence the level of and changes in the level of the money supply was seen in chapter 1.

Questions/ *chapter 2*

1. How would you characterize the type of businesses that rely most heavily on loans from commercial banks to finance their operations? Does a bank's specialization in this kind of loan cause any problems? Explain.

2. If an individual bank finds itself short of reserves, it can borrow the needed reserves for a short period of time either from other banks through the Federal Funds Market or directly from the Federal Reserve. Historical data indicate that the rate of interest on Federal funds is generally several percentage points *above* the Federal Reserve discount rate. Yet banks often borrow in that market rather than at the discount window. Explain why this is so.

3. Relate the analysis of this chapter to the models developed in chapter 1 by explaining the effects that increased volatility in bank demand deposits would have on the money supply.

4. In addition to "profit" and "reluctance" as important factors in the explanation of commercial bank borrowing, some writers include a third factor: the degree of surveillance of bank borrowing patterns at the discount window of the Federal Reserve. Explain how this factor would affect the volume of bank borrowing and the influence this may have on the money stock.

5. Given the premises about bank portfolio behavior outlined in this chapter, what effects do you think the Federal Reserve regulation allowing banks to count their vault cash as part of their legal reserves had upon bank excess reserve holdings and on their liquidity management in general? (*See* Milton Friedman, "Vault Cash and Free Reserves," *Journal of Political Economy*, Vol. 69, April 1961).

6. Several authors have suggested abolishing the discount mechanism. Relate the bank borrowing "privilege" to the last model developed in chapter 1 and explain why some people might feel that this mechanism weakens the monetary authorities' ability to control the money supply.

Bibliography/ *chapter 2*

Board of Governors of the Federal Reserve System, "Reappraisal of the Federal Reserve Discount Mechanism," *Federal Reserve Bulletin* (July 1968), pp. 545-551.

Bowsher, Norman M., "Excess Reserves," *Federal Reserve Bank of St. Louis, Review*, Vol. 45 (April 1963), pp. 11-15.

_____ , "Bank Loans and Investments 1951-1963," *Federal Reserve Bank of St. Louis Review*, Vol. 45 (October 1963), pp. 3-7.

Brechling, F. P. R. and **George Clayton**, "Commercial Banks' Portfolio Behavior," *Economic Journal*, Vol. 75 (June 1955), pp. 290-316.

Carson, Deane and **Ira Scott**, "Commercial Bank Attributes and Aversion to Risk," *Banking and Monetary Studies*, edited by Deane Carson. Homewood, Illinois: Richard D. Irwin, 1963, pp. 420-433.

Cohen, Jacob, "What Do Bank Loans Really Finance," *Banking and Monetary Studies*, edited by Deane Carson. Homewood, Illinois: Richard D. Irwin, 1963, pp. 387-407.

Cooper, J. L., "Continuous Borrowing From the Federal Reserve System: Some Empirical Evidence," *Journal of Finance*, Vol. 24 (March 1969), pp. 33-48.

Federal Reserve Bank of Cleveland, "Sources of Commercial Bank Funds: An Example of 'Creative Response'," *Federal Reserve Bank of Cleveland Economic Review* (November 1965).

Goldfeld, Stephen M., *Commercial Bank Behavior and Economic Activity*. Amsterdam: North Holland Publishing Company, 1966.

Goldfeld, Steven M. and **Edward J. Kane**, "The Determinants of Member

Bank Borrowing: An Econometric Study," *Journal of Finance*, Vol. 21 (September 1966), pp. 499-514.

Guttentag, Jack M. and **Richard G. Davis**, "Compensating Balances," *Essays in Money and Credit*, Federal Reserve Bank of New York, 1964.

Hester, Donald D. and **J. F. Zoellner**, "The Relation Between Bank Portfolios and Earnings: An Econometric Analysis," *Review of Economics and Statistics*, Vol. 48 (November 1966), pp. 372–386.

Hodgman, Donald R., "The Deposit Relationship and Commercial Bank Investment Behavior," *Review of Economics and Statistics*, Vol. 43 (August 1961), pp. 257–268.

——, *Commercial Bank Loans and Investment Policy.* Champaign, Illinois: University of Illinois Bureau of Economic and Business Research, 1963.

Jessup, Paul F., ed., *Innovations in Bank Management.* New York: Holt, Rhinehart and Winston, Inc. 1969.

Jones, David M., "A Review of Recent Academic Literature on the Discount Mechanism," Fundamental Reappraisal of the Discount Mechanism, Project #9, Board of Governors of the Federal Reserve System, (February, 1968).

Luttrell, C. B., "Member Bank Borrowing, Its Origin and Function," *Quarterly Review of Economics and Business*, Vol. 8 (Autumn 1968), pp. 55–66.

Malkiel, Burton G. and **Edward J. Kane**, "Bank Portfolio Allocation, Deposit Variability and the Availability Doctrine," *Quarterly Journal of Economics*, Vol. 79 (February 1965), pp. 113–134.

Moore, Basil J., *An Introduction to the Theory of Finance* (New York: The Free Press, 1968)

Morrison, George, "Liquidity Preferences of Commercial Banks," Doctoral Dissertation, University of Chicago, 1963. Unpublished.

Pierce, James, "Commercial Bank Liquidity," *Federal Reserve Bulletin* (August 1966), pp. 1093-1101.

Robinson, Roland I., *The Management of Bank Funds* (New York: McGraw-Hill Book Company, 1962).

Russell, William R. "Commercial Bank Portfolio Adjustments," *American Economic Review, Papers and Proceedings*, Vol. 54 (May 1964), pp. 544–553.

READINGS/ *part 1*

MONEY SUPPLY

Introduction to Readings / *part 1*

In chapter 1, we specified an analytical framework that may be employed to examine the behavior of the public, commercial banks, and the monetary authorities, as this behavior relates to the determination of the size of the money stock. In chapter 2, one of the critical elements in that process—the portfolio behavior of commercial banks—was studied in greater detail. The following readings extend the material of these chapters into some specific areas relevant to recent controversies in monetary policy.

The first two readings use the kind of models developed in chapter 1 to examine the desirability and feasibility of policies that direct the monetary authority to control actively the size or growth rate of the money stock. George Kaufman's article reviews the recommendation of the Joint Economic Committee of Congress that the Federal Reserve ". . . undertake to attain growth in the money supply at an annual rate of between two and six percent." Kaufman briefly considers some of the potential problems implicit in such a policy and their probable effects on the Federal Reserve's traditional objective of maintaining orderly financial markets.

The second article, by David I. Fand, addresses a similar problem in greater detail. Fand briefly surveys the money supply theories which form the basis of recent empirical work in this field and examines the implications of these theories for the use of the money stock as an instrument of stabilization policy. In analyzing this problem, Fand raises important questions about the speed of the statistical feedback determining the length of the time period required for the monetary authority to determine accurately the size of the monetary stock.

The next two articles in this section deal with some disputed issues raised in chapter 2. The article published by the Federal Reserve Bank of Cleveland describes the innovative response of commercial banks to the changed money-market conditions of the 1960s. In particular, it examines the creation of CD's as an innovation in portfolio management elicited by the necessity for commercial banks to remain competitive in the markets for borrowed funds.

In the final article, James L. Pierce examines some of the difficulties in measuring bank liquidity. He questions the focus of portfolio analysts on certain commonly employed asset/liability ratios as measures of bank liquidity positions. New techniques developed by banks—such as endogenous deposit creation through CD's and other instruments—require a rethinking of the traditional means of measuring the liquidity of commercial bank portfolios. Pierce suggests that an appropriate gauge of liquidity must consider, in addition to the usual elements discussed in chapter 2, the time dimension with respect to selling an asset.

1/ GEORGE G. KAUFMAN

Proposed Experiment In Monetary Policy

A bold new experiment in monetary policy has been proposed by the Joint Economic Committee of the Congress. In a report issued recently, the Committee suggests that the Federal Reserve System undertake to attain growth in the money supply at an annual rate of between two and six percent.[1] The Committee believes that this range centers on the estimated long-run growth potential of the U.S. economy. Money supply growth greater than four percent is recommended when the economy is expanding at less than its potential, and less than four percent when prices are rising rapidly.

The Committee's recommendations represent a sharp break with traditional conduct of monetary policy in the U.S. or elsewhere in the world. Central banks historically have directed monetary policy mainly at attaining fairly stable conditions in financial markets, that is, moderating fluctuations in interest rates. Shifting primary emphasis from changes in interest rates to changes in the supply of money could reasonably be expected to result in greater short-run swings in interest rates.

The view that money and economic activity are closely related is an old one in economics. Even before Adam Smith, abrupt changes in prices were noted to be accompanied more often than not by abrupt changes in the amount of money in circulation. This observation led to the general view that a change in the supply of money induced a proportionate change in the price level in the same direction. Through the passage of

Reprinted from *Financial Analysts' Journal*, November–December 1968, pp. 90-93 by permission of the author and the publisher. George G. Kaufman is Professor of Finance at the University of Oregon.

[1] *Standards for Guiding Monetary Action*, Report of the Joint Economic Committee, Congress of the United States, 1968.

time this view was modified to recognize that changes in the amount of money affect aggregate levels of production of goods and services as well as prices and that people vary the intensity with which they use money to purchase goods and services. As a consequence, a change in money was no longer considered to result in a strictly proportionate change in prices. Nevertheless, the amount of money in circulation continued to hold a prominent position in explaining changes in economic activity. In large measure because of its relative simplicity, the quantity theory of money has attracted a significant number of proponents.

In proposing that the supply of money be the primary guide to monetary policy, the Committee had to consider a number of important questions:

1. What is money?
2. Does the Federal Reserve System have the ability to control the amount of money?
3. How close is the relationship between the amount of money and economic activity?
4. To what extent are the monetary officials constrained in their policy actions by considerations other than economic activity?

WHAT IS MONEY

Although money is an everyday word in nearly everyone's vocabulary, everyone is not agreed on its definition. Generally, money is used to designate instruments commonly used as means of payment. Traditionally, money includes coin, currency and demand deposits at commercial banks. But these are not necessarily equally good means of payment at all times. One may encounter difficulty in buying a daily newspaper with a $100 bill or in paying for even a small purchase by check in a store in which one is not known. In addition, there are financial assets such as savings deposits, savings and loan shares and U.S. savings bonds which, although they do not serve as generally accepted media of exchange, are quickly convertible into coin, currency or demand deposits. Some would include one or more of these in their concept of what constitutes money.

In proposing money as a guide to policy, it is necessary to be specific with respect to its definition. Changes in the amounts of the various financial assets do not always follow the same patterns (Table 1). The Committee has accepted the most commonly used measure of money— coin, currency and demand deposits other than those of the U.S. Government.

TABLE 1

Quarterly Changes in Selected Measures of Money Supply
1966 I–1968 II
(percent, seasonally adjusted annual rate)

Quarter	M_1	M_2	M_3	M_4
1966 I	6.4	8.0	9.2	8.4
II	4.4	8.0	7.6	6.0
III	−0.8	4.0	6.8	2.8
IV	0.4	0.8	1.6	4.8
1967 I	3.6	9.2	8.4	5.6
II	6.0	11.2	9.6	6.8
III	10.0	12.8	12.4	6.8
IV	4.8	8.0	11.2	9.6
1968 I	4.4	6.0	8.0	9.6
I1	7.2	6.0	5.6	5.6
Average	4.6	7.4	8.0	6.6

M_1 = Coin, currency and demand deposits
M_2 = M_1 + time deposits at commercial banks
M_3 = Bank credit
M_4 = Federal Reserve liquid assets series

CONTROL OF THE MONEY SUPPLY

The amount of money outstanding at any time is dependent both on the amount of assets the public wants to hold as money and on the actions of the Federal Reserve System and the commercial banks. Since money does not include all financial assets, the public can readily shift back and forth between, say, demand deposits and time deposits. Financial assets other than coin, currency and demand deposits typically provide an interest return. As interest rates on the different types of financial assets change, the public tends to reshuffle its liquid assets so as to maximize the over-all return in value. The higher the yield obtainable on money substitutes, the weaker is the incentive to hold money. The amount of money the public wants to hold also is determined by its income; the greater income, the greater is the need for money balances. Therefore, the public's demand for money balances changes through time in response to changes in its income and the return available on interest bearing financial assets.

The amount of money outstanding is affected also by factors influencing its supply. The most important of these is the total amount of reserves available to member commercial banks. This amount is determined by the Federal Reserve System. To a lesser extent, the amount of demand deposits (the major component of the money supply) is affected by the actions of the commercial banks. Many banks prefer to hold some reserves in excess to those legally required and the amount of these excess reserves may change. When banks change their holdings of excess reserves, they simultaneously change their total loans and investments and consequently their deposits. Generally banks tend to hold only minimal amounts of excess reserves since they produce no income. However, because the amount of income sacrificed as a result of holding excess reserves varies with interest rates, banks hold somewhat more excess reserves when interest rates are low.

As a result of the independent behavior of the public and the banks, a given amount of total reserves provided by the Federal Reserve may be consistent with a large range of different money supplies. Thus, to control the supply of money, the Federal Reserve would need to predict the behavior of the public and the banks. With the present state of knowledge, this is difficult and the results are far from perfect. Nevertheless, the Committee believes it is easier to forecast changes in the forces affecting the supply of money than in the forces affecting interest rates. Consequently, it concludes that "the capacity of the monetary authority to achieve a chosen pattern of interest rates is . . . substantially less than its control over the supply of money or of bank credit." Moreover, "in normal times and with few exceptions, the Federal Reserve could . . . reach with reasonable accuracy any given preferred level of money supply."

Prediction of the forces affecting the money supply is even more difficult the shorter the time period in which it is desired to achieve a specified money supply and the results poorer. The financial markets are consistently buffeted by many types of short-run disturbances reflecting sizable changes in both the demand and supply for money. Some of these forces are seasonal and can be forecasted with reasonable precision. For example, credit demands typically rise before major holidays. At the same time, the public increases its preference for currency to finance holiday spending and travel. Households and business firms also increase their borrowings in preparation of income tax payments. Other forces are less regular and more difficult to project. The U. S. Treasury and major business firms sell large amounts of new securities at irregular intervals. Furthermore, balances held by the Treasury are excluded from the traditional definition of the money supply. These balances are typically highly volatile and the shift of deposits from private to Treasury ownership and vice-versa results in wide fluctuations in the money supply.

Even if completely predictable, these forces produce sharp short-term fluctuations in interest rates which may discourage maximum use of these markets. Since a smoothly functioning financial market is a requisite for an efficient transfer of funds from savers to investors, dampening of abrupt changes in interest rates is a generally accepted objective of central

bank policy. For this reason, the Committee does not impose limits on
short-run changes in the money supply. Instead, it recommends that the
Federal Reserve undertake to restrict changes in the money supply, on the
average, to within the prescribed range on a quarter-to-quarter basis.

MONEY AND INCOME

The Committee is least sure of itself in describing the relationship between
money and income. While it believes that "a steadily growing economy
with stable prices was likely to be best assisted by a comparable steady
growth of money supply," it recognizes that the inverse does not necessarily follow. "To say that steady growth in the money supply is a necessary
condition for the maintenance of general economic stability and growth is,
however, not to say that a policy of creating steady growth in the money
supply will be sufficient to induce steady growth in the economy."

This uncertainty reflects the lack of persuasive evidence available on
the precise characteristics of the relation between the amount of money
and economic activity. The Committee notes that "the least satisfactory

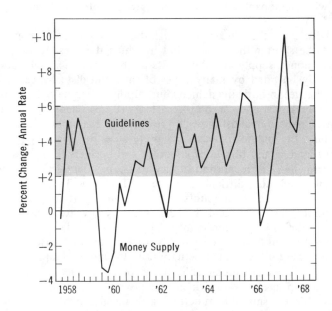

Figure 1. Quarterly Changes in Money Supply 1958–1968

aspect of the problem was that neither the monetary authority itself nor the private witnesses were able to outline in any but the most general terms the manner in which the credit flow generated a flow of real output over time."

The evidence and views presented to the Committee by economists and others was largely contradictory. Some witnesses argued that there was no strong or regular relation between the amount of money and levels of economic activity, others reported the existence of a strong correlation between the two, while still a third group testified that, while the relationship may not always be close, abrupt changes in the amount of money are closely related with succeeding abrupt changes in income, prices, or both.

By proposing a range which restricts abrupt changes in the growth of the money supply but permits more moderate changes, the Committee appears to have embraced the third view. If it had accepted the first view, it would not have proposed a money supply guide. If it had espoused the views of the second group, it would have proposed a steady and unchanging rate of monetary growth.

OTHER CONSTRAINTS

While the primary objective of monetary policy is to affect aggregate levels of economic activity, "it is clear ... that the monetary authority, in adhering to some policy rule—for example, of steady growth of money supply—cannot wholly ignore the side effects of such a policy on interest rates." Changes in interest rates tend to have differential impacts on different sectors of the economy. In particular, the Committee notes "the monetary authority cannot be indifferent if its policy threatens to create such stringency that the mortgage and municipal bond markets verge on collapse. Nor can it ignore the deterioration of monetary contracts in any important market." The Federal Reserve also has an obligation to "maintain the quality of the Federal Government's debt."

Consideration of these objectives may at times constrain the Federal Reserve System from undertaking changes in the supply of money directed solely at final levels of production and prices. In recognition, the Committee provides leeway for the System to operate outside the proposed two to six percent range but requires that the reasons for any such divergences be reported promptly to Congress.

STATUS OF THE RECOMMENDATIONS

The Joint Economic Committee was created by the Employment Act of 1946 and consists of 20 members, an equal number from both the House of Representatives and the Senate. The Act spelled out for the first time the economic responsibilities of the Federal Government. Among other things, these include providing conditions conducive to "maximum employment, production and purchasing power." The President was instructed to transmit an annual economic report to Congress describing his economic program. A Council of Economic Advisors was created to assist and advise the President in this responsibility. The Joint Economic Committee was established to study matters relating to the report, assist other committees of Congress and conduct hearings and make recommendations on economic developments.

The Committee's recommendations are just that, recommendations. The Committee is not empowered to initiate legislation. Nevertheless, the Committee has over the years attracted dedicated members and its reports have earned the respect of Congress. Its recommendations, therefore, cannot be dismissed lightly.

Adherence to the proposed guide presumably would have resulted in somewhat different monetary policy in recent years. Quarter-to-quarter changes in the money supply have been outside the two to six percent range almost 40 percent of the time since 1957 (Figure 1). Of these, rates of growth less than two percent occurred in 12 quarters and rates of growth in excess of six percent in four quarters—all after 1964. Slower rates of monetary growth in the latter periods most likely would have resulted in immediately higher rates of interest and intensified pressures on the money, capital and mortgage markets. However, to the extent the slower rates of growth may have restrained demand and tempered inflationary pressures, lower interest rates may have resulted eventually. Unfortunately, the rudimentary state of current knowledge in economics does not permit more positive statements of the precise effects of alternative policies to be made with great certainty.

Despite the lack of general agreement on many issues, the Joint Economic Committee feels that the Federal Reserve System should subject the proposed guide or some modification thereof to operational testing. In economics, controlled laboratory experiments are not possible and new ideas can only be tested operationally. Operational tests of alternative policy actions involve considerable risk of inflicting, at best, temporary damage on the economy without guaranteeing that the results of the experiment even can be measured accurately. It is the opinion of the Committee that there exists sufficient knowledge to justify taking these risks in the search for means of improving the economic performance of the country.

2/ DAVID I. FAND

Can the Central Bank Control the Nominal Money Stock?

The money stock at any moment in time is the result of portfolio decisions by the central bank, by the commercial banks, and by the public (including the nonbank intermediaries):[1] the central bank determines the amount of high-powered money or monetary base, that is, currency plus bank reserves, that it will supply;[2] the commercial banks determine the volume of loans and other assets that they will acquire and the quantity of reserves they will hold as excess (and free) reserves; and the public determines how

Reprinted with permission of the author and the publisher from the Federal Reserve Bank of St. Louis *Review*, January 1970. David Fand is Professor of Economics at Wayne State University.

[1] For a discussion of the determinants of the money stock see M. Friedman and A. Schwartz, *A Monetary History of the U.S. 1867-1960* (Princeton, 1963), Appendix B on "Proximate Determinants of the Nominal Stock of Money"; P. Cagan, *Determinants and Effects of Changes in the Stock of Money 1875-1960* (Columbia, 1965), Chapter I on "The Money Stock and Its Three Determinants"; K. Brunner, "A Schema for the Supply Theory of Money," *International Economic Review*, January 1961; D. Fand, "Some Implications of Money Supply Analysis," *American Economic Review*, May 1967.

[2] The high-powered money concept used by M. Friedman, A. Schwartz and P. Cagan is essentially the monetary base concept used by K. Brunner, A. Meltzer, and others. The monetary base may be defined either in terms of the sources (Federal Reserve credit, gold stock, Treasury items, etc.) or *uses* (member bank reserves and currency). To compare movements in the monetary base over time, we need to make a correction for changes in reserve requirements. As used here, the monetary base includes a reserve adjustment; that is, it is equal to the source base plus the reserve adjustment.

For a very clear exposition see L. Andersen and J. Jordan, "The Monetary Base— Explanations and Analytical Use" in the August 1968 issue of the St. Louis Federal Reserve Bank *Review*.

to allocate their holdings of monetary wealth among currency, demand, time and savings deposits, CD's, intermediary claims, and other financial assets. The money stock that emerges reflects all these decisions.

It is a natural question to consider whether the central bank, by controlling the monetary base, can actually achieve fairly precise control over the money stock. This depends on whether the link between the monetary base and bank reserves, and between bank reserves and the money stock (the *monetary base—bank reserves—money stock* linkage) is fairly tight and therefore predictable. If there is a tight linkage the monetary authorities can formulate their policies and achieve any particular target for the money stock; on the other hand, if there is significant and unpredictable slippage, and the central bank control over the money stock is not sufficiently precise to achieve a given target, it will necessarily have to formulate its policies in terms of other variables that it can control. The variable used to express (or define) the central bank's objective, or to implement its policy decisions, must therefore be one that it can control within reasonable limits.[3]

The recently recurring idea that the money stock is perhaps best viewed as an endogenous variable, although not a new idea (it would have been acceptable to "real bill" theorists), has received new and powerful support from those who follow the "New View" approach in monetary economics.[4] New View theorists have questioned the validity of much of classical monetary theory concerning the importance of money relative to other liquid assets, the uniqueness of commercial banks relative to other intermediaries, and the extent to which the central bank can control the nominal money stock.[5] They argue that the central bank can control

[3]It is presumably for this reason that some models treat unborrowed reserves as the policy variable (the practice followed in the FRB–MIT model and other econometric models). These model builders believe that some components of the monetary base, and perhaps the entire base, behave as endogenous variables—as the variables that respond to income changes, and are not directly (or completely) under the control of the central bank. They do believe that the Federal Reserve can control the volume of unborrowed reserves.

[4]For the development of the New View see J. Gurley and E. Shaw, *Money in a Theory of Finance* (Brookings, 1959); D. Fand, "Intermediary Claims and the Adequacy of Our Monetary Controls" and J. Tobin, "Commercial Banks as Creators of 'Money,'" in D. Carson (ed), *Banking and Monetary Studies* (Irwin, 1963); H. Johnson, *Essays in Monetary Economics* (Allen and Unwin, 1967), Chapters 1 and 2; W. Brainard, "Financial Intermediaries and a Theory of Monetary Control," in D. Hester and J. Tobin (eds.), *Financial Markets and Economic Activity* (Wiley, 1967); and K. Brunner, "The Role of Money and Monetary Policy," in the July 1968 issue of the St. Louis Federal Reserve Bank *Review*.

[5]Tobin offers the following description of the New View: "A more recent development in monetary economics tends to blur the sharp traditional distinctions between money and other assets and between commercial banks and other financial intermediaries; to focus on demands for and supplies of the whole spectrum of assets

its instruments (open market operations, reserve requirements, discount rate) and some money market variables (free reserves, Treasury bill rate); that the commercial banks supply deposits at a fixed rate; and that the stock of money and liquid assets which emerge—at least in the short-run—largely reflect the public's preference for demand and time deposits, intermediary claims, and other financial assets.[6]

Two schools of monetary economics differ on the use of the money stock as an indicator or target variable, and on the extent to which it is an endogenous variable and therefore not available to the monetary authorities as a stabilization instrument. The *nonmonetarists* believe that the central bank should formulate its policies in terms of money market variables and implement them through operations on the instrument variables. They view the money stock as (in part) an endogenous variable, and do not conceive of it as a proper instrument or target variable. The *monetarists* believe that the central bank can, and should, define its objectives and implement its policies in terms of the money stock. Indeed, these two conceptions of the money stock and its role in monetary policy decisions summarize some important substantive differences that have emerged in monetary economics:

(1) between the *monetarist* view that changes in the nominal money stock may be a causal, active, and independent factor in influencing aggregate demand and the price level, and the *nonmonetarist* views ranging from (a) the older "real bills" doctrine that the money stock responds primarily to changes in the real economy; (b) the Income-Expenditure theories (associated with the 45° diagram) which view money as an accommodating factor; and (c) the more recent New View doctrine

---

rather than on the quantity and velocity of 'money'; and to regard the structure of interest rates, asset yields, and credit availabilities rather than the quantity of money as the linkage between monetary and financial institutions and policies on the one hand and the real economy on the other."

He also suggests that this general equilibrium approach to the financial sector tends to question the presumed uniqueness of commercial banks:

"Neither individually nor collectively do commercial banks possess a widow's cruse. Quite apart from legal reserve requirements, commercial banks are limited in scale by the same kinds of economic processes that determine the aggregate size of other intermediaries."

J. Tobin, "Commercial Banks as Creators of "Money,' " *op. cit.*, pp. 410–412.

[6]Some monetary theorists have argued that while a skillful central bank can manipulate its controls to keep the nominal money stock (M) on target, it is preferable nevertheless to think of (M) as an endogenous variable. They argue that a "theory which takes as data the instruments of control rather than M, will not break down if and when there are changes in the targets or the marksmanship of the authorities." See J. Tobin, "Money, Capital and Other Stores of Value," *American Economic Review*, May 1961.

that the money stock is best viewed as one of several endogenous liquidity aggregates;

(2) between the monetarist view that the money stock—using either the conventional or the broader definition—is a reasonably well-behaved quantity, and the Radcliffe-type view that rejects these measures as narrow and inappropriate, and argues for a broader liquidity aggregate; and

(3) between the monetarist view that the monetary policy posture should be gauged by the behavior of a monetary aggregate, and the Income-Expenditure theories viewing market interest rates as the proper indicator variable.

Many who question the advisability of operating monetary policy in terms of money stock guidelines also question whether the central bank control is precise enough to comply with the guideline requirements. The extent of this control is therefore a key question. Is the money stock best viewed as an endogenous variable—determined by the interaction of the financial and real sectors—and outside the direct control of the central bank? Or is it more nearly correct to view it as an exogenous variable—as a policy instrument—that the authorities can control, and whose behavior can be made to conform to the stabilization guidelines?

This issue is essentially an empirical one: Does control over the monetary base and other instruments provide the central bank with sufficient powers to fit the behavior of the money stock into a given stabilization program? The *monetarists*, in assigning an important role for the money stock in stabilization policy, assume that the central bank can engineer the desired behavior of the money stock. The substantive issue can be reformulated in terms of an empirically refutable hypothesis, as follows: Do changes in commercial bank free reserve behavior, and do portfolio shifts by the public involving currency, demand and time deposits, and other financial assets, introduce enough variability and enough "noise" to break the *monetary base—bank reserves—money stock* linkage, and justify treating the money stock as an endogenous variable—and essentially outside the control of the central bank?

The empirical examination of this issue fits in naturally to a framework of money supply analysis which I have described in an earlier article.[7] The analysis developed there defines four money supply functions which incorporate alternative assumptions concerning portfolio adjustments.

If we let

M = the nominal money stock

[7]See D. Fand, "Some Implications of Money Supply Analysis," *American Economic Review*, May 1967.

X = a vector of Federal Reserve (monetary policy) instruments variables (the monetary base, reserve requirements, discount rate, Regulation Q)

r_b = a vector of endogenous financial variables (e.g., the Treasury bill rate, the Federal funds rate, the Eurodollar rate, the rate on time deposits and other intermediary claims)

T, C = time deposits, currency, shares and other financial assets that are close substitutes for demand deposits

Y = a vector of real sector variables (GNP, business investment, durables, etc.)

a money supply ($M.S.$) function may be written as:

$$M = f(X, r_b; T, C: Y).$$

The four *M.S.* functions that follow reflect alternative *ceteris paribus* conditions changing the portfolio adjustments that we permit for both the banks and the public:

(1) $M.S.$(I) is a short-run supply concept. It gives the money supply response to a change in reserves on the assumption that while banks may choose to adjust their free reserves, the public can only carry out a limited adjustment with respect to currency, time deposits and other financial assets. There are several ways to impose *certeris paribus* conditions on the public's holdings of currency, time deposits, and other financial assets. Some investigators hold *levels* of these assets constant, others hold *ratios* constant, and different investigators impose this *ceteris paribus* condition in a manner most compatible with their model. $M.S.$(I) is of the form $M = f(X, r_b; T, C : Y)$, where T and C specify our assumptions for currency, time deposits, and other close substitutes. To use it as a short-run concept we assume that all variables in the real sector of the economy, including stocks of real assets and flows such as consumption and investment, are held constant, so that it is primarily a function of the monetary policy instrument variables. Accordingly, if $M.S.$(I) is fairly stable it provides some support for the view that the monetary authorities can achieve fairly precise control over the money stock.

(2) To construct $M.S.$(II) we remove some of these portfolio restrictions by permitting the public to adjust their holdings of currency and time deposits, and the terms on which banks supply time deposits to reflect the underlying preferences. This function is of the form $f(X, r_b : Y)$, and does not contain any arbitrary assumptions about currency, time deposits, or the rate paid on time deposits. It is derived by assuming: (a) that

the banks may adjust their free reserves and the rate paid on time deposits; and (b) that the public's holdings of currency and time deposits will be determined by their demand function for these assets. Although $M.S.$(II) does permit a greater degree of portfolio adjustment, it still is a short-run and restricted function because it assumes that the real sector variables and all other financial assets are held constant.

(3) To construct $M.S.$(III) we permit portfolio adjustments throughout the entire financial sector and solve all the equations in the financial sector simultaneously. The Treasury bill rate and other rates which are endogenous variables in the financial sector will therefore be determined, and no longer enter as independent arguments in the money supply function. $M.S.$(III) is a reduced form equation of the form $M = g(X:Y)$ where all endogenous financial variables will have values determined by the simultaneous solution of the behavior equations in the financial sector. This function measures the supply response due to a change in the monetary base or some other policy instrument, assuming that all the variables in the financial sector adjust simultaneously.

(4) Finally, we define $M.S.$(IV) in the form of $M = g(X)$, a reduced-form equation which measures the movements in the money stock in response to adjustments in both the real and the financial sector. To derive this money supply we must solve all the structural equations in the financial and real sectors simultaneously to obtain the reduced form. The real sector variables are no longer treated as exogenous variables, but are now determined simultaneously with all the endogenous financial sector variables. This reduced-form $M.S.$ gives the equilibrium stocks of money as a function of the monetary base and other monetary policy instrument variables. This is the natural $M.S.$ function to construct for those who view the money stock as passive and responding to real sector developments, and to those who view the money stock as an accommodating variable, whose changes may be necessary in order to validate changes in the real economy.[8]

This brief review of the four money supply functions suggests that it is possible to test some of the substantive points that have come up in the recent "control over the money stock" discussions. For example, $M.S.$(I) postulates that we can predict the effect of changes in the monetary base

---

[8] The $M.S.$(IV) function as written implies that an increase in the monetary base will affect the money supply if it induces some real sector changes. A "real bills" proponent might therefore prefer to write it as follows:

$$M = f(Y) \text{ and } X = g(Y);$$

where M and X are both determined by the real sector variables in Y.

(and other instruments) on the money stock, assuming that the public's portfolio adjustments are restricted; *M.S.*(II) postulates that we can predict the effect of a change in the monetary base (and other instruments) on the money stock, even allowing the public to adjust their currency and holdings of demand and time deposits; while *M.S.*(III) postulates that we can predict the money stock response, even allowing the public to adjust their entire portfolios. These three *M.S.* functions assume that commercial bank free reserve behavior and the public's behavior with respect to currency, demand and time deposits are stable; and that the substitution of intermediary claims and liquid assets for money conforms to behavior that can be incorporated into a stable *M.S.* function. Econometric estimates of these three functions provide some evidence for testing the reliability of the *monetary base–bank reserve–money stock* linkage.[9]

Those who follow the "real bills" view—that the money stock is determined by the real sector variables—or the view in many income-expenditure models—that the money stock is an accommodating or permissive variable—presumably deny the possibility of constructing such functions. In their view these three *M.S.* functions do not allow any changes in fiscal policy or in the real sector variables; they permit only restricted changes in the financial sector variables, and they emphasize the monetary base and the central bank's instrument variables. Accordingly, they should predict that the first three *M.S.* functions highlighting the instrument variables are unstable and lack content; indeed, their approach to monetary theory implies that only *M.S.*(IV), which incorporates changes in the real sector, contains the relevant independent variables.

An analysis of these four money supply functions has implications for the use of the money stock as an independent and major instrument in stabilization. Those who argue that money is, at least in part, an endogenous variable, and who question the precision with which it can be controlled, assume (implicitly perhaps) that no statistically significant supply function can be estimated relating the money stock to the monetary base and other instrument variables. Moreover, if such a function is estimated it would have to be a reduced-form function, and a variant of the *M.S.*(IV) concept, incorporating feedbacks from the real sector.

In an earlier study, we compared estimates of the *M.S.* functions calculated from different econometric models. We found that the elasticities and multipliers for the first three *M.S.* functions based primarily on finan-

---

[9] A comparison of the three *M.S.* functions enables us to evaluate the quantitative effects of these portfolio shifts on the money stock. Consider a given change in the monetary base, or any other instrument variable, and compare the money stock response in these three functions. The calculated differences reflect the portfolio adjustments that we introduce as we move from *M.S.*(I) to *M.S.*(III)—i.e., shifts among currency, demand and time deposits, and the substitution of intermediary claims for money—and thus provide a measure of these effects on the money stock.

cial variables appear to be stable enough to justify further effort towards their refinement and improvement. We also found that: "There are at present too few studies available to calculate reliable *M.S.*(IV) elasticities. But the available evidence, meager though it may be, does not point to any superiority of *M.S.*(IV) over *M.S.*(I), and does not appear to favor a real view over a monetary view. Those who take the view that money is passive, responding primarily to the real economy, have to recognize that this is an assumption rather than a proposition derived from empirical evidence."[10]

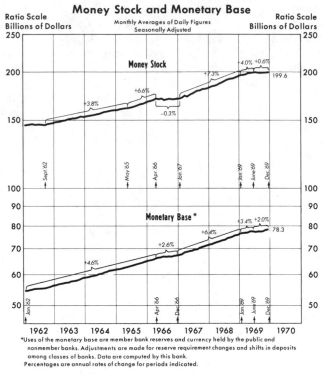

Figure 1.

[10]See D. Fand, "Some Implications of Money Supply Analysis," *op. cit.*, p. 392. The calculated elasticities and multipliers suggest that the short run *M.S.* functions—such as the *M.S.*(I) and *M.S.*(II)—are reasonably stable. These are preliminary findings, derived by using the steady-state solutions to simplify the analysis; they are subject to revision and require the construction of significance tests.

Our findings also suggest that the money stock behavior could be made to conform to a specified stabilization program. For example, by controlling movements in the monetary base, monetary authorities can control quite adequately movements in the money stock. Figure 1 illustrates a rather close relationship between the monetary base and the money stock.

While this research is far from conclusive it is consistent with a number of other findings.[11] It is difficult to maintain the view that the money stock is sufficiently endogenous so that it is outside the *direct* control of the authorities, without getting dangerously close to a "real bills" position. Accordingly, the focus of the "control over the money stock" discussion will shift, in my opinion, to the more interesting question—and the more relevant and less ideological question—concerning the length of the period needed to give the Federal Reserve System sufficient control to achieve a given money stock guideline. Assuming that a "reasonable" degree of precision has been defined, can the particular guideline requirements be achieved in a week? a month? a quarter? Or must we extend the period in order to overcome false signals, "noise," forecasting errors and other disturbances."[12] It would appear that the degree of precision desired is not independent of the time period required for the execution of policy, and it is reassuring to note that recent discussions have been directed increasingly at these points.

[11] See the references to Andersen, Brunner, Cagan, Friedman and Schwartz, and Meltzer in footnotes 1 and 4.

[12] This formulation of the problem has come up in several recent papers. Governor Maisel emphasizes this point as follows:

"This growth of money supply in any period is the result of actions taken by the Federal Reserve, the Treasury, the commercial banks and the public. Over a longer period, the Fed may play a paramount role, but this is definitely not the case in the short run. To the best of my knowledge, the Fed has not and probably would have great difficulties controlling within rather wide limits the growth of the narrowly defined money supply in any week or month."

See Sherman J. Maisel, "Controlling Monetary Aggregates," *op. cit.* For some other discussions of this issue, see A. J. Meigs, "The Case for Simple Rules," *op. cit.*; L. Gramley, "Guidelines for Monetary Policy—The Case Against Simple Rules," *op. cit.*; the Hearings on Standards for Guiding Monetary Action, *op. cit.*; A. Meltzer, "Controlling Money," *op. cit.* See also L. Kalish, "A Study of Money Stock Control," *Working Paper No. 11*, Federal Reserve Bank of St. Louis, for an interesting attempt to develop confidence limits for measuring the money managers' success in controlling the money stock.

3/ FEDERAL RESERVE BANK OF CLEVELAND

Sources of Commercial Bank Funds: An Example of "Creative Response"

This article considers the growing importance of newly innovated sources of commercial bank funds. It thus is concerned with the "creative response"[1] of an industry—in this case, commercial banking—to a new environment in which old or traditional ways of conducting business will no longer produce the same results. In other words, the article examines what banks have done to attract funds in a period when traditional ways proved less than adequate.

Innovation, which is doing something new or doing something old in a new way, arises usually out of need. This is true of innovations in managerial structure, in production, in marketing, and in finance—to mention only a few areas of activity closely associated with the economic process. The case of commercial banking conforms to the pattern of doing something new or doing something old in a new way.

COMMERCIAL BANKING SINCE WORLD WAR II

Since the end of World War II, commercial banks have declined in importance relative to other financial institutions, continuing a trend that

Reprinted with the permission of the Federal Reserve Bank of Cleveland from *Economic Review*, November 1965.

[1] The term is borrowed from Joseph A. Schumpeter, "The Creative Response in Economic History," *Journal of Economic History*, Vol. VII, November 1947.

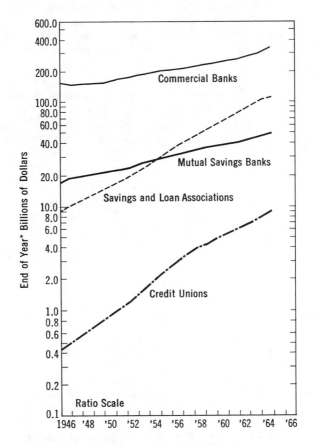

Figure 1. Total sources of funds
Deposit-type financial institutions.

*Last call report of year for commercial banks.
Sources of data: Federal Deposit Insurance Corporation; U.S.
Savings and Loan League; National Association of Mutual Saving
Banks; Credit Union National Association data.

originated around the turn of the century.[2] While commercial banks have
grown in size and are still the nation's leading financial intermediary, their
growth has not kept pace with that of other private deposit-type financial

[2] See Raymond W. Goldsmith, *Financial Intermediaries in the American Economy
Since 1900* (Princeton, New Jersey: Princeton University Press, 1958).

institutions.[3]   This is shown in Figure 1. Whereas over the 20-year period
since World War II, total sources of funds of commercial banks rose about
120 percent, those of mutual savings banks more than tripled, those of
savings and loan associations increased more than twelvefold, and those of
credit unions, though still relatively small in absolute size, increased some
twentyfold.

Put otherwise, while commercial banks at the end of 1945 had held 86
percent of the financial resources of all deposit-type financial institutions,
the share had dropped to 65 percent at the end of 1964. In each year
through 1963, as shown in Figure 2, financial resources of commercial

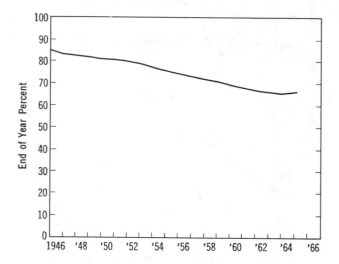

Figure 2. **Proportion of total funds of deposit-type financial
institutions accounted for by commercial banks**
Source of data: Federal Deposit Insurance Corporation.

banks—the total of liabilities and capital—constituted a smaller proportion
of the total resources of all deposit-type institutions. In 1964, however,
there was the first sign of a change in this pattern. Thus, in 1964 for the
only time since World War II, commercial banks succeeded in maintaining
—in fact, slightly improving—their relative position. As a result, at the end

---

[3]In this article, commercial banks are compared only with other deposit-type institutions.   A broader comparison with nondeposit-type financial institutions, for
example, insurance companies and pension funds, would yield conclusions similar to
those of this article.

of the year, sources of funds of commercial banks comprised a slightly larger portion of the total resources commanded by all deposit-type institutions than at the end of 1963—65.37 percent in 1964 against 65.35 percent in 1963.

The primary factor underlying the relatively poor showing of commercial banks in the postwar period perhaps has been the change in at-

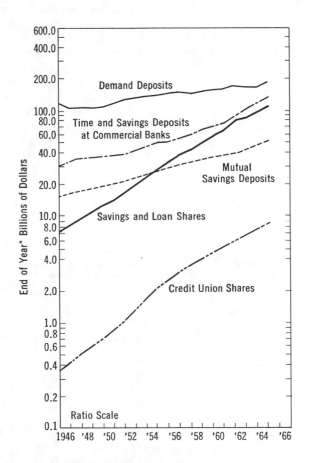

Figure 3. Deposits and shares

Deposit-type financial institutions.

*Last call report for commercial banks.
Sources of data: Federal Deposit Insurance Corporation; U.S. Savings and Loan League; National Association of Mutual Savings Banks; Credit Union National Association data.

titude of both businesses and individuals toward holding demand deposit balances. Both have become increasingly aware of the income foregone by holding temporarily idle funds in the form of "money" or, more specifically, as demand deposits; both have correspondingly become increasingly disinclined to do so. This is evidenced, in part, by the rapid growth of other deposit-type claims, which in turn reflects the public's desire to hold liquidity in income earning forms. Thus, as indicated in Figure 3, demand deposit liabilities of commercial banks over the last 20 years have grown at an average annual rate of only 2.1 percent; this contrasts sharply to average annual growth rates of 7.5 percent for time and savings deposits at commercial banks, 6 percent for mutual savings deposits, 14 percent for savings and loan shares, and nearly 17 percent for credit union shares. On the other side of the ledger, and as shown in Table 1, demand deposit and currency holdings of nonfinancial corporations have grown less rapidly than have their holdings of total financial assets (which include demand deposits and currency). Thus, the ratio of demand deposits and currency to total financial assets of nonfinancial corporations declined from nearly 29 percent in 1946 to 12.5 percent in 1964.

TABLE 1

Holdings of Financial Assets by Nonfinancial Corporations

Year	1 Demand Deposits and Currency (billions of dollars)	2 Total Financial Assets (billions of dollars)	3 One as a Percent of Two
1946	$21.2	$ 74.0	28.6%
1947	23.4	81.2	28.8
1948	23.6	86.6	27.3
1949	24.7	90.7	27.2
1950	26.2	107.5	24.4
1951	27.9	116.1	24.0
1952	28.7	122.1	23.5
1953	28.8	125.2	23.0
1954	30.9	130.3	23.7
1955	31.9	147.7	21.6
1956	32.1	153.0	21.0
1957	32.1	158.1	20.3
1958	33.5	170.0	19.7
1959	32.5	183.4	17.7
1960	32.1	191.4	16.8
1961	33.7	208.4	16.2
1962	34.5	224.4	15.4
1963	32.0	241.7	13.2
1964	32.5	260.7	12.5

Source: Flow of funds data, Board of Governors of the Federal Reserve System.

FACTORS ASSOCIATED WITH THE DECLINING DEMAND FOR CASH

The slower growth of demand deposits, reflecting as it does greater reluctance on the part of the public to hold idle money, is due in part to relatively high and generally rising interest rates that have characterized much of the postwar period.[4] An additional influence in this connection has been the absence of severe alternations in the level of economic activity since the end of World War II. Unlike the previous past when financial and industrial crises periodically gripped the nation's economy, the relative stability characterizing the two most recent decades has enabled businesses to plan their financial affairs better and hence to minimize unprofitable idle cash balances. Other factors might perhaps be cited, but whatever the causes of slower growth of demand deposits, commercial banks had to find ways of holding on to existing deposits[5] and of attracting newly generated funds.

TRADITIONAL RESPONSE

Though commercial banks did react to the changing environment, responses—until the past few years—were pretty much along traditional lines. As a general matter, commercial banks tended to limit their competition for loanable funds—to the extent possible under limitations imposed by Regulation Q—to raising interest rates paid on time and savings deposits, and to narrowing the differential between interest rates paid on such deposits and on deposit-type claims issued by other financial institutions as well as to advertising. That commercial banks did compete in terms of interest rates is seen in Figure 4. In each year from 1952 through 1964, the effective rate paid on interest-bearing claims issued by deposit-type financial

---

[4]Lower and/or declining interest rates would not necessarily reverse the trend. One observer of the financial scene is probably correct in arguing that "once companies and individuals begin to economize on cash and place surplus funds into earning assets, the process is hard to reverse even though the return available from this economizing of cash may decline." See Paul S. Nadler, *Time Deposits and Debentures: The New Sources of Bank Funds* (New York: C. J. Devine Institute of Finance, Graduate School of Business Administration of New York University, 1964), p. 30.

[5]Shifts of funds out of demand deposits and into interest-bearing claims issued by nonbank financial intermediaries do not result in a decline in the demand deposits of the banking system—only a transfer of ownership. But, such shifts create losses for *particular* banks and increase the *volatility* of deposit balances in general. Moreover, if carried to an extreme, commercial banks would evolve into check clearing facilities —not a useless function, but certainly not one that is particularly profitable.

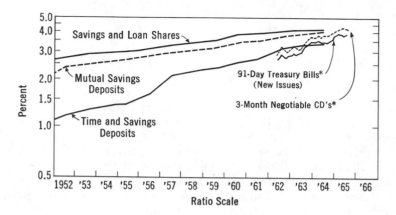

Figure 4. Selected interest rates
*Monthly averages.

Sources of data: Federal Deposit Insurance Corporation; U.S. Savings and Loan League; National Association of Mutual Savings Banks; Salomon Brothers and Hutzler.

institutions exceeded the rate of the previous year. Commercial banks conformed to this pattern, reflecting both a willingness to compete for funds—albeit along traditional lines—and permissive actions by the regulatory authorities in progressively raising the ceiling on Regulation Q.

Banks were successful, after 1956, in narrowing the unfavorable differential between interest rates paid on their claims and interest rates paid on the claims of major competitors. Thus, whereas rates paid by savings and loan associations between 1952 and 1956 exceeded rates paid on time and savings deposits of commercial banks by more than 1.5 percentage points, this differential had narrowed to about ¾ of a percentage point by the end of 1964.[6]

Commercial banks have also sought to compete in the money market for the highly mobile short-term funds of both corporations and well-to-do individuals. The willingness to compete is also evident from Figure 4, where it can be seen that the rate paid on negotiable time certificates of

[6]Various factors enable commercial banks to compete successfully for loanable funds (particularly long-term savings) despite payment of lower effective rates of interest. One reason, for example, is that only commercial banks offer complete banking services and, hence, convenience.

deposit has tended to be above the bid rate on 91-day U.S. Treasury bills, as well as to correlate closely with variations in that rate.[7]

Thus, as it became increasingly apparent that corporations and individuals were less likely to continue to hold large demand deposit balances, commercial banks attempted, as a second best alternative, to induce such depositors to keep funds on deposit as either time or savings deposits by making interest rates more attractive. In these efforts, particularly in the period beginning in 1957, some success was achieved.[8] Commercial banks were able to retain, often with the same deposit ownership, a portion of the funds formerly held in demand balances that might have sought profitable investment outside banks, as well as to attract a share of newly generated loanable funds.

It is evident from Figure 5, which shows the various sources of commercial bank funds, that total time and savings deposits have increased at a much faster rate since the end of 1956 than have demand deposits—the former increased by 1.5 times as compared with the less than 25 percent increase of the latter. At the end of 1956, demand deposits contributed almost 67 percent of total sources of funds of commercial banks; by the end of 1964 the proportion had dropped to only slightly more than 50 percent. Time and savings deposits, on the other hand, gained in relative importance, rising from less than 25 percent to 37 percent over the same period.[9] No particularly pronounced changes in the magnitudes of bank capital and other miscellaneous liabilities appeared in this period; at the

[7] The behavior of commercial banks in setting interest rates for different forms of deposits is rather interesting, and reveals a keen understanding of the advantages of money market segmentation. It is apparent from Figure 4 that the secondary market rate paid on three-month negotiable CDs has moved up considerably faster than the rate paid on total time and savings deposits. Moreover, the former rate has moved much more in sympathy with money market rates than has the effective rate paid on all time and savings deposits. The major portion of time and savings deposits is held by individuals as long-term savings. Though such savings are by no means insensitive to relative interest rate differentials and levels, they are thought to be less sensitive than the short-term idle funds of corporations and well-to-do individuals. Thus, rather than competing for the marginal liquidity of such spending units by raising interest rates across-the-board, commercial banks have issued negotiable CDs in large denominations, especially for acquisition by this segment of the market.

[8] From 1936 through the end of 1956, maximum interest rates payable on commercial bank time and savings deposits under Regulation Q remained unchanged. As of January 1, 1957, maximum interest rate ceilings were raised on all types of time and savings deposits, excepting 30- to 89-day time deposits. This action by the regulatory authorities was initiated in recognition of the general rise in interest rates beginning in 1951.

[9] These percentages are for *total* demand and *total* time and savings deposits, as reported on bank balance sheets. The proportions thus differ from those usually derived from adjusted deposit data. Both sets of data, however, reveal similar patterns over time.

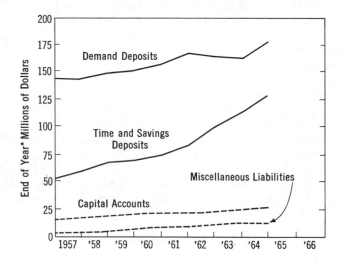

Figure 5. Sources of commercial bank funds
*Last call report of year for commercial banks.
Source of data: Federal Deposit Insurance Corporation.

end of 1956, the two components combined accounted for 9.1 percent of
total sources of funds of commercial banks as compared with 11.2 percent
at the end of 1964. However, recent innovations affecting these sources of
funds have potentially important implications for the future, which are
discussed later.

CREATIVE RESPONSE

To date, the 1960's have seen commercial banks become considerably more
aggressive in their competitive efforts. This has been made possible in part
by the greater leeway given by the monetary authority to commercial
banks in the setting of interest rates.[10] But, in addition, commercial banks
have found new ways of competing for funds—ways which likely will play
a major role in determining the fortunes of commercial banking in coming
years.

[10] Permission to raise rates payable on various types of time and savings deposits
has been granted in every year since 1961. Thus, changes in maximum rates payable
under Regulation Q were made effective as of January 1, 1962, July 17, 1963, and
November 24, 1964. As of this writing, there has been no change in 1965.

Prior to the early 1960's, commercial banks, as a general matter, apparently had been content to attract funds from traditional sources and by traditional means, with rising interest rates as the primary lure. The past four years, however, have witnessed a considerable change, with innovation now playing a dominant role in terms of both characteristics of claims issued by banks and the markets to which these claims are meant to have appeal.

Most important thus far of the debt instruments recently introduced by commercial banks—at least in terms of magnitude—is the negotiable certificate of deposit. In sharp contrast to the past when many banks discouraged or refused corporate-owned time deposits,[11] negotiable CDs were issued primarily to halt the movement of demand deposit funds from large commercial banks by corporate money managers into investment in various money market instruments, for example, Treasury bills, commercial paper, and bankers' acceptances. Certificates of deposit were not unknown prior to 1961, when leading New York City banks announced that they would offer such instruments to both corporate and noncorporate customers and a leading Government securities dealer indicated that it would maintain a secondary market for such instruments. But, as seen from Figure 6,

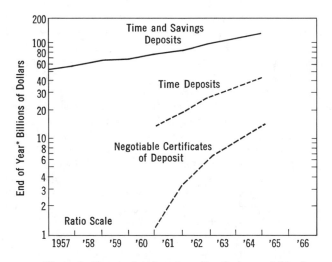

Figure 6. Time and savings deposits of commercial banks
Sources of data: Board of Governors of the Federal Reserve System and Federal Deposit Insurance Corporation.

[11] A view in the past often was (and in some cases still is) that the buildup of interest-earning time deposits owned by corporations would be at the expense of demand deposits which earn no interest.

negotiable CDs totaled only slightly in excess of $1 billion at the end of 1960. By the end of 1964, this almost insignificant figure had grown to more than $12.5 billion—by August of this year to over $16 billion.

Negotiable CDs clearly have grown considerably faster than the total of time and savings deposits. While at the end of 1960, negotiable CDs constituted just 1.5 percent of total time and savings deposits, by the end of 1964 they accounted for almost 10 percent. Of the $54-billion increase in time and savings deposits between the end of 1960 and the end of 1964, negotiable CDs contributed more than one-fifth. Since negotiable CDs are a form of time deposit (as distinct from savings deposits[12]), their increase has contributed far more significantly to the growth of time deposits. And it is the time deposit component in recent years that has evidenced most of the growth recorded in the total of time and savings deposits. From the end of 1961 to the end of 1964, time and savings deposits together increased by about 55 percent. Time deposits alone, however, expanded about 2.3 times. The growing volume of negotiable CDs accounted for almost 45 percent of the nearly $26 billion increase in time deposits over the period.

The appeal of negotiable CDs reflects in part their attractive yields; it also reflects their marketability, something the traditional time deposit lacked. However, while having much appeal to money managers, negotiable CDs are not necessarily as pleasing to bankers. For one thing, CDs tend to be highly sensitive to interest rates—to the extent that the adverse differentials between interest rates paid on CDs and on other money market instruments could cause a loss of CDs and, hence, a source of funds to the banks involved.

Interest rate considerations aside, there also exists the possibility of holders failing to renew maturing CDs, for example, because holders may want back their funds for working capital purposes. This is not a surprising situation in that, in many cases, CDs represent *temporarily* idle funds which in former years might have contentedly remained in demand balances. Negotiable CDs are therefore a potentially volatile source of funds, in contrast to the traditional savings, or even time, deposit. In this respect, CDs bear a strong resemblance to demand deposits.[13] Moreover, not only must legally required reserves and adequate capital be kept against CDs (as in the case of other deposits), but bankers may often feel queasy about investing such funds in high-yielding though relatively illiquid assets. In

[12] Time deposits are generally held by businesses and well-to-do individuals, and include: time deposits open account, time CDs (negotiable and non-negotiable), and other special accounts. Savings deposits, as evidenced by the ownership of a passbook, represent generally the savings of the public-at-large.

[13] See George R. Morrison and Richard T. Selden, *Time Deposit Growth and the Employment of Bank Funds* (Association of Reserve City Bankers, 1965), Chapter III.

short, negotiable CDs can easily become a rather volatile and expensive source of funds.

The issuance of negotiable CDs has probably been the most widely discussed aspect of the renewed vigor with which commercial banks have sought to strengthen their commanding position as a financial intermediary. Of less quantitative importance thus far—but also possessing significant implications for the future—are new sources of funds showing up in the capital and miscellaneous liability accounts of commercial banks. Of particular interest are subordinated debentures and capital notes, and more recently unsecured short-term promissory notes, which were first issued in September 1964 by The First National Bank of Boston. As seen in Figure 7, the outstanding volume of subordinated debentures and capital notes rose from a level of only $21 million in mid-1963 to over $800 million at the end of 1964. In relation to total bank capital of nearly $28 billion at the end of 1964, $800 million is an inconsiderable amount. Yet, in the absence of regulatory restraints, there is reason for believing that the total could increase sharply and to significant proportions.

From a bank's point of view, debentures and capital notes have much to recommend as a source of funds. To the extent that they substitute for additional sales of common stock, and to the extent that the rate of interest on these funds is less than the rate of return on invested capital, present stockholders stand to benefit from higher earnings per share and possibly

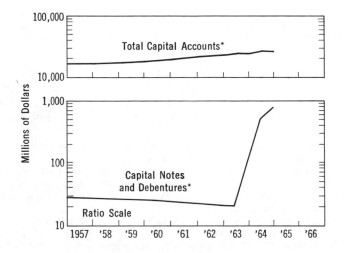

Figure 7. Capital accounts of commercial banks
*End of year through 1962; semiannually beginning 1963.
Source of data: Federal Deposit Insurance Corporation.

higher market values of their equity holdings.[14]   But, aside from use as a substitute for the issuance of additional common stock, unsecured debentures and capital notes may also substitute for and/or supplement deposits (demand and time and savings) as a source of loanable funds to commercial banks.

Compared with negotiable CDs, for example, debentures and capital notes possess several distinct and widely accepted advantages. First, neither debentures nor capital notes require the maintenance of legal reserves, while as a deposit liability, CDs require such reserves. Second, debentures or capital notes do not require supporting equity capital or, at least, not to the extent that CDs or the more traditional deposit liabilities would require it. Third, neither debentures nor capital notes are subject to a Federal Deposit Insurance Corporation assessment; as a form of time deposit, CDs are subject to a $1/12$ of one percent annual assessment. Finally, because funds secured through debentures and capital notes are likely to remain for a relatively long period of time, there is less need for maintaining secondary reserves, such as Treasury bills and other low-yielding though highly liquid assets. Thus, nearly all the proceeds from debentures and capital notes can be placed in loans and longer maturity investments.

In the absence of regulatory restraint, it is likely that unsecured short-term notes will become an increasingly important source of funds for commercial banks. Having some of the advantages of debentures and capital notes, short-term notes, in addition, are not burdened with similar marketing problems.[15]

CONCLUDING COMMENTS

Having said this, however, it should be remembered that, if not handled properly, that is, with full appreciation of the costs and risks involved, these "new" sources of funds could present serious problems to commercial banks.[16] Thus, it should not be surprising that the supervisory author-

[14] For discussion and illustration of this, see Nadler, *Time Deposits and Debentures: The New Sources of Bank Funds*, pp. 20–24.

[15] On August 26, 1965, the Banking Department of the State of New York gave state chartered banks permission to offer non-negotiable promissory notes (in amounts exceeding $1,000,000) to corporate customers. As of this writing, six large New York banks have issued such notes.

[16] Acquisition of substantial amounts of loanable funds through the issuance of capital notes and debentures commits the issuing bank to fixed interest payments over extended periods of time. Should market rates of interest subsequently decline, the bank's earning power may become jeopardized. An additional source of possible difficulty arises from the relatively high interest rate paid on these sources of funds. At, say, a 5 percent rate of interest on debentures, proceeds from this source could hardly be placed in shorter-term loans and investments. Thus, it might become

ities have demonstrated prudent caution in evaluating such sources of funds. Nevertheless, the fact that new sources of funds have been "innovated" does suggest that commercial banks are seriously seeking to revitalize their position as a financial intermediary. The ultimate success of any single innovation is perhaps not important. What is important is that creative innovation has been reintroduced to commercial banking. And this virtually guarantees that the business of banking will never again be the same—as it probably should not since change happens all the time in various segments of U. S. business and financial enterprise.

---

necessary to place these funds in longer-term and less liquid loans and investments. At some point the desire for profit might conflict with prudent behavior. For additional discussion see L. Wayne Dobson, *The Issuance of Capital Notes and Debentures by Commercial Banks* (Kentucky Bankers Association, 1965), pp.22–26.

4/ JAMES L. PIERCE

Commercial Bank Liquidity

Bank liquidity is of concern because of its direct connection with two different, but related, problems. Inadequate liquidity of the banking system, on the one hand, raises the possibility that a number of banks more or less simultaneously may discover that they are incapable of meeting deposit withdrawals by selling assets or by other means. On the other hand, the liquidity of the banking system may be regarded as a basic factor shaping the lending policies of banks, and consequently as a principal determinant of the cost and availability of bank credit to borrowers.

This study deals only with the second of these two problems. The first problem is concerned with the adequacy of the powers of a central bank to cope with major crises, and is outside the scope of the study.

Of obvious and justifiable concern, however, is the problem of bank liquidity and its relation to lending policies of commercial banks. Because these policies cannot be observed directly, statistics such as ratios of loans to deposits or ratios of liquid assets to total assets are often used to measure variations in the willingness of banks to lend.

In this study, it is argued that, although liquidity is an important element in an individual bank's decisions regarding the composition of its asset portfolio, no liquidity ratio provides an unambiguous picture of either

Reprinted with permission of the author from the *Federal Reserve Bulletin*, August 1966. James L. Pierce is Chief, Special Studies Section, Board of Governors of the Federal Reserve System. As in all staff studies, the author is responsible for the analyses and conclusions set forth, and the views expressed are not necessarily those of his colleagues or of the Board of Governors.

Note.—An earlier draft of this paper was presented at a meeting of the Federal Reserve System Committee on Financial Analysis, Philadelphia, Pennsylvania, on Apr. 19–21, 1966. The author would like to thank Lyle E. Gramley for the many useful suggestions offered on the earlier draft.

asset characteristics or lending behavior. The study also points out that recent developments in banking have reduced—but not eliminated—the importance of asset liquidity in the determination of bank lending practices. Before considering the role of liquidity in bank portfolio management, it is desirable to develop a precise definition of asset liquidity. This requires careful consideration of the characteristics of assets, and in particular of the ease and speed with which assets can be sold.

A CONCEPT OF ASSET LIQUIDITY[1]

At any given time, t, an asset has a maximum expected market price, which may be designated P_t^*. P_t^* is the highest price the owner of the asset expects to obtain by liquidating one unit of the asset if he is allowed all useful preparation prior to its disposal. If the unit of the asset must be sold more quickly, the owner at time t can expect to receive an actual price designated P_t that is less than P_t^*. "Quick" sales require acceptance of less than the full market value of the asset; this is the essence of illiquidity.

The value of the ratio P_t/P_t^* is thus determined by the length of time available between the decision to sell a unit of the asset and its actual sale. The longer is this interval, the higher is the ratio P_t/P_t^*. Let n be the number of units of time required to obtain P_t^*, and let i be a variable representing the number of units of time available $(i = 0, \ldots, n)$. If the decision to sell an asset is made in period t, and if the sale is made in period $t + i$, the price received may be designated P_{t+i}; $P_{t+i} < P_t^*$ for all $i < n$ and $P_{t+n} = P_t^*$. The ratio P_{t+i}/P_t^* then shows the relation between actual and full realizable sales price at any given time of sale, $t + i$, when a single unit of the asset is sold. That ratio may be plotted graphically to show its relation with the length of time for sale, as in Figure 1.

Figure 1 portrays a hypothetical situation in which the relationship between P_{t+i}/P_t^* and i is continuous. It is assumed that at time t $(i = 0)$, the seller can obtain no positive price for the asset. If the holder spends m periods finding a buyer, he realizes 50 percent of the maximum price, P_t^*. Finally, if he spends n periods prior to the disposal of the asset, he realizes the maximum price.

The shape of the relationship between P_{t+i}/P_t^* and i, for any asset, depends upon the characteristics of the market in which the asset is traded. Cash is a perfectly liquid asset; its ratio of P_{t+i}/P_t^* is always unity. Treas-

---

[1] The treatment of liquidity provided here is an elaboration and extension of that provided by Professor James Tobin, of Yale University, in his unpublished book on monetary theory, Ch. II, "Properties of Assets."

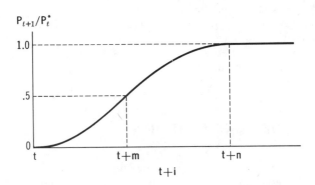

Figure 1.

ury bills can be sold quickly at low cost; the actual sales price P_{t+i} rises rapidly to P_t^*. Mortgages often can be sold, but the market is sufficiently imperfect to require that the holder shop around to avoid low values of P_{t+i}/P_t^*. Many types of bank loans normally are not traded on secondary markets, and as a limiting case it may be supposed that they can be liquidated only at maturity. For these loans $P_{t+i}/P_t^* = 0$ for all $i < n$ and $P_{t+n}/P_t^* = 1$, where n is time to maturity.

The liquidity of an asset is defined in terms of the function describing the relationship between the ratio P_{t+i}/P_t^* and the time available for disposal. At any given point in the horizontal time scale of Figure 1, an asset is the more liquid the higher is its ratio of P_{t+i}/P_t^*. But apart from those assets that are perfectly liquid and those for which sale prior to maturity is impossible, assets cannot be uniquely ranked by degrees of liquidity. Liquidity curves of two assets similar to that shown in Figure 1 may cross at some value of $i < n$.

Whether or not a commercial bank's portfolio is liquid thus depends upon the time period being considered. Knowledge of the relationship between the ratio P_{t+i}/P_t^* and i for each asset in the portfolio would permit construction of a liquidity index for a given value of i. For any fixed time horizon (any given value of i), a liquidity index I^i would weight each asset's liquidity by the share of that asset in the total portfolio. Let P_{kt}^* be the maximum price of the kth asset and a_{kt} be the number of units of that asset held at time t ($k = 1, \ldots, N$). The value of the index is given by

$$I^i = \sum_{k=1}^{N} [(W_k)(P_{kt+i}/P_{kt}^*)]$$

where

$$W_k = a_{kt}(P_{kt}^*)/ \sum_{k=1}^{N} a_{kt}(P_{kt}^*), \sum_{k=1}^{N} W_k = 1, \text{ and } 0 \leqslant I^i \leqslant 1.$$

A vector of liquidity indices could be constructed from the I^i for each value of i from 0 to the value of n for the longest term asset. The elements of this vector would obviously bear only a loose relation to conventional liquidity ratios; liquidity measures cannot be compressed into a single number.

Such a vector of liquidity indices would have only limited usefulness, however, because it does not recognize that, for some assets, the price per unit depends on the number of units sold. For example, it might be possible to dispose of a single mortgage loan quickly and at relatively low cost. But the larger the number of mortgages to be sold, the longer the time needed to find buyers and the lower the ratio P_{t+i}/P_t^* for any given value of i. The relationship between P_{t+i}/P_t^* and the time to disposal for different sizes of transactions, s ($s = 1, 2, \ldots , S$), is shown in Figure 2, where $s_1 < s_2 < s_3$.

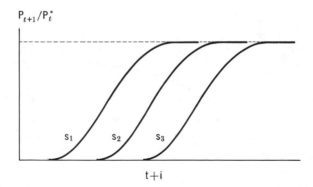

Figure 2.

Thus the price that can be obtained by liquidating an asset depends on both the time available prior to its disposal and the number of units to be sold. For each asset in the portfolio there is a matrix of possible prices with elements defined for given values of i and s. An index of total portfolio liquidity implied by combining the N individual asset matrices could be constructed, but it would be of dubious operational significance.

The concept of liquidity used here provides a clear distinction between liquidity and solvency. Solvency measures the difference between the value of a bank's assets at maximum expected prices and its liabilities. Liquidity refers to realizable value of the asset portfolio for a given time to sale and a given size of the actual sale. A bank can be illiquid and still be solvent.

Brokerage fees, although not an element of liquidity as defined for this study, are important in determining the net return on an asset. Brokerage fees are defined to include all fees charged by middlemen in asset markets, and are assumed to be collected only when assets are sold. If an asset is sold prior to maturity, the brokerage fee must be deducted from P_t^*. Payment of the fee reduces realized rates of return. If an asset is purchased and then sold quickly, brokerage costs could exceed the accumulated interest on the asset, and the rate of return would then be negative. In general, the greater the fee, the longer an asset must be held to yield any given rate of return. Because it is imposed only once, the brokerage fee becomes less important as a determinant of the realized rate of return the longer an asset is held. A hypothetical relationship between the length of time an asset is held, t, and its rate of return, R—given the brokerage fee, the purchase price, the sale price, and the coupon rate—is shown in Figure 3.

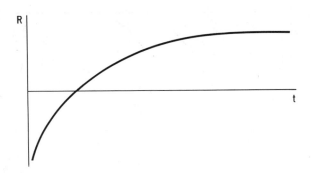

Figure 3.

By definition, brokerage fees are independent of the length of time an asset is held and of the number of units sold. They are, therefore, different in concept from liquidity. Nevertheless, both liquidity and brokerage fees represent sources of inertia in the sale of assets.

THE ROLE OF LIQUIDITY IN BANK PORTFOLIO MANAGEMENT

This concept of liquidity permits a more careful consideration of the role of liquidity in a bank's decisions to make loans. To simplify the analysis and to focus sharply on the role of liquidity in decision-making, the analysis that follows ignores brokerage costs, expected rates of return, predictability of return, and similar matters. It also assumes that all deposit liabilities are demand balances and are exogenously determined.[2] Thus, banks are assumed to stand ready to issue demand deposits at a given and constant yield to anyone willing to hold them. The amount of demand deposits issued by any bank at a given point in time is assumed to be a random variable with constant mean and variance. Also for simplicity, it is assumed that the only other type of bank liability available is a loan from the Federal Reserve obtained at an interest rate exceeding the return on any asset.

The analysis is simplified greatly by assuming also that total assets can be separated arbitrarily into two homogeneous groups called "loans" and "liquid assets." Though salable prior to maturity, a unit of loans is assumed to command a smaller proportion of its full value for a given value of i ($i < n$) than a unit of liquid assets.

The portfolio of liquid assets serves as a buffer that insulates loans from unexpected variations in deposits. When a bank experiences an unexpected loss of funds, it can meet at least part of the loss from its liquid assets.[3] Ownership of liquid assets reduces the probability that the bank has to sell loans under unfavorable terms.

Similarly, when a bank experiences an unexpected net inflow of deposits, the inflow might be viewed as transitory and the funds held in liquid form. Generally speaking, it is not profitable to invest funds in loans if there is reason to believe that an inflow soon will be reversed.[4]

With this simple division of bank assets into two categories, the determinants of loans and of the buffer stock of liquid assets are one and the

---

[2] This assumption will be relaxed later.

[3] Assets in the buffer stock need not and typically are not in cash form. Interest-bearing liquid assets provide some current income and they can be sold quickly at low cost should the need arise.

[4] Many of the considerations involved in liquidity and asset sales are also involved in asset purchases. The price a bank pays for an asset is, in part, a function of the time available to find the most eager seller and of the size of the transaction. For an extended discussion of the role of costs of asset acquisition in bank portfolio management, see James L. Pierce, "A Cross Section Analysis of Commercial Bank Portfolio Management," presented before the 1965 winter meetings of the Econometric Society.

same. Before considering these determinants, it may be helpful to digress a bit to discuss the institutional approach to commercial banking.[5]

The institutional approach asserts that banks assign priorities to the use of their funds. Liquidity receives first priority, and each bank has a subjective liquidity standard which it attempts to meet at all times. The standard for each bank depends upon its deposit stability and upon its preferences, and is fixed in the short run. Loans are accorded second priority. Once the fixed liquidity ratio is attained, each bank stands ready to grant loans to all borrowers who qualify as acceptable loan customers and are willing to pay a given and constant loan rate. For a bank with "adequate" capital and "healthy" loans, the conceptual limits to the size of the loan account are the value of the bank's resources (deposits and capital) and its invariate commitment to liquidity. The ratio of loans to total assets is thought to be limited, under most circumstances, by the paucity of acceptable loans. If a paucity exists, banks move on to their third priority, the purchase of securities for income.

If banks did behave this way, simple liquidity ratios would be useful. Each bank would have a maximum loan-to-deposit ratio determined by its liquidity standard, the size of its capital, and the quality of available loans. A bank could be fully "loaned up" before all its resources were devoted to loans, since the bank would refuse to grant new loans to acceptable customers if its liquidity standard were not met. Differences among banks in liquidity standards, and variations from one bank to another in the strength of loan demands, would alter the significance of an aggregate loan-to-deposit ratio—even during periods of high aggregate loan demand. However, unless subjective preferences for liquidity were highly variable from bank to bank, a higher aggregate ratio of loans to deposits at all banks would generally imply a greater number of banks turning away loan customers.

While the use of an aggregate loan-to-deposit ratio is defensible in this context, the assumption that banks behave in the manner contemplated by the institutional approach is not compelling. Asset returns are not constant over a period of time, and the liquidity standard is unlikely to be independent of alternative rates of return. Decision-making at commercial banks is more complex than the institutional approach assumes.

In the last few years, several efforts have been made to bring a higher level of economic analysis to bear on bank decision-making.[6] A primary

[5] One of the most coherent statements of this position is found in Roland Robinson, *The Management of Bank Funds*, 2nd ed., McGraw-Hill, 1962.

[6] The references most relevant to this paper are as follows: Richard C. Porter, "A Model of Bank Portfolio Selection," *Yale Economic Essays* (Fall 1961), pp. 323–59. Daniel Orr and W. Mellon, "Stochastic Reserve Losses and Expansion of Bank Credit," *American Economic Review* (Sept. 1961), pp. 614–23. David Chambers and Abraham Charnes, "Inter-Temporal Analysis and Optimization of Bank Portfolios," *Management Science* (July 1961), pp. 393–410.

feature of the new approach is the treatment of banks as economic units interested in maximizing profits. The theory of the firm and the theory of portfolio management have been combined to analyze the financial firm. The results obtained are quite different from those of the institutional approach.

The new approach argues that banks seek to maximize some function of their discounted future stream of profits over a period of time for which neither future deposit levels nor future rates of return are known with certainty.[7] Since the only absolutely safe liquidity standard is to hold all deposits in cash, the size of the liquid asset portfolio is inseparably related to the size of the bank's total portfolio.[8] The contribution to current and future profits provided by the flexibility of liquid assets is balanced against the relatively high expected return on less liquid assets. A profit-maximizing assumption implies that the balance point depends both upon deposit levels expected in the future and upon expected rates of return on liquid and illiquid assets.

In this approach, an increase in the expected return on loans relative to liquid assets encourages banks to shift funds into loans. Even though this shift of funds reduces the liquidity of the asset portfolio, a bank is willing to accept an increased probability of either unforeseen asset sales or borrowing from its Reserve Bank if it is sufficiently compensated by an increased rate of return on loans.[9] Liquidity is relevant to the contribution that it makes to profits. Liquid asset purchases are not made independently of profit considerations.

Viewed in this context, the relation between the maintenance of liquidity and the decision to lend is but one part of the more general problem of specifying a function describing a bank's desired allocation of funds to loans, that is, a loan-supply function. The approach clearly does not imply that the willingness to lend is unrelated to the existing ratio of loans to deposits. Rather it suggests that there is no fixed loan limit for a given value of deposits, but there is a limit that is related to the rate of return on loans. With given deposit characteristics, the greater the share of loans in total assets, the greater the probability that a bank will have to dispose of some part of its loan portfolio at unfavorable terms. Consequently, if a bank is to be induced to hold more loans relative to total assets, it must be compensated for the increased probability of loan sales.

---

[7]The models that deal explicitly with stochastic deposit losses are restricted to static, single-period, expected-profit maximization problems. Dynamic models that allow for covariances of asset returns are difficult to solve, but some work is being conducted in this area.

[8]A possible rationalization of the fixed liquidity standard of the institutional approach is to assume that banks seek to maximize expected profit subject to a liquidity constraint.

[9]This "free choice" can, of course, clash with bank examination rules. To the extent that it does, profit maxima are constrained by the rules.

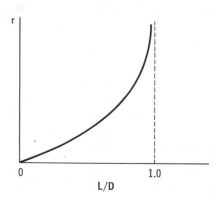

Figure 4.

To illustrate, assume for the moment that the terms on which loans are supplied (and demanded) can be represented by a single interest rate, r. Let L represent loans, and D deposits. The approach discussed here suggests a supply-of-loans function of the sort depicted in Figure 4, where the quantity of deposits, D, and the rate of return on liquid assets are given.

The actual shape of this functional relation is by no means obvious.[10] It depends upon such factors as the characteristics of the bank's deposits, the liquidity characteristics of its loans, and the cost of borrowing as a means of adjusting to deposit withdrawals. Nevertheless, there are some reasons for believing that the supply of loans function would have the generally nonlinear shape depicted in Figure 4.

This shape is indicated because the higher is a bank's loan-to-deposit ratio, the greater is the probability that a loss of deposits would force the bank to dispose of loans on unfavorable terms. Consequently, the higher is the value of L/D, the greater is the increase in r required to induce the bank to supply an additional unit of loans.[11]

At least one further reason exists for believing that the supply-of-loans function has the shape described. The lack of insurance on the greater part of large deposit accounts may induce these depositors to favor banks with higher degrees of liquidity. The higher the value of L/D for any given bank, the greater the probability that a marginal rise in the ratio would in-

---

[10] The quantity of loans supplied at various rates is deflated by deposits so as to present the argument in terms of the loan-to-deposit ratio.

[11] This condition appears to hold even for banks that are risk neutral, that is, for banks guided solely by expected profit.

duce these depositors to move their funds elsewhere. If this is true, a rise in L/D increases the risk of a deposit loss, and banks must be compensated for this added risk.

The position of the loan-supply function in Figure 4 depends upon expected rates of return on liquid assets, the degree of deposit variability, and other factors. The loan-to-deposit ratio expresses its influence on the slope of the loan-supply function, but it is only one element among the several that determine a bank's lending policies. To isolate the role of L/D in the lending decision, it is necessary to specify a loan-supply function that explicitly takes these other elements into account. Before turning to this matter, the discussion must first consider the effects of introducing endogenous liabilities into the argument.

SIGNIFICANCE OF ENDOGENOUS DEPOSIT DETERMINATION

The role of liquidity in a bank's decision to lend is complicated further when the assumption is relaxed that deposits are determined exogenously, but the significance of endogenous deposit determination is well worth pursuing. Markets have developed in recent years that permit banks, within rather wide limits, to obtain funds if they are willing to pay the price.[12] By varying the rates they pay for Federal funds and for certificates of deposit, banks can—within limits—determine the size of their total liabilities.[13] To draw out the implications of these markets for liquidity and lending decisions, it may be supposed that the only form of endogenous deposit liability is a certificate of deposit that has a single maturity, on which banks can pay any interest rate they choose.

Banks are not assumed to be strictly price takers in markets for endogenous deposit liabilities. The rate paid by an individual bank is an increasing function of the average rate prevailing in the market, of the amount of CD's that the bank has outstanding, and of the size of the new issue offered by the bank. Banks, like other borrowers, do not face perfectly elastic demand schedules for their liabilities.

As its most significant feature for the problem at hand, the CD market provides banks with an alternative method of portfolio adjustment. To meet an exogenous loss of funds, banks may sell assets or issue new

[12] For purposes of the present discussion it is assumed that all banks have equal access to liability markets. It is further assumed that there are no legal maxima on the rates paid for these liabilities. Both assumptions are relaxed in the section on loan-supply function (p. 123).

[13] The stochastic processes which generate exogenous deposit liabilities prevent this control from being complete.

liabilities, or both. Profit-maximizing banks would make adjustments by the method that costs the least. For any given loss of deposits there is a particular least-cost combination of asset and liability sales. Since the mere existence of a CD market does not remove the option of selling assets, this mix must be at least as inexpensive as relying strictly on asset sales to meet deposit losses. Thus, the development of markets permitting endogenous determination of liabilities tends to reduce the costs of portfolio adjustment. The existence of such markets also reduces the size of the desired buffer of liquid assets.

But endogenous liabilities also allow a bank to determine the total size, as well as composition, of its asset protfolio. A positive differential between the expected return on loans and the existing CD rate—if it is large enough—would induce a bank to issue CD's and purchase new loans.[14] Issuance of new CD's tends to raise the marginal cost of liabilities, and the acquisition of new loans tends to depress the return expected on loans. Equilibrium is achieved when there is no longer any net advantage to issuing CD's to acquire additional loans.

Sales of liabilities to purchase assets, however, are not likely to be carried to the point at which the marginal cost of new CD's equals the marginal expected return on new loans. When a bank issues a CD and purchases a loan, it runs the risk that CD rates will rise prior to the maturity date of the loan. Most banks would require compensation for this risk.[15]

Endogenous liabilities appear to have some clear qualitative implications for lending practices of banks. The ability of banks to market their liabilities induces them to desire a higher loan-to-deposit ratio for every value of the terms on new loans. The loan-supply relation in Figure 4 shifts down and to the right. The constraint on the volume of loans is no longer determined by the value of D, the level of exogenous deposits, but by the total size of the bank's portfolio.[16]

More important, the function also becomes less steeply sloped. The probability of costly adjustments through large asset sales rises less rapidly when adjustments are permitted in liability markets. Since the market for CD's is relatively well developed (as is the market for Federal funds), adjustment costs for the individual bank are likely to rise less rapidly with the scale of transactions than in markets for assets other than Treasury bills. It is very unlikely that the interest-rate elasticity of demand for CD's facing an individual bank is low enough to produce the sharply rising costs of ad-

---

[14]The possibility is ignored that yield relationships might permit banks profitably to issue CD's and purchase liquid assets.

[15]If ceiling rates on CD's are introduced, the bank runs the risk that the rate will rise to the ceiling. If it does, CD's become exogenous and the bank must rely upon liquid assets for short-term portfolio adjustments.

[16]This implies, of course, that the maximum value of L/D could exceed unity.

justments to deposit losses implied in Figure 4. The slope of the function tends to be reduced by the introduction of endogenous liabilities.

It was observed earlier that bank liquidity is a relative term, even in a world of exogenous liabilities. And when endogenous liabilities are introduced, asset liquidity loses much of its crucial importance. Markets for CD's and other endogenous liabilities bear part of the burden of adjustment to exogenous deposit losses. Conventional measures of liquidity that focus on the share of liquid assets in the total portfolio tend to lose their significance. Statistics such as aggregate loan-to-deposit ratios and ratios of liquid assets to total assets provide at best only incomplete information, and this information may often be quite misleading. To analyze decision-making in today's sophisticated financial markets, more sophisticated measuring techniques are needed.

LOAN-SUPPLY FUNCTION

Although the above remarks are admittedly rather negative, they point to the direction in which further research might illuminate the relation between bank liquidity and bank lending practices. The procedure by which this relation expresses itself is properly formulated in terms of a loan-supply function in which considerations of asset liquidity and costs of making adjustments in endogenous deposit markets are treated explicitly.

Knowledge of the aggregate loan-supply function is of great importance, but almost nothing is known about it. Attempts to obtain statistical estimates of the parameters of the loan-supply function have been thwarted by an almost total lack of information on the terms on which these loans are granted.[17]

Availability of information on loan terms would permit the estimation of the loan-supply function. At any given point in time the following variables might be assumed to enter into the function for a bank: the size and composition of its exogenous liabilities, the rates it pays for endogenous liabilities, the expected rates of return and covariance of return on assets other than loans, the "liquidity" of its portfolio, and finally the set of loan terms. Data on loan terms, coupled with estimates of the extent to which lenders and borrowers trade off elements in the vector of terms in

[17] Loan size, maturity, guarantee, and interest rate are examples of important loan terms. For a discussion of the role of such terms in bank loan decisions, see Donald Hester, "An Empirical Examination of a Commercial Bank Loan Offer Function," *Yale Economic Essays* (Spring 1962), pp. 3–57, and Jack Guttentag, "Credit Availability, Interest Rates, and Monetary Policy," *The Southern Economic Journal* (Jan. 1960), pp. 219–28.

their negotiations, would provide a basis for an approximate identification of the supply-of-loans function.

The specification and estimation of a loan-supply function would be difficult and costly.[18] But the impact of liquidity and other variables on bank lending behavior cannot be known until this supply function is estimated.

[18] A second possible approach lies in a technique which statistically imputes marginal net rates of return to bank assets on a cross section basis. See D. Hester and J. Zoellner, "The Relation Between Bank Portfolios and Earnings: An Econometric Study," a paper presented before the 1964 winter meetings of the Econometric Society. Some preliminary attempts to obtain time series of net loan returns have not been very encouraging, but further efforts are justified.

MONEY DEMAND

PART 2

3

The Transactions Demand for Money

INTRODUCTION

In previous chapters we have examined some alternative specifications of the asset-holding behavior of the public and the banks and the effects of this behavior on the supply of money. Only recently have economists done much research on the money supply relation despite the importance of the money stock in most hypotheses about aggregate economic behavior. In contrast, the *demand* for money has been more thoroughly studied, largely because the implications and predictions that follow from alternative demand-for-money hypotheses have been recognized to generate widely contrasting prescriptions for economic policy.

There are various theoretical approaches to the demand for money. The present chapter focuses on the view that money, as the generally acceptable medium of exchange, is held in the interval between the receipt and disbursement of income primarily because there is some cost associated with both the purchase of interest-earning assets out of income and the sale of these assets to make disbursements. This chapter begins with a review of the basic determinants of this, the transactions demand for money and then examines William Baumol's inventory-theoretic treatment of the subject (1952).

Chapter 4 suggests that an individual also holds money, as one of several financial assets in his wealth portfolio, because he may thereby avoid losses from decreases in the market value of other, income-earning, assets. It describes John Maynard Keynes' original Liquidity Preference Theory (1936) and then develops James Tobin's approach to the subject (1958).

Chapter 5 considers the classical demand for money together with its modern (neoclassical) reformulation.* The classical demand for money inspired Keynes' work and is an important antecedent of the modern neoclassical reconsideration of money demand. The latter stresses neither the role of money in facilitating transactions nor its usefulness as a hedge against the risk of loss from holding other assets, but rather treats the demand for money as part of the general theory of demand.

While, in principle, these approaches are not always incompatible with one another, they will generate different models of the demand for money and different prescriptions for economic policy.** In the survey of empirical tests of various demand-for-money hypotheses which follows chapter 5 we shall see how well the factors suggested by each hypothesis explain variations in the demand for money.

THE TRANSACTIONS MOTIVE FOR HOLDING MONEY

Most modern economists believe that money is demanded, like any asset, because of the flow of services it renders. With most assets, the value of this flow of services is approximated by a dollar yield. With money, however, the income stream is usually not measurable by a simple nominal dollar return; commercial bank demand deposits, for instance, yield no interest return, yet provide a valuable flow of services to their owners. Economists have found it useful to associate this flow of services with the functions that money performs. Money is commonly said to function as a medium of exchange, a store of value and a unit of account.***

*Throughout this book we use the rubrics *classical* and *neoclassical* in a manner common to many monetary economists but perhaps disconcerting to historians of economic thought. We mean by the classical—neoclassical distinction not the difference between the labor-theory-of-value and marginalist schools but rather the historical hiatus between the pre- and post-Keynesian proponents of the Quantity Theory of Money.

**See, for instance, the implications that different demand-for-money functions have for monetary and fiscal policy, discussed in chapters 6 through 9.

***The services associated with the store of value function of money are discussed in the next chapter. The unit of account function of money simply means that money is used commonly as a denominator or *numeraire* in which the prices of all other goods or services are reckoned. We devote no further discussion to the unit of account function of money.

As a medium of exchange money is held between the receipt and disbursement of income because of the costs (brokerage fees, inconvenience, etc.) of converting into and out of other, earning, assets which themselves are not generally acceptable as media of exchange. The amount of money demanded to finance expenditures, in principle, thus depends on these conversion *costs* as well as on the *size* of the expenditures and how far in the future they will be made. Most economists, nevertheless, have emphasized the *size* of expenditures as the primary constraint affecting the demand for money as a medium of exchange. In fact, the transactions demand for money, associated with its use as a medium of exchange, is usually depicted as varying in direct proportion with the level of expenditures.* Following this tradition, where:

M_i/P_T = the average quantity of real transactions balances demanded by the ith individual**

T_i = the level of the ith individual's total real expenditures over a period of time, and

k_i = the proportionality factor, with a magnitude $0 < k_i < 1$ for long periods of time such as a month,

the individual's transactions demand function is $M_i/P_T = k_i T_i$.   (1)

The order of magnitude of k_i relates the size of the average money stock needed to finance a flow of expenditures to the size of that total flow. For instance, suppose an individual is paid a monthly income of $300 on the first day of each month. Assume further that he spends this income at a uniform rate of $10 per day for 30 days until he is paid again on the first day of the next month. His average transactions balance will be $150, i.e., since his holdings are $300 on the first day of the month and zero on the last day and since these balances decline uniformly over the course of the 30 day month, the average value of his transactions balances

---

*Keynes also postulated a demand for money to be held as a reserve against future contingencies such as personal emergencies or unforseen expenditures. Here again the existence of conversion costs explains why money is held to satisfy these needs even though it pays no dollar return. In this book, as in much of the professional literature, this precautionary demand for money is included with the transactions demand and is viewed as varying directly with the size of income and inversely with the market rate of interest.

**The concept of real expenditures, real income, real money balances, etc., is one that abstracts from price changes and measures what the dollar totals would be if prices remained constant. Real measures may be expressed by dividing ("deflating") a nominal measure by a price index; in the present case we deflate the nominal money stock by P_T, an index of the average price level of all goods and services exchanged in the economy over a given period of time.

is the mean of these two figures:

$$\frac{\$300 + 0}{2} = \$150.$$

Therefore,

$$k_i = \frac{M_i/P_T}{T_i} = \frac{\$150}{\$300/\text{mo.}} = \frac{1}{2}\,\text{month.}$$

If we were to measure this individual's total expenditures on a yearly basis, but continue to assume he is paid once each month and spends his income uniformly over the course of each month:

$$k_i = \frac{\$150}{\$3600/\text{yr.}} = \frac{1}{24}\,\text{year} = \frac{1}{2}\,\text{month.}$$

Therefore, we may view k_i as either the average period of time over which the individual holds a unit of money or, more usefully, as the average proportion of his total expenditures which an individual holds in the form of transactions balances.

This example can be used to illustrate the effect of a change in the frequency of receipts (for example, a change in the length of the pay period) or the effect of a change in the frequency of cash disbursements (stemming, for example, from an increased use of credit) on the average size of transactions balances. Consider first a change in the frequency of receipts. continue to assume that this individual *earns* $300 per month and spends his income at a rate of $10 per day. However, now assume that he is *paid* every fifteen days rather than once a month. He will receive $150 on the first and sixteenth days of each month. His average transactions balance will be:

$$\frac{\$150 + 0}{2} = \$75$$

and k_i will equal ¼ ;

$$k_i = \frac{\$75}{\$300/\text{mo.}} = \frac{1}{4}\,\text{month.}$$

Thus an increase in the frequency of receipts reduces the average amount of money which individuals must hold to facilitate a given volume of expenditures (k_i).

Now consider an example of the effect of a change in the frequency of disbursements. Assume the above individual is again being paid $300 on the first day of each month but now assume that he makes lump sum disbursements of $100 every 10 days. His transactions balances will be $300 for the first 10 days, $200 for the next 10 days, and $100 for the last 10 days of the month. His average money holdings will be

$$\frac{(\$300 \cdot 10 \text{ days}) + (\$200 \cdot 10 \text{ days}) + (\$100 \cdot 10 \text{ days})}{30 \text{ days}} = \$200$$

and k_i will equal $2/3$:

$$k_i = \frac{\$200}{\$300} \text{ mo.} = \frac{2}{3} \text{ month.}$$

In this particular case, the decrease in the frequency of disbursements increases the average amount of money (k_i) which individuals must hold to facilitate a given volume of expenditures (T_i).

Other aspects of individual payments and spending habits, such as different coincidences of receipts and disbursements, non-uniform rates of disbursement and the desire to maintain idle balances, influence the size of k_i. The role of individual payments and spending habits is discussed again in chapter 5. For the moment let us simply posit that k_i will always be a positive fraction of the flow of total expenditures measured over periods of time as long as a month.

Since our major concern in later chapters will be the analysis of aggregate economic behavior, we must aggregate over all individuals in the economy and show what determines the value of k for the economy as whole. The fraction that measures the individual's average transactions balance for a given flow of total expenditures over a period of time can be expressed by dividing each side of (1) by T_i

$$k_i = \frac{M_i/P_T}{T_i} \ . \tag{2}$$

For the economy as a whole let the average aggregate transactions balance for a given flow of aggregate total expenditures be

$$k_T = \frac{M/P_T}{T} \ . \tag{3}$$

Now to show the relationship between the individual k_i and the aggregate

k_T first we sum over individual holdings of real money balances where there are n individuals in the economy

$$M/P_T = \sum_{i=1}^{n} M_i/P_T .$$ (4)

Summing equation (1) over i and substituting equation (4) into the result yields

$$M/P_T = \sum_{i=1}^{n} k_i T_i .$$ (5)

Substituting this result into (3) gives

$$k_T = \sum_{i=1}^{n} k_i \frac{T_i}{T}$$

The value of k_T for the entire economy is the summation of the individual k_i each weighted by that individual's share of aggregate total expenditures for a given period of time.

At the outset of the book we noted that theories about the demand for money are considered important because money is widely believed to affect the level of production and employment. Therefore, it will be useful to reformulate the demand for transactions balances as a function of the level of output of newly produced goods and services (real income)* rather than the level of total expenditures. In any economy total expenditures exceed expenditures on the aggregate output of newly produced goods and services, since total expenditures include expenditures on everything exchanged in the economy, including transactions involving financial assets (e.g., stock market transactions) and second-hand physical assets, as well as intermediate transactions between business firms which do not directly add to the level of aggregate output.

---

*We shall assume that the ratio of aggregate total expenditures to aggregate income does not change systematically with real income in the short run even though in the long run such things as the vertical integration of business firms and increased specialization (both of which alter the level of intermediate transactions in the economy) will change this ratio. We shall assume that the ratio of the price indices also does not change systematically with real income in the short run.

Define k_o as the ratio of real aggregate transactions balances to the level of aggregate output,

$$k_o = \frac{M/P_o}{O} \quad . \tag{6}$$

This can be rewritten as

$$k_o = \frac{M/P_T}{T} \cdot \frac{T}{O} \cdot \frac{P_T}{P_o} \quad .$$

Using equation (5) gives

$$k_o = \sum_{i=1}^{n} k_i \frac{T_i}{T} \cdot \frac{T}{O} \cdot \frac{P_T}{P_o} \quad . \tag{7}$$

We can now see how k_o, a term which is used extensively in later chapters, depends on ratio of individuals' money holdings to their total real expenditures (as discussed above, the k_i reflect habits of payment and disbursement in the economy), the individuals' shares of aggregate total expenditures (T_i/T), the ratio of aggregate total expenditures to aggregate real income (T/O), and the ratio of the price index for total expenditures to the price index for newly-produced goods and services (P_T/P_o). Since none of these ratios is expected to change systematically as the level of aggregate real income changes, k_o is usually treated as a constant and the demand for transactions balances is viewed as varying in direct proportion with

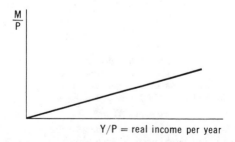

Figure 1. The Aggregate Transactions Demand for Money as a Function
of the Level of Aggregate Real Income, $0 < k_o < 1$

the level of real income. This relation is depicted in Figure 1 as a straight line through the origin with a slope of k_o.

THE INTEREST RATE AND THE TRANSACTIONS DEMAND FOR MONEY

While many earlier economists, including Fisher and Keynes, pointed out that income was not the only variable affecting the transactions demand for money, it took some time for economists to develop rigorously a rather sophisticated hypothesis of how conversion costs might affect transactions demand. Simply conceived, as the interest rate on other financial assets rises, the net cost of converting into and out of money balances for a given period of time is reduced and individuals will reduce their demand for transactions balances.

Consider our earlier example. Assume a bank raises its interest rate on time deposits from 2 percent to 6 percent per annum, payable on the 20th of the month. The individual who formerly held all $300 in transactions balances on the first day of the month, may now be induced to put $100 in the bank as a time deposit for the first 20 days of the month. He would do so because the interest income on $100 for 20 days rose from 11 cents to 33$\frac{1}{3}$ cents, assumed to be enough to compensate him for the cost (inconvenience) of two monthly trips to the bank. The average transactions balance is $100 for the first 20 days and $50 for the last 10 days of the month or 83.33\frac{1}{3}$ for the entire period.

In a similar fashion Keynes in *The General Theory . . .* (1936)*, Hansen in *Monetary Theory and Fiscal Policy* (1949)** and others, rationalized that a relatively high yield on liquid non-money assets could effect an economization in the demand for transaction balances. We write the transactions demand for real money balances as***

*Keynes, *op. cit.*

**Alvin Hansen, *Monetary Theory and Fiscal Policy* (New York: McGraw-Hill, 1949).

****Nominal*, as opposed to *real*, income is defined as being equal to the general price level of newly produced goods and services times the level of output, $Y = P \cdot O$, and the level of nominal money balances demanded as a function of the level of nominal income and the rate of interest (*i*) may be written as

$$M = f(Y, i).$$

While we use the demand for *real* money balances in the rest of this book, equation (8) is not the original Keynesian version since Keynes was rightfully accused of having a "money illusion" in his total money demand function which added together the transactions and precautionary (L_1) and the speculative (L_2) demands. Keynes wrote the total demand for money as

$$M = L_1(P \cdot O) + L_2(i).$$

$$M/p = f(O,i) \tag{8}$$

In this expression, M/p is postulated to vary *directly* with the level of output (O), as discussed above, and *inversely* with the market rate of interest, i. The latter relationship may hold only at "very high" interest rate levels.

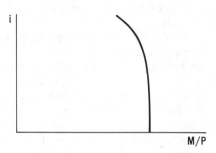

Figure 2. The Aggregate Transactions Demand for Real Money Balances as a Function of the Yield on Liquid Non-Money Assets

The relation between aggregate real transactions balances demanded and the rate of interest is shown in Figure 2 where the level of aggregate real income and other variables which could affect transactions demand are assumed constant. The function is drawn as it traditionally appears in money and banking and macroeconomic theory text books and is premised on the idea that some minimum interest rate is necessary to cover the minimum possible transactions cost in the economy.

BAUMOL'S APPROACH TO THE TRANSACTIONS DEMAND FOR MONEY

While the earlier work of Keynes, Hansen and others is important, it was William Baumol who first precisely systematized the interest rate into the

---

In the above formulation a rise in the general price level could not affect the demand for money for speculative purposes. Hence if P and M increase proportionately at a constant i, individuals have the "illusion" that they are "better off" even though their "real" money balances are unchanged.

It would be proper to include an expression for total wealth in this demand function since, as we shall see in chapter 4, Keynesians view the speculative demand for money in terms of the proportion of total financial wealth individuals will hold in the form of money. In addition, in the reading by John Boorman, which follows chapter 5, wealth (or some measure of permanent income) is shown to explain more of the variation in money demand than current income. Nevertheless, since we restrict the macroeconomic models in this book to short-run, static models where total wealth does not change, this argument may be ignored and we continue to use current income.

demand for transactions balances.* Baumol proceeds from the assumption that the stock of cash is the holder's inventory of the medium of exchange, and that the rational individual will attempt to minimize the cost of holding this inventory by holding the proper proportions of money and bonds. He assumes that transactions are perfectly foreseen and occur in a steady stream over a given time period. Real income per period is T dollars and, by assumption, the individual pays out all of his T dollars per period at a constant rate. Thus, all during the period, he will be holding an ever-diminishing stock of assets.

In what form will these assets be held, bonds or money? If the individual holds money, he will lose the interest income he could have earned on bonds. If he holds bonds, it will cost him something every time he "cashes" one in.

The individual is to begin the period holding all of his income in bonds. He is assumed to withdraw (disinvest) the money from bonds in lot-sized units of C dollars evenly spaced. For example, if an individual's T is $600 per month, C might be $600 every 30 days, $300 every 15 days, $150 every 7½ days, or $20 per day. Whatever the value of C there will be T/C withdrawals made during the period. For each withdrawal he must pay a unit real transactions cost of b dollars. The expression $b \cdot \dfrac{T}{C}$ is a kind of "inventory replenishment cost" which includes not only the explicit costs (brokerage fees) of selling assets to get cash but also the implicit cost (the inconvenience) of doing so.

On the assumption that his withdrawal of C dollars is expended at a constant rate, the individual's average cash balance is $C/2$, the amount of C dollars he holds half way through the interval from one withdrawal to another. The cost of holding cash is equal to the return (i) foregone by holding part of his portfolio in the form of an asset that does not bear a monetary yield.

The expression $i \cdot \dfrac{C}{2}$ represents the "interest opportunity cost" from holding transactions balances in the form of cash. The total cost of holding the inventory of cash (X) is, therefore,

$$X = b \cdot \frac{T}{C} + i \cdot \frac{C}{2} \cdot \qquad\qquad (9)$$

The problem then becomes one of picking the value of the disinvestment lot-size (C) which minimizes the total cost (transactions costs plus interest foregone) cost of holding the inventory of cash. At one extreme a single massive withdrawal (or disinvestment) from bonds at the outset of the

*William Baumol, "The Transactions Demand for Cash: An Inventory Theoretic Approach", *Quarterly Journal of Economics*, 66 (November 1952). For a somewhat more difficult but equally important treatment, *see* James Tobin's "The Interest Elasticity of the Transactions Demand for Cash," *Review of Economics and Statistics*, 38 (August 1956).

period means a high interest opportunity cost, at the other extreme numerous small withdrawals mean a high inventory replenishment cost. At some point between these extremes, the *increase* in interest opportunity cost from slightly increasing C is just equal to the *decrease* in inventory replenishment cost from slightly increasing C, i.e., the increment to total cost is zero. This (first-order) condition is satisfied where $dX/dC = 0$. Solving the resulting expression for optimal C, i.e., the value of C at which $dX/dC = 0$ gives*

$$C = \sqrt{(2bT)/i} \qquad (10)$$

which seems to indicate that a rational individual, acting to minimize the cost of holding his transactions balances, will demand cash in proportion to the square root of the value of his transactions.

Since the optimal average balance was said to be $C/2$,

$$C/2 = 1/2\sqrt{(2bT)/i} \; . \qquad (11)$$

Now let $k = 1/2\sqrt{2b}$ and let P be the general price level introduced to convert the expression into a demand for nominal balances. The above expression may be rewritten:

$$M = kT^{1/2} i^{-1/2} P \; . \qquad (12)$$

The result shows (1) the transactions demand for money does not generally vary in proportion to the level of total expenditures (T), i.e., instead, there should be economies of scale in the management of cash balances,**(2) that the quantity of transactions balances (C) varies inversely with the interest rate (i),*** and (3) that because of the trans-

---

*$dX/dC = -\dfrac{bT}{C^2} + \dfrac{i}{2} = 0.$

This is rearranged to get equation (10) above. The second-order condition for a minimum is likewise met:

$$d^2 X/dC^2 = \frac{2bT}{C^3} > 0.$$

**From equation (12) it can be seen that
$$\delta M/\delta T = 1/2 kT^{-1/2} i^{-1/2} P \neq k$$
and
$$\delta^2 M/\delta T^2 = -1/4\, kT^{-3/2} i^{-1/2} P < 0$$

Notice that when T increases, the demand for money does *not* increase by the factor of proportionality, k. This result (falsified by empirical work, reported following Part 2) would indicate a lack of classical proportionality between the demand for money and the level of income.

***Taking the transactions demand for money
$$M = kT^{1/2} i^{-1/2} P$$
The inverse relationship is shown by
$$\delta M/\delta i = -1/2\, kT^{1/2} i^{-3/2} P < 0.$$

actions cost of exchanging cash for bonds ($b > 0$) it generally pays to hold cash, i.e., in a perfectly frictionless world where purchases and sales of assets are costless, $b = 0$, there is *no* transactions demand for cash, because it costs absolutely nothing to switch from bonds to cash when expenditures must be made.

Baumol's model is extremely suggestive and has implications for the macroeconomic models we develop in chapters 6–9. Two implications are of foremost concern: first, the demand for money can, in principle, depend upon the interest rate (as well as the level of income) without considering the speculative demand for money. The interest rate, as it affects the demand for money and therefore is affected by monetary policy, is of crucial import for policymakers. (For instance, the model in chapter 6 suggests that if monetary policy cannot influence the interest rate, it is less powerful.)*

Secondly, if the demand for money varies less than in proportion to the level of income, a given change in the money supply will, *ceteris paribus*, require a relatively large change in income to increase money demand and bring the money market into equilibrium. The Baumol model lends credence to the belief that monetary policy is a potent way to influence the level of income.

Since. an examination of the effectiveness of monetary policy requires some knowledge of the total demand for money, not just the transactions demand, before these matters can be fully appreciated, we need to develop the speculative demand for money (chapter 4). In chapter 5 we view the demand for money from another theoretical perspective, that of the classical and modern Quantity Theorists. Then, as indicated above, in chapters 6 through 9, we employ alternative demand-for-money hypotheses in a series of macroeconomic models.

---

*These implications, along with tests of hypotheses regarding more general questions (such as which interest rate and which measure of income, if any, best explains variations in the demand for money) are surveyed in the reading by John Boorman which follows chapter 5.

Questions/ *chapter 3*

1. "Keynes did not allow uncertainty to enter his transactions demand for money, reserving its effects entirely for his liquidity preference hypothesis." Evaluate this statement. How could uncertainty enter into the Baumol model?

2. Explain the effects which the development of an extensive credit card system would have on the transactions demand for money.

3. What are some of the ways in which a corporate treasurer could conserve on his transactions balances in order to minimize the opportunity cost of holding such balances?

4. Explain the role of the interest rate in Baumol's "inventory theoretic" hypothesis of the demand for money.

5. "As income becomes more equitably distributed in our economy, Baumol's square root rule suggests monetary policy will be more effective." Evaluate.

6. Prove that the interest elasticity of the demand for money in the Baumol model is equal to $-1/2$.

Bibliography / *chapter 3*

Baumol, William J., "The Transactions Demand for Cash: An Inventory Theoretic Approach," *Quarterly Journal of Economics*, Vol. 66 (November 1952), pp. 545–556.

Brunner, Karl, and Allan H. Meltzer, "Economies of Scale in Cash Balances Reconsidered," *Quarterly Journal of Economics*, Vol. 81 (August 1967).

Hansen, Alvin H., *Monetary Theory and Fiscal Policy*. New York: McGraw-Hill, 1949.

Johnson, Harry G., "Notes on the Theory of the Transactions Demand for Cash," *Indian Journal of Economics*, Vol. 44 (July 1963), pp. 1–11.

Johnson, Harry G., "A Note on the Theory of Transactions Demand for Cash," *Journal of Money Credit and Banking*, Vol. 3 (August 1970), pp. 383–384.

Keynes, John Maynard, *The General Theory of Employment, Interest and Money*. London: Harcourt Brace and World, Inc., 1936.

Miller, H. Lawrence, "On Liquidity and Transactions Costs," *Southern Economic Journal*, Vol. 32 (1965), pp. 43–48.

Smith, P.E., "Probabilistic Demand for Cash Balances and (s,S) Inventory Policies," *Weltwirtschaft. Archiv.*, Vol. 93 (March 1961), pp. 72–83.

Sprenkle, Case, "The Uselessness of Transactions Demand Models," *Journal of Finance*, Vol. 24 (December 1969).

Tobin, James, "The Interest-Elasticity of Transactions Demand for Cash," *Review of Economics and Statistics*, Vol. 38 (August 1956), pp. 241–247.

Tsiang, S. C., "The Precautionary Demand for Money: An Inventory Theoretical Analysis," *Journal of Political Economy*, Vol. 77 (January-February 1969), pp. 99–117.

Whalen, E. L., "An Extension of the Baumol-Tobin Approach to the Transactions Demand for Cash," *Journal of Finance*, Vol. 23 (March 1968), pp. 113–134.

4

The Keynesian Speculative Demand for Money

INTRODUCTION

In the previous chapter we examined the transactions demand for money. In a world where the costs of buying and selling interest-earning assets (to be held in the interval between the receipt and disbursement of income) are not negligible, money, the generally accepted medium of exchange, will be held.

In this chapter we show that money is also held because it functions as a liquid store of wealth whose market value may be less variable than other wealth forms. (Individuals may demand money merely to hold it "idle.")*

At first blush it seems irrational to hold financial wealth in a non-earning form. Yet, as discussed in the next chapter, the earlier Cambridge economists indicated that an individual's uncertainty about future market prices of earning assets, among other things, could induce him to forego these earnings and to hold money. The market value of money may be less variable. Keynes articulated this in his Liquidity Preference Theory, one subject of this chapter.

---

*Thus, total money demand, M_d, consists of transactions (plus precautionary) balances, M_1 and speculative balances, M_2.

As discussed in this chapter, Keynes asserted* that the lower the market rate of interest relative to an expected future rate, the greater the expected decline in the prices of earning assets. Therefore, at low rates of interest liquid money balances are a preferable hedge against the expected capital loss of holding earning assets. In a subsequent section of this chapter James Tobin's version of this hypothesis is considered. Tobin indicated that even if the expected capital loss is zero, some risk of capital loss is always present. He further stated that the lower the rate of interest, the less the individual's preference to hold earning assets and assume this risk, and the greater his preference for liquidity (money balances).

Because of these Keynesian contributions and Baumol's inventory-theoretic approach to transactions demand, economists are inclined to concede, in principle, that the total demand for money depends on the rates of interest (yields) on financial assets as well as on the level of income and/or wealth. However, the extent to which any of these variables explain variations in the demand for money is largely an empirical question. After a look at the Keynesian contributions in this chapter, those of the Quantity Theorists in the next chapter, and, in the readings which follow Part 2, a survey by David Fand of modern Keynesian approaches to monetary theory (including the Radcliffe money-capital model, Tobin's portfolio balance model which emphasizes monetary wealth and the supply price of capital and the Tobin and Gurley-Shaw "new view" of monetary theory), we shall present a survey of empirical work on the demand for money.

THE RELATIONSHIP BETWEEN INTEREST RATES AND BOND PRICES

Before we begin our analysis, it is necessary to explain the relationship between interest rates and the prices of existing debt instruments which promise to pay the holder certain periodic interest payments and to repay the principal value at maturity.

When we speak of the *yield* on debt instruments such as bonds we shall mean the "yield-to-maturity." One measure of the yield of an obligation may be calculated simply by dividing the dollar amount of the interest paid per year by the current market price of the instrument. However, this is not a completely satisfactory measure, for it fails to consider the capital gain or loss to be incurred if that obligation is held to maturity.

---

*What we develop here is a contemporary interpretation of the Liquidity Preference Theory of John Maynard Keynes' *The General Theory of Employment, Interest and Money* (London: Harcourt Brace, 1936). The work will be more rigorous than the usual undergraduate macroeconomic theory or money and banking textbook version but more simplified than the professional literature.

For example, the current yield on an obligation selling for $950 and paying $50.00 per year is $50/$950 = .0526 or 5.26%. But if the face value of this bond is $1000 it will return an additional $50 above purchase price to the owner upon redemption at maturity. Thus, if the bond is held to maturity the owner will realize a capital gain of $50 on his investment in addition to the yearly interest return. This capital gain must be included in the complete return when calculating the total yield to maturity on the security.

Yield-to-maturity may be calculated by means of a formula for computing the present value of a future stream of returns. If one wishes to calculate the present value of a single $50 payment to be made one year from today, he "discounts" that $50 according to the simple formula:

$$\text{Present Value} = P = \frac{50}{(1 + i)}$$

where i is the interest (or discount) rate. For example the present value of $50 discounted at 2% for one year is:

$$P = \frac{\$50}{(1 + .02)} = \frac{\$50}{1.02} = \$49.02.$$

In other words $49.02 invested for one year at 2% yields $50. In general a single payment of Y dollars to be received two years in the future is currently valued at:

$$P = \frac{Y}{(1 + i)^2} .$$

At 2%, then, the present value of this *single* $50 payment to be made two years from today is:

$$P = \frac{\$50}{(1 + i)^2} = \frac{\$50}{(1 + .02)^2} = \frac{\$50}{(1.0404)} = \$48.06.$$

If we generalize this formula, the present value of any payment, Y_n, to be made n years from now is

$$P = \frac{Y_n}{(1 + i)^n} . \qquad (1)$$

Therefore, if a debt instrument carries an obligation to pay $50 *per year* for the next five years and a final repayment of principal of $1000.00 at the end of the five year period, the present value of that stream of returns discounted at a rate of $100i\%$ per year is:

$$P = \frac{Y_1}{(1+i)} + \frac{Y_2}{(1+i)^2} + \frac{Y_3}{(1+i)^3} + \frac{Y_4}{(1+i)^4} + \frac{Y_5}{(1+i)^5} + \frac{Principal}{(1+i)^5} \quad (2)$$

where $Y_1 = Y_2 = Y_3 = Y_4 = Y_5 = \$50$.

For example, if the return demanded by the lender is six percent per year, he would be willing to pay $957.87 for a bond with these characteristics.

$$P = \frac{\$50}{(1.06)} + \frac{\$50}{(1.06)^2} + \frac{\$50}{(1.06)^3} + \frac{\$50}{(1.06)^4} + \frac{\$50}{(1.06)^5} + \frac{\$1000}{(1.06)^5}$$

$$= \$47.17 + \$44.50 + \$41.98 + \$39.60 + \$37.36 + \$747.26$$

$$= \$957.87.$$

Alternatively, knowing the current market price of the instrument, we may use the formula to calculate its yield to maturity. For example, if the obligation is currently selling for $950.00, the yield is given by the formula:

$$\$950 = \frac{\$50}{(1+i)} + \frac{\$50}{(1+i)^2} + \frac{\$50}{(1+i)^3} + \frac{\$50}{(1+i)^4} + \frac{\$50}{(1+i)^5} + \frac{\$1000}{(1+i)^5}$$

$$i = .0619 \qquad 100i = 6.19\%$$

It is clear from the formula that the higher the (interest) rate at which future expected returns are discounted (in the denominators) the lower will be the present value of that income (the market value of the obligation) and, conversely, the lower the rate of discount, the higher will be the present value.

It is through variations in the market price of outstanding securities that the yield on those instruments is adjusted to current market conditions.

The formula suggests that when the market rate in the denominator is equal to the 5% *coupon rate* (the $50 annual interest payment divided by the $1000 principal), the bond sells in the market at "par," i.e., its market price is equal to its principal value. When the market rate is greater than the coupon rate the bond sells below par, and when the market rate is less than the coupon rate the bond sells above par.

This shows that bond prices will always adjust, in the market where bonds are traded, to bring a bond's yield-to-maturity into line with the market rate of interest. It indicates that bond prices vary inversely with the market rate of interest.

Finally, the formula indicates that the market prices of longer-term debt instruments are more affected by a change in the market rate than the prices of shorter-term debt instruments, since instruments with a longer term-to-maturity contain larger powers of $(1 + i)$ in the formula. This is important because it means longer-term bonds are more subject to capital gains and losses than shorter-term bonds.

In this chapter we deal exclusively with *consol bonds* because the relationship between the market price of a consol bond and the market rate of interest can be reduced to a very convenient expression. A consol continues to pay interest indefinitely but does not repay principal. Therefore, the general present value formula, equation (2), is written without the final term for the repayment of principal,

$$P = \frac{Y_1}{(1 + i)^1} + \frac{Y_2}{(1 + i)^2} + \frac{Y_3}{(1 + i)^3} + \cdots + \frac{Y_n}{(1 + i)^n} \ . \tag{3}$$

Now multiply both sides of this equation by $1/1 + i$,

$$\frac{1}{1 + i} P = \frac{Y_1}{(1 + i)^2} + \frac{Y_2}{(1 + i)^3} + \cdots + \frac{Y_n}{(1 + i)^{n+1}} \tag{4}$$

Assume that $Y_1 = Y_2 = Y_3 = \cdots = Y_n$ and subtract equation (4) from equation (3)

$$P \left[1 - \frac{1}{1 + i} \right] = \frac{Y}{1 + i} - \frac{Y}{(1 + i)^{n+1}} \ .$$

Multiply both sides by $(1 + i)$ and rearrange terms,

$$P = \frac{Y}{i} \left[1 - \frac{1}{(1 + i)^n} \right] . \tag{5}$$

This is a general expression for the present value of a stream of future interest payments. If we add an expression for repayment of principal it is often a convenient way to reformulate the present value formula, equation (2).

To derive the expression for the present value of a consol simply let the maturity of the bond n become infinite, so that the expression $(1 + i)^n$ becomes infinitely large and the term $\frac{1}{(1 + i)^n}$ becomes zero as n approaches infinity. This gives

$$P = \frac{Y}{i} \tag{6}$$

which says that the present value of a consol is inversely proportional to the rate of interest.

Now we are ready to begin our analysis of the speculative demand for money. If we ignore physical assets and equities (which have roughly similar portfolio properties as physical assets),* an individual may hold his wealth in two forms, debt instruments and money. As discussed earlier, money has the advantage of being generally acceptable as a medium of exchange. In addition, the market value of money may be subject to less volatile swings than the market value of debt instruments. Economists traditionally have said that the confluence of these two properties make money a unique, most "liquid" financial asset.

THE EARLY KEYNESIAN APPROACH TO LIQUIDITY PREFERENCE

In *The General Theory of Employment, Interest and Money,*** Keynes assumes that all individuals wish to avoid losses and that the gains or losses they anticipate from holding debt instruments (bonds) depend solely on the rate of interest i_e which they are certain will occur at some uncertain date within the forthcoming time period t.***

Capital losses would be expected if the current rate of interest i were less than the expected rate i_e because, as discussed above, as bond yields rise, bond prices fall. If the current rate i were sufficiently lower than the

---

*Both debt and money differ from physical assets and equities in that their values do not fluctuate with the price level and in that they are unattractive investments when the price level is expected to rise. In chapter 5 the effect of price expectations on the demand for money and debt is examined as part of a discussion of the relation between nominal and real rates of interest. For the present our analysis abstracts from changes in the general price level.

**Ibid.*

***The expected rate is forecasted by the individual. For analytical simplicity, we overlook the behavior that generates the rate expected to occur within the forthcoming time period. We assume it occurs independently of the level of the current rate, that is, we assume perfectly inelastic interest rate expectations. Keynes had in mind inelastic, but not perfectly inelastic, interest rate expectations (Keynes, *Ibid.*, 202). They were tied to his concept of the "normal" rate. The "normal" rate of interest, according to Keynes, is the level toward which the expected rate gravitates over time. *The further the current rate diverges from normal, the more it would be expected to bounce back in the forthcoming time period.*

expected rate i_e, it would be unprofitable for the individual firm or household to hold bonds now. Rather, if capital losses were greater than interest income, the individual would hold money balances until the rate i rises to its expected level (and bond prices fall). At that time he would buy bonds. Conversely, if the rate of capital loss were less than the current interest rate i (or if capital gains were expected), the individual would hold bonds now.* Thus the *individual's* financial wealth will consist of either all bonds or all money in Keynes' model.

Keynes proposed that the *economy's* speculative demand for money slopes downward because, as the current rate falls, increasingly more individuals become convinced that the rate of capital loss outweighs the interest rate; that is, as the current rate falls, more and more individuals feel that the current rate is sufficiently below their expected rate to warrant holding all of their speculative financial wealth in the form of money balances.

Mathematically the sufficient condition for the financial investor's holding all of his speculative portfolio as money is:

$$i + g < 0 \qquad \text{where } g < 0 \tag{7}$$

Let:

P_e = expected bond price

P = current bond price.

The definition of the rate of capital loss is:

$$g = \frac{P_e - P}{P} \qquad \text{where } P_e < P. \tag{8}$$

Substituting (8) into (7):

$$i + \frac{P_e - P}{P} < 0$$

or

$$i + \frac{P_e}{P} - 1 < 0.$$

---

*Contrast this analysis, where the *expected value* of the capital gain or loss is nonzero and known with certainty, to Tobin's approach (in the next section) where the *expected value* of the capital gain and loss in a probability distribution is zero, and yet the individual will still be wary of holding bonds because there is a "risk" of holding bonds. "Risk," in Tobin's analysis, is measured by the spread or *dispersion* of *possible* capital losses and gains about this zero *expected value*.

Assume for purposes of analytical convenience that all bonds are *consols* (bonds paying a fixed income in perpetuity). This makes bond prices and bond yields inversely proportional, as shown in equation (6) above, so that the last expression may be re-written as:

$$i + \frac{i}{i_e} - 1 < 0.$$

Multiplying through by i_e, we get

$$i \cdot i_e + i - i_e < 0.$$

The condition for holding all financial wealth as money is then

$$i \cdot i_e + i < i_e.$$

As an example, assume a consol paying $50 a year is currently priced at $1000, so that $i = .05$. But it is expected to attain a market price of $950 sometime within the forthcoming period; by equation (6) the expected rate i_e is .05263. At this rate it follows that

$$i \cdot i_e + i = i_e$$

and the individual is indifferent between bonds or money. If the expected rate (i_e) were higher, he would hold all money; if it were lower, he would hold all bonds. The reader may calculate that where the income per year is $40 on the same bond, the current rate is .04 and the critical expected rate is .04166. A convenient (though slightly inaccurate) rule of thumb is that the expected rate which would induce an individual to hold all money, must be greater than the current rate i plus its square i^2, that is, if

$$i + i^2 < i_e$$

one would hold all money; and if

$$i + i^2 > i_e$$

one would hold all bonds.

Now if Keynes' hypothesis obtains, the individual demand for real speculative money balances (M_2)* may be depicted as the following discontinuous function:

---

*In future chapters we refer, as did Keynes, to transactions balances as M_1 and speculative balances as M_2. It must be pointed out now, as we do in detail in chapter 5, that the usefulness of the concept of separable money demand components is challenged by many economists.

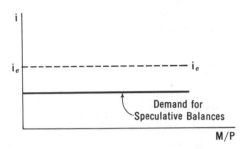

Figure 1. The Individual's Demand for Speculative Money Balances

When the market rate of interest i is sufficiently below the expected rate i_e as discussed above, the individual holds all of his speculative portfolio in the form of real money balances. Otherwise, he holds all of his speculative portfolio in the form of bonds.*

To derive the demand curve for speculative balances for the entire economy, we simply sum across all individual demand curves. A necessary condition for the smooth downward-sloping of this aggregate curve, as depicted in Figure 2,** is that as the market rate i falls, successively greater numbers of individuals feel that this rate is sufficiently below their expected rate to warrant holding all of their speculative portfolio in the form of real money balances.

This analysis carries several crucial implications. First, Keynes suggested that at some low interest rate, practically everyone will feel the current rate is sufficiently below their expected rate to warrant holding their portfolio in the form of money balances. At this point, the economy's demand-for-money function approaches an infinite interest elasticity as shown in Figure 2. No matter how large the increase in the money supply, only a very small decrease in the interest rate is sufficient to convince individuals to hold all of their portfolio in the form of money balances. As

---

*Where future rates are not assumed to be expected with certainty, the individual may actually mix his bond-money holdings. The more the current rate departs from the "normal" rate, the greater the probability with which the individual expects the rate to move back to its "normal" level. In this case, the greater the rise in the current rate, the greater the proportion of financial wealth held in the form of bonds and the greater the decline in the current rate, the greater the proportion held in the form of money. Unlike the Tobin approach, this variation of Keynes' analysis still ties *risk* to the expected rate.

**Again, as in chapter 3, to avoid Keynes' error of money illusion, we depict the demand for *real* money balances. *See* the second section of chapter 3, "The Interest Rate and the Transactions Demand for Money," for a discussion of this problem.

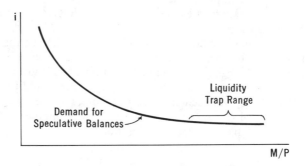

Figure 2. The Demand for Speculative Balances in the Economy

discussed in detail in chapter 6, if the economy is in this "liquidity trap," it may make monetary policy completely ineffective.

Notice that Keynes did not introduce earning assets of very short maturity into his analysis. In the *real* world these assets *might* be held until bond prices fell, and then would be liquidated, the funds being used for purchase of low-priced bonds. The financial investor need not hold money bearing no explicit yield. Nevertheless, Keynes' purposeful omission of such "money substitutes" does not vitiate his hypothesis that the rate of interest affects the demand for money, because, as discussed in chapter 3, earning assets have explicit and implicit conversion costs as they are purchased and liquidated, and therefore, the rational individual will generally hold some of his speculative wealth in the form of money balances. Also, as Keynes assumes that the exact date of the bond price decline is not known with certainty, an individual holding even short-term assets would surely incur some (albeit a small) capital loss. Therefore, money substitutes may not be a profitable hedge against the expected loss from holding long-term bonds.

Finally, if as many critics believe, Keynes suggested the expected rate was subject to change, the demand for money would be statistically unstable. In contrast (as reported in the survey of empirical tests of the demand for money function following Part 2), the function appears to be quite stable statistically.

One might then attempt to preserve Keynes' hypothesis, in light of this evidence, by assuming that the expected rate is relatively constant. There has been considerable criticism of this assumption's lack of realism. In fact, in a world where all individuals have learned to expect the same or very similar "normal" rates,* the speculative demand schedule would have

*The role of the normal rate in Keynes' analysis is discussed at the beginning of this section.

a nearly angular (convex) shape. This shape is not revealed by statistical tests reported in the empirical survey.

The primary weakness of Keynes' original Liquidity Preference hypothesis then is its assumption of a *certain* expected rate. In order to get the stable money demand function revealed by statistical tests, this rate must be relatively fixed by the individual. At the same time, in order to obtain the typical smooth aggregate money demand function (shown in Figure 2) that seems to fit the actual data*, the expected rate would have to differ between individuals, and each individual's holdings would have to be small relative to the total for the economy. This clearly imposes severe restrictions on an already barely tenable assumption.

THE TOBIN APPROACH TO LIQUIDITY PREFERENCE

Introduction. A major advance in monetary theory was the explanation of the inverse relationship between the rate of interest and the quantity of money demanded, without the restrictive rate-forecasting assumption of Keynes. We shall now present an abbreviated, simplified version of James Tobin's hypothesis.**

Definitions. Assume a two asset economy where portfolios are comprised of money and/or consol bonds with an annual market rate of interest of i percent; also assume that each financial investor is *uncertain* about the value of the market rate in the next period. Each investor believes that the probability that the market rate will fall by k percent is equal to the probability that it will rise by k percent, and no rate is any riskier, in and of itself, than any other. (Notice how these two assumptions differ from Keynes' original necessary assumption of a *certain* expected rate that differed between individuals and resulted in their portfolios consisting of either bonds *or* money).

Let:

A_1 = the fraction of total assets which the investor holds as money, where $0 \leqslant A_1 \leqslant 1$

A_2 = the fraction of total assets which the investor holds as consols, where $0 \leqslant A_2 \leqslant 1$

---

*As reported in the survey of empirical work that follows Part 2, most statistical tests do not indicate the presence of the liquidity trap.

**For all points requiring further detail, *see* James Tobin, "Liquidity Preference As Behavior Toward Risk," *Review of Economic Studies*, Vol. 25 (1958). For the reader who would like to go further in investigating modern Keynesian monetary theory, the readings following chapter 5 contain a survey article by David Fand, covering some of the more recent approaches to this topic.

$A_1 + A_2 = 1$ by the above assumption

E = the expected percentage increase in the value of the portfolio during a year (which by the assumption above excludes probable capital gains or losses)*, that is,

$$E = A_2 \cdot i \qquad (9)$$

R = the risk associated with an increase in consol holdings, measured as a percentage, that is

$$R = A_2 \cdot s \qquad (10)$$

where $s \, (0 \leqslant s \leqslant 1)$ is a fixed coefficient measuring the risk of capital loss from holding a bond and is subjectively determined by each investor.**

Note that unlike Keynes' original hypothesis, the capital loss from holding a bond is assumed independent of the *level* of the interest rate.

Utility. Now the individual's problem is this: each bond held increases expected earnings, but it also increases the risk (possible fluctuation of value) of the portfolio. Earnings, viewed here as additions to wealth, are "good"; they add to utility; risk is "bad"; it subtracts from utility. What combination of expected earnings and risk will make the individual "happiest." To answer this question we turn to a tool of elementary economic theory, the *indifference curve*.

Assume that every combination of expected increases in the value of the portfolio E and risk R gives the financial investor a certain amount of expected utility or "satisfaction" I. Further assume that there are numerous sets of possible combinations of E and R that give the investor *equal* amounts of expected utility, $I_1, I_2, I_3, \ldots, I_n$. In the graph below, expected utility is constant along each line I.

Assume that for every level of risk R, the associated value of expected earnings, E, along I_2 is greater than the corresponding E along I_1. Hence

---

*For the reader with some knowledge of elementary mathematical statistics, the individual assesses the *expected value* of probable capital gains and losses as zero and therefore the expected value of holding a bond is just its interest yield.

**Again, for the reader with some knowledge of mathematical statistics, the risk from holding bonds is not the *expected value* of the capital gain or loss (which is assumed to be zero), but rather the standard deviation of the probability distribution of expected future bond prices. Thus, $s = \sigma$.

Other measures of risk have been used in models of portfolio behavior. An important treatise on portfolio theory shows the Tobin model presented here to be a special case of a more general theory of asset choice. *See*, Bernell K. Stone, *Risk, Return and Equilibrium* (M.I.T. Press, Cambridge, 1970).

I_2 represents a greater amount of utility than does I_1; therefore I_2 and I_1 cannot intersect in the graph.

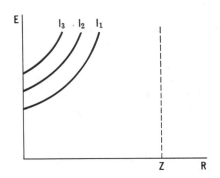

Figure 3. An Indifference Map

Assume that as expected earnings, E, increase by consecutive, equal amounts, increasingly less addition risk, R, is accepted by the individual who chooses to remain at the same level of expected utility I. In Figure 3 it is seen that dR/dE is positive and as E increases dR/dE decreases. Thus, the investor is said to be "risk averse."*

Note also that R total risk has a limiting value Z, which is reached when A_2 equals unity. The portfolio can become no riskier.

Objective constraints. We have now mapped out lines of equal utility called indifference curves. The individual is indifferent between any combinations of E and R along any one curve, but prefers combinations along a higher curve to those along a lower one. The problem faced by the financial investor is to maximize his expected utility by finding, among all points available to him, the combination of E and R that gives him the greatest level of expected utility. There are, however, two factors that constrain this process: the market rate of interest i and the risk coefficient s.

The market rate of interest i relates the expected percentage increase in portfolio value E that the investor can realize by increasing A_2 (that is, (9) $E = A_2 \cdot i$). The risk coefficient s relates the increase in risk R that is a

---

*Tobin mapped out the behavior of "risk lovers" and "plungers" as well. The tradeoff between risk and earnings is quite different for these individuals. However, the concept of the "risk averter" will suffice in developing the conventional asset demand for money.

concomitant of the increase in A_2 (that is, (10) $R = A_2 \cdot s$) and not, as in Keynes, a concomitant of the level of i.

Solving (9) and (10) for A_2, equating the results and solving for E we get

$$E = \frac{R}{s} \cdot i. \tag{11}$$

This expression denotes what the market allows the investor to do as opposed to what he would desire to do as shown by his indifference map. He can get a higher (or lower) expected return E by accepting a greater (or lesser) degree of risk R. The first derivative of (11) with respect to R is:

$$\frac{dE}{dR} = \frac{i}{s} \tag{12}$$

It is seen that the successive amounts of additional E that can be obtained by accepting greater R are constant and equal to i/s.

Maximization. The investor must reconcile his desires as expressed by the indifference or equal-utility curves, $I_1, I_2, \ldots, I_n$, to the objective limitations (constraints) imposed by the market. He must choose the desired combinations of E and R that give maximum total utility subject to the known values of i and s. This may be demonstrated by plotting equation (11) on the same diagram as the indifference map.

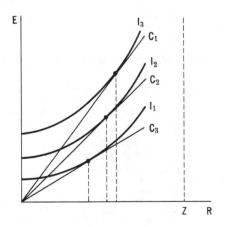

Figure 4. Utility Maximization

As can be seen from (11), the slope of the constraint OC is the ratio i/s. Every time the market rate i falls the OC constraint will move downwards (less return can be obtained by accepting more risk).

Tangency between an objective constraint and an indifference curve depicts the first order condition for a maximization of expected utility.* Each indifference curve (I_1, I_2, I_3) shows how the individual *desires* to exchange E for R. Each constraint (OC_1, OC_2, OC_3) shows how the market *permits* the individual to exchange E for R. A financial investor maximizes his expected utility when the desired increase in expected return E relative to the desired increase in risk R along I is equal to the tradeoff between E and R permitted by the market OC. In short, the investor increases the proportion of consols in his portfolio by successive increments until it is no longer possible to gain more utility from increased expected earnings than to lose utility from increased risk. This is the point where the constraint is tangent to the indifference curve.**

The demand for idle money balances. As the market rate i falls and the risk coefficient of the investor s remains constant, the OC constraint pivots downward, and risk R may either rise or fall depending on how the financial investor desires to exchange E for R. If, as shown in Figure 4, the preferences of the investor are such that the equilibrium value of R falls, from equation (10) it can be seen that the equilibrium value of the fraction of the investor's wealth held as consols A_2 also falls, and hence (as $1 = A_1 + A_2$), the fraction of the investor's wealth held in the form of money balances A_1 rises.

---

*Second order conditions are satisfied by the convexity of the indifference curve.

**This may be expressed mathematically. Let the utility function in general notation be:

$$U = U(E,R).$$

To specify movement along an indifference curve, take the total differential of this function and set it equal to zero,

$$dU = (\partial U/\partial E)dE + (\partial U/\partial R)dR = 0.$$

The "tradeoff" or marginal rate of substitution is derived by rearranging this expression to get

$$\frac{dE}{dR} = -\frac{\partial U/\partial R}{\partial U/\partial E}.$$

Set this equal to the constraint imposed by the market (equation 12) and the first-order condition for a maximum is satisfied,

$$\frac{i}{s} = -\frac{\partial U/\partial R}{\partial U/\partial E}.$$

The second-order condition is satisfied by the convexity of the indifference curve. If the utility function were more fully specified the demand for money could be directly derived.

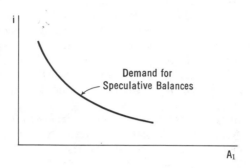

Figure 5. The Risk Averse Individual's Speculative Demand for Money

Therefore, if less risk R is acceptable at a lower market rate i, the quantity of money demanded as a proportion of total speculative wealth varies inversely with the rate of interest as shown in Figure 5.

Does R fall as i falls? In this analysis, as with the usual indifference analysis, there is an income (more properly, a wealth) and a substitution effect associated with a shift in the constraint.

First consider the substitution effect. Given an increase in i (a fall in bond prices), risk R becomes less expensive to acquire, and the investor can increase his expected earnings E by reducing A_1 his proportionate holdings of money. An increase in the rate of interest is an incentive to take more risk; in terms of the substitution effect, it means a shift from security to yield. Given a fall in i, risk R becomes more expensive and he can reduce R (and E) by increasing A_1. These changes are labeled as responses to the substitution effect. In essence, this is the substitution of less risk A_1 for more risk A_2 as the relative "price" of risk rises.

Now consider the income effect. As the price of any commodity falls, the individual may buy more of all commodities (i.e., an "income effect") because he is "better off." Keynesian models usually assume an income elasticity of the demand for money of unity. Under this assumption, a rise in the interest rate raises expected earnings, the individual desires the same proportion of money and bonds, and the income effect would not counteract the substitution effect. The latter will always insure that as the interest rate rises, the quantity of money demanded as a proportion of speculative wealth decreases.

Now relax the usual assumption and assume that risk R is an inferior good. In this case, because he is "better off," he will buy less of an "inferior" good as his income rises. Suppose there is a rise in i (a fall in the price of risk). Clearly, by equation (9) expected earnings increase. In this case, the income effect will dictate that the individual hold less risk.

Equation (10) shows that he can only do this by reducing A_2 and increasing A_1. If risk is an "inferior" good, the income effect will require that the investor hold proportionately fewer bonds as he is "better off."

Conversely, if there is a decrease in i (a decrease in expected earnings), the income effect will require that an individual hold more of the inferior good. In order to acquire more risk, the proportion A_2 must increase. In a sense, as i falls, the individual is increasing his proportionate bond holdings A_2, and reducing his proportionate money holdings A_1, in order to maintain his income level.

If the equilibrium value of R increases as i decreases (and vice versa), the income effect (in this special case) dominates the substitution effect. If R decreases as i decreases (and vice versa), the substitution effect dominates the income effect. Under the assumption that risk is an inferior good, to obtain an inverse relation between the market rate of interest and the fraction of the financial investor's wealth held in the form of money balances, the substitution effect must dominate.

SUMMARY

Keynes asserted that the quantity of speculative balances demanded would vary inversely with the market interest rate. For the individual, the lower the market rate relative to his expected rate, the greater his expected capital loss (the greater his *risk* of holding earning assets). At some level a decline in the market rate would induce the rational individual to switch from holding all of his speculative wealth in the form of bonds to holding it in the form of money balances.

Statistical findings impose two severely restrictive conditions on Keynes' hypothesis of money demand. A smooth, downward-sloping speculative demand function as revealed by most statistical tests, requires the condition that individuals have different expected rates. Statistical tests that show the money demand function to be stable, require the condition that these rates be relatively fixed.

James Tobin's more sophisticated liquidity preference hypothesis is a vast improvement because it disposes of Keynes' assumption of a certain, expected rate and the concomitant restrictions that it be fixed by the individual and differ between individuals.* Tobin shows that even if the expected capital loss is independent of the current interest rate (i.e., is nothing if risk is unchanged), an inverse relation between the interest rate and the demand for speculative balances will obtain as long as individuals are less willing to accept risk as the market rate declines.

*The Tobin analysis is important also because it is a precursor of the portfolio balance approach to monetary theory. The portfolio balance approach introduces many financial assets and as many interest rates as there are imperfect substitutes among these assets. This somewhat more complicated slant is discussed in the survey article by David Fand that appears in the readings that follow chapter 5.

Questions/ *chapter 4*

1. In a world of numerous money substitutes, individuals will never hold speculative balances. True or False?

2. Either Keynes' speculative demand is unstable or else it must be perfectly convex to the origin (L-shaped). Evaluate.

3. What shape would the speculative demand for money take if individuals felt risk were not an inferior good? (As the "price" of risk rises, the individual chooses more risk.)

4. Relate the speculative demand for money to the bank's demand for excess reserves discussed in chapter 2.

5. Explain why the market prices of long-term bonds are more influenced by interest rate changes than the prices of short-term bonds.

6. "If the income elasticity of the demand for money is constrained to unity the proportion of speculative wealth held in the form of money balances will always vary inversely with the interest rate." Evaluate

7. Explain the relation between the market rate and the coupon rate when a bond sells "above par."

Bibliography / *chapter 4*

Chow, Gregory C., "On the Long-Run and Short-Run Demand for Money," *Journal of Political Economy*, Vol. 74 (April 1966), pp. 111–131.

Duesenberry, James S., "The Portfolio Approach to the Demand for Money and Other Assets," *Review of Economics and Statistics*, Vol. 45 (February 1963), Supplement, pp. 9–24.

Keynes, John Maynard, *The General Theory of Employment Interest and Money*. London: Harcourt Brace and World, Inc., 1936.

Konstas, Panos, and Mohmad W. Khouja, "The Keynesian Demand-for-Money Function," *Journal of Money*, *Credit and Banking*, Vol. 1 (November 1969), pp. 765–775.

Leijonhufvud, Axel, *On Keynesian Economics and the Economics of Keynes*. New York: Oxford, 1968.

Laidler, D. A., "The Rate of Interest and the Demand for Money—Some Empirical Evidence," *Journal of Political Economy*, Vol. 74 (December 1966), pp. 543–555.

Latané, Henry A., "Income Velocity and Interest Rates: A Pragmatic Approach," *Review of Economics and Statistics*, Vol. 42 (November 1953), pp. 445–449.

Lee, T. H., "Alternative Interest Rates and the Demand for Money: The Empirical Evidence," *American Economic Review*, Vol. 57 (December 1967), pp. 1168–1181.

Lintner, John, "Security Prices, Risk and Maximal Gains from Diversification," *Journal of Finance* (December 1965).

Markowitz, Harry, *Portfolio Selection*, Cowles Foundation Monograph. John Wiley: New York 1959.

Mayer, Thomas, and Martin Bronfenbrenner, "Liquidity Functions in the American Economy," *Econometrica*, Vol. 28 (October 1960), pp. 810–834.

Meltzer, Allan H., "The Demand for Money: The Evidence from the Time Series," *Journal of Political Economy*, Vol. 71 (June 1963), pp. 219–246, pp. 768–783.

Mossin, Jan, "Equilibrium in a Capital Asset Market," *Econometrica* (October 1966), pp. 768-783.

Sharpe, William, "Capital Asset Prices: A Theory of Market Equilibrium Under Conditions of Risk," *Journal of Finance* (September 1964), pp. 425–442.

Starleaf, D. R. and R. Reimer, "The Keynesian Demand Function for Money: Some Statistical Tests," *Journal of Finance*, Vol. 22 (March 1967), pp. 71–76.

Stedrey, Andrew C., "A Note on Interest Rates and the Demand for Money," *Review of Economics and Statistics*, Vol. 41 (August 1959), pp. 303–307.

Stone, Bernell K., *Risk, Return and Equilibrium*. Cambridge: M.I.T. Press, 1970.

Tobin, James, "Liquidity Preference as Behavior Towards Risk," *Review of Economic Studies*, Vol. 25 (February 1958), pp. 65–86.

Tobin, James, "Money, Capital, and Other Stores of Value," *American Economic Review, Papers and Proceedings*, Vol. 51, (May 1961), pp. 26–37.

Tobin, James, "The Theory of Portfolio Selection" in F. H. Hahn and F. P. Brechling (eds.), *The Theory of Interest Rates*. New York: St. Martin's Press, 1965.

5

The Quantity Theory of Money

INTRODUCTION

In chapters 3 and 4, we examined several theories of the demand for money. Chapter 3 presented the basic analysis of the transactions demand for money, using both the traditional Keynesian approach as well as the somewhat more complex inventory-theoretic analysis of William Baumol. Two variants of the asset demand for money were described in chapter 4: the *liquidity preference theory* of J. M. Keynes and the *risk aversion theory* of James Tobin.

In this chapter, the classical view of the demand for money is surveyed. We shall present the major outlines of the theories of Irving Fisher, A. C. Pigou, Alfred Marshall, and J. M. Keynes. The analytic approach taken by these writers in the works cited is generally referred to as the *Quantity Theory of Money*. We shall also describe the modern reformulation of the Quantity Theory by Milton Friedman, and relate his conclusions to those implicit in the older presentations of this doctrine.

In the following chapters, we shall see that the classical approach to the demand for money* results in a model of the aggregate economy which contrasts markedly with the more familiar Keynesian Model.** In particular, we shall see that very different policy prescriptions are derived from these alternative forms.

TRADITIONAL FORMULATIONS OF THE QUANTITY THEORY OF MONEY

It may safely be said that the Quantity Theory was the theory of the value of money held by virtually all classical economists.*** This theory is believed by many to have had its origin in the sixteenth century in the writings of Jean Bodin, an official of the French court, and a philosopher as well. The impetus for his work was the great rise in prices which took place in France and in most of Western Europe during the latter part of the sixteenth century. Though Bodin recognized several possible causes for these price increases, he laid greatest stress on the rising "stocks of coin" to be found in the country as a result of the huge inflows of "precious" monetary metals from the newly settled colonies in America. His statement was far from a complete analysis of all the forces at work influencing the determination of the absolute price level (a task which has still not been completed by economists), but it did represent the first clear analysis of the relationship between *variations in the price level and changes in the stock of money*.

Though many writers, notably John Locke, David Hume, David Ricardo, and John Stuart Mill contributed to the development of the Quantity Theory during the 18th and 19th centuries, it reached its highest level of sophistication in the works of Irving Fisher, Alfred Marshall, A. C. Pigou and J. M. Keynes in the early part of this century.

*It must be emphasized that dissimilarity in money demand functions is not the *only* distinction between the classical and the Keynesian models.

**The "Keynesian model" referred to in this context is the familiar textbook model that derives originally from Keynes' major theoretical work *The General Theory of Employment, Interest and Money* (London: Harcourt, Brace and World, 1936). This model is discussed in chapter 6 and elaborated upon in chapter 7. Keynes' earlier work, as represented in his other major works, *A Tract on Monetary Reform* (London: Harcourt, Brace and World, 1923), and *A Treatise on Money* (London: Harcourt, Brace and World, 1930), is more squarely in the tradition of the classical Quantity Theory of Money.

***By "the value of money" we mean the exchange value or the purchasing power of a unit of the monetary stock, the quantity of real goods and services commanded by one unit of "money" however defined.

IRVING FISHER'S EQUATION OF EXCHANGE

Fisher's formulation of the Quantity Theory of Money is summarized in his "equation of exchange." In this equation Fisher relates the circulation of the money stock to the amount of money expended in the economy during a given period of time. If (p_i) is the average price of a particular commodity (the ith commodity) and (q_i) is the total quantity of that commodity sold, $(p_i \cdot q_i)$ is the total money value spent on that commodity during that time period. For all (n) commodities in the economy, then,

$$p_1q_1 + p_2q_2 + \cdots + p_nq_n = \sum_{i=1}^{n} p_iq_i = P \cdot Q$$

where P is an index of prices (the average price of all goods sold in the economy) and Q is an index of the quantity of goods sold. The product $P \cdot Q$ will be a measure of total monetary expenditures on goods sold in the economy. If we divide this total level of expenditure $(P \cdot Q)$ by the average quantity of money in the economy during the period in which those expenditures took place, this measure, $(P \cdot Q)/M$, will be the average rate of turnover of money in the exchange of those goods. Fisher terms this "average rate of turnover" the velocity of circulation of money, V. Therefore

$$V = (P \cdot Q)/M \quad \text{or} \quad M \cdot V = P \cdot Q. \tag{1}$$

The velocity of circulation represents the number of times an average dollar in the total money stock must change hands (during the period in which the flow of goods is measured) for that money stock to finance a given level of transactions. For example, if a money stock of 200 billion dollars serves to facilitate the transfer of 800 billion dollars in goods and services during a given period of time, the velocity of circulation of that money stock is four.

$$V = (P \cdot Q)/M = \frac{800 \text{ billion dollars/year}}{200 \text{ billion dollars}} = 4 \text{ times per year.}$$

Though the relation embodied in the equation of exchange must always hold true if V is viewed as a residual term defined to insure equality between the two sides of the equation $(\dot{V} = (P \cdot Q)/M)$, this truism is *not meaningless*. Rather, the equation represents an algebraic statement of the proximate influences on the value of money ". . . through which all others (influences) whatsoever must operate."* (parentheses added) In addition, where V is not defined residually but is instead a variable determined by forces at work in the economy, the equation of exchange may be viewed as an equilibrium condition, summarizing the primary factors which influence the determination of the absolute price level P, i.e., $P = (M \cdot V)/Q$.

Within the framework provided by this equation, Fisher examined the Quantity Theory of Money. His analysis of the factors specified within the equation led him to conclude that since an increase in the quantity of money, M, would generally not be expected, of itself, to change either the velocity of circulation, V, or the volume of transactions in the economy, Q, we could expect that the price level, P, would vary directly with the quantity of money in circulation. As he stated it ". . . the normal effects of an increase in the quantity of money is an exactly proportional increase in the general level of prices."** This result, to Fisher, was the basis of the Quantity Theory:

> . . . we find then that, under the conditions assumed, the price level varies (1) directly as the quantity of money in circulation (M), (2) directly as the velocity of its circulation (V), (3) inversely as the volume of trade done by it. . . . The first of these three relations is worth emphasis. It constitutes the "quantity theory of money."***

It is clear from his own writings that Fisher did not mean to imply that V and Q would never change. He viewed V, the velocity of circulation, as an institutionally determined factor influenced primarily by such things as the public's payment habits, the extent of the use of credit, the speed of transportation and communication as it influences the time required to make a payment, and other technical factors that ". . . bear no discoverable relation to the quantity of money in circulation."† Likewise, the volume of trade, Q, was determined by factors other than the quantity of money, factors such as the supply of natural resources and the technical conditions of production and distribution.†† Thus, as any of these secondary influ-

---

*Irving Fisher, *The Purchasing Power of Money* (New York: The Macmillan Company, 1911), p. 150.

**Ibid., p. 157.

***Ibid., p. 29.

†Ibid., p. 152. *See* also the discussion in the second section of Chapter 3.

††More specifically, the level of real income was assumed to be determined outside the system of equations represented by the equation of exchange. The body of economic theory summarized in Walrasian equations of general equilibrium is held to explain the determination of the level of output. *See* Milton Friedman, "A Theoretical Framework for Monetary Analysis," *Journal of Political Economy*, Vol. 78, (March/April 1970).

ences changed, V and Q could indeed change and this could affect the general level of prices. For example, if Q, the volume of trade produced by the economy, were to change significantly while the money stock, M, and the velocity of circulation, V, remained relatively constant, the price level, P, would have to change to insure the equality embodied in the equation of exchange.

History provides us with many examples of this phenomenon: for instance, during the latter part of the 19th century, the secular expansion of production and trade in this country (Q) outpaced the growth of the money stock (M). With Q increasing faster than M and with a relatively stable V, there was a continual decline in the average price level, arrested only by the discovery of new gold deposits and the rapid expansion in the use of the checking account towards the end of the century.

But Fisher was mainly interested in the results of a particular change in the stock of money at a particular time. His conclusion on this point was that such a change would cause a proportionate change in the equilibrium price level (P), *not* because V and Q never change, but rather because there is no reason to believe that the equilibrium values of those variables would change *in response to* the given change in M. Thus, the directly predictable result of a doubling, say, of the money stock, would be unchanged values of V and Q, and doubled P.

Although the equation of exchange, by itself, is a somewhat mechanical formulation of the factors involved in the determination of the absolute price level, in the hands of an analyst as skilled as Irving Fisher, who emphasized the multitude of secondary factors influencing the level of the variables explicitly displayed in this equation, it was a useful analytical tool. In the hands of the less skillful and more dogmatic, who did not appreciate the subtleties of the complete Fisherian model, however, V and sometimes even Q, degenerated into constants and the equation of exchange became a rigid tool which purported a *necessary* proportionality between M and P.

Fisher's view of the role of the equation of exchange as an analytical device was stated clearly in *The Purchasing Power of Money*.

> One of the objectors to the quantity theory attempts to dispose of equation of exchange . . . by calling it a mere truism. While the equation of exchange is, if we choose, a mere "truism," based on the equivalence, in all purchases, of the money or check expended, on the one hand, and what they buy, on the other, . . . this equation is a means of demonstrating the fact that normally the P's (price levels) vary directly as M, that is, demonstrating the quantity theory. "Truisms" should never be neglected. The greatest generalizations of physical science, such as that forces are proportional to mass and acceleration, are truisms, but, when duly supplemented by specific

>   data, these truisms are the most fruitful sources of useful mechanical
>   knowledge.*

The flexibility of Fisher's use of the equation of exchange is evidenced
by two of his most important contributions to the development of the
Quantity Theory: his discussion of the events that occur during a "transition period" which follows a monetary change,** and his detailed statistical investigations of the determinants and behavior of the velocity of circulation. On the former point he notes

>   . . . that a sudden change in the quantity of money and deposits will
>   temporarily affect their velocities of circulation and the volume of
>   trade. . . .   Therefore, the "quantity theory" will not hold true
>   strictly and absolutely during transition periods.***

Thus the quantity theory conclusions refer only to the effects on the
equilibrium values of the variables in the model that occur in response to a
monetary change.†   Fisher's emphasis on this point was lost on many
analysts. On the latter point, the data presented in *The Purchasing Power
of Money* show clearly, however, that Fisher himself was under no illusion
about the variability of the velocity of circulation.

The emphasis in Fisher's model of the Quantity Theory of Money is on
the *supply of money* and on the institutional and technical factors that influence the level of production and the value of the velocity of circulation.
He had little to say about the psychological factors that influence the
"individual habits" that determine an individual's (and society's) velocity
of money. He viewed money as a commodity that yields *no utility* to the
holder, and that is held simply to facilitate exchange. He notes that

>   The Quantity Theory of Money rests, ultimately, upon the funda-
>   mental peculiarity which money alone of all goods possesses,—the
>   fact that it has *no power to satisfy* human wants except a power *to
>   purchase* things which do have such power.††

*Fisher, *op. cit.,* page 157.

**The "transition period" analysis that Fisher presents is basically a discussion of
the dynamics of moving from one monetary equilibrium to another. He recognized,
for example, that although a doubling of the money supply may be expected to
double the price level, this result will not occur immediately or automatically. The
economy will go through a transition period during which the price level increases
to its new value. During that period, other variables in the economy (such as the rate
of interest) may very well be affected.

Fisher's discussion of the events that may occur during a transition period is reprinted in the readings at the end of Part 2.

***Fisher, *op. cit.,* p. 161.

†This point is discussed in greater detail in chapters 8 and 9.

††Fisher, *op. cit.,* p. 32.

A. C. PIGOU AND THE CAMBRIDGE EQUATION

An alternative view of the functions performed by money was advanced by Alfred Marshall, A. C. Pigou and other "Cambridge" economists. In this view, which is now generally accepted by most economists, *money is capable of yielding utility or satisfaction in and of itself*, since it satisfies two particular needs for the person who possesses it. The first is the provision of convenience and the second, the provision of security. As Pigou notes:

> . . . everybody is anxious to hold enough of his resources in the form of titles to legal tender (money) both to enable him to effect the ordinary transactions of life without trouble, and to secure him against unexpected demands, due to a sudden need, or to a rise in the price of something he cannot easily dispense with.*

The major motivation for holding money in the Cambridge version of the Quantity Theory remains the use it provides to the holder in facilitating transactions. If all receipts and expenditures could be perfectly synchronized as they could be in a perfectly static, timeless model, there would be no need for anyone to hold positive money balances. Even when a disparity does exist between receipts (income flows) and expenditures, in the absence of transactions costs—costs such as brokers' fees and transfer taxes incurred in switching from money to interest-yielding assets—there may still be no net demand for money balances. The absence of transactions costs would allow a person to channel his money income into interest bearing assets immediately upon receipt, and convert those assets into money only at the exact moment the money was required in exchange. In this instance, average money balances held by individuals would be zero. However, when finite transactions costs are introduced into the analysis, it becomes evident that although one could earn interest by purchasing income producing assets and divesting oneself of money balances, the cost involved in purchasing and selling these assets may well exceed the short-term return from the investment. In such a case, money balances actually yield a higher *net* rate of return than the interest-yielding security. Consequently, the randomness of the timing of receipts and expenditures and the possibility of unforeseen contingencies, together with the finite transactions costs incurred in switching between money and earning assets, leads individuals to hold money rather than to convert all cash balances into income-earning assets upon receipt of those balances.**

---

*A. C. Pigou, "The Value of Money," *The Quarterly Journal of Economics,* Vol. 32 (November 1917), p. 41.

**For a more complete discussion of the role of transactions costs in determining the demand for money, *see* chapter 3.

In the Cambridge formulation, the quantity of money demanded for these purposes was postulated to vary proportionately with the volume of final transactions or the level of money income; i.e.,

$$M_d = k \cdot Y = k \cdot P \cdot O \tag{2}$$

where:

M_d = the quantity of money demanded

Y = the level of money income = $(P \cdot O)$

P = an index of the general price level

O = an index of the level of real output in the economy

k = the factor of proportionality, the "Cambridge" k.

Since, in equilibrium, the quantity of money demanded must equal the quantity supplied, we may equate this formula for the demand for money with the given money supply, M_s, determined exogenously by the authorities. This substitution yields the famous Cambridge equation:

$$M = k \cdot Y. \tag{3}$$

This formulation can be reconciled with Fisher's equation of exchange quite simply. Let Q' be the level of real output in the economy (real *GNP*) rather than a measure of *total* transactions (which include transfers of used goods, financial assets, etc.). This latter measure was represented by Q in Fisher's model. Therefore $Q' < Q$. Also, call V' the income velocity of circulation of money. Then we may write the equation of exchange to refer only to transactions in final goods and services.*

$$M \cdot V' = P \cdot Q' \tag{4}$$

Since $Q' = O$ in the Cambridge version:

$$M = k \cdot Y = k \cdot P \cdot O = k \cdot P \cdot Q'$$

and

$$M(1/k) = P \cdot Q'. \tag{5}$$

Therefore, the reciprocal of k, the proportionality factor, is equal to V',

---

*We assume that the prices of all goods in the economy change in the same proportion as the price index. In this way, we need not distinguish between the price index of all goods (in Fisher's equation of exchange) and the index of currently produced goods (in the Cambridge equation).

the income velocity of circulation or the "rate of turnover" of money in the purchase of currently produced goods and services. Thus, while Fisher was concerned with the length of time an average unit of the money stock would be held, Pigou focused on the proportion of income (or expenditures) which would be held in the form of money. Just as V, the velocity of circulation of money, may be viewed either as a residual measure defined to insure the equality expressed in Fisher's equation of exchange, or as a measure of the velocity of circulation of money balances *desired* by the public, i.e., as a volitional measure of the public's demand for money, so too, k, the ratio of money balances to income, may be viewed either as an ". . . observed ratio so calculated as to make equation (3) an identity, or as the 'desired' ratio so that M is the 'desired' amount of money . . ."* Equilibrium in the money market then requires an equality between the desired and observed magnitudes in each of these models so as to equate the supply of and the demand for real money balances.

Pigou has commented on the relation between his own analysis and that which focuses on the velocity of circulation of money. As he notes,

> . . . there is no conflict between my formula and that embodied in the quantity theory. But it does not follow that there is nothing to choose between them. . . . The claim that I make on behalf of mine is that it is a somewhat more effective engine of analysis. It focusses attention on the proportion of their resources that people choose to hold in the form of legal tender instead of focussing it on "velocity of circulation." This fact gives it, as I think, a real advantage, because it brings us at once into relation with volition—an ultimate cause of demand—instead of with something that seems at first sight accidental and arbitrary.**

Thus, the "Cambridge" contribution involves much more than the renaming of variables. First of all, whereas the emphasis in the Fisherian version is on changes in the *supply of money* and on a (primarily) institutionally determined "rate of turnover" of that money stock, the focus in the Cambridge version is placed equally on *money supply* and *money demand*. Second, the *volitional* element on the demand side of the market is more obvious in the Cambridge equation and leads one to consider the specific motivations involved in an individual's demand for money balances. Given the institutional framework outlined by Fisher, for example, the size of k depends on the strength of the public's motivations for holding money.

This orientation led the Cambridge economists to formulate a fresh line of monetary inquiry from which emanates many of the modern develop-

*Friedman, "A Theoretical Framework . . . ,"*op. cit.*, p. 200.
**Pigou, *op. cit.*, p. 54.

ments in monetary economics. By emphasizing the individual's demand for money and the utility which money balances may yield, Cambridge economists were led to examine choices facing the individual. For example, with Pigou the individual determined the size of his desired money balances by equating the marginal returns from holding those money balances with the marginal returns from the alternative use of his resources, capital investment.

The more recent manifestation of this tradition views money as simply one among many assets, both physical and financial, that an individual may hold. As a result, the determination of desired money balances involves equating the marginal returns from all these assets in the individual's portfolio. We shall return to this development later in this chapter.

Let us consider more thoroughly the determinants of k, the proportion of money income people desire to hold in the form of money balances. The historical and institutional factors that influenced Fisher's V may be viewed as characteristics of the socio-economic framework within which the Cambridge economists studied the behavioral determinants of k.* These relatively objective institutional factors included: (1) the length of the period between wage and salary payments; (2) the degree of sophistication of the population in the use of credit; and (3) the degree of vertical integration of business firms. The more subjective behavioral determinants of the size of k which were emphasized by the Cambridge economists included: (1) the public's degree of preference for present consumption over future consumption; (2) their expectations concerning the future return from investment in "industrial activity"; and (3) their expectations about price movements. On the last point, for example, Pigou notes that ". . . any expectation that general prices are going to fall increases people's desire to hold (money); and any expectation that they are going to rise has the contrary effect."**

In short, the Cambridge Theory recognizes the same institutional factors that Fisher discussed as determinants of V, but adds to them a very strong emphasis on individual psychological factors such as preferences and expectations. In the Cambridge version, $M = k \cdot Y$, just as in the Fisherian version, $M \cdot V' = P \cdot Q'$, if we assume that a change in the stock of money has no direct effect upon any of the factors except P, the price level, we arrive at the familiar Quantity Theory conclusion that the price

---

*In chapter 3 there is considerable discussion of the effect of these factors on the order of magnitude of k.

**Pigou, *op. cit.,* p. 48. Fisher also placed great emphasis on the role of price expectations in the determination of velocity, particularly in his analysis of the transition period. The Cambridge formulation of the Quantity Theory is better suited to the explicit inclusion of this factor into the analysis, however. For an examination of the price expectation effect and its role in the determination of the level of interest rates, *see* "Factors Affecting the Level of Interest Rates," by Milton Friedman, reprinted in the readings at the end of Part 2.

level will vary in direct proportion to the size of the money stock. However, the emphasis on the volatile volitional determinants of k in the Cambridge formulation left no doubt that this result would be somewhat less than certain. For a change in the public's preferences and expectations could easily nullify the simple Quantity Theory result.

Consequently, the less obvious forces in Fisher's model, which are introduced only in his discussion of "transition periods," are brought to the fore in the Cambridge theory and made an integral part of the analysis. Though the conclusions of the models often appeared identical and indeed were thought identical by their architects, it is far more obvious in the Cambridge version that the price level or the level of money income merely *tends* to follow the size of the money stock, and that strict proportionality between these variables is highly unlikely.

The flexible Cambridge formulation of the Quantity Theory, as the foundation of much modern monetary theory, has proven more viable than the Fisherian version. However, this was not its major contribution. The most important result of the work of the Cambridge economists (and one that has not yet been completely exploited) was the fact that it provided a more promising line of inquiry than the model of Irving Fisher. It led economists to consider a utility analysis of the demand for money balances and to view money as simply one asset in a multi-asset portfolio. In this way the analysis of the demand for money came to be viewed simply as the application of the general theory of demand to a specific problem. The results of this orientation were the development of Keynes' Liquidity Preference Theory as reviewed in chapter 4 and the reformulation of the Fisherian model by Milton Friedman.

THE NEOCLASSICAL REFORMULATION

Very few economists today accept either the Cambridge or the Fisherian Quantity Theories in their original form. In fact, the Liquidity Preference Theory as presented in chapter 4 and its role in the general equilibrium macroeconomic models to be presented in chapters 6 and 8, represents today's most widely accepted theoretical paradigm. However, the Quantity Theory approach remains an important analytical tool in the work of a few very influential theorists, most notably Milton Friedman of the University of Chicago.*

*Friedman's major works in this field include: "The Quantity Theory of Money— A Restatement" in *Studies in the Quantity Theory of Money*, Milton Friedman, ed. (Chicago: University of Chicago Press, 1956); "The Demand for Money: Some Theoretical and Empirical Results," *The Journal of Political Economy*, Vol. 67 (August, 1959); and "Money and Business Cycles," with Anna J. Schwartz in *The Review of Economics and Statistics*, Vol. 45 (Supplement: February 1963). These

Friedman's Quantity Theory* is more sophisticated than the theories of Fisher and the Cambridge economists, yet it remains in their tradition. Like the earlier Quantity Theorists, he maintains the hypothesis that the demand for money function is the most stable macroeconomic relation economists have discovered, and he promotes it as the most reliable basis for aggregate economic analysis and policy decisions. In contrast to those who favor the familiar Keynesian analytic framework, he explicitly rejects the idea that the consumption function (more specifically, multipliers derived from models based on the Keynesian consumption function) represents a more stable and reliable function. The theoretical money demand function which Friedman postulates appears quite different from the simple equation of exchange of Irving Fisher. Nevertheless, the final empirical form of this function, which incorporates the conclusions of his statistical analysis, supports the major conclusions of the classical Quantity Theory.**

In his analysis of the demand for money, Friedman does not separate the individual's money stock into analytically distinct components, such as "active" and "idle" balances, as is a common practice in some versions of the Liquidity Preference Theory. Rather, he views money as *one kind of asset*, in which a wealth-owning unit may hold a part of its wealth, or as a *capital good*, which yields productive services that a business enterprise can combine with the services of other productive assets or labor to produce an output. Money, therefore, is seen as a commodity which yields utility to its holder according to the functions it performs. As Friedman notes: ". . . the most fruitful approach is to regard money as one of a sequence of assets, on a par with bonds, equities, houses, consumer durable goods, and the like."***

Friedman's procedure, then, is to develop a theory of the demand for money on the basis of an examination of the services that money performs for wealth-owning units and business enterprises. He is not primarily con-

---

works and an essay entitled "The Optimum Quantity of Money" are reprinted in *The Optimum Quantity of Money and Other Essays*, Milton Friedman (Chicago: Aldine Publishing Co., 1969).

*The classification of Friedman's work as part of the "Quantity Theory tradition" has recently been challenged by Don Patinkin. *See* "The Chicago Tradition, The Quantity Theory and Friedman," *Journal of Money, Credit and Banking*, Vol. 1 (February, 1969), pp. 46–70.

**For a more complete discussion of the differences between the pre-Keynesian quantity theory and its post-Keynesian reformulation, and the relationship of these theories to Keynesian liquidity preference, see David Fand, "Keynesian Monetary Theories, Stabilization Policy and the Recent Inflation," *Journal of Money, Credit and Banking*, Vol. 1 (August 1969), pages 561-565. This article is reprinted in the readings following Part 2.

***Friedman, "The Demand for Money: Some Theoretical and Empirical Results," *op. cit.*, p. 349.

cerned with the motives that lead people to hold money. Rather, it is taken as given that money is held by households and business firms, and the principles of traditional demand theory are applied to determine the factors that may influence the size of the money balances that these groups desire. As he notes, "To the ultimate wealth-owning units in the economy, money is one kind of asset, one way of holding wealth. To the productive enterprise, money is a capital good, a source of productive services that are combined with other productive services to yield the products that the enterprise sells."*

Friedman's analysis of the demand for money by the ultimate wealth-owning unit is based on the theory of the demand for a consumption service. The major factors suggested by this theory as important in the determination of money demand include: the total wealth of the unit; the division of wealth between human and non-human forms; the relative returns on alternative wealth forms, including money; and the tastes and preferences of individuals. For the business enterprise, the theory of the demand for the services of productive resources suggests that the demand for money is determined by the cost of services yielded by money balances—that is, the cost of raising funds by borrowing or by other means, the cost of substitute productive services, and the contribution of money as a productive factor to the value of the output of the production process.

In his restatement of the Quantity Theory, Friedman writes the following (approximate) demand for money function:**

$$\frac{M_d}{P} = f\left(i_m, i_b, i_e, \frac{1}{P}\frac{dP}{dt}, W, n\right) \tag{6}$$

where

i_m = the rate of return on money
i_b = the rate of return on bonds
i_e = the rate of return on equities (stocks)
P = an index of the general price level
$\dfrac{1}{P}\dfrac{dP}{dt}$ = the rate of change of the price index, P, over time

---

*Friedman, "The Quantity Theory of Money—A Restatement," in *Studies on the Quantity Theory of Money, op. cit.,* p. 4.

**A velocity function can be derived from a demand-for-money function by setting nominal money demand equal to nominal money supply, inverting the functions and multiplying by income:

$$M_s = M_d = f\left(i_m, i_b, i_e, \frac{1}{P}\frac{dP}{dt}, W, n\right)$$

$$Y/M_s = Y/f\left(i_m, i_b, i_e, \frac{1}{P}\frac{dP}{dt}, W, n\right).$$

$$\frac{M_d}{P} = \text{the } \textit{real} \text{ quantity of money demanded}$$

W = wealth

n = the ratio of non-human to human wealth.

The presence of the terms i_m, i_e, i_b and $(1/P)\,(dP/dt)$ reflects the influence of the rates of return on alternative wealth forms in the determination of the desired level of money balances. For example, i_e, measures the nominal return on equities and $(1/P)\,(dP/dt)$ measures (in part) the change in the real value of that return as the general price level changes. The term W is a measure of wealth and reflects the constraint imposed on an asset holder by the size of his portfolio. This variable plays a role analogous to that of the income constraint in the traditional theory of the demand for consumer goods.

The final term, n, is a measure of the "human wealth" component in an individual's total wealth. Since wealth is simply the discounted present value of a future stream of returns (or income) to be received from a certain stock of capital, Friedman recognizes that an individual can increase this flow of income (and his wealth) by "investing" in education or by other activities which increase the value of his labor power. To account for the human factor in the total wealth stock, Friedman includes the ratio of non-human to human wealth in his money demand function. We may expect that the larger the "human" component of an individual's total stock of wealth, the greater will be his demand for money, since holding a larger stock of money balances is one means of balancing the illiquidity or non-marketability of human wealth.

The demand for money by business firms can be explained, as Friedman suggests, by the same variables that explain the demand for money by other wealth-owning units. Consequently, the demand-for-money function—or velocity function—for the entire economy will have the same form as equation (6) and will include interest rate terms, wealth measures, and price factors as independent variables. Friedman indicates that the influence of both the interest rate variables and price variations on the volume of money balances demanded will be negative, while the relation between wealth and money demand is positive.

Few economists could disagree with Friedman on the general lines of his formal analysis or even his abstract formulation of the money demand (velocity) function. Nonetheless, when his theory suggests that it is some measure of *wealth* rather than *current income* that is the basic constraint on the public's desired money holdings, it contrasts with the money demand theories discussed in the previous chapters and the earlier sections of this chapter.* Friedman notes that "The emphasis on income as a surrogate

---

*However, Keynesian-type models of recent vintage do often incorporate a wealth constraint.

for wealth, rather than as a measure of the 'work' to be done by money, is conceptually perhaps the basic difference between more recent work and the earlier versions of the quantity theory."*

Friedman's theory gives little indication of the relative importance of the variables included in the money demand function. Consequently, critical appraisal of Friedman's Quantity Theory of Money must rest on empirical analysis of the public's money holding behavior, and it is on this point (the interpretation of empirical evidence) that most of the disagreements surrounding Friedman's theories arise.

The most important questions which empirical analysis can help to answer concern

      (1) the actual importance of the various interest rates in the money demand function;

      (2) the relative explanatory power of income and wealth in such a function; and

      (3) the stability of the function over time.**

Friedman himself has presented evidence relevant to these questions.*** However, other investigators have often disagreed both with his methods and with his conclusions. Specifically, though his reformulated Quantity Theory explicitly recognizes several interest rates as independent variables, Professor Friedman concludes from his empirical studies that no statistical significance can be attached to them.† In other words, though *economic theory* would lead one to expect that interest rates influence the public's desired money balances, Friedman claims that the *empirical evidence* he presents shows that this influence, if present at all, is of minor importance. As he states it, he was unable ". . . to find any close connection between changes in velocity (or desired money balances) from cycle to cycle and any of a number of interest rates."††(parentheses added)

Of much more importance, according to Friedman's interpretation of the available evidence, is the response of the volume of real money balances demanded, to changes in the level of "permanent income." Permanent income is a concept he developed in connection with a study of the consumption function.††† It is a measure of a long-run income concept

---

*Friedman, "A Theoretical Framework . . . ," *op. cit.*, p. 203.

**These questions are dealt with in detail in the survey of the empirical work done in this field which appears in the readings at the end of this chapter.

***Friedman, "The Demand for Money: Some Theoretical and Empirical Results," *op. cit.*

†Statistical significance means that the relationships discussed have been subjected to empirical tests and have been found "significant" or "nonsignificant" by the usual 95% interval tests applied to the coefficients in regression analysis.

††Friedman, "The Demand for Money . . ." *op. cit.*, p. 349.

†††Milton Friedman, *A Theory of the Consumption Function* (Princeton: Princeton University Press, 1957).

thought to be the most important factor relevant to consumer spending decisions. Empirically, this figure is constructed as a weighted average of past values of "measured" income (net national product, for example).*

Friedman's empirical analysis leads him to conclude that a satisfactory explanation of money demand behavior can be achieved through the application of the following equation to aggregate data:

$$\frac{M_d}{NP} = \gamma \left(\frac{Y_p}{NP} \right)^\delta$$

where M_d and P are as defined above and

N = population

Y_p = permanent income

γ and δ are behavioral parameters.

This equation indicates that real per capita money balances demanded are an exponential function of real per capita permanent income. Thus, the interest rate and the price change terms have been dropped from the empirical function as explanatory variables. As Friedman notes: "In our experiments, *the rate of interest* had an effect in the direction to be expected from theoretical considerations but too small to be statistically significant. We have not as yet been able to isolate by correlation techniques any effect of the rate of change of prices, though a historical analysis persuades us that such an effect is present.** Consequently, only the permanent income variable employed as a proxy measure for the theoretically more relevant concept of wealth remains in the final form of the equation, and it assumes a form similar to Fisher's "equation of exchange."

MONEY DEMAND, THE INTEREST RATE, AND PRICE EXPECTATIONS

Although many variables are included in his theoretical money demand function, Friedman concludes that a single measure of income (a wealth

---

*Friedman's use of this concept is partly the result of inadequate data on alternative wealth measures. As he notes, "In practice, estimates of total wealth are seldom available. Instead, income may serve as an index of wealth. However, it should be recognized that income as measured by statisticians may be a defective index of wealth because it is subject to erratic year-to-year fluctuations, and a longer-term concept, like the concept of permanent income . . . , may be useful." Friedman, "A Theoretical Framework . . . ," *op. cit.*, p. 203.

**Friedman, "The Demand for Money . . . ," *op. cit.*, p. 329. The italics have been added to the original by the authors.

proxy) is sufficient to explain most changes in the demand for money.*
This conclusion is disputed in much of the recent empirical literature on
the demand for money.** Most analysts find that when the empirical
money demand function includes some interest rate measure, the explanatory power and predictive capability of that equation is significantly improved. However, the presence of a statistically significant interest rate
term in the money demand function is not sufficient cause, by itself, to
reject the quantity theorists' formulation of the demand for money or
their analysis of the aggregate economy. Quantity theorists have long
recognized that the demand for money may be influenced by interest
rates. Nonetheless, in many quantity theorists' models of the aggregate
economy although the interest rate may enter the money demand function, adjustments in the monetary sector (changes in the supply of money,
for example) do not in turn influence the *equilibrium* level of interest
rates.** They merely exert *temporary effects* on interest rates during what
Fisher referred to as "transition periods." As seen in chapter 8, the
equilibrium interest rate in neo-classical aggregate models is determined
solely by "real" factors in the economy—productivity (investment) and
thrift (saving).

One aspect of these transitional effects, which has been the subject of
detailed analysis, involves the relationship between changes in the average
level of prices in the economy and changes in the level of interest rates.
For example, while maintaining the conclusion that the equilibrium level
of interest rates is determined by "real" phenomena, Friedman has emphasized the means by which price level changes caused by a monetary
disturbance temporarily may influence market interest rates.

Friedman's analysis begins with a discussion of the three effects that a
monetary change ultimately may have on the level of interest rates.
These include: (1) the liquidity effect, (2) an income-and-price-level
effect and (3) a price-anticipation effect. *The liquidity effect* refers to
the initial short-run influence which a change in the money stock (or
the rate of change of the money stock in a dynamic framework) will have
on interest rates. It is recognized, for example, that an increase in the

---

*Some of the doubts concerning the meaning of Friedman's empirical results cen-
ter on his use of the permanent income measure. His critics contend that this empirical measure ". . . combines wealth, interest rates, population, and lagged income in a
single variable and thus combines their separate effects." Allan H. Meltzer, "The Demand for Money: The Evidence from the Time Series," *The Journal of Political
Economy* (June, 1963), p. 221.

**See the survey of the empirical literature on the demand for money reprinted
with the readings following Part 2.

***See chapter 8 for complete discussion of the assumptions which must be in-
corporated into the Quantity Theorists' model of the aggregate economy to generate
these results.

money stock, since it disturbs the equilibrium of the public's asset portfolio, will induce individuals who find themselves holding excess cash to readjust their portfolios by purchasing securities. This action will bid up security prices and temporarily decrease interest rates. This response is similar to that described in the Keynesian literature on liquidity preference. Quantity theorists emphasize, however, that this is only a "first round" effect and that the lower interest rates which may follow an increase in the money stock do not represent the final adjustment to a new equilibrium. This change is simply a manifestation of the transition period. For, under certain conditions, as interest rates fall, there will be an increase in expenditures and current income.* This, in turn, will increase the demand for loanable funds and for transactions balances, reversing the fall in interest rates and pushing them back up to their previous level. This is referred to as *the income effect.*

The *price anticipation effect* may actually drive interest rates beyond their previous level.** This reaction is suggested in the work of Irving Fisher. Fisher distinguished sharply between two components in observed (nominal) interest rates: ". . . the 'real' rate of interest, to which real saving and investment respond, and a premium based on expected changes in the price level."*** During periods of rising prices, for example, the premium component reflects an attempt on the part of lenders to recoup through an interest return an amount equal to the loss of real purchasing power which they expect to suffer from the deterioration of the real principle value of their assets. During periods of relative price stability, when no change was anticipated in future prices, there would be no premium and the real rate and the nominal rate would be the same. However, during periods of rapidly changing prices, the nominal rate could diverge sharply from the real rate even for a long period of time.

Thus, it is this *price-adjustment premium* that is likely to push market interest rates beyond their previous level. As the initial monetary increase lowers interest rates and induces a rise in spending and nominal income, it also may induce an increase in prices. After prices have been rising for some time, individuals will eventually come to anticipate that prices will continue to rise. In these circumstances, lenders ". . . would hedge against changes in the real value of their loan principle by adding the percentage change in prices over the life of the loan to the interest charge"; and

---

*For a more complete explanation of this mechanism, *see* William E. Gibson, "Interest Rates and Monetary Policy," *Journal of Political Economy*, Vol. 78 (May/ June 1970) pp. 431–455.

**Milton Friedman, "Factors Affecting the Level of Interest Rates," *Savings and Residential Financing,* 1968 Conference Proceedings, United States Savings and Loan League (May 1968), reprinted with the readings following Part 2.

***William P. Yohe and Denis Karnosky, "Interest Rates and Price Level Changes, 1952–69," Federal Reserve Bank of St. Louis *Review* (December 1969), p. 18.

borrowers, ". . . expecting money income to change in proportion to prices, would readily accept the higher rate."*

A study by William Yohe and Denis Karnosky indicates that just such a price anticipation effect may be the critical element in the explanation of the recent rise in interest rates (1952-69). In particular, they conclude that ". . . price level changes since 1952 have evidently come to have a prompt and substantial effect on price expectations and nominal interest rates . . . . Most significant is the finding that price level changes, rather than (changes in) "real" rates, account for nearly all the variation in nominal interest rates since 1961."**

This discussion indicates the scope of the work currently being done by writers in the quantity theory tradition. The Quantity Theory of Money in its modern reformulation is not simply a static theory of the demand for money. Rather, building on the path-breaking work of Irving Fisher, the post-Keynesian quantity theory represents a theory of money income based on an analysis of money demand. It is a theory that incorporates Fisher's detailed analysis of the determinants of the velocity of circulation, the Cambridge analysis of the psychological factors influencing the public's desire for money balances, and the dynamic analysis that begins with Fisher's discussion of the "transition period."

CONCLUDING REMARKS

We have presented a review of the major theoretical formulations of the Quantity Theory of Money as developed by Fisher, Pigou, Friedman, and others. Though seemingly diverse, each begins from the same focal point in analyzing the aggregate economy. Furthermore, they each come to similar conclusions about the role of money in the economy and the relative efficiency of monetary and fiscal policy for control of the economy. Friedman has provided the best description of what it means to be a "quantity theorist." As he states it:

> The quantity theorist accepts the empirical hypothesis that the demand for money is highly stable—more stable than functions such as the consumption function that are offered as alternative key relations . . . . The quantity theorist not only regards the demand for money function as stable; he also regards it as playing a vital role in determining variables that he regards as of great importance for the analysis of the economy as a whole, such as the level of money income or of prices. . . . The quantity theorist also holds that there

Ibid, p. 19.
**Ibid*, p. 35-36.

are important factors affecting the supply of money that do not affect the demand for money.*

This last point is crucial, since "A stable demand function is useful precisely in order to trace out the effects of changes in supply, which means that it is useful only if supply is affected by at least some factors other than those regarded as affecting demand."**

This chapter has been limited almost exclusively to an examination of the demand for money function (the equation of exchange or the velocity function, in alternative formulations) as developed in the literature on the Quantity Theory of Money. We have not discussed at length the contributions made by the writers in this tradition to the broader aspects of macroeconomic analysis. However, some of these topics are dealt with in the readings which follow Part 2. Specifically, our brief discussion of the dynamic adjustment process incorporated in the quantity theorists' analysis of the aggregate economy is extended in Fisher's discussion of the "transition period" and in Friedman's discussion of the factors determining the level of interest rates.

In chapter 7, we shall incorporate the quantity theorists' formulation of the demand for money function into a general equilibrium model of the aggregate economy. At that point, we shall examine the differing conclusions deriving from such a model when the quantity theory formulation of the money demand relation replaces the more familiar Keynesian Liquidity Preference Theory.

---

*Milton Friedman, "The Quantity Theory of Money—A Restatement" in *Studies in the Quantity Theory of Money*, *op. cit.*, p. 16. This description of "The Quantity Theorist" has recently been challenged by Don Patinkin. *See* "The Chicago Tradition, The Quantity Theory, and Friedman," *Journal of Money, Credit and Banking*, Vol. 1 (February 1969), pp. 46–70).

**Friedman, "The Quantity Theory of Money—A Restatement," in *Studies in the Quantity Theory of Money*, *op. cit.*, pp. 16–17.

Questions/ *chapter 5*

1. a. What is the equation of exchange? Define each variable that appears in this equation. What does it mean to say that the equation of exchange may be viewed as an "identity"?

   b. "To say that $MV = PT$ is to espouse the Quantity Theory." True or false? Explain.

2. What two assumptions are necessary to make the Fisher and/or Cambridge versions strict quantity theories of money?

3. a. Why does the Cambridge formulation of the Quantity Theory represent more than a simple renaming of the variables of the Fisherian equation of exchange?

   b. "Unmistakably Keynes' monetary theory bore the Cambridge imprint!" Do you agree or disagree?

4. List the basic institutional factors which determine V, the velocity of circulation of money. What additional influences were stressed by the Cambridge economists in discussing the determinants of k, the proportionality factor in the money demand equation?

5. How does Milton Friedman's analysis of the factors affecting the demand for money differ from the Keynesian liquidity preference analysis?

6. Explain the rationale by which Friedman includes an interest rate term in his theoretical demand for money function. What is his empirical finding about this factor as a determinant of money demand?

Bibliography / *chapter 5*

Allais, Maurice, "A Restatement of the Quantity Theory of Money," *American Economic Review,* Vol. 56 (December 1966), pp. 1123-1157.

Chow, Gregory C., "On the Long-Run and Short-Run Demand for Money," *Journal of Political Economy,* Vol. 74 (April 1966), pp. 111–113.

Fand, David I., "A Monetarist Model of the Monetary Process," *The Journal of Finance,* Vol. 25 (May 1970), pp. 275–289.

Fisher, Irving, *The Purchasing Power of Money.* New York: Augustus M. Kelley, Bookseller, 1963. Reprint of new and revised edition, 1922.

Friedman, Milton, "The Quantity Theory of Money—A Restatement," *Studies in the Quantity Theory of Money,* edited by Milton Friedman. Chicago: University of Chicago Press, 1956, pp. 1–21.

————, "The supply of Money and Changes in Prices and Output," *The Relationship of Prices to Economic Stability and Growth: Compendium of Papers Submitted to the Joint Economic Committee,* 85th Congress, 2nd Session, March 31, 1958. Washington: Government Printing Office, 1958.

————, "The Demand for Money: Some Theoretical and Empirical Results," *Journal of Political Economy,* Vol. 67 (August 1959), pp. 327–351.

————, "The Demand for Money," *American Philosophical Society Proceedings,* Vol. 105 (June 1961), pp. 259–264.

————, "Postwar Trends in Monetary Theory and Policy," *The National Banking Review,* Vol. 2 (September 1964), pp. 1–10.

————, "Interest Rates and the Demand for Money," *Journal of Law and Economics,* Vol. 9 (October 1966), pp. 71–85.

_____, *The Optimum Quantity of Money and Other Essays.* Chicago: Aldine Publishing Company, 1969.

_____,"A Theoretical Framework for Monetary Analysis," *Journal of Political Economy*, Vol. 78 (March/April 1970), pp. 193–238.

_____, and Anna Schwartz; "Money and Business Cycles," *The Review of Economics and Statistics*, Vol. 45 (Supplement), February 1963.

_____, "Comment on Tobin," *Quarterly Journal of Economics*, Vol. 84 (May 1970), pp. 318–327.

Gibson, W. E., "Interest Rates and Monetary Policy," *Journal of Political Economy*, Vol. 78 (May/June 1970), pp. 431–455.

_____, "The Lag in the Effect of Monetary Policy on Income and Interest Rates," *Quarterly Journal of Economics*, Vol. 84 (May 1970), pp. 288–300.

_____, "Price-Expectations Effects on Interest Rates," *Journal of Finance*, Vol. 25 (March 1970), pp. 19–34.

Johnson, Harry G., "A Quantity Theorist's Monetary History of the U. S.," *Economic Journal*, Vol. 75 (June 1965), pp. 388–396.

Keynes, John Maynard, *The General Theory of Employment, Interest, and Money.* London: Harcourt, Brace and World, 1936.

_____, *A Tract on Monetary Reform.* London: Harcourt, Brace and World, 1923.

_____, *A Treatise on Money.* London: Harcourt, Brace and World, 1930.

Meltzer, Allan H., "Irving Fisher and the Quantity Theory of Money," *Orbis* (March 1967), pp. 32–38.

Patinkin, Don, "The Chicago Tradition, the Quantity Theory, and Friedman," *The Journal of Money, Credit and Banking*, Vol. 1 (February 1969), pp. 46–70.

Pigou, A. C., "The Value of Money," *The Quarterly Journal of Economics,* Vol. 32 (November 1917).

Samuelson, Paul, "What Classical and Neoclassical Monetary Theory Really Was," *Canadian Journal of Economics*, Vol. 1 (February 1968).

Sargent, Thomas J., "Commodity Price Expectations and the Interest Rate," *Quarterly Journal of Economics*, Vol. 83 (February 1969), pp. 127–140.

Tobin, James, "Money and Income: Post Hoc Ergo Propter Hoc?" *Quarterly Journal of Economics*, Vol. 84 (May 1970), pp. 301–317.

Yohe, William P., and Denis S. Karnosky, "Interest Rates and Price Level Changes, 1952–1969," *Federal Reserve Bank of St. Louis Review* (December 1969).

READINGS/ *part 2*

MONEY DEMAND

Introduction to Readings/ *part 2*

The chapters in this section were concerned with the theories of the demand for money. We have examined several models formulated to explain the behavior of the public in holding money balances. In the next part of the text we shall relate the implications of those models to the broader questions of the determination of macroeconomic aggregates—the level of income, the interest rate, and the price level.

The readings in this section begin with an excerpt from Irving Fisher's *The Purchasing Power of Money*. In this piece, Fisher examines the temporary effect of a change in the quantity of money—the effects which take place during the period of transition from one monetary equilibrium to another. The analysis in this article, though it was written before 1911, remains remarkably relevant and fresh today, and forms the basis of much of the modern "monetarist" analysis of inflationary processes and the factors determining the level of interest rates as discussed in chapter 5.

The implications of the quantity theory formulation of the demand for money for the theories of the determination of the price level and the interest rate which were examined in chapter 5 are explored in greater detail in the next article, by Milton Friedman. This work rests firmly on Fisher's original analysis of transition periods, his distinction between the real and nominal rates of interest, and his careful discussion of the shorter-term and longer-term effects of a change in the money stock. Friedman's article demonstrates the continuity of the quantity theory tradition and the debt of modern "monetarist" analysis to the ingenious work of Irving Fisher.

Several of the issues raised by Fisher are reviewed with an eye towards policy by David Fand in his "Keynesian Monetary Theories, Stabilization, and the Recent Inflation." Fand begins with a consideration of the theoretical underpinnings of the current policy dilemma encountered in the United States. He then compares the Keynesian and quantity theories of the demand for money (as presented in chapters 4 and 5) and analyses the implications of these theories for the processes which determine the levels of the interest rate, prices, and real cash balances. Especially useful for the reader is Fand's examination of the alternative liquidity-preference theories developed in the literature—those of the modern Keynesians, the Radcliffe Committee, and Tobin—and their implications for theories of the interest rate and the price level. Fand's review demonstrates the influence of much of the original work of Fisher and Keynes in modern monetary analysis.

We conclude this section with a survey of the recent empirical literature on the demand for money. In this article, John Boorman surveys several formulations of the money demand function and compares the results of alternative tests of these relations which have been presented in the literature. This survey provides a summary statement of the current consensus which has been achieved on the elements deemed most important in the determination of the public's demand for money.

1/ IRVING FISHER

Disturbance of Equation (of Exchange) and of Purchasing Power During Transition Periods

1

In the last chapter it was shown that the quantity of bank deposits normally maintains a definite ratio to the quantity of money in circulation and to the amount of bank reserves. As long as this normal relation holds, the existence of bank deposits merely *magnifies* the effect on the level of prices produced by the quantity of money in circulation and does not in the least *distort* that effect. Moreover, changes in velocity or trade will have the same effect on prices, whether bank deposits are included or not.

But during periods of transition this relation between money (M) and deposits (M') is by no means rigid.

We are now ready to study these periods of transition. The change which constitutes a transition may be a change in the quantity of money, or in any other factor of the equation of exchange, or in all. Usually all are involved, but the chief factor which we shall select for study (together with its effect on the other factors) is quantity of money. If the quantity of money were suddenly doubled, the effect of the change would not be the same at first as later. The ultimate effect is, as we have seen, to double prices; but before this happens, the prices oscillate up and down. In this chapter we shall consider the *temporary effects during the period of transition* separately from the *permanent or ultimate effects* which were con-

This reading originally appeared as chapter 4 in *The Purchasing Power of Money*. New and revised edition, Reprints of Economic Classics, Augustus M. Kelley, Bookseller, New York, 1963. (Reprinted from the second revised edition, 1922.) We reprint this article with the permission of the publisher, Augustus M. Kelley.

sidered in the last chapter. These permanent or ultimate effects follow after a new equilibrium is established,—if, indeed, such a condition as equilibrium may be said ever to be established. What we are concerned with in this chapter is the temporary effects, *i.e.* those in the transition period.

The transition periods may be characterized either by rising prices or by falling prices. *Rising* prices must be clearly distinguished from *high* prices, and *falling* from *low*. With stationary levels, high or low, we have in this chapter nothing to do. Our concern is with rising or falling prices. Rising prices mark the transition between a low and a high level of prices, just as a hill marks the transition between flat lowlands and flat highlands.

Since the study of these acclivities and declivities is bound up with that of the adjustment of interest rates, our first task is to present a brief statement regarding the effects of rising and falling prices[1] on *the rate of interest*. Indeed, the chief object of this chapter is to show that the peculiar behavior of the rate of interest during transition periods is largely responsible for the crises and depressions in which price movements end.

It must be borne in mind that although business loans are made in the form of money, yet whenever a man borrows money, he does not do this in order to hoard the money, but to purchase goods with it. To all intents and purposes, therefore, when A borrows one hundred dollars from B in order to purchase, say, one hundred units of a given commodity at one dollar per unit, it may be said that B is virtually lending A one hundred units of that commodity. And if at the end of a year A returns one hundred dollars to B, but the price of the commodity has meanwhile advanced, then B has lost a fraction of the purchasing power originally loaned to A. For even though A should happen to return to B the identical coins in which the loan was made, these coins represent somewhat less than the original quantity of purchasable commodities. Bearing this in mind in our investigation of interest rates, let us suppose that prices are rising at the rate of 3 per cent each year. It is plain that the man who lends $100 at the beginning of the year must, in order to get 5 per cent interest in purchasing power, receive back both $103 (then the equivalent of the $100 lent) plus 5 per cent of this, or a total of $108.15. That is, in order to get 5 per cent interest in *actual purchasing power*, he must receive a little more than 8 per cent interest in *money*. The 3 per cent rise of prices thus ought to add approximately 3 per cent to the rate of interest. Rising prices, therefore, in order that the relations between creditor and debtor shall be the same during the rise as before and after, require higher money interest than stationary prices require.

Not only will lenders require, but borrowers can afford to pay higher

[1]For a fuller statement, see Irving Fisher, *The Rate of Interest*, New York (Macmillan), 1907, Chapters V, XIV.

interest in terms of money; and to some extent competition will gradually force them to do so.[2] Yet we are so accustomed in our business dealings to consider money as the one thing stable,—to think of a "dollar as a dollar" regardless of the passage of time, that we reluctantly yield to this process of readjustment, thus rendering it very slow and imperfect. When prices are rising at the rate of 3 per cent a year, and the normal rate of interest—*i.e.* the rate which would exist were prices stationary—is 5 per cent, the actual rate, though it ought (in order to make up for the rising prices) to be 8.15 per cent, will not ordinarily reach that figure; but it may reach, say, 6 per cent, and later, 7 per cent. This inadequacy and tardiness of adjustment are fostered, moreover, by law and custom, which arbitrarily tend to keep down the rate of interest.

A similar inadequacy of adjustment is observed when prices are falling. Suppose that, by the end of a year, $97 will buy as much as $100 at the beginning. In that case the lender, in order to get back a purchasing power equivalent to his principal and 5 per cent interest, should get, not $105, but only $97 + 5 per cent of $97 or $101.85. Thus the rate of interest in money should in this case be 1.85 per cent, or less than 2 per cent, instead of the original 5 per cent. In other words, the 3 per cent fall of prices should reduce the rate of interest by approximately 3 per cent. But as a matter of fact, such a perfect adjustment is seldom reached, and money interest keeps far above 2 per cent for a considerable time.[3]

2

We are now ready to study temporary or transitional changes in the factors of our equation of exchange. Let us begin by assuming a slight initial disturbance, such as would be produced, for instance, by an increase in the quantity of gold. This, through the equation of exchange, will cause a rise in prices. As prices rise, profits of business men, measured in money, will rise also, even if the costs of business were to rise in the same proportion. Thus, if a man who sold $10,000 of goods at a cost of $6000, thus clearing $4000, could get double prices at double cost, his profit would be double also, being $20,000 − $12,000, which is $8000. Of course such a rise of prices would be purely nominal, as it would merely keep pace with the rise in price level. The business man would gain no advantage, for his larger money profits would buy no more than his former smaller money profits bought before. But, as a matter of fact, the business man's profits will rise more than this because the rate of interest he has to pay will not adjust itself immediately. Among his costs is interest, and this cost will not, at first, rise. Thus the profits *will* rise faster than prices. Con-

[2]Rate of Interest, Chapter XIV.
[3]Rate of Interest, loc. cit.

sequently, he will find himself making greater profits than usual, and be encouraged to expand his business by increasing his borrowings. These borrowings are mostly in the form of short-time loans from banks; and, as we have seen, short-time loans engender deposits. As is well known, the correspondence between loans and deposits is remarkably exact.[4] Therefore, deposit currency (M') will increase, but this extension of deposit currency tends further to raise the general level of prices, just as the increase of gold raised it in the first place.[5] Hence prices, which were already outstripping the rate of interest, tend to outstrip it still further, enabling borrowers, who were already increasing their profits, to increase them still further. More loans are demanded, and although nominal interest may be forced up somewhat, still it keeps lagging below the normal level. Yet nominally the rate of interest *has* increased; and hence the lenders, too, including banks, are led to become more enterprising. Beguiled by the higher nominal rates into the belief that fairly high interest is being realized, they extend their loans, and with the resulting expansion of bank loans, deposit currency (M'), already expanded, expands still more. Also, if prices are rising, the money value of collateral may be greater, making it easier for borrowers to get large credit.[6] Hence prices rise still further.[7] This sequence of events may be briefly stated as follows:

1. Prices rise (whatever the first cause may be; but we have chosen for illustration an increase in the amount of gold).

2. The rate of interest rises, but not sufficiently.

3. Enterprisers (to use Professor Fetter's term), encouraged by large profits, expand their loans.

4. Deposit currency (M') expands relatively to money (M).

5. Prices continue to rise, that is, phenomenon No. 1 is repeated. Then No. 2 is repeated, and so on.

In other words, a slight initial rise of prices sets in motion a train of events which tends to repeat itself. Rise of prices generates rise of prices, and continues to do so as long *as the interest rate lags behind its normal figure*.

----

[4] See J. Pease Norton, *Statistical Studies in the New York Money Market* (Macmillan), 1902, chart at end.

[5] See article by Knut Wicksell in the *Jahrbücher für Nationalökonomie*, 1897 (Bank 68), pp. 228-243, entitled "Der Bankzins als Regulator der Warenpreise." This article, while not dealing directly with credit cycles as related to panics, points out the connection between the rate of interest on bank loans and changes in the level of prices due to the resulting expansion and contraction of such loans.

[6] See Kinley, *Money*, New York (Macmillan), 1904, p. 223.

[7] See Wicksell, *op. cit.*

3

The expansion of deposit currency indicated in this cumulative movement abnormally increases the ratio of M' to M. This is evident if the rise of prices begins in a change in some element or elements in the equation other than the quantity of money; for if M remains constant and M' increases, the ratio M' to M must increase also. If M increases in any ratio, M' will increase in a greater ratio. If it increased only in the same ratio, prices would increase in that ratio (assuming velocities and quantities unchanged); and if prices increased in that ratio, loans (which being made to buy goods must be adjusted to the prices of goods) would have to be increased in that ratio in order to secure merely the same goods as before. But enterprisers, wishing to profit by the lag in interest, would extend the loans beyond this old or original point. Therefore, deposits based on loans would increase in a greater ratio. That is, the ratio M' to M would increase. In other words, during the period while M is increasing, M' increases still faster, thus disturbing the normal ratio between these two forms of currency.

This, however, is not the only disturbance caused by the increase in M. There are disturbances in the Q's (or in other words T) in V, and in V'. These will be taken up in order. Trade (the Q's) will be stimulated by the easy terms for loans. This effect is always observed during rising prices, and people note approvingly that "business is good" and "times are booming." Such statements represent the point of view of the ordinary business man who is an "enterpriser-borrower." They do not represent the sentiments of the creditor, the salaried man, or the laborer, most of whom are silent but long-suffering,—paying higher prices, but not getting proportionally higher incomes.

The first cause of the unhealthy increase in trade lies in the fact that prices, like interest, lag behind their full adjustment and have to be pushed up, so to speak, by increased purchases. This is especially true in cases where the original impetus came from an increase in money. The surplus money is first expended at nearly the old price level, but its continued expenditure gradually raises prices. In the meantime the volume of purchases will be somewhat greater than it would have been had prices risen more promptly. In fact, from the point of view of those who are selling goods, it is the possibility of a greater volume of sales at the old prices which gives encouragement to an increase of prices. Seeing that they can find purchasers for more goods than before at the previously prevailing prices, or for as many goods as before at higher prices, they will charge these higher prices.

But the amount of trade is dependent, almost entirely, on other things than the quantity of currency, so that an increase of currency cannot, even temporarily, very greatly increase trade. In ordinarily good times practically the whole community is engaged in labor, producing, transporting, and exchanging goods. The increase of currency of a "boom" period cannot, of itself, increase the population, extend invention, or increase the efficiency of labor. These factors pretty definitely limit the amount of trade which can be reasonably carried on. So, although the gains of the enterpriser-borrower may exert a psychological stimulus on trade, though a few unemployed may be employed, and some others in a few lines induced to work overtime, and although there may be some additional buying and selling which is speculative, yet almost the entire effect of an increase of deposits must be seen in a change of prices. Normally the entire effect would so express itself, but transitionally there will be also some increase in the Q's.

We next observe that the rise in prices—fall in the purchasing power of money—will accelerate the circulation of money. We all hasten to get rid of any commodity which, like ripe fruit, is spoiling on our hands.[8] Money is no exception; when it is depreciating, holders will get rid of it as fast as possible. As they view it, their motive is to buy goods which appreciate in terms of money in order to profit by the rise in their value. The inevitable result is that these goods rise in price still further. The series of changes, then, initiated by rising prices, expressed more fully than before, is as follows:

1. Prices rise.
2. Velocities of circulation (V and V') increase; the rate of interest rises, but not sufficiently.
3. Profits increase, loans expand, and the Q's increase.
4. Deposit currency (M') expands relatively to money (M).
5. Prices continue to rise; that is, phenomenon No. 1 is repeated. Then No. 2 is repeated, and so on.

It will be noticed that these changes now involve all the magnitudes in the equation of exchange. They are temporary changes, pertaining only to the transition period. They are like temporary increases in power and readjustments in an automobile climbing a hill.

4

Evidently the expansion coming from this cycle of causes cannot proceed forever. It must ultimately spend itself. The check upon its continued

---

[8]For statistical proof, see Pierre des Essars, *Journal de la Société de Statistique de Paris,* April, 1895, p. 143. The figures relate only to velocity of bank deposits. No corresponding figures for velocity of circulation of money exist. Pierre des Essars has shown that in European banks V' reaches a maximum in crisis years almost without fail. The same I find true in this country as shown by the ratio of clearings to deposits in New York, Boston, and Philadelphia.

operation lies in the rate of interest. It was the tardiness of the rise in interest that was responsible for the abnormal condition. But the rise in interest, though belated, is progressive, and, as soon as it overtakes the rate of rise in prices, the whole situation is changed. If prices are rising at the rate of 2 per cent per annum, the boom will continue only until interest becomes 2 per cent higher. It then offsets the rate of rise in prices. The banks are forced in self-defense to raise interest because they cannot stand so abnormal an expansion of loans relatively to reserves. As soon as the interest rate becomes adjusted, borrowers can no longer hope to make great profits, and the demand for loans ceases to expand.

There are also other forces placing a limitation on further expansion of deposit currency and introducing a tendency to contraction. Not only is the amount of deposit currency limited both by law and by prudence to a certain maximum multiple of the amount of bank reserves; but bank reserves are themselves limited by the amount of money available for use as reserves. Further, with the rise of interest, the value of certain collateral securities, such as bonds, on the basis of which loans are made, begins to fall. Such securities, being worth the discounted value of fixed sums, fall as interest rises; and therefore they cannot be used as collateral for loans as large as before. This check to loans is, as previously explained, a check to deposits also.

With the rise of interest, those who have counted on renewing their loans at the former rates and for the former amounts are unable to do so. It follows that some of them are destined to fail. The failure (or prospect of failure) of firms that have borrowed heavily from banks induces fear on the part of many depositors that the banks will not be able to realize on these loans. Hence the banks themselves fall under suspicion, and for this reason depositors demand cash. Then occur "runs on the banks," which deplete the bank reserves at the very moment they are most needed.[9] Being short of reserves, the banks have to curtail their loans. It is then that the rate of interest rises to a panic figure. Those enterprisers who are caught *must* have currency[10] to liquidate their obligations, and to get it are willing to pay high interest. Some of them are destined to become bankrupt, and, with their failure, the demand for loans is correspondingly reduced. This culmination of an upward price movement is what is called a crises,[11] —a condition characterized by bankruptcies, and the bankruptcies being due to a lack of cash when it is most needed.

---

[9] A part of the theory of crises here presented is similarly explained in a paper by Harry G. Brown, *Yale Review*, August, 1910, entitled "Typical Commercial Crises *versus* a Money Panic."

[10] Irving Fisher, *Rate of Interest*, pp. 325–326.

[11] This is the definition of a crisis given by Juglar and the history of crisis which he gives in detail corresponds to the description. See Juglar, *Des Crises Commerciales*

It is generally recognized that the collapse of bank credit brought about by loss of confidence is the essential fact of every crisis, be the cause of the loss of confidence what it may. What is not generally recognized, and what it is desired in this chapter to emphasize, is that this loss of confidence (in the typical commercial crisis here described) is a consequence of a belated adjustment in the interest rate.

It is not our purpose here to discuss nonmonetary causes of crises, further than to say that the monetary causes are the most important *when taken in connection with the maladjustments in the rate of interest.* The other factors often emphasized are merely effects of this maladjustment. "Overconsumption" and "overinvestment" are cases in point. The reason many people spend more than they can afford is that they are relying on the dollar as a stable unit when as a matter of fact its purchasing power is rapidly falling. The bondholder, for instance, is beguiled into trenching on his capital. He never dreams that he ought to lay by a sinking fund because the decrease in purchasing power of money is reducing the real value of his principal. Again, the stockholder and enterpriser generally are beguiled by a vain reliance on the stability of the rate of interest, and so they overinvest. It is true that for a time they are gaining what the bondholder is losing and are therefore justified in both spending and investing more than if prices were not rising; and at first they prosper. But sooner or later the rate of interest rises above what they had reckoned on, and they awake to the fact that they have embarked on enterprises which cannot pay these high rates.

Then a curious thing happens: borrowers, unable to get easy loans, blame the high rate of interest for conditions which were really due to the fact that the previous rate of interest was not high enough. Had the previous rate been high enough, the borrowers never would have overinvested.

5

The contraction of loans and deposits is accompanied by a decrease in velocities, and these conspire to prevent a further rise of prices and tend toward a fall. The crest of the wave is reached and a reaction sets in. Since prices have stopped rising, the rate of interest, which has risen to compensate the rise of prices, *should* fall again. But just as at first it was slow to rise, so now it is slow to fall. In fact, it tends for a time to rise still further.

The mistakes of the past of overborrowing compel the unfortunate

---

et de leur retour périodique en France en Angleterre et aux Etats-Unis. 2d ed., Paris (Guillaumin), 1889, pp. 4 and 5. See also translation of part dealing with the United States, by De Courcey W. Thom, *A Brief History of Panics in the United States,* New York (Putnam), 1893, pp. 7-10.

victims of these mistakes to borrow still further to protect their solvency. It is this special abnormality which marks the period as a "crisis." Loans are wanted to continue old debts or to pay these debts by creating new ones. They are not wanted because of new investments but because of obligations connected with old (and ill-fated) investments. The problem is how to get extricated from the meshes of past commitments. It is the problem of liquidation. Even when interest begins to fall, it falls slowly, and failures continue to occur. Borrowers now find that interest, though nominally low, is still hard to meet. Especially do they find this true in the case of contracts made just before prices ceased rising or just before they began to fall. The rate of interest in these cases is agreed upon before the change in conditions takes place. There will, in consequence, be little if any adjustment in lowering nominal interest. Because interest is hard to pay, failures continue to occur. There comes to be a greater hesitation in lending on any but the best security, and a hesitation to borrow save when the prospects of success are the greatest. Bank loans tend to be low, and consequently deposits (M') are reduced. The contraction of deposit currency makes prices fall still more. Those who have borrowed for the purpose of buying stocks of goods now find they cannot sell them for enough even to pay back what they have borrowed. Owing to this tardiness of the interest rate in falling to a lower and a normal level, the sequence of events is now the opposite of what it was before:—

1. Prices fall.
2. The rate of interest falls, but not sufficiently.
3. Enterpriser-borrowers, discouraged by small profits, contract their borrowings.
4. Deposit currency (M') contracts relatively to money (M).
5. Prices continue to fall; that is, phenomenon No. 1 is repeated. Then No. 2 is repeated, and so on.

Thus a fall of prices generates a further fall of prices. The cycle evidently repeats itself as long as the rate of interest lags behind. The man who loses most is the business man in debt. He is the typical business man, and he now complains that "business is bad." There is a "depression of trade."

During this depression, velocities (V and V') are abnormally low. People are less hasty to spend money or checks when the dollars they represent are rising in purchasing power. The Q's (or quantities in trade) decline because (1) the initiators of trade—the enterpriser-borrowers—are discouraged; (2) the inertia of high prices can be overcome only by a falling off of expenditures; (3) trade against money which alone the Q's represent gives way somewhat to barter. For a time there is not enough money to do the business which has to be done at existing prices, for these prices are still high and will not immediately adjust themselves to the sudden contraction. When such a "money famine" exists, there is no way of doing all the business except by eking out money transactions with barter. But while recourse to barter eases the first fall of prices, the inconvenience of barter immediately begins to operate as an additional force tending to reduce prices by inducing sellers to sell at a sacrifice if only money can be secured and barter avoided; although this effect is partly neutralized for a time by a decrease in the amount of business which people will attempt under such adverse conditions. A statement including these factors is:—

1. Prices fall.
2. Velocities of circulation (V and V') fall; the rate of interest falls, but not sufficiently.
3. Profits decrease; loans and the Q's decrease.
4. Deposit currency (M') contracts relatively to money (M).
5. Prices continue to fall; that is, phenomenon No. 1 is repeated. Then No. 2 is repeated, and so on.

The contraction brought about by this cycle of causes becomes self-limiting as soon as the rate of interest overtakes the rate of fall in prices. After a time, normal conditions begin to return. The weakest producers have been forced out, or have at least been prevented from expanding their business by increased loans. The strongest firms are left to build up a new credit structure. The continuous fall of prices has made it impossible for most borrowers to pay the old high rates of interest; the demand for loans diminishes, and interest falls to a point such that borrowers can at last pay it. Borrowers again become willing to take ventures; failures decrease in number; bank loans cease to decrease; prices cease to fall; borrowing and carrying on business become profitable; loans are again demanded; prices again begin to rise, and there occurs a repetition of the upward movement already described.

We have considered the rise, culmination, fall, and recovery of prices. These changes are abnormal oscillations, due to some initial disturbance. The upward and downward movements taken together constitute a complete credit cycle, which resembles the forward and backward movements of a pendulum.[12] In most cases the time occupied by the swing of the commercial pendulum to and fro is about ten years. While the pendulum is continually seeking a stable position, practically there is almost always some occurrence to prevent perfect equilibrium. Oscillations are set up

[12]For a mathematical treatment of this analogy, see Pareto, *Cours d'économie politique,* Lausanne, 1897, pp. 282–284.

which, though tending to be self-corrective, are continually perpetuated by fresh disturbances. Any cause which disturbs equilibrium will suffice to set up oscillations. One of the most common of such causes is an increase in the quantity of money.[13] Another is a shock to business confidence (affecting enterprise, loans, and deposits). A third is short crops, affecting the Q's. A fourth is invention.

The factors in the equation of exchange are therefore continually seeking normal adjustment. A ship in a calm sea will "pitch" only a few times before coming to rest, but in a high sea the pitching never ceases. While continually seeking equilibrium, the ship continually encounters causes which accentuate the oscillation. The factors seeking mutual adjustment are money in circulation, deposits, their velocities, the Q's and the p's. These magnitudes must always be linked together by the equation $MV + M'V' = \Sigma pQ$. This represents the mechanism of exchange. But in order to conform to such a relation the displacement of any one part of the mechanism spreads its effects during the transition period over all parts. Since periods of transition are the rule and those of equilibrium the exception, the mechanism of exchange is almost always in a dynamic rather than a static condition.

It must not be assumed that every credit cycle is so marked as to produce artificially excessive business activity at one time and "hard times" at another. The rhythm may be more or less extreme in the width of its fluctuations. If banks are conservative in making loans during the periods of rising prices, and the expansion of credit currency is therefore limited, the rise of prices is likewise limited, and the succeeding fall is apt to be less and to take place more gradually. If there were a better appreciation of the meaning of changes in the price level and an endeavor to balance these changes by adjustment in the rate of interest, the oscillations might be very greatly mitigated. It is the lagging behind of the rate of interest which allows the oscillations to reach so great proportions. On this point Marshall well says: "The cause of alternating periods of inflation and depression of commercial activity . . . is intimately connected with those variations in the real rate of interest which are caused by changes in the purchasing power of money. For when prices are likely to rise, people rush to borrow money and buy goods, and thus help prices to rise; business is inflated, and is managed recklessly and wastefully; those working on borrowed capital pay back less real value than they borrowed, and enrich themselves at the expense of the community. When afterwards credit is shaken and prices begin to fall, every one wants to get rid of commodities which are falling in value and to get hold of money which is rapidly rising; this makes

[13]Such would seem to be the explanation of the panic of 1907. Cf. Irving Fisher, *Rate of Interest*, p. 336.

prices fall all the faster, and the further fall makes credit shrink even more, and thus for a long time prices fall because prices have fallen."[14]

A somewhat different sort of cycle is the seasonal fluctuation which occurs annually. Such fluctuations, for the most part, are due, not to the departure from a state of equilibrium, but rather to a continuous adjustment to conditions, which, though changing, are normal and expected. As the autumn periods of harvesting and crop moving approach, there is a tendency toward a lower level of prices, followed after the passing of this period and the approach of winter by a rise of prices.

6

In the present chapter we have analyzed the phenomena characteristic of periods of transition. We have found that one such "boom" period leads to a reaction, and that the action and reaction complete a cycle of "prosperity" and "depression."

It has been seen that rising prices tend towards a higher nominal interest, and falling prices tend towards a lower, but that in general the adjustment is incomplete. With any initial rise of prices comes an expansion of loans, owing to the fact that interest does not at once adjust itself. This produces profits for the enterpriser-borrower, and his demand for loans further extends deposit currency. This extention still further raises prices, a result accentuated by a rise in velocities though somewhat mitigated by an increase in trade. When interest has become adjusted to rising prices, and loans and deposits have reached the limit set for them by the bank reserves and other conditions, the fact that prices no longer are rising necessitates a new adjustment. Those whose business has been unduly extended now find the high rates of interest oppressive. Failures result, constituting a commercial crisis. A reaction sets in; a reverse movement is initiated. A fall of prices, once begun, tends to be accelerated for reasons exactly corresponding to those which operate in the opposite situation.

[14]Marshall, *Principles of Economics*, 5th ed., London (Macmillan), 1907, Vol. I, p. 594.

2/ MILTON FRIEDMAN

Factors Affecting the Level of Interest Rates

There is a problem in terminology that is worth commenting on at the outset. In all sorts of monetary discussions, there is a tendency to use the word "money" in three different senses. We speak of a man making money when we mean that he is earning income. We speak of a man borrowing money when we mean that he is engaging in a credit transaction. Similarly, we speak of the money market in the sense of a credit market. Finally, we talk about money when we mean those green pieces of paper we carry in our pocket or the deposits to our credit at banks.

CONFUSION OF CREDIT WITH MONEY

Much of the misunderstanding about the relationship between money and interest rates comes from a failure to keep those three senses of the term "money" distinct, in particular to keep "credit" distinct from "quantity of money." In discussing credit, it is natural and correct to say that the interest rate is the price of credit. General price theory tells us that the price of anything will be lowered by an increase in supply and will be raised by a reduction in supply. Therefore it is natural to say that an increase in credit will reduce the rate of interest. That is correct. A shift to the right of the supply curve of loanable funds—that is, an increase in the supply of loanable funds at each interest rate—will, other things being

Reprinted by permission of the author and publisher from the *Proceedings* of the 1968 Conference on Savings and Residential Financing, sponsored by the United States Savings and Loan League. Milton Friedman is Professor of Economics at the University of Chicago.

the same, tend to reduce the interest rate. A decrease in supply will tend to raise it.

The tendency to confuse credit with money leads to the further belief that an increase in the quantity of money will tend to reduce interest rates, and a reduction in the quantity of money will tend to increase interest rates.

Because of this confusion, there is also a tendency to regard the term "monetary ease" as unambiguous, as meaning either a more rapid increase in the quantity of money or lower interest rates and, similarly, monetary tightness as meaning either a reduction in the quantity of money or higher interest rates.

INTEREST RATE PRICE OF CREDIT, NOT MONEY

My main thesis is that this is wrong, that the relation between the quantity of money and the level and movement of interest is much more complicated than the relation that is suggested by the identification of money with credit. It is more complicated because the interest rate is not the price of money. The interest rate is the price of credit. The price level or the inverse of the price level is the price of money. What is to be expected from general price theory is what the quantity theory says, namely, that a rapid increase in the quantity of money means an increase in prices of goods and services, and that a decrease in the quantity of money means a decrease in the price of goods and services. Therefore, to see what effect changes in the quantity of money have on interest rates, it is necessary to look more deeply beneath the surface.

Before going into the detailed analysis, let me prepare the groundwork by discussing some facts. If you ask most economists, or most noneconomists for that matter, certainly if you ask most people at savings and loan institutions or in banks, whether an increased quantity of money will mean higher or lower interest rates, everybody will say lower interest rates; but looking at broad facts shows the reverse.

If I ask in what countries in the world are interest rates high, there will be widespread agreement that they are high in Brazil, Argentina and Chile. If I say, "I take it that in those countries there are very low rates of increase in the quantity of money and that interest rates are high because money has been tight," you will laugh at me. Those are countries which have had very rapid increase in the quantity of money and inflation.

If I ask in what countries of the world are interest rates low, you will tell me in countries like Switzerland. On the usual view, this would imply that they have been having rapid increases in the quantity of money. Yet we all know that the situation is precisely the reverse. Switzerland is a country which has held down the quantity of money.

Let us turn to the United States. Suppose I said, "What is the period in the United States when interest rates fell most rapidly?" There is not the slightest doubt when that was. It was the period from about 1929 to the mid-1930s. Would you then say, "That must have been the period when the quantity of money was increasing." Obviously not. We all know that it is the opposite. From 1929 to 1933, the quantity of money fell by one-third and, as I shall proceed later to say, therefore interest rates fell, although in terms of the usual presumptions that economists have and which are enshrined in our elementary textbooks, one would say precisely the opposite.

Similarly, interest rates are high now in the United States in nominal terms. Nominal interest rates are far higher than they were in the mid-'30s, far higher than they were just after the war. Yet, in the past five or six years, the quantity of money has been increasing relatively rapidly.

The point of this crude and rough survey of experience is to bring home that the broadest factual evidence runs precisely contrary to what most of us teach our students and what is accepted almost without question by the Federal Reserve System, by bankers, by the savings and loan business.

So far I have mentioned one set of broad facts, namely, the relation between the level of interest rates and the rate of change in the quantity of money. When the quantity of money has been increasing very rapidly, there is a tendency to have high interest rates; when it has been decreasing very rapidly or increasing slowly, there is a tendency to have low interest rates.

GIBSON PARADOX: PRICES, INTEREST RATES MOVE TOGETHER

Another empirical regularity, which was pointed out many years ago, exists not between money and interest rates but between prices and interest rates. The Gibson paradox is the observed empirical tendency for prices and interest rates to move together. When prices are rising, interest rates tend to be rising; when prices are falling, interest rates tend to be falling.

This was regarded as a paradox because of the orthodox view I have been questioning. Ordinarily, prices would be expected to be rising because the quantity of money is increasing. If the quantity of money is increasing, the orthodox view is that interest rates should be falling. Yet we find that when prices are rising, interest rates are rising, and when prices are falling, interest rates are falling.

That is another piece of empirical evidence which needs to be interpreted by any theory which tries to explain the relationship between the changes in the quantity of money on the one hand and the level or direction of movement in interest rates on the other hand.

Let me turn from this background to a theoretical analysis of the relationship between money and interest rates. This analysis is one which has been developed over the past few years, and in that period three different empirical pieces of work have been done which I am going to summarize for you. To the best of my knowledge, none is yet published.

The first is some work that Anna Schwartz and I have done in studying the relationships between longer term movements in the quantity of money and in interest rates. The second is some work that Phillip Cagan has done at the National Bureau on shorter term movements in interest rates within the cycle. Anna's and my work uses as the basic unit a half-cycle, so it has to do with the inter-cycle movement. Phil Cagan's work has to do with the intra-cycle movement.

The third is a doctoral dissertation just recently completed at the University of Chicago by William Gibson, who is now at the University of California in Los Angeles, which also deals with the shorter period relationships between money and interest rates.

The new work in this area is an interesting phenomenon because it reflects a very long cycle. Irving Fisher worked on this problem back in the '20s and '30s. What the three of us have done is to redo Fisher and find that he was right after all. While there has been considerable work done in these past three years, it owes a great deal to the much earlier work done by Fisher. This is particularly true of the analysis of the Gibson paradox.

ANALYSIS OF CHANGES IN MONEY, INTEREST RATES

I should like to present to you what seems to me now to be the correct theoretical analysis of the relationship between changes in the quantity of money and interest rates. I shall argue that there are three sets of effects which have to be distinguished. The first is the liquidity effect. The second is what I shall call the income effect. The third is the price anticipations effect. I shall argue that, of these three effects, the first one works in the direction which has been generally expected, but the second and the third work in the opposite direction. If the effect of monetary change on interest rates is to be understood, all three have to be taken into account.

The liquidity effect in its simplest form is the usual textbook relationship between the quantity of money and the interest rate which says that the larger the quantity of money, the lower the interest rate will have to

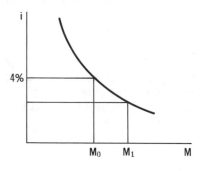

Figure 1.

be to induce people to hold it. I have drawn it in that form in Figure 1, but no one who is careful writes it in that form and this is one of the slips in the analysis. What really should be measured on the horizontal axis is not M, the nominal quantity of money, but $\dfrac{M}{P}$, the real quantity of money.

Part of the story of tracing the effect of a change in money is going from a change in the nominal quantity of money to what happens to the real quantity of money. For the moment, however, let us waive that. We shall come back to it because it is in the second set of effects—the income effect or income-and-price effect. Let us stay here for the moment with the liquidity effect.

Consider now Figure 2, in which time is measured on the horizontal axis. Let us suppose that up to some moment of time, t_0, there has been a constant rate of increase in the quantity of money, say 3% per year. At a certain time it suddenly starts increasing at 5% a year. Let us suppose that interest rates prior to t_0 have been 4%, as shown on Figure 2. What should we expect to be the pattern of behavior of interest rates as a result of this one-shot change in monetary growth as it works itself out through time? That is the central theoretical problem.

The first tendency of any economist, in terms of our present literature, is to stress the fact that in order to get people to hold the large quantity of money, interest rates will have to go down. As shown in Figure 1, people were willing to hold M_0 at a rate of interest of 4%. To get them to hold more, there will have to be a movement along the curve to lower interest rates. There is an implicit assumption in that analysis that needs to be brought to the surface. The implicit assumption is that prices are not in the first instance affected by the change in the quantity of money.

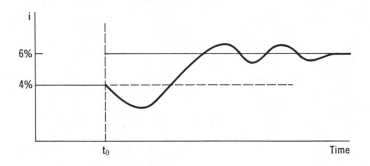

Figure 2.

Let us suppose that prior to this time, prices were stable. Let us suppose for a moment that 3% corresponds to the rate of output increase in the economy and that velocity is constant, just to keep matters simple. None of these assumptions really affects the essence of what I am saying. If, when the quantity of money started increasing at 5% per year instead of 3%, prices suddenly started increasing at 2% per year, you would stay exactly in the same place on the curve in Figure 1 (if the horizontal axis is interpreted as M/P), and there would be no tendency for interest rates to go down. The implicit assumption that, in the first instance, the effect is not likely to be on prices, is consistent with much empirical evidence. I should qualify this statement. The implicit assumption seems correct *if* this jump from 3% to 5% is an unanticipated jump. If it were announced that the jump was going to occur, it would be more plausible that it would have an immediate effect on prices.

LIQUIDITY EFFECT: PRICE OF SECURITIES UP, INTEREST RATE DOWN

If this is an unanticipated jump in the rate of monetary increase, it is reasonable to suppose that its first impact will be that people will find the composition of their portfolios disturbed. Holders of cash will find that they have more cash than they planned to have. Their first impulse will be to attempt to readjust the portfolios by replacing cash with other securities. This will bid up the price of other securities and lower the rate of interest. This would be the liquidity effect.

This is the effect which explains why academic economists in general will say offhand that an increase in the quantity of money will lower interest rates. In economic terminology, we would call this an effect through stocks. The financial economist or Federal Reserve economist will argue a little differently. He would expect an immediate effect through flows. He would say, "How is the rate of increase in the quantity of money stepped up?" He would say that in our kind of financial system ordinarily it will be stepped up by an increased rate of purchase of securities by the central banks, which in turn will add to the reserves of commercial banks which will expand by making additional loans. He would say that the very process of stepping up the quantity of money in our kind of financial system operates to raise the supply of loanable funds. That is entirely true for our kind of financial system.

It is interesting to note that discussions of the problem in earlier literature, for example, in John Stuart Mill's *Principles of Political Economy*, written over a century ago, very clearly stated that the first-round effect which was to be expected from a change in the quantity of money would be different as it occurred through the credit market or as it occurred through a change in gold production. It was argued that if it occurred through gold production, its first-order effect would be not on interest rates but on the wages of gold miners and the prices of commodities they bought and that it would spread from there. On the other hand, if the increase in the quantity of money occurred through the credit market, its first-round effect would be on interest rates.

These two factors—the effect on stocks and the effect through flows—would work in the same direction. However, the title "liquidity effect" under which I have included both is not an entirely descriptive term. Both factors tend to make for an initial decline in the rate of interest—the stock effect because of a movement along the liquidity curve and the flow effect because of a movement to the right in the supply of loanable funds. There is a difference. The flow effect would produce a decline in the interest rate which might be expected to happen immediately. As long as prices do not react, the effect through stocks will exert a continuing downward pressure on the interest rate. So it is not clear whether the liquidity effect would produce simply a sudden drop to a new level, or a period during which interest rates fall, as I have shown it on Figure 2. That is the first effect—a liquidity effect.

INCOME-AND-PRICE LEVEL EFFECT

The next effect is the income-and-price level effect. As cash balances are built up, people's attempts to acquire other assets raise the prices of assets and drive down the interest rate. That will tend to produce an increase in spending. Along standard income and expenditure lines, it will tend to increase business investment. Alternatively, to look at it more broadly, the prices of sources of services will be raised relative to the prices of the service flows themselves. This leads to an increase in spending on the service flow, and therefore to an increase in current income. In addition, it leads to an increase in spending on producing sources of services in response to the higher price which can now be obtained for them.

The existence and character of this effect does not depend on any doctrinal position about the way in which monetary forces affect the economy. Whether monetary forces are considered as affecting the economy through the interest rate and thence through investment spending or whether, as I believe, reported interest rates are only a few of a large set of rates of interest and the effect of monetary change is exerted much more broadly, in either case the effect of the more rapid rate of monetary growth will tend to be a rise in nominal income.

For the moment, let us hold prices constant and suppose that the rise in nominal income is entirely a result of rising output. What effect will that have? It will raise the demand curve for loanable funds. A business expansion is in process and the increasing level of income will raise the demand for loanable funds. This will exert a force tending to raise interest rates, or at least to counteract the downward pressure from the increasing stock of money. In addition, the rising incomes will tend to shift to the right the liquidity preference curve of Figure 1, since the higher the income, the larger the quantity of money demanded at each interest rate. (Strictly speaking, under our assumptions that the initial position was one of a 3% per year rate of growth in real income, the effect will be a still more rapid shift of the liquidity preference curve. Alternatively, we can interpret Figure 1 as representing a trend-corrected curve.)

Suppose the expansion in income takes the form in part of rising prices. This will not alter the tendency for the demand for loanable funds, expressed in nominal terms, to rise. But, if we measure the real quantity of money $\left(\dfrac{M}{P}\right)$ on the horizontal axis of Figure 1, this tendency will affect that figure. Suppose prices go up as rapidly as the increased rate of monetary growth, in our assumed case, 2%. The real quantity of money will remain constant. If prices go up more rapidly than that, you will tend to move back along the curve. As income rises, whether or not prices rise, interest rates will turn around and go up, as a result of the rising demand for loanable funds, the shift of the liquidity preference curve and the possible movement along it.

There are many reasons to believe that this rise in interest rates will go too far. It will overshoot. I cannot cover this point in full here but let me suggest some reasons to expect even this short-run effect to overshoot.

In the first place, we started out by saying that prices will be slow to react and that the initial effect is the disturbance of portfolios. That means that there is some catching up to do. We can see what is involved most readily by looking at the ultimate long-run position.

If the rate of monetary growth stayed at 5%, the long-run equilibrium position would involve nominal income rising at 2% per year more than it did prior to the increase in the monetary growth rate. In Figure 3, Line C is a continuation of the original trend of rising income, let us say, at 3% a year. Line B shows a trend linked to the initial trend but with a rate of rise of 5%. If at first income proceeds along C but ultimately has to proceed along B, then for some period income will have risen more rapidly in order to catch up. That is one reason for a tendency to overshoot.

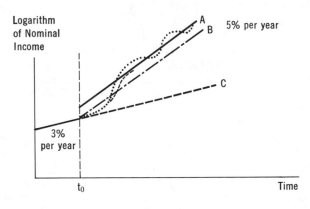

Figure 3.

A second reason is a little more complicated. The true long-run equilibrium position of income will not be Line B but a higher line, say Line A. It will be a higher line because the amount of real balances that people want to hold will be smaller when prices are rising at 2% per year than when they are stable.

PRICE ANTICIPATION EFFECT

This brings us to our third effect, the price anticipation effect. When prices are rising at 2% a year and people come to anticipate that they will continue to, this raises the cost of holding cash. Consequently, they will want to hold smaller balances relative to income. This is clearly the case and has been well-documented for hyper-inflation and substantial inflation. Phil Cagan's study on hyper-inflation, which is by now a classic, documents very clearly that in such episodes, the higher the rate of change of prices, the higher is monetary velocity or the lower are real balances.

Studies for countries like Argentina and Brazil and Chile, countries that have had very substantial inflation, show the same phenomenon. For the United States, it has been much harder to pin down that phenomenon because our price movements have been mild.

In the study by Anna Schwartz and me, using averages for half-cycles, referred to earlier, we have been able for the first time to extract from the American data the same kind of response to the rate of change in prices as had been extracted for the more extreme inflationary episodes.

As a theoretical matter, the higher the rate of change of prices, the higher the velocity expected. This shows up as an empirical phenomenon. This is why the long period equilibrium will be a path like A in Figure 3 rather than like B. Therefore, even if there were no lag in the initial adjustment, at some time or other income or prices have to rise faster than the ultimate equilibrium rate of 2% per year in order to get up to this higher level. To digress for a moment, the phenomenon I have been describing is, in my opinion, the fundamental reason why a shift in the quantity of money tends to produce cyclical reaction patterns and not smooth movements. The dotted lines show two possible paths, one involving damped oscillations, the other a direct approach to equilibrium. But note that even the latter involves a cyclical reaction in the rate of change of income.

The price anticipation effect is the one that is most closely linked to Irving Fisher, that he investigated statistically, and that he introduced to explain the Gibson paradox.

If I may go back a moment, I am sliding over one point that I ought to make explicit. For simplicity, I have been talking as if the initial position we started from was one where there was reasonably full employment, so that while in the interim there can be a period with income increasing and prices stable, sooner or later the higher rate of rise in income will be translated into a higher rate of price increase. That really is not essential for my story at all.

It may be that part of the effect will be taken up in output rather than in prices. All that is essential is that there be some tendency for prices to rise somewhat more than they otherwise would, although I may say that, as an empirical matter, I would expect a shift from one fairly steady rate of monetary growth to another to be reflected fully, sooner or later, in prices.

DISTINGUISH BETWEEN NOMINAL, REAL RATE OF INTEREST

As long as there is some tendency for part of the increase in the rate of growth of the quantity of money to end up in a higher rate of price rise, sooner or later people will come to anticipate it. As people come to anticipate it, we introduce a distinction that I have so far kept out of the picture, namely, the distinction between the nominal rate of interest and the real rate of interest.

We are all very much aware of the distinction right now. It is also a distinction that goes back in our literature, at least to Irving Fisher who analyzed it most exhaustively. If the nominal interest rate is 4% per year and if prices over any period rise at the rate of 2% per year, then the realized real yield will be 2%, not 4%.

However, what matters for the market is not the *ex post* yield which is realized after the event but what people anticipate in advance. People today are buying bonds or other securities or making loans for the long-term future on the basis of what they anticipate will happen.

Let us designate the nominal interest rate by R_B (the B for bonds) and the real rate by R_E (E for equity). Now $\frac{1}{P}\frac{dP}{dt}$ is the percentage rate at which prices are changing at time t. Let an asterisk attached to it stand for an anticipated rate, so $\left(\frac{1}{P}\frac{dP}{dt}\right)^*$ is the anticipated rate of change in prices. Then, the relation Fisher developed is $R_B = R_E + \left(\frac{1}{P}\frac{dP}{dt}\right)^*$. In other words, the nominal rate of interest on the market will be equal to the real rate of interest plus the anticipated rate of price change. Therefore, if R_E stays the same but the anticipated rate of price change goes up, the nominal interest rate will also go up. That is the third effect.

Returning to Figure 2, we see that if the whole of this 2% higher rate of monetary growth goes into prices, and if the initial equilibrium interest rate was 4%, then the new long-run equilibrium rate will be 6%. The interest rate pattern then will be something like that shown in Figure 2 and will ultimately get up to 6%.

WHAT THEORETICAL ANALYSIS DETERMINES

That is the whole of the theoretical analysis that leads to tracing out a path of reaction in interest rates. I have exaggerated somewhat what can be traced out from the theoretical analysis alone since the fluctuations I have put in are not well determined. What is really determined by the theoretical analysis is an initial decline, a subsequent rise and an ultimate attainment of a level about 2% higher than the initial one.

Let me give this theoretical analysis some empirical content. How long are these periods? What is their duration? Of the three studies that I have described, the one that Anna and I have done traces out the time pattern at the end, while Cagan's and Gibson's studies trace out the time pattern at the beginning. So far we have a missing link in between. The empirical work all three of us have done is entirely consistent with the pattern traced out in Figure 2. Empirically, there is a tendency for a rapid rate of monetary growth to be followed by a decline in interest rates and, after a lag, by a rise and then a final ultimate movement to a level higher than the starting point. The major patterns are recorded in the empirical evidence and do come out very clearly.

I have been talking about an increase in the rate of monetary expansion. Obviously, everything is reversed for a decrease, and our empirical studies, of course, cover both increases and decreases.

It turns out that the initial decline in interest rates after an acceleration of monetary growth lasts about six months. Clearly, there is variation but the average period is about six months. The time it takes to get back to the initial level is something like 18 months.

LONG PERIOD TO FINAL EQUILIBRIUM LEVEL

The period it takes to get to the final equilibrium level is very long. Fisher came out with a period of something like 20 years. He did a number of different studies which gave him estimates of 20 or 30 years. Our own estimates are about the same. They make a distinction which Fisher's did not. They suggest that the period is different for short rates than it is for long rates. Fisher did his studies for long rates and did not make that distinction.

As a purely theoretical matter, one would expect that it would take longer for long rates than for short rates. When you are buying a security with a short life, you are really interested in extrapolating price movements over a shorter future period of time than when you are buying a very long-term security. It seems not unreasonable that if you are extrapolating for a short period, you will look back for a shorter period than when you are extrapolating for a longer period.

I regard it as very strong empirical confirmation of this interpretation of the evidence that it does turn out that the period it takes to get full adjustment tends to be much longer for long rates than it does for short rates.

In Figure 2, the time it takes to get to the final equilibrium level depends on how long it takes for a change in the rate of monetary change to produce general anticipation of further price rises. That implicitly means that it depends on how far back people look in forming their anticipations. The mean period of price anticipation turns out to be something like 10 years for short rates and 20 years for long rates. Since these are the average periods, they imply that people take an even longer period of past history into account. These results are wholly consistent with Fisher's.

One more interesting point—and here I am much more tentative— such evidence as I have seen suggests what is to be expected, namely, that the period it takes is much longer in a country which has experienced mild price movements than in a country which has experienced rapid price movements. In one of the South American countries where prices have moved much more rapidly, the period it takes appears to be much shorter. That is what is to be expected in a more variable world where anticipations would be formed over a briefer period of time.

RELATIONSHIP BETWEEN ANALYSIS AND GIBSON PARADOX

Let me tie this in to the Gibson paradox and show how this analysis is related to that. The explanation that Fisher offered for the Gibson paradox was the same as what I have called the third-effect, but it hinges very much on how long it takes for people to form their anticipations. If price change were perfectly anticipated, if people instantaneously anticipated what was actually going to happen, high interest rates would be associated with rapid rates of price rise, and low interest rates would be associated with low rates of price rise or with price declines, but there would be no reason to expect a connection between rising prices and rising interest rates.

Let me see if I can make this clear. Suppose that the historical record of prices was like that plotted in Figure 4, where the ordinate is the logarithm of the price, so that straight lines correspond to constant rates of price increase or decrease. If people fully anticipated this, the result would be that for periods a and c the interest rate would be high, for periods b and d the interest rate would be low—as shown by the dashed steps. There is no reason why rising prices should be associated with rising interest rates. Rising prices would be associated with high interest rates; falling prices with low interest rates. Yet the Gibson paradox is that rising prices are associated with rising interest rates and falling prices with falling interest rates.

In order to explain the Gibson paradox on this basis, Fisher says that if prices start to rise, people do not really believe it. It takes a long time before they accept the idea that prices are rising. Therefore, if we plot on Figure 4 not what the actual rate of change of prices is but what the anticipated rate of change of prices is, we find that it behaves like the wavy dotted line; the anticipated rate of change of prices starts being low, and only gradually rises, and keeps on rising for a time after actual prices start declining. Only after a lag, will it start to decline and then it will decline only gradually.

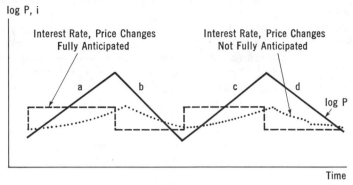

Figure 4.

So, said Fisher, let prices start to rise when those prices have been stable. As prices rise, people gradually come to anticipate the rise. Only after prices have been rising for a long time will people take full account of the actual rate of rise.

PRICE SAVINGS AND ANTICIPATION TIME

In order for this delayed formation of anticipations to explain Gibson's paradox empirically, it is clear that there has to be a particular relation between the length of the period that it takes for people to form their anticipations and the actual long swings in prices. If people formed their anticipations very rapidly—much more rapidly than the length of a price rise or fall—then interest rates would rise for only a short period along with prices and soon would be high but constant. When prices started declining, interest rates would be low but constant. They would look more like the steps in Figure 4 than like the wavy dotted line. In order to have a close correlation between rising prices and rising interest rates, there must be a particular relation among the periods. It must be that the period of the long swings in prices is roughly comparable to the period of time which it takes for people to form anticipations.

That is what Fisher found. Indeed, that is the way in which he estimates the period it takes to form anticipation and it is the way we have done it as well.

Fisher's conclusions as he presented them in the 1920s tended to be disregarded by almost all economists. Very few people paid any attention to him. The explanation is simple. People said, "That's a silly theory, why should it take people 20 to 30 years to form anticipations about price changes? Surely, a theory which requires such a long period must be wrong."

What Anna Schwartz and I did was to recalculate the correlations for an additional 40 years or so beyond the period for which Fisher had data. The correlations are just as good for the additional 40 years as they were for the period before. This is a rare event in applied economics. All of us have had problems with spurious results. We try a dozen different correlations and finally get one that is satisfactory. How do we know it will hold for the future? It usually does not. But in this case, it so happens that Fisher studied this up through the '20s and we have about 40 more years of experience. Nobody since has paid any attention to this particular aspect of the data. Yet they show exactly the same thing for the period since then that they showed before, namely, a high correlation between the rate of change of prices and the rate of change of interest rates. The correlation is higher than the correlation between the level of interest rates and the rate of change of prices. That is to say, it is not the step relation in Figure 4 that dominates but the wavy one.

It is interesting to ask the question, "Why is it that it should take people so long to form anticipations?" I think another feature of the work that Anna and I did gives a very important clue to the answer and has importance beyond this particular problem. You will recall that I mentioned the repeated failure in former work to find a relationship between the rate of price change and velocity in the United States. In the study we made, we found it for the first time. The reason we did, I believe, is that we used as our unit of analysis the half-cycle. Ordinarily, in most such work when we introduce lags we tend to introduce constant chronological lags—one year, two years, three years.

When we started to work on this problem, we found ourselves introducing variable lags without intending to do so because if economic series are averaged over half-cycles, some half-cycles are short, some are long. Consequently, when we related velocity today to price change in a prior cycle phase, we implicitly had a lag that was long when the cycle phases were long and short when the cycle phases were short.

DISTINCTION BETWEEN PSYCHOLOGICAL, CHRONOLOGICAL TIME

What led me to continue along this line was the work that Maurice Allais described in his "A Restatement of the Quantity Theory of Money," recently published in the *American Economic Review* and in which he made a very basic and important distinction between psychological time and chronological time.

Let me translate this idea without going into Allais' particular way of putting it—though I believe his paper is one of the most important and original that has been written for a long time, not particularly because of its treatment of the demand for money but for its consideration of the problem of the formation of expectations.

People who are trying to form anticipations have some understanding of the nature of the society. They know that the economy goes in cycles and has its ups and downs. Suppose you are trying to form an anticipation about what is going to happen to prices. You will say, "I had better average out over these cycles. I had better look back to what was happening in a corresponding phase of the last cycle." If you are examining past history with the idea that there is some kind of cyclical pattern, it is perfectly reasonable for you to go back a roughly fixed number of cycles, not years.

That is exactly what our results suggested. Better results were obtained by taking as a unit of measurement the cycle and not the year. Let us apply this idea to the present problem. Let us say that you are going to buy a 40- or 50-year bond. You want to make a prediction for a long period on the basis of the past. It is reasonable for you to form your anticipation not on the basis of short-period data of the last few years but of a period that will encompass, as it were, full economic episodes.

Because of limitations of time, I am proceeding very dogmatically and sketchily, but this establishes a theoretical reason why it is not surprising to find that the period over which the anticipation is formed bears a relationship to the observed period of long swings in prices.

CORRELATION BETWEEN ANTICIPATION PERIOD, FLUCTUATIONS

You might say that Fisher's result is a pure coincidence. His result depends on the periods of formation of anticipations being roughly as long as the periods of sustained price movements. Why should they be? If people are intelligently forming anticipations about the future on the basis of an analysis of the past, it is not a foolish thing for them to behave that way. That is why I believe that you will find that this period of anticipation is shorter in those countries which have sharper and more rapid fluctuations than in those which have slower and longer fluctuations.

I was very much struck with this point the other day when I was in New York acting as a representative of many of you at a College Retirement Equity Fund lunch. Some financial people started talking about the difference between the behavior of young people today and of their own behavior with respect to borrowing on credit. These people's behavior today was being very much influenced by what had happened in the 1930s. This was over a 30-year lag in their behavior.

Now of course the actual lag for the society is an average over all age classes and this is the longest lag, but once you start to look at it in that way, it does not seem to me too surprising that the lag should be so long.

Let me give you another empirical illustration. There is little doubt in my mind that the widespread expectation that prevailed in the United States after World War II that there would be a price fall involved using data going back roughly 150 years.

You ask yourself, "How shall I form an anticipation about what happens after a major war?" There is no use looking at what happened during peace time. It is better to look at what happened after earlier major wars. People who were forming these anticipations after World War II looked back at what happened after World War I, what happened after the Civil War, what happened after the War of 1812, and they found that in each of these cases, within about 10 or 15 years after the end of the war, prices were half what they had been at the end of the war. So it was not at all absurd for people to form their anticipations on the basis of a period stretching back over 100 years.

RECENT EXPERIENCE ILLUSTRATES ANALYSIS

Let me conclude simply by applying this analysis to recent experience because it applies beautifully. When I say this analysis, I really am talking mostly about the short period analysis, not Fisher's long period analysis. Consider what happened in 1966 and 1967, because it was almost a perfect representation of the relationship I have shown in Figure 2.

There was a rapid rate of growth in money until April 1966. (The exact rate depends on whether you use a narrow or a broad definition of money but nothing I say will be affected by that, because the patterns of behavior of the different rates are the same although the quantitative rates of change are different.) From April 1966 to about December 1966 there was a brief but sharp decline in the rate of monetary change.

From December 1966 or January 1967 through most of 1967, to something like October or November of 1967, there was an even more rapid rate of increase than before April 1966. Since about November 1967, there has been a tapering off in the rate of growth.

DELAYED IMPACT OF EARLIER MONETARY GROWTH

What happened to interest rates during that period? Prior to April 1966 interest rates were rising. Why were they rising? This was the delayed impact of the earlier high rate of monetary growth.

Suddenly there was a tightening of money—a sharp decrease in the rate of growth of the quantity of money. What does our theory say? Turn Figure 2 upside down. It says a rapid increase in interest rates would be expected because the delayed effect of earlier monetary ease is reinforced by the impact effect of monetary tightness. That, of course, is what happened. There was a very sharp rise in interest rates culminating in the so-called credit crunch.

The interesting thing is when did that culminate? In September or October 1966, several months before the reversal in monetary growth. That is exactly what our analysis would lead you to expect—a turnaround about six months after the shift in monetary growth.

At this point the tight money was having a depressing effect on interest rates. The liquidity effect had shot its bolt, the income effect was beginning to take over. That income effect resulted in a slowdown in the economy in the first half of 1967 which reduced the demand for loanable funds and so interest rates fell.

Then what happened? After monetary growth accelerated in January 1967, the short-term effects of easy money reinforced the delayed effect of the tighter money and so interest rates continued to fall. But this time the short-term effect was abnormally short—less than six months. Interest rates turned around some time in March or April that year and started to go up. These delayed effects of easy money were then reinforced in November 1967 by the tapering off of monetary growth.

MANY FACTORS AFFECT INTEREST RATES

Obviously, I am not trying to say for a moment that monetary change is the only thing that affects interest rates. Do not misunderstand me. I am trying to isolate that part of the interest rate movement which is determined by monetary change. Many, many other things affect interest rates.

In particular, I have no reason to doubt that the sharp increase in the federal government's deficit, which meant an increase in the demand for borrowing by the federal government was a factor which was raising interest rates through most of 1967. It may be that is why there was an abnormally short delay before the initial impact of easy money was reversed.

I should have made this qualification about other factors earlier. Our squared correlations are perhaps on the order of about .5 which means they account for half of the fluctuations in nominal interest rates. I do not for a moment want to suggest that if you understand the effect of monetary change on interest rates, you therefore have a theory of interest rates. In the first place, there are other forces which will change real interest rates. In the second place, there are undoubtedly other forces changing nominal interest rates, but it so happens that the major movements of nominal interest rates in 1966 and 1967 seem to have been dominated by the monetary effects so they serve to bring out very clearly the relations I have described.

One more word about the longer term relations. If this analysis is right, our present interest rates of 6% or 6½% are still on the way up because they are still reflecting the building up of anticipations of price increases. Our present interest rates are extremely low—if you subtract the rate of price change, you have very low real interest rates. Therefore, if this analysis is right, the long-term trend of interest rates ought still to be up.

3/ DAVID I. FAND

Keynesian Monetary Theories, Stabilization Policy, and the Recent Inflation

THE DEMAND FOR MONEY AND LIQUIDITY PREFERENCE: REAL BALANCES AND INTEREST RATES

The quantity theory, in its post-Keynesian reformulation, is a theory of the demand for money and a theory of money income. As a theory of demand it is based on the hypothesis that the demand for real cash balances is highly stable, and that the factors affecting the demand for real balances are independent of those affecting the supply of nominal balances; as a theory of money income it differs from other aggregative income theories in its characterization of the demand function and in the variables that it stresses.[19,20]

This reading is excerpted from the *Journal of Money, Credit and Banking,* Vol. 1 (August 1969), and is reprinted with the permission of the author and the publisher. David I. Fand is Professor of Economics at Wayne State University.

[19] Friedman, in his formulation of the modern quantity theory, points out that the statement concerning the stability of the demand for money needs both elaboration and qualification, as follows: "The quantity theorist must sharply limit, and be prepared to specify explicitly, the variables that it is empirically important to include in the function. For to expand the number of variables regarded as significant is to empty the hypothesis of its empirical content; there is indeed little if any difference between asserting that the demand for money is highly unstable and asserting that it is a perfectly stable function of an indefinitely large number of variables.

The quantity theorist not only regards the demand function for money as stable; he also regards it as playing a vital role in determining variables that he regards as of great importance for the analysis of the economy as a whole, such as the level of money income or of prices. It is this that leads him to put greater emphasis on the demand for money than on, let us say, the demand for pins, even though the latter might be as stable as the former. It is not easy to state this point precisely, and I cannot pretend to have done so." See Friedman [30, 31], Cagan [14], Meltzer [65], Patinkin [71], Allais [2] and Johnson [55, pp. 15–103].

[20] We shall not examine the historical evidence to determine whether quantity

The pre-Keynesian and the constant velocity quantity theories, and the post-Keynesian quantity theories share a number of important common features. They all assume that the money stock, together with the demand for money, determines (in some sense) the equilibrium stock of real balances and not the interest rate, and further, that if the demand for money is stable, the resulting velocity function provides a link between money, income and prices. The Keynesian aggregative theories interpret the demand for money as a liquidity preference function which, given the stock of real cash balances, determines the interest rate.

In the pre-Keynesian quantity theory the demand for money was used either as a monetary theory of *changes* in the price level (if output is constant) or as a theory of the price level (if output and velocity are both constant), while the post-Keynesian quantity theory uses the demand for money as a theory of changes in money income, assuming that both output and velocity may change in response to changes in the money stock. In contrast to these theories, Keynesian analysis views the demand for money as providing a monetary theory of interest rates, or of *changes* in interest rates, assuming that prices are constant. The treatment of the demand for money is therefore a useful way to bring out the differences between the quantity and the Keynesian theories.[21]

Although the pre-Keynesian quantity theorists acknowledged that the demand for money balances is affected by interest rates, they did not generally allow for the influence of portfolio decisions on interest rates. Productivity and thrift determined interest rates and thereby shaped the demand for money, but adjustments in the monetary sector did not, in

---

theorists always distinguished the theory from the equation of exchange, whether they treated velocity as a numerical constant, whether they distinguished clearly between the demand for real cash balances (a behavior relation), and a technical relation between money and income related to the payments mechanism, and whether the quantity theory association of money and income is a useful approach to the stabilization problem. We shall also abstract from the problems discussed by Patinkin concerning the analytical foundation of the quantity theory involving the related issues of homogeneity, dichotomy, and neutrality, the introduction of money in the utility function, and the derivation of the real balance effect.

The point we do wish to emphasize is that the quantity theory—at least as it is currently formulated—is, in the first instance, concerned with defining the demand function for real cash balances. Whether this money demand theory is used in an aggregative model to predict the absolute price level, changes in the price level, money income, or changes in money income depends in large measure on auxiliary assumptions. For further discussion of these issues see Ball [3], Brunner [6], Brunner and Meltzer [7], Cagan [15], Friedman and Schwartz [33, 34], Johnson [52, 55], Modigliani [67], Patinkin [71], and Samuelson [80].

[21] The pre-Keynesian quantity theory is often identified with the constant velocity theory and interpreted as a theory of the price level. A more general approach allows for changes in velocity in response to significant changes in the money stock. So interpreted, the pre-Keynesian theory is a monetary theory of *changes* in the price level.

turn, affect these equilibrium interest rates. They did, however, recognize that changes in either the demand or supply of money would have *temporary* effects on interest rates.

The pre-Keynesian quantity theory assumed that the demand for money was stable, that substantial changes in velocity did not occur unless they were induced by prior changes in M, and that changes in the monetary sector did not permanently influence the interest rates determined in the real sector, except for possible velocity changes during transition periods.[22] Although they were aware that interest rates and prices often move together, and although they distinguished between *nominal* and *real* interest rates, they nevertheless abstracted from short run changes in employment and output and from independent changes in velocity.[23] The pre-Keynesian quantity theory assumed a given level of output, concluded that changes in prices were related to changes in money, and used the demand for money to predict *changes* in price levels.

The modern formulation of the quantity theory has been heavily influenced by the Keynesian liquidity preference analysis emphasizing portfolio choices and the substitutability of money, bonds, and other assets. Unlike the payments relations of the transactions approach, or even as a store of value relations of the Cambridge approach, it treats the demand for money as a problem in capital theory, focusing on the composition of the balance sheet and the selection of assets.

The post-Keynesian quantity theory assumes (1) that the demand for real cash balances is a function of interest rates and other variables, (2) that the quantity of real cash balances is an endogenous variable and not always under the control of the monetary authorities, (3) that changes in nominal balances will generally have effects on interest rates, on income and on prices, (4) that the interest rate effect is a compound effect including a short run liquidity (Keynes) effect, and a longer run (Fisher) price expectation effect, and (5) that although marginal and average velocity differ, the velocity function is sufficiently stable to provide a relation between changes in money and changes in money income.[24] The equilibrium quantity of real balances M/P is therefore an endogenous variable, with a solution value that must satisfy the demand function.[25]

---

[22] See Mints [66], Chapter 3 on "The Propensity to Hoard and Unemployment," and especially the Appendix for the views of Thornton, Marshall and Fisher.

[23] See Fisher [28], Chapter 4, for his analysis of transition periods.

[24] There is an assumption that the monetary sector is *almost*, or *nearly*, decomposable from the real sector, at least when dealing with successive equilibrium positions. For this reason a change in nominal M, or a change in its rate of growth, is not assumed to have a significant, and permanent, effect on real balances or interest rates, except possibly when dealing with an economy that has substantial unemployed resources.

[25] See Friedman's restatement of the Quantity Theory [30] and Cagan's analysis of Hyperinflation [14].

Although the monetary authorities can always vary nominal M, they do not control the equilibrium interest rates or the equilibrium quantity of real balances; at the same time, since real balances provide the link relating nominal M with prices, the nominal quantity of money is nevertheless the dominant variable in predicting money income.[26,27] In the modern quantity theory, the demand for money is used to predict *changes* in money income.[28]

The theory of demand for money underwent radical change in the Keynesian theory. Instead of defining a demand for real (or nominal) balances, money balances were treated as a datum, and the demand function was thereby transformed into the liquidity preference theory of interest rates. In the Keynesian theory the exogenously given quantity of money, together with the liquidity preference function, determines the interest rate. But if liquidity preference is not just a theory of short run *changes* in interest rates but a theory of interest rates (i.e., an equilibrium relation between money and interest rates), it implies that the monetary sector is determining interest rates, or that the monetary sector and the real sector mutually determine interest rates in some as yet unspecified simultaneous determination. In any event, the demand for money as a liquidity preference function no longer serves to determine the price level or equilibrium stock of real cash balances, and does not, therefore, support the notion of a velocity function or of a stable relation between money and income.[29] The Keynesian treatment of real balances as a datum, rather than as an endogenous variable to be explained by the model, tends to rule out any systematic behavior relations involving money, prices, and income.[30]

The quantity theory relates money M, prices P, and income through the quantity of real balances given by the money demand function, while the Keynesian theory relates M, or M/P and interest rates i via the liquidity preference theory. Accordingly, the quantity theory focuses on discrepancies between actual and desired real balances to explain movements

[26] A demand function or a velocity function that is stable with respect to permanent, and equilibrium, quantities does not necessarily imply that we can use it to make short run predictions. This is an empirical question. See Friedman [31, 32] and Johnson [55, pp. 31–34].

[27] See, however, Friedman and Schwartz [34], Chapter 12 on the "Postwar Rise in Velocity," and the criticism of Tobin [94].

[28] This limitation is emphasized by Friedman.

[29] Even if the authorities can treat real balances as a policy variable and change the quantity over a fairly wide range, we can still define an equilibrium stock of real balances in the sense that we can divide the stock of nominal M by the price level. But this quantity is viewed as a policy variable rather than an equilibrium value of an endogenous variable.

[30] Such a relation may nevertheless still show up in the reduced form, even though it is not explicitly introduced as one of the behavior equations.

in income and in the price level, and highlights *M* as the operational policy variable; the Keynesians assume a given price level, focus on discrepancies between actual and full employment output, and highlight interest rates *i;* and since *i* may not always respond to changes in *M*, other policy variables are sometimes needed.

This shift in emphasis from the price level to the level of employment, from a money demand function to a liquidity preference function, from viewing real balances as a quantity to be explained to treating it as an autonomous factor, are all related to the change in roles of real balances *M/P* and interest rates *i*. Whereas real cash balances was a key endogenous variable in the quantity theory, providing a direct link from money to spending, *i* is the key variable in Keynesian theory, and *M/P* is treated almost as a policy instrument. This relative neglect of real balances as an endogenous variable, the assumption that, barring significant inflation, it can be controlled by the authorities, and the highlighting of interest rate movements are all prominent in the recent Keynesian theories of money, of the price level, and of inflation; and they also help explain why current stabilization policy is interest rate oriented, and apt to overlook, or minimize, the price level consequences.

Finally, we should also note that while the modern quantity theory focuses on the price level it does not have a satisfactory theory of price level movements in mild (or creeping) inflation.[31] Indeed, neither the Keynesians, nor the quantity theorists, have a satisfactory theory of the proportions in which a change in money income is divided between a change in prices and a change in income. Friedman [36] in a discussion of the Keynesian and the quantity theories states:

> The Keynesian tendency is frequently to regard ... output as perfectly elastic with respect to a change in the general price level up to a point and then as perfectly inelastic; to have an L-shaped supply curve of output. The quantity theory tendency is frequently to regard output as throughout inelastic with respect to a change in the price level and hence to regard the whole of a change in money income as reflected in prices. In practice neither of these extremes is valid.

THREE KEYNESIAN LIQUIDITY PREFERENCE THEORIES

Keynes rejected the quantity theory emphasis on real cash balances as an endogenous variable, assumed that, in an economy with unused resources, the authorities can control both nominal and real balances, and

---

[31] I am distinguishing between the quantity theory viewed as a theory of demand for real cash balances or as a theory of money income, and a monetary rule of increasing the money supply by a fixed percent each year. See Wallich [98].

developed from the money demand function his famous liquidity preference theory of interest. Keynesian monetary economists, following his example, have used the liquidity preference theories to analyze the long term rate, the availability of funds, the structure of interest rates, liquidity and, most recently, asset yields and rates of return.

The earlier Keynesians, concerned with the interest elasticity of investment demand, saw a major role for monetary policy in facilitating capital formation by keeping the long term rate low.[32]   After the revival of monetary policy in the early 1950's, many of the economists responsible for the conduct of monetary policy emphasized its impact on the supply of funds and on availability; at the end of the 1950's there was widespread disenchantment with monetary policy, and many economists expressed this analytically by framing their analysis in terms of liquidity, and by emphasizing the structure as well as the level of interest rates.[33]   Finally, the most recent writers analyze the impact of monetary action primarily in terms of portfolio changes, wealth effects and the required rate of return on capital, and only secondarily concern themselves with changes in interest rates, availability and supply of funds.[34]

[32]Okun [69] has formulated this Keynesian theory as follows: "The Keynesian model of short-run income determination provides a clear specification of the way in which central bank instruments affect the level of output. A change in the volume of money alters the rate of interest so as to equate the demand for cash with the supply; the change in interest affects the level of investment; the change in investment has a multiplied effect on equilibrium income."

[33]Samuelson [78] explains the background of this disenchantment: "In 1939 Oxford questionnaires were sent to businessmen and investors generally asking whether interest rates were of any importance to them and whether availability of credit was of any importance to them. To a man they all answered: 'No, no importance whatsoever.' So, this is coffin nail No. 1 on the importance of money. At the Harvard Business School, the late Professor Ebersole did case studies on finance, and what do you think they all showed, every one of them? They showed that money and finance were of no importance. If that doesn't convince you, let's turn to econometrics. Professor Tinbergen of Rotterdam did the first econometric studies—giant computer models for an economy. He tried regression coefficients, and no matter how he regressed investment on the interest rate, he always got a zero coefficient.

"Finally, if more is necessary, economic theory came to the rescue of this view and people like Sir John Hicks said that as far as short-term investment is concerned, interest is of no consequence as a cost; and as far as long-term investment is concerned, uncertainty is so great that it completely swamps interest, which leaves you with only a miniscule of intermediate investment that is interest elastic. Well, that was the 1939 view. Unfortunately, some people get frozen into what they learned in their youth, and those views still prevail in some circles. Still, those fellows are dying out in this country. The Radcliffe Committee in England held extensive investigations and the majority view pretty much came out, I would say, with the conclusion that money doesn't matter."

[34]Tobin [91] has described this approach as follows: "The course of economic activity, then, depends on the difference between two rates of return on ownership of capital. One is the anticipated marginal productivity of capital, determined by

These successive views as to the relative importance of (1) the long rate, (2) availability, the level and structure of interest rates and liquidity, and (3) the yield on capital, reflect three theories of the transmission process: the initial Keynes theory that the long term rate is crucial and that monetary policy can influence it; the second, the Radcliffe-type theory that interest rates may or may not be important, and monetary policy may or may not be able to influence the level and structure of interest rates; and Tobin's theory, which emphasizes the required yield on capital rather than interest rates, and in which the authorities can influence this required yield through wealth and money and liquid asset effects.[35]

These three transmission theories derive largely from their different analyses of liquidity preference: the Keynesian theory, from a money-bond model in which authorities can affect the long rate; the Radcliffe theory, from a money-capital model in which the authorities may have more effect on the relative supplies of assets, on intermediation or disintermediation, on the structure of rates, rather than on the level of interest rates or yields; and Tobin's theory, from his money-bond-capital model, in which the authorities may, at times, influence the expected, or required, rate of return on capital, and which increases the potential influence of monetary action in one sense, but also limits it in another sense.[36,37,38]

In presenting the three Keynesian liquidity preference theories we fol-

---

technology, factor supplies, and expectations about the economy. This cannot be controlled by the managers of money and public debt, except in the indirect sense that if they somehow successfully control the economy they control all economic magnitudes. The second rate of return on capital equity is that rate at which the public would be willing to hold the existing stock of capital, valued at current prices. It is this rate of return, the *supply price of capital*, which the monetary and debt authorities may hope to influence through changing the supplies and yields of assets and debts that compete with real capital for place in the portfolios and balance sheets of economic units."

[35]The distinction between the *wealth* and *money* and *liquid asset* effects will be developed below in our discussion of Tobin's theory.

[36]This limitation is emphasized in his formulation of the "New View," in which the *money* effect is identified with a *liquid asset* effect.

[37]Differences among Keynesians in their attitudes towards interest rates are not unrelated to the ambiguous attitude of a pre-Keynesian quantity theorist toward money. These quantity theorists thought of money as a veil but, at the same time, also saw money as the key to controlling major fluctuations in employment and output. The quantity theorists' ambivalence toward money carried over, to some extent, in the range of different attitudes toward interest rates among Keynesian writers. While some saw a major role for monetary policy because it could help keep the long rate down, others, for reasons that appeared compelling at the time, tended to dismiss interest rates and monetary policy as important factors. The Keynesian liquidity preference theories reflect this range of views. See Ball [3] and Johnson [52, pp. 107–147].

[38]It may also be interesting to note that the Keynes and Tobin liquidity prefer-

low Tobin's (1961) illuminating analysis of an aggregative model with three assets: money, bonds, and real capital (physical assets). Each of these three assets is viewed as a broad aggregate; money may include near monies, bonds may include other market instruments.[39] The extent to which the monetary authorities can affect the long term rate, or the marginal efficiency of capital, or the supply price of capital will depend, in these three liquidity preference theories, on the asset substitution assumptions. As outlined by Tobin, the three theories incorporate the following Keynesian substantive assumptions: (1) they assume that there is no real balance effect in the commodity market (an increase in money balances does not directly affect the demand for commodities);[40] (2) they separate the analysis of the income flow, emphasizing consumption and investment expenditures, from the analysis of the capital account, emphasizing portfolio adjustments of assets and liabilities,[41] (3) they incorporate the (Keynesian) hypothesis that yield differentials depend systematically on relative supplies, in contrast to the classical theory of portfolio selection in perfect markets;[42] (4) they assume that monetary action may influence the rate structure at which both the monetary and the real sectors will be in equilibrium, and reject the view that the monetary sector adjusts to yields determined in the real sector.[43]

---

ence theories, in which money may have a substantial impact, share an important feature with the modern quantity theory (reflecting Keynes' analysis) in treating money as an asset in a capital theoretic framework. The Radcliffe theory, which is pessimistic about the monetary impact, concentrates on the credit aspect of money, on lending and borrowing, on sources of liquidity and availability, and does not focus directly on the portfolio impact of changes in cash balances on other assets. See Ball [3, pp. 163–65].

[39] If the differential between two assets is constant and does not vary with changes in relative supplies we consider them perfect substitutes, and aggregate them into one asset. The precise content of these three assets will thus vary with the substitution relations postulated in the model.

[40] The distinction between the credit effects and monetary effects can be formulated in terms of the real-balance effect. The emphasis on credit follows the Keynesian tradition in assuming that the real-balance effect operates primarily in the bond market, while the emphasis on monetary effects follows the hypothesis that there is also a real-balance effect in the commodity market. See Patinkin [71, p. 664].

[41] One implication of this assumption for monetary theory is made explicit in Tobin's distinction between money (means of payment) and monetary wealth (net private claims against the government).

[42] In his analysis of the Keynes model, Tobin [90] writes as follows: "Keynes departed from the classical model of portfolio choice and asset yield to explain money holdings, applying and developing an innovation borrowed from his own *Treatise*, a rate differential that depends systematically on relative asset supplies."

[43] The significance of this point in terms of price level behavior will be discussed below.

THE KEYNES MONEY-BOND MODEL

Keynes abstracted from the obvious differences among non-monetary assets and assumed that bond and real assets may be usefully treated as perfect substitutes, and that any yield differentials between two non-monetary assets are independent of their relative supplies. By means of this simplification he was able to focus his analysis on two assets, money and bonds, in which the rate of interest, the marginal efficiency of capital and other rates of return are either equal, or differ by a given differential.

Since the yield on money is zero, there is only one yield differential, that between money and bonds, to explain. In Keynes' liquidity preference theory, the premium of bond yields over the zero yield on money is made a function of the supply of money (relative to bonds). Keynes' liquidity preference is thus, in the first instance, a theory of the long rate; but when this rate is fixed yields on other assets can differ only by the given differential (i.e., to allow for risk or for price changes). Once we have determined the long rate, in this money-bond model, we have also determined all other rates, including the marginal efficiency of capital.

This long term rate is therefore the key to investment and capital formation in two senses: first it is the relevant rate for an individual to use in planning a long term undertaking; second, it is also the rate which the central bank can control in its open market operations. Moreover, from the assumption that bonds are perfect substitutes for real (physical) capital, it follows that monetary action, i.e., an open market purchase of bonds, is equivalent to the central bank taking away part of the capital stock (i.e., non-monetary assets) from the public, and so it is not entirely surprising that the monetary authority may help determine the long rate.

This analysis assumes a set of conditions in which monetary action can permanently influence interest rates, and needs modification, if intended to apply to a world of "classical" full employment, or one in which the productivity of capital is very elastic.[44]   For the Keynes money-bond model, interest rates are a natural indicator of monetary action, and so is the money stock. Indeed, the two indicators are highly correlated, both deriving their relevance from the same liquidity preference function. Nevertheless, in this model, there are a number of conditions that must be satisfied before we can conclude, as a general statement, that the monetary authorities can permanently affect the interest rate.

---

[44] In addition, the relevance of this liquidity preference theory for analyzing monetary action in a more complex economy will depend on (1) whether bonds are, in fact, very good substitutes for real capital, and (2) whether money refers to the means of payment (inside money), or to the net value of private claims (outside money), or some other "net money" concept.

THE CAMBRIDGE-RADCLIFFE MONEY-CAPITAL MODEL

The Cambridge Money-Capital Model. To introduce the money-capital version of the three-asset model, it is instructive to review Tobin's treatment of the Cambridge cash balance quantity theory model, consisting of two assets, money and capital. Although the Cambridge economists assumed that direct capital investment was the alternative to holding money, they did not *explicitly* incorporate the yield on capital as one of the variables in the demand for money. They assumed that the yield on capital was already determined (in the real sector) and that the monetary sector would adjust to this rate.

The motivation for this money-capital model was to formulate a demand for money derived from the hypothesis that real cash balances, at the margin, must adjust to the return on capital. They also assumed, perhaps somewhat inconsistently, that when the rate of return is given the quantity of real balances would move proportionately with real income. The constant velocity model follows naturally from this particular assumption.

Although the Cambridge cash balance model represented a significant advance in formulating the quantity theory as a theory of demand for real balances, it was nevertheless a primitive model: it assumed that the yield on capital is given; it did not contain assets which the central bank and the banking system can buy or sell to change the quantity of money; and it did not consider the effect of money substitutes, other than real capital, on the demand for money. But it did emphasize the yield on capital and the money-capital margin, and thereby initiated the treatment of money as an asset—subject to portfolio analysis. The later Keynesian and post-Keynesian quantity theories are best seen as attempts to reformulate and extend the Cambridge theory.

The Radcliffe Three-Asset Money-Capital Model. While still retaining the Cambridge hypothesis of a money-capital margin, let us extend this two-asset model to include a third asset, government debt, and let us also adopt a Radcliffe-type view that bonds are perfect substitutes for money.[45] This Radcliffe money-capital model is the antithesis of Keynes' money-

---

[45] I associate the Radcliffe view with the following hypotheses: (1) that traditional central bank action primarily involves changes in the composition of liquid assets; (2) that while changes in total liquidity may affect private spending, compositional changes may not; and (3) that velocity is a number given by arithmetic computation, but having no necessary volitional content. See the Radcliffe Report [73], Gurley's Review [44] and Sayers [83]. This analysis of the Radcliffe-Cambridge model was inspired by Tobin's Analysis [90], but it may not accord with his own interpretation of the Cambridge or the Radcliffe Model, and I would like to absolve him of any responsibility.

bond model, which treats bonds (and all non-monetary assets) as perfect substitutes for capital. If we remove the restrictive Cambridge assumption that yields are given, and assume that we can apply the Keynesian liquidity preference theory to the money-capital margin, the yield differential between money and capital will depend on relative supplies. An open market operation—a sale or purchase of bonds—changes the proportions of these two assets in private portfolios. But if bonds are a perfect substitute for money and part of the money stock, and if the money stock and total liquidity are therefore identical, the open market operation is then merely a change in the composition of money (or liquidity) but does not change the ratio of money to capital, which is needed in order to affect the yield on capital. Consequently, if the authorities wish to influence the expected, or required, yield on capital they will have to conduct open market operations in real assets, or change the proportions of money and capital in other ways.

The implications of the Radcliffe money-capital model are quite different from those of the Keynes' money-bond model in which monetary action can affect the long rate, the marginal efficiency of capital and other rates by changing the proportion of money and bonds. In the Radcliffe model, monetary action affects the composition but not necessarily the aggregate of the public's liquidity, and will have its main effects on the flow of funds in credit markets, on intermediation and disintermediation, on the structure of rates and, at times, even on the level of interest rates; and while these are not unimportant effects, they do not point to any obvious stabilization role for monetary policy.

Consequently, if we are concerned with stabilization, neither the interest rate nor the money stock is a relevant measure of the monetary impact on aggregate demand. An open market operation involving money and bonds is very much like exchanging $5 bills for $1 bills, and even if it affects the structure of interest rates it may have very little impact on the expected yield on capital. The interest rates that the central bank can control through conventional open market transactions may influence the composition of liquid assets in private portfolios. But if we are interested in aggregate demand and stabilization we must operate on the money-capital margin and affect the expected yield on capital.

TOBIN'S KEYNES-CAMBRIDGE SYNTHESIS: MONEY AND MONETARY WEALTH

The most carefully articulated Keynesian monetary model is due to Tobin, who presents a synthesis of these polar Keynes and Cambridge approaches: the assets of his model—money, government debt, private debts, physical capital—are not perfect substitutes; interest rates and yields will vary from the zero (own) rate on currency up to the marginal productivity of capital; and among assets that are not perfect substitutes, yields will depend on relative supplies.[46]

Unlike the earlier Keynesian models, which take interest rates as a key variable in the transmission mechanism, Tobin builds on the Cambridge model—with its emphasis on the money-capital margin. In his synthesis, it is the supply price of capital that links the monetary and real sectors, and the liquidity preference function is a relation between the proportion of monetary and real wealth and the supply price of capital. Before stating his liquidity preference theory we shall first define his concept of the supply price of capital, and his distinction between money and monetary wealth.[47]

The Supply Price of Capital (SPC). Tobin follows the Keynesian hypothesis in assuming that changes in interest rates and other rates of return will influence aggregate demand only if they affect investment. But he rejects the Keynesian interest rate as the link between the monetary and the real sectors, and emphasizes that:

> The strategic variable—the ultimate gauge of expansion or deflation, of monetary tightness or ease—is the rate of return that the community of wealth owners require in order to absorb the existing capital stock (valued at current prices), no more, no less, into their portfolios and balance sheets. This rate may be termed the supply price of capital.

Tobin follows the Cambridge money-capital model in defining the supply price of capital (SPC) as the relevant measure of monetary action, and this provides him with a different framework for analyzing and interpreting policy actions.[48]

[46] "In general, an increase in the supply of an asset—e.g., long term bonds—will cause its rate to rise relative to other rates, but less in relation to assets for which it is directly or indirectly a close substitute—in the example, short term securities and money—than in relation to other assets—in the example, capital." See Tobin [90].

[47] The model is described in Tobin's 1961 article [90]. For a more elaborate and definitive treatment of the key ideas see "An Essay on the Principles of Debt Management," [91] which applies this theory to analyzing debt management policy. Monetary policy in this theory is concerned with changing the amount of demand debt relative to other government debt, while debt management policy deals with changes in the composition of government debt. This brilliant essay provides the most carefully articulated statement of the theory and its implication for stabilization policy, and I have treated this essay as the most influential statement of Tobin's Synthesis. Additional material may be found in his ms. on *Monetary Theory*.

[48] Accordingly, the Keynesian long term rate—the interest rate on long term bonds—is not a reliable indicator, since its movements are not always correlated with movements in the SPC (e.g., debt retirement, where long term rates may decline while the SPC may rise). Similarly, the quantity of money may be a misleading indicator. There is no substitute for the SPC that can be used to analyze or assess policy actions.

Money and Monetary Wealth. Tobin suggests that we should differentiate between a change in money (means of payments) which can be accomplished quickly, and a change in the monetary components of net private wealth, since an increase (decrease) in wealth takes time and requires an increase (decrease) in private saving. He therefore distinguishes between the stock of money (means of payment) and monetary wealth (MW)—the net value of private claims on the central government. Tobin's monetary wealth is therefore related to the concepts of "outside money" or "net money," developed by Gurley and Shaw [45], and it consists of several forms of government debt.[49,50]

The money stock (means of payment) may increase without any change in MW; similarly, MW may increase without any change in the money stock. An increase in MW, whether or not it is associated with an increase in the money stock, changes the proportions of MW to real physical assets, lowers the SPC, stimulating investment expenditures. This is the *wealth* effect on the SPC.[51]

An increase in the money stock, holding MW constant, will lead to changes in asset prices, a restructuring of yields and rates of return, and substitutions among assets. Consequently, such an increase in money is expansionary only if these changes bring about a desired reduction in the ratio of MW to real assets. This is the *money* effect on the SPC.[52]

This distinction between the *wealth* effect and the *money* effect rests on the choice of an "outside money" (or a "net money") concept to measure monetary wealth MW, thus sharply distinguishing between MW and the means of payment. On the other hand, if we use inside money (a "gross money" concept) to measure monetary wealth, the *wealth* effect and the *money* effect are almost identical and difficult to separate out in practice. The use of inside money as a proxy for monetary wealth in Tobin's Synthesis brings it quite close to a quantity theory type of approach.[53,54]

[49] For a discussion of "outside money" and the "net money" doctrine, and an analysis favoring the use of "gross money," an "inside money" concept, see Gurley and Shaw [45, pp. 132–49].

[50] Monetary wealth (MW) is the sum of demand debt plus government securities. Demand debt is the sum of currency and unborrowed bank reserves, and is equivalent to unborrowed high-powered money or to the monetary base (adjusted for borrowing). See his *Debt Management Essay* [91], especially Sections 1 and 2.

[51] The *wealth* effect is therefore the permanent monetary effect of a fiscal deficit.

[52] The liquidity preference function may be drawn as a curve relating the stock of MW to the SPC for a given stock real assets: the *wealth* effect corresponds to a movement *along* the curve; the *money* effect to a downward *shift* in the liquidity preference function.

[53] I do not want to give the impression that the *money* effect, when MW is defined as outside money, is necessarily a weak one. The neoclassical synthesis, which Tobin favors, is an example where the indirect *money* effect dominates the direct *wealth* effect.

[54] I am not suggesting that "inside money" will satisfy Tobin's requirement for

The Liquidity Preference Theory of the Supply Price of Capital (SPC). The demand function relating *MW* and the SPC, together with the stock of *MW*, determine the SPC in Tobin's model in conditions where the yields in the real sector can adjust to the monetary sector. Accordingly, the demand for *MW* may be viewed as a liquidity preference theory of the SPC; and an increase in *MW* relative to physical assets will lower the SPC.

An open market transaction changing the proportion of demand debt (high-powered money) in *MW*, and a debt management swap operation changing the relative proportions of short and long government debt, do not effect the relative proportions of *MW* to real assets. Consequently, the effects of these changes in the *composition* of *MW* on the SPC must be associated with shifts in the liquidity preference function. A relative increase in demand debt through an open market purchase will lower the liquidity preference function, and similarly for a relative increase in short debt through a debt management swap operation.

An increase in the money stock due to a lowering of reserve requirements does not change the volume or composition of *MW*. Its effects on the SPC must also derive from induced shifts in the liquidity preference function. An increase in the stock of money changes the composition of assets and liabilities in private portfolios (the public's net monetary position), and will have effects similar to those of open market and debt management operations changing the composition of *MW*. Consequently, while the liquidity preference theory relates the SPC to changes in *MW*, there is no direct way to relate changes in the money stock with the SPC, with the long term rate, or with the structure of yields. Changes in the money stock will affect aggregate demand only through a chain of asset substitutions; and if we take the Radcliffe view that money and other liquid assets are fairly good substitutes, this may be a negligible effect.[55]

---

monetary wealth in all relevant respects. Obviously it does not. But the effect of "inside money" on aggregate demand is not only a theoretical question but also an empirical one, and it may be that "inside money" has effects on aggregate demand very similar to those of monetary wealth. The question of the relevant concept of money, including the inside-outside money issues, have been discussed recently by Pesek and Saving [72], by Friedman and Schwartz [40], and by Johnson [56], in addition to the Gurley-Shaw [45] discussion mentioned earlier.

[55]The demand relation between *MW* and the SPC is assumed to be sufficiently stable, so that we could use it as a liquidity preference theory of the SPC. But this does not necessarily imply that the differential between money and bonds can be explained by a liquidity preference function for money in terms of the long rate, unless we make some special assumptions about all liquid assets other than money. If, as postulated in the Radcliffe model, money and other liquid assets are good substitutes, we would not expect any such stable liquidity preference function between money and bonds.

KEYNESIAN THEORIES OF MONEY AND INTEREST RATES

In Keynes' model, since bonds are perfect substitutes for all non-monetary assets, the demand for money—the liquidity preference function—relates the long term rate to the changing proportions of money and non-monetary wealth. An open market operation is equivalent to a change in the composition of privately held wealth and, in some circumstances, enables the central bank to influence the interest rate, the marginal efficiency of capital, and other rates of return. This Keynesian liquidity preference theory of the interest rate is presumably not intended to apply to an economy in classical full-employment equilibrium, where prices are flexible, where the real wage is equal to both the demand price and the supply price of labor, and where desired and actual real balances are in equilibrium. Under these conditions, where prices adjust fairly quickly, changes in M do not necessarily result in corresponding changes in real balances.[56]

In those circumstances where the monetary authorities can permanently affect interest rates, the long rate is a good indicator—a reliable gauge—of monetary action; similarly, the money stock and velocity are also useful indicators. Indeed all three variables—the long rate, money and velocity—derive their relevance from the same liquidity preference function. For if the demand for money is stable relative to a given portfolio, velocity behavior is also stable. Moreover, even if calculated velocity changes with changes in M, because marginal and average velocity differ, such differences are consistent with a reasonably well-behaved velocity function.[57] The stability of the velocity function, in turn, depends on the relations between money and wealth and between wealth and income.

In the Radcliffe model, an open market operation will affect the composition of liquid assets and it may affect yield differentials, but it need not bring about any changes in total liquidity, in aggregate demand, or in spending. Moreover, even if the demand for total liquidity should happen to be fairly stable, there is no reason to expect this stability to carry over to the demand for money. Consequently, if we are interested in stabilization it is necessary to look at the money capital margin and analyze what is happening to total liquidity and to the required rate of return on capital. Alternatively, if we are concerned with the equity aspects of monetary action, and with the effects of intermediation and disintermediation, we must analyze the impact of monetary action on the availability of funds,

[56] Those who follow the Keynes or the Money-Capital models may argue that real balances should be deflated by asset prices and not by commodity prices.

[57] Following the assumption that the money demand function is homogenous of degree one in real income.

on interest rates, and on maturities and down-payments in the important credit markets. Movements in the long-term rate and changes in the money stock are not likely to provide useful insights for either of these two problems though the level and structure of interest rates may, at times, be useful.

If one should attempt to relate money and income it would not be surprising to find that velocity is very erratic, depending, of course, on the elasticities of substitution among liquid assets. The equilibrium stock of real cash balances may be quite variable since liquid assets are assumed to be good substitutes for each other; the velocity function would also be quite unstable—a ratio of two basically unrelated quantities.

Tobin's synthesis of the Keynes money-bond and the Cambridge money-capital models rejects the long rate as an indicator or gauge of monetary action.[58] Interest rates and rates of return are, nevertheless, important in the transmission mechanism, insofar as they may reflect movements in the SPC and link portfolio decisions (in the capital account) with investment decisions (in the income flow). Although a rate is emphasized as in the Keynes model, it is not the long rate that has the unique and strategic importance as an indicator of policy. Similarly, Tobin's synthesis also incorporates features of the Cambridge model by emphasizing the money-capital margin, the SPC, and by stressing the substitutability of money and bonds relative to physical assets. The SPC is the strategic variable and the relevant gauge of monetary action; and while changes in interest rates and in the money stock are essential parts of the transmission mechanism, their movements do not always provide unambiguous inferences as to the changes in the SPC. The demand for *MW* is the liquidity preference function and a determinant of the SPC, and if this demand is stable, then it is also a basis for a velocity function relating money income and *MW*.

Our analysis of the three Keynesian theories, in specified circumstances where the monetary authorities can influence interest rates and other rates of return, leaves us with the following paradox: the Keynes model, which emphasizes the long rate, also emphasizes money; the Radcliffe model, which minimizes the significance of changes in money, also de-emphasizes the long rate and other rates as well; the Tobin model, which stresses the importance of *MW* and the SPC, argues against using either interest rates or the money stock as the relevant indicator of monetary action.[59]

[58] I am distinguishing Tobin's theory (based on the Keynes—Cambridge Synthesis), which I interpret as a liquidity preference theory of the supply price of capital, from a "New View" approach to monetary theory, which may be interpreted as a synthesis of the Keynes-Radcliffe models, emphasizing the *liquid asset* effect.

[59] Suppose that we can substitute inside money for *MW*, and that the liquidity preference is now a relation between the money stock and the SPC. Under these assumptions that inside money is viewed as private wealth, changes in the money stock may be a good indicator of movements in the SPC, and may be better than any of the rates.

It would appear that while the Keynes model can motivate the concern with the long rate, none of these three theories can justify the emphasis on interest rates and the relative disregard of M that is so typical of contemporary Keynesian thinking. Our analysis of these models seems to suggest that when interest rates are relevant, so is the money stock; conversely, if the money stock is irrelevant, or misleading, this will also be true of interest rates. Consequently, even in the special conditions when the authorities can influence interest rates, the current treatment of the money stock and interest rates does not appear justified.

Suppose we move away from underemployed economies and consider one that is close to, but not necessarily at, full employment. Consider a situation where prices are just beginning to rise, where the productivity curve of capital may be relatively flat, where employment and output cannot be increased very easily, and where we do not expect any permanent effects of monetary action on interest rates. An increase in nominal M in this economy will have its permanent effect on prices rather than on interest rates.

Moreover, if the real balance effect is operative and if prices are rising, it may not be possible for the authorities to increase the quantity of real balances to generate a decline in interest rates, except possibly for a temporary effect. Indeed, we would expect to find that movements in interest rates and money are positively correlated, and that rising (and high) interest rates and rising prices are associated with acceleration in the growth rate of the money stock, as described in the Gibson Paradox. This sequence of events is sufficiently well known, that Fisher (with his hypothesis that nominal rates are adjusting to the inflation), Wicksell and Keynes, have all offered different explanations for the paradox.[60] This suggests that when money, interest rates, and prices are all moving together the money stock may be a more reliable indicator of the policy thrust. While the explicit introduction of price level movements does complicate the interpretation of interest rate movements, it also enables us to see that rising market rates may be associated with monetary inflation. Also, when we introduce prices explicitly and distinguish between nominal and real rates the differences between the long rate and the SPC in the Keynes-Cambridge models recedes. The real bond rate or the long rate corrected for inflation may, in fact, be a fairly good measure of the SPC. The relation of Fisher's *real* interest rates to nominal market rates may therefore provide a useful analytical device for defining the conditions in which bonds are perfect substitutes for physical assets.

Fisher's concept of real rates and his treatment of price level changes helps narrow some of the differences between the Keynesian and classical models. In a high-employment economy, and especially when prices are

---

[60] See Fisher [27, 28, 29], the summary of the Wicksell and Keynes analysis of the Gibson Paradox in Cagan [15] and Meiselman [63].

rising, the monetary sector has a more limited influence on real interest rates, and it is for this reason that Keynesian analysis typically focuses on an underemployed economy. But as we get closer to a world of high employment, and especially if interest rates and prices are both rising, the money stock may be a better (less misleading) indicator or target variable than interest rates.[61] Paradoxically, the current tendency to emphasize interest rates and to ignore changes in the money stock would seem more relevant to a society where interest rates and prices are falling while the money stock is constant, or rising at a lower rate than output.

In basing policy on Keynesian models we are, in effect, identifying monetary actions with interest rate movements, questioning the direct link from money to spending that quantity theorists assume, de-emphasizing the real balance effect in the commodity market, and highlighting the interest rate aspects, the credit effects, and the indirect effects of monetary change. Keynesian theory as applied in current policy discussions assigns, in effect, three important roles to interest rates: first, they are viewed as an *indicator* of monetary policy—so that rising interest rates are associated with monetary restriction and vice versa; second, they are also viewed as a measure of the *cost* of capital, so that rising interest rates are expected to discourage investment; finally, they are also viewed as playing a key role in initiating the *transmission mechanism*, going from money to interest rates to investment and to consumption via the multiplier mechanism. Paradoxically, in situations where prices are rising, such as we have experienced since 1965, market interest rates cannot serve any of these roles properly. They may be faulty indicators of monetary policy and misleading measures of the cost of capital, and may seriously misrepresent the impact of monetary policy when they are viewed as the key element in the transmission mechanism; and this may have been especially pronounced in the 1966–67 period of rising prices.[62]

Thus far we have argued that Keynesian liquidity preference theory does not justify the almost exclusive attention given to interest rates in assessing monetary policy. There is, however, another related question as to whether the Keynesian theory is a useful approximation to reality, and whether the Keynesian hypothesis that monetary expansion causes interest rates to fall, while obviously an incomplete analysis, is nevertheless sufficiently accurate to serve as a useful approximation.[63] Cagan [15, 16], Meiselman [63], Gibson [41], Friedman and Schwartz [39] have, in a number of recent studies, raised questions about the interest rate behavior that is postulated in Keynesian theories. These authors depart from the

---

[61] See the discussion of target and indicators by Brunner and Meltzer [8].

[62] For further elaboration of this point see Fand [26].

[63] See Fand [24] for some evidence that movements in the long rate may be independent of movements in the short rate for periods of six to eight months.

Keynesian tradition and introduce an income effect and a price expectation effect (in addition to Keynesian liquidity effect), assume that the
monetary effect on interest rates is not instantaneous, and attempt to
allow for the different kinds of lags.

Their findings are in sharp contrast to the Keynesian analysis. De-
parting from the Keynesian hypothesis of negative association between
money and interest rates, these studies find evidence of offsetting income
effects, including a positive price expectation effect of the kind referred
to in the Gibson Paradox. The Keynesian assumption of a negative
association is a *ceteris paribus* result while the actual relation between
money and interest rates reflects induced income and price expectation
effects, in addition to the initial, and temporary, liquidity effect. Some
of the evidence seems to suggest that while the lag for the income effect
may be fairly short (less than one year), the price expectation lag may be
fairly long. These studies seem to suggest that a higher rate of monetary
expansion can be expected to be associated with a higher level of *nominal*
interest rates, though not necessarily a higher level of *real* interest rates.

THE "NEW VIEW" OF MONEY AND LIQUID ASSETS

Johnson [55, p. 35] in his thorough survey of monetary theory and
policy lists the following four schools of monetary thought, classified by
their treatment of money: (1) those who find the distinguishing characteristics of money in its function as a means of exchange; (2) those who
define money as a temporary abode of purchasing power; (3) those who
reject money in favor of some broader concept such as the total amount
of credit outstanding, or of total liquidity; and (4) those who focus on the
effect of money substitutes on the demand for money and on velocity.
Johnson also points out that though initially concerned with the impact
of short term debt, this last school has since the mid-fifties concentrated
on intermediary claims.[64]

This emphasis on privately created liquid assets is identified with
Gurley and Shaw who, in their major theoretical work, analyze the implications of non-bank intermediaries for monetary theory, and suggest
that the growth of these liquid assets may reduce the demand for money.
One implication of their analysis is that the quantity of money relevant
for monetary theory and policy should, perhaps, include some of these
intermediary claims. In subsequent work Gurley has suggested that
interest rates in the postwar period can be explained on the assumption

---

[64]For the development of the "New View" see Gurley and Shaw [45]. See also
Brainard [4], Fand [23], Tobin [92], Johnson [55], Chaps. 1 and 2, and Brunner
[5].

that the growth in liquid assets has reduced the demand for money by approximately one-half. He uses a weighted sum of money and liquid assets to represent the quantity of money although, as he himself points out, money alone could also have been used.

Gurley and Shaw's reformulation of monetary theory emphasized the importance of financial structure and financial development, and some similarities between banks and non-bank intermediaries, and this led subsequently to the emergence of a "new view" in monetary theory. Recent literature expounding the new view suggests that it is associated with the following kinds of propositions; (1) "that deposits are attracted and not created"; (2) that "the public is given a significant role in determining the total amount of bank liabilities"; (3) that the "substitution between time deposits and securities may be an important source of procyclical variation in the stock of money, even in face of counter-cyclical central bank policy"; (4) that "received money supply theory" is inadequate because we need to construct a theory of an individual bank as a firm; and (5) "that there is no essential difference between the manner in which the liabilities of banks and non-banks are determined."[65]

Individual expressions of the new view do, of course, differ, but almost all revolve around the related questions of whether money is unique or just one of a group of liquid assets, and whether commercial banks are basically different from other financial intermediaries. These are the issues highlighted by Tobin in his statement of the "new view," which I shall now take up.

THE KEYNES-RADCLIFFE SYNTHESIS

A change in the quantity of money will affect investment expenditures if the resulting chain of asset substitutions ultimately affects the terms on which the public will acquire capital.[66] But is money the only liquid asset that can do this? Is it possible for other liquid assets to have this effect in changing the desired proportion of physical capital in net private wealth?

Changes in the money stock have effects, in Tobin's model, that are similar to changes in other privately created liquid assets and different from changes in monetary wealth. But to say that the *money* effect and the *liquid asset* effect operate through the same channels, that both effects are felt only insofar as they influence the desire to acquire capital, is to say very little about their relative impacts. An increase in demand deposits

---

[65] See Brunner [5] for detailed references to individual writers.

[66] Following Tobin's theory, I am using the SPC and not the long term rate as the relevant gauge of the monetary impact.

may have a much greater impact on the SPC than an equivalent increase in, say, other intermediary claims; and such quantitative differences, if sufficiently large, may be viewed as qualitative differences.

As formulated by Tobin, the new view may be interpreted as a synthesis of the Keynes-Radcliffe models. It hypothesizes: that money and other intermediary claims operate through the same channels; that differences among liquid assets can easily be exaggerated; that so far as the SPC effects are concerned, the special features of money (means of payment) recede relative to those features shared by all financial claims; and that the traditional distinction between commercial banks and other financial intermediaries needs to be deemphasized because all intermediaries (including commercial banks) are limited in the creation of liabilities by the public's preferences (i.e., demand functions) for liquid assets.[67,68]

The new view stresses the need to consider the demand and supply functions for the whole spectrum of liquid assets, unlike the quantity theory which typically abstracts from these financial claims and is, therefore, skeptical as to whether the velocity function is a useful tool for monetary theory. The new view also questions whether we should think of M as an exogenous variable controlled by the central bank, and whether it is not more realistic to think of the quantity of money as an endogenous variable.[69]

This new view approach to monetary theory incorporates a key hypothesis of the Radcliffe model in questioning (or denying) the uniqueness of money as a liquid asset, and it may be viewed as an attempt to synthesize the Keynes-Radcliffe models, giving thereby a more precise formulation of the Radcliffe hypothesis. The Radcliffe hypothesis is sometimes stated in terms of "velocity is capable of great variation," sometimes, that a change

---

[67]Tobin [92] defines this approach as follows: "A more recent development in monetary economics tends to blur the sharp traditional distinctions between money and other assets and between commercial banks and other financial intermediaries; to focus on demands for and supplies of the whole spectrum of assets rather than on the quantity and velocity of 'money'; and to regard the structure of interest rates, asset yields, and credit availabilities rather than the quantity of money as the linkage between monetary and financial institutions and policies on the one hand and the real economy on the other."

[68]"Neither individually nor collectively do commercial banks possess a widow's cruse. Quite apart from legal reserve requirements, commercial banks are limited in scale by the same kinds of economic processes that determine the aggregate size of other intermediaries." Tobin [92].

[69]He acknowledges, of course, that a skillful central bank can generally manipulate its controls to keep M on target, but argues nevertheless that the true exogenous variables are the instruments of monetary control—the volume of bank reserves, the discount rate, and the required reserve ratios. Monetary policy, in this view, is concerned with determining the size of demand debt—the quantity of high-powered money—which it can affect by means of open market operations and through changes in the discount rate. See Tobin [90].

in the quantity of money may produce offsetting changes in other liquid assets, or that money is just one of many liquid assets. In terms of the SPC and the liquidity preference theory, the new view reformulation of the Radcliffe hypothesis identifies the *money* effect with the *liquid asset* effect.

The new view as articulated by Tobin is, therefore, intended as a working hypothesis and a prolegomena to future work rather than a substantive statement concerning monetary policy. Indeed, Tobin is quite explicit in stating that he does not wish to draw policy conclusions from his exposition of the "new view".[70]

IMPLICATIONS FOR VELOCITY

Although the new view acknowledges that the central bank can fix the money stock within fairly close limits, it nevertheless prefers to think of money as an endogenous variable, and seeks to develop a theory of monetary policy in terms of the exogenous variables—the instruments of monetary control. Accordingly, the new view interprets a quantity theory relation between money and income as involving the reduced form equations, and does not conceive of a velocity function as reflecting any behavior relation. The great emphasis on money substitutes in the new view discussions certainly builds up an expectation that the demand for money is not a stable function, and that the equilibrium quantity of real balances is neither unique nor stable, but subject to substantial variation. Nevertheless, these are basically empirical questions, depending on whether liquid assets are indeed close substitutes for money, and whether the velocity function—or the reduced form equation relating income to money—is stable enough to be used for predicting changes in money income.

The empirically implemented "new view" monetary theory can yield policy implications as divergent as the Radcliffe and the quantity theories, depending on the empirical substitution elasticities. The Radcliffe Hypotheses, that monetary action will often have its primary impact on composition of liquid assets, that the substitution elasticities are large, that the demand for money and the velocity function are unstable, and the sharply contrasting substantive hypotheses in the quantity theory are both refutable. Consequently, when the new view has achieved the

---

[70] "I draw no policy morals from these observations. That is quite another story, to which analysis of the type presented here is only the preface. The reader will misunderstand my purpose if he jumps to attribute to me the conclusion that existing differences in the regulatory treatment of banks and competing intermediaries should be diminished, either by relaxing constraints on the one or by tightening controls on the other." See Tobin [92].

empirical results and parameter estimates it is seeking, it will have more definite implications for monetary policy.

Although many statements of the new view can be interpreted as an acceptance of the Radcliffe hypothesis, it is more nearly correct to think of the new view as expressing skepticism about the quantity theory, and doubts about the quantity theory approach to monetary policy, rather than affirming a Radcliffe hypothesis.[71] Gurley [44] has questioned the Radcliffe approach to monetary policy, while Tobin presents the new view as a general equilibrium approach to the determination of asset yields and interest rates. But while the substantive content of the new view may be free of any monetary policy implications, the tone of new view writing shades into Radcliffism, and some of the recent advocates of the new view may have mistaken this tone for acceptance of Radcliffe substantive content. It is quite possible that those who concern themselves with changes in the composition of liquidity, with intermediation and disintermediation, with liquidity rather than money, and who assume that desired real cash balances and velocity are neither useful nor relevant concepts, may well believe that they are espousing the monetary theory of the "new view."[72]

[71] See Fand [23].

[72] The "new view" does tend to perpetuate a tendency in some Keynesian theories to treat the price level as an institutional datum. Even the post-1965 expositions of the "new view" fail to distinguish between *nominal* and *real* quantities, although they were written at a time when price level movements were significant and the inflation problem paramount. And these more recent statements of the "new view" also tend to treat the *initial* (and immediate) effect as if it were the *long run* equilibrium (and permanent) effect. These two tendencies coexist and are related to a basic objective of the "new view"; this is to develop a sophisticated general equilibrium model of the monetary sector that can be formulated mathematically in a manner satisfactory to the theorists and, at the same time, maintain a high degree of institutional realism—a theoretical model with a system of equations geared to the concepts (and language) of money market professionals. The attempt to satisfy these (somewhat contradictory) objectives simultaneously may result in a general model with considerable institutional realism but little content.

Bibliography/ *keynesian monetary theories*

1. **Ando, A.** and **F. Modigliani,** "The Relative Stability of Monetary Velocity and the Investment Multiplier," *AER* (September, 1965).

2. **Allais, M.,** "A Restatement of the Quantity Theory of Money," *AER* (December, 1966).

3. **Ball, R. J.,** *Inflation and the Theory of Money.* Aldine, 1964.

4. **Brainard, W. C.,** "Financial Intermediaries and a Theory of Monetary Control," in *Financial Markets and Economic Activity*, ed. Hester and Tobin.

5. **Brunner, K.,** "The Role of Money and Monetary Policy," *Review*, Federal Reserve Bank of St. Louis (July 1968).

6. _____ . "A Reconsideration of the Quantity Theory of Money." Unpublished manuscript, 1968.

7. **Brunner, K.** and **A. H. Meltzer,** "Predicting Velocity Implication for Theory and Policy," *JOF* (May 1963).

8. _____ . *Targets and Indicators of Monetary Policy.* San Francisco: Chandler Publishing, 1969.

9. **Burns, A. F.,** "The New Stagnation Theory and our Current Economic Policies," *Morgan Guaranty Survey* (May 1961).

10. _____ . "A Second Look at the Council Economic Theory," *Morgan Guaranty Survey* (August 1961).

11. _____ . *The Management of Prosperity.* New York: Columbia University Press, 1966.

12. **Burns, A. F.** and **P. A. Samuelson,** *Full Employment, Guideposts and Economic Stability.* Washington, 1967.

13. **Burns, A. F.,** "The Perils of Inflation." Unpublished manuscript, 1968.

14. **Cagan, P.,** "The Monetary Dynamics of Hyperinflation," in *Studies in the Quantity Theory of Money*, ed. M. Friedman. Chicago: University of Chacago Press, 1958.

15. ____ . *Determinants and Effects of Changes in the Stock of Money.* New York: Columbia University Press, 1965.

16. ____ . *The Channels of Monetary Effects on Interest Rates* (forthcoming, 1968).

17. **Carson, D.,** ed. *Banking and Monetary Studies* (Irwin, Comptroller of the Currency, 1963).

18. **Council of Economic Advisors,** *The American Economy in 1961: Problems and Policies.* Washington, 1961.

19. ____ . "The Council's View," *Morgan Guaranty Survey* (August 1961).

20. **Denison, E. F.,** *The Sources of Economic Growth in the United States.* C.E.D., 1962.

21. ____ . *Guideposts for Wages and Prices: Criteria and Consistency.* Ann Arbor. 1968.

22. **Duesenberry, J. S.,** "The Portfolio Approach to the Demand for Money and Other Assets," *RES* (February 1963).

23. **Fand, D. I.,** "Intermediary Claims and the Adequacy of our Monetary Controls," in *Banking and Monetary Studies*, ed. D. Carson, 1963.

24. ____ . "A Time Series Analysis of the 'Bills only' Theory of Interest Rates," *RES* (November 1966).

25. ____ . "Some Implications of Money Supply Analysis," *AER* (May 1967).

26. ____ . "The Impact of Monetary Policy in 1966," *JPE* (August 1968).

27. **Fisher, I.,** *Appreciation and Interest.* Macmillan, 1896.

28. ____ . *The Purchasing Power of Money* (*Revised*). Macmillan, 1913.

29. ____ . *The Theory of Interest.* Macmillan, 1930.

30. **Friedman, M.** "The Quantity Theory of Money: A Restatement," in *Studies in the Quantity Theory of Money*, ed. Milton Friedman. Chicago: University of Chicago Press, 1958.

31. ____ . "The Demand for Money: Some Theoretical and Empirical Results," *JPE* (August 1959).

32. ____ . "The Lag in Effect of Monetary Policy," *JPE* (1961).

33. **Friedman, M.** and **A. Schwartz**, "Money and Business Cycles," *The State of Monetary Economics*, *RES* (February 1963).

34. _____ . *A Monetary History of the U.S. 1867–1960.* Princeton: Princeton University Press, 1963.

35. **Friedman, M.** and **D. Meiselman,** "The Relative Stability of Monetary Velocity and the Investment Multiplier in the U.S. 1897–1958," in *Stabilization Policies.* Englewood Cliffs, N. J.: Prentice-Hall, Inc., 1963.

36. **Friedman, M.,** "The Present State of Monetary Theory," *Economic Studies Quarterly* (September 1963).

37. _____ . "The Monetary Studies of the National Bureau," *NBER Annual Report, 1964.*

38. _____ . "The Role of Monetary Policy," *AER* (March, 1968).

39. **Friedman, M.** and **A. Schwartz,** "Trends in Money, Income and Prices 1867–1966." Unpublished manuscript, 1968.

40. _____ . "Monetary Statistics of the U.S." Unpublished manuscript, 1968.

41. **Gibson, W. E.,** "Effects of Money on Interest Rates," Federal Reserve System, *Staff Economic Studies,* #43 (1968).

42. **Griliches, Z.,** "The Brookings Model Volume: A Review Article," *RES* (May 1968).

43. **Gurley, J. G.,** *Liquidity and Financial Institutions in the Postwar Economy.*

44. _____ . "The Radcliffe Report and Evidence," *AER* (September 1960).

45. **Gurley, J. G.** and **E. S. Shaw,** *Money in a Theory of Finance* (Brookings, 1960).

46. **Haberler, G.,** *Money in the International Economy.* Cambridge: Harvard University Press, 1965.

47. _____ . *Inflation: Its Causes and Cures* (*Revised Edition*). Washington: 1966.

48. **Heller, W. W.,** *New Dimensions of Political Economy.* New York: W. W. Norton and Co., 1966.

49. _____ , ed. *Perspectives on Economic Growth.* New York: Random House, 1968.

50. **Hester, D.** and **J. Tobin,** eds. *Financial Markets and Economic Activity.* New York: John Wiley and Sons, 1967.

51. **Horwich, G.,** ed. *Monetary Process and Policy.* Homewood, Ill.: Richard D. Irwin, 1967.

52. **Johnson, H. G.,** *Money, Trade and Economic Growth.* Cambridge: Harvard University Press, 1962.

53. _____ . *The Canadian Quandary.* New York: McGraw-Hill, 1964.

54. _____ . *The World Economy at the Crossroads.* London: Oxford, 1965.

55. _____ . *Essays in Monetary Economics.* London: Allen and Unwin, 1967.

56. _____ . "Inside Money, Outside Money, Income Wealth and Welfare in Monetary Theory." Unpublished manuscript, 1968.

57. **Joint Economic Committee,** *The Relationship of Prices to Economic Stability and Growth.* Washington, 1958.

58. _____ . *Staff Report on Employment, Growth, and Price Levels.* Washington, 1959.

59. _____ . *Twentieth Anniversary of the Employment Act of 1946.* Washington, 1966.

60. **Leijonhufvud, A.,** "Keynes and the Keynesians: A Suggested Interpretation," *AER* (May, 1967).

61. _____ . *On Keynesian Economics and the Economics of Keynes* (forthcoming, 1968).

62. **McCracken, P. W.,** "Price-Cost Behavior and Employment Act Objectives," in *Twentieth Anniversary Symposium,* Joint Economic Committee.

63. **Meiselman, D.,** "Bonds Yields and the Price Level: The Gibson Paradox Regained," in *Banking and Monetary Studies.*

64. **Meigs, A. J.,** "Inflation and Financial Stability." Unpublished manuscript, 1968.

65. **Meltzer, A. H.,** "The Demand for Money: The Evidence From the Time Series," *JPE* (June, 1963).

66. **Mints, L. W.,** *Monetary Policy for a Competitive Society.* New York: McGraw-Hill, 1950.

67. **Modigliani, F.,** "The Monetary Mechanism and its Interaction with Real Phenomena," *RES* (February, 1963).

68. **Morton, W.,** Keynesianism and Inflation," *JPE* (June, 1951).

69. **Okun, A. M.,** "Monetary Policy, Debt Management and Interest Rates: A Quantitative Appraisal," *Stabilization Policies.* Englewood Cliffs, N.J.: Prentice-Hall, Inc., 1963.

70. _____ . "Measuring the Impact of the 1964 Tax Reduction," in *Perspectives on Economic Growth,* ed. W. Heller. 1965.

71. **Patinkin, D. M.,** *Money, Interest and Prices,* 2nd ed. New York: Harper and Row, 1965.

72. **Pesek, B. P.** and **T. R. Saving,** *Money, Wealth and Economic Theory.* New York: Macmillan, 1967.

73. Radcliffe Report, *Committee on the Working of the Monetary System.* London 1959.

74. **Samuelson, P. A.**, "Stability, Growth and Stagnation," 2nd Wicksell Lecture. *Collected Scientific Papers*, 1962. Pp. 1693–1728.

75. ———. "Reflections on Central Banking," in *Collected Papers*, 1962–63. Pp. 1361–86.

76. ———. "A Brief Survey of Post-Keynesian Developments," in *Collected Papers.* 1963. Pp. 1534–50.

77. ———. "Stabilization Policies in the Contemporary U. S. Economy," in *Monetary Process and Policy*, ed. G. Horwich. 1965.

78. ———. "Money, Interest Rates, and Economic Activity," in *Proceedings of a Symposium of Money, Interest Rates and Economic Activity.* 1967.

79. ———. "Irving Fisher and the Theory of Capital," *Ten Economic Studies in the Tradition of I. Fisher.* New York: John Wiley and Sons, 1967.

80. ———. "What Classical and Neo-Classical Monetary Theory Really Was," *The Canadian Journal of Economics*, February 1968.

81. **Samuelson, P. A.** and **A. F. Burns**, (see Burns [12]). *Full Employment, Guideposts, and Economic Stability.* Washington, 1967.

82. **Saulnier, R. J.**, *The Strategy of Economic Policy.* New York: Fordham University Press, 1963.

83. **Sayers, R. S.**, "Monetary Thought and Monetary Policy in England," *Economic Journal* (December 1960).

84. **Shonfield, A.**, "Stabilization Policies in the West: From Demand to Supply Management," *Issues in Monetary Economics, 1966, JPE* (Supp., August 1967).

85. **Sprinkel, B. W.**, "Highly Expansionary Economic Policies in the Midst of Inflation," *Journal of Business* (January 1968).

86. **Thorn, R. G.**, *Monetary Theory and Policy.* New York: Random House, Inc., 1966.

87. **Tobin, J.**, "Monetary Policy and the Management of the Public Debt: The Patman Inquiry," *RES* (May 1953).

88. ———. "A Dynamic Aggregative Model," *JPE* (April 1955).

89. ———. "Liquidity Preference as Behavior Toward Risk," *RES* (February 1958).

90. ———. "Money, Capital and Other Stores of Value," *AER* (May 1961).

91. ———. "An Essay on the Principles of Debt Management," in *Fiscal and Debt Management Policies.* Englewood Cliffs, N.J.: Prentice-Hall, 1963.

92. ———. "Commercial Banks as Creators of 'Money'," *Banking and Monetary Studies* (1963).

93. **Tobin, J.** and **W. C. Brainard,** "Financial Intermediaries and the Effectiveness of Monetary Control," *AER* (May 1963).

94. **Tobin, J.,** "The Monetary Interpretation of History," *AER* (June 1965).

95. _____ . *The Intellectual Revolution in U.S. Economic Policy-Making.* The University of Essex, 1966.

96. _____ . *National Economic Policy.* Yale University Press, 1966.

97. _____ . "Monetary Theory," ms.

98. **Wallich, H.,** "The Quantity Theory and Quantity Policy" in *Ten Economic Studies in the Tradition of I. Fisher.* New York: John Wiley and Sons, 1967.

4/ JOHN T. BOORMAN

The Evidence on the Demand for Money: Theoretical Formulations and Empirical Results

INTRODUCTION

In the previous three chapters (Part 2), we have examined theories attempting to explain the public's demand for money. Though the range of hypotheses implicit in these theories is extremely broad, there are certain important elements common to all of them. Most significantly, almost all of these theories propose a stable relationship between a few important economic variables and the stock of money demanded. Nevertheless, while these theories often posit similar variables to explain the demand for money, most differ in the emphasis they give to them.

For example, in the simplest version of the transactions demand theory as outlined in chapter 3, the stock of money demanded is strictly proportional to a single variable—the volume of transactions to be facilitated by that money stock. In comparison, the inventory theoretic view, which recognizes the interest rate as an opportunity cost of holding money balances and brokerage fees and other charges as explicit costs of switching assets between bonds and money, denies this proportionality between money and income. In this model, the minimization of the total cost of managing money balances leads to a solution which suggests the possibility of substantial economies of scale in the demand for money.

As another example, in the liquidity preference theories of Keynes and Tobin, discussed in chapter 4, the role of money as an asset is stressed and the *motives* for holding money examined. An analysis of the costs (income foregone) and benefits (risks avoided) of holding wealth in the form of money balances leads to a hypothesis in which income and the interest rate on some alternative financial asset are suggested as the primary deter-

I should like to thank my coauthor, Tom Havrilesky, for reading several drafts of this paper, and for making numerous valuable detailed comments each time, and my colleagues Paul Meyer and Lloyd Atkinson for reading an early version of this paper and making many helpful comments. They bear no responsibility for any errors that may remain.

minants of desired money balances. In comparison, Friedman's "Restatement"* of the Quantity Theory, discussed in chapter 5, does not focus exclusively on the "roles" of money or the "motives" of individuals in holding money balances. Instead, defining money as a somewhat broader measure than that employed by other analysts, Friedman emphasizes the services yielded by money in individual and business portfolios. In this view, "money" is simply one among the many assets held by the public. This leads to the hypothesis that *all* the alternatives available to the wealth holder (including physical assets) may influence his desired money balances.

These examples of alternative money demand hypotheses indicate some of the major questions that have been the focus of empirical investigation. A more complete list would include the following specific problems:

(1) What empirical measure ought to be used to represent our theoretical concept of "money"?

(2) What is the role of the interest rate in the money demand function? This issue raises several related questions:
   (a) If the interest rate is statistically important in the determination of the demand for money, what is the interest elasticity of the demand for money balances?
   (b) Given that the interest rate is important in the money demand function, has evidence been presented which would support the existence (historical or potential) of a "liquidity trap"?
   (c) Which one of all the alternative interest rate measures available is most relevant to the determination of the demand for money?

(3) What is the significance of income, wealth, expectational factors and other economic variables suggested as determinants of the demand for money? How successfully can we specify a single function, including the interest rate and one or more of these additional factors, to explain the historical variations in the level of the demand for money?

These are the major issues raised in the empirical literature on the demand for money. Let us consider each of them in turn.

THE EMPIRICAL DEFINITION OF MONEY

What assets ought to be included in our measure of "the money stock"? If we focus on those theories which emphasize the transactions motive for

*Milton Friedman, "The Quantity Theory of Money, A Restatement," in Milton Friedman (ed.), *Studies in the Quantity Theory of Money*, Chicago, 1956. See Don Patinkin, "The Chicago Tradition, the Quantity Theory, and Friedman," *The Journal of Money, Credit, and Banking*, 1 (February, 1969), pp. 46–70.

holding money, the proper definition of money is not a profound problem. Money should be defined to consist only of those assets which serve as generally acceptable media of exchange. It is widely agreed that only commercial bank demand deposits and currency in circulation provide this service. If we view the money demand of the public as arising from a speculative motive, however, the list of assets in our definition of money must be expanded to include those assets which are stable in value, i.e., fixed-dollar assets whose value is independent of variations in the interest rate. Finally, when the demand for money is approached as part of the general theory of demand, those assets which are very close substitutes (and hence respond to the same yields in the demand function) should be included in the definition. This approach clearly indicates that the proper definition of money is largely an empirical question.

Allen H. Meltzer has enunciated one possible criterion for selecting the appropriate definition of money.

> The problem is one of defining money so that a stable demand function can be shown to have existed under differing institutional arrangements, changes in social and political environment, and changes in economic conditions, or to explain the effects of such changes on the function.*

Let us briefly consider the implications of this criterion for the degree of control that the monetary authority has over crucial macroeconomic variables.** The money stock and interest rates are thought to have a strong effect upon aggregate demand, employment, and the price level in the economy. If the demand for money is unstable (shifts unpredictably), the effect of policy actions on the equilibrium money stock and interest rates will be uncertain. In short, stability of the money demand function, together with a capability on the part of the monetary authority to influence closely the stock of assets corresponding to the theoretical con-

---

*Allan H. Meltzer, "The Demand for Money: The Evidence from the Time Series," *Journal of Political Economy*, 71 (June 1963), p. 222.

**There are, of course, many additional possible criteria by which to define a measure of the money stock. George Kaufman, following Milton Friedman and David Meiselman, defines money according to its correlation with income (taking into consideration the possible lead-lag relationship between money and income). In selecting the set of financial assets to be included in the money supply, he employs two criteria: choose that set which (1) has the highest correlation with income and (2) has a higher correlation with income than any of the components separately. This alternative operational approach, unlike the Meltzer criterion, derives from the proposition that the equilibrium nominal money stock can be controlled by the monetary authority, and suggests a rather special theoretical model on which to base monetary policy. The Meltzer criterion is preferred here since it relates closely to the interest elasticity of the demand for money. See George G. Kaufman, "More On An Empirical Definition of Money," *American Economic Review*, 59 (March 1969), pp. 78–87.

cept of money employed in that function, would seem to be necessary conditions for the successful implementation of monetary policy.* These conditions will allow the authorities to exert a predictable influence over the equilibrium stock of money, the interest rate, and other variables in the money demand function.

Economists traditionally have defined money in the "narrow" sense as the sum of demand deposit liabilities of commercial banks and currency held by the public. However, a number of analysts include time deposits at commercial banks within their measure of the money stock. Milton Friedman, for example, views time deposits as ". . . a temporary abode of purchasing power . . ." and includes them in the "broad" measure of money which he employs in his empirical work. A few researchers go beyond even this "broad" concept to include such things as savings and loan shares, mutual savings bank deposits, and claims against other financial intermediaries in their measure of "money." Conceptually, of course, it is possible to go even further and include still other financial assets (or even some measure of credit availability such as commercial bank "lines of credit") in a measure of "money."**

Ultimately the question of the best definition of money must be satisfied in accord with the Meltzer criterion. The stability of the money demand function is closely linked to the degree of substitutability that exists between money, as it is defined in that function, and other financial assets. For example, if the secular and cyclical changes in the competitive position of financial intermediaries makes available substitutes for currency in circulation and demand deposits held by the nonbank public (the narrowly defined money stock), the demand for money, so defined, may shift as these substitutes appear. In such a case, a demand function for some broader measure of money, one which includes these close substitutes, would be more stable, and would shift less over time.*** Under these conditions, monetary policy actions that concentrate on the narrower measure of money would be focusing on an unstable, shifting target. Policy actions that focus on broader measures of money would be more appropriate. On the other hand, if claims against nonbank financial intermediaries are not

*See Sherman J. Maisel, "Controlling Monetary Aggregates" in *Controlling Monetary Aggregates*: *Proceedings* of the Monetary Conference of the Federal Reserve Bank of Boston (June 1969), pp. 152–174.

**See Arthur B. Laffer, "Trade Credit and The Money Market," *Journal of Political Economy*, 78 (March/April 1970), pp. 239–267.

***Gurley and Shaw, for example emphasize the substitutability between claims on certain financial intermediaries and demand deposits at commercial banks, and argue that "money" must be defined so as to include these substitutes. Evidence supporting this position is presented below. See John G. Gurley and Edward S. Shaw, *Money in a Theory of Finance* (Washington, D. C.: The Brookings Institution, 1960).

This view is also embodied in the report of the Radcliffe Committee, which views "liquidity" and "the stock of liquid assets" held by the public as the relevant concept

good substitutes for currency and demand deposits, the broader measures of money may be quite volatile and policy actions which focus on the narrow measure of money would be preferable.

Let us examine some of the evidence which has been presented on this issue. Specifically, are assets such as commercial bank time deposits, savings and loan shares, mutual savings bank deposits, and others which have been suggested for inclusion in a measure of "money," sufficiently close substitutes for commercial bank demand deposits to warrant treating them in a single measure.* We employ the concept of substitutability because it relates directly to the Meltzer criterion, i.e., which definition of money allows us to identify and estimate the most stable demand function. In examining the empirical evidence, we identify one function as more stable than another if it allows us more accurately and more easily to predict the effects of changes in monetary policy on the equilibrium values in our model. As David Laidler expresses it:

> A "more stable demand for money function" may be taken to be one that requires knowledge of fewer variables and their parameters in order to predict the demand for money with a given degree of accuracy or, which amounts to the same thing, one that yields parameter estimates that are less subject to variation when the same arguments are included in the function and hence enables more accurate prediction of the demand for money to be made.**

---

on which to focus in monetary theory and policy. In this view, only policy actions which change the *total liquidity* of the public—and not simply the *composition* of the public's stock of liquid assets—are likely to lead to predictable results. This is so because of the high degree of substitutability that exists between the narrowly defined money stock and near-monies. *See The Radcliffe Report*, Committee on the Working of the Monetary System, London, 1959, and the reading by David I. Fand in this section.

*The cross elasticity of demand measures the extent to which two commodities or assets are related to each other, and is the most frequently used measure of substitutability. If we consider two assets X and Y, and the returns on each, i_x and i_y, respectively, the cross elasticity of X with respect to Y equals the percentage change in the quantity of X demanded, divided by the percentage change in the return on Y.

$$\eta_{x \cdot y} = \frac{\Delta x/x}{\Delta i_y/i_y}$$

If an increase in the return on asset Y (Δi_y positive) causes a switch in holdings from X to Y, Δx will be negative and the cross elasticity will be negative. In this case, the assets X and Y are said to be "substitutes." If $\eta_{x \cdot y}$ is positive, indicating a *direct* relationship between the return on Y and holdings of asset X, these assets are said to be "complements."

**David Laidler, "The Definition of Money: Theoretical and Empirical Problems," *The Journal of Money, Credit and Banking*, 1 (August 1968), p. 516.

In a recent empirical study Laidler (37) contends that the most stable money demand function he has been able to isolate is one employing Friedman's broad definition of money. This contrasts with earlier results presented by Karl Brunner and Allan Meltzer (4), both of whom found that the narrow measure—demand deposits plus currency—yielded the best statistical results.

What accounts for these starkly contrasting conclusions? First of all, these two studies specify different explanatory variables in their money demand equations. Secondly, they use data from different time periods to estimate the parameters of these relations. Finally, they employ different procedures to test their hypotheses. Since the relative performance of these measures of the money stock in empirical money demand functions is likely to be highly sensitive to all of these considerations, it may be impossible to choose the better measure of money on the basis of these studies alone.

However, additional evidence on this problem is available in those studies that attempt to derive explicit estimates of the degree of substitutability between demand deposits, time deposits, and other financial assets. For a "monetary" measure that includes commercial bank time deposits or some other assets to be more stably related to the variables that appear in the demand function, these assets must be close substitutes for demand deposits.

In a study on the demand for liquid assets by the public, Edgar Feige (14) measured the cross-elasticities of demand between various assets. Using data on the volume of liquid assets held by households in each state of the United States for each year during the period from 1949 to 1959, he found that the yields on nonbank intermediary liabilities (savings and loan shares etc.) did not affect the demand for money. Ownership of each of these assets was found to be highly sensitive only to its "own-rate" of interest. In his results, there appears to be no very high degree of substitutability between demand deposits, time deposits, savings and loan shares, or mutual savings bank deposits. In fact, demand deposits were found to be mildly *complementary* with savings and loan shares and mutual savings bank deposits; commercial bank demand and time deposits were only very weak substitutes for each other. From this and other evidence, Feige concludes that the narrow definition of money is the preferred definition when estimating money demand functions, and that analysts need not concern themselves with the effects of the activities of other intermediaries on the public's demand for money.

The methods used by Feige in deriving these results are subject to several criticisms. First of all, there are serious questions as to whether the way in which he measures the rate of return on commercial bank demand deposits reflects the relevant return considered by asset holders in making allocation decisions relating to their respective portfolios. Secondly, he uses data on assets owned in a state by residents of all states when, in fact, the relevant measure for his purposes is that on assets owned by the residents of each state. His data probably require the inclusion of rates on out-of-state assets in order to capture effects of ownership that crosses state lines. These problems detract from Feige's results.

Feige's conclusions are disputed by T. H. Lee (42) and V. K. Chetty (9). Lee's work will be described in detail in the next section in connection with our survey of the relevance of alternative interest rates in the money demand function. Briefly, Lee suggests that the liabilities of financial intermediaries, particularly savings and loan shares, are indeed very good *substitutes* for money. Rather than supporting Friedman's "broad" definition of money, however, he claims that the definition should be extended to encompass an even broader collection of assets, including as a minimum, shares in savings and loan associations.

Chetty makes a similar proposal. In his article, a technique originally developed in production theory to measure the substitutability between capital and labor in the production process, is employed to measure the substitutability between assets in the consumer's utility function.* Chetty assumes that consumers attempt to maximize their utility (subject to the budget constraint) by combining money (demand deposits plus currency in circulation), time deposits, and other assets to produce desired levels of liquidity at the lowest cost. By combining the conditions required for utility maximization with the budget constraint, he derives an equation which contains parameters that, when estimated, yield measures of the partial elasticities of substitution between money and other assets.

On the basis of these estimates, Chetty concludes that while savings and loan shares and mutual savings bank deposits are rather good substitutes for money, time deposits appear to be virtually perfect substitutes. This last finding supports Friedman's use of the "broad" definition of money. Nevertheless, as with Lee, Chetty suggests that an even broader measure of money may be more appropriate and shows how such a measure may be calculated. Employing weights that measure the "moneyness" of assets as implied by their substitutability with demand deposits and currency, he constructs a weighted average of demand deposits and currency (with weights constrained to unity), time deposits, saving and loan shares (SL), and mutual savings bank deposits (MS). The final form of the equation defining this average "money" stock is:

$$M_a' = M + TD + .615SL + .88MS$$

Note that the coefficient (unity) on the time deposit variable stems from

---

*See K. J. Arrow, H. B. Chenery, B. S. Minhas, and R. M. Solow, "Capital-Labor Substitution and Economic Efficiency," *Review of Economics and Statistics*, 63 (August 1961), pp. 225–250.

his conclusion of perfect substitutability between these deposits and money (demand deposits plus currency in circulation).

Chetty's findings represent persuasive evidence in favor of a broader measure of money.* Nonetheless, many economists feel that this issue is still unresolved, and further evidence is sought. In the remainder of this survey, therefore, whenever we are reporting on empirical work, we shall cite the specific definition of money used by a particular analyst.

Let us now turn to the role of the interest rate in the demand for money. As we shall see in chapters 6–9, this particular issue has critical implications for national economic policy.

THE EVIDENCE ON THE ROLE OF THE INTEREST RATE IN THE MONEY DEMAND FUNCTION

In the United States, most studies on the demand for money have focused primarily on the explanatory role of the interest rate as a determinant of desired money balances. The stimulus for much of this work derives from Keynes' presentation of the Liquidity Preference Theory in *The General Theory of Employment, Interest, and Money* (1936) discussed in chapter 4. Although Pigou, as early as 1917, suggested that the interest rate was a potentially important factor determining the public's money holding behavior, it was Keynes' full explication of the "speculative" motive for holding "idle" money balances which provided the major impetus for testing this hypothesis. Research has been further encouraged by the work of Milton Friedman (19). Contrary to the findings of most other investigators, Friedman finds little basis for assigning a significant role for the interest rate in determining the demand for money.

SINGLE EQUATION MODELS OF THE DEMAND FOR MONEY

Most of the following studies reviewed use similar statistical techniques. In general, the authors develop a model of the demand for money specified as a single equation that relates the stock of real money balances demanded to the interest rate and other variables.

This equation is usually either linear or exponential in form:

*This evidence also lends support to the broad measure of money used by Lydall in his empirical study of the demand for money in Britain and increases the importance of Lydall's conclusions on the issues discussed below. See H. Lydall, "Income, Assets, and the Demand for Money," *Review of Economics and Statistics* (February 1958), pp. 1–14.

$$\frac{M_d}{P} = a_1 + a_2 \, i + a_3 \, X \tag{1}$$

$$\frac{M_d}{P} = \alpha i^{\beta_1} \, X^{\beta_2} \tag{2}$$

where M_d/P is the stock of real money balances demanded*, i is an interest rate, and X represents the other variables such as wealth, permanent income, or current income included in specific money demand equations. When equation (2) is employed, a logarithmic transformation is made so that the equation is *linear* in the logarithms of the variables. Thus, taking logs of both sides of the equation:

$$\log \frac{M_d}{P} = \log \alpha + \beta_1 \, \log i + \beta_2 \log X **$$

*Money demand functions are generally cast in real terms on the assumption that the price elasticity of nominal money balances is unity. This assumption is made by most authors. The implication of this assumption is that price level changes alone will cause no change in the demand for *real* money balances or, alternatively, that the demand for nominal balances is proportional to the price level. Let us examine this assumption further. Let X in equation (2) above be a measure of real wealth. Then:

$$M_d/P = \alpha \cdot i^{\beta_1} \cdot W^{\beta_2}.$$

If *nominal* money balances were specified as a function of *nominal* wealth, this equation would be

$$M_d = \alpha \cdot i^{\beta_1} \cdot (P \cdot W)^{\beta_2}.$$

But these two equations are quite different. The first equation implies that the price-level elasticity is unity—the exponent of P equals one—and β_2 is the wealth elasticity of money balances. But in the latter form, β_2 is some *average* of the price level and wealth elasticities. Consequently, if the price level elasticity is really unity, but the true wealth elasticity is not equal to one, β_2 will be *biased* towards that value and will not be a good estimate of the true wealth elasticity. To avoid that bias, investigators have generally chosen to work with functions cast in real terms.

The validity of this procedure is supported by evidence presented by Allan Meltzer (45). His work indicates that when the price variable is included as a separate argument in a log-linear equation, its coefficient is very close to unity. Furthermore, if nominal wealth is employed in an equation with nominal balances specified as the dependent variable, the wealth elasticity is closer to unity than if these measures are cast in real terms. Hence, the assumed proportionality of nominal money balances to the price level would appear to have a firm basis in empirical analysis.

**In this form, the coefficients β_1 and β_2 can be directly estimated by linear regression techniques and those coefficients will be elasticities. This may be shown as follows: Let $\eta_{M \cdot i}$ denote the interest elasticity of money demand (let M in this instance represent *real* money balances demanded); then,

$$\eta_{M \cdot i} = \frac{\partial M/M}{\partial i/i} = \frac{\partial M}{\partial i} \cdot \frac{i}{M}$$

These simple linear (in the coefficients) models may be fitted to empirical observations of variables if, and only if, two additional assumptions are made: first, we must assume that the money market is always in equilibrium so that desired money balances, M_d, equal the actual money stock reported in the statistical series, M; secondly, we must assume that there exist exact empirical counterparts to the theoretical variables specified; for example, the average of daily rates quoted by the New York Federal Reserve Bank on U.S. Treasury Bills may be chosen as the empirical measure of "the interest rate." With data on each of the variables specified in the equation, multiple regression methods may be employed to derive estimates of the coefficients in these single equation models.* On the basis of the statistical characteristics of the estimates derived by these techniques, judgments have been made about the relative importance of the variables in the money demand function. More specifically, the results may give some indication of the interest sensitivity of the public's demand for money.

Henry Latané carried out one of the earliest studies along these lines. Latané specified and tested three alternative models of the demand for money. In his first test, he proposed a constant ratio of total money balances to nominal national income, $M/Y = k$. This hypothesis represented a crude form of the Quantity Theory discussed in chapter 5. By showing graphically that this ratio was highly variable, fluctuating be-

---

but, from equation (2),

$$\partial M / \partial i = \beta_1 (\alpha X^{\beta_2}) \cdot i^{(\beta_1 - 1)}$$

therefore,

$$\eta_{M \cdot i} = \beta_1 (\alpha X^{\beta_2}) \cdot i^{(\beta_1 - 1)} \cdot \frac{i}{\alpha X^{\beta_2} \cdot i^{\beta_1}} = \frac{\beta_1 i^{\beta_1}}{i^{\beta_1}} = \beta_1 .$$

Consequently, elasticities may be estimated directly by employing the log-linear form of equation (2) in the regression procedure.

*Least squares regression analysis may be defined as a procedure whereby an hypothesized relationship may be confronted with actual data in order to derive numerical estimates of the parameters specified in that relationship. Under specified conditions concerning the nature of the hypothesized relationship and the characteristics of the data employed, these techniques will yield estimates with certain desirable statistical properties. In the models above, for example, data on the size of the money stock, the value of the interest rate, and, say, national wealth, may be employed in regression analysis to derive estimates of β_1, the interest elasticity of money demand, and β_2, the wealth elasticity of money demand. For a discussion of the mechanics of least squares regression and the properties of least squares estimators, see Saul Hymans, *Probability Theory* (New York: Prentice Hall Inc., 1966) chapter 8, or Karl A. Fox, *Intermediate Economic Statistics* (New York: John Wiley and Sons, 1968) chapter 4.

tween a low of .26 to a high of .50 in the period from 1919 to 1952, Latané rejected this hypothesis.

In his second test, he proposed a Keynesian-type money demand function such as the one presented in chapter 4. In this formulation, the total demand for money balances is seen as the sum of a transactions component dependent on the level of income, and an asset or speculative component dependent on the rate of interest:

$$M = a\,(1/i) + bY + c \tag{3}$$

Latané showed that this form implies a continually declining ratio of money balances to income as income increases (and the interest rate remains constant).* Since empirical evidence indicated that this was not the case, Latané also rejected this form.

Latané's last model proposed that the ratio of money balances to (nominal) national income was dependent upon the rate of interest:

$$\frac{M}{Y} = f(i) \tag{4}$$

In testing this model, he specified a linear form,

$$\frac{M}{Y} = c\,(1/i) + d$$

and derived the following estimates of the parameters (c) and (d) from his regression:

$$\frac{M}{Y} = .0074\,(1/i) + .1088$$

This equation was then used to predict values of the dependent variable for dates not included in the original data. The success of these predictions prompted Latané to conclude that he had identified a stable behavioral relation between cash balances, income, and the long-term rate of interest. Specifically, "In the past thirty years each 1.0% change

---

*This may be seen by dividing both sides of equation (3) by Y:
$$M/Y = a/(i \cdot Y) + b + c/Y.$$

If Y increases, a/Y and c/Y will decline. Thus, with the interest rate constant, the proportion of income held in the form of money balances would decline as income increased.

in $(1/i)$ has tended to be associated with a change of 0.8% in gross national product held as currency and demand deposits."[*]

One characteristic of Latané's last model should be cited, since this characteristic is shared by the money demand functions tested by several other authors. The equation form chosen by Latané to test the interest sensitivity of the cash balance ratio constrains the income elasticity of the demand for money to equal unity. This may be shown as follows: Let $\eta_{M \cdot Y}$ denote the income elasticity of money balances. Then:

$$\eta_{M \cdot Y} = \frac{\Delta M/M}{\Delta Y/Y} = \frac{\Delta M}{\Delta Y} \cdot \frac{Y}{M}$$

But from the basic model (eq. 4), we may write $\Delta M = f(i) \cdot \Delta Y$. Therefore,

$$\eta_{M \cdot Y} = f(i) \cdot \frac{Y}{M} = \frac{f(i) \cdot Y}{f(i) \cdot Y} = 1.$$

The effects of this arbitrary restriction on the order of magnitude of the income elasticity of money balances can only be judged by comparing the results of this model with those derived from models which are not so constrained.

Other investigators, in testing the Liquidity Preference Theory, have attempted to isolate "asset" or "idle" balances held by the public, that is, money balances held other than for transactions purposes. James Tobin (58), in an early study, and Martin Bronfenbrenner and Thomas Mayer (3) in subsequent work, tested the influence of the interest rate on the volume of such balances held by the public.

In calculating the idle balance component of total money balances, Tobin assumed (like Latané) that desired *transactions* balances are proportional to the level of income. To determine the exact factor of proportionality between transaction balances and income, Tobin further assumed that during periods of very high interest rates and high economic activity, when the ratio of total money holdings to income is at its lowest level, idle balances are zero and the money stock is held only in transactions balances. The minimum value for this ratio was found to occur in 1929. Therefore, Tobin asserted that this 1929 ratio actually measures the constant factor of proportionality between transactions balances and income. This may be seen symbolically. Let

$$M_{\text{total}} = M_{\text{idle}} + M_{\text{trans}} = f(i) + kY$$

[*]H. A. Latané, "Cash Balances and the Interest Rate—A Pragmatic Approach," *Review of Economics and Statistics*, 36 (November 1954), p. 460.

where

$$M_{idle} = f(i) \text{ and } M_{trans} = kY$$

If $M_{idle} = f(i) = O$, as Tobin asserts for 1929, then $M_{total} = kY$ and

$$M_{total}/Y = k \text{ in 1929.}$$

Since k (the reciprocal of the transactions velocity of circulation of money, V_t) was assumed to be a constant, this allowed a calculation of idle balances for other years as:

$$(M_{idle})_t = (M_{total})_t - (M_{trans})_t = (M_{total})_t - k_{1929}(Y)_t$$

Tobin plotted idle balances calculated in this manner for each year against interest rates. For the period ending in 1945, he obtained excellent representations of what appeared to be Keynesian liquidity preference functions—the roughly hyperbolic functions depicted in the discussion of Keynesian theory in chapter 4. Although the scatter diagrams did not appear to yield such well-behaved relations for subsequent years, it did appear that Tobin had isolated a statistical liquidity preference function.

In their work, Bronfenbrenner and Mayer (3) estimated regression coefficients in equations that contained a wealth measure and lagged money balances as explanatory variables, in addition to the interest rate. As the dependent variable, they alternately used total money balances and a measure of idle balances, similar to the one originally defined by Tobin. The equation they tested in log-linear form was:

$$\log (M/P)_t = \alpha_1 + \alpha_2 \log i + \alpha_3 \log W + \alpha_4 \log (M/P)_{t-1}$$

In the equations employing idle balances as well as in those specifying total money balances as the dependent variable, the coefficient of the interest rate had a negative sign attached to it, and was statistically significantly different from zero at the one per cent level.*

In further tests based on equations similar to the one above, Bronfenbrenner and Mayer concluded that the liquidity preference hypothesis did a better job of predicting the movement of money balances from year to

*To say that a coefficient is "statistically significantly different from zero" at the one percent level of significance is to imply that there is less than one chance in a hundred that the estimated coefficient differs from zero solely because of random (chance) factors affecting the data from which the estimate was derived. If we cannot judge a coefficient to be significantly different from zero at the one per cent level or five per cent level of significance, we generally have little confidence in the hypothesized relation which that coefficient represents.

year than did a "naive" model which simply assumed that there would be no relation (or random relation) between movements in the interest rate and money balances. This again appeared as evidence favorable to the liquidity preference hypothesis.

Virtually all of the work presented since the Bronfenbrenner and Mayer study has wisely avoided the arbitrary classification of money balances into active and idle components. Even earlier authors, such as Latané, felt that such a distinction did not allow for the possible effect of the interest rate on "active balances."[*] As indicated in chapter 5, many economists believe that such a dichotomy is unreasonable since *total money balances* are simply one of many assets held for the services they provide, and cannot be separated into unique components.[**]

Among studies specifying total money balances as the dependent variable, are those by Meltzer (45), Brunner and Meltzer (4, 5), Laidler (37, 38), Heller (28), and Chow (10). These studies use different time periods to test their basic hypotheses; they use variables other than the interest rate in the money demand equation; and often they differ in the empirical measure chosen to represent "the interest rate," some specifying the rate on U.S. Treasury Bills or short-term commercial paper, while others employ the rate on long-term government bonds or corporate securities. Yet, in spite of these many differences, these studies, like the ones above, show that the interest rate measure is an important factor in explaining variations in the demand for money. Some of the more important characteristics of these studies are summarized in Table 1.

In addition to the unanimous conclusion that the interest rate is an important determinant of the demand for money, these studies also demonstrate a strong consistency in their estimates of the interest elasticity of money balances. (Such consistency over different periods of time suggests a rather stable demand function for money, as discussed above). Those studies employing a long-term rate of interest, report elasticities in the range of -.4 to -.9. However, the estimates in the lower half of this range occur only when money is defined in a "broad" sense (inclusive of commercial bank time deposits). Considering only those studies that use the more common measure of money $(DD + C)$, the range of elasticity estimates narrows to -.7 to -.9.

When the short-term rate of interest is employed, the estimated elasticities range from -.1 to -.5. However, all the estimates in the upper part of this range derive from those studies which specify "idle" balances as the dependent variable. If we exclude these results and consider only total money balances as the dependent variable, the elasticity of money balances

---

*Latané, *op. cit.*, pp. 456–457.

**Milton Friedman, "The Demand for Money—Some Theoretical and Empirical Results," *Journal of Political Economy*, 67 (June 1959), pp. 327–351.

TABLE 1

The Demand for Money in Single Equations Studies

Study	Interest Rate Elasticity of M		Interest Rate Measure Employed	Other Variables in M_D Function	Data and Time Period
1. Latané		-0.7 (M1)	R_B	GNP	1919–1952 (A)
2. Bronfenbrenner and Mayer	a)	$-.3 - -.5$ (M_{Idle})	R_{4-6}	GNP, Wealth	1919–1956 (A)
	b)	approx -0.1 (M1)	R_{4-6}	GNP, Wealth	1919–1956 (A)
3. Meltzer	a)	$-.7 - -.9$ (M1)	$R_{20\ yr}$	Net Non-human Wealth	1900–1958 (A)
	b)	$-.5 - -.6$ (M2)	$R_{20\ yr}$	Net Non-human Wealth	1900–1958 (A)
	c)	$-.4$ (M3)	$R_{20\ yr}$	Net Non-human Wealth	1900–1949 (A)
4. Heller	a)	$-.1$ (M1)	R_{60-80}	GNP	1947–1958 (Q)
	b)	$-.1$ (M2)	R_{60-80}	Private Non-human Wealth	1947–1958 (Q)
5. Laidler (Feb. '66)	a)	not available (M1)	R_{4-6}	Permanent Income	1920–1960 (A)
	b)	not available (M2)	R_{4-6}	Permanent Income	1892–1960 (A)
6. Laidler (Dec. '66)	a)	$-.18 - -.20$ (M1)	R_{4-6}	Permanent Income	1919–1960 and subperiods (A)
	b)	$-.5 - -.8$ (M1)	$R_{20\ yr}$	Permanent Income	1919–1960 and subperiods (A)
	c)	approx $-.15$ (M2)	R_{4-6}	Permanent Income	1892–1960 and subperiods (A)
	d)	$-.3 - -.5$ (M2)	$R_{20\ yr}$	Permanent Income	1892–1960 and subperiods (A)
7. Chow	a)	approx $-.75$ (M1)	$R_{20\ yr}$	Permanent Income	1897–1958 (excl. war years) (A)
	b)	approx $-.79$ (M1)	$R_{20\ yr}$	Current Income and Lagged Money Stock	1897–1958 (excl. war years) (A)

Notes: $M_1 = DD + C$; $M_2 = M_1 + TD$; $M_3 = M_2 +$ Deposits at Mutual Savings Banks and the Postal Savings System; $R_B =$ interest rate on high grade corporate bonds; $R_{20\ yr} =$ rate on 20 year corporate bonds; $R_{4-6} =$ rate on 4–6 month prime commercial paper; $R_{60-80} =$ rate on 60–80 day commercial paper; A = annual; Q = quarterly.

with respect to the short-term interest rate lies in the range from −.1 to −.2. This result holds whether money is defined in the "narrow" or "broad" sense. The difference between the long-rate and the short-rate elasticities may be an indication of the different rates of adjustment by the public to what they consider to be temporary versus long-term movements in financial variables. It may also reflect the fact that the long term rate fluctuates less than the short term rate. We shall soon consider this point again.

THE EVIDENCE FROM SIMULTANEOUS EQUATION MODELS

All of the studies reported in Table 1 have one basic, and perhaps unfortunate, characteristic in common. All of the estimates of interest elasticities are derived from single equation models.

Elementary statistics teaches that in order for estimated coefficients derived by least squares regression methods to have certain desirable characteristics (unbiasedness, efficiency, etc.), there must be a one-way causation from the independent to the dependent variable, with no direct feedback. Thus, in the single equation models specified above, the interest rate and other explanatory variables must be assumed to influence the stock of money, the dependent variable, but the stock of money must not in turn influence these variables.

In contrast, if the conventional aggregate economic model is considered (such as any of those developed in chapters 6 to 9), it is obvious that the causation between interest rates, real factors, and the money stock is not unidirectional. There is simultaneous interrelation between both the supply of and demand for money as well as between the monetary and real factors. This leads to what is commonly referred to as an "identification" problem.*

*The source and nature of "simultaneous equations bias" may be illustrated as follows: consider the usual supply-demand relationship as drawn below.

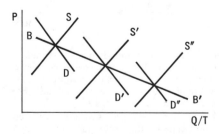

time (t) supply S demand D
time ($t + 1$) supply S' demand D'
time ($t + 2$) supply S'' demand D''

Observed price-quantity figures are A, B, C at times t, $t + 1$, $t + 2$, respectively.

Fortunately, some empirical work does assume simultaneity either between money supply and money demand or, more generally, between the monetary and the real expenditure sectors of the economy. These studies employ statistical techniques designed to correct for the interaction among "dependent" and "independent" variables specified within a single equation and to derive estimates which have certain desirable statistical properties. In these studies, the money demand function is estimated as one element in a multi-equation model. Some of the results of these studies are presented in Table 2.*

An attempt to fit a statistical demand or supply curve to empirical observations will not, in fact, yield the desired relationships except in very special circumstances. The usual time series observations of prices and quantities do not correspond to either any one demand curve or any one supply curve, but rather, they are intersection points of various supply and demand curves which are almost continuously shifting either randomly or systematically due to the influence of outside factors.

Attempts to derive single equation estimates of these curves on the basis of observed data will actually result in a statistical construct which is neither a supply curve nor a demand curve. For example, the least squares regression line which could be fitted to the data above would be BB'. This line would have a negative slope in the situation drawn here only because of the tendency for the supply curve to shift relatively more than the demand curve. Yet a statistical study of the data involved could easily be misunderstood by the unwary to represent the true demand relation. This would lead one to accept a meaningless estimate of the slope and, thus, of the elasticity of the demand curve.

The only way in which such time series data could readily yield true structural estimates of the parameters of either the supply curve or the demand curve would be in the very special circumstances where one of the curves is stable and the shifting of the other curve traces out points along the desired curve. This is pictured below.

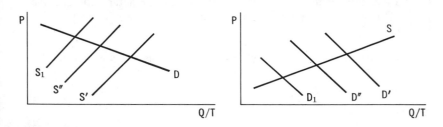

To get around this problem, the true interaction of supply-demand relations in determining price-quantity figures must be considered. This may be done by specifying a simultaneous equation model including both a supply equation and a demand equation, and taking care to observe the familiar rules for "identification." See Gerhard Tintner, *Econometrics* (New York: John Wiley and Sons, 1962) ch. 6.

*All of the studies reported in Table 2 employ two-stage least squares in the estimating process. For a discussion of the mechanics of this technique and the characteristics of the estimates derived from it, see J. Johnston, *Econometric Methods*, (New York, 1963), chapter 9.

TABLE 2

Money and Deposit Demand in Simultaneous-Equation Models

Study	Representative Equation (seasonal dummies omitted where appropriate)	Interest Elasticity	Interest Rate Measure	Data
1. Brunner and Meltzer	$M1 = -18.994\, r^* + .201\, W/Pa - 54.72\, Y/Y_p + .347 P_y$ W/Pa = real public wealth P_y = price index Y/Y_p = ratio of current to permanent income	−0.75	r = bond yield	1930–1959 (A)
	$M2 = -16.806\, r^* + .340\, W/Pa - 44.81\, Y/Y_p + .290 P_y$	−0.42	r = bond yield	1930–1959 (A)
2. Teigen (1966)	$\Delta D = 3.101 + .0719 Y^* - .0018\, r_b^* Y^* - .0066\, r_p Y^*$	−0.10	r_b = Treas. bill rate	1953–1964 (Q)
	$-.1895\, D_{T-1}$	−0.43	r_p = rate on bank time deposits	
	D = demand deposits adjusted at commercial banks Y = gross national product			
3. deLeeuw (Brookings)	$\dfrac{\Delta D}{W} = .0067 - 0.158 \left(\dfrac{D}{W}\right) r_{-1} - 0.00355\, r_s^*$	−0.35	r_s = yield on private securities	1948–1962 (Q)
	$-0.0451\, r_p^* - .140\, \dfrac{Inv}{W_{r-1}} +$ other terms	−0.17	r_p = rate on bank time deposits	
	W = wealth measure, Inv. = bus. investment			
4. Goldfeld	$\Delta D = -.270 - 0.127\, D_{T-1} + 0.140\, Y^*$	−0.11	r_b = Treas. bill rate	1950–1962 (Q)
	$-0.0066\, r_b^* Y^* - 0.012\, r_p Y^*$	−0.18	r_p = rate on bank time deposits	
	Y = gross national product			

*An asterisk is used to denote an independent variable used in the money (or D) demand function which is treated as endogenously determined within the multi-equation model as a whole.

The results derived from simultaneous-equation models generally confirm the single-equation results reported above. Those studies employing a short-term rate of interest in the money or demand deposit demand equation, report elasticities in the range of -.10 to -.12. This compares with the -.1 to -.2 range reported from Table 1. The elasticity measures based on long-term rates are again substantially higher than the short-term rate elasticities. They range from -.35 in de Leeuw's work to -.75 in Brunner and Meltzer's model. Since de Leeuw's measure is a weighted average of rates on private securities of different maturities, and not a long-rate comparable to the corporate bond yields used in the other studies, these results are not inconsistent with the evidence presented in Table 1. Furthermore, since these estimates are less likely to be biased because of the simultaneous nature of the relations involved, they lend strong support to the earlier single-equation work and indicate that in this case the identification problem may not be particularly serious.

In summary, let us emphasize that both those studies based on single-equation models as well as those which employ multi-equation models and simultaneous-equation estimation techniques, appear to support the hypothesis that the interest rate is an important determinant of the demand for money.

MILTON FRIEDMAN AND THE DEMAND FOR MONEY

As you will recall from chapter 5, in his "Restatement" of the Quantity Theory of Money, Milton Friedman develops a theoretical money demand function that includes several interest rate terms as explanatory variables. However, his empirical work leads him to question the significance of the interest rate effect on desired money balances.

Friedman's empirical work begins with an observation on the behavior of the income velocity of money. He notes that from 1870 to 1954, over long periods of time, the income velocity of circulation (Y/M) moved in an opposite direction from real income, but over shorter periods of time, during business cycles, these variables moved in the same direction. He attempts to reconcile these observations by explaining the public's behavior regarding the demand for real money balances.

Friedman argues that the *nominal* stock of money in the economy is determined in the first instance on the supply side of the market by the monetary authorities, and that "Holders of money cannot alter this amount directly." In contrast, however, the holders of money " . . . can make the *real* amount of money anything in the aggregate they want to."* For, if

---

*Milton Friedman, "The Demand for Money: Some Theoretical and Empirical Results," *Journal of Political Economy* 67 (August 1959), p. 330.

individuals find themselves holding too large a stock of nominal money balances, their attempt to decrease these balances by increasing expenditures will reduce the real quantity of money to the desired level by raising money income and prices. Conversely, lowering expenditures to increase money holdings will lower money income and prices thereby raising the real quantity of money to the desired equilibrium level.

This analysis suggests that since the *nominal* stock of money is predetermined by the monetary authorities, an explanation of the observed behavior of the *real* volume of money balances and the income velocity of money requires an examination of the demand for money.* It may be possible to explain the patterns exhibited by velocity through an analysis of the historical behavior of the explanatory variables that enter a stable demand-for-money function. Friedman's attempt to find variables in addition to income which enter the money demand function and which ". . . exert an influence opposite to that of income . . . sufficiently potent to dominate the (cyclical) movement of velocity"** is unsuccessful, however. As he reports,

> Our secular results render this implausible for we there found that income appeared to be the dominant variable affecting the demand for real cash balances. Moreover, the other variables that come first to mind are interest rates, and these display cyclical patterns that seem most unlikely to account for the sizable, highly consistent, and roughly synchronous cyclical pattern in velocity.***

As an alternative approach, suggested by his work on the consumption function, Friedman employs the concept of permanent income in the money demand function to reconcile the cyclical and secular behavior of velocity. This attempt starts by viewing " . . . the statistical magnitude called 'real income' as corresponding to a different theoretical construct in the cyclical than in the secular analysis."† This reconciliation depends on the relation between measured and permanent income. If permanent income rises less than measured income during cyclical expansions, and falls less than measured income in contractions, and if money balances are adapted to permanent income " . . . they might rise and fall more than in proportion to permanent income, as is required by our secular results, yet

---

*Following Fisher in employing the equation of exchange, Friedman often couches his analytical discussion in terms of the velocity of circulation of money rather than the demand function for money balances. But since $V = (Y/M)$, an increase in the demand for nominal balances relative to income will be reflected in a decrease in the income velocity of circulation of money and, conversely, a decrease in the demand for money will reflect an increase in velocity.

**Ibid.*, p. 332.

***Ibid.*, p. 332.

†*Ibid.*, p. 332.

less than in proportion to measured income, as is required by our cyclical results."*

On the basis of his theoretical reconciliation of the conflicting behavior of observed velocity, Friedman turns to an empirical examination of this phenomenon. For, as he notes, " . . . an interpretation in terms of interest rates can also rationalize the qualitative results; (but) we reject it because it appears likely to be contradicted on a more detailed quantitative level."**

In his empirical tests, Friedman measures both money balances and permanent income in real, i.e., deflated, per capita form and specifies the following exponential money demand function:

$$M/NP = \alpha(Y_p/NP)^\delta$$

or, in logarithmic form,

$$\ln(M/NP) = \ln\alpha + \delta \ln(Y_p/NP)$$

where, P is an index of (permanent) prices
       N is population, and
       Y_p is permanent income.***

Friedman fits this function to cycle-average data for the period 1869–1957. His estimate of δ, the permanent income elasticity of money balances, is 1.8. Using this relationship, he calculates annual, within-cycle projections of the velocity of circulation of money and finds that his formulation predicts actual velocity figures extremely well. Most importantly, however, he also finds that *the errors which are evident in these predictions are almost completely unrelated to the level of interest rates.* Thus, he concludes that there is little role for the interest rate, in addition to permanent income, in explaining variations in the velocity of circulation of money or the variation in money balances.

Friedman achieves these results by using some statistical techniques not generally used by other investigators. His use of cycle-average data,† for

Ibid., p. 334.

**Ibid.*, p. 335.

***Friedman originally derived his permanent income concept in connection with his studies on the consumption function. Permanent income is calculated as a weighted average of past income levels with the weights attached to the income levels of the more distant past declining geometrically. See Milton Friedman, *A Theory of the Consumption Function*, (Princeton: Princeton University Press 1957), pp. 142–147.

†An annual time-series of observations on a given variable, X, represents a list of

example, contrasts with the more common practice of using chronologically determined, annual or quarterly data in regression studies. Also, his use of the broad definition of money is claimed by many to bias his results against finding any role for the interest rate in the determination of money demand.

This contention may be explained as follows: if demand deposit balances are negatively related to interest rates, but time deposits are positively related to the rate paid on such deposits by commercial banks—a rate which generally follows market rates—a general increase in interest rates will decrease the demand for demand deposits and increase the demand for time deposits. If these two assets are added together in a single measure, these movements will tend to cancel out and the sum, $DD + TD$, may appear to be completely interest-inelastic.

Laidler (38) has pointed out that over the period covered by Friedman's study there was a slight downward trend in interest rates and that by omitting an interest rate term from his regression equation, some of the (trend) influence of the interest rate on money balances was attributed to the trend in the permanent income variable. It follows then that if money balances are negatively related to the rate of interest, the decline in rates over this period would cause a relative increase in money balances. However, without an interest rate term in the equation, this increase in money balances would be attributed to the increasing level of permanent income. This may help to explain the rather high (1.8) income elasticity derived from Friedman's tests.

Friedman's results have been even more seriously challenged in the work of other analysts. Let us review this other evidence briefly.

Several of the studies reported in Table 1 employ interest rates along with Friedman's permanent income measure in a log-linear money demand function. Meltzer (45), for example, employing the long term rate of interest, showed that this measure generally appears as a highly significant variable in his regressions. Similarly, Brunner and Meltzer (4) find that the interest rate plays an important role in the several alternative money demand (velocity) functions examined in their empirical work. In their words:

> ... the data suggest that interest rates enter significantly in the velocity equations and in the demand for money equations from

---

values for that variable for each year over a specified period of time. Cycle-average data on the other hand relies not on calendar years to generate observations, but rather on the cyclical swings in economic activity as defined by the National Bureau of Economic Research. Those who use cycle-average data argue that such a choice of values is economically more meaningful than the arbitrary designation of the calendar (or fiscal) year as the standard measure of time used to generate statistical data.

which the velocity equations are derived. Including interest rates as an additional variable in Friedman's permanent income model improves the prediction of measured velocity from the model.*

The results obtained by Chow (10) and Laidler (38) reported in Table 1 lend further support to this interpretation of the available data.

This evidence also casts suspicion on the high permanent income elasticity of money balances indicated in Friedman's results. Meltzer claims that Friedman's use of the permanent income measure combines the influence of income, wealth and interest rates into a single measure. He shows that when the money demand function is specified to include the interest rate as a separate variable, the (permanent) income elasticity is closer to unity than to Friedman's estimate of 1.8. He reports that he can find " . . . almost no evidence of diseconomies of scale which approach in magnitude those which Friedman has suggested."**

One important point with respect to these studies must be mentioned in defense of Professor Friedman. The studies by Brunner and Meltzer and Chow use annual time series data and these data are not strictly comparable

---

*Karl Brunner and Allan H. Meltzer, "Predicting Velocity: Implications for Theory and Policy," *Journal of Finance*, 18 (May 1963) p. 350.

**Friedman's estimate of 1.8 for the permanent income elasticity of money balances may be interpreted as suggesting the existence of diseconomies of scale in holding money. It suggests that as permanent income rises, desired money balances increase by a more than proportionate amount. This assertion contrasts sharply with the conclusions of William Baumol (2) and James Tobin (58). In their theories, rational behavior implies the possibility of substantial economies of scale in the demand for money by business firms.

As you will recall from chapter 3, Baumol's model for the minimization of the cost of holding cash balances leads to the familiar square root inventory formula:

$$\frac{C}{2} = \frac{1}{2} \sqrt{\frac{2bT}{i}}$$

where, $C/2$ is the average volume of transactions balances demanded
        T is the volume of transactions
        b represents the costs of switching from bonds to money, and
        i is the rate of interest on bonds.

The income (transactions) elasticity of cash balances in this formula is 1/2.

The evidence presented by Meltzer (45, 46) which fails to support Friedman's assertion also casts doubt on the Baumol-Tobin theses. In addition, Brunner and Meltzer (6) have shown that "Neither the Baumol nor the Tobin formulations are inconsistent with the quantity theory of money . . . as a first approximation to the cross-section demand for money by business firms" (p. 423). They demonstrate that in an extended and more general form of the Baumol model, the elasticity of money balances with respect to transactions volume approaches unity for large values of T. As we have shown above, that is the value suggested by the quantity theory.

to Friedman's (perhaps more subtle) cycle-average data. Consequently, their results do not represent a satisfactory refutation of his findings. However, David Laidler (38), employing cycle-average data for the period 1891-1957, refitted Friedman's original equation and compared the results with those obtained when an interest rate term was included in the equation. (Laidler employs a short-term rate of interest in these tests.) His results are reported below:

$$\log (M/NP) = -2.017 + 1.618 \log (Y_p/NP) \tag{5}$$

$$\log (M/NP) = -1.403 + 1.430 \log (Y_p/NP) - .158 \log i_e \tag{6}$$

where i_e is the rate on 4–6 month commercial paper.

Laidler then used these estimates to predict annual levels of per capita real money balances—a procedure very similar to Friedman's use of his equation to predict annual, within-cycle values for the velocity of circulation of money. The mean error of prediction* for the equation which includes the interest rate is less than half that for the equation which contains only permanent income. Since the interest rate equation explains the data significantly better than Friedman's original equation, Laidler concludes that " . . . the difference in the intercept and coefficient of the logarithm of permanent income that results from the omission of the interest rate is sufficient to produce misleading results (about the relation between prediction errors and the level of the rate of interest)." It appears that there was indeed " . . . some secular (long term) correlation between permanent income and interest rates which caused permanent income to pick up part of the effect of interest rates in the regression from which the latter variable was omitted."** The decrease in the estimate of the coefficient of permanent income that occurs when interest rates are included in Laidler's regression on cycle-average data lends some support to the similar finding by Meltzer reported above.

As Laidler points out, then, the evidence coming from so many different sources is so persuasive that "it is probably safe to conclude that the rate of interest must be included in the demand function for money."*** Professor Friedman's results may be attributed in large part to his rather special statistical technique.

*The mean error of prediction is the arithmetic average of the absolute value of *f* the difference between the actual and predicted values of a given variable for all points for which a prediction is obtained.

**David Laidler, "The Rate of Interest and the Demand for Money-Some Empirical Evidence," *Journal of Political Economy*, 74 (December 1966), p. 546.

***Ibid., p. 546.

INTEREST ELASTICITY AND THE LIQUIDITY TRAP

The evidence reviewed above clearly supports the Keynesian notion of an interest sensitive demand for money or liquidity preference function. However, as noted in chapter 4, Keynes went further than merely to posit the interest rate as a determinant of the public's demand for money. In *The General Theory*, he also speculated briefly about the shape of the liquidity preference function. Specifically, he noted that

> There is the possibility . . . , that, after the rate of interest has fallen to a certain level, liquidity preference may become virtually absolute in the sense that almost everyone prefers cash to holding a debt which yields so low a rate of interest. In this event the monetary authority would have lost effective control over the rate of interest. But while this limiting case might become practically important in the future, I know of no example of it hitherto.*

In spite of Keynes' disclaimer, his suggestion that the liquidity preference curve *may* become perfectly interest elastic at some low level of the interest rate, attracted much attention and stimulated a moderate amount of "searching" for this phenomenon. His suggestion is also responsible for the shape given the liquidity preference curve in most texts (as shown in Figure 1).

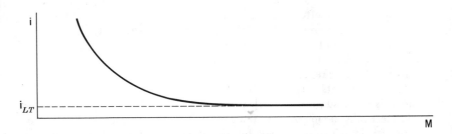

Figure 1.

The implication of this hypothesis, which is eminently suitable for empirical testing, is that the interest elasticity of the liquidity preference function should be found to increase as the interest rate declines. This proposition has been tested by Bronfenbrenner and Mayer (3), by Meltzer (45), by David Laidler (38), by Konstas and Khouja (35) and by others.

*J.M. Keynes, *The General Theory of Employment, Interest, and Money*, (London and New York 1936), p. 207.

Bronfenbrenner and Mayer, after examining the relation between the short-term interest rate and the Cambridge k, (M/Y), tested to see if the elasticity of their estimated liquidity functions increased as the interest rate fell. Specifically, they calculated the "rank" correlation coefficient between elasticities and the level of interest rates. This involves ordering the level of interest rates from highest to lowest and comparing the ordering of the elasticities associated with those rates. If the highest rate was associated with the lowest elasticity, the lowest rate with the highest elasticity and so on for all rates in between, there would be perfect negative rank correlation between these two measures. Bronfenbrenner and Mayer calculate a coefficient of +.16 which is not only not statistically significant, but is of the wrong sign. They conclude: "This does not mean, of course, that the liquidity schedule could never become completely elastic even at a zero interest rate. However, the absence of a negative correlation in a period when interest rates were at times quite low, casts doubt on, if not the truth, then at least the relevance of the liquidity trap proposition . . ."*

Other investigators have supported these conclusions. In 1963, Meltzer (45) fitted velocity functions (the dependent variable in his relations was $V_1 = Y'/M1$, where Y' defines an income measure: $Y' = r \cdot W$)** for the six decades from 1900 to 1958. His results deny that the interest elasticity of the demand for money increased during periods of low interest rates such as the 1930's. As he notes, "The data deny that the interest elasticity of the demand for money or velocity became exceptionally large during that decade (the 1930's). Indeed, the interest elasticity of V_1 was slightly below the average for the (entire) fifty-nine years."*** This evidence of a lower than average interest elasticity during periods of low interest rates is perfectly consistent with Bronfenbrenner and Mayer's positive rank-correlation coefficient.

Meltzer's work with Karl Brunner (4) adds additional support to this position. Using estimates derived from data for the 1930's, they were able to predict the velocity of circulation for the 1950's with sufficiently small mean errors to conclude that the velocity function remained highly stable over these periods of differing interest rate levels. They conclude that " . . . the liquidity trap proposition is denied by the evidence."†

David Laidler (38) has reported evidence from a test somewhat similar

---

*M. Bronfenbrenner and T. Mayer, "Liquidity Functions in the American Economy," *Econometrica*, 28 (October 1960), p. 831.

**For the purpose of these tests Meltzer defines income as the return on wealth, i.e., the interest rate or rate of return, r, times the wealth stock, W. The wealth measure used to calculate income in this formula is net non-human wealth of the public—the same variable employed in his money demand functions. $M1$ is the customary measure of money balances ($DD + C$).

***Meltzer, *op. cit.*, p. 243.

†Brunner and Meltzer, *op. cit.*, p. 350.

to Bronfenbrenner and Mayer's. Employing both the narrow $(M1)$ and the broad $(M2)$ definitions of money and testing both the long-rate and the short-rate of interest in separate regressions, Laidler divided the observations for the period 1892–1960 into two subsets: those years in which the relevant interest rate was above the mean and those in which it was below the mean. The general equation tested was:

$$\log_e M = a + b_1 \log_e Y_p + b_2 \log_e i$$

where M was either narrowly or broadly defined, i was defined as either the short-term rate or the long-term rate and Y_p is permanent income. Laidler's results, using both logarithms and first differences of the logarithms of the variables defined above demonstrated very little tendency for the interest elasticity (b_2) to be higher for the low interest rate observations than it was in the equations fitted to the high interest rate observations. As he notes, " . . . the elasticity with respect to the short rate seems to fall a little at low rates of interest, though the elasticity with respect to the long rate rises slightly at low interest rates. . . . Thus, the hypothesis of the liquidity trap, as it is usually presented, appears to be refuted."*

An interesting article by Konstas and Khouja reports on statistical tests relevant to this issue. In their study, the authors attempt to specify a functional form for the demand for money relation which accurately portrays the characteristics originally suggested by Keynes.** In their model

> The transactions demand for money is taken to be a homogeneous linear function of observed income (Y), i.e., (1) $M1 = \gamma Y$, $\gamma > 0$, which implies unitary elasticity of $M1$ with respect to Y. In regard to the speculative part of the demand for money, however, we believe that the function which is consistent with Keynesian requirements must be stated in the following manner:
>
> $$M2 = \frac{\beta}{r - \alpha}; \quad \beta > 0, \quad \alpha > 0$$
>
> . . . The relevant properties of this function are: (a) As r falls, the quantity of idle balances demanded $M2$ rises and, in accordance with

---

*Laidler, "The Rate of Interest . . . ." *op. cit.*, p. 550.

**For another study that claims to formulate and test Keynes' original liquidity preference hypothesis more accurately than is done in some of the literature cited above, see Dennis R. Starleaf and Richard Reimer, "The Keynesian Demand Function for Money: Some Statistical Tests," *Journal of Finance*, 22 (March 1967), pp. 71–76.

the liquidity trap hypothesis, as r approaches α, M_2 approaches infinity. (b) The elasticity Ei of M_2 with respect to r,

$$Ei = \frac{\partial M_2}{\partial r} \cdot \frac{r}{M_2} = -\frac{\beta}{(r-\alpha)^2} \cdot \frac{r}{\beta/(r-\alpha)} = \frac{r}{r-\alpha},$$

is inversely related to r.*

This formulation quite accurately reflects the properties of the function shown diagrammatically in Figure 1. In particular, it allows for a minimum interest rate level, α, and increasing interest elasticity of money balances as interest rates decline. The authors estimate the parameters of this model using annual observations for the period 1919–1965. In general the data seem to fit this relationship rather closely.

Konstas and Khouja use their estimated relation to examine the claim that the U.S. economy was in a liquidity trap in the 1930's. Specifically, they calculate an estimate of the speculative component of total money balances by subtracting estimated transactions balances from (actual) total money balances for each of the years 1919–1965. The pattern indicated in the relation between the long-term interest rate and calculated idle balances fails to confirm the claim that monetary policy was impotent in the 1930's because of the very high interest elasticity of the demand for money. They conclude that their test " . . . does not seem to offer much evidence in support of this claim."** Although this is not a direct test of the liquidity trap hypothesis, these results are consistent with those reported by most other analysts and adds to the weight of the evidence reported above.

Most of the individual tests cited in this section approach the question of the liquidity trap indirectly. Furthermore, some of the results of Laidler's tests with the long-term rate of interest could be taken as very weak support for the existence of the low level trap. However, the weight of all these studies together seems sufficient to allow a rather firm judgment against the historical existence of the liquidity trap. In addition, recent work by Brunner and Meltzer*** has shown that the necessary and sufficient conditions for the occurrence of a liquidity trap in the demand function for money are extremely restrictive. Consequently, our conclusion on the absence of a liquidity trap would seem warranted by the absence of any falsifying evidence.

*Konstas, Panos, and Mohamad W. Khouja, "The Keynesian Demand-for-Money Function," *Journal of Money, Credit and Banking* 1 (November 1969), pp. 766–767.

**Ibid., p. 774.

***Karl Brunner and Allan H. Meltzer, "Liquidity Traps for Money, Bank Credit, and Interest Rates," *Journal of Political Economy*, 76 (February 1968) 1–37.

ALTERNATIVE INTEREST RATE MEASURES IN THE EMPIRICAL MONEY DEMAND EQUATION

While it is generally accepted that "an" interest rate should appear in the demand for money function, there is little agreement as to which empirical measure should be used to represent that rate. Much of the available evidence that attempts to determine which rate best explains the demand for money is inconsistent. Furthermore, since the various tests employ data from different time periods, specify different dependent variables, and often include dissimilar constraints within the function, comparisons among these empirical studies must remain rather tenuous.

The problem may stem partly from the fact that the theoretical work available provides little guidance on this issue. Some writers, like Brunner and Meltzer, argue that the demand for money should be treated within the broad theory of portfolio selection, and suggest that this demand depends on the yield on equities as well as on bonds. Others, like Bronfenbrenner and Mayer (3), Laidler (37, 38), and Heller (28), argue that some short-term interest rate is the more relevant determinant since it measures the opportunity cost of holding money as the rate of return on what they consider to be money's closest substitutes. Still others, including Gurley and Shaw, emphasize the liquidity of money and the minimal risks associated with changes in its nominal value. They argue that the closest substitutes for money are assets with similar characteristics, such as the liabilities of financial intermediaries, e.g., savings and loan associations, and that it is the rates on these assets which are most relevant to the money demand function.*

One attempt to present direct evidence on this issue was made by Heller in 1965 (28). In alternative money demand equations, Heller compared the performance of the long-term rate of interest as measured by the rate on U. S. government bonds with that of a short-term rate, measured as the yield on 60–90 day commercial paper. Regression coefficients were estimated for equations in log-linear form using quarterly observations for the period 1947–1958. Both $M1$ (money, narrowly defined) and $M2$ (money, broadly defined) were tried as dependent variables with the interest rate and current income or non-human wealth specified as alternative constraints. In these regressions, the long-term rate of interest *never* appeared as a statistically important explanatory variable,** while the short-term rate was important in all equations but one. Consequently, Heller con-

---

*See the first section of this article for some implications of this view.

**The long-term rate was never significant at the 5% level and in some of the equations it even appeared with the wrong sign.

cluded that

> The short-term rate is of greater importance (than the long-term rate) in the money function. The closest substitute for money available, a 60 to 90 day commercial paper, is most influential in deciding whether to hold assets in the form of money or not. Long-term interest rates do not influence the quantity of money demanded . . .*

The results of a much more extensive test which support Heller's general conclusions were reported by David Laidler (38) in 1966. Laidler's basic test involves the examination of evidence derived from equations fit to annual data for the period 1892-1960, and sub-periods therein. He bases his analysis on the following proposition:

> Given that the interest rate is an important variable in the demand function for money, and that movements of various interest rates are related to one another, one would expect almost any rate chosen at random to show some relationship to cash balances. . . . however, though all interest rates are interrelated there is no reason to suppose that the nature of their interrelationship remains unchanged for all time. Thus, if the demand function for money is stable, one would expect the "right" interest rate to show the same relationship to the demand for money in different time periods while the "wrong" one need not.**

Laidler uses the rate on 4–6 month commercial paper and the yield on twenty year bonds as his alternative interest rate measures. His equations are in log-linear form and include only permanent income as an additional explanatory variable. When his dependent variable is $M2$, he claims that "there is little question of the superior explanatory power of the shorter interest rate."*** The short rate consistently explains more of the variation in the dependent variable than does the long rate, and its coefficient is highly stable in all the sub-period regressions.

When the dependent variable is specified as $M1$ in Laidler's tests, his results are somewhat contradictory. When he employs levels of the logarithms of the variables, the long-term rate explains more of the variation in $M1$ for most periods than does the short rate. Nonetheless, he maintains his original conclusion that a short-term rate is the relevant rate measure in

---

*H.R. Heller, "The Demand for Money—The Evidence from the Short-Run Data," *Quarterly Journal of Economics,* 79 (May 1965) p. 297.

**Laidler, "The Rate of Interest . . . , " *op. cit.,* p. 547.

****Ibid.,* p. 547.

the money demand function. He argues that "... the contradictory conclusions obtained with the narrower definition reflect only the fact that that definition is an unsatisfactory one."* The basis for his conclusion on this matter is to be found in our comments on his previous work (37), reported in the first section of this survey.

The conclusions derived from this work by Heller and Laidler are challenged by Michael Hamburger. In his study of the demand for money by households, Hamburger (26) concludes that long-term interest rates are the relevant determinants of the demand for money. Employing a model which includes distributed lags to measure the rate of adjustment of households to changed market conditions, he finds that in the household demand for money function "... for short-run analysis (of the household money demand function), it is useful to include two yields—one on debts and one on equities—and that the elasticities of the demand for money are approximately the same with respect to both of these rates."** His findings show that government bills (short-term securities) may be *poorer* substitutes for money for the household sector than longer-term securities.

These results are in direct contrast to Heller's findings reported above. Hamburger claims that Heller's conclusions depend on his choice of time period. During the 1947–1951 period included within the time series employed by Heller, the Federal Reserve pegged interest rates. When Hamburger re-runs Heller's regressions excluding these years, he find that the long-term rate and the short-term rate appear equally important.

Additional evidence has been reported by T. H. Lee (42). Lee criticizes the previous work done by the cited authors because they restrict their comparisons to only two alternative rate measures. Furthermore, he believes that the *differentials* between interest rates and the yield on money, rather than simply interest rate *levels*, are the relevant measures that should appear in money demand functions.

Like Laidler, Lee specifies a Friedman-type permanent income money demand model as the basic framework for his tests. He tries both $M1$ and $M2$ as dependent variables and, in addition to his alternative interest rate measures, either permanent income or permanent income and lagged money balances as explanatory variables. His regression estimates show "... the yield on nonbank intermediary liabilities is the most significant interest rate variable in affirming the demand for money." Specifically "... the yield on savings and loan shares performs the best in terms of R^2 among respective regressions of static or dynamic formulations."*** Fur-

---

Ibid., p. 553.

**The rates he used were Moody's Aaa rate on long-term corporate bonds and Moody's dividend yield. M.J. Hamburger, "The Demand for Money by Households ... ," *Journal of Political Economy*, 74 (December 1966), p. 608.

***T.H. Lee, "Alternative Interest Rates and the Demand for Money: the Empirical Evidence," *American Economic Review*, 57 (December 1967), p. 1171.

thermore, while the closest substitutes for money are savings and loan shares, time deposits at commercial banks appear to be only modest substitutes for money.

The tentative nature of these conclusions should not be evident. While Heller and Laidler argue that the short-term rate is the relevant interest rate measure in the money demand function, this conclusion is challenged by both Hamburger and Lee. Lee's results further indicate that it may be the differential between the yield on money (defined as $M1$ or $M2$) and the yield on the liabilities of some financial intermediary rather than a market interest rate which is the most appropriate constraint on desired money balances. But Lee's conclusions on the substitutability between money and time deposits conflicts with Chetty's findings surveyed in the first part of this paper. Additional work in which a serious attempt is made to make new results comparable to the results of previous investigators will be required before any firm conclusions are possible on this critical empirical issue.

OTHER VARIABLES IN THE DEMAND-FOR–MONEY FUNCTION

The results surveyed above lead us to observe that the performance of any given interest rate measure in an empirical money demand function depends on the definition of money (the dependent variable) as well as on the choice of other explanatory variables included in the equation. Throughout this paper, we have mentioned variables besides the interest rate which were included in the empirical money demand equations. We must now examine the relative importance of these other variables in determining the public's demand for money balances.

In addition to the interest rate, the other variables generally specified in theoretical money demand functions are income and wealth. The use of income as a constraint on the volume of money balances demanded is generally related to the role of money as a medium of exchange. This is stated explicitly in the Keynesian demand function, $M_d = L_1 (Y) + L_2 (i)$ presented in chapter 4 and in the Cambridge equation, $M = kY$, discussed in chapter 5. In these formulations, a part or all of money demand is viewed as a linear function of income or the volume of transactions.

On the other hand, when the role of money as a productive asset or a durable consumer good is stressed, a wealth measure is generally proposed as the relevant explanatory variable in the demand-for-money function. In this view, attention is focussed on ". . . the equilibrium of the balance sheet, the allocation of assets, and the services that money provides."[*]

*Meltzer, *op. cit.*, p. 232.

And as stressed in our discussion of Professor Friedman's theory of the demand for money in chapter 5, "Effecting a volume of transactions is but one of these services."*

Wealth or income, which is the more relevant variable in the money demand function? Let us summarize the evidence available on this important issue by surveying those works which are similar, except for their specification of the wealth or income constraint.

Three measures may be considered: current income, proposed as a proxy for the volume of transactions to be effected by the money stock; non-human wealth, measured as consolidated net worth in the balance sheets of the public; and permanent income, proposed as a proxy for a wealth concept that includes the present value of future labor income as well as the value of real physical assets. This last measure, originally derived by Friedman, includes the value of both human and non-human wealth.**

Meltzer (45) tests all three of these variables in log-linear equations which specify both $M1$ and $M2$ as dependent variables and include the yield on corporate bonds as the measure of the interest rate. Meltzer's basic model proposes non-human wealth (W) as the relevant constraint on money demand. He finds the elasticity of "narrow" money $(M1)$ with respect to this measure of wealth to be close to unity. This contrasts with Friedman's finding of an elasticity of "broad" money balances with respect to permanent income ("total" wealth) of 1.8.

Meltzer attempts to reconcile these results. His findings, which are confirmed by those of Laidler (reported earlier), suggest that Friedman's use of "broad" money as the dependent variable in his equation and the absence of an interest rate term from that equation are responsible for his very high estimate of this parameter. Thus, Meltzer contends that it is time deposits which are highly elastic with respect to wealth, and that by including these deposits in his measure of "money," Friedman has overstated the wealth elasticity of money defined as $(DD + C)$. More importantly, Meltzer claims that his measure of non-human wealth*** produces

---

Ibid., p. 232.

**Permanent income may be interpreted as " . . . reflecting the effect of those factors that the unit regards as determining its capital value or wealth: the nonhuman wealth it owns; the personal attributes of the earners in the unit, such as their training, ability, personality; the attributes of the economic activity of the earners, such as the occupation followed, the location of the economic activity, and so on. It is analogous to the "expected" value of a probability distribution." Milton Friedman, *A Theory of the Consumption Function* (Princeton 1957), p. 21.

***Meltzer's basic "wealth" definition includes "Total Wealth" as estimated by Goldsmith, adjusted to exclude government securities, inventories, public land, and the monetary gold and silver stock, and to include the monetary and non-monetary debt of state, local, and federal governments. R. W. Goldsmith, *A Study of Savings in the United States* (Princeton 1956).

an empirical money demand function which explains a slightly higher proportion of the variance of money balances (defined as $M1$ or $M2$) than does Friedman's permanent income measure.

Meltzer also finds his wealth measure "superior" to current income in the empirical demand-for-money function. For, when both wealth and income are included in the equation, the income variable appears to play no significant role in explaining the variation in money balances, whereas the wealth variable maintains approximately the same size coefficient (and significance) in all tests. Thus, Meltzer concludes that a non-human wealth measure is slightly superior to Friedman's permanent income variable and far more important than current, measured income in explaining variations in the demand for money.

These results are supported in further tests carried out by Brunner and Meltzer (4). Their experiments involved comparisons of the predictions of measured velocity made by various formulations of the money demand function. In their words

> . . . the tests sharply discriminate between the effects of income and wealth on the demand for money. . . . income appears to play a much smaller role than wealth as a determinant of desired money balances. The evidence from a number of Keynesian type equations that take income as a constraint and ignore the effect of wealth suggests that, in general, such equations will not predict velocity or desired money balances as well as a "naive" model.*

Their tests on human versus non-human wealth measures as explanatory variables in the money demand function yield less certain results. They conclude that the relative importance of these two measures remains an "open question" in their work.

Further evidence has been put forward by Heller (28), Laidler (37), and Chow (10). Employing quarterly data for the postwar period, Heller calculates the regression coefficient for six alternative relations. Both $M1$ and $M2$ are specified as dependent variables in equations that include income and the short-term rate of interest, wealth and the short-term rate, or both income and wealth and the short-term rate as explanatory variables. The coefficients of both GNP and wealth are statistically significant in all equations in which only one of these variables appears with the short-term interest rate. However, when both of these constraints are included in the same equation, only one of them retains its significance: GNP in the $M1$ equation and wealth in the $M2$ equation.

Heller attributes this result to the fact that time deposits (included in

---

*Brunner and Meltzer, *op. cit.*, p. 350. The "naive" model referred to by the authors is a model which assumes that velocity in any one year will be the same as actual velocity in the previous period.

the $M2$ measure), are related positively to wealth and negatively to income. A negative income coefficient results when time deposits are regressed against both income and wealth in a single equation. This indicates a substitution effect between time deposits and demand deposits: i.e., with wealth constant, an increase in GNP will cause a fall in the volume of time deposits and a rise in the quantity of currency and demand deposits. Heller interprets this evidence as showing that time deposits and demand deposits are demanded for different reasons: ". . . the transactions motives for cash and demand deposits and the speculative or precautionary motive for time deposits."*

Assume, for the moment, the importance of measured income as a relevant argument in explaining the transactions demand for cash. In chapter 3 we mentioned the possibility of economies of scale in the transactions demand function. Unfortunately the work of Meltzer (45), Whalen (64) and others gives little support to this hypothesis.

An important test of the importance of measured income, permanent income, or wealth in the money demand function was performed by Laidler. He set out to compare the explanatory power of four alternative money demand hypotheses. These include: (1) the textbook equation with current income and an interest rate as constraints; (2) a Friedman-type permanent income formulation; (3) a model that includes permanent income as a proxy for the volume of transactions, and a measure of accumulated transitory income and negative transitory consumption to account for the allocation of funds from these sources to money balances; and (4) a model which includes the last factor specified above and a non-human wealth measure defined as accumulated savings out of permanent income.

Implicit in his tests of these hypotheses is a comparison of the explanatory power of current income, permanent income, and his indirect measure of non-human wealth (accumulated savings out of Y_p) as explanatory variables in the money demand function. From his regressions, which employ first differences of annual observations, Laidler finds that "Though the results are not absolutely decisive, they strongly suggest that permanent income provides a better theory of the demand for money than does either non-human wealth or any other set of variables tested."**

Specifically, the third hypothesis, which includes a measure of transitory income in the money demand equation, performs the least satisfactorily over the period covered by his data. Although both the non-human wealth (4) and the permanent income (2) hypotheses explain the variation in the dependent variable quite satisfactorily, Laidler judges the results with permanent income to be marginally superior. More importantly, both

---

*Heller, *op. cit.*, p. 300.

**David Laidler, "Some Evidence on the Demand for Money," *Journal of Political Economy*, 74 (February 1966), p. 63.

wealth and permanent income explain more of the variation in the dependent variable than does current income. Furthermore, this last finding obtains regardless of the definition of money employed. Thus, using annual data rather than quarterly figures, Laidler challenges Heller's assertion that current income is the relevant constraint on money balances when these balances are defined as $M1$.

A very interesting set of experiments performed by Chow may shed some light on the inconsistencies in these results. Chow attempts to isolate two different sets of factors not generally specified by other investigators: those which determine the long-run equilibrium demand for money and those which influence the rate at which people will make short-run adjustments to restore equilibrium. These adjustments take place when a discrepancy exists between the long-run *desired* level of money balances and *actual* money holdings.

Chow reasons that money may be treated as a consumer durable good. He applies to the analysis of the demand for money, a model originally developed to explain the demand for automobiles. In this model, the long-run demand for money is posited to depend on some measure of the individual's total assets (a wealth measure) and the opportunity cost of holding those balances, the interest rate. The short-run demand for money, however, will depend on the rate at which individuals try to adjust their actual money balances to this long-run desired level. This speed of adjustment in turn depends on the actual size of any discrepancy between actual and desired balances and the rate of change of the individual's total assets (or the rate of savings)—the source from which money balances may be accumulated. Chow summarizes these factors as follows:

> . . . three sets of factors govern the demand for money. The first set is derived from considering the demand for services from holding money in the long-run. The second is due to time lags in the adjustment of demand to equilibrium. The third is from treating the change in the money stock as a part of saving.*

Chow tests his hypothesis by fitting annual data for the period 1897–1958. In the long-run equilibrium demand function, permanent income always performs far better than current income but, as in Laidler's work, only marginally better than a wealth measure.** However, in the short-run functions which attempt to measure the speed of adjustment to equilibrium, current income is preferable to either wealth or permanent income.

A word of caution is in order in interpreting these results. Since perma-

---

*Gregory Chow, "On the Long-Run and Short-Run Demand for Money," *Journal of Political Economy*, 74 (April 1966), p. 115.

**Chow uses the same measure of net non-human wealth as was employed by Meltzer.

nent income is calculated as a weighted average of past levels of measured income, we may write the long-run demand for money function in linear form as follows (ignoring interest rates):

$$\left(\frac{M_d}{P}\right)_T = f(Y_P) = b(Y_P)_T = b\left[\beta_0 Y_T + \beta_1 Y_{T-1} \ldots \beta_n Y_{T-n}\right]$$

Assuming the weights, β_i, follow a geometrically declining lag function (following Friedman), we may write

$$\left(\frac{M_d}{P}\right)_T = b\left[\beta_o Y_T + \beta_o(1 - \beta_o)Y_{T-1}\right.$$

$$\left. + \beta_o(1 - \beta_o)^2 Y_{T-2} \ldots \beta_o(1 - \beta_o)^n Y_{T-n}\right]$$

But if $(1 - \beta_o)^j \longrightarrow 0$ as $j \longrightarrow n$, by a Koyck Transformation,* this can be shown equivalent to

$$\left(\frac{M_d}{P}\right)_T = (1 - \beta_o)\left(\frac{M_d}{P}\right)_{T-1} + b\beta_o Y_T$$

On the other hand, if we posit that the public only partially adjusts their current money holdings to the desired level and that this level depends on current measured income, we would write the following relation:

$$\left(\frac{M}{P}\right)_T - \left(\frac{M}{P}\right)_{T-1} = \lambda\left[\left(\frac{M}{P}\right)^*_T - \left(\frac{M}{P}\right)_{T-1}\right]$$

where $\left(\frac{M}{P}\right)^*_T$ is the desired level of money balances and

$$\left(\frac{M}{P}\right)^*_T = a\, Y_T$$

Substituting

$$\left(\frac{M}{P}\right)_T - \left(\frac{M}{P}\right)_{T-1} = \lambda\left[a\, Y_T - \left(\frac{M}{P}\right)_{T-1}\right]$$

$$\left(\frac{M}{P}\right)_T = (1 - \lambda)\left(\frac{M}{P}\right)_{T-1} + \lambda a\, Y_T$$

*See Wonnacott, Ronald J., and Thomas H. Wonnacott, *Econometrics.* (New York: John Wiley & Sons, Inc., 1970), pp. 145-146.

But this form, derived from a partial adjustment model in which desired money balances depend on current measured income, is indistinguishable from the model above which postulates that the demand for money depends on permanent income.

These relationships make unique interpretation of Chow's results impossible. They suggest that in his short-run adjustment relation, from which he concludes that current income is the appropriate explanatory variable in the demand for money function, he may simply have been measuring an equilibrium relation between desired money balances and permanent income. In short, this test is not sufficient to distinguish between a permanent income hypothesis and the hypothesis that the demand for money balances depends on current measured income but that the public is slow to adjust to its long-run desired level.

However, if there is any validity to his results, they suggest a possible reconciliation of the conflict between those obtained by Heller using quarterly data and those presented by Laidler based on annual data. Heller's method may have picked up the influence of short-run adjustment factors which dominate the quarterly figures, but are less important in the longer-run annual observations.

In summary, the bulk of the evidence available on this issue seems to indicate clearly that some measure of wealth rather than measured income is the most relevant constraint on the *equilibrium level* of the demand for money balances. Whether this constraint is best represented by a permanent income measure which purports to include a human wealth component, or by a non-human wealth measure, such as that employed by Chow and Meltzer, is much less apparent.* However, this evidence does indicate that current income may be related to the demand for money through short-run adjustments made to bring *actual* money balances in line with *desired* money holdings.

CONCLUDING COMMENTS

The first, and perhaps most important finding reported by almost all of the empirical works surveyed is that the interest rate plays a significant role in the determination of the public's demand for money. Furthermore, the range of estimates for the interest elasticity of money balances has been fairly narrowly circumscribed, with the best results suggesting an elasticity of about -0.1 to -0.2 for the short rate, and approximately -0.7 with respect to the long rate.

Secondly, studies generally conclude that there is no empirical basis for

---

*Both of these measures involve statistical difficulties, and are very difficult to interpret.

the liquidity trap hypothesis: the proposition that the demand for money function becomes infinitely elastic at some low level of interest rates.

Thirdly, it is not yet possible to state confidently which particular interest rate measure is the relevant constraint on money balances. Moreover, this question is so intimately connected with the problem of the "correct" definition of money to be used in these studies, that until additional results are reported, we feel that a judgment on these matters must be suspended.

Finally, the best evidence to date suggests that, in addition to an interest rate measure, some measure of wealth—either a direct balance sheet measure or a proxy variable such as permanent income—would seem to be most relevant to the public's long-run decision to hold money balances. Wealth measures seem superior to current income measures. However, some evidence suggests that short-run movements in money balances, determined by the speed at which people adjust their actual money holdings to the long-run equilibrium level, may well be dependent on the flow of current money income.

The conclusions stated above rest primarily on the evidence cited in this study. Other important works, most of which are cited in the bibliography, could have been referenced to support some of these conclusions. The studies we chose to review were selected because of their historical importance in the debate on the issues to which we have directed our attention or because we believe that they represent the best starting point for students of these problems. In short, no claim is made that this survey represents an exhaustive review of all the literature in this field.

Some of the policy implications of these conclusions will be analyzed in chapters 6 through 9.

Bibliography / *the evidence on the demand for money*

1. Barro, Robert J., "Inflation, the Payments Period, and the Demand for Money," *Journal of Political Economy*, 78 (November/December 1970), pp. 1228–1263.
2. Baumol, W., "The Transactions Demand for Cash: An Inventory Theoretic Approach," *The Quarterly Journal of Economics*, 66 (November 1952).
3. Bronfenbrenner, Martin, and Thomas Mayer, "Liquidity Functions in the American Economy," *Econometrica*, 28 (October 1960), pp. 810–834.
4. Brunner, Karl, and Allan H. Meltzer, "Predicting Velocity: Implications for Theory and Policy," *Journal of Finance*, 18 (May 1963), pp. 319–354.
5. _____, "Some Further Evidence on Supply and Demand Functions for Money," *Journal of Finance*, 19 (May 1964), pp. 240–283.
6. _____, "Economics of Scale in Cash Balances Reconsidered," *Quarterly Journal of Economics*, 81 (August 1967), pp. 422–436.
7. _____, "Liquidity Traps for Money, Bank Credit, and Interest Rates," *Journal of Political Economy*, 76 (February 1968), pp. 1–37.
8. _____, "Comment on the Long-Run and Short-Run Demand for Money," *Journal of Political Economy*, 76 (November/December 1968), pp. 1234–1239.
9. Chetty, V. K., "On Measuring the Nearness of Near-Moneys," *American Economic Review*, 59 (June 1969), pp. 270–281.

10. Chow, Gregory, "On the Short-Run and Long-Run Demand for Money," *Journal of Political Economy*, 74 (April 1966), pp. 111–131.

11. _____, "Long-Run and Short-Run Demand for Money: Reply and Further Notes," *Journal of Political Economy*, 76 (November/December 1968), pp. 1240–1243.

12. Courchene, Thomas J., and Alex K. Kelly, "Money Supply and Money Demand: An Econometric Analysis for Canada," *Journal of Money, Credit and Banking*, 3 (May 1971), pp. 219–244.

13. Eisner, Robert, "Another Look at Liquidity Preference," *Econometrica*, 31 (July 1963), pp. 531–538.

14. Feige, Edgar, *The Demand for Liquid Assets: A Temporal Cross Section Analysis*. Englewood Cliffs Company, 1964.

15. _____, "Expectations and Adjustments in the Monetary Sector," *American Economic Review*, 57 (May 1967), pp. 462–473.

16. Fisher, Douglas, "Real Balances and the Demand for Money," *Journal of Political Economy* 78 (November/December 1970), pp. 1340–1354.

17. Friedman, Milton, *A Theory of the Consumption Function*.Princeton: Princeton University Press, 1957.

18. _____, "The Quantity Theory of Money, A Restatement," in Milton Friedman (ed.), *Studies in the Quantity Theory of Money*.Chicago: 1956.

19. _____, "The Demand for Money–Some Theoretical and Empirical Results," *Journal of Political Economy*, 67 (June 1959), pp. 327–351.

20. _____, and Anna J. Schwartz, *A Monetary History of the United States, 1867–1960*. Princeton: National Bureau of Economic Research, 1963.

21. _____, and David Meiselman, "Relative Stability of Monetary Velocity and the Investment Multiplier in the United States 1897–1957," Commission on Money and Credit, *Stabilization Policies*, Englewood Cliffs, 1963.

22. Galper, Harvey, "Alternative Interest Rates and the Demand for Money: Comment," *American Economic Review*, 59 (June 1969), pp. 401–407.

23. Griliches, Zvi., "Distributed Lags: A Survey," *Econometrica*, 35 (January 1967), pp. 16–49.

24. Goldfeld, Stephen, *Commercial Bank Behavior and Economic Activity*. Amsterdam: North-Holland Publishing Company, 1966.

25. Gurley, John, and Edward Shaw, *Money in a Theory of Finance*. Washington, D. C.: The Brookings Institution, 1960.

26. Hamburger, Michael J., "The Demand for Money by Households,

Money Substitutes, and Monetary Policy," *Journal of Political Economy*, 74 (December 1966), pp. 600–623.

27. _____ , "Alternative Interest Rates and the Demand for Money: Comment," *American Economic Review*, 59 (June 1969), pp. 407–412.

28. **Heller, H. R.**, "The Demand for Money–The Evidence from the Short-Run Data," *Quarterly Journal of Economics*, 79 (June 1965), pp. 291–303.

29. **Hu, Teh-wei,** "Hyperinflation and the Dynamics of the Demand for Money in China, 1945–1949," *Journal of Political Economy*, 79 (January/February 1971), pp. 186–195.

30. **Jones, David,** "The Demand for Money: A Review of the Empirical Literature," Staff Economic Studies of the Federal Reserve System, paper presented to the Federal Reserve System Committee on Financial Analysis in St. Louis (October 1965).

31. **Johnson, Harry G.**, "Monetary Theory and Policy," *American Economic Review*, 52 (June 1962), pp. 335–384.

32. **Kaminow, I. P.**, "The Household Demand for Money: An Empirical Study," *Journal of Finance*, 24 (September 1969).

33. **Kaufman, George G.**, "More on an Empirical Definition of Money," *American Economic Review*, 59 (March 1969), pp. 78–87.

34. **Keynes, John Maynard,** *The General Theory of Employment, Interest, and Money.* New York: Harcourt, Brace and World, First Harbinger Edition, 1964.

35. **Konstas, Panos** and **Mohamad W. Khouja,** "The Keynesian Demand-for-Money Function: Another Look and Some Additional Evidence," *Journal of Money, Credit and Banking*, 1 (November 1969), pp. 765–777.

36. **Laffer, Arthur B.**, "Trade Credit and the Money Market," *Journal of Political Economy*, 78 (March/April 1970), pp. 239–267.

37. **Laidler, David,** "Some Evidence on the Demand for Money," *Journal of Political Economy*, 74 (February 1966), pp. 55–68.

38. _____ , "The Rate of Interest and the Demand for Money–Some Empirical Evidence," *Journal of Political Economy*, 74 (December 1966), pp. 545–555.

39. _____ , *The Demand for Money: Theories and Evidence.* Scranton: International Textbook Company, 1969.

40. _____ , "The Definition of Money: Theoretical and Empirical Problems," *Journal of Money, Credit and Banking*, 1 (August 1969), pp. 509–525.

41. **Latané, Henry A.**, "Cash Balances and the Interest Rate–A Pragmatic Approach," *Review of Economics and Statistics*, 36 (November 1954), pp. 456–460.

42. **Lee, T. H.**, "Alternative Interest Rates and the Demand for Money: The Empirical Evidence," *American Economic Review*, 57 (December 1967), pp. 1168–1181.

43. **de Leeuw, Frank**, "A Model of Financial Behavior," in *The Brookings Quarterly Econometric Model of the United States*. James Duesenberry, Gary Fromm, Lawrence Klein, and Edwin Kuh (eds.). Chicago: Rand McNally and Company, 1965, pp. 464–530.

44. **Lydall, Harold**, "Income, Assets, and the Demand for Money," *Review of Economics and Statistics*, 40 (February 1958), pp. 1–14.

45. **Meltzer, Allan H.**, "The Demand for Money: The Evidence from the Time Series," *Journal of Political Economy*, 71 (June 1963), pp. 219–246.

46. _____, "The Demand for Money: A Cross Section Study of Business Firms," *Quarterly Journal of Economics*, 77 (August 1963), pp. 405–422.

47. **Miller, M. H.**, and **D. Orr**, "A Model of the Demand for Money by Firms," *Quarterly Journal of Economics*, 80 (August 1966) pp. 413–435.

48. **Motley, Brian**, "A Demand-for-Money Function for the Household Sector—Some Preliminary Findings," *Journal of Finance*, 22 (September 1967), pp. 405–418.

49. _____, "The Consumer's Demand for Money: A Neoclassical Approach," *Journal of Political Economy*, 77 (September/October 1969), pp. 817–826.

50. **Ochs, J.**, "The Transaction Demand for Money and Choices Involving Risk," *Journal of Political Economy*, 76 (March/April 1968), pp. 289–291.

51. **Patinkin, Don**, "The Chicago Tradition, The Quantity Theory and Friedman," *The Journal of Money, Credit and Banking*, 1 (February 1969), pp. 46–70.

52. **Shapiro, Harold**, "Distributed Lags, Interest Rate Expectations, and the Impact of Monetary Policy: An Econometric Analysis of a Canadian Experience," *American Economic Review*, 57 (May 1967), pp. 444–461.

53. **Starleaf, D. R.**, and **R. Reimer**, "The Keynesian Demand Function for Money: Some Statistical Tests," *Journal of Finance*, 22 (March 1967), pp. 71–76.

54. **Stedrey, Andrew**, "A Note on Interest Rates and the Demand for Money," *Review of Economics and Statistics*, 41 (August 1959), pp. 303–307.

55. **Teigen, Ronald**, "Demand and Supply Functions for Money in the United States, Some Structural Estimates," *Econometrica*, 32 (October 1964), pp. 477–509.

56. _____ , "An Aggregated Quarterly Model of the U.S. Monetary Sector, 1953–1964," unpublished manuscript presented to the Conference on Targets and Indicators of Monetary Policy, University of California at Los Angeles (April 1966).

57. **Tobin, James**, "Liquidity Preference and Monetary Policy," *Review of Economics and Statistics*, 29 (May 1947), pp. 124–131.

58. _____ , "The Interest Elasticity of Transaction Demand for Cash," *Review of Economics and Statistics*, 38 (August 1956), pp. 241–247.

59. _____ , "Liquidity Preference as Behavior Towards Risk," *Review of Economic Studies*, 25 (February 1958), pp. 65–86.

60. **Taylor, L. D.**, and **J. P. Newhouse**, "On the Long-Run and Short-Run Demand for Money: A Comment," *Journal of Political Economy*, 77 (September/October 1969), pp. 851–856.

61. **Tsiang, S. C.**, "The Precautionary Demand for Money: An Inventory Theoretical Analysis," *Journal of Political Economy*, 77 (January/February 1969), pp. 99–117.

62. **Turnovsky, Stephen J.**, "The Demand for Money and the Determination of the Rate of Interest Under Uncertainty," *Journal of Money, Credit and Banking*, 3 (May 1971), pp. 183–204.

63. **Walters, Alan A.**, "The Demand for Money—The Dynamic Properties of the Multiplier," *Journal of Political Economy*, 75 (June 1967), pp. 293–298.

64. **Whalen, Edward L.**, "A Cross Section Study of Business Demand for Cash," *Journal of Finance*, 20 (September 1965), pp. 423–443.

65. **Zarembka, P.**, "Functional Form in the Demand for Money," *Journal of the American Statistical Association*, 63 (June 1968), pp. 502–511.

EFFECTS OF MONEY SUPPLY AND MONEY DEMAND ON MACROECONOMIC MODELS

PART *3*

6

Macroeconomic Models:
Aggregate Demand*

INTRODUCTION

In previous chapters some modern theories of money supply and money demand were developed. We are now prepared to examine how this monetary behavior interacts with and affects spending behavior in the economy. It is assumed that the reader has some familiarity with elementary models of income determination and the simple expenditures multiplier.

Elementary macroeconomic theory develops the theory of income determination on the assumption of a given level of interest rates. In the present chapter the interest rate is treated as a variable whose equilibrium value is determined simultaneously with that of the level of income. This

---

*The ideas capsuled here originate in Alvin Hansen's *A Guide to Keynes* (1953) and in Sir John R. Hicks' "Mr. Keynes and the 'Classics,' A Suggested Interpretation," *Econometrica*, Vol. 5 (1937). Among the early mathematical treatments is Lawrence Klein's *The Keynesian Revolution* (New York: Macmillan, 1947). As a teaching device, this piece draws inspiration from Edward C. Budd's *Note on Money, Interest and Income* (unpublished).

rate is the long-term rate.* It is assumed that money wage and price levels are constant, so that all quantities are expressed in dollars of constant purchasing power. Government expenditures, taxation and transfers are assumed to be zero.

THE *IS* (INCOME-EXPENDITURE EQUILIBRIUM) CURVE

Saving is current income not allocated to the purchase of consumption goods. Elementary economic theory teaches that planned saving and planned consumption vary directly with the level of income, and that the level of planned investment varies inversely with the market rate of interest. These propositions, together with the familiar condition that planned saving must equal planned investment in equilibrium, suggest equilibrium combinations of the four variables (income, saving or consumption, investment, and the interest rate).

The set of equilibrium relationships between the interest rate and the level of spending (consumption and investment) is called the *IS* curve. The *IS* curve shows, for a given interest rate, the level of income that makes planned saving equal to planned investment. Some economists call this relationship the income-expenditure equilibrium curve, since for any level of production (or income), it shows the interest rate required to generate total aggregate expenditures (investment plus consumption expenditures) sufficient to absorb this output (or real income). In other words, with *given* commodity prices, there are unique combinations of interest rates and income levels which would clear the relevant markets without excess demand or supply, and hence without unplanned inventory change or unplanned saving.

The *IS* curve is derived from the investment and consumption functions and the condition that the economy must be in equilibrium. Figure 1 demonstrates this derivation (where *positive* quantities are measured along all axes).

Saving is an increasing of the level of income (quadrant 4 of Figure 1). For purposes of construction, the saving function replaces the consumption

---

*The article by David I. Fand in the preceding readings revealed that economists often incorporate the effects of interest rates on *many* assets into their models. The article by Warren L. Smith in the readings following chapter 9 discusses how monetary impulses are transmitted in such models. The survey of empirical work on the demand for money in the preceding readings indicated that there are many interest rates in the real world which are closely interrelated. This interrelation deserves investigation, but is beyond the scope of the present book. For a survey of studies in this area, *see* J. Michaelson, *The Term Structure of Interest Rates* (Intext: Scranton, 1970).

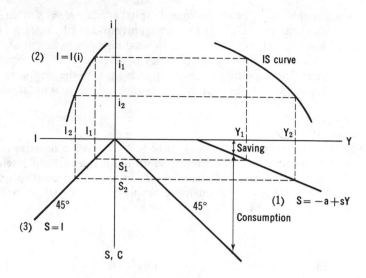

Figure 1. Income-Expenditures Equilibria

function (it will be recalled from elementary macroeconomic theory that they can be used interchangeably).* The saving function is assumed to be linear in Figure 1 and may be represented as follows:

$$S = -a + sY \qquad (1)$$

where s is the marginal propensity to save, $(0 < s < 1)$ and $-a$ is the level of dissaving or negative saving which occurs autonomously of the level of income (i.e., it is constant at all levels of income), $(a > 0)$. Consumption expenditures are measured as the distance between the 45-degree line and the saving function.

Investment is a decreasing function of the rate of interest (quadrant 2 of Figure 1) as expressed in equation (2). This is consistent with elementary economic theory. The principle of diminishing returns holds that as

---

*In elementary theory
$$C = a + bY$$
where $a > 0$, $0 < b < 1$ and saving is defined as
$$S = Y - C.$$
Substitution gives
$$S = -a + (1 - b)Y$$
where $(1 - b) = s$ above.

businesses acquire more newly-produced capital goods, *ceteris paribus*, the expected marginal internal rate of return on investment (the marginal efficiency of investment) falls.* In order to maximize profits businesses will invest until the expected marginal efficiency of investment or the expected marginal internal rate of return on investment is equal to the market rate of interest. The investment function can be expressed in general notation as

$$I = I(i). \tag{2}$$

In Figure 1, the investment demand curve is drawn with a negative slope (the level of investment varies inversely with the market rate of interest) and concave to the origin. (Remember all axes measure positive quantities.) We present the equation more simply in our model by writing this function as the linear relationship

$$I = a' + hi \tag{2'}$$

where h and a' are parameters and $h < 0$ and $a' > 0$.

The condition for equilibrium in the commodity (non-monetary) sector of the economy is that planned (or intended) saving equal planned (or intended) investment (quadrant 3 of Figure 1).

$$S = I. \tag{3}$$

To determine a point on the *IS* curve, assume an arbitrary level of income (say Y_1), and from equation (1) derive the amount of planned saving (S_1) concomitant with that income level. From (3) determine the amount of planned investment (I_1) that necessarily must equal planned saving (S_1) in order to maintain income-expenditure equilibrium. The line drawn in Figure 1 to represent equation (2) discloses that this amount of investment will result only if the rate of interest is i_1. Hence, i_1 and Y_1 represent a point of income-expenditures equilibrium which must lie on the *IS* curve and is therefore consistent with all three equations. Other points, e.g., i_2 and Y_2, are similarly derived.

The *IS* curve depicts a crucial macroeconomic relationship between the interest rate and the level of income in the income-expenditures sector of the economy. As the interest rate declines, planned investment spending increases (equation 2). As investment spending increases, the level of income will rise; the rise in the level of income will generate sufficient

---

*At the margin of production, each newly-produced capital good in the economy will have a successively smaller future income stream. Thus, as the flow of future income to the marginal investment good declines, its marginal internal rate of return (or yield) declines. The relationship between the future income stream from an asset and its yield is thoroughly discussed in the second section of chapter 4.

planned saving (equation 1), such that planned saving will equal planned investment and the non-monetary (income-expenditures) sector of the economy will be in equilibrium (equation 3).* The *IS* curve is not a demand or a supply curve, but an income-expenditures equilibrium curve.

Substituting equations (1) and (2') into equation (3), we may solve for the level of income (*Y*) in terms of all parameters and the rate of interest (*i*). Because equation (2') indicates that the level of investment (*I*) is a linear function of the market rate of interest (*i*), the income-expenditures' equilibrium curve will be linear, its slope being constant and equal to *h/s*.

$$Y = \frac{a + a'}{s} + \frac{h}{s} \cdot i. \tag{4}$$

THE *LM* (MONEY MARKET EQUILIBRIUM) CURVE

In the previous section, we developed three linear equations to express income-expenditure equilibria in the economy. Yet within this system there are four unknowns: investment (*I*), saving (*S*), the interest rate (*i*), and the level of income (*Y*). Clearly, unless one of the variables is given in a fourth equation (say the interest rate, $i = i_o$), one cannot find the equilibrium level of income, saving, or investment for the economy. Therefore, we would have to add *n* equations in *n* − 1 unknowns to make a formal solution for this model possible.

Nevertheless, it would be unrealistic in the extreme to assume that the interest rate is given by dictate of the monetary authority. In the more general case, let us assume the monetary authority attempts to control total reserves or the monetary base in the banking system, thereby affecting the supply of money in existence, as discussed in chapter 1. Indeed, the interest rate, instead of being dictated, is the "price" which equates the supply of money (so determined) to the demand for money. The demand for money is, in turn, an increasing function of the level of income, as well as a decreasing function of the interest rate.

In short, three additional behavioral equations (money supply, money demand, and the money market equilibrium condition) may be specified for the monetary sector of the economy. It is then possible to derive an equilibrium curve that combines these three equations and relates, for any given level of income, the rate of interest necessary to equate the demand and supply of money. This curve, the "money market equilibrium curve," is denoted by *LM*, and, in conjunction with the *IS* curve,

---

*As elementary macroeconomic theory teaches, the presence of equilibrium in a Keynesian model does not necessarily indicate a *full-employment* equilibrium.

expresses a complete general equilibrium model of aggregate demand in six equations and six unknowns. The *LM* curve is derived from these three basic relations relating to monetary behavior as shown in Figure 2. The total demand for money is considered to be a function of the level of income and the interest rate. The demand-for-money function used in this model derives from the analysis presented in chapters 3 and 4. It is treated as consisting of two separate components. The first component of

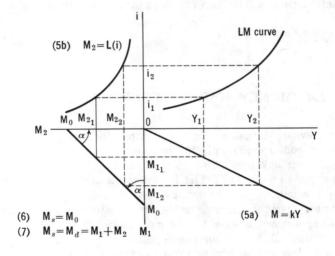

Figure 2. Money Market Equilibria

the demand for money is a function of the level of income and is drawn in quadrant 4 of Figure 2. This demand for "active" money balances is identified with the transactions motive for holding money. A high interest rate has been shown to bring about an economization of transactions balances. Accordingly, as discussed in chapter 3, it is reasonable to indicate the transactions demand will vary inversely with the interest rate, and will vary less than in proportion to Y. Nevertheless, for the time being, in the interest of analytical simplicity, the interest rate variable will be ignored in this portion of the total demand function for money, and the quantity of transactions balances demanded will be represented as varying in direct proportion to the level of current income

$$M_1 = kY \tag{5a}$$

where k is a parameter and the reciprocal of the income velocity of "active" money balances. As the price level is assumed constant, this represents a demand for real money balances. (In this discussion the precautionary motive for holding money is not explicitly related to any variable, but may be assumed in all cases to be related to the same variables as the transactions motive).

The second component of the demand for money is a function of the interest rate (M_2) and is shown in quadrant 2 of Figure 2, where again all axes measure positive quantities. This portion of the total demand is identified with the speculative motive for holding money (or the "asset" demand for money). It is sometimes called the demand for "idle" balances, and is inversely related to the rate of interest; the liquidity preference function shown in quadrant 2 of Figure 2 is negatively sloped. In Figure 2, the function is convex to the origin. For simplicity's sake, the equation of the liquidity preference curve can be expressed in general notation as

$$M_2 = L(i). \tag{5b}$$

The reasons for the negative slope of the liquidity preference curve, as drawn in Figure 2 and described above, were examined in chapter 4. In Tobin's analysis a larger percentage of financial wealth is held in the form of money as the interest rate declines, because the lower the interest rate the less attractive the risk of holding bonds. Later in this discussion it will be useful to write this portion of the total demand for money (M_2) as the linear function

$$M_2 = m + ui \tag{5b'}$$

where u and m are parameters and where $u < 0, m > 0$.

The quantity of money supplied (M) is assumed to be determined by the monetary authority and the banking system as M_o in a manner similar to that discussed in chapter 1.

$$M_s = M_o. \tag{6}$$

In quadrant 3 of Figure 2 the quantity of money supplied is measured as both the directed distance M_o on the M_1 (y) axis, and the directed distance M_o on the M_2 (x) axis. By geometry it may be seen that where the angle α equals the angle α' in the 3rd quadrant, that portion of the money supply *not* held as transactions balances on the M_1 axis must be held as speculative balances on the M_2 axis. For instance, the directed distance on the M_1 axis, $M_{1_1} M_o$, is equal to the directed distance on the M_2 axis, OM_{2_1}, and the directed distance on the M_1 axis, $M_{1_2} M_o$, is equal to the directed distance on the M_2 axis, OM_{2_2}. Thus the 3rd quadrant of Figure 2 depicts the condition that the supply of money (M_o) must equal the quantity of money demanded $(M_1 + M_2)$.

$$M_s = M_1 + M_2 = M_d. \tag{7}$$

To determine a point on the LM curve, assume an arbitrary level of income (say Y_1) and derive from equation (5a) the amount of M_1 (i.e., M_{1_1}) concomitant with that level of income, i.e., necessary to satisfy the transactions demand or to "finance" the level of income (Y_1). If M_{1_1} is desired as transactions balances and M_o is the fixed money supply, by geometry it may be seen that only the amount M_{2_1} is available to satisfy the speculative demand for money. Given the liquidity preference function (5b), the interest rate i_1 is required to ration the supply of idle balances (M_{2_1}) among asset holders. Therefore, i_1 is necessary to equate demand for $(M_{1_1} + M_{2_1})$ and supply of (M_o) money at an income level of Y_1. The point i_1, Y_1 represents a point of money market equilibrium which must lie on the LM curve and is therefore consistent with all three equations. Other points, e.g., i_2, Y_2, are similarly derived.

The LM curve is then a set of equilibria in the money sector of the economy. Each point is consistent with the demand for money (equations (5a) and (5b')), the supply of money (equation 6), and money market equilibrium (equation 7).

The LM curve depicts a crucial macroeconomic relationship between the interest rate and the level of income in the monetary sector of the economy. As the level of income (Y) rises, the quantity of transactions balances desired (M_1) rises (equation 5a). Given a fixed money supply (M_o) (equation 6), individuals who desire more transactions balances must acquire them from those who hold idle balances (M_2), i.e., they must sell "bonds" to holders of idle balances. Holders of idle balances will only relinquish them for bonds when "bribed" by a higher interest rate, i.e., a lower bond price (equation 5b). Therefore, as the level of income rises, the interest rate must rise in order to maintain equilibrium between the supply and demand for money (equation 7) and the monetary sector of the economy will be in equilibrium. The LM curve is not a supply or demand curve but rather it is a money market equilibrium curve.

Substituting linear approximations (5a), (5b'), and (6) into equation (7), we may solve for the level of income (Y) in terms of all parameters and the market rate of interest (i). Because equation (5b'), shows the quantity of speculative balances demanded (M_2) as a linear function of the market rate of interest (i), the money market equilibrium curve will be linear, and its slope will be constant and equal to u/k.

$$Y = \frac{M_o - m}{k} - \frac{u}{k} \cdot i. \tag{8}$$

The unique equilibrium level of income and the equilibrium rate of interest can be determined by the intersection of the IS and the LM curves when both are plotted on the same graph in Figure 3. At this point both the money and income-expenditures sectors are in equilibrium. Every point on LM represents a position of money market equilibrium; every point on IS represents a position of income-expenditure equilibrium. Where the two curves intersect, both sectors, and hence the entire model, are in equilibrium.

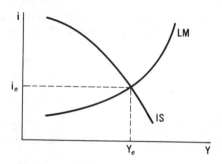

Figure 3. Aggregate Equilibrium: the *LM* **and** *IS* **Curves**

Where equations (2) and (5b) are linear as ($2'$) and ($5b'$), the solution for income is derived from six equations in six unknowns (Y, i, M_d, M_s, S, I) by rearranging both equations (4) and (8) with the interest rate on the left-hand side, setting them equal and solving for the equilibrium level of income:

$$Y_e = \frac{u(a + a') + h(M_o - m)}{su + hk} \tag{9}$$

HOW FISCAL POLICY INFLUENCES THE *IS* CURVE

We now relax the assumption made in the introduction to this chapter that government expenditures and government transfers and taxes are zero.

Since each of these is a part of spending and income flows respectively, they influence the *IS* curve rather than the *LM* curve.*

As in elementary macroeconomic theory, autonomous government expenditures may be treated as autonomous aggregate demand similar to autonomous investment expenditure or autonomous consumption expenditure. Hence, an increase in government expenditures can be reflected in Figure 1 either by moving the investment schedule horizontally to the. left, or by shifting the saving schedule upward (an increase in autonomous consumption is identical to a decrease in autonomous saving). Thus, at each point along the old *IS* curve there will be an excess aggregate demand for newly-produced goods and services. Only a rise in the level of income (or a rise in the interest rate) will increase output (or reduce aggregate demand) sufficiently to keep the income-expenditure sector in equilibrium.

An increase in autonomous expenditure will, therefore, shift the *IS* curve to the right to *IS'*. Measured horizontally (in Figure 4) the *IS* curve shifts by the amount of the increase in autonomous aggregate demand times $1/s$. The rationale for this is quite clear. Take any level of income on the *IS* curve,

$$Y_o = \frac{a + a'}{s} + \frac{h}{s} \cdot i_o .$$ (4)

Now change autonomous expenditures and observe the new level of income (Y_1) which keeps the income-expenditures sector in equilibrium when the interest rate is held constant at i_o:

$$Y_1 = Y_o + \Delta Y = \frac{a + a' + \Delta a'}{s} + \frac{h}{s} (i_o).$$

Only if income increases by ΔY,

$$\Delta Y = Y_1 - Y_o = \Delta a' \frac{1}{s}$$

at a fixed interest rate will sufficient saving (ΔS) be generated to equal the increase in autonomous investment, $\Delta a'$ (or decrease in autonomous saving),

$$\Delta a' = \Delta S = \Delta Y \cdot s,$$

---

*Deficit financing could affect the *LM* curve. This is discussed later in the present chapter.

thus keeping the income-expenditures sector in equilibrium and satisfying equation (3),

$$S + \Delta S = I + \Delta a'.$$

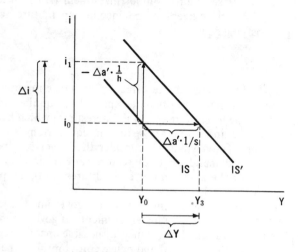

Figure 4. A Change in Income-Expenditure Equilibrium

Conversely, measured vertically in Figure 4 the shift in the *IS* curve is $\Delta a'(1/h)$. This may be readily seen. Rewrite equation (4) with the interest rate on the left-hand side and take any interest rate on the *IS* curve,

$$i_o = \frac{-(a + a')}{h} + \frac{s}{h} \cdot Y_o . \tag{4'}$$

Now change autonomous expenditures and observe the new level of the interest rate (i_1) which keeps the income-expenditure sector in equilibrium if the level of income is held constant at (Y_o):

$$i_1 = i_o + \Delta i = \frac{-(a + a' + \Delta a')}{h} + \frac{s}{h} \cdot Y_o .$$

Only when the interest rate rises by Δi,

$$\Delta i = i_1 - i_o = -\Delta a' \frac{1}{h} ,$$

at a fixed income level will investment spending be *reduced* sufficiently,

$$\Delta i \cdot h = -\Delta I,$$

to offset the initial increase in autonomous investment $(\Delta a')$ (or decrease in autonomous saving), thus keeping the income-expenditure sector in equilibrium and satisfying equation (3),

$$S = I + \Delta a' - \Delta I.$$

So far we have only discussed the effect of a change in autonomous aggregate demand upon the entire income-expenditure equilibrium curve. The effect on the unique level of income and interest rate which keep *both* the income-expenditure and monetary sectors in equilibrium is discussed later in this chapter. Only when we consider the effect of changes in autonomous aggregate demand on both sectors can we develop a more sophisticated version of the autonomous expenditures multiplier principle of elementary macroeconomic theory.

In elementary macroeconomic models with a government sector the presence of total tax receipts less transfer payments of government (= net government receipts) is assumed to reduce disposable income (aggregate income less net government receipts) and hence consumption expenditure. In this model for purposes of analytical convenience we do not introduce a government sector explicitly. Rather we assume that government expenditures and net government receipts are both autonomous and are reflected as changes in the intercept terms of the saving and investment functions, a and a'. Thus, changes in autonomous taxation or transfer payments will shift the saving function (by the change in autonomous taxation or autonomous transfer payments times the marginal propensity to consume) and hence will shift the *IS* curve, as discussed above. The directed distance between the horizontal axis and the saving function will then show the sum of personal saving and net government receipts. Changes in autonomous government expenditures will shift the investment function and the *IS* curve as discussed above.

HOW MONETARY POLICY INFLUENCES THE *LM* CURVE

Because money is a stock and not part of the flow of spending and income, monetary policy influences the *LM* curve. An increase in the quantity of money supplied, a process described in chapter 1, will be shown as an increase in the length of the legs of the triangle in quadrant 3 of Figure 2. Thus, at each point along the old *LM* curve, there will be an excess supply of money (which will be used by individuals to acquire bonds or goods and services) and only a lowering of the interest rate and/or a raising of the level of income will cause the increased money supply to be absorbed into transactions (M_1) and/or speculative balances (M_2) and keep the money market in equilibrium.

An increase in the money supply will, therefore, shift the *LM* curve to the right to *LM'* in Figure 5 by the amount of the increase in the money supply (ΔM_s) times $1/k$. This may be seen as follows: Take any level of income on the *LM* curve (Y_o),

$$Y_o = \frac{M_o - m}{k} - \frac{u}{k} \cdot i \ . \tag{8}$$

Now increase the money supply (ΔM_s) and observe the effect on the level of income (Y_1) which keeps the money market in equilibrium where the interest rate is held constant at i_o:

$$Y_1 = Y_o + \Delta Y = \frac{M_o - m + \Delta M_s}{k} - \frac{u}{k} \cdot i_o \ .$$

We see that only if income increases by ΔY,

$$\Delta Y = Y_1 - Y_o = \Delta M_s \frac{1}{k} \ ,$$

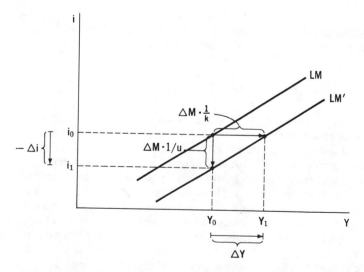

Figure 5. A Change in Money Market Equilibrium

at an unchanged interest rate will the increased money supply be absorbed in transactions balances, thus keeping the money market in equilibrium,

$$\Delta Y \cdot k = \Delta M_d = \Delta M_s.$$

Conversely, we may measure vertically the shift from LM to LM' in Figure 5 by $\Delta M_s(1/u)$. Rewrite equation (8) with the interest rate on the left-hand side and take any interest rate on the LM curve (i_o),

$$i_o = \frac{M_o - m}{u} - \frac{k}{u} \cdot Y_o . \qquad (8')$$

Now increase the money supply (ΔM_s) and observe the new interest rate (i_1) which keeps the money market in equilibrium if the level of income is held constant at Y_o:

$$i_1 = i_o - \Delta i = \frac{M_o - m + \Delta M_s}{u} - \frac{k}{u} \cdot Y_o .$$

Only if the interest rate falls by $-\Delta i$,

$$-\Delta i = i_1 - i_o = \Delta M_s \frac{1}{u} ,$$

at an unchanged level of income, will the increased money supply be absorbed in speculative balances, thus keeping the money market in equilibrium,

$$-\Delta i \cdot u = \Delta M_d = \Delta M_s.$$

Thus far, we have discussed only how an increase in the money supply affects the entire money market equilibrium curve. The effect on the *unique* level of income and interest rate which keep *both* the money and commodity market in equilibrium is discussed later in this chapter.

This analysis overlooks the process by which total reserves (and/or the monetary base) are increased and results in a variable money supply expansion depending on the portfolio behavior of the banks and the public. The reader may want to study chapter 1 which elaborates on these factors in the money supply expansion process. However, for the immediate purposes of this analysis, the effects in the monetary sector of a simple, discrete expansion of the money supply is illustrated in Figure 5.

MULTIPLIERS AND THE SLOPES OF THE BASIC FUNCTIONS: AN INCREASE IN AUTONOMOUS EXPENDITURES

The two previous sections showed us how changes in the policy parameters of our model disturbed the equilibrium in the money and income-expenditure sectors *separately*, and shifted the *IS* or *LM* curves. Now let us examine how monetary and fiscal policy affect *aggregate* equilibrium. In Part 2, we saw that a good deal of theoretical and empirical controversy centered around hypotheses about the manner in which the interest rate and a measure of income affect the demand for money.* Now we shall see the crucial influence of these hypotheses on the strength of monetary and fiscal policy in our macroeconomic model.

The inclusion of money market behavior and the rate of interest in this model modifies the form of the autonomous expenditure multiplier of elementary macroeconomic theory. The solution for income in the linear model was

$$Y_e = \frac{u(a + a') + h(M_o - m)}{su + hk}. \tag{9}$$

The autonomous expenditure multiplier shows the change in income caused by a change in "autonomous" expenditures (a), which shifts the *IS* curve. In Figure 6, the new equilibrium level of income (Y'_e) will be

$$Y'_e = Y_e + \Delta Y = \frac{u(a + a' + \Delta a) + h(M_o - m)}{su + hk}.$$

Therefore, the change in income is

$$\Delta Y = \frac{u(\Delta a)}{su + hk}.$$

*In the survey of the empirical literature of the demand for money following chapter 5, we pointed out that permanent income explained more of the variation in the demand for money than current income. It was shown that the use of permanent income, as a weighted average of past and present levels of measured income, does not remove current income from the money demand (and consumption) functions but rather adds a *lagged* value of income as a new explanatory variable in these relations. This modification of the basic model of this chapter simply means that while changes in the money supply or autonomous expenditures still affect income in the same direction, they would not *immediately* work their full multiplier effect. Instead, since past changes in income would also affect current income, any monetary or expenditures stimulus would take *time* to develop the full multiplier effect on income.

The autonomous expenditures multiplier is a function of the slopes of the basic functions, or

$$\frac{\Delta Y}{\Delta a} = \frac{u}{su + hk} \,. \tag{10}$$

One can readily see that the autonomous expenditures multiplier of elementary macroeconomic theory $(1/s)$ is considerably larger than the autonomous expenditures multiplier in this general equilibrium model containing a money market.*

The effect of monetary phenomena on the autonomous expenditures multiplier is illustrated in Figure 6. The *IS* curve is drawn on the assumption that $a = 0$ and $0 < s < 1$. The marginal efficiency of investment schedule is located in the same quadrant as is the *IS* curve. The initial equilibrium position is at A, where equilibrium income (Y_e) is equal to OF; investment, OD; consumption, DF; and the rate of interest, OK. If the investment schedule shifts to the right by an amount ΔI ($=CE$) and if the rate of interest were fixed at OK, the equilibrium level of income would

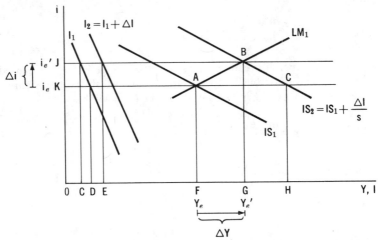

Figure 6. An Increase in Autonomous Expenditures Affects Aggregate General Equilibrium

rise by $FH\left(\dfrac{1}{s}CE\right)$ to OH (*see* the preceding section on fiscal policy). However, the increase in aggregate income will force the rate of interest up

---

*Those contemporary economists who believe that the effectiveness of fiscal policy has been overrated often contend that the proponents of fiscal policy overlook this salient point. *See,* for instance, the reading by David I. Fand which follows chapter 9.

to OJ. The new equilibrium level of income (Y'_e) will be OG, and the increase in the level of income (ΔY) will only be FG rather than FH. The increase in the rate of interest has reduced investment spending by CD and hence the level of income by $GH \left(\dfrac{1}{s} CD\right)$.

This occurs because as the level of income increases, the demand for transactions balances (M_1) increases and can only be satisfied given a fixed money supply (M_o) if speculative balances (M_2) are relinquished. Speculative balances will only be relinquished and bonds accepted if the rate of interest rises. Because of the rise in the rate of interest, the level of investment spending falls by CD and the level of income may only rise to G. (This may be shown roughly as the movement from C to B along the IS curve).

Clearly, the rise in the interest rate reduces the size of the autonomous expenditures multiplier. The size of the multiplier depends on the slopes of the IS and LM curves which, in turn, depend upon the slopes of the basic functions from which they are derived. The slope of the saving schedule (1) is s, and reflects the increase in saving, given a unit increase in the level of income. The slope of the investment schedule in linear form ($2'$) is h, and reflects the amount by which investment must fall, given a unit increase in the interest rate, i.e., $h = dI/di$.

The slope of the transactions demand for money schedule (5a) is k, and reflects the increase in transactions balances demanded, given a unit increase in the level of income. The slope of the liquidity preference curve in linear form ($5b'$) is u, and reflects the amount by which the quantity of speculative balances demanded must increase, given a unit decrease in the rate of interest, i.e., $u = dM_2/di$. Hence, the effect of the interest rate and the level of income on the demand for money greatly influences the results brought about by a change in autonomous expenditures.

In reality, these slopes may not be constant for all points in the schedules (the functions may not be linear), although we assumed they were for purposes of deriving, most simply, the solution for the level of income. As explained for the more general case in equations (2) and (5b), the absolute value of h falls as we move down along the investment schedule, and the absolute value of u rises as we move down along the liquidity preference schedule.* As discussed in chapter 3, where the transactions demand is less than proportional, e.g., Baumol's square root rule, the interest rate will not be "bid up" much as income increases (the LM curve will be flatter), and as can be seen in equation (10), the autonomous expenditures multiplier will be greater in magnitude.

*To the extent that low interest rates are associated with massive unemployment, fiscal policy is a more reasonable stabilization tool during periods of unemployment (and monetary policy more reasonable during periods of nearly full employment). *See* the readings by Fand and Cagan, which follow chapter 9.

Within the more convenient linear framework the slope of the *IS* curve is equal to h/s and the slope of the *LM* curve is then equal to $-u/k$. This may be verified by examining the mathematical expressions for the *IS* and *LM* curves, equations (4) and (8). (Remember $u, h < 0$ and $1 > k_1 s > 0$.)

In order to compare the new *LM-IS* autonomous expenditures multiplier to the simple autonomous expenditures multiplier of the elementary Keynesian model, $(1/s)$, it is instructive to rewrite it as

$$\frac{\Delta Y}{\Delta a} = \frac{1}{s + \dfrac{hk}{u}}. \tag{10}$$

If $dM_2/di = u = -\infty$ (a perfectly interest elastic liquidity preference schedule and hence *a horizontal LM curve*), or if $dI/di = h = 0$ (a completely interest inelastic investment schedule, and hence *a vertical IS curve*), then (10) reduces to the simple autonomous expenditures multiplier. Aggregate demand would not be "choked off" by a rise in interest rates as income rose, either because the interest rate would not be bid upward ($u = -\infty$), or else because the rise in the rate would not affect spending ($h = 0$).

On the other hand, if $dM_2/di = u = 0$ (a completely interest inelastic speculative demand schedule, and hence *a vertical LM curve*), or if $dI/di = h = -\infty$ (a completely interest elastic investment schedule and hence *a horizontal IS curve*), any increase in autonomous expenditures would *not* affect the level of income because the rise in the interest rate would "choke off" all of the increased aggregate demand, i.e., the autonomous expenditures multiplier would be zero either because the rise in the interest rate would be immense as idle balances were sought to finance increased expenditures ($u = 0$) or else because any rise in the rate would completely "choke off" spending ($h = -\infty$). In this case only an increase in the quantity of money, affecting a horizontal shift in the *LM* curve, could cause the level of income to rise.

The existence of a very interest inelastic demand curve for money ($u \longrightarrow 0$) or a very interest elastic investment demand schedule ($h \longrightarrow -\infty$) makes the change in the level of income following from a change in autonomous expenditure insignificant. This may be seen from (10). Therefore, when the liquidity preference schedule is relatively interest inelastic or when investment spending is very interest sensitive, fiscal policy is considered relatively less powerful.

Conversely, when the speculative demand schedule is very interest elastic ($u \longrightarrow -\infty$) or when investment demand is very interest inelastic ($h \longrightarrow 0$) as can be seen in (10), the change in the level of income following from a change in autonomous expenditures approaches the value of the simple multiplier $(1/s)$ of elementary Keynesian models without a monetary sector. Therefore, when investment spending is very interest insensitive or when the liquidity preference schedule is relatively interest elastic, fiscal policy is considered relatively more powerful.

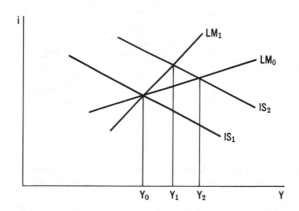

Figure 7. The Greater the Interest Sensitivity of the Demand for Money, the Greater the Autonomous Expenditures Multiplier

Thus, we see that the order of magnitude of the autonomous expenditures multiplier is related to the orders of magnitude of the four slope parameters of our model, h, u, s and k. The greater the absolute value of u, the greater the magnitude of the autonomous expenditures multiplier in equation (10). This is illustrated in Figure 7 which compares the orders of magnitude of the increases in income which follow from an increase in autonomous expenditures (shown as a shift in the *IS* curve from IS_1 to IS_2), given two alternative *LM* curves. The steeper *LM* curve (LM_1) reflects a lesser absolute value of u, a less interest sensitive demand-for-money function; the less steep *LM* curve (LM_o) represents a more interest sensitive demand-for-money function. The curve with a greater absolute value of u (LM_o) will give a larger equilibrium level of income (Y_2) where it intersects IS_2.

The less the absolute value of h, the greater the size of the autonomous expenditures multiplier in equation (10). This is illustrated in Figure 8, which compares the orders of magnitude of the increases in income which follow from an increase in autonomous expenditures shown alternatively as a shift in the *IS* curve either from IS_1 to IS_2 or from IS'_1 to IS'_2 with a given *LM* curve. The steeper pair of *IS* curves (IS'_1, IS'_2) reflect a lesser absolute value of h, a less interest sensitive investment spending function; the less steep pair of *IS* curves (IS_1, IS_2) represents a more interest sensitive

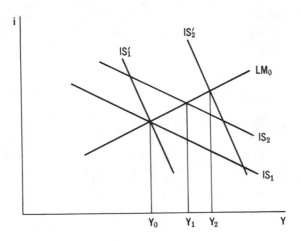

Figure 8. The Less the Interest Sensitivity of the Investment Demand, the Greater the Autonomous Expenditures Multiplier

investment function. The steeper *IS* curves, the ones with a lesser absolute value of h, will give a larger equilibrium value of income (Y_2) where IS_2' intersects LM_o.

Note also that as in the autonomous expenditures multiplier of elementary macroeconomics, the smaller the marginal propensity to save, s, the larger is the multiplier in equation 10. Finally the smaller the proportionality factor in the transactions demand for money, k, the larger is the autonomous expenditures multiplier in equation (10).*

MULTIPLIERS AND THE SLOPES OF THE BASIC FUNCTIONS: AN INCREASE IN THE MONEY SUPPLY

The multiplier concept applies also to a shift in the *LM* curve caused by a change in the quantity of money supplied or a shift in the money demand function. In Figure 9 the new equilibrium level of income (Y''), caused by a change in the quantity of money supplied (ΔM), is:

$$Y_e'' = Y_e + \Delta Y = \frac{u(a + a') + h(M_o - m + \Delta M)}{su + hk}.$$

Therefore, the change in income is

*In more complex models, additional leakages such as induced taxation, induced business saving (retained earnings), and induced imports would reduce the magnitude of the multiplier.

$$\Delta Y = \frac{h\Delta M}{su + hk}.$$

The correct multiplier is a function of the slopes of the basic functions, or

$$\frac{\Delta Y}{\Delta M} = \frac{h}{su + hk}$$

or, written in a form which can be compared with previous multiplier expressions:

$$\frac{\Delta Y}{\Delta M} = \frac{h}{u}\left[\frac{1}{s + \dfrac{hk}{u}}\right]. \tag{11}$$

The difference between (10) and (11) lies only in the term h/u.* An increase in autonomous expenditures as depicted by (10), raises aggregate income by the multiple $[1/(s + hk/u)]$. The autonomous expenditures multiplier portion of (11), which is the term in brackets, is the same as equation (10). But an increase in M, as depicted by (11), increases the level of income only insofar as it reduces the market rate of interest (i), and increases the level of investment spending (I). The reduction in the market rate depends on the size of u, (the fall in i with respect to an increase in M_s). The rise in investment spending depends on the size of h (the rise in I with respect to a fall in i). By calculus

$$\frac{dY}{dM} = \frac{di}{dM} \cdot \frac{dI}{di} \cdot \frac{dY}{dI}.$$

The existence of a very interest inelastic investment demand schedule $(h \longrightarrow 0)$ makes the change in the level of income following from a change in the quantity of money supplied, (M), insignificant. This can be seen from (11). Even though monetary policy affects the interest rate, the rate has little effect on investment. Therefore, if investment is interest insensitive, as it may well be in many sectors of the economy, monetary policy is relatively less powerful.**

Also, the existence of a very interest elastic speculative demand schedule $(u \longrightarrow -\infty)$ makes the change in the level of income following from a change in the quantity of money supplied, (M), insignificant. This can be seen from (11). Even if investment is interest sensitive, under these circum-

---

*A decrease either in the order of magnitude of (s) or (k) increases *both* the monetary and fiscal policy multipliers.

**The readings by Warren Smith and Phillip Cagan following chapter 9 consider the interest sensitivity of investment spending in various sectors of the economy.

stances the money supply may be increased without much effect on the rate of interest, as individuals can be "bribed" to hold additional speculative money balances without much decline in the interest rate. Therefore, when the speculative demand schedule is relatively interest elastic, monetary policy is less powerful.*

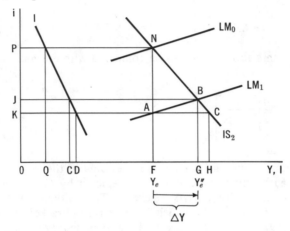

Figure 9. An Increase in the Money Supply Affects Aggregate General Equilibrium

The effect of change in the money supply on the level of income, as shown in equation (11), is illustrated in Figure 9. The initial equilibrium at N is disturbed by an increase in the quantity of money supplied (ΔM). As discussed earlier, the LM curve shifts horizontally to the right by an amount equal to $\Delta M/k$. At the initial equilibrium level of income OF, the rate of interest will fall by PK ($= (1/u)\Delta M$), i.e., as excess money balances are used to acquire "bonds", the price of bonds rises and the interest rate falls. At the lower interest rate, investment is stimulated by QD ($= (h/u)\Delta M$). If the interest rate were fixed at OK, the simple multiplier process would move the economy to C and the level of income would rise by FH. However, as discussed earlier in this section and illustrated in Figure 6, an increase in the level of income will force the interest rate back up to OJ as transactions balances must be obtained at the expense of speculative balances. The increase in the level of income will be limited to FG and the increase in the level of investment will be limited to QC.

Thus, we see that the size of the monetary policy multiplier is related to the orders of magnitude of the four slope parameters of our model, h, u, s

*Estimated interest elasticities of the demand for money are reported in Tables 1 and 2 of the survey of empirical tests of the money demand function that follows chapter 5.

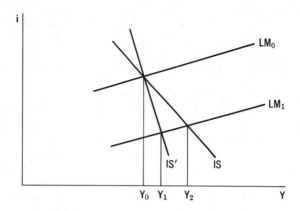

Figure 10. The Greater the Interest Sensitivity of the Investment
Demand Function, the Greater the Monetary Policy Multiplier

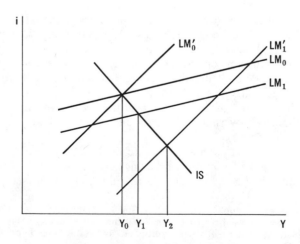

Figure 11. The Less the Interest Sensitivity of the Demand for Money
the Greater the Monetary Policy Multiplier

and k. The greater the absolute value of h the greater the size of the monetary policy multiplier in equation (11). This is illustrated in Figure 10,
which compares the orders of magnitude of the increases in income which
follow from an increase in the money supply (shown as a shift in the LM
curve from LM_0 to LM_1) given two alternative IS curves. The steeper IS
curve (IS') reflects a lesser absolute value of h, a less interest sensitive investment demand function; the less steep IS curve (IS) represents a more
interest sensitive investment function. The IS curve with a greater absolute
value of h (IS) will give a larger equilibrium value of income (Y_2) where it
intersects LM_1.

The less the absolute value of u the greater the size of the monetary policy multiplier in equation (11). This is illustrated in Figure 11 which compares the orders of magnitude of the increases in income which follow from
an increase in the money supply, shown alternatively as a shift in the LM
curve either from LM_0 to LM_1 or from LM_0' to LM'_1 with a given IS
curve. The steeper pair of LM curves (LM_0' LM'_1) reflect a lesser absolute
value of u, a less interest sensitive demand-for-money function; the less
steep pair of LM curves (LM_0 LM_1) represent a more interest sensitive
demand-for-money function. The steeper LM curves, the ones with a lesser
absolute value of u, will give a larger equilibrium value of income (Y_2)
where LM'_1 intersects IS.

DEFICIT FINANCING

To this point it has been assumed that monetary policy affects the LM
curve and fiscal policy affects the IS curve. If expansionary fiscal policy requires a deficit*, however, the Treasury's method of financing the deficit
could have repercussions on the money market and be reflected in the LM
curve. Indeed, those contemporary economists who believe that the effectiveness of fiscal policy has been overrated, contend that much of the effect ostensibly exerted by fiscal policy on the level of income obtains because of the way government deficits and surpluses cause the money
supply to change.**

If the Treasury sells bonds to private nonbank investors, the money
supply and hence the LM curve will be unchanged, and the combination of
the fiscal and debt policy will cause a rise in the rate of interest as well as

---

*This discussion overlooks analysis of the small expansionary effect of increased
government expenditures financed by an equal increase in taxes. This analysis is
usually labelled "the balanced budget multiplier" and is discussed on pp. 444-446 of
the reading by Spencer and Yohe.

**See, for instance, the contribution by David Fand included in the readings at
the end of Part 3. See also, Carl Christ, "A Simple Macroeconomic Model with a
Government Budget Restraint," *Journal of Political Economy* (January 1968).

in the level of income.* As the income level rises because of fiscal policy (reflected as a shift in the *IS* curve), an increase in the quantity of transactions balances demanded (ΔM_1) causes individuals either to sell their bonds or to issue new ones (loans) to obtain additional money balances. Because the deficit was financed without an increase in the money supply, bond prices must fall (the interest rate rises) to a level that will wipe out the excess demand for money. (The increase in the interest rate chokes off part of the private investment that would otherwise have been made, and income does not rise as much as it would have without the induced increase in the interest rate.)

On the other hand, bonds sold by the Treasury may be purchased by Federal Reserve Banks (as a matter of deliberate policy). Such a policy would increase total reserves** and cause the money supply to rise by a multiple of the initial bond sale, thereby shifting the *LM* curve to the right. The rate of interest would not rise as much because the *LM* curve is shifted.

The preceding analysis has shown that there will be a money supply-expanding effect of deficit financing if bonds are sold to the central bank. In contrast, if bonds are sold to the public, the money supply will not expand and the government's deficit will not be as expansionary.

Some economists*** have argued that a government deficit financed by bond sales to the public could actually have a contractionary monetary effect; it will shift the *LM* curve to the left. Such an effect could occur by recognition of the effect of an increased supply of bonds on the demand for money. While the present model is not sufficiently sophisticated to handle this case rigorously, it could be introduced simply by adding a variable representing net financial wealth (including bonds) to the demand-for-money function (equation (5b) of our model).† If bond wealth in the hands of the public increases, in order to maintain balance in their port-

---

*It is important not to confuse *Treasury* deficit financing through the sale of securities with *Federal Reserve open market* sales and purchases of government securities. The former relates to the U.S. government's issuance of (retirement of) its own indebtedness because of its budget deficit (or surplus). The latter refers to the Federal Reserve purchase and sale of outstanding debt as a means of influencing the level of total bank reserves.

**Barring defensive Fed operations discussed in the fifth section of chapter 1.

***See, for instance, James Tobin, "An Essay on the Principles of Debt Management," in *Fiscal and Debt Management Policies*, Commission on Money and Credit (Englewood Cliffs, N. J.: Prentice-Hall, 1963); Karl Brunner and Allan H. Meltzer, "The Place of Financial Intermediaries in the Transmission of Monetary Policy," *American Economic Review*, Vol. 53 (May 1963), page 381; Richard H. Timberlake, "The Stock of Money and Money Substitutes," *Southern Economic Journal*, Vol. 30 (January 1964), page 255.

†The conditions under which bonds represent net financial wealth are discussed in the third section of chapter 9.

folios (to maintain the same proportion between money and bonds), individuals must increase their demand for money. This may be viewed as an increase in the parameter, m, in the linear form of the money demand curve, equation (5b'). Given this shift in money demand, it can easily be seen that the *LM* curve would shift leftward.

If such claims are realistic they would cast doubt on the heralded effectiveness of fiscal policy. Even though deficit spending causes the *IS* curve to shift rightward, if it is financed by bond sales to the public it could cause the *LM* curve to shift leftward. The result would be an even higher equilibrium interest rate than shown in Figure 6 (because the *LM* curve shifts leftward as the *IS* curve shifts rightward). In addition, the equilibrium level of income would not rise as much as depicted in Figure 6. These theoretical allegations support the critics who point with distress to the ineffectiveness of fiscal policy.*

SUMMARY

This chapter has shown that the rate of interest and the level of aggregate income are variables that are simultaneously determined as part of a "general equilibrium" system rather than separately, as the elementary theory of income determination or a partial equilibrium theory of the rate of interest might suggest.

It often will be useful to discuss the operation of the economy, and monetary (and fiscal) policy with this paradigm in mind. However, like any theory, the present model has limitations. For example, prices are assumed given, and a single interest rate rather than a series of interest rates is assumed. Therefore, subsequent chapters will examine macroeconomic models with flexible prices and, in the readings which follow chapter 9, an article by Warren L. Smith will offer a variant of the basic Keynesian model of this chapter which considers flexible prices and many interest rates.

*In the readings which follow chapter 9 several authors, but especially Roger Spencer and William Yohe provide a good deal more detail on these allegations.

Questions/ *chapter 6*

1. Assume the Council of Economic Advisors (CEA) announces the marginal propensity to save has fallen. Using the *LM - IS* model of this chapter, would you be encouraged about the strength of monetary policy, fiscal policy, neither, or both?

2. Assume the CEA announces that the amount of transactions balances held as a proportion of income has risen. Again, would you be encouraged about the strength of monetary policy, fiscal policy, neither, or both?

3. Assume the CEA announces the interest elasticity of investment demand has increased. Would you be encouraged about the strength of monetary policy, fiscal policy, neither, or both?

4. Assume the CEA announces the interest elasticity of the speculative demand for money has increased. Would you be encouraged about the strength of monetary policy, fiscal policy, neither, or both?

5. Suppose the U.S. Treasury finances a 10 billion dollar increase in government expenditures through the sale of government securities to the Federal Reserve (i.e., tax receipts remain constant as expenditures increase by $10 billion). Is this monetary policy or fiscal policy? Show the effect of these actions by means of *LM* and *IS* curves.

6. Explain completely (without the aid of graphs) why the size of the autonomous expenditures multiplier depends upon the interest sensitivity of the demand for money function.

Bibliography / *chapter 6*

Ando, A., and **Stephen Goldfeld,** "An Econometric Model for Evaluating Stabilization Policies," Albert Ando, Edgar C. Brown, and Ann Friedlander (eds.), *Studies in Economic Stabilization.* Washington: The Brookings Institution, 1968, pp. 215–287.

Budd, Edward C., *Note on Money, Interest, and Income* (unpublished).

Cagan, Phillip, "Current Issues in The Theory of Monetary Policy," in *Patterns of Market Behavior: Essays in Honor of Philip Taft,* edited by Michael J. Brennan (Providence: Brown University Press, 1965), pp. 135-154.

Carlson, K. and **D. Karnosky,** "The Influence of Fiscal and Monetary Actions on Aggregate Demand," Working Paper No. 4, Federal Reserve Bank of St. Louis (March 1969).

Chow, Gregory, "Multiplier Accelerator and Liquidity Preference in the Determination of the National Income of the United States," *Review of Economics and Statistics* (February 1967), pp. 1–15.

Christ, Carl, "A Short-Run Aggregate-Demand Model of the Interdependence and Effects of Monetary and Fiscal Policies With Keynesian and Classical Interest Elasticities," *The American Economic Review,* Vol. 57 (May 1967), pp. 434–443.

———, "A Simple Macroeconomic Model With A Government Budget Restraint," *Journal of Political Economy* (January 1968).

Eisner, R., "Fiscal and Monetary Policy Reconsidered," *The American Economic Review,* Vol. 59 (December 1969), pp. 897–905.

Hansen, Alvin H., *A Guide to Keynes.* New York: McGraw-Hill, 1953.

Hicks, J. R., "Mr. Keynes and the Classics: A Suggested Interpretation," *Econometrica*, Vol. 5 (1937), pp. 147–159.

Keynes, John Maynard, *The General Theory of Employment, Interest, and Money*. London: Harcourt, Brace and World, 1936.

Klein Lawrence, *The Keynesian Revolution*. New York: The Macmillan Company, 1947.

Leijonhufvud, Axel, *On Keynesian Economics and the Economics of Keynes* (Oxford University Press, 1968).

Musgrave, Richard, *The Theory of Public Finance* (New York: McGraw-Hill, 1959).

Ritter, Lawrence, "The Role of Money in Keynesian Theory," *Banking and Monetary Studies*, edited by Deane Carson. Homewood, Illinois: Richard D. Irwin, 1963, pp. 134–150.

Scott, Robert H., "Estimates of Hicksian *IS* and *LM* Curves for the United States," *Journal of Finance*, Vol. 21, (September 1966), pp. 479–487.

Silber, William L., "Fiscal Policy in *IS-LM* Analysis: A Correction," *Journal of Money, Credit and Banking* Vol. II (November, 1970) pp. 461–472.

Smith, Warren, "A Graphical Exposition of the Complete Keynesian System," Warren Smith and Ronald Teigen (eds.), *Readings in Money, National Income, and Stabilization Policy*. Homewood, Illinois: Richard D. Irwin, Inc., 1970, pp. 66–73.

Spencer, Roger W., and William P. Yohe, "The Crowding Out of Private Expenditures by Fiscal Policy," Federal Reserve Bank of St. Louis *Review* (October, 1970), pp. 12-24.

7

Alternative Formulations of
Money Demand in
Aggregate Economic Models

In chapter 5 we examined several formulations of the Quantity Theory of Money. At that time we quoted Milton Friedman to the effect that a "quantity theorist" could be distinguished by his emphasis on the stability of the demand-for-money function, the independence of the factors affecting the supply of and the demand for money and the crucial role of the money demand function in the determination of the equilibrium values of several important aggregate economic variables. In this chapter we shall assume a money demand function of the form presented by the quantity theorists, and examine the implications in $LM - IS$ analysis of using this functional form in place of the familiar Keynesian liquidity preference function.*

*We must emphasize that this analysis never goes beyond the realm of "statics," and thus leaves out much of the richness of the quantity theorists' approach, as represented in Fisher's analysis of "transition periods" and Friedman's discussion of the monetary "transmission" mechanism. Furthermore, the assumption of perfect interest inelasticity of the money demand function is made for convenience of exposition and is not absolutely necessary to arrive at the general conclusions presented here.

We begin by rewriting the Fisherian equation of exchange (1), the Cambridge equation (2) and the final empirical money demand equation presented by Friedman (3).

$$M \cdot V' = P \cdot Q' = Y \tag{1}$$

$$M = kY \tag{2}$$

$$M_d/(N \cdot P) = \gamma \, [Y_p/(N \cdot P)]^{\delta}. \tag{3}$$

A distinguishing characteristic of these equations is that each one contains some measure of income as the primary variable explaining the quantity of money balances demanded, and each excludes the interest rate as an explanatory variable. In the Quantity Theory tradition, then, the demand for money is viewed as a function of the level of income. In Liquidity Preference Theory, on the other hand, the rate of interest is included as a significant determinant of desired money balances. An obvious point of dispute among advocates of these theories then centers on the empirical significance of the interest rate in the money demand function.*

The role of the Liquidity Preference Theory in the determination of national income was demonstrated in chapter 6 through the use of *LM – IS* curves. That analysis affirmed the feasibility of both monetary and fiscal policies as means of influencing the level of national income. Let us re-examine this model after substituting a classical money demand function for the Keynesian one. In terms of the basic static model, this simply eliminates the interest rate term from the money demand function. Here, as in chapter 6, we assume that the price level remains constant. Therefore, quantities are expressed in dollars of constant purchasing power and nominal and real values may be assumed to be the same.**

The essentials of the analysis of chapter 6 is reviewed in Figure 1 and in the linear equations (4) to (9).

The Expenditure Equations	The Money Market Equations
$S = S(Y) = -a + sY$ (4)	$M_d = M_1 + M_2 = kY + m + ui$ (7)
$I = I(i) = a' + hi$ (5)	$M_s = M_o$ (8)
$S = I$ (6)	$M_d = M_s$ (9)

The necessity for the simultaneous solution of the equilibrium level of

---

*This issue is considered in greater detail in chapter 6, in the empirical survey following chapter 5, and in the readings that follow chapter 9.

**This Keynesian assumption is made to preserve continuity with chapter 6, and is relaxed in chapter 8. The Quantity Theory frequently assumes, as shown in chapter 8 and the first reading by David Fand following chapter 9, that *real* income is constrained to full employment, that *real* money balances are demanded, and that nominal money balances are supplied and determine the level of nominal income. Therefore, the present analysis is firmly Keynesian except for the money demand function.

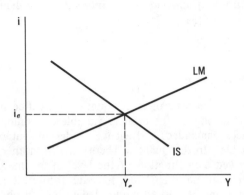

Figure 1. Income-Expenditure and Monetary Sector Equilibrium

income (Y_e) and the equilibrium rate of interest (i_e) results from the fact that in both the income-expenditure sector (equations (4)-(6)), and the monetary sector (equations (7)-(9)), there are only three equations and four unknowns. In general, there must be as many equations as there are unknowns to be able to solve a set of simultaneous linear equations.* Since *two* of the four unknowns in each of the markets are the same, however, we may combine the models of each market to derive a complete six equation model in exactly six unknowns $(S, I, Y, i, M_d,$ and $M_s)$. The global model may be solved for these unknowns. This is demonstrated graphically in Figure 1.

In the Quantity Theory formulation, the income-expenditure sector may be represented exactly as above. Therefore, we retain equations (4) to (6) and we employ the same *IS* curve as in Figure 1. Yet, the income-expenditure sector is still indeterminate by itself. Equations (4) to (6) can only yield various combinations of Y and i which establish equilibrium in this sector. The equations cannot yield unique solutions for these variables.

Eliminating the Liquidity Preference equation and substituting a Quantity Theory relation (specifically, the Cambridge equation) into the money market model provides the following set of equations:

$$M_d = k \cdot Y \tag{7'}$$

$$M_s = M_o \tag{8}$$

$$M_s = M_d. \tag{9}$$

*More specifically, unique solutions for n unknowns can be derived from a system of n linear equations if these equations are consistent, independent, and non-homogeneous.

But with this specification the money market is no longer indeterminate. It is, instead, a separable (segmentable) subsystem. There are now only three unknowns (M_d, M_s and Y) in these three linear equations, since the interest rate no longer appears in the money demand function. Therefore, rather than deriving an *LM* curve that relates various possible combinations of Y and i which will establish equilibrium in the money market, we may solve equations (7′), (8) and (9) directly for a unique level of income.

$$M_s = M_d$$
$$M_o = k \cdot Y$$
$$Y = M_o/k. \tag{15}$$

Adding this solution as a fourth equation in the income-expenditure sector (equations (4) to (6)), we may derive solutions for the remaining unknowns (i, S, I):

$$S = -a + sY = -a + s(M_o/k)$$
$$S = I$$
$$-a + s(M_o/k) = a' + hi$$
$$i_e = (1/h)\,[s(M_o/k) - a - a']\,.* \tag{16}$$

Consequently, in the classical formulation, the level of income is determined in the money market without reference to the income-expenditure sector. This is the level of *real* income, since the price level is assumed to remain constant. Simultaneous methods employing the models of both sectors are no longer necessary to derive an equilibrium solution for the level of income. Rather, a unique solution for the income variable can be derived from the monetary sector alone. This value can then be assumed given in the expenditure equations which then yield solution values for the remaining variables ($S, I,$ and i). In this way, the system is solved *recursively*—one separable subsystem at a time, yielding solutions which then determine equilibrium values in other subsystems.

In the current framework, the interest rate serves only to assure equilibrium between saving and investment in the income-expenditure sector. This may be demonstrated graphically:

---

*Equations (15) and (16) are "reduced form" equations derived from the structural equations of our model. Each of these equations yields a solution for one of the endogenous variables—variables whose equilibrium values are determined within the model—in terms of parameters and exogenous variables—variables whose value is assumed to be known from outside our model, e.g., the money stock.

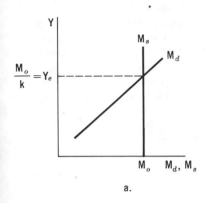

a.

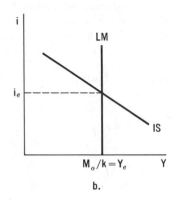

b.

Figure 2a. The Money Market

Figure 2b. Aggregate Equilibrium in the "Classical" Model

Figure 2(a) shows that the intersection of the money supply curve (fixed at M_o by the authorities) and the money demand curve determine a unique equilibrium level of income (Y_e). That is, given the constant, k, in the money demand function (or V, the velocity of circulation in Fisher's formulation), there is only one income level, Y_e, which will assure that the public will desire to hold the entire money stock supplied by the monetary authorities. In Figure 2(b), the vertical *LM* curve drawn at the equilibrium level of income determined in part (a), indicates that the level of income is the only "real" variable that can affect conditions in the money market. The interest rate has no influence in that market. The intersection of the *LM – IS* curves serves only to determine the equilibrium interest rate. The level of income is predetermined by the position of the *LM* curve as determined in part (a). Thus, the interest rate serves only to induce a level of investment spending sufficient to offset the level of saving that will be forthcoming at the level of income predetermined in the money market.*

*In chapter 8 we shall see that when complete price-wage flexibility is assumed in a classical model such as this one, equilibrium in the economy will occur only at full employment. Consequently, the money income level determined in the monetary sector in this model, Y_e, will represent the product of a full employment level of output, O_f, and the equilibrium price level, P_e; i.e., $Y_e = O_f \cdot P_e$. In effect, then, the money market of this model serves to determine only the equilibrium price level. However, with the price level assumed constant—as it is in the traditional *LM – IS* analysis—the equilibrium money income level, Y_e, may not represent full employment. In this case, the money market serves to determine more than simply the absolute price level. This distinction has important implications for the issue of the "neutrality" of money discussed in chapter 9. *See* Milton Friedman, "A Theoretical Framework For Monetary Analysis," *Journal of Political Economy*, Vol. 78, (March/April 1970).

The importance of these conclusions can be seen as follows. Suppose that the government, through a change in taxation or expenditures, causes a shift in the saving function or the investment demand schedule. This will cause a shift in the *IS* curve (*see* chapter 6). As Figure 3 demonstrates, a shift in the *IS* curve in a classical model will affect only the interest rate and not the level of income.

This can also be demonstrated by use of the reduced form equations for the equilibrium interest rate (16) and the equilibrium level of income (15) presented above. Note that since none of the expenditure equation parameters $(a, a', s, \text{ or } h)$ enter the reduced form equation for the equilibrium level of income, no change in these parameters induced through fiscal policy can affect that income level. From equation (16), however, it is clear that such changes will affect the equilibrium interest rate. Furthermore, as equation (15) clearly indicates, only changes in the money supply (M_O) or the parameters of the money demand function (k) can bring about a change in the equilibrium level of income. Consequently, within the Quantity Theory framework, government fiscal policy by itself is powerless to influence the *level* of aggregate income; it can only influence the allocation of resources between the government and the private community. Consequently, higher government outlays would not mean greater national income, but only less consumer and investment goods. Only a change in money market conditions, such as a change in the supply of money or a change in the parameter k (or V, the velocity of circulation) which would shift the *LM* curve to the right, can bring about a change in the level of income. In short, only monetary policy instruments can be used effectively to manage the level of national income.

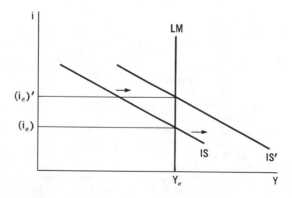

Figure 3. Money Market Determination of the Level of Income

This kind of analysis leads Milton Friedman to propose that we de-emphasize fiscal policy and concentrate primarily on monetary policy. Nevertheless, he does not approve of monetary policy as currently conducted. He feels that our knowledge of the time lags involved in monetary processes and of the "transmission mechanism" through which monetary changes affect their results is much too limited for us to manage the economy on a day to day or even month to month basis. He is convinced that acceleration or deceleration of the rate of growth of the money supply is an important cause of instability.* Hence, he proposes that we simply establish a fixed rule for the monetary authorities to follow: increase the money supply at a steady, predetermined rate. He suggests 3 to 5 percent per year as an appropriate range. He would hope by this technique to induce a steady increase in the level of national income with minimum disturbance caused by fluctuating federal taxation and expenditure levels.

This discussion indicates the importance of the dispute over the role of interest rates in the public's money demand behavior. A great deal of empirical work has been carried out to provide information on this question. Most of the studies have taken the form of regression analysis, in which money balances are the dependent variables and various interest rates, measures of income, and measures of wealth are independent variables. Though Friedman's work supports the classical Quantity Theory tradition, few other investigators agree with his interpretation of his results. Most empirical studies indicate that the interest rate is an important argument in the money demand function and that variations in the quantity of money balances demanded can be more completely explained by assigning a critical role to the interest rate. The evidence to date seems to favor the Liquidity Preference Theory in its general outlines. More importantly, these results indicate that *both* monetary and fiscal measures have an important role to play in the array of policy tools with which the government can manage the aggregate economy.**

*See Milton Friedman and Anna Schwartz, "Money and Business Cycles," Conference on the State of Monetary Economics, *Review of Economics and Statistics*, Supplement (February 1963) and Milton Friedman, "The Lag Effect in Monetary Policy," *Journal of Political Economy* (October 1961), pp. 447–466, and "The Role of Monetary Policy," *American Economic Review*, Vol. 58 (March 1968), pp. 1–17. The role of acceleration and deceleration of money supply growth as a causal factor in economic fluctuations is discussed in readings by Brunner, Cagan, Meltzer, and Smith that follow chapter 9.

**For the results of some interesting tests carried out to measure the relative effectiveness of monetary and fiscal actions in stabilization policies, *see* L. Andersen and J. Jordan, "Monetary and Fiscal Actions: A Test of Their Relative Importance in Economic Stabilization," The Federal Reserve Bank of St. Louis *Review* (November 1968). *See* also the survey of empirical tests of the demand for money function which appears as one of the readings following chapter 5. Evidence from various econometric models is discussed in the readings by Brunner, Fand, Meltzer, and Smith that follow chapter 9.

Questions/ *chapter 7*

1. What determines the level of income in the classical model of the aggregate economy?

2. Explain (without the aid of graphs) why governmental fiscal policy may be totally ineffective in changing the level of income in the economy if the demand-for-money function is interest insensitive.

3. Suppose all expenditure demand functions in the economy were completely unresponsive to changes in the rate of interest. What would the basic *LM–IS* graphical portrayal of this model look like? What would be the relative efficacy of monetary and fiscal policies in such an economy? Explain.

4. Did the classical economists believe that monetary factors could never influence the rate of interest? What do Fisher's "transition periods" and Friedman's "transmission mechanism" have to do with the analysis of this chapter?

Bibliography / chapter 7

Andersen, L. C., and J. Jordan, "Monetary and Fiscal Actions: A Test of Their Relative Importance in Economic Stabilization," *The Federal Reserve Bank of St. Louis Review* (November 1968), pp. 11-24.

Andersen, L. C., "Additional Empirical Evidence on the Reverse-Causation Argument," The Federal Reserve Bank of St. Louis *Review* (August 1969), pp. 19-23.

Brunner, Karl, "The Role of Money and Monetary Policy," Federal Reserve Bank of St. Louis *Review*, Vol. 50 (July 1968), pp. 9-24.

Davis, Richard, "How Much Does Money Matter? A Look at Some Recent Evidence," *Monthly Review*, Federal Reserve Bank of New York (June 1969).

deLeeuw, F., and J. Kalchbrenner, "Comment" on "Monetary and Fiscal Actions: A Test of Their Relative Importance in Economic Stabilization," by L. Andersen and J. Jordan, The Federal Reserve Bank of St. Louis *Review* (April 1969), pp. 6–11.

DePrano, Michael, and Thomas Mayer, "Tests of the Relative Importance of Autonomous Expenditures and Money," *American Economic Review*, Vol. 55 (September 1965), pp. 729-752.

Fand, David, "Some Issues in Monetary Economics," Federal Reserve Bank of St. Louis *Review* (January 1970), pp. 12-27.

Friedman, Milton, "The Role of Monetary Policy," *American Economic Review*, Vol. 58 (March 1968), pp. 1-17.

Friedman, Milton, and David Meiselman, "Relative Stability of Monetary Velocity and the Investment Multiplier in the U.S., 1897-1958," in

Commission on Money and Credit, *Stabilization Policies.* Englewood Cliffs, New Jersey: Prentice-Hall Inc., 1963, pp. 105-268.

Hester, Donald D., "Keynes and the Quantity Theory: A Comment on the Friedman-Meiselman CMC Paper," *Review of Economics and Statistics*, Vol. 46 (November 1964), pp. 376-377.

Meltzer, Allan H., "Comment on the Role of Money in National Economic Policy," in *Controlling Monetary Aggregates*: Proceedings of a Monetary Conference of the Federal Reserve Bank of Boston (June 1969).

Modigliani, Franco, and Albert Ando, "The Relative Stability of Monetary Velocity and the Investment Multiplier," *American Economic Review*, Vol. 55 (September 1965), pp. 693-728.

Patinkin, Don, "Keynesian Economics and the Quantity Theory," *Post Keynesian Economics*, edited by K. Kurihara. New Brunswick, New Jersey: Rutgers University Press, 1954, pp. 123-152.

8

Macroeconomic Models: Aggregate Supply and Aggregate Demand

INTRODUCTION

In chapter 6 we introduced a basic $LM - IS$ analysis of the Keynesian model of the aggregate economy. In that model the income-expenditure sector was represented by three linear equations: a saving (consumption) function, an investment demand function and an equilibrium condition. Three linear equations also served to describe the monetary sector: a money demand function, a money supply equation, and the market equilibrium condition. The aggregate economy was said to be in "equilibrium" when these six equations were solved simultaneously for values of income and the interest rate which would satisfy the equilibrium conditions in both sectors.

Two crucial assumptions were made in the development of that model. First, the price level was assumed to be constant, so that changes in nominal values were also changes in real values. Secondly, equilibrium in aggregate demand (i.e., in the income-expenditure sector and the monetary sector simultaneously) was referred to as equilibrium for the aggregate economy as a whole. No explicit reference was made to the supply (production and labor market) sector of the economy.

In this chapter, we expand that analysis of the aggregate economy. To accomplish this, four major modifications are made in the traditional *LM* – *IS* model presented in chapter 6. First, the money supply is made an endogenous variable, as suggested in chapter 1; secondly, additional behavioral influences on consumption and investment expenditures are included; thirdly, the price level and the level of money wages are introduced as explicit variables in the analysis; and fourthly, a supply (labor market) sector is added.

The order of presentation is based on the historical development of the theories attempting to explain the operation of the aggregate economy. We begin with a neoclassical model from which the Quantity Theory conclusions are derived. "Keynesian" factors such as wage rigidity, the liquidity trap, and interest-insensitive investment demand are then introduced. In chapter 9, we will introduce the real-balance effect and examine the role of this mechanism in the neoclassical response to the Keynesian critique.

AGGREGATE DEMAND*

THE INCOME-EXPENDITURE SECTOR

All behavioral relations in the income-expenditure sector of our model are specified to be relations between *real variables*, i.e., neither consumers nor investors suffer from money illusion. Money illusion refers to the notion that an equiproportionate change in both the nominal money stock and the prices of all commodities, even though it leaves all relative prices, real wealth, and the real value of money balances, $\frac{M}{P}$, unchanged, will nonetheless cause a change in some *real* aspect of an individual's economic behavior. As Don Patinkin notes ". . . if the initial paper-money endowment of an *illusion free* individual were suddenly increased and he were simultaneously confronted in the market by new money prices, all of which had increased in the same proportion, he would once again have *no reason* for

---

*The development of this model closely relates to the following works: Martin Bailey, *National Income and the Price Level* (New York: McGraw-Hill, 1962), chapters 2 and 3; Boris Pesek and Thomas Saving, *Money, Wealth and Economic Theory* (New York: Macmillan, 1967), chapters 1 and 2; and Warren Smith, "A Graphical Exposition of the Complete Keynesian System," *The Southern Economic Journal*, Vol. 23 (October 1956), pp. 115–125.

changing the amount demanded of any commodity."* (italics added) An individual whose demand for some commodity *would change* in these circumstances would be said to be suffering from money illusion. We assume that both consumption and investment expenditure decisions depend on the level of income and the interest rate.** The absence of money illusion implies that at given levels of *real income* and the *interest rate*, people will spend the same amount on *real* consumption and *real* investment regardless of the prevailing price level.*** The expenditure relations embodying these assumptions may be written as follows:†

$$\frac{C}{P} = C\left(\frac{Y}{P}, i\right) = \frac{a}{P} + b \cdot \frac{Y}{P} + \frac{e}{P} \cdot i \; ; \tag{1}$$

$$0 < \frac{\partial C/P}{\partial Y/P} < 1;$$

the sign of $\dfrac{\partial C/P}{\partial i}$ is not restricted *a priori* ;

$$\frac{I}{P} = I\left(\frac{Y}{P}, i\right) = \frac{a'}{P} + g \cdot \frac{Y}{P} + \frac{h}{P} \cdot i \; \dagger\dagger; \tag{2}$$

$$0 < \frac{\partial I/P}{\partial Y/P} < 1 \text{ and } \frac{\partial I/P}{\partial i} < 0.$$

*Don Patinkin, *Money, Interest and Prices*, 2nd edition (New York: Harper and Row, 1965) p. 22.

**For analytical simplicity, we abstract from government expenditure and taxation for the time being. Alternatively, they may be assumed to be subsumed in the autonomous components of the investment demand and consumption functions.

***This is most easily rationalized if we assume unitary elasticity of price expectations. This implies that people expect the current price level to prevail in the future; but if prices change (unexpectedly), the public will then expect the new price level to prevail, i.e., they would expect neither a return to the old price level nor a continuation of the rate of price change in its current direction. This concept was introduced by J. R. Hicks in *Value and Capital* (Oxford: The Clarendon Press, 1939), p. 205. As he states: "If the elasticity of expectations is unity, a change in current prices will change expected prices in the same direction and in the same proportion; if prices were previously expected to be constant at the old level, they are now expected to be constant at the new level; changes in prices are expected to be permanent."

†A glossary of the symbols used in the following model appears at the end of this chapter.

††The expression $g(Y/P)$ shows that investment spending can be induced by an increase in real income where g is the marginal propensity to invest. As in chapter 6, we assume some familiarity with the behavior indicated by equations (1) and (2) from elementary macroeconomics.

All variables other than P , the price level, and i, the interest rate, and all parameters other than b and g, are stated in nominal dollar terms, but are deflated by the index of the average price level to yield *real* values. Thus, the terms a/P, a'/P, Y/P, etc., represent *real values* as implied by the assumed absence of any money illusion. This assumption further implies that if the price level should double, a, a', Y and the other nominal values would have to double in order to maintain a/P, a'/P, Y/P and the other real variables at *constant real levels*. This makes the linear consumption and investment demand equations homogeneous of degree zero in nominal values and prices.*

By expressing the behavioral (expenditure) relations in this form, the average price level (P) is eliminated as a separate variable in these equations. Regardless of changes in the price level, real expenditure decisions remain unchanged. Consequently, the unknowns in these equations are specified as (C/P), (I/P), (Y/P) and (i).

When these two expenditure demand functions are combined with the equilibrium condition for income and output (for a closed economy)

$$\frac{Y}{P} = \frac{C}{P} + \frac{I}{P}, \tag{3}$$

we derive a three equation model in *four* unknowns. This linear system cannot be solved for equilibrium values of all four variables but it can, through substitution, be reduced to one equation in two unknowns.

Substituting equations (1) and (2) into (3) yields:

$$\frac{Y}{P} = \frac{a}{P} + b \cdot \frac{Y}{P} + \frac{e}{P} (i) + \frac{a'}{P} + g \cdot \frac{Y}{P} + \frac{h}{P} (i)$$

$$\frac{Y}{P} = \frac{(a/P + a'/P) + (e/P + h/P)i}{1 - b - g} = \frac{a/P + a'/P}{1 - (b + g)} + \frac{(e/P + h/P)i}{1 - (b + g)}. \tag{4}$$

This is a linear form only slightly more complicated than the equation of the *IS* curve in chapters 6 and 7. The intercept term is

$$(a/P + a'/P)/[1 - (b + g)]$$

and the slope is:

$$(e/P + h/P)/[1 - (b + g)].$$

*We shall not consider certain distributional effects of a changing price level in this discussion. Instead, we assume that when the average price level, P, changes, the prices of all goods and services in the economy change in the same proportion.

We may expect $(b + g) < 1$, i.e., the marginal propensity to spend out of real income is less than one. Thus, $1 - (b + g) > 0$. Likewise, h/P is likely to be negative while e/P, through possibly positive, can be expected to be small. Therefore, $(e/P + h/P) < 0$. As a result, the slope of this equation, which represents all combinations of real income, Y/P, and the interest rate, i, which bring equilibrium to the income-expenditure sector (i.e., which equate planned saving and planned investment) will be negative. This equation may be graphed as follows:

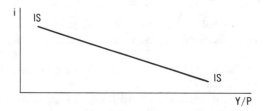

Figure 1. The Income-Expenditure Equilibrium Curve (*IS*)

Recalling our assumptions about the absence of money illusion, examination of equation (4) indicates that the *position of this curve is independent of the price level.* If the price level should increase, for example, all nominal values increase in the same proportion, and the slope and intercept terms in equation (4) remain unchanged.

THE MONETARY SECTOR

Our analysis of the monetary sector begins with the assumption that the *nominal* stock of money supplied to the economy is an increasing function of the interest rate. As we have seen in chapters 1 and 2, institutional and legal conditions establish the framework within which the public, commercial banks, and the monetary authorities interact to determine the actual money supply. For example, the monetary authorities set the reserve requirements determining the volume of legal reserves that member banks must hold against their demand and time deposit liabilities. Also, they have the power to determine the size of the monetary base. The public, on the other hand, determines its preferred asset ratios, which influence the allocation of the monetary base among its alternative uses either as reserves against demand deposits, reserves against time deposits or as currency holdings of the public (*see* chapter 1).

Given these factors, commercial banks determine the final volume of money which will be created on the basis of the unborrowed monetary base. Bank borrowing from the central bank can increase reserve holdings and expand the deposit creating capabilities of the banks. Holding reserve balances in excess of requirements tends to absorb legal reserves and to decrease the money creating abilities of banks. In this way, the money stock depends on the behavior of banks relating to their desired holdings of excess and borrowed reserves.

One of the important factors affecting this aspect of bank behavior is the market interest rate. If the market rate is high, banks will be induced to hold a relatively small volume of reserves in excess of legal requirements, since the interest rate represents the alternative cost of holding these reserves. But the lower their desired excess legal reserves, the greater the volume of loans banks will extend and the larger the volume of deposit liabilities they will have outstanding for a given monetary base. Therefore, as holdings of excess legal reserves vary inversely with the market interest rate, the money stock can be expected to vary directly with variations in that rate.*

Similarly, banks will increase their borrowing from the Federal Reserve when the differential between the market rate and the discount rate increases. As a result, for a given discount rate, the higher the market rate, the greater the volume of bank borrowing and the larger the stock of liabilities created by the commercial banks.

Therefore, given the monetary base, the required reserve ratios set by the authorities and the preferred asset ratios of the public, the nominal money supply can be expected to vary directly with the rate of interest, i.e.,

$$M_s = \gamma(i) \qquad \frac{\partial M_s}{\partial i} > 0 . \tag{5}$$

This relationship is shown in the figure below:

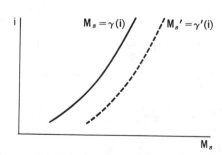

Figure 2. The Supply of Money Function

*A money supply model that incorporates this relation in a structural equation is presented in chapter 1. Note that having the money supply depend on the (endogenous) interest rate causes the money stock *to be affected* by economic activity as well as *to affect* that activity. It is this point that lies at the center of much of the so-called reverse causation controversy over the econometric models which purport that the money supply is a statistically exogenous variable. For further discussion of this matter see the second reading by Fand and the readings by Brunner, Smith, and Meltzer, which follow chapter 9.

The position of this curve is assumed to depend on all the factors listed above. For example, if the monetary authorities *increase* the monetary base, the curve will shift from M_s to M_s'. The slope of the curve will depend on the marginal responses of desired excess and borrowed reserve levels of commercial bankers to changes in the interest rate.

On the demand side of the money market, we assume that the desire for money balances on the part of the public stems from two sources: first, a desire for *real* transactions balances to facilitate a *real* volume of trade; and secondly, a desire to maintain some percentage of their real financial wealth in the form of money balances.* In other words, the public demands a *real* stock of money balances both to facilitate *transactions* and to hold as *speculative* (asset) balances. Following the discussion in chapters 3–5, we express the transactions demand for money as an increasing function of the level of real income, Y/P, and the speculative demand for money as a decreasing function of the market rate of interest, i. These two components of total money demand are assumed to be additive, and the public's behavior is again assumed free of money illusion.

$$M_d/P = L_1(Y/P) + L_2(i).** \qquad \frac{\partial M_d/P}{\partial Y/P} > 0 \qquad \frac{\partial M_d/P}{\partial i} < 0 \qquad (6)$$

Equilibrium in the money market requires that the *real* volume of money in circulation be just sufficient to satisfy the public's real demand for money balances.

$$\frac{M_s}{P} = \frac{M_d}{P}. \qquad (7)$$

To make equation (5) consistent with the equilibrium condition, we divide both sides by the price level, P. Substitution of equations (5) and (6) into (7) then yields the money market equilibrium equation:

$$\frac{1}{P} \cdot \gamma(i) = L_1\left(\frac{Y}{P}\right) + L_2(i) \qquad (8)$$

---

*See Alfred Marshall, *Money, Credit and Commerce* (London: Macmillan and Company, Ltd., 1923).

**Differing demand-for-money hypotheses lead to the same *general* functional form for the money demand relation. Our structural analysis is completely compatible with these alternative formulations. It is the *a priori* restrictions placed on the partial derivative of these forms and the empirical specification of these equations that we would expect to differ under varying formulations of the theory of money demand. *See* chapters 3 and 4 and the survey of empirical money demand literature in the readings which follow chapter 5 for a detailed analysis of the alternative hypotheses that yield these specifications.

In order to solve this system of equations for equilibrium solutions in terms of the exogenous variables and the parameters of the model, let us assume linear functional forms to represent the relations between the nominal stock of money supplied and the interest rate and between the real stock of money demanded and real income and the interest rate. Thus,

$$M_s = \gamma(i) = j + d \cdot i \ * \quad \text{and} \tag{9}$$

$$\frac{M_d}{P} = L_1(Y/P) + L_2(i) = \frac{m}{P} + k\frac{Y}{P} + \frac{u}{P}i \ . \quad \text{Then, in equilibrium:} \tag{10}$$

$$\frac{1}{P} \cdot M_s = \frac{M_d}{P}$$

$$\frac{1}{P} \cdot (j + di) = \frac{m}{P} + k\frac{Y}{P} + \frac{u}{P}i$$

$$\frac{Y}{P} = \frac{1}{k}\left[\left(\frac{1}{P} \cdot j - \frac{m}{P}\right) + \left(\frac{1}{P} \cdot d - \frac{u}{P}\right)i\right] \tag{11}$$

It is extremely important to note that the parameters j and d from the (nominal) money supply equation *do not* react to price changes in the same way as the parameters m and u from the (real) money demand relation. Our assumption of no money illusion on the part of individuals who demand real money balances implies that when the price level, P, changes, the nominal values m and u change by the same proportion, leaving the ratios m/P and u/P unchanged. The supply of money, however, is specified in nominal terms. It follows then, that there is no reason for the parameters j and d to change when the price level changes. Consequently, in the money market equilibrium equation (eq. 11) there are three unknowns: real income, Y/P, the interest rate, i, and the price level, P. The presence of the price level as a distinct variable in this equation reflects our assumption that the behavior of the public, the banks, and the monetary authorities determines the *nominal* money stock.

The equilibrium condition in this market can be depicted as a family of market equilibrium curves. The graphical derivation of these curves is shown on page 342.

---

*Compare this formulation to the linear functional forms of chapter 1; here the monetary base may be assumed to be incorporated in the intercept term (j). This explains how the variable base could appear as an exogenous variable in reduced form equations such as the one on page 346 and the ones discussed in several of the readings which follow chapter 9.

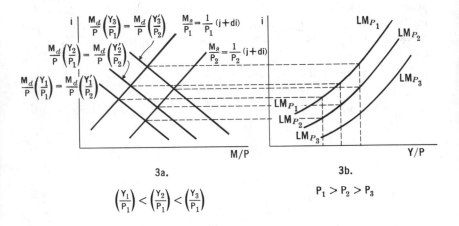

3a.   3b.

$$\left(\frac{Y_1}{P_1}\right) < \left(\frac{Y_2}{P_1}\right) < \left(\frac{Y_3}{P_1}\right)$$ $$P_1 > P_2 > P_3$$

Figure 3. Monetary Sector Equilibrium Curves (*LM*)

In Figure 3a, real money balances $\left(\dfrac{M}{P}\right)$ are measured along the horizontal axis. Since the demand for money depends upon both the level of real income and the interest rate, a family of money demand curves appears in the real money balances-interest rate plane. Each curve shows the volume of real money balances demanded at every level of the interest rate for a given level of real income. For example, $\dfrac{M_d}{P}(Y_1/P_1)$ shows how the demand for real money balances varies with the interest rate when real income is assumed to be $\dfrac{Y_1}{P_1}$. For any given level of the interest rate, real money balances demanded will be greater the greater level of real income. As a result, $\dfrac{M_d}{P}(Y_2/P_1)$, representing the demand for real money balances at income level

$$\frac{Y_2}{P_1} > \frac{Y_1}{P_1}$$

lies to the right of $\dfrac{M_d}{P}(Y_1/P_1)$.

A given *real* income level $\left(\dfrac{Y_1}{P_1}\right)$ represents any one of an infinite number of nominal income-price level combinations. For example, if nominal income is Y_1 and the price level is P_1, real income will be $\dfrac{Y_1}{P_1}$. But this same real income level would also result from a nominal income level of $2Y_1$ and a price level of $2P_1$, i.e., $\dfrac{2Y_1}{2P_1} = \dfrac{Y_1}{P_1}$.

Let us assume an initial price level of P_1. If

$$Y_1 < Y_2 < Y_3, \quad \text{then} \quad \frac{Y_1}{P_1} < \frac{Y_2}{P_1} < \frac{Y_3}{P_1}.$$

Three curves showing how the demand for real money balances varies with the interest rate at these real income levels are drawn in Figure 3a.

Since the money supply relation is expressed in nominal terms, it must be modified to depict the real values reflected in our diagram. This is done simply by dividing the nominal money supply function by the average price level. Thus, for an assumed initial price level, P_1, the money supply relation, $\dfrac{M_s}{P_1} = \dfrac{1}{P_1}\,(j + di)$, is shown in Figure 3a as an upward sloping line.

Given the price level, the intersection point of the single money supply curve with the family of money demand curves yields combinations of the interest rate and the level of real income which equate the supply of and demand for real money balances. These points may be used to locate the money market equilibrium curve LM_{P_1} in Figure 3b. This curve, derived under the assumption of a constant price level, P_1, is similar to the LM curve employed in the analysis of chapter 6 (also derived under the assumption of a constant level of prices).

What happens to the money demand curve if the price level should change? Suppose, for example that the price level falls to $P_2 < P_1$. There is some nominal income level $Y_1' < Y_1$ such that $\dfrac{Y_1'}{P_2} = \dfrac{Y_1}{P_1}$. Therefore, the money demand curve $\dfrac{M_d}{P}\left(\dfrac{Y_1'}{P_2}\right)$ coincides with $\dfrac{M_d}{P}\left(\dfrac{Y_1}{P_1}\right)$; both curves showing the relation between real money balances demanded, and the interest rate at a given level of *real* income. But what happens to the money supply curve if the price level should change? Since the money supply function is specified in nominal terms, when the price level falls, the same volume of nominal balances supplied by the monetary system will represent a greater volume of *real* money balances. Therefore, at each interest rate $\dfrac{M_s}{P_2} = \dfrac{1}{P_2}\,(j + di)$ lies to the right of $\dfrac{M_s}{P_1} = \dfrac{1}{P_1}\,(j + di)$.

The new money supply curve together with the family of money demand curves generates a new money market equilibrium curve, LM_{P_2}. The new curve lies to the right of LM_{P_1}, indicating that in money market equilibrium at the lower price level, P_2, each interest rate level will now be associated with a higher level of *real* income and each real income level will now be associated with a lower interest rate. Along the new money market equilibrium curve, LM_{P_2}, nominal money balances supplied to the economy at each interest rate represent a larger stock of real balances at the lower price level. Therefore, at unchanged interest rate levels, only a higher level of real income can cause the nonbank public to demand these additional real money balances (for transactions purposes), thereby bringing the money market into equilibrium. As a consequence, at each interest rate level, the new money market equilibrium curve (LM_{P_2}) lies *to the right* of the old money market equilibrium curve (LM_{P_1}).

As another way of looking at this, at unchanged real income levels only a lower interest rate can cause the nonbank public to demand the additional real money balances (for speculative purposes) thereby bringing the money market into equilibrium. As a consequence, at each real income level the new money market equilibrium curve (LM_{P_2}) lies *below* the old money market equilibrium curve (LM_{P_1}). (The simple analytics of a shift in the LM curve are discussed in more detail in chapter 6.)

Proceeding in this manner, we can derive a family of money market equilibrium curves—one for each possible price level. For example, in figure 3b, LM_{P_3} represents a money market equilibrium curve for a still lower level of prices than LM_{P_2}.

Now consider the equilibrium curve for the monetary sector (equation 11) together with the equilibrium curve for the income-expenditure sector (equation 4). If, as in chapters 6 and 7, we assume that the price level is constant, we are restricted to just one of the family of money market equilibrium curves. In Figure 4, where the two curves intersect, there is equilibrium in both the income-expenditure sector and the monetary sector.

Analytically, this is equivalent to solving equations (4) and (11) simultaneously for the level of income and the interest rate at an assumed (constant) level of prices. This solution is presented below for an assumed price level P_2.

$$\frac{Y}{P_2} = \frac{a/P_2 + a'/P_2}{1 - (b + g)} + \frac{(e/P_2 + h/P_2)}{1 - (b + g)} \cdot i \tag{4}$$

$$\frac{Y}{P_2} = \frac{1}{k}\left[\left(\frac{1}{P_2} \cdot j - \frac{m}{P_2}\right) + \left(\frac{1}{P_2} \cdot d - \frac{u}{P_2}\right) \cdot i\right] \tag{11}$$

Solving each of these equations for the interest rate, i, yields

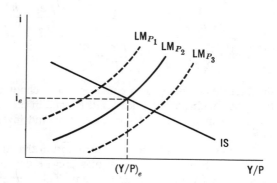

Figure 4. Expenditure and Money Market Equilibrium at Fixed Prices

$$i = \frac{(1 - (b + g))}{(e/P_2 + h/P_2)} \cdot \frac{Y}{P_2} - \frac{(a/P_2 + a'/P_2)}{(e/P_2 + h/P_2)} \tag{4'}$$

and

$$i = \frac{k}{\left(\dfrac{1}{P_2} \cdot d - \dfrac{u}{P_2}\right)} \cdot \frac{Y}{P_2} - \frac{\left(\dfrac{1}{P_2} \cdot j - \dfrac{m}{P_2}\right)}{\left(\dfrac{1}{P_2} \cdot d - \dfrac{u}{P_2}\right)} \tag{11'}$$

Substitution then yields the solution (in terms of the parameters of the model) for the equilibrium level of income:

$$\frac{Y}{P_2}\left[\frac{1 - (b + g)}{e/P_2 + h/P_2} - \frac{k}{\left(\dfrac{1}{P_2} \cdot d - \dfrac{u}{P_2}\right)}\right] = \frac{(a/P_2 + a'/P_2)}{(e/P_2 + h/P_2)} - \frac{\left(\dfrac{1}{P_2} \cdot j - \dfrac{m}{P_2}\right)}{\left(\dfrac{1}{P_2} \cdot d - \dfrac{u}{P_2}\right)}$$

$$\frac{Y}{P_2} = \frac{\left[\dfrac{a/P_2 + a'/P_2}{e/P_2 + h/P_2} - \dfrac{\dfrac{1}{P_2} \cdot j - \dfrac{m}{P_2}}{\dfrac{1}{P_2} \cdot d - \dfrac{u}{P_2}}\right]}{\left[\dfrac{1 - (b + g)}{(e/P_2 + h/P_2)} - \dfrac{k}{\left(\dfrac{1}{P_2} \cdot d - \dfrac{u}{P_2}\right)}\right]}$$

Simplifying:

$$\frac{Y}{P_2} = \frac{(a/P_2 + a'/P_2)\left(\dfrac{1}{P_2} \cdot d - \dfrac{u}{P_2}\right) - \left(\dfrac{1}{P_2} \cdot j - \dfrac{m}{P_2}\right)\left(\dfrac{e}{P_2} + \dfrac{h}{P_2}\right)}{(1 - (b + g))\left(\dfrac{1}{P_2} \cdot d - \dfrac{u}{P_2}\right) - k\left(\dfrac{e}{P_2} + \dfrac{h}{P_2}\right)}$$

This equation is directly comparable to equation (9) in chapter 6. It differs only in its explicit inclusion of price level, P_2, and in the inclusion of the new behavioral parameters from the consumption and investment demand functions.*

Implicit in the analysis so far has been the assumption that the response of aggregate supply to changes in the level of aggregate demand consists exclusively of a quantity (real output) adjustment. This is implied by our assumption of a constant, exogenously determined, general price level. In contrast, if we assume instead that the response of aggregate supply to changes in aggregate demand is not constrained to a pure quantity adjustment, then the general price level becomes a variable endogenous to our model.

With a variable price level, no single *LM* curve can be isolated to represent the locus of money market equilibrium values for the level of real in-

---

*The effects of a change in some component of autonomous expenditures may be seen in this equation. For example, assume the volume of autonomous investment spending, a'/P, increases and shifts the *IS* curve.

$$\frac{\partial Y/P_2}{\partial a'/P_2} = \frac{(1/P_2) \cdot d - (u/P_2)}{[1 - (b + g)] \, [(1/P_2) \cdot d - (u/P_2)] - k(e/P_2 + h/P_2)}$$

$$= \frac{1}{[1 - (b + g)] - \dfrac{k(e/P_2 + h/P_2)}{(1/P_2 \cdot d - u/P_2)}}$$

This derivative indicates the order of magnitude of the change in real income caused by an increase in autonomous investment expenditures. It may be employed in a strictly qualitative way to determine the direction of the effect of an increase in autonomous investment expenditures on the level of income. Since

$$1 > [1 - (b + g)] > 0$$
$$1 > k > 0$$
$$(e/P_2 + h/P_2) < 0$$
$$\frac{u}{P_2} < 0, \text{ and } \frac{1}{P_2} \cdot d > 0$$

the last term in the denominator

$$\frac{k(e/P_2 + h/P_2)}{\left(\dfrac{1}{P_2} \cdot d - \dfrac{u}{P_2}\right)} \text{ will be } \textit{negative.}$$

As a result, the derivative is seen to be *positive* and an *increase* in investment expenditures will *increase* the level of income.

come and the level of the interest rate, and no unique solution for these variables can be found in the *LM-IS* quadrant. This is illustrated in Figure 4. In other words, the aggregate demand sector (*LM* and *IS* curves) are not sufficient by themselves to provide a determinate solution for our model because we will have added to our aggregate demand sector a new variable, the general price level, but no new equations. Therefore, in order to be able to discuss the determination of the general price level jointly with the determination of the level of real income, the interest rate, and all the other variables of the model, we now add a set of be-havioral relations describing the aggregate supply (production and labor market) sector of the economy.

AGGREGATE SUPPLY

We first explicitly introduce the labor market and a production function into this model and examine its comparative-static characteristics under the classical assumption of perfect price-wage flexibility. Pure competi-tion is assumed in all markets.

The Supply of Labor. Assume that individuals attempt to balance the mar-ginal disutility of labor with the marginal utility of income. Since the util-ity to be derived from money income depends on its real value or purchas-ing power, the quantity of labor supplied will depend primarily on the *real* return from offering one's labor services—the real wage rate (w/P). Under the joint assumptions of diminishing marginal utility of consumption (out of earned income) and increasing marginal disutility of work, the labor sup-ply function will have a positive slope indicating that laborers will only supply more labor at higher real wage rates. We may express this as follows:

$$N_s = N_s(w/P) \tag{12}$$

$$\frac{\partial N_s}{\partial(w/P)} > 0.$$

The Demand for Labor. On the demand side of the market, profit maxi-mizing conditions indicate that firms hire workers up to the point where the real wage they must pay the employee is equal to the marginal produc-tivity of labor.* Assume a simple aggregate production function:

---

*For the individual firm, given its production function, the demand curve for its product and the labor supply curve it faces, and where capital costs are invariate in the short run, profit may be defined as $\pi = P \cdot O - w \cdot N - c$, where c represents con-stant capital costs. The first order condition for profit maximization requires

$$\frac{\partial \pi}{\partial N} = \left[\frac{dP}{dO} \cdot O + P\right]\frac{\partial O}{\partial N} - \left[\frac{\partial w}{\partial N} \cdot N + w\right] = 0$$

which simplifies to the general proposition that the profit-maximizing firm will hire labor until its marginal revenue product equals its marginal factor cost,

$$O = Y/P = \ell(N,K) \tag{13}$$

where O is the real volume of output from production and K is the capital stock used in the production process. Then

$$\frac{w}{P} = \frac{\partial O}{\partial N} = \ell'(N, K) \tag{14}$$

where $\ell'(N, K)$ is the first derivative of the aggregate production function with respect to labor input. Diminishing marginal productivity of labor (derived from the aggregate production function under the assumption that the stock of capital, K, and level of technology are held constant and that the function increases monotonically over the relevant domain) implies a downward sloping demand for labor curve. These relations are represented graphically in Figure 5:

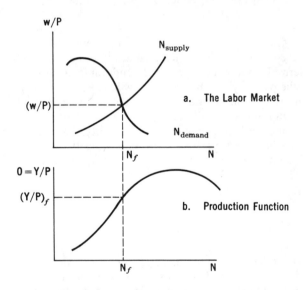

Figure 5. The Labor Market

$$\frac{\partial O}{\partial N}\left[P\left(1 + \frac{O}{P} \cdot \frac{dP}{dO}\right)\right] = w\left(1 + \frac{N}{w} \cdot \frac{\partial w}{\partial N}\right).$$

The reciprocals of the final terms on either side of the equation represent the price elasticity of product demand and the wage elasticity of labor supply, respectively. In pure competition, these terms are equal to zero, and the expression simplifies to the condition that the profit-maximizing firm will hire labor until its marginal physical product is equal to the real wage, $\dfrac{\partial O}{\partial N} = \dfrac{w}{P}$.

If we assume price-wage flexibility and perfectly competitive conditions in the labor market, the money wage rate will be bid to a level which, together with the current price level, will establish a real wage which equates the supply of and demand for labor. This is the position of intersection shown in Figure 5a. Since everyone who is willing to offer his labor services at this wage rate will be employed, this position is defined as full employment. When this level of employment is substituted into the production function (in Figure 5b) the full employment level of real output $(Y/P)_f$ is determined.*

This may be shown symbolically. We may represent the aggregate supply sector as a system of four equations—labor supply, labor demand, the equilibrium condition and the production function—in four unknowns—$N_s, N_d, Y/P$, and w/P. These relations are shown below.

$$N_s = N_s(w/P) \tag{12}$$

$$N_d = N_d(w/P) \tag{14}$$

$$N_s = N_d \tag{15}$$

$$Y/P = \ell(N, K) \tag{13}$$

K, the capital stock, is assumed fixed. By substitution we can solve equations (12), (14) and (15) for the level of employment, N:

$$N_f = N(w/P)$$

Then from the production function (equation (13)), we may solve for the full employment volume of output, (Y/P).

$$(Y/P)_f = \ell(N(w/P), K) = \phi(w/P) \tag{16}$$

*The reader will note that we have associated full employment with the equilibrium solution in the labor market. Likewise, involuntary unemployment will be associated with disequilibrium or with points off the supply curve of labor. In discussing these definitions, Don Patinkin notes: "The norm of reference to be used in defining involuntary unemployment is the supply curve of labor; for this curve shows the amount of employment which the workers of the economy want to obtain in the light of the money wage, price level, and budget restraints with which they are confronted. Hence as long as workers are "on their supply curve"—that is, as long as they succeed in selling all the labor they want to at the prevailing real wage rate—a state of full employment will be said to exist in the economy. . . . Thus, by definition, the extent of involuntary unemployment is identical with the extent of the excess supply of labor which exists at the prevailing wage rate." Don Patinkin, *Money, Interest and Prices*, 2nd edition (New York: Harper and Row, 1965), pp. 314-315.

Recently, the effects of accelerating and decelerating price inflation as causes of changes in employment have been analyzed by R. E. Lucas and L. A. Rapping in "Real Wages, Employment, and Inflation," *Journal of Political Economy*, Vol. 77 (Sept./Oct. 1969), pp. 721-754.

THE EQUILIBRIUM SOLUTION
FOR ALL THREE MARKETS

The solution for the equilibrium values of all the variables in our model may be viewed as follows. The labor market represents a fully determinate (i. e., separable) subset of the global model. There are four equations (labor demand, labor supply, the equilibrium condition, and the production function) and four unknowns (N_s, N_d, w/P, Y/P). This subset is sufficient to determine the level of employment, the volume of real output, and the real wage rate (as shown in Figure 5). The substitution of this solution for the volume of real output into the income-expenditure equilibrium equation (equation (4)) determines the rate of interest (that rate which will equate planned saving (S) and planned investment (I) at the full employment level of output.

The subsequent substitution of these solution values for Y/P and i into the money market equilibrium equation (equation (11)) determines the price level. Prices will be at that level sufficient to equate the *real* value of the *nominal* supply of money balances provided through the monetary system with the *real* volume of money balances demanded at the levels of Y/P and i determined in the labor market and the income-expenditure sector, respectively. Finally, the money wage rate, w, will be set at that level which, together with the absolute price level determined in the money market, will equal the real wage, w/P, determined in the labor market. This model is presented graphically in Figure 6.*

Let us examine some of the characteristics of this model.

(1) The levels of employment (N), real output (Y/P) and the real wage rate (w/P) are determined in the labor market (in conjunction with the production function).

(2) The interest rate (i) is a "real" phenomenon determined in the income-expenditure sector (by the intersection of the IS curve with the vertical line S constructed over the full employment level of output in Figure 6. It is that rate which is just sufficient to

---

*This model is said to be solved *recursively*. One subset of the model, the labor market, is isolated and solved for the equilibrium values of the variables that enter the equations of that subset. One of these variables, real income, Y/P, may then be treated as predetermined or "known" in another subset of the global model, the income-expenditure sector. Solution values for the remaining variables in the equations of that subset may now be determined. Again, one of the variables from that subset, the interest rate i, together with the level of real income, may be treated as predetermined or "known" in the money market equations, and those equations may be solved for the equilibrium values of the remaining variables—the price level and the quantity of money supplied and demanded in the economy.

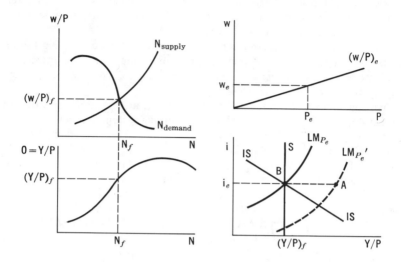

Figure 6. Aggregate General Equilibrium

equate the *real* supply of saving with the *real* volume of investment demand at full employment.

(3) The absolute price level is determined in the monetary sector. Prices will adjust to that level necessary to make the nominal money supply equal to the real quantity of money balances demanded at the level of real income and interest rate determined in the labor market and the income-expenditure sector, respectively. Graphically, the determination of the absolute price level isolates LMP_e from the entire family of money market equilibrium curves (as shown in Figure 3b).

(4) The money wage rate will adjust to that level necessary to make $(w/P)_e = (w/P)_f$; i.e., the real wage and the absolute price level determine the equilibrium money wage rate.

These conclusions reflect the classical tenets that the interest rate is a *real* variable determined by *productivity* (investment) and *thrift* (saving), and that the Quantity Theory of Money is a theory of the value of money (the absolute price level), rather than a theory of income determination or employment (see chapter 5, The Quantity Theory of Money). In this neoclassical model, the monetary variables (the absolute price level, the money wage rate, and the money stock) are determined solely by the monetary relations in the model. Thus, the equilibrium values of the *real* variables are independent of both the supply of and the demand for money.* In this way the classical economists indicated that monetary forces determined not the value of real variables in the economy, but rather only the absolute price level, i.e., the value of money.**

Let us demonstrate these quantity theory results by examining the effects of an increase in the money supply. For example, suppose there is an exogenous increase in bank reserves which causes a shift in the money-supply curve from $M_s = \gamma(i)$ to $M_s' = \gamma_2(i)$.

Now assume further that at each interest rate the nominal stock of money which would be supplied by the banking system is exactly twice as large as before. At each and every interest rate-real income level combination along the old money market equilibrium curve there exists an excess supply of money. The family of money market equilibrium curves shifts to the right since some combination of a higher level of real income or a lower interest rate is necessary to generate an increase in the demand for money to absorb the increase in supply thereby maintaining money market equilibrium. As a result, in Figure 6, LM_{P_e} shifts out to LM_{P_e}'.

In terms of economic behavior, the increased supply of bank reserves at existing price and interest rate levels will provide banks with undesired excess reserves. As banks expand loans and increase their deposit liabilities, the nonbank public finds itself with excess real money balances. As mentioned above, the excess supply of money can only be absorbed if there occurs some combination of an increase in real income or a decline in the interest rate.

However, in the present model real income cannot increase because the economy is at a full employment capacity level. Therefore, as individuals use their excess real money balances either (1) to purchase goods and services or (2) to purchase financial assets, only the general price level can rise. If the excess supply of money is spent directly on goods and services there will be an immediate excess demand for goods and services. If the excess supply of money is spent on financial assets, there will be an increase

---

*This may be seen from the recursive nature of our equation system. Since the equilibrium values of all real variables are in a sense "predetermined" in the production and expenditure sectors, if we change either the supply of or demand for money *only* those variables determined in the monetary subset (P and w) will be affected. All variables predetermined in the production and expenditure subsets remain unchanged (in equilibrium).

**The equilibrium solution of this neoclassical model may be contrasted to that of a crude classical model. In the crude classical model the equations are the same as above except that the level of real income does not enter the saving-investment equations and the interest rate does not enter the money market equations. This results in the labor market determining the real wage, employment and real income as above; the saving-investment sector determining real saving, real investment and the interest rate; and the monetary sector (given the level of real income) determining the equilibrium money stock and the general price level.

in the price of those assets and a decrease in the market rate of interest which stimulates an increase in the demand for investment goods (and consumer durables). Either way, the excess demand for goods and services will exert upward pressure on the general price level. The inflation will cease only when the price level has *exactly doubled* so as to restore real money balances to their previous equilibrium level. Finally, with real money balances restored to their former level, in Figure 6 $LM_{P_e'}$ shifts back to its original position but with prices and all nominal values exactly doubled. At the new equilibrium, *all real variables* will have the same values they had prior to the increase in the money supply. They will have been "neutral" to this increase in the money stock.*

With the interest rate at its original level, the nominal money stock will be exactly twice as high as before $(M_s' = \gamma_2(i))$. Therefore, if prices exactly double, real money balances will be the same as in the initial equilibrium,

$$\frac{2M_s}{2P} = \frac{M_s}{P}.$$

The economy adjusts to a higher nominal money stock simply by reducing the value of that money stock to the equilibrium real value (M/P). This adjustment requires a change in the price level but no change in any *real* variables.

We should note explicitly that the interest rate may diverge from its equilibrium value during the period of changing prices, while the economy is adjusting to the new higher stock of money. Although the equilibrium rate of interest is determined by real factors (productivity and thrift) during transition periods** (the period during which the economy is adjusting to a new monetary equilibrium) the interest rate may be influenced by monetary forces. In the final equilibrium, however, the interest rate will have returned to its previous value.

Consequently, we see that in this model *with perfect price-wage flexibility*, the economy *tends* towards full employment through the competitive bidding for labor and jobs in the labor market; the interest rate is a *real* phenomenon determined by productivity and thrift; and the absolute price level (P) will be proportional to the nominal money stock (the Quantity Theory holds). This analysis may be presented by means of an alternative graphical technique—a technique that makes the determination of the

---

*"Monetary neutrality" defines a situation in which the equilibrium values of the real variables are independent of changes in the *money supply*. In chapter 9 we shall examine this question more completely.

**See Irving Fisher, *The Purchasing Power of Money* (New York: Augustus M. Kelly, Bookseller, Reprints of Economic Classics, 1963) chapter 4, reprinted in the readings following chapter 5.

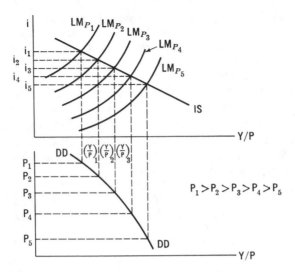

Figure 7. The Derivation of the Aggregate Demand Curve

equilibrium price level more explicit. Let us consider first the demand subset (the income-expenditure sector and the money market).

For the aggregate demand subset (equations (1) through (4), and (9) through (11), Figure 7 shows how the family of *LM* curves (reproduced from Figure 3) may be combined with the *IS* curve to yield a single aggregate demand curve (*DD*) in the *P*, *Y/P* plane. This curve shows the level of aggregate demand for real output at various price levels. For example, for the nominal money stock which would be supplied at interest rate *i*, to be sufficient to induce a level of aggregate demand equal to $(Y/P)_1$, the price level would have to be P_1. At any *lower* price level, fewer *nominal* transactions balances would be required, more money would be available for asset holding purposes by the public, leading to a lower interest rate and higher investment demand, and a higher level of real aggregate demand. Thus, the *DD* curve slopes downward to the right. *

Let us derive the equation for this aggregate demand curve in the *P*, *Y/P* plane. For analytical simplicity, assume that the nominal money stock is fixed by the authorites: $M_s = M_o$. Continue to assume a linear demand for money function.

$$\frac{M_d}{P} = \frac{m}{P} + k \cdot \frac{Y}{P} + \frac{u}{P} \cdot i \ .$$

*The *DD* curve is drawn concave to the origin to maintain consistency with the graphs presented later in the chapter when non-linearities are introduced into the basic relationships. This does not influence our essential conclusions in any way.

In equilibrium $\quad\dfrac{1}{P}M_s = \dfrac{M_d}{P}$

Substituting $\quad\dfrac{1}{P}M_o = \dfrac{m}{P} + k\,\dfrac{Y}{P} + \dfrac{u}{P}\,i$

$$\frac{Y}{P} = \frac{1}{k}\left[\frac{1}{P}M_o - \frac{m}{P} - \frac{u}{P}\,(i)\right] \tag{17}$$

Solving equation (4), the market equilibrium equation for the income-expenditure sector, for the interest rate yields

$$i = \frac{(1 - (b + g))}{(e/P + h/P)}\cdot\frac{Y}{P} - \frac{a/P + a'/P}{(e/P + h/P)} \tag{4'}$$

Substitution of this result into equation (17) yields:

$$\frac{Y}{P} = \frac{1}{k}\left(\frac{1}{P}\cdot M_0 - \frac{m}{P}\right) - \frac{1}{k}\cdot\frac{u}{P}\left[\frac{1 - (b + g)}{e/P + h/P}\cdot\frac{Y}{P} - \frac{a/P + a'/P}{e/P + h/P}\right]$$

$$\frac{Y}{P}\left[k + \frac{u}{P}\left(\frac{1 - (b + g)}{e/P + h/P}\right)\right] = \left(\frac{1}{P}\cdot M_0 - \frac{m}{P}\right) + \frac{u}{P}\left(\frac{a/P + a'P}{e/P + h/P}\right)$$

$$\frac{Y}{P} = \frac{(e/P + h/P)\,((1/P)\cdot M_0 - m/P)) + u/P\,(a/P + a'/P)}{k(e/P + h/P) + u/P\,(1 - (b + g))} \tag{18}$$

This equation is represented by the *DD* curve in Figure 7.

In accord with our initial assumptions, when the price level, P, changes, all the nominal values a, a', m, etc. change in equal proportion, leaving the *real* values $a/P, a'/P, m/P$ etc. unchanged. However, M_o is determined by the monetary authorities. Therefore, when P increases (decreases), M_o/P will decrease (increase) causing a decrease (increase) in Y/P, i. e., in equation (18)

$$\frac{\partial\,Y/P}{\partial\,P} < 0\,*$$

There are two unknowns, Y/P and P, in the equation. We may solve for equilibrium values of these variables by introducing the aggregate supply sector.

Just as discussed at the outset of this section, in the aggregate supply subset (equations (12) through (15)), if prices and money wages are *per-*

---

*This derivative is written out on page 362.

fectly flexible, the money wage rate will always adjust to assure full employment, regardless of the absolute price level. Therefore, regardless of the price level, the full employment volume of output, $(Y/P)_f$, will be supplied and the aggregate supply curve will appear as SS in Figure 8. Thus, aggregate supply (SS) and aggregate demand (DD) together determine the equilibrium price level. More correctly, conditions in the money market determine the price level *given* the volume of output supplied. This equilibrium occurs at point A in Figure 8. This represents the solution value obtained by substituting the full employment level of output determined in equation (16),

$$(Y/P)_f = \phi(w/P)$$

into equation (18) and solving for the average price level, P.

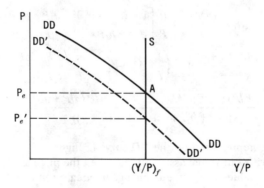

Figure 8. The Determination of the Price Level

A KEYNESIAN RIGID WAGE MODEL

Let us modify our assumption about the degree of price-wage flexibility in the economy and examine the case of rigid money wages within the framework of our global model. Laborers may suffer from a money illusion in the labor market; that is, they may determine the volume of labor services they are willing to supply on the basis of the *money* wage rate rather than the *real* wage rate. Alternatively, because of the contract structure in the labor market, or minimum wage laws, or some other institutional rigidity, money wages may be inflexible *downward*. In either case, the assumption of downward money wage rigidity will modify the conclusions of our model.

In the previous (price flexibility) model, a decrease in aggregate demand (caused by a drop in autonomous investment expenditures, for example) would cause a decrease in the price and wage level and a decrease in the interest rate sufficient to restore aggregate demand to its previous full employment level. Graphically, the decrease in autonomous aggregate demand would cause a downward shift in the *IS* curve and, therefore, the *DD* curve. But full employment equilibrium would be restored at $P_e' < P_e$ (*see* Figure 8). Excess aggregate supply at P_e would cause prices and wages to fall, increasing *real M*. This in turn would lead to a decrease in the interest rate and stimulate induced investment spending so as to restore aggregate demand to the full employment level. In this situation, there are no restraints on the flexibility of money wages, prices or the interest rate. As a result, the absolute price level can always decrease sufficiently to allow whatever fall in the interest rate necessary to induce a volume of aggregate demand equal to the full employment volume of aggregate supply. The money wage rate will adjust to allow w/P_e to equal $(w/P)_f$, the full employment equilibrium wage rate.

If money wage rates are fixed at their current level (w_o in Figure 9), however, this adjustment mechanism cannot work. For with w_o fixed, as prices fall because of the decrease in autonomous aggregate demand, real wages (w_o/P) would rise. This increase in the real wage rate would discourage the hiring of laborers by employers and would reduce the volume of employment and output.

Graphically, this inflexibility of money wage rates changes the shape of the labor supply curve and the aggregate supply curve. At the current money wage rate, w_o, the labor supply curve becomes horizontal. This implies either that money wages cannot be lowered (for institutional reasons) or that laborers will not continue to supply their services if the rate is reduced below this level. The rigidity in the structure of money wages causes the aggregate supply curve (*SS*) to slope upward to the right (this can be seen in Figure 9).*

---

*The slope of this curve depends on the slope of the production function and, implicitly, on the slope of the demand for labor curve. Assuming the money wage rate fixed at w_o, equation (16) becomes

$$(Y/P) = \phi(w_o/P) \quad \text{where} \quad \frac{\partial(Y/P)}{\partial P} > 0$$

This can be simply proven.

Assume $w = w_o$

Profit maximization by employers, under conditions of pure competition, yields the condition that the real wage equals the marginal physical product of labor.

$$w_o/P = \varrho'(N, \overline{K})$$

Rearranging terms and recalling that pure competition in the goods market means that price equals a marginal cost

$$P = MC = w_o/\varrho'(N, \overline{K}).$$

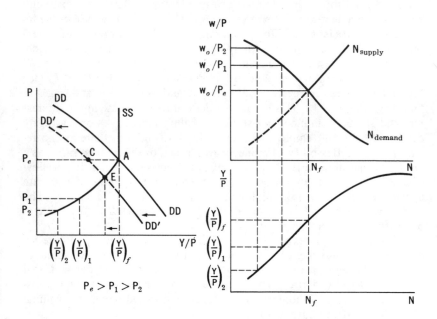

Figure 9. Aggregate General Equilibrium with Rigid Wages

Then the slope of the aggregate supply curve (SS) is

$$\frac{\partial P}{\partial (Y/P)} = \frac{\partial P}{\partial \ell'(N,K)} \cdot \frac{\partial \ell'(N,K)}{\partial N} \cdot \frac{\partial N}{\partial Y/P}$$

Since a decline in the marginal physical product causes an increase in marginal cost and hence the price of output,

$$\frac{\partial P}{\partial \ell'(N,K)} < 0,$$

since an increase in labor input causes a decrease in its marginal physical product,

$$\frac{\partial \ell'(N,K)}{\partial N} < 0,$$

and since output varies directly with labor input,

$$\frac{\partial N}{\partial (Y/P)} > 0.$$

Therefore,

$$\therefore \frac{\partial P}{\partial (Y/P)} > 0.$$

Here, as assumed in our earlier discussion of aggregate supply, the production function increases monotonically over the relevant domain.

The presence of a fixed money wage implies that the labor market is not

Under these conditions a decrease in aggregate demand *from the full employment equilibrium* described above (Figure 8) will result in a new comparative static equilibrium at less than full employment. The aggregate demand curves (DD and DD') are reproduced from the previous figure. The decrease in aggregate demand from DD to DD' leads to a condition of excess aggregate supply at the old equilibrium price level P_e (point C in Figure 9). Therefore, prices begin to fall and, in accordance with the discussion in the fourth section of this chapter, real aggregate demand is stimulated as we move downward along DD' from C. But with rigid money wages (w_o) as the price level falls, the real wage (w_o/P) will increase and employment will decrease. This causes aggregate supply to decrease as prices fall and we move downward along SS from A. The final equilibrium in the income-expenditure sector, the labor market, and the money market will occur at point E. Though the economy is at less than full employment, since aggregate demand is equal to aggregate supply, there is no further stimulus for prices to fall or *for the "automatic" mechanism to restore full employment. This conclusion rests firmly on Keynes' assumption of rigid money wages.*

It should be noted that the final "equilibrium" values of the real variables in the model (N, Y/P, I, S, etc.) are no longer independent of the absolute level of money wages and prices as they were in our original model, which assumed perfect price and wage flexibility. In contrast to the neoclassical flexible-wage model discussed earlier in this chapter, there are, in the solution of this Keynesian system, no separable subsets of the global model which may be solved recursively. All (labor market, saving investment sector and monetary sector) equations are solved simultaneously.

The influence of monetary conditions on the final equilibrium can be

---

automatically at full employment equilibrium and that the above relation

$$\left(\frac{Y}{P}\right) = \phi\left(\frac{w_0}{P}\right)$$

will not always represent a full employment solution.

*At this point the traditional classical prescription was to promote once and for all money wage cuts which would shift the cost and supply curves of business firms (and hence SS in Figure 9) downward. Whether the concomitant reduction in the price level would stimulate aggregate demand is a moot point. In the case of DD' in Figure 9, a downward shift of SS would stimulate aggregate demand along DD'. Real output and employment would rise. Consistent with the increase in output and employment and decrease in the marginal product of labor, the real wage rate would fall. With the increase in output, there is therefore some upward pressure on marginal costs and prices and therefore the decrease in money wages exceeds the decrease in prices. For reasons developed in the next section, aggregate demand may not be price sensitive; in fact it may be perfectly price inelastic. In this case, if money wages fall, output does not increase, prices fall proportionately, and the system remains unchanged in real terms. The aggressive demand function in the P, Y/P plane would be a vertical line through E.

seen in Figure 9. Since a change in the nominal money supply causes a shift in the family of *LM* curves and thereby in the aggregate demand curve (*DD'*), this purely monetary change will affect the intersection of *DD'* and *SS* and, thereby, change the "equilibrium" values of real income and employment. In short, money is no longer "neutral." Modigliani stated this nicely:

> Systems with rigid wages share the common property that the equilibrium value of the "real" variables is determined essentially by monetary conditions rather than by "real" factors . . . . The monetary conditions are sufficient to determine money income and, under fixed (money) wages and given technical conditions, to each money income there corresponds a definite equilibrium level of employment. This equilibrium level does not tend to coincide with full employment except by mere chance.*

OTHER SOURCES OF INCONSISTENCY IN THE AGGREGATE MODEL

The likelihood of a rigid money wage structure in modern industrialized economies was not the only problem posed by Keynes in his criticism of the market economy for its failure to maintain full employment. In fact, even under a regime of perfect price-wage flexibility, certain conditions may preclude the economy from automatically attaining a full employment level of output. Consequently, although the assumption of rigidity in the wage-price structure may be realistic when analyzing the short-run behavior of the aggregate economy, *let us restore our original assumption of perfect price-wage flexibility and examine some of the problems that may arise even under these circumstances.*

Keynes suggested two possible features that could lead to unemployment within the framework of our static model, even though wages and prices were perfectly flexible. One of these is the liquidity trap and the other is a special case of insufficient investment demand. Each of these possibilities involves a situation in which the full employment level of saving is greater than the level of investment which could be induced at any *attainable* interest rate. In short, aggregate demand at full employment is less than aggregate supply at all attainable interest rates.

In the case of the *liquidity trap*, money demand becomes perfectly elastic at some positive interest rate. For example, when conditions are

---

*Franco Modigliani, "Liquidity Preference and the Theory of Interest and Money," *Econometrica* (January, 1944).   Reprinted in *Readings in Monetary Theory*, Friedrich A. Lutz and Lloyd W. Mints, eds. (Homewood, Ill.: Richard D. Irwin, Inc., 1951), p. 211.

such that virtually everyone expects bond prices to fall, people will prefer money to bonds. They will absorb any increase in the money stock into asset balances without requiring a reduction in the interest rate (see chapter 4). Therefore, regardless of how large the supply of money may be, the market rate cannot fall below the level determined by money demand. Hence, even if sufficient investment could be induced to offset full employment saving at some low rate of interest, the rate will never attain that low level, and investment will remain insufficient at the attainable rate.

In the case of insufficient investment demand (with no liquidity trap) investment expenditures may be so unresponsive to changes in the interest rate that even at a near zero rate of interest, sufficient investment cannot be generated to match full employment saving.

Graphically, we may present these two cases in terms of our original *LM – IS* curves.

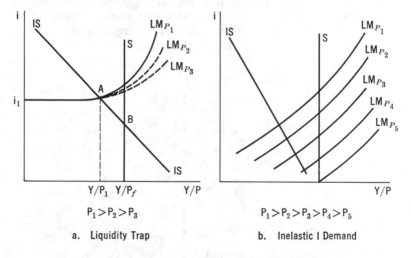

a. Liquidity Trap   b. Inelastic I Demand

Figure 10. Inconsistent Aggregate Models with Flexible Prices

Note that in the case of the liquidity trap (*a*), full employment equilibrium could be attained if the money market equilibrium curve could be shifted down so as to intersect the expenditure and full employment supply curves at point *B* (Figure 10a). However, because of the liquidity trap, there is a floor in the level of the interest rate at (i_1) and hence sufficient investment spending is not forthcoming at that rate to match full employment saving. Thus, at point *A*, aggregate demand is below aggregate supply and prices will continually fall. Though decreasing prices shift the upward-sloping portion of the money market equilibrium curve out to the right (as shown by the dotted *LM* curves), they leave the horizontal section of the curve around point *A* unaffected. Hence, as the model is constructed, *falling prices are not sufficient to restore equilibrium in a liquidity trap situation.*

In the case of inelastic investment demand (*b*), the interest rate can be reduced as prices fall. Price deflation shifts the money market curve so it intersects the expenditure curve at consecutively lower interest rates. Nevertheless, even if the interest rate is reduced to near zero, investment will be insufficient to match full employment saving. Again we have a situation in which *prices will fall continually, and yet are not capable of reducing the interest rate to the level necessary to restore full employment.*

These two cases are demonstrated in terms of aggregate supply and demand relations in Figure 11. Since we are assuming complete price-wage flexibility, the aggregate supply curve is again a vertical line at the full employment level of income. However, at some price level the aggregate demand curve becomes vertical at a level of aggregate demand for real output which is short of the full employment level. Because of the liquidity trap and inelastic investment demand, aggregate demand does not respond to price changes; it is relatively price inelastic.*

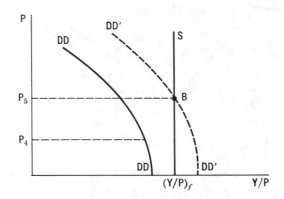

Figure 11. Liquidity Traps and Interest Insensitive Investment
Demand in Terms of Aggregate Supply and Demand Curves

*This may be seen in terms of equation (18). That equation, you will recall, represents the aggregate demand relation depicted by the *DD* curve in Figure 11. In equation (18),

$$\frac{\partial Y/P}{\partial P} = \frac{-(e/P + h/P)M_0(1/P^2)}{k(e/P + h/P) + u/P(1 - (b + g))}$$

In our original model, a fall in prices was always sufficient to free some money balances from use in transactions and make them available for asset-holding (speculative) purposes. Price level reductions were always sufficient to lower the interest rate and thereby stimulate additional investment expenditures and increase aggregate demand. As a result, the aggregate demand curve (DD) sloped downward to the right over its entire range. In the present models, however, there is some price level (P_1 in the liquidity trap case, Figure 10a, and P_4 in the interest insensitive investment demand case, Figure 10b) below which further price declines have no effect on the interest rate and, therefore, cannot induce additional investment spending in order to increase aggregate demand. Consequently, in Figure 11 the DD curve becomes vertical at those price levels.

The policy implications of these cases are very important. Since monetary policy (changes in the stock of money) works through shifts in the money market equilibrium curve, monetary policy is no longer effective in restoring full employment. (This was previously demonstrated.) Therefore, only a policy that can bring about a positive shift in the expenditure sector curve (and, thus, the aggregate demand curve, DD) can restore full employment. Since government expenditures are a part of aggregate demand, and government tax policy can affect aggregate demand indirectly through its influence on private expenditure decisions, government fiscal policy alone may be sufficient to stimulate the volume of expenditures necessary to generate full employment. In the case above, for example (Figure 11), an increase in aggregate demand brought about by fiscal policy would shift DD to DD′ and would restore full employment at price level P_5 (point B).*

In the case of the liquidity trap, the interest rate coefficient in the money demand relation, u/P, becomes infinite (the public demonstrates an unlimited preference for liquidity). Consequently, as

$$u/P \longrightarrow \infty, \frac{\partial Y/P}{\partial P} \longrightarrow 0$$

and changes in the price level become ineffective as a force for changes in aggregate demand.

In the case of perfectly interest insensitive expenditure demand functions, (h/P), the interest rate coefficient in the investment demand equation goes to zero. If consumption expenditures are also perfectly interest inelastic, $(e/P) = 0$ and

$$\frac{\partial Y/P}{\partial P} = 0$$

Again, price level changes cannot induce an increase in aggregate demand. Under these conditions, the DD curve becomes vertical over some range as depicted in Figure 11.

*We may again employ equation (18), the aggregate demand relation, to demonstrate this point. Government fiscal policy (an increase in government expenditures, for example) affects our model through its impact on the autonomous

Therefore, even with complete wage-price flexibility, certain cases may arise which prevent the economy from automatically reaching full employment equilibrium.* Furthermore, in these cases, it is possible to restore full employment *only* by the positive intervention of the government through its fiscal policy.

The destruction of the assumed automaticity of the market economy (even under the assumption of price-wage flexibility) together with the summoning of governmental fiscal intervention into the economy to maintain full employment, were serious blows both to the foundations of classical analysis and to laissez-faire ideology. It is not suprising, therefore, that attempts have been made to restore the automaticity of the classical model of the aggregate economy. In the next chapter, chapter 9, we shall examine the outstanding effort in the classical counter-attack, the Pigou Real-Balance Effect.

---

expenditure parameters, (a/P) and (a'/P). In equation (18),

$$\frac{\partial Y/P}{\partial(a/P)} = \frac{\partial Y/P}{\partial(a'/P)} = \frac{u/P}{k(e/P + h/P) + u/P(1 - (b + g))} > 0$$

Thus, an increase in autonomous expenditures will increase aggregate demand. The relative response in aggregate demand to a given change in autonomous expenditures will be determined by the parameters in the equation above. Most importantly, the numerically larger is u/P, the interest rate coefficient in the money demand function and a determinant of the interest elasticity of the demand for money balances, the greater will be the change in aggregate demand. Likewise, the smaller the sum of the interest coefficients in the expenditure demand equations $(e/P + h/P)$, the less will induced expenditure be cut back as the interest rate rises in response to the increase in *autonomous* demand, and the greater will be the net increase in aggregate demand in the economy. These principles were discussed in chapter 6.

*The survey of empirical tests of the money demand function which follows chapter 5 shows little evidence of the liquidity trap.

Glossary / *chapter 8*

Symbols employed in this chapter:

P	an index of the average price level in the economy
C	aggregate consumption expenditures in nominal dollars
Y	aggregate income (national income) in nominal dollars
i	an index of relevant interest rates in the economy
I	aggregate investment expenditures in nominal dollars
M_S	money supply
M_d	the demand for money
N_S	the supply of labor
N_D	the demand for labor
w	the *money* wage rate
O	the real volume of output (or measure of production)
K	capital stock
DD	aggregate demand in the economy
SS	aggregate supply

Questions/ *chapter 8*

1. Evaluate: Given a position of unemployment, a once and for all cut in money wages will increase real output and employment because lower prices will:
   a. lower directly the real interest rate.
   b. increase real income and hence real consumption.
   c. increase real money balances and hence lower the interest rate.
   d. lower real wages and hence the quantity of labor supplied will decrease.
   e. increase exports.
   f. cause anticipations of further price declines.

2. Rank the following Keynesian propositions in the order of their importance to the result of underemployment equilibrium:
   a. a high interest elasticity of the speculative demand for money.
   b. the absence of an international sector in many models.
   c. rigid money wages.
   d. the concept of income induced consumption spending.
   e. a low interest elasticity of investment demand.

3. If a disequilibrium situation (characterized by an excess supply of or excess demand for money) exists in the money market *in the "classical" model* through what exact mechanism will the market (and the aggregate economy) be restored to equilibrium? (Be sure to emphasize the behavior of the public which is induced by the disequilibrium and which brings about the changes necessary to restore equilibrium.)

4. Is there any role for monetary and/or fiscal policy *in the classical model* of the aggregate economy? Explain and give examples.

Bibliography/ *chapter 8*

Aschheim, Joseph, and **Ching-Yao Hsieh,** *Macroeconomics: Income and Monetary Theory.* Columbus, Ohio: Charles E. Merrill Publishing Company, 1969.

Ackley, Gardner, *Macroeconomic Theory.* New York: The Macmillan Company, 1961, chapter 14.

Andersen, Leonall C., and **Keith M. Carlson,** "A Monetarist Model for Economic Stabilization," Federal Reserve Bank of St. Louis *Review,* Vol. 52, No. 4 (April 1970), pp. 7-25.

Bailey, Martin, *National Income and the Price Level.* New York: McGraw-Hill Book Company, 1962, chapters 2 and 3.

Christ, Carl F., "A Model of Monetary and Fiscal Policy Effects on the Money Stock, Price Level and Real Output," *Journal of Money, Credit and Banking,* Vol. 1 (November 1969), pp. 683-705.

Fisher, Irving, *The Purchasing Power of Money.* New York: Augustus M. Kelly, Bookseller, Reprints of Economic Classics, 1963.

Hicks, J. R., "Mr. Keynes and the Classics: A Suggested Interpretation," in The American Economic Association, *Readings in the Theory of Income Distribution.* New York: McGraw-Hill–Blakiston, 1946, pp. 461–472.

Johnson, Harry G., "Monetary Theory and Keynesian Economics," *Pakistan Economic Journal,* Vol, 8 (June 1958), pp. 56-70. Reprinted in Warren Smith and Ronald Teigen, *Readings in Money, National Income, and Stabilization Policy.* Homewood, Illinois: Richard D. Irwin, Inc., 1965, pp. 32–43.

Keynes, J. M., *The General Theory of Employment, Interest and Money.* London: Macmillan, 1936.

Leontief, Wassily, "Postulates: Keynes' General Theory and the Classicists," *The New Economics*, edited by Seymour E. Harris. New York: Alfred A. Knopf, Inc., 1947, pp. 232–242.

Lucas, Robert E., Jr., and **Leonard A. Rapping**, "Real Wages, Employment, and Inflation," *Journal of Political Economy*, Vol. 77 (September/October 1969), pp. 721–754.

Marshall, Alfred, *Money, Credit and Commerce.* London: Macmillan and Company, Ltd., 1923.

Metzler, Lloyd A., "Wealth, Saving and the Rate of Interest," *Journal of Political Economy*, Vol. 59 (April 1951), pp. 93–116.

Modigliani, Franco, "Liquidity Preference and the Theory of Interest and Money," in American Economic Association, *Readings in Monetary Theory* (New York: McGraw-Hill–Blakiston, 1951), chapter 11.

———, "The Monetary Mechanism and Its Interaction with Real Phenomena," *Review of Economics and Statistics*, Vol. 45 (February 1963), pp. 79–107.

Patinkin, Don, "Price Flexibility and Full Employment," *American Economic Review*, Vol. 38 (September 1948), pp. 543–564.

———, *Money, Interest and Prices*, 2nd edition. New York: Harper and Row, 1965.

Pesek, Boris, and **Thomas Saving,** *Money, Wealth, and Economic Theory.* New York: The Macmillan Company, 1967, chapters 1–3.

Tobin, James, "Money Wage Rates and Employment," *The New Economics*, edited by Seymour E. Harris. New York: Alfred A. Knopf, Inc., 1947, pp. 572–587.

Tucker, Donald P., "Macroeconomic Models and The Demand for Money under Market Disequilibrium," *Journal of Money, Credit and Banking* Vol. 3 (February 1971), pp. 57–83.

9

Real Balances and the Wealth Effect in Macroeconomic Models

In chapter 8 we expanded the basic *LM-IS* model of macroeconomic theory to include flexible money-wage rates and prices, an endogenous money supply, additional behavioral influences on consumption and investment expenditures, and a very simple production (labor market) supply sector. In this chapter, we will continue the modification and expansion of that model. In particular, we introduce a wealth effect into our analysis and examine its effect on the conclusions derived in the previous chapter. We begin our analysis with an examination of the *Pigou* or real-balance effect.

THE REAL-BALANCE EFFECT IN A STATIC MODEL

The introduction of the Pigou effect into the model of chapter 8 requires a reformulation of the consumption function to include the *net real value of financial wealth* or "real balances" as an independent variable. The

Pigou or real-balance effect refers to the hypothesis that saving varies inversely (and therefore consumption varies directly) with the current net real value of financial wealth held by individuals.

Assume for the moment that there are only two financial assets in the economy: bonds issued and purchased solely by the public and fiat money spent into circulation by the government.* In this economy the *net* value of bond holdings is zero since the holdings of debtors and creditors within the private sector of the economy cancel out. Under these assumptions, the total value of net financial wealth *held by the public* is equal to the value of the government fiat money in circulation. The nominal value of this money stock is designated by the symbol M_g. Thus:

M_g/P = real money balances = net real financial wealth of the public.

Assume that the public is influenced by the *real* value of these money balances when making its consumption (and saving) decisions.** Thus, the consumption function of the previous chapter is modified to include this new variable.

$$\frac{C}{P} = C\left(\frac{Y}{P}, i, \frac{M_g}{P}\right) = \frac{a}{P} + b \cdot \frac{Y}{P} + \frac{e}{P} \cdot i + d \cdot \frac{M_g}{P} \tag{1}$$

$$\frac{\partial C/P}{\partial M_g/P} > 0.$$

The specific hypothesis implied by the real-balance effect is that there is a direct relationship between the value of net real financial wealth held by the public (M_g/P) and the level of real consumption expenditures. For any given level of real income and the interest rate, the greater the value of an individual's current real money balances, the less his desire to save and add to his wealth and therefore the greater his consumption expenditures.

---

*The money stock in this model will consist solely of government fiat money spent into circulation for the purchase of goods and services by the government. By assumption, then, there are no demand deposit liabilities issued by the commercial banking system, and the net financial wealth of the public consists solely of monetary claims against the government. The rationale of these assumptions will become clear in the following discussion. We relax these restrictions in the third section of this chapter.

**Here we consider only price-induced wealth effects; there are, in addition, interest-induced wealth effects which are reflected by including a total net worth (outside money plus outside bonds *plus the present value of capital goods*) term in the consumption function and money demand function.

In this way, an open market operation (a swap of outside money for outside bonds) might affect wealth if it affected the interest rate, and hence the present (discounted) value of capital goods. The interest-induced wealth effect is discussed by Warren L. Smith in one of the readings that follow this chapter.

Let us examine the effects this new variable has on our previous conclusions. Substitution of the modified consumption function together with the investment demand function of chapter 8 into the equilibrium condition yields the following income-expenditure sector equilibrium (*IS*) equation:

$$\frac{Y}{P} = \frac{a}{P} + b \cdot \frac{Y}{P} + \frac{e}{P} \cdot i + d \cdot \frac{M_g}{P} + \frac{a'}{P} + g \cdot \frac{Y}{P} + \frac{h}{P} \cdot i \qquad (2)$$

$$\frac{Y}{P} = \left[\frac{1}{1-(b+g)}\right] \left[\frac{a}{P} + \frac{a'}{P} + \left(\frac{e}{P} + \frac{h}{P}\right)(i) + d\left(\frac{M_g}{P}\right)\right]. \qquad (3)$$

In the model of the previous chapter, the income-expenditure equilibrium equation was linear in two unknowns, Y/P and i. Therefore, we were able to represent it graphically as a straight line in the real income (Y/P) – interest rate (i) quadrant, as in Figure 1. The equation was assumed to be homogeneous of degree zero in all nominal values (Y, a, a', etc.) and prices. Since we assumed no money illusion, the price level appeared only as a deflator of nominal values (which varied proportionately with prices) and not as an independent argument in the equation. Consequently, a change in the price level, *by itself*, could not change the form of the income-expenditure equilibrium equation.

This will no longer be true. The *nominal* money stock (M_g) is assumed to be controlled by the authorities and to remain unchanged when the price level changes. Under these circumstances, M_g/P, the *real* value of net financial wealth held by the public, will be decreased by a rise in the price level. As a result, an increase (decrease) in P will tend to lower (raise) the level of consumption expenditures and aggregate demand.

In the new income-expenditure equilibrium equation (3), P is now a separate variable. We now have a single equation in three unknowns. This relation can no longer be represented as a single curve in two dimensions. Instead, we must represent this relation as a family of curves similar to the family of money market equilibrium curves presented in chapter 8. There will be one income-expenditure equilibrium curve in the (Y/P, i) quadrant for each different level of prices.

Since $\dfrac{\partial(C/P)}{\partial(M_g/P)} > 0$,

and M_g/P is inversely related to the level of prices,

$$\frac{\partial(Y/P)}{\partial P} < 0,$$

and the income-expenditure equilibrium curve will shift to the right when the price level decreases. This is shown graphically in Figure 1.

Let us combine this new analysis of the income-expenditure sector with an analysis of the monetary sector and the supply sector. All relations except the money supply equation are assumed to be the same as in the model of chapter 8. The stock of fiat money in circulation is assumed to be exogenously determined by the government, $M_s = M_g$. This modification changes (the absolute value of) the slope and elasticity of the family of money market equilibrium curves but leaves all its other significant characteristics unchanged.

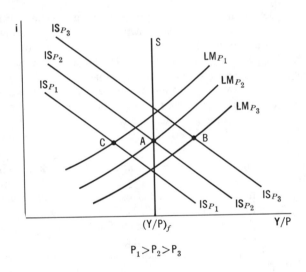

Figure 1. **Aggregate General Equilibrium**

As can be seen in Figure 1, equilibrium will occur in this model at point A, at the full employment level of output and price level P_2. In order to see that this point is truly a point of equilibrium, let us assume that prices are at some level other than P_2, say P_3. At price level P_3, the money market and income-expenditure equilibrium curves intersect at point B. But point B lies to the *right* of the full employment real income line (S) indicating a condition of excess aggregate demand. This condition will lead to an increase in prices (as the economy is assumed to be at full employment). The increase in the price level will decrease the *real* stock of money in circulation, thereby shifting back the family of money market equilibrium curves (LM_{P_i}) to the left (just as in the original model). But this price movement will also decrease consumption expenditures and increase saving because of the reduction it causes in the *real* value of money balances (M_g/P). As a result, there will also be a leftward movement of the family of income-expenditure equilibrium curves (IS_{P_i}). These shifts will continue until prices have increased to P_2. At this higher price level, P_2, real money balances will have shrunk sufficiently to decrease aggregate demand enough to eliminate excess demand in the economy.

Similarly, if the price level were P_1 (point C), excess aggregate supply would lead to a decrease in the price level, an increase in *real* money balances, and an increase in aggregate demand. Again, prices will fall to the level P_2 where expenditures are sufficient to eliminate excess supply and restore the economy to full employment.

A COMPARATIVE STATIC ANALYSIS OF THE REAL-BALANCE MODEL

Let us examine the comparative static characteristics of the equilibrium solution of the real-balance model. Assume that the initial equilibrium at point A in Figure 1 is disturbed by an increase, say a doubling, of the nominal quantity of money. The effects of this change are demonstrated in Figure 2. The increase in the money stock will cause a rightward shift of the entire family of money-market equilibrium curves. The curve relevant to equilibrium at point A, LM_{P_2}, will shift out to LM'_{P_2}.

In addition, due to the influence of real money balances on consumption expenditures, the increase in nominal money balances, M_g, will increase the net real wealth of the public and cause a rightward shift in the family of income-expenditure equilibrium curves. The curve relevant to

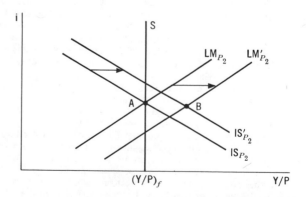

Figure 2. The Initial Effect of an Increase in the Nominal Stock of Money

equlibrium at A, IS_{P_2}, will shift out to IS'_{P_2}. The immediate effect of the increase in the nominal money stock will be to increase aggregate demand (point B in Figure 2). Since the economy is already at full employment, the result will be inflation. As prices rise, the real money stock (M_g/P) will decrease and both the relevant money-market equilibrium curve $(LM_{P'_2})$ and the relevant income-expenditure equilibrium curve (IS'_{P_2}) will shift back to the left. Equilibrium will be restored only when prices have exactly doubled to a new equilibrium level $2P_2 = P_e$, the real money stock has been reduced to its initial level, $(2M_g/2P_2 = M_g/P_2)$, and both the money market equilibrium curve and the income-expenditure equilibrium curve have moved back to their initial positions.* In the real-balance model, then, just as in our original neoclassical model with flexible wages and prices, an increase in the nominal money stock causes a proportionate increase in the price level, restoring real money balances to the level at which they stood prior to the monetary disturbance.

Although A. C. Pigou and Gottfried Haberler were among the first to indicate the role of real money balances in affecting expenditures, it was Don Patinkin in his *Money, Interest and Prices* who incorporated and refined their suggestions in a complete analytical framework, and fully examined the properties and implications of this model. Specifically, he demonstrated that through the introduction of real money balances as a determinant of aggregate demand in a regime of complete price-wage flexibility:

*The logical necessity of this result may be demonstrated as follows: if the price level increases by a smaller proportion than the nominal money stock in the assumed new "equilibrium," *real* money balances, $(2M_g/P'_e)$, will be *greater* than they were before the increase in the money stock $(M_g/P_e$ in Figure 2). This net increase in real wealth will induce additional consumption expenditures. Consequently, for this to represent a new equilibrium, the interest rates would have to be *higher* than before to discourage an amount of investment spending equal to the increase in consumption spending (i.e., to decrease I by an amount equivalent to the decrease in full employment S). At the same time, the larger stock of money balances will be absorbed into the public's portfolio (as indicated in the money demand function) only at a *lower* interest rate. Thus, there is a logical contradiction between the conditions required for equilibrium in the income-expenditure sector and those required for a new equilibrium in the money market. As a result, this cannot be a general equilibrium solution. In a similar fashion, if prices increased by a greater proportion than the money stock, real money balances, $(2M_g/P'_e)$, would be less than in the initial equilibrium. To generate a new equilibrium in the income-expenditure sector under these conditions, interest rates would have to *fall* to induce investment expenditures to offset the decrease in consumption caused by the decrease in the value of net real wealth. But the public will willingly hold fewer real money balances only at an increased interest rate. Therefore, in the money market the interest rate would have to *rise*. Consequently, if prices can change by neither a greater nor lesser amount than the money stock, they must change by an exactly proportionate amount.

(1) the Quantity Theory conclusions (that prices vary directly and proportionately with the nominal money stock, and that equilibrium values of the "real" variables are independent of the size of that money stock) could be maintained; and

(2) the full employment solution was the only "equilibrium" solution within a static framework.

We shall return to this latter point subsequently. Now, let us carefully examine the first point made above: the question of the "neutrality" of money and the conditions under which that neutrality will hold.

THE CONDITIONS FOR THE NEUTRALITY OF MONEY

In the wage-price flexibility models of chapter 8 and in the model of this chapter which takes account of the real-balance effect, money is neutral. This means that changes in the supply of nominal money balances cause equiproportionate changes in the absolute price level and in all nominal values, but leave the equilibrium values of all real variables in the model, e.g., the level of real income, employment, and the interest rate—unaffected. This result depends on six important assumptions. Four of these were discussed in chapter 8. They are:

(1) there is complete price-wage flexibility in all markets;

(2) there is no money illusion in the expenditure or money demand relations in these models;

(3) there are no distributional effects caused by changes in the absolute price level; and

(4) the elasticity of price expectations is unity. *

Two additional assumptions necessary to demonstrate the neutrality of money in a real-balance model were introduced in this chapter. These were:

(5) all money is "outside" money; and

(6) there is no interest-bearing government debt outstanding.

---

*While the present model is essentially static in nature, recently more attention is being paid to the policy implications of anticipated and unanticipated rates of price change (induced perhaps by acceleration and deceleration of the growth rate of the money supply). The readings by Karl Brunner, Allan Meltzer, and Warren Smith, which follow this chapter, and the reading by Milton Friedman, which follows chapter 5, reflect on the policy implications of these considerations. *See* also Milton Friedman, "The Role of Monetary Policy," *American Economic Review,* Vol. 58 (March 1968), pp. 1-17.

If all money is outside money*, this means it is issued by the government in payment for the goods and services it purchases. In this connection, the government, in its spending and taxing decisions, ignores the existence of this money as a claim against itself, i.e., the government ignores the real burden of this debt in making its fiscal decisions.

If there is no interest-bearing government debt outstanding, all bonds in the system are issued and held only by individuals in the private sector. Under this assumption, the bonds of the private sector cancel out when the individual balance sheets of that sector are consolidated. Consequently, these assets do not contribute to private net wealth.

Given these assumptions, "private net financial wealth" consists solely of the monetary claims against the government held by the public. We designated the real value of this stock as M_g/P and included it within the real-balance model as a determinant of private consumption spending. As demonstrated in the second section of this chapter, an increase, say a doubling to $2M_g$, in this stock of nominal outside money in the economy, leads to an equiproportionate rise in the average price level, P. Initially, the increase in nominal money balances increases real private financial wealth. This, in turn, increases aggregate demand. However, since the economy is already at full employment, excess aggregate demand leads to an increase in the price level. Prices continue to rise until the *real* value of the stock of nominal balances is reduced to its initial level. In this case $2M_g/2P_e = M_g/P_e$. Furthermore, the equilibrium values of all real variables in the model are restored to their original levels.

---

*"Outside" money may be defined as a monetary claim against an agent "external" to the economic system i.e., "outside" the private sector in our model (the government). This is in contrast to "inside" money which consists of claims against an institution or an individual internal to the economic system (the commercial banks of the private sector). The essence of this distinction lies in the response of holders and issuers of monetary claims to changes in the real value of these claims.

In the case of outside money, the government, the issuer of outside money, is assumed to be unaffected by a change in the real value of its monetary debt. In making its expenditure decisions, the government does not consider the burden of its outstanding liabilities. The public, on the other hand, is sensitive to the net real value of its financial wealth. As a result, changes in the price level which affect the real value of its monetary claims against the government, will influence private expenditure decisions. A price rise, for example, will decrease the real value of the public's claims against the government, thereby decreasing private expenditures; the government, however, will not react to the change in the real value of its liabilities. Consequently, the change in prices will induce a net change in *total* real expenditures in the economy.

In the case of inside money, changes in the price level change the real value of both assets and liabilities of the private sector by an equivalent amount and leave the net real financial wealth of the public unaffected. Therefore, changes in the value of inside money caused by variations in prices will not generally be expected to influence net expenditures in the economy.

The implications of these distinctions will be explained in greater detail later.

If any of these assumptions are relaxed, money may not be neutral in the system. For example, let us relax the assumption that only private securities are issued and held in the economy, and introduce interest-bearing government debt into the analysis. In this instance, "net private financial wealth," (W_f/P), will equal the real value of (outside) money issued by the government (as in our previous model) *plus* the real value of bonds issued by the government and held by the public: $W_f/P = M_g/P + B/P$, where B is the nominal value of government debt outstanding. The consumption function of our real-balance model must now be specified to include this additional component of private net wealth:

$$\frac{C}{P} = \frac{a}{P} + b\,\frac{Y}{P} + \frac{e}{P}\,i + d\left(\frac{M_g}{P} + \frac{B}{P}\right).\text{*}$$

The effect of this modification on our model has been succinctly stated by Patinkin:

> ... since the net financial assets of the private sector no longer coincide with its real money holdings, the wealth effect of a change in the price level no longer coincides with the "real balance" effect. Correspondingly, the impact of such a change on the demands for various goods should no longer be analyzed in terms of this latter effect but in terms of an analogous "net-real-financial-asset effect."**

Let us examine the effects of a change in the nominal money stock in this system. When nominal money balances are increased (by deficit financing, for example), net real financial wealth increases. This will stimulate an increase in aggregate demand above its initial full employment level

---

*Implicit in this statement is the assumption that the public does not fully discount the value of its future tax liabilities, i.e., the tax liabilities which will arise due to the necessity of paying interest on the public debt. If the full value of these future tax liabilities were considered by the public, the *net* value of its bond holdings would be zero and they would not represent net wealth. Although we proceed in our analysis as if the public does not recognize any burden to the future taxes which will be levied to finance the public debt, the essence of our conclusions requires only that the public not discount the burden of future tax liabilities *completely*.

Through the influence of this new factor, a government deficit may cause consumption expenditures to increase and, hence, the *IS* curve to shift further toward the right. However, the issuance of outside bonds for outside money could cause the interest rate to rise and a (negative) interest induced wealth effect, mentioned above, could counteract this movement. Moreover, the *LM* curve may shift toward the left as the demand for money increases with the level of wealth. Thus, as Yohe and Spencer point out in the readings that follow chapter 9, deficit spending need be only mildly expansionary.

**Don Patinkin, *Money, Interest and Prices*, 2nd edition (New York: Harper and Row, 1965), p. 290.

and prices will begin to rise. However, an exactly proportionate increase in the price level which leaves the initial equilibrium values of the real variables unchanged, will not restore equilibrium.

This may be demonstrated as follows: suppose the nominal stock of outside money is doubled to $2M_g$ by a purchase of goods and services by the government. Since the real (and nominal) stock of money balances is now greater than initially, the equilibrium of the private sector is disturbed. The public finds itself with excess money balances. This disequilibrium in the relative proportions of bonds and money held by the public will be marked by an excess demand for bonds (i.e., at the initial price and interest rate levels, the public will try to restore the original balance between its holdings of bonds and money), and an excess demand for commodities. In either case, as discussed in chapter 8, the increase in expenditures will create excess aggregate demand and prices will rise.

A rise in prices proportional to the increase in money balances will not restore equilibrium, however. Assume a doubling of both the stock of outside money and the general price level. Since the nominal value of bonds held by the public, B, has not increased, the real value of bonds has decreased $(B/2P < B/P)$ and the net real financial wealth held by the public $(2M_g/2P + B/2P)$ has decreased from its initial equilibrium level. This will induce a reduction in the volume of consumption expenditures as individuals save more of their income in an attempt to restore their initial real wealth position.

Consequently, in the absence of a change in the real variables besides consumption spending, a doubling of the price level would represent an over-reaction to a doubling of the nominal stock of outside money and would not restore equilibrium. The decline in net real financial wealth would cause a decline in aggregate demand and the general price level would have to fall from its doubled level. As prices fell, real money balances, M_g/P, and net real financial wealth would increase. The creation of an excess supply of real money balances would lead to a decline in interest rates inducing additional consumption and investment expenditures until aggregate demand was again equal to aggregate supply.

In the final equilibrium, then, the interest rate will be below its initial equilibrium level, consumption will have declined (because of the decline in net real financial wealth) and investment expenditures will have increased (induced by the fall in interest rates.) Finally, the price level will have increased by some proportion smaller than the increase in the nominal money stock. Therefore, in a system which contains both outside money and bonds issued by the government, money is not neutral.

As a final example, consider the effects of introducing "inside" money into the analysis. Inside money consists of monetary claims issued by individuals in the private sector. It may be thought to consist primarily of demand deposit liabilities of commercial banks. In this case, total money balances in the system will equal the sum of the public's monetary claims against the government (outside money, M_g) and the public's monetary claims against the banks (inside money, M_b) i.e., $M/P = M_g/P + M_b/P$. However, since the debt of the nonbank public to the banking system (in the form of loans and securities issued by the public and held by the banks) cancels out against the demand deposit liabilities of the banks in the consolidated balance sheet of the private sector, the *net* real financial wealth of the public consists solely of its claims against the government, in this case, its monetary claims. Therefore, $W_f/P = M_g/P$.*

In this instance, money will not be neutral, since an increase in one of the types of money in the system will not lead to a proportionate increase in the price level. This may be indicated as follows: if outside money, M_g, is increased to $2M_g$ and the price level doubles, net real financial wealth will be restored to its initial equilibrium level,

$$\frac{W_f}{P} = \frac{M_g}{P} = \frac{2M_g}{2P}$$

but the real value of total money balances will have decreased:

$$\frac{2M_g}{2P} + \frac{M_b}{2P} < \frac{M_g}{P} + \frac{M_b}{P}**$$

This reduction in real money balances, with all other variables assumed to be at their initial equilibrium levels, will create an excess demand for

*Boris Pesek and Thomas Saving in *Money, Wealth and Economic Theory* (New York: The Macmillan Company, 1967) have argued that bank money—monetary claims issued by the banking system—should be included in our measure of the public's net financial wealth. They claim that "inside" money does represent net wealth and ought to be included in any measure of wealth specified in the consumption function. As they state:

> . . . *money in real terms, measured in terms of its purchasing power, is a part of the net wealth of the community . . . money yields income to the owner without yielding a negative income to the producer of it or to anybody else. Consequently, money must be part of the net wealth of the community; it is not a debt.* (pp. 245–246)

For a critique of their position, which shows that inside money is net wealth only in the case of monopoly banking franchise, *see* Don Patinkin, "Money and Wealth: A Review Article," *Journal of Economic Literature*, Vol. 7 (December 1969), pp. 1140–1160.

**There is one important exception to this analysis, the case in which the institutional framework and the behavior of the banking system are such that a fixed proportionate relationship is maintained between the stock of outside money (bank reserves, for example) and the volume of inside money created by the banking system. For a discussion of this point, *see* Don Patinkin, *Money, Interest and Prices*, op. cit., pp. 298–302.

money. Thus, equilibrium will be restored only when this excess demand is eliminated. Restoration of equilibrium will involve an increase in the interest rate and a subsequent decline in investment expenditures. The decline in investment spending will reduce aggregate demand and the rise in prices will be reversed. As prices begin to fall, net real financial wealth will increase, inducing a rise in consumption.

In the final equilibrium, then, interest rates will have increased (decreasing investment by an amount equal to the increase in consumption), net real financial wealth and consumption will have increased, and the price level will have risen less than in proportion to the initial increase in the nominal stock of money. Again, since the equilibrium values of real variables change in response to a change in the nominal stock of money, money is not neutral.*

There are many other special cases we could examine to determine those conditions under which money is neutral. The most exhaustive analysis of this issue is contained in Don Patinkin's book *Money, Interest and Prices* and we refer the interested reader to his volume, especially to chapter 12. We shall turn now to the other characteristic of the real-balance model, the unique equilibrium at full employment.

FULL EMPLOYMENT EQUILIBRIUM IN THE REAL-BALANCE MODEL

In order to demonstrate that the "full employment" solution is the only equilibrium solution in a real-balance model that assumes price-wage flexibility, we must reexamine the two situations discussed in chapter 8 which could lead to less-than-full-employment solutions in our model of the aggregate economy. We must show that even under the conditions described by the liquidity trap and interest-insensitive investment demand, the real-balance model yields a consistent solution only at full employment.**

---

*The general framework developed in this example may be employed to demonstrate the results of other assumptions. For example, in a "pure outside money" economy, $M_b = 0$. Therefore $M/P = M_g/P$ and $W_f/P = M_g/P$ and our model reduces to that developed in the first part of this chapter. At the other extreme, if all money is of the inside variety, $M_g = 0$. In this case, $M/P = M_b/P$ and $W_f/P = 0$, and our model reduces to that discussed in the early sections of chapter 8, i.e., there will be no Real-Balance Effect.

In both of these instances, where the money stock consists solely of "inside" money or solely of "outside" money, the neutrality of money is easily established as long as the assumptions cited above hold.

**In the rest of this discussion, we shall assume an economy in which all money is of the outside variety.

As the reader will recall from the previous chapter, those situations led to "equilibrium" at less than full employment because price adjustments could in no way induce a full employment level of aggregate demand. Price adjustments shifted only the money market equilibrium curve, but such movements could not induce sufficient investment through interest rate reductions to offset the full employment level of saving. In the case of the absolute liquidity trap, additional real money balances created by falling prices were simply absorbed by the public at the current interest rate (i_e) and no rate reduction was forthcoming. In the case of interest insensitive investment demand, although price declines could decrease interest rates, those lowered rates were insufficient to generate a level of investment capable of offsetting the full employment volume of savings.

In the present model, however, since price reductions increase the value of real money balances, they increase *consumption* and decrease saving at every level of income. This is represented by the rightward shift of the IS_p curves in Figure 3. In this way, continual deflation reduces the full employment level of saving to any level necessary to match the volume of investment forthcoming at some attainable positive rate of interest. (This solution occurs at price level P_3 and interest rate i_e in Figure 3a and P_3 and i_0 in Figure 3b). Therefore, the Pigou real-balance effect would seem to counter the Keynesian attack on the ability of the market economy to automatically produce full employment under conditions of

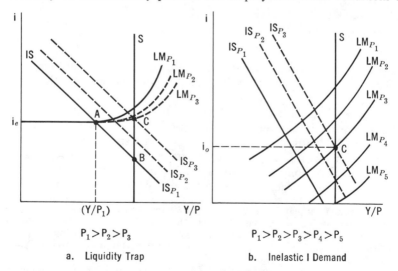

P_1 > P_2 > P_3

a. Liquidity Trap

P_1 > P_2 > P_3 > P_4 > P_5

b. Inelastic I Demand

Figure 3. The Real-Balance Effect in Price-Flexible Models with a. Liquidity Trap or b. Interest Insensitive Investment Demand

perfect price-wage flexibility.* *Neither the liquidity trap nor interest inelastic investment demand would seem to be sufficient to bring about a static equilibrium at less than full employment.*

Therefore, on the basis of this analysis, we state the following proposition: if the Pigou effect is operative, there will exist (even in the case of a liquidity trap or insufficient investment demand) some price level which is sufficient to induce the proper level of consumption expenditures (aggregate demand) to assure full employment. Most importantly, *the introduction of the real-balance effect appears to restore the automatic character of the market economy under the assumption of price-wage flexibility.* Within a static analysis, then, the Keynesian case of a less than full employment equilibrium rests *squarely* and *completely* on his assumption of rigid money wages. This conclusion is maintained in a "real-balance" model. If rigid wages are in effect, the *modus operandi* of the Pigou effect, falling prices, has been removed. Aggregate demand cannot be increased by increasing the real value of the public's money balances through falling prices. This is the only case, however, in which we can generate a less than full employment static equilibrium in our model. *Underemployment static equilibrium, therefore, depends on Keynes' assumption of rigid money wages.* **

THE PIGOU OR REAL-BALANCE EFFECT IN DYNAMIC ANALYSIS

These conclusions raise two very important questions. First, what are the policy implications of this analysis? Secondly, if we are dealing with a rigid wage economy, what is the relevance of the Pigou effect?

It appears from the preceding discussion that the Pigou effect restores automaticity to the market economy under conditions of perfect price-wage flexibility. However, our analysis has been restricted to a static and comparative static framework. If we are to consider policy matters, our analysis must consider the dynamics of the Pigou effect. The introduction of dynamic factors likely to be operative in the real economy

*The Pigou effect may be viewed as increasing the price sensitivity of real aggregate demand in such a way that a full employment equilibrium is always possible in the P, Y/P plane of Figure 11, chapter 8. However, we must recall at this point our previous assumptions about the elasticity of price expectations, as well as other necessary factors.

**See Harry G. Johnson, "Monetary Theory and Keynesian Economics," *Pakistan Economic Journal*, Vol. 8 (June 1958), pp. 56–70, reprinted in Warren Smith and Ronald Teigen (eds.), *Readings in Money, National Income and Stabilization Policy* (Homewood, Illinois: Richard D. Irwin, Inc., 1965).

greatly weaken the case for price flexibility as a tool of practical policy. Let us examine three considerations that reduce the viability of the Pigou effect as a basis for economic policy in a dynamic world.

First, and most simply, the decrease in prices and wages required to restore full employment may take too long to be economically and/or socially acceptable. Secondly, even if prices can be made to adjust fairly rapidly, the Pigou effect may be so weak that a very large and possibly disruptive price deflation may be necessary to induce the required increase in aggregate demand.* In the extreme, the Pigou effect may be completely inoperative (the coefficient d in the consumption function and the elasticity of consumption expenditures with respect to real money balances—net real financial wealth—may be zero). Another possibility involves the situation in which initial price declines have the desired result but, after a certain amount of adjustment, the marginal utility of increased consumption out of money balances eventually decreases sufficiently to again make the effect inoperative. Thirdly, a falling price and wage level may set up adverse anticipations which lead to decreases rather than increases in aggregate demand. For example, as prices fall, though real money balances are increasing, consumers may postpone expenditures in the hope of buying the desired items at a later time at lower prices. Likewise, investors may postpone investment projects in the hope of further price declines. Construction, for example, may be postponed in the hope that wages of construction workers will decline further and decrease the cost of the investment project. Falling prices may also discourage investment because of the uncertainty of the future selling price of newly produced goods. Building factories at today's high prices for the sale of goods at tomorrow's low prices is not a prospect likely to stimulate businessmen's confidence in their profit margins.**

Any one of these arguments represents a rather serious attack on the potential usefulness of using price flexibility as a basis for policy making. Together, these arguments have been sufficiently persuasive to convince us that the Pigou effect is primarily a theoretical curiosity rather than a mechanism for managing the aggregate economy.***

*See Thomas Mayer, "The Empirical Significance of the Real Balance Effect," *The Quarterly Journal of Economics*, Vol. 73 (May 1959), pp. 275–291, and Don Patinkin, *Money, Interest and Prices*, 2nd edition (New York: Harper and Row, 1965) pp. 651–664.

**See Don Patinkin, "Price Flexibility and Full Employment," *American Economic Review*, Vol. 38 (September 1948), pp. 543–564.

***Pigou himself writes ". . . The puzzles we have been considering . . . are academic exercises, of some slight use perhaps for clarifying thought, but with very little chance of ever being posed on the chequerboard of actual life." "Economic Progress in a Stable Environment," *Economica*, 14 (1947), p. 188.

THE PIGOU OR REAL-BALANCE EFFECT IN MODERN ANALYSIS

If the Pigou effect is likely to be very weak or inoperative in a depression economy, or if wages and/or prices are really inflexible downward in our modern industrialized economies, what, if any, is the relevance of the Pigou effect to modern analysis? There are two main points to be made in this connection: First, the Pigou effect, if significant, remains an important analytical tool in the analysis of inflationary economies. Upward price flexibility involves a Pigou effect through the decrease in money balances affected by rising prices. This may be significant to the stability of economies in times of rapidly rising prices. Secondly, under certain conditions imposed on the models of the previous chapter, monetary policy was shown to be totally ineffective as a means of increasing aggregate demand. With the insertion of the Pigou effect into these models, this conclusion no longer holds. Under the circumstances assumed in those models, monetary policy was ineffective because increases in the money stock could not decrease interest rates and stimulate *investment*. Under these same circumstances, the insertion of the Pigou effect allows monetary policy to become effective through the influence of real money balances on *consumption*. Though it may be impossible to decrease P because of rigidities in the economy, M/P can still be increased by changing M. Thus, monetary policy is effective in our model as long as a significant Pigou effect can be demonstrated.

CONCLUDING REMARKS

This chapter is a brief survey of some of the more important issues centering on the wealth effect in macroeconomic models; it in no way represents a complete presentation of the development of economic models of the aggregate economy. However, the models presented here represent a significant advance over the $LM - IS$ model of chapter 6 and function as expedient tools in the analysis of many current economic problems.

Questions/ *chapter 9*

1. a. What is the Pigou effect?

  b. How does the insertion of a variable into a model of the aggregate economy to account for the Pigou effect modify the structural form of that model (i.e., which behavioral equations are affected and in what specific ways)?

2. The liquidity trap and the interest insensitive investment demand function are often presented as specific cases that make possible a "Keynesian" underemployment equilibrium. Yet Harry Johnson notes: "In my opinion . . . the Pigou effect finally disposes of the Keynesian contention that underemployment equilibrium does not depend on the assumption of wage rigidity. *It does.*"

  a. How does the Pigou effect guarantee full employment equilibrium in an economy with complete price-wage flexibility? Consider, for example, the case of an economy at less than full employment and in a situation in which full employment saving is greater than investment at all positive interest rates. Demonstrate this situation graphically. Explain and show how the real balance mechanism is supposed to restore the economy to full employment.

  b. Granting Johnson's statement is true, demonstrate graphically how rigid money wages within the framework of a *real* balance model could lead to a situation of less than full employment (equilibrium).

3. Again, granting the truth of Johnson's statement above, on the basis of the analysis of the real balance effect, should we press for the restoration of complete price-wage flexibility to restore "the self-regulating and self-correcting mechanism" of the market economy (i.e., is downward

price-wage flexibility likely to be an acceptable and successful policy for the restoration of full-employment from a below full employment position)? Why or why not?

4. Has the "real-balance" effect any significance or importance in the analysis of an economy in which there is no downward flexibility in wage and price levels?

5. Assume government calculates that its real indebtedness increases when prices fall. Further assume that government raises taxes or reduces spending accordingly. What effect will this have on the real-balance effect?

Bibliography / *chapter 9*

Friedman, Milton, "The Role of Monetary Policy," *American Economic Review*, Vol. 58 (March 1968), pp. 1-17.

Friedman, Milton, and Anna J. Schwartz, "The Definition of Money," *Journal of Money, Credit and Banking*, Vol. 1 (February 1969), pp. 1-14.

Haberler, Gottfried, *Prosperity and Depression*. Geneva: The League of Nations, 1941, 3rd edition, pp. 491-503.

_____ , "The Pigou Effect Once More," *Journal of Political Economy*, Vol. 60 (June 1952), pp. 240-246.

Johnson, Harry G., "Monetary Theory and Keynesian Economics," *Pakistan Economic Journal*, Vol. 8 (June 1958), reprinted in *Money, National Income, and Stabilization Policy*, Warren Smith and Ronald Teigen (eds.), Homewood, Illinois: Richard D. Irwin, Inc., 1965.

_____ , "Inside Money, Outside Money, Income, Wealth and Welfare in Monetary Theory," *Journal of Money, Credit and Banking,* Vol. 1 (February 1969), pp. 30-45.

Lange, Oscar, "Say's Law: Restatement and Criticism," *Studies in Mathematical Economics and Econometrics*, Chicago, 1942.

Marty, Alvin, "Inside Money, Outside Money, and The Wealth Effect: A Review Essay," *Journal of Money, Credit and Banking*, Vol. 1 (February 1969), pp. 101-111.

Mayer, Thomas, "The Empirical Significance of the Real Balance Effect," *Quarterly Journal of Economics*, Vol. 73 (May 1959), pp. 275-291.

Patinkin, Don, "Price Flexibility and Full Employment," *The American Economic Review*, Vol. 38 (September 1948), pp. 543–564.

———, "Money and Wealth: A Review Article," *Journal of Economic Literature*, Vol. 7 (December 1969), pp. 1140–1160.

———, *Money, Interest and Prices*, 2nd edition, New York: Harper and Row, 1965.

Pesek, Boris, and **Thomas Saving,** *Money, Wealth and Economic Theory.* New York: The Macmillan Company, 1967, chapters 2 and 3.

Pigou, A. C., "The Classical Stationary State," *Economic Journal*, Vol. 53 (1943), pp. 343–351.

———, "Economic Progress in a Stable Environment," *Economica*, Vol. 14 (1947), pp. 180–190.

Samuelson, Paul, "Money, Interest Rates and Economic Activity: Their Interrelationship in a Market Economy," *Proceedings of a Symposium of Money Interest Rates and Economic Activity.* New York: American Bankers Association, 1967, pp. 45–57.

Schotta, Charles R., "The Real Balance Effect in the United States, 1947–1963," *Journal of Finance*, Vol. 19 (December 1964), pp. 619–630.

Smith, Warren L., "A Graphical Exposition of the Complete Keynesian System," *The Southern Economic Journal*, Vol. 23 (October 1956), pp. 115–125.

———, "A Neo-Keynesian View of Monetary Policy," *Proceedings* of a Monetary Conference of the Federal Reserve Bank of Boston (June 1969), pp. 105-126.

Timberlake, Richard Henry, "Patinkin and the Pigou Effect: A Comment," *Review of Economics and Statistics*, Vol. 39 (August 1957), pp. 346–348.

Tydall, H. F., "Savings and Wealth," *Australian Economic Papers*, Vol. 2 (December 1963), pp. 228–250.

READINGS/ *part 3*

EFFECTS OF MONEY SUPPLY AND MONEY DEMAND ON MACROECONOMIC MODELS

389

Introduction to Readings/ *part 3*

The four chapters of Part 3, beginning with the Hicks-Hansen *IS-LM* formulation of the basic Keynesian model, have brought us to a discussion of the monetary characteristics of a fully specified real-balance model of the aggregate economy. The readings we include in this section review the development of some of the more important policy issues surrounding these models and describe the alternatives facing the policy maker who uses one of these models in the formulation of macroeconomic and, particularly, monetary policy.

The first essay is a survey of "Current Issues in the Theory of Monetary Policy" by Phillip Cagan. This article brings together many elements from all three parts of this text. Cagan considers the policy implications of the interest sensitivity of the demand to hold money balances, and the effects of the presence of financial intermediaries (the availability of money substitutes) in the economy. In addition, he relates the Keynesian emphasis on government deficits as a pivotal determinant of aggregate demand to the monetary effects of the financing of those deficits. Cagan reiterates the warning in chapter 6 that monetary and fiscal effects must be considered together.

The following two selections are excerpts from an article by David Fand. The first article is a critique of the failure of post-Keynesian aggregate economic models to distinguish carefully between "nominal" and "real" values. Fand contrasts the postulates of the modern quantity theory with those of the post-Keynesian income-expenditure theories, and calls for a reconciliation between them. In particular, he suggests an integration of the quantity theorists' analysis of the Fisher effects of monetary changes with the Keynesian income-expenditure model. In the second article, Fand restates the criticism raised in chapter 6 and in the Cagan article, of those who omit capital market and money market effects from their analysis of fiscal policy. He emphasizes the need to specify the exact monetary and fiscal effects of a given policy, and to devise better ways to measure these effects.

This issue is examined in greater detail in the article by Roger Spencer and William Yohe. Their contribution provides a brief survey of economic theory pertaining to the influence of fiscal actions on economic activity, from Adam Smith to the present. They find that "crowding out" has been the dominant view during the past two hundred years. Moreover, the emphasis on the simple Keynesian multiplier analysis in developing economic stabilization programs during the 1960's is not in general agreement with Keynes' own views or with post-Keynesian economics.

We continue this section with readings by Warren Smith and Allan Meltzer. Meltzer reviews the forecasts made by some of the larger econometric models for the first and second quarters of 1969, and suggests that the magnitude of the errors involved in these forecasts can be explained by the failure of these models to assign an important role to money as a causal factor in the economy. Meltzer, like Fand, calls for an explicit introduction of the important distinction between "real" and "nominal" values into the income-expenditure analysis that characterizes these models.

Warren Smith's article serves as a summary statement of many of the issues raised throughout this text. He considers the transmission mechanism through which monetary policy influences the aggregate economy; he renews the discussion of the role of money in judging the effectiveness of fiscal policy, and, finally, he raises the question first considered in Part 1 concerning the particular guidelines the monetary authorities should use in conducting monetary policy to achieve their stated aims.

To emphasize the disagreement that currently exists over many of the foremost policy issues raised in the text and surveyed by Warren Smith, we conclude this section with an article by Karl Brunner. In this piece, Brunner provides a particularly comprehensive review of the "New View" and "Monetarist" positions. This includes a critical examination of several articles representative of the "New View" approved and labeled as part of the countercritique of the Monetarist position. Brunner presents evidence on the relative importance of the behavior of the banks and the public versus the actions of the monetary authorities in determining cyclical movements in the money stock. Finally, he compares the transmission mechanisms of monetary policy in various formulations of the monetarist and Keynesian models and takes up the question of what decision variables guide Federal Reserve policy actions and how these actions accord with their stated objectives.

1/ PHILLIP CAGAN

Current Issues in the Theory of Monetary Policy

BACKGROUND OF CURRENT ISSUES

Monetary theory is often ridiculed for lagging a decade behind the problem actually faced by the economy. While theory grapples with the problems of one decade and gradually influences public policy in one direction, conditions change and the policy forged for one problem muddles up another. Yet despite the swings in policy views, work in monetary theory has always pursued the same objective: to discover how and to what extent monetary factors affect prices and output. Nor has the nature of problems of policy changed basically, if one looks back more than a decade or two. It is just the answers that change. Whether they have also evolved and improved over time is less clear. In any event, interest in problems of monetary policy is currently high, reversing a long period of widespread indifference. In the latter 1930's and early 1940's many felt that money was unimportant, and then in the latter 1940's and early 1950's it was decided that money did matter after all, though how far monetary measures can stabilize the economy remains in dispute. Criticism has shifted ground from time to time but continues at full force, with the efficacy and proper role of monetary policy still the subject of most current work in the field.

The criticism intensified and took a new direction with Keynes' *General Theory*. Monetary theory is still trying to assimilate or cast off—as you prefer—his influence. Keynes initiated the modern emphasis in monetary

Reprinted from *Patterns of Market Behavior: Essays in Honor of Philip Taft*, ed. Michael J. Brennan (Providence: Brown University Press, 1965), pp. 135–154, by permission of the author and publisher. Phillip Cagan is Professor of Economics at Columbia University and is on the Research Staff of the National Bureau of Economic Research. Copyright © 1965 by Brown University.

theory on how money enters or leaves the economy. New money received by the public in exchange for other forms of wealth affects spending differently from new money received as additional income. The first has no immediate effect on spending, while the second has an effect over and above the initiating expenditure. Examples of the distinction appear in earlier writings, but it had little influence on theory. Increases in the money stock, regardless of how produced, were typically viewed before Keynes as simply providing excess cash balances, which increased spending of all kinds.

In line with Keynes' shift in emphasis, theory now distinguishes between monetary and fiscal measures for increasing the money stock. In open-market operations by the central bank, money is exchanged for bonds on wealth account, while financing Treasury expenditures with new money augments national income. An increase in income will in large part be spent, and fairly soon, while exchanging money for bonds increases liquidity but affects spending only when those who initially become more liquid—generally banks and financial institutions, not the public at large—find borrowers for the extra funds. An expansion of borrowing takes time; hence by this route the effects on spending are slow and uncertain. That, it seems to me, is the essential and valid point for monetary policy of the "Keynesian revolution."

From this point of view, an open-market operation raises two questions: (1) How will a change in the liquidity of their portfolios affect the terms on which banks and the public offer loans to borrowers? (2) Under what terms and conditions will potential borrowers accept and spend the funds? The operation of financial markets is complicated. To simplify, current theory answers the first question by a liquidity-preference or demand-to-hold-money function, and the second by an investment function. The main variable in these functions is the rate of interest, though admittedly it stands as proxy for a host of factors at play. As a first approximation in theoretical models, these functions represent the main channel through which monetary measures affect spending. In bare outline the theory is that an open-market purchase of bonds by the central bank raises their price and lowers the yield. Because national income is not directly changed by the purchase,[1] no increase in aggregate spending will result except indirectly from the lower yield on bonds and on other securities to which the change spreads. Since the 1930's monetary econo-

---

[1] Although the sellers of bonds have less earning assets and interest income, the Federal Reserve has more; hence, society's income has not changed. The redistribution of income between the public as taxpayers and as interest recipients is usually ignored.

Capital gains or losses from a change in bond prices affect wealth but not income. There are conflicting views on whether a change in wealth affects spending, but most agree the effect, if any in an ordinary operation, is small.

mists have wrestled with the question of how, and whether, spending responds to such changes in interest rates. An extreme view was that an increase in the money stock through open-market operations might not increase spending at all because investment expenditures would not respond to lower costs of borrowing. Even though banks acquired excess reserves and could expand deposits by buying bonds, the new money might sit idly in the bond sellers' cash balances.

My commentary on the development of these issues will be critical of the early criticisms of monetary policy, on the ground that the evidence affords them only limited support. The next section covers the response of investment expenditures to changes in interest rates. The third and fourth turn to the related question of whether the demand to hold money is affected by changes in interest rates. The fifth explores some of the implications for policy. The Keynesian approach emphasizes government deficits as a pivotal determinant of aggregate spending, with little attention to whether they are financed by bonds or new money. This ignores the temporary effects of deficits financed by bonds and leads to misinterpretation of their impact, a point taken up in the last section.

MONETARY EFFECTS ON INVESTMENT EXPENDITURES

In the *General Theory* Keynes contended that investment opportunities—in depression at least—might appear unattractive even at very low rates of interest. Of the many statistical studies carried out subsequently, most agreed with Keynes and claimed to find no effect of interest rates on investment, even for normal times. The initial studies seemed to support a widespread opinion at the time that lowering interest rates by monetary measures could not stimulate investment in a business recession. Later, the lack of response was also applied to restraining investment in a boom. Here the argument rested on much weaker ground: A sufficiently tight monetary policy could always force cuts in aggregate investment through inability to obtain financing; in a theoretical sense, borrowing costs would then rise to whatever level was necessary to bring the amount of funds demanded down to the limited supply. Nevertheless, it was maintained that only extreme tightening would have much effect, at which point there was allegedly danger of going too far and precipitating recession.

The view that interest rates do not influence investment swayed majority opinion for a time, but is now greeted with increasing scepticism. It proves too much. How could money then affect prices and output at all? Yet over the long run such effects can be shown to exist.[2] Studies of in-

[2] See my discussion of the evidence in chapter 6 of P. Cagan, *Determinants and Effects of Changes in the Money Stock 1875-1960* (National Bureau of Economic Research, 1965).

vestment have demonstrated only that its response to interest rates is elusive and difficult to measure.[3] Negative results may reflect an insignificant response or simply failure to identify it. Since investment and interest rates rise and fall over the business cycle together with sales and profits, time series analysis has difficulty disentangling their separate effects, particularly if profit expectations—as is likely—play a dominant role.

Earlier discussion of monetary effects was deficient because of lack of evidence to back up the theory. One of the first to write in detail about the effects was Hawtrey,[4] who thought that changes in bank loan rates mainly affect short-term borrowing for carrying inventory stock. His view was criticized for overlooking that interest charges are a small part of the total cost of carrying stocks, and hence that borrowing for that purpose may depend very little on interest rates.[5] Interest charges appear to be relatively large only on long-term capital investments. Yet here, too, it has been argued that the large risks involved and the uncertainties surrounding the prospective return may render interest costs of minor importance.[6]

These theoretical arguments were far from conclusive, and the inflationary conditions during and after World War II added doubts, for the accompanying easy-money policies appeared to stimulate the high and rising level of spending. It is now widely accepted, with more empirical justification, that interest rates affect spending on a wide range of products,

---

[3]In recent years an increasing number of studies point to an interest effect. See, for example, L. Klein, "Studies in Investment Behavior," in *Conference on Business Cycles* (National Bureau of Economic Research, 1951), pp. 233–304; S. J. Maisel, "A Theory of Fluctuations in Residential Construction Starts," *American Economic Review*, 53 (June, 1963), 359–383; J. Meyer and E. Kuh, *The Investment Decision* (Cambridge, Mass.: Harvard University Press, 1960); Y. Grunfeld, "A Study of Corporate Investment" in A. Harberger (ed.), *The Demand for Durable Goods* (Chicago: University of Chicago Press, 1960); W. Roberts, "Business Cycles, Residential Construction Cycles, and the Mortgage Market," *Journal of Political Economy*, 70 (June, 1962), 263–281; G. Stigler, *Capital and Rates of Return in Manufacturing Industries* (National Bureau of Economic Research, 1963). (The last reference deals with the rate of return on capital rather than the rate of interest.)

For a criticism of evidence from survey studies which claim to find no effect, see W. H. White, "Interest Inelasticity of Investment Demand—The Case from Business Attitude Surveys Re-examined," *American Economic Review*, 46 (September, 1956), 565–587.

[4]R. G. Hawtrey, *Currency and Credit* (4th ed.; London: Longmans, Green and Co., 1950), ch. 4; J. R. Hicks, "Mr. Hawtrey on Bank Rate and the Long-term Rate of Interest," *The Manchester School*, 10 (1939).

[5]R. S. Sayers, *Modern Banking* (1st ed.; Oxford: Clarendon Press, 1938), ch. 6; J. M. Keynes, *A Treatise on Money* (London: Macmillan, 1930), Vol. 1, pp. 185–200.

[6]Such arguments, even if valid, do not necessarily imply, contrary to a widespread view, that the response of investment to changes in interest rates is low. Uncertainties may affect the mean and variance of expected returns, but not the density of potential projects arrayed along the schedule, which is all that is relevant for the elasticity of investment to changes in interest cost. See L. Tarshis, "The Elasticity of the Marginal Efficiency of Capital Function," *American Economic Review*, 51 (December, 1961), 958–985.

including housing and many other consumer durables. By implication, the meaning of "investment" expenditures in monetary theory needs re-examination. It has typically meant purchases of capital goods, while in some models it represents autonomous expenditures (that is, expenditures not related to changes in income), and in many empirical studies it measures business expenditures on plant and equipment and changes in inventories. The various meanings are not identical. For monetary theory, the meaning of investment has broadened to comprise spending on the full range of durable goods as well as some services like business research, all of which can be influenced by the cost of borrowing. Such a definition may throw national income statisticians into despair, but that is another matter.

Interest-rate effects are also likely to be distributed over a long period of time, since investment expenditures by their nature require at least some and often extensive advance planning. Such lags are a further reason, perhaps, why empirical studies have trouble spotting the effects, in addition to the identification problem already mentioned. Another reason is that quoted interest rates are not entirely representative. They do not cover many kinds of negotiated loans on real estate and other physical capital. They also fail to reflect fully the availability of loanable funds,[7] which can influence indirect costs of borrowing, such as compensatory balances and other terms of loan contracts. Changes in these terms or in the ease of borrowing affect the "true" cost but are not reflected in quoted average rates paid and are probably not perfectly correlated with them. Nonprice rationing of funds is often important. In a tight money period like 1955–1956, banks shave down many applications for loans. It is sometimes overlooked that the purpose of monetary measures is to affect spending, not quoted interest rates, and that these rates may not fully register the effects being achieved, notwithstanding the simplified assumptions of theoretical models.

For various reasons, therefore, monetary effects are hard to trace. Evidence of an indirect nature points to long lags. Mayer[8] analyzed different kinds of investment expenditure for the time normally taken to plan and make payment after the initial decision to go ahead. He estimated that a change in direction of monetary policy takes a year or more to become ef-

[7] R. Roosa, "Interest Rates and the Central Bank," in *Money, Trade, and Economic Growth, Essays in Honor of J. H. Williams* (New York: Macmillan, 1951), pp. 270–295.

[8] T. Mayer, "The Inflexibility of Monetary Policy," *Review of Economics and Statistics*, 40 (November 1958), 358–374, and "Dr. White on the Inflexibility of Monetary Policy," *Review of Economics and Statistics*, 45 (May 1963), 209–211; W. H. White, "The Flexibility of Anticyclical Monetary Policy," *Review of Economics and Statistics*, 43 (May 1961), 142–147.

fective. On a quite different approach, Friedman and Schwartz[9] have compared fluctuations in business activity and in the rate of growth of the money stock over a long period. They find a close correspondence between the two, with turns in monetary cycles leading turns in activity on the average by twelve months at troughs and sixteen months at peaks, though the lead varies considerably from cycle to cycle.

These findings help to reconcile two traditionally opposing views in monetary theory: One holds that changes in the money stock are an important source of instability in the economy, while the other claims that control over such changes is ineffective for promoting economic stability. According to the first view, if monetary effects occurred with little or no lag central banks ought—at least in principle—to be able to stabilize activity. If there are long lags, however, the two views are no longer inconsistent.

It is therefore somewhat surprising, though perhaps in keeping with tradition, that monetary controversy now rages hotter than ever. The interpretation of the evidence by Friedman and Schwartz is disputed. Two points are at issue. The first is their interpretation of the association between fluctuations in monetary growth and economic activity, which implies an effect running from money to activity. Though once quite popular, this proposition meets resistance today. To avoid that implication, one must argue that the response of the money stock to business cycles is fully responsible for the observed association. Over many mild business cycles—and particularly recent cycles—monetary growth has a synchronous, inverted cyclical pattern; that is, the growth tapers off and declines during business expansions, then revives and increases during business contractions.[10] The inverted pattern can indeed be attributed to the effects of business activity and of countercyclical monetary policies. Conceivably such effects can account for the impression that monetary growth has a long lead when compared with business cycles on a positive basis, that is, expansions in money with subsequent business expansions and similarly for contractions. Friedman and Schwartz, while not denying that business activity affects the money stock, claim that the association between the two is much closer for a positive than for an inverted comparison. If they are right, the positive association cannot be merely a reflection of the inverted one. There must be a mutual interaction, with money affecting activity after a long lag. The evidence for this interpretation is admittedly

[9] M. Friedman and A. Schwartz, "Money and Business Cycles," in *The State of Monetary Economics*, supplement to *Review of Economics and Statistics*, 45 (February, 1963), 32–64.

[10] Cagan, *op. cit.*

of a tentative nature; it is neither so crushing nor so weak as to stop all further research on the question.

The second point at issue concerns the appropriateness of relating changes in the rate of monetary growth to cycles in the *level* of economic activity, as Friedman and Schwartz do, rather than to cycles in the *rate of growth* of activity. The criticism is that the former comparison gives a spurious lead to money, on the ground that the rate of growth of economic time series generally has a cyclical turn before the level of the series does.[11] The lead is spurious, however, only if the mode of comparison is inappropriate. The evidence, to be sure, indicates that, over the long run, changes in the average rate of monetary growth tend to produce changes of equal amount in the average rate of change of prices. Suppose, however, that price adjustments lack the flexibility to match short-run cyclical changes in the monetary growth rate, though these cyclical changes still have an effect on aggregate spending: if prices do not adjust, real output bears the brunt of the spending effects. The pattern of the disturbance thus produced in real output is not obvious. Changes in the *level* of output may measure the disturbance more accurately than changes in its *rate of change*. Or the effects may be more complex than such simple relationships can handle. If monetary effects are distributed over time rather than discretely lumped at a point in time, and if there is feedback, the beginning of a movement is arbitrary and has no special significance. Yet the Friedman-Schwartz method need not for that reason be inappropriate. More elaborate analysis may, however, be necessary to bring out the timing relations in full clarity. How best to measure the relationship is yet to be settled.

Much of this controversy veers away from the main issue. Supposing that monetary effects had on the average only a moderate lag, substantial (and unpredictable) variability in the length of the lag would still cast serious doubt on our ability to use monetary controls effectively. Even though the method of dating turning points followed by Friedman and Schwartz may not appropriately measure the average length of the lag if it is distributed over time, their estimate of the lag could provide a reliable measure of the variability in its length, provided, of course, that the association does reflect the influence of money on activity. Their finding of large variability levels a severe criticism at traditional monetary policy, different in nature from the earlier charges of impotence but the same in the implication of ineffectiveness.

---

[11] One study—E. C. Brown, R. M. Solow, A. Ando, and J. Kareken, "Lags in Fiscal and Monetary Policy," in Commission on Money and Credit, *Stabilization Policies* (1963)—using quarterly data finds no difference in timing between turns in the rate of change of the money stock and of economic activity. The proper interpretation of this result is not clear, for the implied lag of less than three months is incredibly short.

THE EFFECT OF INTEREST RATES ON THE DEMAND TO HOLD MONEY

Since open-market operations exchange money for bonds in someone's portfolio but do not immediately increase anyone's income or spending, there must be some inducement to acquire and to hold the new money, at least temporarily. The inducement in theory is a rise in price of bonds outstanding, which reduces their yield and hence the opportunity cost of holding money. In technical terms, there is a movement down along the demand-to-hold-money schedule. At first the additional money is excessive relative to other forms of wealth held; the attempt by money holders to exchange their excess balances for other assets raises asset prices and lowers rates of return across the board. The decline in rates thus spreads to all financial and physical assets, so that an increase in the money stock may eventually stimulate new investment spending in many directions. The dependence of money holdings on interest rates and the slope of this relation have received considerable empirical study.

Many of the first studies correlating money holdings and interest rates left much to be desired. Since the nominal amount of money balances demanded is partly determined by individuals' wealth and volume of transactions, the demand can only be meaningfully measured relative to money national income or wealth. Many studies, following Keynes, assumed that one part of an individual's money holdings is actively used for transactions and is proportional to his income. The temporarily idle remainder was treated as unrelated to income and dependent only on interest rates. It is doubtful, however, that the dichotomy between "active" and "idle" balances holds up empirically. It is useful only for pedagogical purposes. The demand for idle balances will also be affected by the level of wealth and income, and the demand for transactions balances also by interest rates. A further difficulty with most of these studies was their coverage of just the four decades since the 1920's. Over that period, monetary velocity (that is, the ratio of national income to the money stock) and interest rates have both had two large movements, first down during the 1930's and early 1940's, then up until the mid-1950's. The two movements are by far the largest over the entire period and so dominate the regressions fitted to the data. The fit is deceptively impressive; one is sceptical of a correlation based essentially on only two movements, particularly since the other smaller movements are less closely related.[12] On this evidence alone, the

---

[12] L. H. Bean, " 'On Interest Rates and the Demand for Money': A Comment," *Review of Economics and Statistics*, 42 (August, 1960), 333–334; C. Warburton, "Monetary Velocity and the Rate of Interest," *Review of Economics and Statistics*, 32 (August, 1950), 256–257.

association between velocity and interest rates may reflect, not a causal relation, but their similar response to depression and war.

Studies by Latané[13] and by Meltzer[14] avoid those difficulties by measuring the demand function for money in more sophisticated forms and by examining two earlier decades. Their results show a high correlation between interest rates and velocity. Moreover, Meltzer obtained consistent results for each decade of the whole period. It is not clear whether these results indicate a long-run or a short-run relation, or both. They are based on annual data and so probably measure a long-run relation, though the similar short-run cyclical fluctuations in velocity and interest rates no doubt add in some degree to the correlations found.[15]

Even if we grant that the demand to hold money depends on interest rates, the difficulties created by this dependence are constantly deplored but never adequately explained. To be sure, if the change in amount demanded for any given change in rates is infinite, as Keynes suggested was possible in deep depression at very low interest rates, rates could not fall lower through increases in the money stock because the public would sell all the bonds the Federal Reserve wanted to buy, at no increase in price. Monetary stimulation of the economy by open-market purchases is then virtually impossible.[16] It is doubtful that the economy has ever entered this strange world, even during the latter 1930's,[17] though no evidence is required to establish the self-evident proposition that such a "liquidity trap" does exist at rates of return of zero or slightly higher on all assets. Money is clearly preferable to any other asset fixed in nominal value and

[13]H. A. Latané, "Cash Balances and the Interest Rate: A Pragmatic Approach," *Review of Economics and Statistics*, 36 (November, 1954), 456–460; "Income Velocity and Interest Rates: A Pragmatic Approach," *Review of Economics and Statistics*, 42 (November, 1960), 445–449.

[14]A. H. Meltzer, "The Demand for Money: The Evidence from the Time Series," *Journal of Political Economy*, 71 (June, 1963), 219–246.

[15]Insofar as they do, there is danger that the effect is overestimated because of the failure to allow for the effect of income on interest rates via the investment-demand function. In statistical terms, this produces single-equation least-squares bias. Unfortunately, it cannot be easily handled until we are successful in specifying the investment-demand function.

There is another difficulty, pertaining to short-run movements, in that independent changes in the demand to hold money can produce changes in the supply of loanable funds and so affect interest rates. If the changes in money demand are produced by cyclical fluctuations in income, there is an appearance of a dependence of velocity on interest rates which actually reflects a relation running in the opposite direction.

[16]Virtually but not entirely, because a sufficiently large increase in the money stock probably would create fears of inflation and greatly reduce the demand to hold money at any given level of interest rates.

[17]A. H. Meltzer, "Yet Another Look at the Low Level Liquidity Trap," *Econometrica*, 31 (July, 1963), 545–549.

offering a negligible return. For interest rates normally prevailing, however, suppose that the response of demand to a change in rates is not infinite. What then? The precise degree of response determines the amount that interest rates will change for a given change in the quantity of money. A greater response requires a commensurately larger open-market operation to produce a given change in interest rates and hence to stimulate investment and aggregate spending. Yet why should this matter? If a certain change in interest rates is thought desirable, an open-market operation can, in principle, be large enough to produce it, whatever the size. Moreover, even if errors in forecasting the demand for money were large because its sensitivity to interest rates was high, the authorities should still be able, by a series of trial-and-error adjustments, to push a selected list of interest rates to any desired level.

The real problem is that the authorities can only guess what level of interest rates is appropriate at any time. This is not their fault. The problem is basically that the effects of open-market operations on spending take time and so cannot be quickly corrected by trial-and-error adjustments. A high interest-sensitivity in the demand to hold money does not itself add any further difficulties.

Having become aware of lags in investment spending, however, we may suspect that they occur in the demand to hold money also. If the response of demand to a change in interest rates is distributed over time, a large open-market operation taken to produce a given change in interest rates may gradually have a larger or smaller effect than is intended. Frequent attempts to offset unintended changes could subject interest rates to large fluctuations, disrupting the very stability that monetary policy is supposed to promote.

How real are such dangers? An assessment should take account of likely differences in behavior of various sectors of the economy. Households hold money as part of their wealth, equalizing the marginal rate of return that each asset offers in income or capital gain, liquidity, and risk. Nonfinancial businesses use money like any other factor of production, demanding more or less with changes in the cost of alternatives. In these two sectors, the interest-sensitivity of the demand to hold money is likely to be zero in the first instance but to increase gradually as a change in rates persists and time is allowed for adjustments.

Financial intermediaries and brokers are in the business of lending and borrowing money and so are expected to respond fairly quickly to a change in interest rates. As the middlemen of the money and capital market, they help to absorb short-run changes in supply. If the Federal Reserve buys bonds and lowers yields, bond dealers immediately provide the securities and then later buy securities on the open market to restock their inventory. If in the meantime yields do not stay down but rise, the dealers make a profit. When the Federal Reserve sells, the opposite behavior also produces a profit. Dealers exhibit what Keynes called the "speculative" motive for holding (or temporarily not holding) money. This is the explanation, perhaps, for the market's ability to absorb changes in the money stock from open-market operations in the very short run with only slight changes in interest rates.

But this short-run response need not last long, and over the intermediate run the response may be quite different. The dealers, together with other speculators, may not always expect interest rates to return to the original level; sometimes they may expect the direction of recent changes to continue and act to reinforce them. Such behavior can be observed from time to time, for example in the first part of 1958, when the Federal Reserve initiated an easy-money policy and professional and amateur speculators started a boom in government securities. That behavior implies, contrary to the usual formulation, that interest rates and the amount of money demanded move in the same direction. This has not been measured by time series studies, presumably because it happens too quickly or too infrequently.

As I interpret the limited evidence, in the short run the interest-sensitivity of the demand to hold money is fairly high, in the intermediate run it is low or sometimes perverse, and in the long run it is high or low depending on the long-run response of households and businesses. The varieties of behavior possible suggest that applying long-run relationships to short- or intermediate-run conditions is apt to mislead. In particular, the well-known cyclical fluctuations in the income velocity of money may not be an intermediate-run response to interest-rate changes at all. The fluctuations may reflect other cyclical factors, such as a temporary willingness to decrease or increase money holdings relative to the volume of expenditures as business prospects brighten or darken (though, to be sure, "business prospects" could be said to represent a rate of return on physical assets). Or, as one study suggests,[18] income velocity might improperly measure changes in the demand to hold money. Relative to wealth or "permanent" income, money balances do not fluctuate much over business cycles, and those quantities may be more appropriate than current income to indicate changes in the demand to hold money. There is therefore some basis for the view that, while the short-run sensitivity of the demand to interest rates is high, the intermediate-run sensitivity, which is of chief concern for counter-cyclical measures, is likely to be low, though it may also be less predictable.

[18] M. Friedman, "The Demand for Money: Some Theoretical and Empirical Results," *Journal of Political Economy*, 67 (August 1959), 327–351.

FINANCIAL INTERMEDIARIES AND SUBSTITUTES FOR MONEY

The main determinant of the interest-sensitivity of the demand to hold money by households and businesses is the availability of substitutes. The growth of money-like claims has lately received considerable attention, attracted by the rapid growth of savings deposits held by households with financial intermediaries and of Treasury bills, commercial paper, and other liquid assets held by businesses. Various questions have been debated. One is the perennial favorite, "Is the traditional definition of money as currency and demand deposits too limited?" The discussion of this question has not progressed far, in part because of an understandable aversion to recognize as money anything for which the data are meager. The basic issue for policy, however, is whether the growth of money substitutes reinforces the sources of instability in the economy, and whether Federal Reserve control over the reserves of commercial banks is adequate. Such questions can be discussed in terms of cyclical swings in velocity, the subject of the preceding section. Financial intermediaries have received so much attention in the literature, however, that a survey of this kind would be remiss not to discuss them explicitly.

Financial intermediaries might increase short-run instability in two different ways. One is by changing their reserve ratios. Lending previously idle reserves puts money into circulation and thus raises spending. Any holder of cash balances can increase spending in the same way. As a matter of fact, the ratio of reserves to liabilities of financial intermediaries other than commercial banks is fairly stable over time.[19] There is no reason to single out such institutions on these grounds.

A second and more important source of short-run instability results from supplying substitutes for commercial bank deposits. Tight money, for example, may induce depositors to shift funds from commercial banks to other financial intermediaries as the latter take advantage of rising market rates to increase the rate of interest paid on deposits. This raises the velocity of commercial bank deposits. Conversely, easy money may bring the opposite shifts. Such shifts diminish the effect on cyclical swings in aggregate spending that tight or easy money is supposed to provide. It is true that the Federal Reserve can still control the supply of loanable funds by changing commercial bank reserves and hence deposits in any amount

---

[19]W. C. Freund. "Financial Intermediaries and Federal Reserve Controls Over the Business Cycle," *Quarterly Review of Economics and Business*, 2 (February 1962), 21–29.

desired,[20] so that the rapid growth of substitutes does not incapacitate traditional monetary controls. Yet the substitutes probably make the demand for commercial bank deposits more sensitive to interest rates than it would otherwise be. As previously said, it is the difficulty of forecasting the distribution of the shifts over time rather than their magnitude that complicates monetary policy.

Concern over substitutes for money is, of course, not new. The Banking School of the mid-1800's in England thought that fluctuations in trade credit vitiated controls over the stock of currency set up by Peel's Act. Later, in this country, Henry Simons warned of the instability created by sudden shifts between demand deposits and short-term claims of all kinds.[21] Simons was mainly concerned about panics, which we now feel will be prevented even with short-term claims galore hanging precariously over the market. The problem now is mild cyclical shifts between those claims and commercial bank deposits.

Shifts between money and other assets have been deplored so much that we tend to forget how little we know about them. We know that savings deposits and other liquid assets have grown rapidly relative to commercial bank deposits. But beyond this we have to conjecture. Much of the long-run increase probably reflects a growing preference by the public for the services of intermediaries over direct holdings of stocks and bonds. Theoretically, the growth of liquid assets need not increase the interest-sensitivity of demand for commercial bank deposits[22] and no one has demonstrated that it does. Yet demand is always affected in this way by the availability of close substitutes, and it seems likely that most liquid assets, including commercial bank deposits, are close substitutes for one another.

Although the interest-sensitivity of demand for these assets may be high, cyclical shifts to and from savings deposits do not appear to present a serious problem. The differential rate paid by savings and loan associations and mutual savings banks over the rate paid by commercial banks displays little cyclical fluctuation.[23] While the rates which commercial banks can pay are subject to a ceiling, the rates of other financial intermediaries, which have no ceiling, adjust to market conditions slowly. Moreover, individuals on the whole seem to respond slowly to changes in rate differentials. Except for a limited amount of "hot money," large and sudden shifts in and out of these assets appear unlikely.

[20] J. Tobin and W. Brainard, "Financial Intermediaries and the Effectiveness of Monetary Controls," *American Economic Review Papers and Proceedings*, 53 (May 1963), 383–400.

[21] H. C. Simons, *Economic Policy for a Free Society* (Chicago: University of Chicago Press, 1948), pp. 166–171.

[22] A. Marty, "Gurley and Shaw on Money in a Theory of Finance," *Journal of Political Economy*, 69 (February, 1961), 56–62.

[23] Cagan, *op. cit.*, 5.

In recent years, it is true, changes in certain rate differentials have been large and the induced shifts in holdings apparently also large. Those were special developments, however, not likely to be often repeated, certainly not as a regular feature of each business cycle. In 1950 Congress made the insurance offered savings and loan depositors virtually identical to the insurance offered commercial and mutual savings bank depositors. Also, during the 1950's, yields on mortgages and other securities rose; while ceilings prevented commercial banks from raising their rates very far, other financial intermediaries offered higher and higher rates. Many savers shifted their funds to the institutions paying more. Then, recently, the ceiling on commercial bank time and savings deposits was lifted, and they experienced rapid growth. These episodes prove that many people are rate-conscious, at least among assets that government insurance makes identical by assuming the risk of loss. There is no evidence, however, that such shifts quickly follow the changes in market rates typical of mild business cycles if government regulations are not altered.[24]

Proposals to moderate the effects of such shifts nevertheless abound. Simons, no man for half measures, would have abolished nearly all short-term claims. Present proposals have less dash. Since no one has devised an easy way to regulate the issue of commercial paper, trade credit, and other short-term claims with elastic supplies, attention has centered on the deposit institutions. Some benefit would come from removing rate ceilings on commercial bank deposits, both time and demand; this price-fixing can be disruptive when changed, as it must be from time to time because competition has a way of seeping into the most tightly regulated markets. Removing the ceiling would also help to keep commercial bank rates in line with the rates paid by other institutions over the cycle. Proposals have also been offered to require all savings banks to hold reserves with a government agency. If fixed as a percentage of deposits, such requirements would hold the total quantity of liquid assets constant whenever depositors shifted (for example) from commercial banks to savings and loan associations, assuming both institutions had to maintain the same reserve ratio. The shift would not then increase aggregate spending, as it can now.

The proposed reserve requirements could, however, introduce other sources of instability which are not now a problem. When the demand for savings deposits increased, savings banks would have to acquire additional reserves at the expense of commercial banks. Supplying savings deposits would therefore force a reduction in the quantity of commercial bank deposits, unless the authorities increased total reserves. The resulting constancy of total liquid assets is appropriate if the shift to savings bank deposits accompanies an equal decline in the demand for commercial bank deposits, but not otherwise. If individuals sold bonds and put the proceeds

[24] Freund, *op. cit.*

into savings deposits, and the purchasers paid with funds acquired from maturing commercial paper or some other asset with a tractable supply, the demand for commercial bank deposits would not change. Because commercial banks are nevertheless forced to contract, aggregate spending is curtailed.

Monetary policy could in principle offset these and other shifts. The point of such proposals is to reduce the sources of instability that require offsetting. The desirability of the reserve proposals for savings banks therefore depends on the importance of the shifts thereby rendered harmless relative to those that become a new source of instability. The difficulty of determining this makes the proposals unattractive, and lately they have received less attention.

THE DILEMMA OF MONETARY POLICY

Substitutes for money create more problems for monetary theory than for policy. Theory is called upon to analyze the demand and supply characteristics of money and its substitutes. Policy can largely overlook the gaps in that analysis and concentrate on supplying or withdrawing funds from the market to stimulate or restrain spending. Policy need not know how monetary measures work, only how to guide them and how to avoid difficulties. To judge from the behavior of rate differentials over cycles, financial intermediaries do not appear to be an important source of cyclical instability. The only real concern is whether they have or will become suppliers of nearly perfect substitutes for money. Contrary to the Radcliffe Report,[25] that danger seems remote, at least for the United States.

The problem faced by policy is rather that the effects of open-market operations on the prices of assets, and of changes in those prices on spending, take a long time. Policy therefore acts in the dark. At best, it lacks perfection, and the authorities are reduced to hoping that cautiously "leaning against the wind" does some good. At worst, policy adds a random source of disturbance to the market; or, if the lags are long enough, it may reinforce the very fluctuations it is piously striving to offset. This criticism goes considerably further than earlier contentions that monetary policy is ineffective. Before, critics admonished policy merely to refrain from extreme actions that might rock the boat; now, they advise it to pack up and go ashore.

[25] *Report of the Committee on the Working of the Monetary System* (Cmnd. 827) (London: H. M. Stationery Office, August, 1959).

An extreme proposal explicitly offered by Friedman[26] and by Shaw[27] advocates a constant rate of growth in the money stock at all times. A rate of 3½ or 4 per cent per year would allow for growth in the demand for money and keep prices roughly constant. Practically the same proposal is made by Angell,[28] who would have bank reserves grow at the estimated rate of growth of economic activity. The purpose of a constant rate is to avoid introducing variations in monetary growth that, though intended to mitigate current fluctuations in activity, may, because of long lags, generate fluctuations later. The Federal Reserve banks undoubtedly could produce a constant growth rate in the money stock except for minor deviations. To be sure, they often complain that they cannot prevent a decline in growth during recessions, when banks lack borrowers and excess reserves accumulate. In recent years, however, the reserve ratio of commercial banks (aside from changes in reserve requirements) exhibits very little fluctuation; banks have quickly purchased Treasury bills or other securities with new reserves when loan demand declined. Unforeseen variations in reserves from fluctuations in float and from currency or gold flows will make a constant growth rate in the money stock from week to week difficult, but from month to month it should be attainable.

The proponents of a constant growth rate do not claim that it would remove all instability from the economy. When for any reason loan demand declines, giving banks the same predetermined amount of reserves allows them to buy short-term securities and (if reserve ratios are not raised) to keep the money stock growing at the same rate. Sellers of the securities may just hold the money acquired, however, and not immediately spend it; in technical terms, the monetary expansion is offset in the first instance by a fall in velocity. Under these conditions it is tempting to favor a more aggressive expansion of bank reserves to try to make spending rise faster. Adhering to a constant rate of monetary growth appears defeatist to proponents of a discretionary countercyclical policy. Yet their position rests squarely on the assumption that a countercyclical policy does some good, which is the point at issue. The proponents of a constant rate argue that cyclical fluctuations in output, though not eliminated under the proposal, would have less amplitude than in the past, because variations in the monetary growth rate are an important source of instability in the economy.

[26] M. Friedman, *A Program for Monetary Stability* (New York: Fordham University Press, 1959).

[27] E. S. Shaw, "Money Supply and Stable Economic Growth," in *U.S. Monetary Policy* (New York: American Assembly, 1958), pp. 49–71.

[28] J. A. Angell, "Appropriate Monetary Policies and Operations in the United States Today," *Review of Economics and Statistics*, 42 (August 1960), 247–252.

One serious difficulty with a predetermined rate of monetary growth is that the selected rate may not keep prices constant over the long run, nor would it force them down when a persistent deficit in the balance of foreign payments required deflation. The rise in velocity during the 1950's, for example, made a lower growth rate of money desirable, although, had monetary policy not held interest rates so low during the 1940's, the postwar rise in interest rates and velocity would presumably have been much smaller. Such long-run swings in velocity may nevertheless occur, and from time to time an adverse balance of payments undoubtedly will. Adjustments required in the rate of monetary growth would have to be carried out in small steps, however, since every change is allegedly a source of instability to be avoided.

One might dislike this particular proposal but still agree that countercyclical monetary actions may be more disruptive than helpful because of lags. At the very least, policy should avoid large and sudden changes in the rate of monetary growth, though in such watered-down form the advice is hardly novel. Federal Reserve actions moved in that direction some time ago. Fluctuations in the monetary growth rate have been smaller since World War II than ever before for an extended period, though the results still fall short of a constant rate of growth.

THE ALTERNATIVE OF FISCAL POLICY

If monetary controls cannot stabilize the economy, it is natural to turn to fiscal measures. Government deficits pour additional dollars directly into the spending stream and so avoid the delays of open-market operations. To spread the dollars widely, tax cuts are superior to increases in federal expenditures on armaments or public works, which by nature mainly stimulate particular sectors of the economy, generally not those needing help the most. Yet obtaining congressional action to cut taxes promptly in a recession has been unsuccessful, and future prospects are bleak.

Even with full congressional co-operation, stabilizing the economy by varying the size of deficits or surpluses is not quite as simple as the "crude multiplier approach" implies. A permanent government deficit financed by selling bonds raises aggregate expenditures *over the long run* to the extent that monetary velocity rises. (For a given money stock, national income and velocity increase proportionately.) In theory, velocity will become moderately higher in the long run through an increase in interest rates produced by the government's sale of bonds to finance the deficit. Except for that effect, the rise in interest rates induces an offsetting reduction in private investment and—to the extent that saving is stimulated—also consumption. The reduction in private spending, resulting from the sale of U.S. bonds, takes time, however. The lag is very similar to the lag in the effect of monetary policy: Selling U.S. bonds raises their market yield, which gradually spreads to other assets and eventually curtails private investment. In the first instance, therefore, the budget deficit stimulates the economy by the full amount of the deficit plus the associated multiplier effects; the offsetting effect of the bond financing on private spending occurs slowly. Over the long run, the effect of a permanent deficit will be far smaller than the initial effects.

To the extent that the Treasury sells bonds to banks having excess reserves, of course, deficits are financed by new money, and while they continue, the effects remain at their initial strength. No offsetting effect on private spending occurs. Banks have not had large excess reserves in recent years, however, and the monetary authorities have generally not provided them specifically to absorb deficits. It may be that the stimulation of deficit spending induces some expansion of bank credit, although there is no evidence that such expansion accompanies deficits as a normal pattern except at special times, such as under the Federal Reserve bond-support program of the 1940's and early 1950's.

The effect of a deficit financed by selling bonds is therefore complicated and easy to misjudge. An accurate judgement must allow for the present and future effects of past levels of the deficit. The effect of a given rate of deficit is highest at first, then gradually fades, so that continued stimulus to the economy of the same initial amount requires a larger and larger deficit. Similarly, reducing a deficit of long standing is equivalent to running a surplus after having balanced the budget for a time. While financing a deficit with new money (by Federal Reserve purchases of the bonds issued by the Treasury) would maintain an undiminished effect, it would serve no purpose. For countercyclical purposes, fiscal measures need not last long, and over the long run their effects on aggregate demand can be achieved just as well by monetary measures.

With its rapid impact on aggregate demand, therefore, fiscal policy is primarily a countercyclical weapon. For that purpose budget policy should, ideally, increase the deficit gradually during business contractions, and at the onset of expansion reduce it gradually and then switch over to a gradually increasing surplus. Such a pattern occurs in part automatically through the interaction of income fluctuations with fixed tax rates and unemployment compensation. Although such automatic stabilizers cannot eliminate business cycles, they have done much in recent years to ameliorate them. We probably cannot, for practical reasons, go farther. Congressional changes in tax rates or in public expenditures are too slow and too often nonreversible.

CONCLUDING REMARKS ON THE USES
OF MONETARY AND FISCAL MEASURES

With monetary theory raising grave warnings about the adequacy and dangers of traditional countercyclical policies and advising retrenchment, events oddly enough have thrust policy into a broader role. Monetary measures, together with what help our clumsy fiscal machinery can provide, are supposed to stabilize the economy, raise the growth rate of output, and stop the outflow of gold. It is enough to ruffle the most composed central banker. Theory helps to clarify the incompatibility of some of these goals. With easy money the authorities may perhaps stimulate investment and hence the growth of capital, but they cannot at the same time indefinitely avoid inflation unless the federal budget runs a substantial surplus. They cannot stimulate investment and at the same time expect to stop an adverse balance of payments unless the dollar exchange rate is allowed to fluctuate on the open market.[29] It is doubtful whether a discretionary monetary policy can do any more to stabilize the economy than has already been done without a more adept fiscal policy, and it might well try doing less. Lately, however, complaints of lagging economic growth outweigh those of instability, so that the goals of monetary policy may be changing, in part perhaps because the traditional goals of stabilization have been partially attained and further achievements appear out of reach.

Confronted with such diverse and conflicting goals, policy makers are susceptible to the appeal of nostrums. Juggling tax rates to spur investment for growth, along with export subsidies and import quotas to alleviate the adverse balance of payments, while deplorable on many grounds, at least help to attain the purposes intended. The policy of public expenditures directed at particular regions to attack pockets of persistent unemployment, though largely only a temporary palliative, at least recognizes that each region poses special problems and that a stimulant fed to the whole economy will not solve them. However, the recent disposition to use budget deficits for long-run problems of growth and unemployment, leaving monetary policy to look after short-run developments, cannot be defended. That disregards their comparative advantages. Budget deficits and surpluses have an immediate impact but (unless continually increased)

---

[29] At present rates of outflow (1964), our gold stock in a few years will be close to minimum requirements. In future thereafter, we shall have to forgo the luxury, now so much appreciated in Washington, of procrastination in dealing with balance-of-payments difficulties.

accomplish little in the long run, while monetary measures affect the economy at large mainly in the long run, very little in the short run. Reliance instead on temporary deficits and surpluses to mitigate business cycles, and on monetary measures for longer-run objectives, will give more dependable results. Assigning separate domains to monetary and fiscal policy will also avoid setting them at cross purposes, an effect which too easily results from the confusing variety of national goals.

2/ DAVID I. FAND

Some Issues in Monetary Economics: The Income-Expenditure Theory and the Quantity Theory: Nominal and Real Quantities

There is considerable agreement on the proposition in monetary theory that the *real* value of the money stock is an *endogenous* variable, determined by the interaction of the financial and real sectors, and therefore outside the control of the monetary authorities. This is in sharp contrast to the theoretical (and practical) disagreements concerning the extent to which the central bank can control the behavior of the (nominal) money stock. In equilibrium, the stock of real cash balances has a value—analogous to, say, the real wage—which the stabilization authorities cannot readily influence, except in those special cases where nominal and real variables move together. Figure 1 demonstrates that such is not always the case. For instance, the nominal money stock was unchanged during the latter half of 1966, while real money balances activity declined.

Income-expenditure theorists in their macroeconomic models often use nominal balances when the analysis requires real balances. This substitution of a nominal quantity (which can be easily changed) for a real quantity (with a determinate equilibrium value) has two consequences: it suggests than an increase in nominal balances will always tend to lower market interest rates; it also implies that changes in market rates correspond to, and reflect, changes in real rates. This procedure is sometimes justified by a special interpretation of the demand for money, an interpretation that is often attributed to Keynes' *General Theory*.

Reprinted with permission of the author and the publisher from the Federal Reserve Bank of St. Louis *Review*, January 1970. David I. Fand is Professor of Economics at Wayne State University.

Nominal and Real Money Stock

Figure 1.

It is therefore useful to recall the transformation of the demand for money in Keynes' *General Theory*. Instead of defining a demand for a *quantity* of real balances, the demand for money (or real balances) was transformed into the liquidity preference function and a basic determinant of the interest rate: the liquidity preference function together with the (real) quantity of money determines the interest rate; and since Keynes assumed explicitly that the price level was given, he could move from nominal to real balances to determine the *market* (or nominal) interest rate, the *real* interest rate (or return on capital), and the equilibrium quantity of real balances.[1]   The post-Keynesian income models follow

---

[1] For an elaboration of this theme see D. Fand, "Keynesian Monetary Theories, Stabilization Policy and the Recent Inflation," *op. cit.*, Section II on "The Demand for Money and Liquidity Preference: Real Balances and Interest Rates," which discusses the changing role of real cash balances in the Keynesian and quantity theories, the shifting emphasis from the price level to the level of employment, and the transformation of the money demand function into a liquidity preference function.

the *General Theory* in treating the demand for money as a liquidity preference function, but they do not determine explicitly the equilibrium quantity of real cash balances. The failure to define an equilibrium value for the real money stock opens up the possibility of treating both the real and nominal money stock as policy variables,[2] and as close substitutes. The substitution of nominal balances for real balances in many post-Keynesian income-expenditure models has extremely important consequences. To assume that nominal and real balances may be interchanged is to assume that the authorities have the power to print real capital and wealth: it exaggerates the control of the authorities over *real* interest rates (and rates of return); and it necessarily abstracts from any *direct* effects of money on prices (note that the link between the money stock and prices requires that we distinguish between nominal and real values). This tendency to abstract from the price level, to freely substitute nominal and real variables, and to equate market interest rates with real rates (of return) reflects the analytical *failure to define equilibrium conditions for real balances*, and is a striking feature of the post-Keynesian income models.

In sharp contrast to the income-expenditure theory, we have the following postulates concerning real balances in the modern quantity theory: (1) the money demand function defines the demand for real cash balances; (2) the quantity of real cash balances is an endogenous variable and not under the control of the monetary authorities (except for the very short run); and (3) changes in nominal balances will generally have effects on market interest rates, on income, and on prices.[3] For the analysis of transition periods it assumes that an increase in nominal balances will have a compound effect on interest rates—including a short-run liquidity (Keynes) effect, an income effect, and a longer-run (Fisher) price expecta-

---

[2] For a penetrating analysis emphasizing the originality and generality of the Keynes theory, in contrast to the rigidities, traps, and elasticity pessimism in many of the post-Keynesian income models, see A. Leijonhufvud, *On Keynesian Economics and the Economics of Keynes* (Oxford, 1968). See also D. Fand, "Keynesian Monetary Theories, Stabilization Policy and the Recent Inflation," *op. cit.*, Section III on "Three Keynesian Liquidity Preference Theories," and J. Tobin's seminal article on "Money, Capital, and Other Stores of Value," *op. cit.*, for his illuminating analysis of an aggregate model with three assets.

[3] See L. Mints, *Monetary Policy for a Competitive Society* (McGraw-Hill, 1950); M. Friedman (ed.), *Studies in the Quantity Theory of Money* (Chicago, 1958), and *The Optimum Quantity of Money* (Aldine, 1969), especially chapters 6-9; H. Johnson, *Essays in Monetary Economics* (Harvard, 1967), chapters 1-3; D. Patinkin, *Money, Interest and Prices*, 2nd ed. (Harper, 1965), chapter 15; and C. Warburton, *Depression, Inflation, and Monetary Policy*, (Johns Hopkins Press, 1966).

tion effect.[4] The modern quantity theory also assumes that the demand for money is quite stable, and that a velocity function (derived from the money demand function) may provide a useful link between (changes in) money and (changes in) money income; and, in contrast to the earlier quantity theory, postulates a stable velocity function, but allows marginal velocity to differ from average velocity.

Taken together, these quantity theory propositions have two important implications. They suggest: (1) that the monetary authorities do not control *real* interest rates or the stock of real balances, even if they can always control the stock of nominal money and thereby influence nominal or market interest rates; (2) that money is an important variable for explaining changes in prices, since the equilibrium quantity of real balances links changes in nominal money with changes in the price level. Accordingly, the modern quantity theory uses the money demand function to predict the level of money income and prices if output is given, or *changes* in money income if output varies with changes in the money stock.

The modern quantity theory and income-expenditure theory thus differ sharply in their analysis of the money demand function. In the modern quantity theory it serves as a velocity function relating either money and money income, or marginal *changes* in money and money income (if both output and marginal velocity vary with the money stock); in the income-expenditure theory, it serves as a liquidity preference theory of interest rates, or of *changes* in interest rates (if the price level is given and determined independently of the monetary sector). Accordingly, the modern quantity theory focuses on discrepancies between actual and desired real balances, distinguishes between (exogenous) nominal balances and (endogenous) real balances, emphasizes monetary aggregates rather than interest rates, and highlights nominal money as the operational policy variable; the income-expenditure theory focuses on discrepancies between actual and full-employment output, abstracts from price level changes, emphasizes an interest rate transmission mechanism, views the monetary

---

[4] For a more explicit statement of the relation between changes in the nominal money stock and interest rates, see M. Friedman and A. Schwartz, *Trends in Money, Income and Prices* (forthcoming); M. Friedman, *Dollars and Deficits* (Prentice Hall, 1968); P. Cagan and A. Gandolfi, "The Channels of Monetary Effects on Interest Rates," *American Economic Review*, May 1969; W. Gibson and G. Kaufman, "The Sensitivity of Interest Rates to Changes in Money and Income," *Journal of Political Economy*, May 1968; D. Meiselman, "Bond Yields and the Price Level: The Gibson Paradox" in *Banking and Monetary Studies, op. cit.*; and D. I. Fand, "A Monetarist Model of the Monetary Process," *The Journal of Finance*, Vol. 25 (May 1970), pp. 275–289.

aggregates as endogenous variables, and highlights the full-employment surplus as the operational policy variable.[5]

Viewed as general theories of income determination, both theories have deficiencies. The modern quantity theory seeks to explain prices, or money income, but often abstracts from the level of employment; the income-expenditure theory seeks to explain the levels of employment, but often abstracts from the price level; this difference in focus mirrors the change in the analytical roles of real balances and interest rates in the two theories. The quantity theory emphasis on real balances as an endogenous variable implies that the attempt by the monetary authorities to raise the money stock may cause prices to rise, and also cause *nominal* and *real* interest rates to diverge. In contrast, the income-expenditure theory, by de-emphasizing the endogeneity of real balances, implies that real balances and interest rates can be controlled (within limits) by the authorities—an impression that is reinforced by their failure to distinguish between nominal and real rates.

The analysis of money, interest rates, and prices in the post-Keynesian income theories may explain several of the troublesome features of recent stabilization policy: the use of market interest rates as an indicator of monetary policy; the tendency to minimize the price level consequences of excessive monetary growth; the failure to recognize the impact of inflationary expectations on market interest rates; the reluctance to distinguish between nominal and real quantities; and the conviction that the

---

[5]The mnemonic statements that money is or is not important do not bring out the essential monetary differences between the income and quantity theories. In some ways the income-expenditure theory attaches greater significance to money than does the quantity theory. Thus, the income-expenditure theory assumes that it is often possible to permanently lower interest rates, or rates of return, by an increase in nominal money, while the quantity theory is more inclined to view nominal money changes as having a permanent effect mainly on money income and prices. Yet because quantity theorists are often analyzing situations where inappropriate monetary policies may have caused severe difficulties (e.g., in the 1930's), they may foster the impression that errors in monetary policy are always associated with such drastic consequences.

One other paradox may be noted. Many income-expenditure theorists treat the nominal money stock as an endogenous variable because they believe that this approach assumes less and is therefore more accurate. But while this treatment of the money stock is most appropriate in this formal sense, it may apparently also lead to substantive errors. For example, the large scale econometric models treat the nominal money stock as an endogenous variable, but do not restrict the movements in real balances by well-defined equilibrium conditions. The assumption that an increase in nominal balances will increase real balances may have been responsible for some of the forecasting errors and policy mistakes in 1968. This assumption may involve a more serious error, substantively and analytically, than treating the nominal money stock, formally, as an exogenous variable.

rise in market interest rates since 1966 was due to an increased demand for money, and not the result of excessive growth in the money supply.[6]

The failure of income-expenditure theorists to consider the impact of accelerated (excessive) monetary growth on rising (or high) market interest rates, and to distinguish between market and real interest rates, is especially relevant for analyzing the post-1965 inflation and the stabilization difficulties since June 1968. The surprising failure of the Revenue and Expenditure Control Act of June 1968 to cool the economy thus far could be explained by noting that the fiscal "refrigeration" effect was offset by the monetary "boiler" effect.[7] The authorities, while fighting inflation with the surcharge, also wished to lower interest rates and move toward a tighter fiscal and easier monetary policy during this period, and this led to a very substantial increase in the monetary aggregates.

Many who favored monetary expansion after the June tax package based their case on the desirability (and social necessity) of lowering market interest rates. In retrospect, it seems difficult to suppose that an increase in nominal money will raise real balances, lower interest rates, curtail disintermediation, facilitate residential construction, and somehow not raise aggregate demand or prices. But an increase in the money stock which takes place in the midst of an inflation will not only raise prices but also raise market interest rates. Nevertheless, if true, it suggests that an incredibly optimistic theory—based on a refusal to acknowledge the endogeneity of real cash balances and its implications for diverging nominal and real rates—may have contributed directly to the inflationary pressures which are still continuing, and it may also have contributed to our 1966 stabilization difficulties, if the authorities believed that monetary expansion would bring about lower interest rates.[8]

[6] For a recent, and very useful, statement of the income theory approach to stabilization, incorporating a commitment to economic growth and viewing it as a key aspect of government policy, see W. Heller (ed.), *Perspectives on Economic Growth* (Random House, 1968). Because the contributors to this volume are outstanding, it may not be inappropriate to mention that the chapters dealing with stabilization policy and monetary theory provide examples illustrating the several questionable tendencies just summarized. Obviously these tendencies are not just limited to those whose understanding of the income theory may be questioned. It is for this reason that I do not regard these characteristics as analytical errors, but think of them as "methodological commitments" that may have become burdensome, and perhaps analytically oppressive.

[7] See the cogent analysis by A. Wojnilower, "Blowing Hot and Cold," First Boston Corporation (September 1968).

[8] The fear of *overkill* articulated by influential sources in the summer of 1968 may have served to reconcile the views of those who favored the tax increase primarily as a stabilization measure to cool the inflation with the views of those who favored the tax increase to shift the policy mix to achieve lower interest rates and stimulate socially desirable capital expenditures.

The stabilization difficulties that we have experienced since 1965 may be related to two questionable propositions about money, which are implicit in many income-expenditure models: (1) that the authorities can affect real balances if they can control the nominal stock of money; and (2) that the authorities can influence *real* rates through central bank operations which change *nominal* market rates. Although both of these propositions are generally accepted, they have only a limited validity, and may lead to serious policy errors when applied to a high-pressure economy such as the United States in the post-1965 period.

In an underemployed economy, *nominal* quantities and *nominal* rates

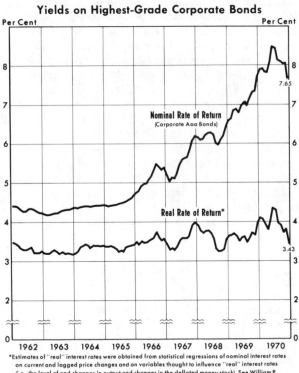

Yields on Highest-Grade Corporate Bonds

*Estimates of "real" interest rates were obtained from statistical regressions of nominal interest rates on current and lagged price changes and on variables thought to influence "real" interest rates (i.e., the level of and changes in output and changes in the deflated money stock). See William P. Yohe and Denis S. Karnosky, "Interest Rates and Price Level Changes, 1952-69," Review, Federal Reserve Bank of St. Louis, December 1969.
Latest data plotted: December

Prepared by Federal Reserve Bank of St. Louis

Figure 2.

may move with *real* quantities and *real* rates, and real balances may be sufficiently flexible to be treated as a policy variable. But in a high-pressure economy with rising prices, nominal and real quantities no longer coincide; the real (value of the) money stock cannot be treated as a policy variable, and an increase in the money stock will not only raise prices but will raise market interest rates as well. A similar question arises regarding the behavior of interest rates. In a slack economy market interest rates and real rates move together; but in a high-employment economy with rising prices, *market* rates and *real* rates may diverge (*see* accompanying Figure 2). Indeed, in a period of price inflation, constant *real* rates are necessarily associated with rising *market* rates, so that movements in the market rates cannot always correspond to real rates.

The endogeneity of the real (value of the) money stock, as indicated by the divergence between nominal and real balances and by the divergence between real and market interest rates, is thus a manifestation of an economy approaching full utilization. And we need to investigate empirically when movements in interest rates and in money balances begin to diverge, and whether the divergence between real and nominal interest rates is related to the divergence between real and nominal balances.[9]

Many investigators have commented on the monetary lag, and have suggested that because of this lag we would expect very sharp movements in interest rates—as the initial response to changes in the money stock. It is not clear how the monetary lag may be affected by the divergence between *market* and *real* interest rates and between nominal and real balances. Knowledge of the conditions when real and nominal balances diverge, of the process that causes interest rates to diverge, and of the mechanism through which the monetary lag operates, should be useful in improving stabilization policy. It would also help reconcile the income-expenditure and modern quantity theories and thus help complete the work initiated by Keynes by providing us with a truly general theory of employment, interest and money.

---

[9] Somewhere between the slack economy and the inflationary high-pressure economy there is a change in the relation between nominal and real balances and between nominal and real rates. Responsible policy officials must therefore identify and take account of the divergence between nominal and real rates, especially if they follow an interest rate criterion and use money market rates in the implementation of monetary policy decisions.

3/ DAVID I. FAND

Some Issues in Monetary Economics: Fiscal Policy Assumptions and Related Multipliers

The theory of fiscal policy highlights the direct income-generating effects of government deficits and surpluses and the stabilization aspects of the cumulative multiplier expansion process; but the theory often ignores the interest rate or capital market effects, and invariably abstracts from any associated money stock effects. The simplest presentation may be summarized as follows: an increase in government spending is viewed as a *direct* demand for goods and services; reductions in tax rates are viewed as *directly* affecting consumer spending, investment, and aggregate demand; and the initial increase in spending is viewed as setting off a cumulative expansion as given by the multiplier process.[1] More advanced discussions go beyond the 45° diagram, introduce the Hicksian *IS-LM* analysis to account for the capital market effects of changes in fiscal policy; but even this more advanced analysis typically abstracts from the money creation aspects that may be associated with a cumulative expansion.

A widely quoted statement describing the "Workings of the Multiplier" in the *Economic Report of the President for 1963* illustrates this tendency

Reprinted with permission of the author and the publisher from the Federal Reserve Bank of St. Louis *Review*, January 1970. David I. Fand is Professor of Economics at Wayne State University.

[1] The volume of readings, *American Fiscal Policy: Experiment for Prosperity* (Prentice-Hall, 1967), edited by L. Thurow, is a good example. With very few exceptions, the individual papers either abstract from, or ignore, monetary factors, and do not cite any empirical evidence to justify the strategic role assigned to discretionary changes in the full-employment surplus. It appears that such justification was not felt necessary, because the very substantial growth in GNP since 1964 was widely interpreted as the result of the 1964 tax cut and reduction in the full-employment surplus.

to omit the capital market and money creation aspects.[2] The direct income-generating effects of the deficit are stressed, but no indication is given whether the rise in income requires stable interest rates, an elastic monetary policy, or a deficit financed through the banking system. Thus, the case for a discretionary tax cut and a reduction in the full-employment surplus, as presented by the Council of Economic Advisers (CEA) in 1963, does not bring in any explicit discussion of the method in which the deficit is financed. Their position is stated as follows:

> Tax reduction will directly increase the disposable income and purchasing power of consumers and business, strengthen incentives and expectations, and raise the net returns on new capital investment. This will lead to initial increases in private consumption and investment expenditures. These increases in spending will set off a cumulative expansion, generating further increases in consumption and investment spending and a general rise in production, income and employment.

The analysis of the 1964 tax cut presented by Arthur Okun in 1965 explicitly justifies the omission of any capital market or monetary effects.[3] Although Okun accepts the view that significant changes in the cost or availability of credit would have an important influence on business investment, he does not make allowance for these factors in his quantitative estimates of the multiplier. He rationalizes his procedure as follows:

> . . . in practice, dealing with the period of the last year and a half, I cannot believe that the omission of monetary variables can make a serious difference. By any measure of interest rates or credit conditions I know, there have been no significant monetary changes that would have either stimulated or restrained investment to a major degree.

He does concede that "the maintenance of stable interest rates and stable credit conditions requires monetary action" and that at least to this extent, "monetary policies have made a major contribution to the advance." But in his view, "that contribution is appropriately viewed as permissive rather than causal." Okun's analysis, presented in August 1965, attributing the GNP expansion to the tax-cut multiplier, was a strict fiscal policy in-

---

[2]See the section, "Workings of the Multiplier" in the *Economic Report of the President for 1963*. This is reprinted in A. M. Okun (ed.), *The Battle Against Unemployment* (Norton, 1965), pp. 88–97.

[3]Okun's analysis of the 1964 tax cut was presented at the 1965 meetings of the American Statistical Association. His paper, "Measuring the Impact of the 1964 Tax Reduction" has been published in W. Heller (ed.), *Perspectives on Economic Growth*, *op. cit.*, pp. 25–51.

terpretation, in contrast to other (monetary and eclectic) interpretations that were presented at that time.[4] His analysis was not modified when it was published in 1968.[5]

If the fiscal approach, with its multiplier analysis, emphasizes the deficit or surplus and relegates both the interest rate and the money creation aspects to a secondary role, the monetary approach emphasizes the money stock effects. To the monetarist, the impact of fiscal actions will depend crucially on *how the government deficit is financed:* expenditures financed either by taxing or borrowing involve a transfer of resources (from the public to the government), with both interest rates and wealth effects on private portfolios, but the net effect of a temporary change in fiscal policy on spending may be ambiguous. Similarly, the effect of a reduction in taxes on private demand, financed through borrowing, will depend on (1) the extent to which it is viewed as a permanent, or temporary, tax cut, and (2) its effect on market interest rates. Accordingly, the direct income-generating effects of a deficit—the pure fiscal effect—may be quite small and uncertain. On the other hand, if the deficit is financed through money creation by the banking system—if the deficit is monetized—the effect is unambiguously expansionary.

Many income theorists recognized that the multiplier analysis based on the 45° diagram was inadequate, and modified their analysis to take account of interest rate effects through the Hicksian *IS-LM* framework. But even this modification, while a step in the right direction, does not really make allowance for the money creation aspects of deficits. What is needed is a macroeconomic model, where the monetary effects of the deficit are taken up by introducing an explicit government budget restraint. Recent studies along these lines suggest many of the standard propositions about the multiplier need to be revised.[6]

---

[4] See D. I. Fand, "Three Views on the Current Expansion" in G. Horwich (ed.), *Monetary Process and Policy: A Symposium* (Irwin, 1967), analyzing the views of the fiscal proponents, the monetary proponents, and those who take an eclectic position. *See also* A. F. Burns, *The Management of Prosperity* (Columbia University Press, 1966); M. Friedman, "The Monetary Studies of the National Bureau," reprinted as chapter 12 in his *The Optimum Quantity of Money*, pp. 261-284; B. Sprinkel, "An Evaluation of Recent Federal Reserve Policy" in the *Financial Analysts Journal*, August 1965; and G. Morrison, "The Influence of Money on Economic Activity," in the 1965 *Proceedings* volume of the American Statistical Association.

[5] Okun, in a note added in June 1967 to his 1965 analysis of the tax cut, does concede that "any analysis of fiscal impact that covered the more recent period could no longer treat monetary policy as a passive supporting force, nor could it continue to ignore the influence of higher levels of aggregate demand on prices." See W. W. Heller (ed.), *op. cit.*, pp. 27-28.

[6] See L. S. Ritter, "Some Monetary Aspects of Multiplier Theory and Fiscal Policy," *Review of Economic Studies*, February 1956; C. Christ, "A Simple Macroeconomic Model with a Government Budget Restraint," *Journal of Political Economy*,

Aside from these theoretical reasons, the need to separate out the monetary effects from the fiscal effects has been highlighted by the recent Andersen-Jordan study, testing the relative effectiveness of monetary and fiscal actions in stabilization.[7] Their results, while preliminary and subject to further testing, do suggest that the theory of fiscal policy (in the income-expenditure framework), with its emphasis on discretionary changes in the full-employment surplus as the key stabilization instrument, may be incorrect or only partially correct. Their findings also suggest that the tax and expenditure multipliers, as estimated in many income models, tend to confound a *ceteris paribus* fiscal action (excluding money stock effects), with a *mutatis mutandis* fiscal action (incorporating both monetary and fiscal effects).

The need to revise the standard multiplier theory and to develop more discriminating empirical tests of the relative effectiveness of monetary and fiscal actions is recognized even among fiscal policy advocates. There is a significant modification of the multiplier theory in the *Economic Report of the President for 1969*, stressing two points in particular: (1) "the results of this multiplier process are affected by the amount of unused resources available in the economy"; and (2) monetary policy does affect the magnitude of the multiplier:

> Developments in financial markets may influence the magnitude of the multiplier. Increases in demands for goods and services will tend to enlarge credit demands. Unless monetary policy permits supplies of funds to expand correspondingly, interest rates will rise and credit will become less readily available. In that event, some offsetting reduction is likely to take place in residential construction and other credit-sensitive expenditures. Generally this will be a partial offset,

---

January 1968; and J. M. Culbertson, *Macroeconomic Theory and Stabilization Policy* (McGraw-Hill, 1968), pp. 462–464.

See also K. M. Carlson and D. S. Karnosky, "The Influence of Fiscal and Monetary Actions on Aggregate Demand: A Quantitative Appraisal," *Working Paper No. 4,* March 1969, Federal Reserve Bank of St. Louis; and K. M. Carlson, "Monetary and Fiscal Actions in Macroeconomic Models: A Balance Sheet Analysis," an unpublished manuscript, for an interesting attempt to define and estimate the monetary effects of fiscal policy actions.

[7]The Andersen-Jordan results are presented in "Monetary and Fiscal Actions: A Test of their Relative Importance in Stabilization," *op. cit.* See also the *Comments* of DeLeeuw and Kalchbrenner, and the *Reply* by Andersen and Jordan, *op. cit.*, and R. G. Davis, "How Much Does Money Matter: A Look at Some Recent Evidence," *op. cit.*; the earlier study by M. Friedman and D. Meiselman on "The Relative Stability of Monetary Velocity and the Investment Multiplier in the United States, 1897-1958" in *Stabilization Policies* (Prentice Hall, 1963), and the subsequent discussion of this study by F. Modigliani and A. Ando, and by T. Mayer and M. DePrano in *American Economic Review*, September 1963.

varying according to how much the supply of credit is permitted to expand.[8]

There is therefore a growing consensus that multiplier theory needs to separate out the monetary effects from the pure fiscal effects, in order to develop meaningful tests of the relative contribution of monetary and fiscal policy in stabilization. In particular, we need to define and measure monetary variables so as to separate out exogenous changes in the money stock, resulting from actions taken by the monetary authorities—from endogenous money stock changes—resulting from shifts in the demand for money, so as to remove the identification problem in a manner that is acceptable to the income-expenditure theorists. We also need to define a pure *ceteris paribus* fiscal action with restrictions on the growth rate for the monetary aggregates that is acceptable to the *monetarists*. A revision of multiplier theory along these lines would enable us to distinguish analytically, and estimate, *ceteris paribus* fiscal and monetary multipliers, and thus bridge some of the gap between the income-expenditure theory and the quantity theory. But it requires that we find an acceptable method to separate out endogenous and exogenous changes in the money stock, and to estimate empirically the money stock effects of deficits and surpluses.

Fiscal deficits are obviously often associated with, if not directly responsible for, substantial increases in the monetary aggregates. Our recent experience reminds us once again that a fiscal deficit, financed by the banking system, will tend to accelerate the growth in the money stock; while a fiscal surplus, whether impounded or used to retire debt, will tend to decelerate the money stock growth. And if the fiscal deficit is financed in part through accelerated monetary expansion, as was the case since the Vietnam escalation in 1965, the growth in GNP reflects the combined effects of fiscal and monetary action.

Monetary policy, measured in terms of the money stock, typically changes in the same direction as fiscal policy. Accordingly, what we observe in most periods (like the 1964 tax cut) is the effect of a combined action incorporating both monetary and fiscal elements. It is therefore fortunate for the development of stabilization theory that they were working in opposite directions on two occasions in recent years—thus providing an interesting test case. In 1966 a sharp increase in the deficit was matched by a very substantial tightening in monetary policy; and the crunch in the latter half of 1966 and the mini-recession in early 1967 clearly demonstrate the power of monetary policy. Similarly in 1968, the very substantial increase in the full-employment surplus enacted in the June 1968 Revenue and Expenditure Control Act (and giving rise to widespread fear of *overkill*) was apparently offset by the preceding and subsequent growth in

[8]See *The Economic Report of the President for 1969*, p. 72.

the monetary aggregates. In these cases, the monetary forces seem to have been the stronger ones, not relatively minor (or permissive) factors that can only accommodate (or validate) fiscal policy actions. Hence there has been renewed interest in their relative contribution to stabilization.

This, then, brings us to our first question: How do we define the *ceteris paribus* fiscal action if monetary policy and fiscal policy often move in the same direction? The income-expenditure theorists, who define this as a fiscal action with interest rates held constant, are calibrating monetary policy in a manner which is consistent with their view of the transmission mechanism. On this definition, a *ceteris paribus* fiscal deficit may require a very substantial increase in the stock of money, and appears to the *monetarist* as a *mutatis mutandis* effect. To the *monetarist*, a *ceteris paribus* deficit requires a given money stock growth rate, which may lead to a rise in the interest rate; and to fiscal policy advocates, this appears as an *offsetting action* since the rise in interest rates (which they use to calibrate the posture of monetary policy) is restrictive and tends to offset the income-generating effects of the deficit. The *ceteris paribus* effect for deficits or surpluses, as defined by the *monetarist*, will necessarily differ from the definition adopted by the fiscal policy advocates. This point is illustrated in a recent study of monetary and fiscal influences on economic activity for the pe-

TABLE 1

Impact of Fiscal Influences (ΔE) On Economic Activity (ΔY)
$$\Delta Y = f_0 + f_1 \Delta E$$
(First Differences—Billions of Dollars)

	Lags*	f_0	$f_1 \Delta E$ (sum)	$R^2 / D\text{-}W$
II/1919–I/1969	t-6	3.83	.81	.13
		(5.16)	(3.01)	.96
II/1919–II/1929	t-7	1.73	3.27	.41
		(2.44)	(2.78)	1.58
III/1929–II/1939	t-10	-3.45	18.28	.14
		(2.25)	(2.18)	1.49
III/1939–IV/1946	t-4	4.29	.53	.61
		(2.91)	(2.11)	1.43
I/1947–IV/1952	t-4	9.38	-1.49	.09
		(3.91)	(1.76)	.81
I/1953–II/1969	t-3	6.08	1.71	.08
		(2.95)	(2.15)	1.13

Note: Regression coefficients are the top figures; their "t" values appear below each coefficient, enclosed by parentheses. R^2 is the percent of variations in the dependent variable which is explained by variations in the independent variable. $D\text{-}W$ is the Durbin-Watson statistic.

*Selected on the basis of minimum standard error of estimate, adjusted for degrees of freedom.

riod 1919-69.[9] The evidence summarized in Table 1 indicates that when we regress economic activity on fiscal policy, the relation is fairly good. If, however, we include a monetary aggregate variable in the regression, we find, as shown in Table 2, that the *ceteris paribus* fiscal effect, as defined by the *monetarist*, is either statistically insignificant or has the wrong sign. The evidence summarized in Tables 1 and 2 illustrates the problem of separating out the fiscal effect from the effect due to the monetary aggregate.

TABLE 2

*Indicators of Monetary (ΔM) and Fiscal (ΔE)
Influences On Economic Activity (ΔY)*

$$\Delta Y = a_0 + a_1 \, \Delta M + a_2 \, \Delta E$$

(Quarterly First Differences—Billions of Dollars)

Time Periods	Lags*	a_0	$a_1 \, \Delta M$ (sum)	$a_2 \, \Delta E$ (sum)	R^2 D-W
II/1919–I/69	t-6	1.92 (2.34)	2.89 (4.31)	-.07 (.28)	.32 1.15
II/1919–II/29	t-3	.36 (.51)	5.62 (3.16)	**	.35 1.58
III/1929–II/39	t-5	-.51 (.54)	5.40 (3.41)	-7.97 (1.95)	.39 1.86
III/1939–IV/4ϵ	t-5	6.32 (1.39)	-1.21 (.59)	.35 (.81)	.66 1.60
I/1947–IV/52	t-10	3.65 (.84)	13.82 (3.51)	-3.37 (4.12)	.72 2.74
I/1953–I/69	t-4	1.42 (.74)	8.85 (4.70)	-.84 (1.07)	.47 1.71

Note: Regression coefficients are the top figures; their "t" statistics appear below each coefficient, enclosed by parentheses. R^2 is the percent of variations in the dependent variable which is explained by variations in the independent variable. D-W is the Durbin-Watson statistic.

*Lags are selected on the basis of minimum standard error, adjusted for degrees of freedom.

**Fiscal variable omitted for 1919–29 because it increased the standard error of the estimate.

This difference in concepts helps explain the existence of a fairly pronounced communications gap. What a monetarist regards as a *ceteris paribus* deficit may entail a rise in interest rates, and will therefore appear as an *offsetting* action to the fiscal advocate; what a fiscal advocate regards as a *ceteris paribus* fiscal effect may entail accelerated growth in the money stock, and will therefore appear as a *mutatis mutandis* monetary effect to the monetarist. This applies especially to the analysis of the 1964 tax cut.

[9] Michael Keran, "Monetary and Fiscal Influences on Economic Activity—The Historical Evidence" in the November 1969 issue of this *Review*.

The money stock effects of deficits and surpluses need to be quantified if we are to obtain a realistic formulation of the government budget restraint. Once this is done we may be able to estimate the differential effects of non-monetized and monetized deficits, and obtain acceptable estimates of fiscal multipliers—for the *ceteris paribus* and for the *mutatis mutandis* cases. We would also like to derive such estimates for the *monetarist* who calibrates monetary actions in terms of the money stock growth, and for the fiscal advocates who calibrate monetary policy in terms of interest rates. Once this is done, we may be able to translate the results obtained in these two frameworks. This should help bridge the communication gap, and it may also help reconcile the two opposing points of view.[10]

CONCLUSION

In this paper we have discussed four issues in monetary theory which seem central to many of the recent discussions and debates concerning monetary policy. The first issue is the extent to which the central bank can control the nominal money stock. This issue has been raised by those who find it more natural to formulate Federal Reserve policy in terms of money market and instrument variables, by those who follow the interest rate transmission mechanism specified by the income-expenditure theory and prefer an interest rate criterion for policy making, and by those who believe that the money stock is, in part, an endogenous variable and therefore question whether it can serve as an indicator or target variable. We have tried to formulate these different viewpoints in terms of a money supply function, and reported results of empirical tests which compared the short-run money supply functions (excluding feedbacks from the real sector) with a longer-run, reduced form money supply function (allowing for feedbacks). Our preliminary findings seem to suggest that the central bank has sufficient control of the money stock to make it conform to a given set of guidelines, but that its control may be weaker (and less pre-

---

[10] A technique that enabled us to separate out exogenous changes in the money stock due to monetary policy from endogenous changes induced by the real sector would also enable us to estimate a *ceteris paribus* fiscal action in terms of exogenous money stock behavior. This approach would, in principle, be acceptable to the fiscal advocates. See K. M. Carlson and D. S. Karnosky, *op. cit.*

The full-employment surplus (or deficit) is generally accepted as the best measure of fiscal policy, in preference to the actual surplus (or deficit), which is affected by the level of activity and behaves therefore more nearly like an endogenous variable. But the full-employment surplus is available only for the income and product budget and is tied to an income-expenditure framework. It may be desirable to experiment with "similar" concepts (separating out endogenous effects) for the cash budget and the new, and comprehensive, liquidity budget, to determine which of these budgets provides the most useful measure of fiscal policy.

cise), the shorter the time period available to achieve a given objective. This would suggest that the degree of precision expected of the monetary authorities is not independent of the time period that they have to achieve the policy guidelines.*

The second question that we have explored is the relation between nominal and real quantities in the income-expenditure theory and modern quantity theory. The stabilization difficulties that we have experienced in the last several years may be related to two propositions about money which have been widely accepted in many of the income models. These are: (1) that the authorities can influence real balances if they can control nominal balances; and (2) that the authorities can influence *real* interest rates (and rates of return) by operations which change nominal market rates. Both of these propositions may lead to serious policy errors when applied to a high-pressure economy such as the United States in the post-1965 period.**

The third topic that we have considered is various theories of the price level and related frameworks for analyzing inflation. We find that there has been a tendency since World War II to divorce money from prices, to stress real factors in explaining the absolute price level, and to neglect even substantial movements in the monetary aggregates. Moreover, when income theorists highlight the short-run effect of money on interest rates—the liquidity effect—and treat it as a permanent effect, they necessarily minimize the effect on prices. This corresponds to treating real balances as if it were a variable that could be influenced by the monetary authorities. Having ruled out any *direct* link between money and prices, income theorists necessarily explain the post-1965 rise in the price level by bringing in aggregate supply variables, other real sector developments, Vietnam escalation, and inappropriate fiscal policy, but continue to abstract from the very substantial growth in the money stock and other monetary aggregates.

The fourth problem that we have considered is that of defining *ceteris paribus* and *mutatis mutandis* fiscal effects. A *ceteris paribus* fiscal deficit—holding money stock growth constant—allows interest rates to rise and will therefore appear as an offsetting action to a fiscal advocate; while a *ceteris paribus* fiscal deficit—holding interest rates constant—allows money stock growth rates to increase, and appears as a *mutatis mutandis* effect to the *monetarist*. These concepts need to be defined both for the monetarists and the fiscal advocates, in order to translate the results obtained in the two frameworks. This may help bridge some of the communications gap in stabilization theory, and also help reconcile the two points of view.

---

*This discussion is included in the readings in Part 1.

**This discussion appears in the previous reading.

4/ ROGER W. SPENCER AND WILLIAM P. YOHE

The "Crowding Out" of Private Expenditures by Fiscal Policy Actions

Fiscal policy provides additional spending in a world of sparse spending opportunities. But it does not provide a new source of finance in a world where spending is constrained by sources of finance. The government expenditures are financed in debt markets in competition with private expenditures. The case least favorable to fiscal policy is that in which the additional government borrowing simply CROWDS OUT of the market an equal (or conceivably even greater) volume of borrowing that would have financed private expenditures.[1] (Italics and capitalization added)

Changes in Government expenditures and taxes, the policy arm of Keynesian economics, have come under attack recently for their apparent failure to secure desired stabilization goals. Several studies, in this *Review* and elsewhere, have concluded that increases in Government expenditures, which are not accompanied by money creation, induce temporary increases in nominal GNP with no net effect over a longer period of time.[2] Monetary actions, in contrast, have been found to exert an important influence

Reprinted from the Federal Reserve Bank of St. Louis *Review*, Vol. 52, No. 10, October 1970, by permission of the authors and the publisher.

The authors wish to acknowledge the helpful comments on earlier drafts of: Leonall C. Andersen, Karl Brunner, Keith M. Carlson, E. G. Corrigan, John M. Culbertson, R. Alton Gilbert, Thomas M. Havrilesky, Jerry L. Jordan, Michael W. Keran, Laurence H. Meyer, and Clark A. Warburton. The authors are solely responsible for the analysis and conclusions presented in the article.

[1] John M. Culbertson, *Macroeconomic Theory and Stabilization Policy* (New York: McGraw-Hill Book Company, 1968), p. 463.

[2] Leonall C. Andersen and Jerry L. Jordan, "Monetary and Fiscal Actions: A

on economic activity quite apart from fiscal developments. Much of the rebuttal of these articles has been focused on debating the strengths of the monetary variables rather than the weaknesses of the fiscal variables.[3]

This article surveys a large body of economic literature, in search of some reasonable rationale which could explain the poor showing of the Government spending multipliers in the previously mentioned reduced-form statistical studies. Two possible reasons why these multipliers fail to achieve the high magnitudes promised by a mathematical derivation of the basic "Keynesian" multiplier are that many Keynesian models do not capture (1) the displacement of private spending by Government spending (the "crowding-out" effect), or (2) leakages associated with consumer or Governmental propensities to spend. The leakages are usually accounted for in the more sophisticated econometric models, resulting in lower multipliers than those derived from the elementary models, but failure to allow for the possibility of crowding out makes even these multipliers higher than warranted.

Worldwide acceptance of the Keynesian theory, and increasing Government intervention in economic affairs, represent the trend of post-depression thinking on stabilization policy.[4] There seems to be a growing

---

Test of Their Relative Importance in Economic Stabilization," this *Review* (November 1968); Leonall C. Andersen and Keith M. Carlson "A Monetarist Model for Economic Stabilization," this *Review* (April 1970); Michael W. Keran, "Monetary and Fiscal Influences on Economic Activity—The Historical Evidence," this *Review* (November 1969), and "Monetary and Fiscal Influences on Economic Activity—The Foreign Experience," this *Review* (February 1970); John Deaver, "Monetary Model Building," *Business Economics* (September 1969). Also, in this vein, *see* Milton Friedman and David Meiselman, "The Relative Stability of Monetary Velocity and the Investment Multiplier in the United States, 1897–1958," in *Stabilization Policies*, Commission on Money and Credit (Englewood Cliffs, N.J.: Prentice-Hall, Inc., 1963).

[3]The monetary variables most often employed in these articles are changes in money and the monetary base. The primary fiscal spending variable is changes in high-employment Government expenditures. For a defense of the fiscal position, *see* Murray Weidenbaum, "Is Fiscal Policy Dead?" *Financial Analysts Journal* (March-April, 1970) and E. G. Corrigan, "The Measurement and Importance of Fiscal Policy Changes," Federal Reserve Bank of New York *Monthly Review* (June 1970).

[4]See, for example, Robert Lekachman, *The Age of Keynes* (New York: Random House, 1966). The difficulty of generalizing "Keynes' view" or "the Keynesians' view" has been pointed out by Axel Leijonhufvud ("Keynes and the Keynesians: A Suggested Interpretation," *American Economic Review*, May 1967, Papers and Proceedings, p. 401).

> *One must be careful in applying the epithet 'Keynesian' nowadays. I propose to use it in the broadest possible sense and let 'Keynesian economics' be synonymous with the 'majority school' macroeconomics which has evolved out of the debates triggered by Keynes's* General Theory . . . .

belief, however, that fiscal policies developed and applied in a society operating at a low level of resource utilization are not necessarily applicable under high-employment, inflationary conditions. Further, the evidence presented by one analyst casts doubt on the efficacy of fiscal policies even during the deflationary 1930's.[5]

Pure fiscal actions, which entail changes only in Government expenditure and tax programs, are rare; most stabilization actions involve a mixture of (1) fiscal (tax-financed Government spending), (2) monetary (Federal Reserve actions) and (3) debt management (changes in the maturity or value of the debt) policies.   For example, the offering of Treasury bonds to finance a deficit constitutes debt management policy (or fiscal policy, by more conventional definitions) at first, but the subsequent purchase of such bonds (or perhaps the failure to purchase such bonds) by the Federal Reserve is generally construed to be monetary policy.   Thus the existence of Government bonds clouds the distinction between the two basic economic stabilization policies—monetary and fiscal.

The method of financing Government expenditures influences economic stabilization efforts.   There are two conflicting views regarding the extent of this influence.   Funds for Government spending are obtained by taxing the public, borrowing from the public, and/or money creation.   Monetarists (those who favor monetary over fiscal stabilization policies) generally assert that Government spending financed by either taxing or borrowing from the public is mainly a resource transfer from the private sector to the Government, with little net effect on total spending.   Monetary expansion, even if unaccompanied by an increase in Government spending, has a strong, stimulative influence on the economy.

Contemporary Keynesian theory holds that all of the three techniques of Government finance involve something more than a simple resource transfer from the private to the Government sector.   An expansionary effect on the economy may be achieved by a rise in Government spending matched by an increase in tax receipts, or by a rise in Government spend-

---

Within the majority school, at least two major factions live in recently peaceful but nonetheless uneasy coexistence. With more brevity than accuracy, they may be labeled the 'Revolutionary Orthodoxy' and the 'Neoclassical Resurgence'. . . . The orthodoxy tends to slight monetary in favor of fiscal stabilization policies. The neoclassical faction may be sufficiently characterized by negating these statements. As described, the orthodoxy is hardly a very reputable position at the present time. Its influence in the currently most fashionable fields has been steadily diminishing, but it seems to have found a refuge in business cycle theory—and, of course, in the teaching of undergraduate macroeconomics.

[5] Keran, "Monetary and Fiscal Influences on Economic Activity—The Historical Evidence," p. 23.

ing financed by bond issuance either to the public or the monetary authorities.

The monetarists' view that Government spending financed by taxes or borrowing from the public merely displaces, or "crowds out," private spending is not a new one. It was, in fact, the dominant view before the Keynesian revolution of the 1930's. Classical economists including Adam Smith and David Ricardo, and neo-classicists including F. A. Hayek and R. G. Hawtrey, found little use for fiscal stabilization efforts. Keynes, at first a fairly orthodox neo-classical economist, altered his views on many issues prior to the publication of *The General Theory of Employment, Interest and Money*, including a downgrading of the fiscal crowding-out concept.[6] Since it was Keynes' theory of the proper use of fiscal policy which eventually became the dominant view, we will develop at some length Keynes' thinking on the subject. Because Keynes was strongly aware of the traditional neo-classical views on fiscal theory, he hedged his arguments more carefully than many of his successors.

Keynes' *General Theory* analysis, in contrast to the focus of the classical school on long-run supply factors, was oriented toward short-run demand considerations. Both views were couched predominantly in real (rather than nominal) terms. Consequently, crowding-out analysis derived from either of these two approaches deals primarily with the displacement of real private spending by Government spending.[7]

A summary of classical, neo-classical and Keynes' early views on fiscal crowding out will be presented first. Next, we will trace Keynes' later fiscal views, underscoring the assumptions on which his final position was built. The subsequent section examines bond- and tax-financed crowding out, based principally on a Keynesian analytical framework outlined by

[6] John Maynard Keynes, *The General Theory of Employment, Interest and Money* (New York: Harcourt, Brace and Company, 1936). His book will be referred to as *The General Theory* throughout the remainder of this article.

[7] The crowding-out phenomenon may be described in conventional mathematical symbols in the following manner.

a) Real crowding out

$$\frac{dY^*}{dG^*}\bigg|_{dM^* = 0} \approx 0$$

b) Nominal crowding out

$$\frac{dY}{dG}\bigg|_{dM = 0} \approx 0$$

These relations imply that:

c) $\dfrac{d(Y^* - G^*)}{dG^*}\bigg|_{dM = 0} \approx -1$

Richard Musgrave. Finally, we discuss alternative frameworks and some empirical evidence bearing on the crowding-out issue.

SUMMARY OF CLASSICAL, NEO-CLASSICAL AND KEYNES' EARLY VIEWS ON FISCAL CROWDING OUT

The mainstream of economic thought prior to the publication of Keynes' *General Theory* in 1936 did not favor Government spending for stabilization purposes.[8]   There was some opposition to an enlarged role for Government spending purely from a philosophical view, but much of the criticism of increased Government intervention was based on crowding-out theory.

Adam Smith, for example, opposed extensive Government involvement for both philosophical and crowding-out reasons. For the most part, Smith (writing in 1776) considered Government labor "unproductive," and condemned the transfer of resources from the private sector, whether through taxation or borrowing. Borrowing funds from the public to finance Government spending was asserted to involve the "destruction of some capital which had before existed in the country; by the perversion of some portion of the annual produce which had before been destined for the maintenance of productive labour, towards that of unproductive labour."[9] Smith believed that "saving is spending," because one man's saving becomes another man's investment. Later classical economists, such as John Stuart Mill and J. B. Say, writing primarily in the first half of the nineteenth century, saw in Adam Smith's maxim a *guarantee* of full employment. That is, Government spending was considered unnecessary as a stabilization tool, because private investment was sufficient to utilize the funds provided by private saving.

The most elementary case for crowding out may be examined in a

---

or

d) $\dfrac{d(Y-G)}{dG}\bigg|_{dM=0} \approx -1$

Y = total spending, G = Government spending, and M = money supply.

Relation (*b*) most closely represents the empirical crowding-out results reported in studies cited in footnote 2.

[8] A more detailed discussion of classical, neo-classical and Keynes' early views on crowding out will be presented in a forthcoming Working Paper of the Federal Reserve Bank of St. Louis.

[9] Adam Smith, *The Wealth of Nations* (New York: Random House, Inc., 1937), p. 878.

"Say's Law" framework. Say's Law is widely known as "supply creates its own demand." More specifically, if output (supply of goods and services) is determined by the behavior of profit maximizing producers, competitive labor markets, the existing stock of capital goods, and the state of technology, then relative prices will tend automatically to adjust so as to eliminate a deficiency or excess of demand. In an economy in which Say's Law is operative, attempts by the Government to increase total spending, by raising Government expenditures and financing the increasing budget by either borrowing from the public or taxation, merely induce changes in relative prices so as to reallocate the same level of real output.

The two cases—bond- and tax-financed Government expenditures—involve changes in the structure of prices (principally interest rates) to restore equilibrium at full employment, so they represent the tendency of a market economy ultimately to neutralize disturbances (in this instance budgetary shocks). Without the Government's presence, private propensities to spend the full-employment level of real income for either consumption or investment sum to one as a consequence of automatic price adjustments; adding a Government propensity to spend correspondingly reduces private propensities, in order to maintain total propensities to spend equaling one.[10]

Neo-classical business cycle theories became an important part of economic stabilization literature in the early twentieth century. One of these theories, over-investment financed by "forced" saving, was equally applicable for any sector favored over others for loan extension by the banking system. If, for example, the Government were to borrow from banks to finance its investment spending, the increased purchasing power of the Government would allow it to bid resources away from other sectors and, under full-employment conditions, drive up the price level. The higher price level would serve as a deterrent to "real" consumer or private investment spending which would otherwise have taken place.

A good example of this view is found in the testimony of the English economist, R. G. Hawtrey, before the Macmillan Committee in 1930. Hawtrey denied the usefulness of Government spending, regardless of financing even under depression conditions:

> On the matter of government spending [to bring England out of her stagnation], Hawtrey stated that whether the spending came out of taxes or loans from savings, *the increased governmental expenditures would merely replace private expenditures.* He even considered the "radical" idea of government spending out of new bank credit, but predicted that the result of such a policy would be inflationary and a

[10] See, for example, Culbertson, p. 333.

threat to the gold standard, thus forcing up the bank rate of interest and causing credit contraction. Such a plan, for him, would only defeat itself, since government expenditures out of bank credit would mean the end of cheap money for free enterprise.[11] (Italics added)

Keynes advocated Government spending as a stimulative economic measure twelve years before the publication of *The General Theory*, but he attached the "rider" that such spending should be financed by monetary expansion.[12] He emphasized (in 1929) that the central bank had the power to defeat expansionary fiscal actions and thus ". . . ensure that the expenditure financed by the Treasury *was* at the expense of other business enterprise."[13] The British Treasury, however, like Hawtrey, took the position that Government spending, regardless of financing, simply displaced private spending.

Keynes continued to press his fiscal policy arguments in the years preceding *The General Theory*, but eventually downgraded the necessity of monetary expansion accompanying increased Government spending in order for such spending to have an expansionary effect. Development of the liquidity preference theory of interest and the fiscal multiplier theory, particularly the latter, were the keys to Keynes' ability to shift money into the background of his analysis. The liquidity preference concept led to the idea that more efficient utilization of the existing money stock (increased velocity) was encouraged by increased Government expenditures, while the mathematical formulation of the multiplier (by R. F. Kahn, a student of Keynes) indicated that the increased taxes and saving generated by the rise in Government-induced income would be *just enough* to cover the financing of the deficit.

[11] Lawrence R. Klein, *The Keynesian Revolution* (London: The Macmillan Company, 1968), pp. 45–46. Hawtrey's business cycle theory was based on easy money creating additional working capital and inducing inventory investment.

[12] Roy Forbes Harrod, *The Life of John Maynard Keynes* (New York: Harcourt, Brace and Company, 1951), p. 441. Keynes was only one of a number of economists of the Twenties and Thirties who advocated governmental deficit spending to spur economic activity. Twelve University of Chicago economists, for example, recommended deficit spending in a 1932 memorandum to a member of Congress: "Convinced that pump-priming deficits would induce at best only temporary revival, the Chicago economists recommended that deficits should continue until recovery was indisputably established. These would be financed by selling new issues of bonds to the reserve banks or by exchanging them for bank deposits and Federal Reserve notes," See J. Ronnie Davis, "Henry Simons, the Radical: Some Documentary Evidence," *History of Political Economy*, Fall, 1969, pp. 389-90.

[13] See John Maynard Keynes, *Essays in Persuasion* (New York: Harcourt, Brace and Company, 1932), p. 126.

KEYNES' *GENERAL THEORY* VIEW OF FISCAL CROWDING OUT

A detailed explanation of the workings of the multiplier was one of the chief contributions of *The General Theory*, as was the discussion of the qualifications of multiplier analysis. The investment multiplier (k), wrote Keynes, "tells us that, when there is an increment of aggregate investment, income will increase by an amount which is k times the increment . . ."[14] The principle of the multiplier provides "an explanation of how fluctuations in the amount of investment, which are a comparatively small proportion of the national income, are capable of generating fluctuations in aggregate employment and income so much greater in amplitude than themselves."[15]

The multiplier concept of an increment of new investment spending being transmitted from pocket to pocket and thereby increasing total spending by some multiple is easier to grasp intuitively than mathematically. Keynes, himself searching for the proper mathematical rationale for his deficit spending ideas, was quick to seize and popularize Kahn's version. He and Kahn realized some of the limitations of their formal multiplier theory, but the scores of articles published during the past three decades, which clarify or repudiate "the Keynesian multiplier," suggest the inadequacy of its treatment in *The General Theory*.

The significance of the multiplier may be examined from the crowding-out point of view, to the extent that the multiplier represents causal relations rather than the *ex post* tautology that the change in income must, by definition, equal some multiplier times the increment of investment.[16] Keynes, in *The General Theory*, provided one of the most cogent and clear crowding-out arguments to be found. Although he wished to move money to a supporting rather than leading role in his *General Theory* analysis, he recognized that monetary influences *could* overcome his newly developed multiplier and liquidity preference constructs.

Contrary to expressions found in the present "conventional wisdom," Keynes hedged his arguments considerably. He pointed out that,

---

[14]Keynes, *The General Theory*, p. 115. The multiplier concept may be formalized as $\Delta Y = k \Delta I$ where ΔY is the change in income, ΔI is the change in investment and k is the multiplier. Investment refers to outlays on newly created plant and equipment and housing, and additions to inventories. A similar multiplier is developed for changes in Government expenditures (ΔG).

[15]*Ibid.*, p. 122.

[16]R. F. Kahn (*Economic Journal*, 1931, p. 188) was quite aware of the causal vs. tautological nature of the equality between the increase in the rate of investment expenditure and the subsequent streams of generated saving. The equality, he wrote, "far from being the logical consequence of summing an infinite geometrical progression, is in reality self-evident in nature . . ."

If, for example, a Government employs 100,000 additional men on public works, and if the multiplier ... is 4, it is not safe to assume that aggregate employment will increase by 400,000. For the new policy may have *adverse reactions on investment* in other directions. . . . The method of financing the policy and the increased working cash, required by the increased employment and the associated rise of prices, may have the effect of increasing the rate of interest and so *retarding investment in other directions,* unless the monetary authority takes steps to the contrary; whilst, at the same time, the increased cost of capital goods will reduce their marginal efficiency to the private investor, and this will require an actual *fall* in the rate of interest to offset it.[17]

The multiplier limitation outlined above by Keynes can be summarized within the conventional *IS – LM* curve framework. In the *IS – LM* system, a set of equations is postulated regarding propensities to spend, to save, and to hold money balances.[18]   The system may be reduced to two equa-

Crowding Out in an IS-LM Framework

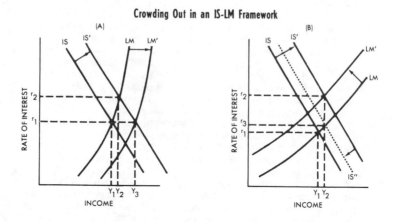

Figure 1.

tions.   One contains various combinations of income (Y) and interest rates (r) at which investment equals saving; this is referred to as the *IS* curve and represents the real sector of the economy.   The other equation contains various combinations of Y and r at which money demanded equals the money stock in existence; this is labeled the *LM* curve and represents the financial sector.   The two equations may then be solved simultaneously to determine equilibrium values of the interest rate and income.

[17]Keynes, *The General Theory*, pp. 119–20.   (Italics added except for "fall")

[18]See, for example, Gardner Ackley, *Macroeconomic Theory* (New York: The Macmillan Company, 1961), pp. 359–98.

If the *LM* curve is steeply sloped as shown in part (*A*) of the accompanying figure, the increase in Government spending reflected in the rightward shift of the *IS* curve affects a sharp rise in interest rates (from r_1 to r_2) and iittle or no change in income (Y_1 to Y_2). A sharply rising *LM* curve implies that the retarding effects of such actions on private investment are substantial. Only by shifting the *LM* curve to the right, through monetary expansion for example, will a significant rise in income occur (from Y_1 to Y_3). Keynes, by mentioning this multiplier limitation, supplied a strong theoretical basis for the crowding-out thesis, and thereby shifted the discussion to a quantitative plane involving determination of the slopes of the *IS-LM* curves and the substitutability of Government and private spending.

Keynes recognized a second way, based on business psychology, in which Government spending could crowd out private spending. "With the confused psychology which often prevails, the Government programme may, through its effect on 'confidence', increase liquidity-preference or diminish the marginal efficiency of capital, which, again, may retard other investment unless measures are taken to offset it."[19]

[19]Keynes, *The General Theory*, p. 120. Daniel Throop Smith, "Is Deficit Spending Practical?", *Harvard Business Review* (Vol. 18, 1939), pp. 38–9, was particularly concerned about the business confidence aspect of the crowding-out thesis.

> A continued experience with deficits which do not produce sustained recovery, as in this country, or a recent inflation and collapse, as in continental European countries, is likely to make a deficit matter for concern and anxiety. And, if there is disbelief in the benefits of a deficit, then the *new money spent by the government may well be more than offset by additional withdrawals of private money which would otherwise be spent.* Likewise, if consumer incomes do increase immediately as a result of the deficit, business *may anticipate that the increase is temporary* and refrain from long-term commitments.
>
> . . . Consumer income arises primarily out of the processes of the production and distribution of goods and services. Therefore, if private spending decreases by as many dollars as government spending increases (and it takes *only a very small proportionate decrease* in private *spending to offset a large proportionate* increase in government spending), then on balance there is no net increase in consumer income. Furthermore, even if there is an immediate net increase in consumer income, there may be enough flexibility in our economic system in the form of idle capacity, especially during a depression, to obviate any necessity of spending on capital goods to provide consumer goods. Also, if there is an actual increase in consumer income and spending but it is believed that the demand is an artificial one dependent upon a continuation of government deficits which cannot last indefinitely, business will be loath to make long-term capital commitments. In such circumstances business at most will make up deferred maintenance and build up inventories creating an artificial "boomlet" which is not likely to develop into a sustained recovery. This seems to have been particularly true in 1936 and 1937. (emphasis added)

This analysis implies that, dependent upon the time period specified, Government spending may not only crowd out an equal magnitude of private spending but an even greater amount. The multiplier would then be negative rather than zero or positive.

If the increase in Government spending (shown by the shift of *IS* to *IS'* in part *B* of Figure 1) has an adverse effect on liquidity preference, the *LM* curve shifts to the left (*LM'*) and income increases only slightly from Y_1 to Y_2. If the marginal efficiency of capital is adversely influenced, this may be shown by a leftward shift of the *IS* curve from *IS'* to *IS"*, also resulting in a small increase in income from Y_1 to Y_2. The magnitude of these shifts of the curves depends, of course, on the assumed response of "business confidence" to increased Government spending.

Keynes also noted a potential multiplier leakage in the hypothesized tendency of the marginal propensity to consume to diminish as employment increases. This introduces the state of economic activity as an influence on the efficacy of the multiplier. Thus Keynes could, without reservation, recommend any sort of public works (pyramid building, wars) during periods of unemployment, "if only from the diminished cost of relief expenditure, provided that we can assume that a smaller proportion of income is saved when unemployment is greater; but they may become a more doubtful proposition as a state of full employment is approached. Furthermore, if our assumption is correct that the marginal propensity to consume falls off steadily as we approach full employment, it follows that it will become more and more troublesome to secure a further given increase of employment by further increasing investment."[20]

A related leakage was that of an increase in employment which tends, "owing to the effect of diminishing returns in the short period, to increase the proportion of aggregate income which accrues to the entrepreneurs, whose individual marginal propensity to consume is probably less than the average for the community as a whole."[21] Moreover, the impact of the multiplier might be reduced by those unemployed consumers formerly existing on negative savings, private or public, whose employment would diminish negative savings, and thereby, the marginal propensity to consume.

An additional *caveat* to those who would mechanistically apply the multiplier was that, "In any case, the multiplier is likely to be greater for a small net increment of investment than for a large increment; so that, where substantial changes are in view, we must be guided by the average value of the multiplier based on the average marginal propensity to consume over the range in question."[22]

These multiplier modifications and many more can be found in the

---

[20]Keynes, *The General Theory*, p. 127. One implication of this analysis is that increased Government spending, for the reasons given, may not only be less effective at stimulating the economy near full employment than at substantially less than full employment, but also relatively ineffective at slowing it.

[21]*Ibid.*, p. 121.

[22]*Ibid.*

post-*General Theory* literature,[23] but enough has been introduced here to indicate that the value of the Government spending multiplier may be positive, zero or negative. It should be pointed out that although Keynes was aware of some of the limitations of the multiplier (as demonstrated above), he did not emphasize them, partly because of his desire to put a simple rationale for Government spending during the depression in the hands of the policy-makers as expeditiously as possible.[24]

A BASIC KEYNESIAN FRAMEWORK FOR CROWDING-OUT ANALYSIS

A number of attempts were made after Keynes to spell out more formally the relationships governing the conditions under which Government spending would add to total spending or crowd out a significant volume of private spending. Richard Musgrave developed one of the most efficient frameworks for analyzing the crowding-out phenomenon of those constructed in the approximately three decades following *The General Theory*.[25]

[23] See Hugo Hegeland, *The Multiplier Theory* (New York: Augustus M. Kelley Publishers, 1966) p. 73: "The basic weakness of the multiplier theory lies in its assumptions, which in fact eliminate the real problems involved and make the theory almost a truism."

One example of post-Keynesian criticism of the mechanical application of the multiplier can be found in Gardner Ackley, "The Multiplier Time Period: Money, Inventories, and Flexibility," *American Economic Review* (June 1951) pp. 350–368. Ackley notes that the existence of inventories serves as a buffer providing a potentially long and variable lag between a change in consumer expenditures and a change in production rates. An argument made by Milton Friedman is that Government expenditure increases may be viewed by consumers as adding only to transitory income (i.e., temporary income.) He argues that the marginal propensity to consume out of transitory income is zero. See Milton Friedman, *A Theory of the Consumption Function* (Princeton: Princeton University Press, 1957), p. 26.

[24] The crowding-out issue emerged in a different context in at least one of Keynes' post-*General Theory* essays. In Paul Davidson, "Keynes's Finance Motive," *Oxford Economic Papers* (March 1965), pp. 48–49, Keynes is quoted from an April 18, 1939, letter to the London *Times*, in which he explains his approach to financing Government expenditures for rearmament: "If an attempt is made to borrow them [the savings which will result from the increased production of non-consumption (war) goods] before they exist, as the Treasury have done once or twice lately, a stringency in the money market must result, since, pending the expenditure, the liquid resources acquired by the Treasury must be at the expense of the normal liquid resources of the banks and of the public."

[25] See Richard A. Musgrave, *The Theory of Public Finance* (New York: McGraw-Hill, Inc., 1959), pp. 526–55.

Others outlining frameworks under which crowding out might be analyzed include

There are three basic sectors of the economy and three basic "effects" in the Musgrave framework.[26] Government, consumer, and investment spending comprise the three sectors, and income, wealth, and substitution are the three effects. Income effects are those related to changes in disposable income. Wealth effects occur with changes in the level of wealth, the ratio of wealth to income or changes in the level or structure of debt claims (money and/or Government bonds). Substitution effects result from saving or spending incentives provided by a particular Governmental tax or expenditure policy. Income and wealth effects are interdependent; the initial effect may be one or the other, but both effects become operative as the adjustment proceeds. For example, an increase in investment may occur as a result of a change in income because of a change in the propensity to invest. The income effect would be followed by a wealth effect as changes in the interest rate and the ratio of wealth to income occur over the period of adjustment.

Musgrave assumes that consumption is altered through income effects and/or wealth effects. Investment is influenced by changes in income and/or (via interest rates) changes in the level or structure of claims, while the substitution effect, which does not appear explicitly in the model, may be operative through changes in profitability due to taxation.

Alvin H. Hansen, *Monetary Theory and Fiscal Policy* (New York: McGraw-Hill Inc., 1949), pp. 167–73, and Abba P. Lerner, "The Burden of the National Debt," in *Income, Employment and Public Policy, Essays in Honor of Alvin H. Hansen* (New York: W. W. Norton and Company, Inc., 1948), pp. 255–75. Lerner, for example (p. 269), states that "The sale of government bonds diminishes liquidity, tends to raise interest rates, and discourages investment. The government should therefore not borrow unless it wishes to bring about these deflationary effects."

[26]The following is the linear form of Musgrave's basic equations:

$$(1) \quad Y = C + I + G$$
$$(2) \quad C = a + c(Y - T) + wM$$
$$(3) \quad I = d - ei$$
$$(4) \quad i = U/M_a \cdot (1 - \beta)/\beta$$
$$(5) \quad M_a = M - M_t$$
$$(6) \quad M_t = 1/V \cdot Y$$
$$(7) \quad G = T$$

Y = income, C = consumption, I = investment, G = Government spending, T = tax yield, M = total money supply, M_a = asset money, M_t = transactions money, V = income velocity, i = "the" market interest rate, c = marginal propensity to consume, w = a wealth parameter, e = an investment parameter, U = bond coupon bill, β = fraction of claims (asset money and Government debt) people wish to hold in form of Government debt, a = intercept term, d = intercept term.

The Government budget constraint, $G = T$, could be modified to permit deficit finance through changes in money or Government bonds. A rough approximation of the Government budget constraint for the above system of equations might take the form $G = T + \Delta M + \Delta U$.

Wealth and income effects are seen most clearly by comparing the private sector's response to a variety of policy actions. The accompanying table illustrates a basic cataloguing of budget policies within the Musgrave framework. It gives various combinations of stabilization actions by arraying changes in the supply of Government debt against changes in the supply of money.

TABLE 1

Cataloguing Fiscal Finance

Change in* Supply of Debt	Change in Supply of Money		
	+	**0**	**−**
+	4 Deficit financed by mix of debt and money	2 Deficit financed by debt	9 Money retirement financed by borrowing
0	3 Deficit financed by new money	1 Equal change in tax yield and expenditures	6 Money retirement financed by current surplus
−	8 Debt retirement financed by new money	5 Debt retirement financed by current surplus	7 Current surplus used to retire mix of money and debt

*Changes in the supply of debt refer to changes in coupon bill or maturity value rather than to changes in the market value of the total debt outstanding.

We assume that the ratio of consumption to income will increase (that is, the ratio of saving to income will fall) with increases in the supply of money, or (with some qualification) the supply of public debt and the level of investment will rise with an increase in the supply of money and *will fall with an increase in the supply of debt.* It is then possible to determine whether each policy mix is expansive or restrictive. Policies 3, 4, and 8 are expansionary, policies 6, 7, and 9 are restrictive, and policies 1, 2, and 5 contain ambiguous effects. Policy 2, a deficit financed by debt issue, most closely approximates the bond-financed crowding-out case. Policy 1 approximates the tax-financed crowding-out case. Note that neither policy 1 or 2 involves changes in the supply of money. These two cases will be examined separately, to ascertain which factors are involved in determining whether purely budgetary actions result in an expansionary effect on the economy, or simply crowd out private spending.

BOND-FINANCED CHANGES IN GOVERNMENT EXPENDITURES

What actually happens in the case of bond-financed Government expenditures depends to a large extent on the movement of the interest rate. There will be an expansionary income effect (Government spending adds directly to income) which may be augmented by a stimulative wealth effect on consumption (more bonds held by the public), if the interest rate remains relatively unresponsive.[27] If the increase in the supply of Government bonds is accompanied by a sharp rise in the interest rate, the expansionary income effect could be countered by: (1) a smaller net wealth effect (since the market value of the Government debt varies inversely with the interest rate); (2) displacement of private investment, which responds negatively to a rise in the bond interest rate; and (3) a diversion of funds from consumption into Government bond purchase (voluntary saving), having an initially restrictive effect.

The response of total spending to bond-financed Government expenditures is ambiguous. If savers are indifferent between the holding of bonds and money, the interest rate does not rise, the net market value of the debt increases by this means of financing, and a strong wealth effect may be realized. At the other extreme, savers insisting on holding a fixed ratio of money and debt would result in a rise in the interest rate, no change in the value of the debt (gains from the acquisition of new bonds being offset by capital losses suffered from the holding of old bonds), and no wealth effect.

Actual conditions, according to Musgrave, fall somewhere in the middle. During a depression, the interest rate is likely to be relatively unresponsive. The implication is that the interest rate is likely to be most responsive during periods of rapid expansion. A more detailed model might consider the effects of price expectations and varying default risks on interest rates (and, consequently, private spending), and present a wider spectrum of private and public assets.

---

[27]The wealth effect, as described by Musgrave, does not consider the issue of future tax liabilities associated with Government debt. Even if the interest rate responds negligibly to an increase in Government bonds, the rise in the value of the debt (positive wealth effect) may be partially offset by the discounted future tax liability required to pay the interest on the debt. The impact of the future tax liability on aggregate demand in the current period depends upon (a) the degree to which the bond-holding public considers future tax liabilities, (b) the maturity of the debt, and (c) the anticipations of the public as to the nature of the future taxes to be levied (on the income from labor or capital) to pay the interest on the debt. See Boris P. Pesek and Thomas R. Saving, *Money, Wealth and Economic Theory* (New York: The Macmillan Company, 1967), chapter 10, who argue that the tax liability offset to the wealth effect is only partial and not total as some analysts have suggested.

The introduction of fractional reserve banking (which is excluded from the above discussion) into the system complicates the argument somewhat, but the essential principles remain unchanged. In practice, as Buchanan points out, commercial bank purchases of Government bonds out of excess reserves permit the full expansionary effect to take place (money creation), but bonds purchased when reserves are not in excess have the same effect as borrowing from the public. In the latter case, "The expansionary effects of the public spending side of the deficit are, to a considerable extent, offset by the reduction in private investment caused by the tightening up of funds available for private securities."[28]

TAX-FINANCED CHANGES IN GOVERNMENT EXPENDITURES

The most obvious crowding out of private expenditures by Government spending, involving the involuntary transfer of funds from the private to the Government sector, is the case in which expenditures are financed by taxation. A balanced-budget multiplier equal to one (total spending increases by an amount equal to an increase in Government spending financed by taxes) is the usual upper limit assigned to tax-financed Government expenditures. This result is generally deduced from the assumption that the Government's propensity to spend for goods and services out of tax revenue is 100 per cent, while private propensities to spend after-tax income are less than 100 per cent.[29]

[28]James M. Buchanan, *The Public Finances* (Homewood, Ill.: Richard D. Irwin, 1965), p. 99.

[29]One observer has relied strongly on a positive balanced-budget multiplier to support his argument for the expansiveness of bond-financed Government expenditures. *See* Robert Eisner, "Fiscal and Monetary Policy Reconsidered," *American Economic Review* (December 1969), pp. 897–905. Eisner finds Government expenditures, regardless of the financing, to be the controlling exogenous variable in slowing or stimulating the economy ("monetary measures are likely ultimately to be as limited in their impact in combating inflation as they have long been recognized to be limited in combating a deep depression . . . . "Public works or, more generally, government investment and consumption, reemerge in their early role as prime weapons in the arsenal against depression and take on analogous importance in any struggle against inflation," p. 904). His model shows that whether Government spending financed by bond issue is expansionary (increase in prices) or offset depends on the interest and wealth elasticities of real money and commodity demand. He presents no empirical justification for his conclusion that bond-financed Government expenditures are expansionary, but concludes that to argue against an expansion "would be to argue that a deficit-financed increase in Government expenditures can be deflationary while the same increase in Government expenditures would be inflationary if fully supported by taxes." (p. 903) His balanced-budget multiplier analysis ignores its numerous limitations as discussed above.

Most simple models, including Musgrave's, do not allow adequately for potential leakages from the Government balanced-budget multiplier, but by injecting debt considerations into the discussion of an increase in Government expenditures met by a rise in taxes, Musgrave uncovers potentially adverse influences on private spending. If an initial rise in income is generated by a balanced-budget change, a drain on asset money would develop (because of the increased transactions demand for money) which tends to have a detrimental effect on investment. The rise in income relative to a constant money supply may have a depressing effect on consumption, especially so the more the drop in net wealth (that is, a fall in the value of the debt) produced by a rising interest rate.

Most observers, however, ignore debt considerations in their analysis of the limitations of the unitary balanced-budget multiplier. The large number of assumptions necessary to the determination of a unitary balanced-budget multiplier, disregarding debt problems, reflects to some extent its implausibility.[30] Baumol and Peston discuss the issue in terms of leakages from the multiplier, and conclude that, in essence, a rise in Government spending financed by taxation may crowd out an equivalent or greater magnitude of private spending.[31] The basis for their reasoning is that, although the Government's marginal propensity to spend exceeds that of the private sector, Government spending is subject to significant leakages before its influence on private spending is realized.

> The existence of these "leakages" in a governmental tax-expenditure program—the nonredistributional effects on private consumption, the purchase of items on capital account and of goods from abroad—is, of course, well known, though no attempt seems to have been made to take account of them in the literature. Possibly some of the writers had them in mind but considered them unimportant, since presumably none of them considered the unit multiplier figure as more than an approximation to the empirical magnitude in view of the recognized qualifications. The magnitude of the leakages may indeed be rather small, and it is very tempting to conclude that if 10 per

[30] James Buchanan provides a list of seven assumptions underlying the unitary balanced-budget multiplier in *The Public Finances*, pp. 78–80. These are: 1) The entire amount of the Government spending change must take the form of purchases of real goods and services currently produced; 2) the balanced-budget change must be financed through taxes having about the same effects as the personal income tax; 3) the public spending must not exert substitution effects on the pattern of private spending; 4) the marginal propensity to save for taxpayers must be equal to the marginal propensity to save for the suppliers of Government goods and services; 5) investment spending must not be altered significantly by the budgetary change; 6) the monetary-banking framework must permit attempted changes in spending to be carried out; 7) individual behavior in earning income must not be directly affected by the budgetary change.

[31] W. J. Baumol and Maurice H. Peston, "More on the Multiplier Effects of a Balanced Budget," *American Economic Review* (March 1955).

cent of the government's balanced budget expenditure is "leaked," the multiplier will be reduced from unity to say about 0.9. However, we argue now that fairly small leakages can even produce a negative balanced budget multiplier.

... Thus the multiplier will be positive, zero, or negative as the marginal propensity to save and import of the private sector is greater than, equal to, or less than k, the government's 'marginal propensity to leak.'[32]

ALTERNATIVE FRAMEWORKS FOR ANALYSIS OF THE CROWDING-OUT EFFECT

If, as has been maintained, the method by which Government spending is financed matters to both private and overall spending, it would seem that current analysis should explicitly account for it in discussions of the Government expenditure multiplier. Quite often, however, current analysis ignores the potential crowding out of private spending when Government expenditures are financed by bond sales or taxation.

One possible reason for this oversight is that the numerous attempts to clarify the principles enunciated in Keynes' *General Theory* have resulted in serious oversimplification of the complete Keynesian doctrine. This oversimplification has taken place at both basic and advanced levels of economic analysis. At the basic level, the "45-degree diagrams" popularized in principles text books leave no room for budget financing considerations.[33] Similarly, the fundamental two-equation Keynesian model popularized in elementary text books, and its usual extensions, encourage the mechanical "cranking out" of fiscal multipliers which omit adequate treatment of the financing issue.[34]

The Hicksian *IS - LM* analysis, formulated to summarize Keynesian macroeconomic theory, represents oversimplification at a fairly advanced level (*see* Figure 1). An increase in Government spending is demonstrated by a rightward shift of the *IS* curve, which, as explained above, may result in a rise in both the interest rate and income. If the analysis stops here (as it frequently does), it is difficult to discern how the increased expenditure

---

[32]*Ibid.*, pp. 144 and 145.

[33]See, for example, Paul Samuelson, *Economics*, 8th edition (New York: McGraw-Hill Book Company, Inc., 1970), p. 317.

[34](1) $C = a + bY$
    (2) $Y = C + I + G$
Substituting (1) into (2) and solving for Y gives:
      $Y = a/1 - b + I/1 - b + G/1 - b$ where
      $\delta Y/\delta G = 1/1 - b$ = Government spending multiplier

is financed. In reality, the shift from an equilibrium to a disequilibrium position may bring about simultaneous changes in income, wealth, interest rate, money demand and money supply variables, and tax functions, depending on the source of finance. An approximation of the effects of movements in the key variables, as a new equilibrium position is established, may be achieved by altering the slopes and positions of the *IS* and *LM* curves, but the framework of analysis, without an explicit Government budget constraint, is not conducive to such shifts.[35]

William L. Silber sets forth conditions under which Government spending can be contractionary in a properly specified *IS-LM* framework.[36] Utilizing a framework of analysis similar to that of Musgrave, he finds that a rise in the supply of Government bonds which increases wealth also increases the demand for money (represented in the *IS-LM* framework by a leftward shift of the *LM* curve). Silber concludes:

> It has been demonstrated that traditional *IS-LM* analysis has not treated the bond-finance and new money-finance cases of government deficits symmetrically. When proper treatment is given to the former case, we found that in the simple world of *IS-LM* analysis government expenditures financed by selling bonds to the public can be contractionary. Even when GNP does go up due to ΔG, the increase that occurs is overstated in the traditional (but incomplete) *IS-LM* model of income determination. The failure to incorporate the monetary effects of *debt* finance into the *LM* function is the major source of confusion. While other studies have treated this question, it has never been formally incorporated into *IS-LM* models. This had led to incorrect conclusions regarding the multiplier affects of government spending.

The many income-expenditure econometric models which have emerged in the 1960's appear to be well-suited to handle the problems of simultaneity and the Government budget constraint. Unfortunately, some explicit provision for the fact that Government expenditures must be financed by taxing, borrowing from the public, or money creation has often been omitted from monetary and fiscal policy simulations of these large models. A model which includes, for example, Government purchases of goods and services, transfer payments, taxation, the change in the sales of Government bonds to the public, and the change in the stock

[35] "The Hicks-Hansen diagram has elegant simplicity which appeals to many. It has the disadvantage, however, that most of the 'works' are out of sight. This means that we need to use another diagram (or an extra mental calculation) to determine the effect of a displacement of the equilibrium on the other variables of our system." See Ackley, p. 372.

[36] William L. Silber, "Fiscal Policy in *IS-LM* Analysis: A Correction," *The Journal of Money, Credit and Banking*, Vol. 2 (November 1970), pp. 461–472.

of high-powered money, should be closed by the specification of the relationship between the items representing Government expenditures and the items representing Government "income."

Closure of the above system implies that in simulating the economy's response to alternative monetary and fiscal actions, it is not possible to change only one of the five variables at a time when evaluating multipliers. Carl Christ provides the following example relating Government expenditures to Government receipts:

> . . . if government purchases are increased, then either transfers must be cut, or tax payments must rise, or government debt must be issued to the private sector, or high powered money must be issued, or some combination of these. The effect of the increase in government purchases will depend upon what combination of them is chosen.[37]

Thus, those models which purport to be able to say something like "A $1 billion increase of Government purchase of goods and services results in a one-quarter increase in income of $2.5 billion" should also make statements regarding another fiscal/monetary variable which changes in order for the statement to have meaning. With no way to determine how the $2.5 billion increase in income is generated, it may be falsely attributed to a fiscal action when, in reality, a monetary action is responsible. That is, if changes in money are not held constant in the analysis, the estimated increase in income arising from a change in the independent fiscal policy variable may not be accurately captured. Consequently, the model would not measure accurately fiscal crowding out.

One analyst gives several examples of how, by failure to incorporate correctly the Government budget constraint, a number of income-expenditure models overestimate the impact of Government actions on income. His own reduced form empirical evidence leads him to conclude that "These results are consistent with a simple Keynesian multiplier from a deficit financed by bond purchases, with respect to the income of the private sector equal to zero."[38]

Neglect of the Government budget constraint is not the only reason why fiscal crowding out has not appeared in some structural econometric models. If such monetary variables as money demand and supply are omitted completely from the model, the "real" sector of the economy—which normally includes Government spending actions—will, by default,

---

[37]Carl Christ, "Monetary and Fiscal Policy in Macroeconomic Models" (Paper presented at the Sixteenth Annual Conference on the Economic Outlook, Ann Arbor, Michigan, November 14–15, 1968), p. 102.

[38]Robert Auerbach, *The Income Effects of the Government Deficit* (Ph.D. Dissertation, University of Chicago, 1969), Appendix A and p. 49.

dominate income changes. In terms of *IS – LM* analysis, omission of the *LM* curve (which reflects money demand and supply functions) would severely restrict the possible emergence of the crowding-out effect.

Evidence presented in this *Review* is consistent with the thesis that failure to identify monetary variables adequately leads to suppression of the crowding-out effect. Michael Keran found that the use of interest rates rather than monetary aggregates as monetary variables in his reduced-form equations resulted in the elimination of the fiscal crowding-out phenomenon.[39] His study suggests that proper specification of monetary actions, in terms of monetary aggregates rather than interest rates, assists empirical estimators in uncovering fiscal crowding-out influences.

Karl Brunner and Allan Meltzer have developed (in a preliminary paper) a framework of equations couched in terms of elasticities of interest rates, prices, wealth, and anticipations. Their approach to macroeconomic analysis, in contrast to the standard Keynesian framework, emphasizes the whole spectrum of relative price adjustments (which includes changes in the prices of goods and services as well as interest rate responses) to monetary and fiscal actions.[40] "The role of the relative price process is particularly examined together with the responses resulting from the interaction of the asset markets. The orthodox Keynesian view of a 'reliable and direct' effect of fiscal policy on income disolves rather thoroughly. The analysis establishes that monetary and fiscal policy are equally 'indirect' and dependent on stimuli conveyed by relative price changes and adjustments in wealth positions."[41]

Brunner and Meltzer believe their analysis "provides a foundation for the proposition that changes in budgetary variables (Government expenditures or taxes) exert by themselves relatively little effect on economic activity or price levels. The crucial effect depends on the financing." They find that the Government expenditures elasticity of aggregate de-

[39] Michael W. Keran, "Selecting a Monetary Indicator—Evidence from the United States and Other Developed Countries" (Federal Reserve Bank of St. Louis *Review*), September 1970.

[40] Crowding out in a relative price context may be illustrated by the following simple example: If a newly issued Government construction contract enables a Government enterprise to bid against private firms for construction and other workers in a near-fully employed community, the private firms must raise wages to retain their workers. Those private firms losing workers will probably have to curtail output, while those retaining workers with higher wages may attempt to pass along the higher costs in the form of price increases. The higher prices would be most noticeable in the construction sector, but, with the general rise in purchasing power, could be transmitted throughout the community. Also, the higher prices of residential construction could cause households to shift expenditures away from housing into less expensive alternatives.

[41] Karl Brunner and Allan Meltzer, "Fiscal and Monetary Policy in a Non-Keynesian World" (paper prepared for private circulation), p. 6.

mand "varies between less than 1/5 up to unity . . ." with the higher values achieved through the injection of base money. "The pure fiscal effect of Government expenditures thus amounts to at most 1/5 measured in terms of elasticities."[42]

Even the more conventional econometric models may uncover crowding-out influences, if interest rate effects are permitted to develop over a substantial period. Private spending is curtailed over time by a rise in interest rates generated by expanded Government spending, but the result is not immediate. This is particularly true of corporations whose decisions to invest are based on the economic climate which exists well before actual outlays are made. The specification of the lags involving interest-sensitive private spending plans may play a strong role in determining the time lag necessary for crowding out to occur.

The FRB-MIT model, which is characterized by rather long lag structures, demonstrated complete crowding out of private spending by Government actions, when model simulations were tracked over a long period. "In the long run, and by this we mean a long run of ten or fifteen years, the [FRB-MIT] model is classical in that the only permanent effect of fiscal policy is to raise prices and the transactions demand for money and, in the presence of a fixed supply of money, interest rates sufficiently to crowd out enough real private expenditures that the ultimate real income effect of Government spending is zero."[43]

Fiscal crowding out emerges in the reduced form equations published in this *Review* only after a period of time, even though it is a much shorter period of time than that of the FRB-MIT model. Government spending, as measured by high-employment expenditures, exercises a strong influence on GNP (assuming a constant money supply) in the current quarter and the next quarter, but the Government-spending effects wash out over approximately a one-year period. These results should not be interpreted to suggest that "Government spending doesn't matter." It matters very much over a certain period. Moreover, if Government spending were to accelerate rapidly rather than be held to a once-and-for-all increase, the impact on GNP would be considerable over the period of acceleration and somewhat beyond.

CONCLUSION

A number of plausible theories have been developed over the years which substantiate the view that Government expenditures, depending on the

[42]*Ibid.*, pp. 57 and 57a.

[43]Edward M. Gramlich, "Recent Experience with the FRB-MIT Model," (paper presented to the Committee on Banking and Credit Policy, New York, November 6, 1969), p. 6.

source of finance, may crowd out a roughly equivalent magnitude of private expenditures. This view, in fact, was the dominant classical and neo-classical view, persisting at least until the publication of Keynes' *General Theory*.

Keynes himself discussed crowding out in detail in *The General Theory*. He indicated that the fiscal multiplier might not generate the increases in employment given by a mechanical manipulation of the equations centering on his consumption function, because of the restrictive assumptions upon which his equations were based. Keynes noted several factors tending to offset the influence of increased Government expenditures: possible adverse reactions on private investment, "confused" business psychology, and a tendency of the marginal propensity to consume to decline with rises in employment.

A significant number of additional limitations to the Keynesian multiplier have been pointed out in the post-*General Theory* literature. One of the most serious deficiencies of the fiscal multiplier appears to be its asymmetry; that is, the crowding out of private spending is theoretically more likely at full-employment than at considerably less than full-employment conditions. Since the unemployment rate has rarely exceeded seven per cent in the past three decades, compared with an average unemployment rate of 18 per cent in the 1930's, the crowding-out effect has probably been much stronger in recent years than during the period in which Keynesian multiplier theory was developed.

Wealth, income, and substitution effects, important factors in the determination of the degree of crowding out, are often incorporated in econometric models, but failure to impose the Government budget constraint or treat adequately the monetary variables in the system of equations probably has led to understatement of the crowding-out effect.

More research on the time interval of crowding-out influences should be conducted to improve stabilization policy recommendations. Articles published in this *Review* suggest that Government expenditures financed by taxes or borrowing from the public are important over a very short period, but their tendency to crowd out private expenditures obviates any significant, lasting influence. This conclusion is supported by other research, which indicates that crowding out does indeed occur, but over a much longer time period.[44] These results suggest that the main dispute regarding the crowding out effect centers on the length of time involved. The rationale and some empirical verification of the existence of crowding out have been established—precise relationships and time periods remain a subject of further research.

[44]*Ibid.*

5/ WARREN L. SMITH

A Neo-Keynesian View of Monetary Policy

Those of us who take an essentially Keynesian view in macroeconomics are often accused, somewhat unjustly, I believe, of minimizing the importance of monetary forces. That contention was probably true 20 years ago for a variety of historical and institutional reasons. But much water has passed over the dam since that time, and I believe it would now be difficult to find an example of the popular stereotype of the Keynesian economist who thinks fiscal policy is all-important and monetary policy is of no consequence. After all, in Keynesian analysis the power of monetary policy depends on the values of certain parameters, and if one is open-minded, he must be prepared to alter his views as empirical evidence accumulates. In some respects, this process has already proceeded quite far—some of the simulations performed with the FRB-MIT model, which is decidedly Keynesian in spirit, show monetary policy having very powerful effects indeed, albeit operating with somewhat disconcerting lags.

Thus, there is nothing inherent in the Keynesian view of the world that commits its adherents to the belief that monetary policy is weak. What is, it seems to me, distinctive about Keynesianism is the view that fiscal policy is capable of exerting very significant independent effects—that there are, broadly speaking, two instruments of stabilization policy, fiscal policy and monetary policy, and that the mix of the two is important. Indeed, I suppose most Keynesians would assign primacy to fiscal policy, although even this need not inevitably be the case. But in a certain fundamental sense, I believe the issue separating the Keynesians and the so-called Monetarist School relates more to fiscal than to monetary policy, since

Reprinted from *Controlling Monetary Aggregates*: Proceedings of a Monetary Conference of the Federal Reserve Bank of Boston, June 1969, pp. 105–126, by permission of the author. Warren L. Smith is Professor of Economics at the University of Michigan.

some Monetarists seem to deny that fiscal policy is capable of exerting any significant independent effects. In addition, the neo-Keynesian view seems to differ significantly from that of the Monetarists with respect to the role played by the stock of money in the process by which monetary policy affects the economy.

In this paper, I shall attempt to sketch what I would describe as a neo-Keynesian view of the process by which monetary and fiscal policy produce their effects on the economy and to evaluate some aspects of the recent controversy regarding stabilization policy in the context of this view. I shall then advance some suggestions concerning the conduct of monetary policy.

THE TRANSMISSION MECHANISM OF MONETARY POLICY

There appear to be several elements involved in the mechanism by which the effects of changes in monetary policy are transmitted to income, employment, and prices.

PORTFOLIO ADJUSTMENTS

The major advance in monetary theory in recent years has been the development of a systematic theory of portfolio adjustments involving financial and physical assets. This theory of portfolio adjustments fits very comfortably within a Keynesian framework and indeed greatly enriches Keynesian analysis and increases its explanatory power. The *General Theory*, itself, embodied a rudimentary theory of portfolio adjustments: the way in which the public divided its financial wealth between bonds and speculative cash balances depended on "the" rate of interest. The interest rate then affected investment expenditure, but Keynes failed to incorporate the stock of real capital into his analysis and relate it to the flow of investment spending. Indeed, many of the undoubted shortcomings of the *General Theory* stem from the failure to take account of capital accumulation.

The way in which monetary policy induces portfolio adjustments which will, in due course, affect income and employment may be described briefly as follows: A purchase of, say, Treasury bills by the Federal Reserve will directly lower the yield on bills and, by a process of arbitrage involving a chain of portfolio substitutions, will exert downward pressure on interest rates on financial assets generally. Moreover—and more important—the expansion of bank reserves will enable the banking system to expand its assets. If the discount rate is unchanged, the banks can be expected to use some portion of the addition to their reserves to strengthen their free reserve position by repaying borrowings at the Federal Reserve and perhaps by adding to their excess reserves. But the bulk of the addition to reserves will ordinarily be used to make loan accommodation available on more favorable terms, and to buy securities, thereby exerting a further downward effect on security yields.

With the expected yield on a unit of real capital initially unchanged, the decline in the yields on financial assets, and the more favorable terms on which new debt can be issued, the balance sheets of households and businesses will be thrown out of equilibrium. The adjustment toward a new equilibrium will take the form of a sale of existing financial assets and the issuance of new debt to acquire real capital and claims thereto. This will raise the price of existing units of real capital—or equity claims against these units—relative to the (initially unchanged) cost of producing new units, thereby opening up a gap between desired and actual stocks of capital, a gap that will gradually be closed by the production of new capital goods. This stock adjustment approach is readily applicable, with some variations to suit the circumstances, to the demands for a wide variety of both business and consumer capital—including plant and equipment, inventories, residential construction, and consumer durable goods.

WEALTH EFFECTS

Since monetary policy operates entirely through voluntary transactions involving swaps of one financial asset for another, it does not add to wealth by creating assets to which there are no corresponding liabilities. Nevertheless, monetary policy does have wealth effects, which may be of considerable importance. An expansionary monetary policy lowers the capitalization rates employed in valuing expected income streams, thereby raising the market value of outstanding bonds as well as real wealth and equity claims thereto. In part, this strengthens the impact on economic activity of the portfolio adjustments, already referred to, by increasing the size of the net portfolios available for allocation. In addition, the increase in household wealth may significantly stimulate consumption. Indeed, in a recent version of the FRB-MIT model, the effect on consumption resulting from the induced change in the value of common stock equities held by households accounts for 35 to 45 percent of the initial impact of monetary policy in some simulations.

CREDIT AVAILABILITY EFFECTS

The portfolio and wealth effects appear to constitute the basic channels through which monetary policy has its initial impact on economic activity.

In addition, however, the institutional arrangements for providing financing to certain sectors of the economy may be such as to give monetary policy a special leverage over the availability of credit to these sectors, thereby affecting their ability to spend. It is perhaps most illuminating to discuss changes in credit availability in the context of a restrictive monetary policy.

No doubt changes in credit availability affect many categories of expenditures to some degree. But the sector in which they are most clearly of major importance is homebuilding. Even in the absence of the rather unique institutional arrangements for its financing, housing demand might be significantly affected by monetary policy as changes in mortgage interest rates altered the desired housing stock. But as postwar experience has repeatedly shown, most dramatically in the "credit crunch" of 1966, changes in mortgage credit availability may greatly strengthen the impact of restrictive monetary policy on homebuilding and cause the effects to occur much more rapidly than the stock-adjustment mechanism would imply. There are three different ways in which mortgage credit availability may be affected by a restrictive monetary policy.

First, commercial banks may raise interest rates on consumer-type time deposits to attract funds to meet the demands of their customers. If savings and loan associations do not raise the rates paid to their depositors or raise them less than the banks raise their rates, households may rechannel their saving flows away from the savings and loan associations and toward the banks—or may even withdraw existing savings from savings and loan associations and shift them to banks. Even if, as has recently been the case, the Regulation Q ceilings are used to prevent the banks from attracting household saving away from savings and loan associations, a rise in short- and intermediate-term open-market interest rates may set in motion a process of "disintermediation," with savers channelling their funds away from fixed-value redeemable claims generally and directly into the securities markets. Either of these processes which cut down the flows of funds to savings and loan associations can have, of course, a powerful effect on housing activity. With frozen portfolios of older mortgages made at lower interest rates than currently prevail, these institutions may find it difficult to pay substantially higher interest rates to attract or hold funds even if the Home Loan Bank Board will allow them to.

Secondly, when commercial banks feel the effects of credit restraint, they normally reduce their mortgage lending in order to be able to accommodate the needs of their business borrowers.

Thirdly, as interest rates rise, yields on corporate bonds typically rise relative to mortgage interest rates, and some institutional investors, such as life insurance companies, shift the composition of their investment flows away from mortgages and toward corporate bonds, which, in any case, have investment properties which make them more attractive than mortgages at equivalent yields. This tendency may be exacerbated by unrealistically low interest rate ceilings on FHA and VA mortgages and by State usury laws applicable to conventional mortgages.

The way in which mortgage credit availability impinges on home-building has changed with the passage of time. In the 1950's, when FHA and VA financing was more important than it has been recently and when the FHA and VA interest rate ceilings were more rigid than they are now, restrictive monetary policy affected housing mainly by diverting the flows of funds coming from investors having diversified portfolios away from mortgages and toward corporate securities. That is, the third effect listed above was the most important. In 1966, when homebuilding was drastically curtailed by monetary restraint, all of the effects were operating, but the first—the drain of funds away from savings and loan associations—was by far the most important. In 1968 and 1969, interest rates have risen sufficiently to arouse concern about a repetition of the 1966 experience. But while housing seems currently to be feeling the effects of tight money, it has proved to be much less vulnerable than was generally expected. There are several reasons for this, but the one most worthy of mention is the adoption by the Federal Reserve and the various Federal housing agencies of a number of measures designed to cushion or offset the effects of high interest rates on housing activity.

SECONDARY EFFECTS

Working through portfolio effects, wealth effects, and credit availability effects, the initial impacts of monetary policy will generate additional income, and this will further increase the demand for consumer non-durable goods and services. It will also expand the demand for the services of durable goods, thereby giving a further boost to the desired stocks of these goods. Thus, the familiar magnification of demand through multiplier and accelerator effects comes into play. It is often overlooked that the sharp reduction in the multiplier since the 1930's as a result of the greatly increased income-sensitivity of the tax-transfer system has presumably had important effects on the working of monetary as well as fiscal policy. Indeed, I would judge this increase in "built-in stability" through the fiscal system to be a major factor making monetary policy less potent today than in earlier times.

A further chain of secondary effects is set in motion as the rise in income increases demands for demand deposits and currency for trans-actions purposes, thereby reversing the initial decline in interest rates. This induced rise in interest rates will exert a dampening effect on the expansion by a partial reversal of the forces that initially triggered the rise in income. Whether or not this secondary effect will carry interest rates all the way back to their initial level (or higher) is an open question, concerning which I shall have some comments later on in this paper.

EFFECTS ON REAL OUTPUT VS. PRICES

I think almost all economists of a Keynesian persuasion would accept the proposition that the way in which the effect of an increase in demand is divided between output response and price-level response depends on the way it impinges on productive capacity. Thus, expansion caused by monetary policy is generally no more or no less inflationary than expansion caused by fiscal policy (or, for that matter, by an autonomous increase in private demand). This statement needs to be qualified in a couple of minor respects. First, monetary expansion might be less inflationary than an equivalent amount of fiscal expansion over the longer run if it resulted in more investment, thereby causing labor productivity to increase more rapidly. Secondly, the impacts of monetary policy are distributed among sectors in a different way from those of fiscal policy; and, with less than perfect mobility of resources, the inflationary effect might depend to some degree on this distribution.

SOME CONTROVERSIAL ISSUES

I would now like to discuss several of the issues that seem to be at the heart of the recent controversy regarding monetary and fiscal policy.

THE EFFECTIVENESS OF FISCAL POLICY

For the purpose of isolating the effects of fiscal policy from those of monetary policy, I believe a "pure" fiscal policy action should be defined as a change in government expenditures or a change in tax rates without any accompanying change in the instruments of monetary policy. Under our present institutional set-up, the instruments of monetary policy are open-market operations, changes in reserve requirements, and changes in the Federal Reserve discount rate. Open-market operations may be viewed as governing unborrowed reserves plus currency, with defensive operations offsetting undesired changes in this total that would result from erratic variations in float, gold stock, etc.

An increase in government purchases of goods and services, with tax rates constant, would affect the economy by three different routes. First, there would be a direct expansionary *income effect* resulting from the purchase of output by the government. Second, there would be an expansionary *wealth effect* as the private sector, experiencing an increment to its wealth entirely in the form of net claims against the government, increased its demand for real capital in an effort to diversify its portfolios.[1] These income and wealth effects would set off a multiplier-accelerator process of economic expansion. This expansion, in turn, would activate a partially offsetting monetary effect as the rise in income increased the demand for money. If the dial settings of the monetary instruments remained unchanged, this would drive up interest rates. The rise in interest rates would cause some reductions in those types of expenditures that were sensitive to interest rates through portfolio, wealth, and availability effects.

The wealth effect of fiscal policy may be quite powerful, particularly because it is cumulative—that is, it continues to operate until the budget has been brought back into balance, thereby shutting off the increase in net claims against the government. But, unfortunately, no effort that I know of has been made to incorporate it in an empirical model; consequently there is no way to formulate even a crude estimate of its importance.

If we neglect the wealth effect simply because we do not know how much weight to give it, we are left with the income effect and the offsetting monetary effect. The monetary effect will be greater (a) the greater the proportion of expenditures in GNP that are affected by interest rates, (b) the greater (in absolute value) is the average interest elasticity of these expenditures, (c) the greater is the income elasticity of demand for money, (d) the smaller (in absolute value) is the interest elasticity of demand for money and (e) the smaller is the interest elasticity of the supply of money.[2]

---

[1] For an extensive theoretical treatment of the wealth effect, see James Tobin, "An Essay on the Principles of Debt Management," in *Fiscal and Debt Management Policies* (Englewood Cliffs, N. J.: Prentice-Hall, Inc., 1963), pp. 142–218.

[2] It is possible to derive a more elaborate version of the static Keynesian multiplier incorporating the monetary effect. The following is such a multiplier equation.

$$\frac{dY}{dG} = \frac{1}{1 - e + \dfrac{\dfrac{I}{Y} \eta_{Ir} \eta_{LY}}{\eta_{Lr} - \eta_{Mr}}}$$

Here Y is GNP; G is government purchases; e is the marginal propensity to spend out of GNP; I/Y is the proportion of GNP that is sensitive to interest rates; $\eta_{Ir}(<0)$ is the average interest elasticity of interest-sensitive expenditures; $\eta_{Lr}(<0)$ is the interest elasticity of demand for money; $\eta_{Mr}(>0)$ is the interest elasticity of supply of money; and $\eta_{LY}(>0)$ is the income elasticity of demand for money. The usual simple Keynesian multiplier without allowance for monetary effect is $1/(1 - e)$. The

Only if the interest elasticities of both the demand for and supply of money are zero will the monetary effect completely cancel out the income effect.[3] That is, there will be some leeway for fiscal policy to increase income if a rise in interest rates either induces economization in the use of demand deposits and currency or causes the supply of such monetary assets to expand (for example, by inducing banks to increase their borrowings at the Federal Reserve). Since the empirical evidence is overwhelming that both money demand and money supply possess some degree of interest elasticity, it seems clear that fiscal policy is capable of exerting an independent effect on income. This conclusion is heavily supported by evidence derived from large structural models of the U.S. economy. For example, while there is no unique multiplier for fiscal policy in the FRB-MIT model, a number of simulations with that model show fiscal policy to have very substantial independent effects on economic activity.

It is often pointed out, especially by those who emphasize the role of money in the economy, that the effect produced by a stimulative fiscal action is dependent on the way in which the resulting deficit is financed. This is in a sense true, but this way of putting it is somewhat misleading. For example, it is sometimes stated that, in order to achieve the full Keynesian multiplier effect, the entire deficit must be financed by creating money—some statements even say high-powered money. What is necessary to achieve this result is to create enough money to satisfy the demand for money at the new higher level of income and the initial level of interest rates.

Ordinarily, the required increase in the supply of money will be only a fraction of the deficit, and the required increase in high-powered money will be an even smaller fraction. Moreover, there is a serious stock-flow problem. When income reaches its new equilibrium in a stable economy, the increased deficit (a flow) will be financed out of the excess of saving over investment generated by the rise in income. Additional demand deposits and currency are needed to meet the increased transaction demand at the higher income level, but this requires only a single increase in the money stock. In reality, there may be further complexities that require

---

monetary effect is incorporated in the third term (taking the form of a fraction) in the denominator of the equation above. Since this term is positive, its presence reduces the size of the multiplier. The statement in the text above regarding the factors determining the size of the monetary effect is based on this expression.

[3] In this case, the supply of money may be regarded as exogenously determined. If the demand for money depends only on income, income will have to change sufficiently to eliminate any discrepancies that arise between the demand for and supply of money. Thus, money controls income, and fiscal policy is incapable of affecting it. The reader will note that if both η_{Mr} and η_{Lr} are zero, the multiplier for fiscal policy given in footnote 2 above becomes zero.

a modification of this principle—for example, if the demand for money depends on wealth as well as income or if the price level is determined by a Phillips Curve mechanism so that prices are not merely higher but are increasing more rapidly at higher levels of income.

Nevertheless, the principle is, I believe, basically correct. Rather than saying that the multiplier depends on how the deficit is financed, I think it is more accurate to say that it depends on the kind of monetary policy that accompanies the fiscal action. If monetary policy is such as to hold interest rates approximately constant, something analogous to the full Keynesian multiplier (with no monetary feedback) will be realized; if it allows interest rates to rise, the multiplier will be somewhat smaller; if it causes interest rates to fall, the multiplier will be somewhat greater.[4]

THE ROLE OF MONEY

Although I have used the term "money" in my discussion above, I am not sure the term is a very useful or meaningful one. Money (in the sense of means of payment) has two components, demand deposits and currency. Those two components are not, however, perfect substitutes—they are held, by and large, by different kinds of spending units; demand for them responds in different ways to different stimuli; and, because they are subject to markedly different reserve requirements, shifts between them alter the total amount of credit that can be supplied by the financial system. They are best regarded as two different financial assets and treated as such.

Moreover, there is no apparent reason why "money"—whether in the form of currency or demand deposits—is more or less important than any of the myriad other financial assets that exist. It is now generally agreed that the demands for demand deposits and currency depend on the yields available on alternative assets and on income or related measures (and possibly, but by no means certainly, on wealth). Thus, the quantities of currency and demand deposits held by the public are generally agreed to be endogenous variables determined in a general equilibrium setting along with the prices and quantities of other financial and real assets.

[4] If fiscal policy has a wealth effect working through changes in the public's holdings of net claims against the government, it seems quite likely that the magnitude of this effect will depend on the form taken by the change in net claims. For example, a change in public holdings of short-term debt may have a larger effect on aggregate demand than an equal change in holdings of long-term debt. To the extent that this is the case, debt management policies which change the maturity composition of the public's holdings of government debt may have important economic effects. But there is no reason to focus special attention on the composition of increments to the debt resulting from deficits, since the increment to the debt in any year is only a tiny fraction of the total debt to be managed. In any case, as indicated earlier, we are entirely neglecting the wealth effect because in the present state of knowledge there is no way of forming a judgment concerning its importance.

Nor is there any appreciable evidence that money—whether in the form of demand deposits or currency—affects peoples' spending on goods and services directly. Such empirical evidence as there is suggests that people change their expenditures on goods and services because (a) their income changes; (b) their wealth changes; (c) their portfolios are thrown out of equilibrium by changes in relative yields on real and financial assets by actions taken by the monetary or fiscal authorities; (d) credit availability changes for institutional reasons altering in one direction or the other their ability to finance expenditures they want to make; or (e) their propensities to spend or their preferences for different kinds of assets change for essentially exogenous reasons, such as changes in tastes, changes in technology, and so on. That changes in the stock of money *per se* would affect spending seems to me highly improbable.

Of course, if changes in stocks of demand deposits and currency—or the combination of the two—were tightly linked to those changes in yields, in wealth, and in credit availability through which monetary policy operates, changes in the stocks of these monetary assets might be highly useful measures of the thrust of policy even though they played no part in the causal nexus. But this, too, I think is unlikely. In a highly sophisticated financial system such as ours, in which new financial instruments and practices are constantly being introduced, it seems highly improbable that the demands for monetary assets are simple and stable functions of a few unchanging variables.

The many empirical studies of the demand for money that have been made in recent years have generally proved incapable of differentiating among alternative hypotheses. Consequently, one is free to choose among a variety of possible theories of the demand for money. The one that appeals to me is the hypothesis that money (i.e., demand deposits and currency) is dominated by time deposits and very short-dated securities, with the result that it is not a significant portion of permanent portfolios. This leaves the demand for monetary assets as an interest-elastic transactions demand along the lines postulated by Baumol and by Tobin.[5]

Such an explanation, however, makes sense only for relatively large business firms and wealthy individuals. It does not seem applicable to smaller units. Among such units, I suspect that the general rise in interest rates that has been going on for the past two decades has pushed these rates successively above the thresholds of awareness of different groups of people, causing them to abandon their careless habit of foregoing income by holding excessive cash balances. If I am right, this behavior is probably not readily reversible if interest rates should fall. It seems to me that there is still a substantial element of mystery about the demand for monetary

---

[5]See W. J. Baumol, "The Transactions Demand for Cash: An Inventory Theoretic Approach," *Quarterly Journal of Economics*, 66, November 1952, pp. 545-56; James Tobin, "The Interest Elasticity of the Transactions Demand for Cash," *Review of Economics and Statistics*, 38, August 1956, pp. 241-47.

assets—mystery that will probably be resolved, if at all, only on the basis of extensive study of the behavior of the cash-holdings of micro-units.

RELATIONSHIP BETWEEN CHANGES IN MONEY AND CHANGES IN INCOME

None of the above should be taken to mean that there is no relation between changes in demand deposits and currency and changes in income. Indeed, I believe there are three such relationships, which are very difficult to disentangle.

First, an expansionary monetary policy that stimulated increased spending and income through portfolio effects, wealth effects, and credit availability effects would bring in its wake an increase in supplies of demand deposits and currency. This would be a sideshow rather than the main event, but it would nevertheless occur. But the size of the increase associated with a given stimulus might vary considerably from one situation to another.

Secondly, a rise in income caused by fiscal policy or by an autonomous shift of private demand, with the monetary dials unchanged, would react back on the money supply in three different ways.[6] (1) The rise in interest rates caused by the rise in income would cause the banks to increase their borrowings from the Federal Reserve and perhaps to economize on excess reserves. (2) The rise in market interest rates would cause investors to shift funds from time deposits and similar claims into securities if, as is likely, the interest rates on these claims did not rise fully in pace with market rates. This would cause the quantity of demand deposits to increase as investors withdrew funds from time accounts and paid them over to sellers of securities for deposit in demand accounts. (3) If banks and related institutions raised rates on time-deposit type claims, some holders of non-interest-bearing demand deposits would be induced to shift funds to time accounts. To the extent that issuers of these claims held cash reserves against them, the amount of reserves available to support demand deposits would be reduced, requiring a contraction in these deposits. Effects (1) and (2) would cause the money supply to increase, while effect (3) would cause it to fall. It seems likely that (1) and (2) would outweigh (3), leading to an increase in the supply of monetary assets. The probability of this outcome would be increased if the Federal Reserve was laggard in adjusting Regulation Q ceilings. Indeed, a rigid Regulation Q ceiling would completely immobilize effect (3) while maximizing the size of effect (2).

---

[6] This discussion is based on an analysis developed in W. L. Smith, "Time Deposits, Free Reserves, and Monetary Policy," in Giulio Pontecoroo, R. P. Shay, and A. G. Hart (eds.), *Issues in Banking and Monetary Analysis* (New York: Holt, Rinehart and Winston, Inc., 1967), pp. 79–113.

Thirdly, under the rubric of "meeting the needs of trade" or "leaning against the wind," the Federal Reserve has, at times, adjusted the supply of reserves to accommodate, or partially accommodate, changes in the demand for money brought about by changes in income, thereby creating a third chain of causation running from income to money supply.

With perhaps three relations between money and income present at the same time—one running from money to income and two running from income to money—it is likely to be almost impossible to tell what is going on by direct observation. And, as Tobin has shown, in such a complex dynamic situation, it is almost impossible to infer anything conclusive about causation by studying the lags.[7]

DOES EASY MONEY CAUSE INTEREST RATES TO RISE?

One of the supposedly startling propositions that has been advanced recently is the notion that an easing of monetary policy—commonly measured in terms of the rate of increase in the money stock—will cause interest rates to rise and, conversely, that a tightening of monetary policy will cause interest rates to fall. To be sure, if the rate of growth of the money stock is accelerated, interest rates will decline at first. But before long, money income will begin to grow so rapidly that the resulting increase in the demand for money will, it is contended, pull interest rates back up above the level from which they originally started.

In the first place, this possibility has long been recognized in Keynesian economics. In a static Keynesian model it is possible for the *IS* curve to have a positive slope, with stability conditions requiring only that this slope be less than that of the *LM* curve. This could happen, for example, if income had a strong effect on investment.[8] In such a situation, a shift to the right of the *LM* curve, which might be caused by an increase in the money stock, would cause the equilibrium interest rate to rise. A more realistic possibility is that the economy contains endogenous cycle-generators of the accelerator or stock-adjustment type, which cause income

---

[7] James Tobin, "Money and Income: Post Hoc Propter Hoc?" (mimeographed); also W. C. Brainard and James Tobin, "Pitfalls in Financial Model Building," *American Economic Review*, 58, May 1968, pp. 99–122.

[8] The actual condition required is that the sum of the marginal propensities to consume and invest must exceed one, but (as a condition for stability) be less than one plus a term measuring the size of the monetary feedback. (Even if the two propensities totaled less than unity, the *IS* curve could slope upward if a rise in interest rates caused total spending to rise. But this could occur only on the remote chance that the income effect dominated the substitution effect in saving behavior so powerfully that a rise in interest rates caused consumption to increase by more than it caused investment to decline.)

to respond so vigorously to a stimulative monetary policy that interest rates rise above their original level at an ensuing cyclical peak.

There is another chain of causation, working through the effects of inflation on nominal interest rates, which might cause a decline in real interest rates to be associated with a rise in nominal interest rates. This possibility has generally been neglected by Keynesians, but it is in no way inconsistent with Keynesian analysis. An expansionary monetary policy, which lowers nominal interest rates (and real interest rates) initially, will push the economy up the Phillips Curve, thus causing prices to rise more rapidly. As the increase in the actual rate of inflation generates a rise in the anticipated future rate of inflation, an inflation premium may get built into interest rates, causing nominal interest rates to rise. It seems possible that nominal interest rates could be pushed above their original level even though real interest rates remain below this level. This outcome would be more likely (a) the greater the expansionary effect of a given fall in the real rate of interest on real income, (b) the greater the decline in unemployment caused by a given increase in real income, (c) the greater the increase in the rate of inflation caused by a given decline in unemployment, and (d) the more sensitive the response of the anticipated rate of inflation to a change in the actual rate of inflation.[9] The probability that nominal interest rates would be pushed above their initial level by this mechanism is very difficult to evaluate, however, primarily because we know very little about the extent to which, and the speed with which, an increase in the actual rate of inflation gets translated into an increase in the anticipated rate of inflation.

Thus, the notion that an expansionary monetary policy would ultimately cause nominal interest rates to rise above their initial level is in no way inconsistent with Keynesian views. Whether such a phenomenon actually occurs is a different matter. With fiscal policy changing and with the strength of private demand changing, it is not safe to conclude that,

---

[9] Beginning with the equation $r = r' + p_e$, which expresses the relation between the nominal interest rate (r), the real interest rate (r') and the anticipated rate of inflation (p_e), the following expression can be rather easily derived.

$$\frac{dr}{dr'} = 1 + m \frac{dI}{dr'} \frac{du}{dY} \frac{dp}{du} \frac{dp_e}{dp}$$

Here m is the multiplier; dI/dr' is the response of interest-sensitive expenditures to a change in the real rate of interest; du/dY is the response of the unemployment rate to a change in real GNP; dp/du is the response of the rate of inflation to a change in the unemployment rate (i.e., the slope of the Phillips Curve); and dp_e/dp is the response of the anticipated rate of inflation to a change in the actual rate of inflation. Since three of the components of the second term on the right-hand side of the equation (dI/dr', du/dY, and dp/du) take on negative values, the second term as a whole is negative. Whether a fall in the real rate of interest will cause the nominal rate of interest to rise or fall depends on whether the second term on the right is larger or smaller than unity.

because an easing of monetary policy was followed at some later time by a rise of interest rates above their initial level, the easing of monetary policy *caused* the rise in interest rates. The best evidence I have seen is from simulations with the FRB-MIT model which show that an injection of bank reserves causes interest rates to fall sharply at first and then rise gradually but only part of the way back to their original level. But, of course, simulations starting from a different initial position might show different results. In all probability, the phenomenon in question occurs under some conditions but not under others.

SUGGESTIONS REGARDING POLICY

At the very beginning of this discussion of the conduct of monetary policy, let me make clear that I am not talking about the issue of rules versus discretion. That is a different subject, which I will discuss briefly at the conclusion of my paper. Assuming that the Federal Reserve will continue to conduct a discretionary policy, let us consider what is the best way to proceed with that task.

It seems to me that much of the recent literature on monetary policy has been obsessed with a search for a magic touchstone—some measure of the impact of monetary forces that can be used as the sole guide in the conduct of policy. Unfortunately, I don't believe there is such a touchstone—the world is too complicated and we know too little about it for that. There is a second related obsession with the problem of characterizing monetary policy. Is it "tight" or "easy"? Is it "tighter" or "easier" today than it was, say, six months ago?

The first of these questions is clearly a matter of judgment and opinion. The second, comparative form of the question sounds more capable of a scientific answer, but in fact I think it is equally unanswerable. Does it mean, "Is monetary policy contributing more to aggregate demand today than it was six months ago?" If it does mean that—and I can think of no other interpretation—I wouldn't have the faintest idea how to go about answering it. The problem facing the Federal Reserve, however, is not how to characterize monetary policy but how to carry it out, and this puts things in a somewhat different light.

Since monetary policy affects economic activity with substantial lags, policy must clearly be based on forecasts of future economic conditions. While our knowledge has improved considerably, we still cannot be very sure about the lags, which undoubtedly depend upon underlying conditions. Moreover, the lags vary from sector to sector. It seems quite clear that monetary policy can affect homebuilding quite rapidly, at least under some conditions, if the dials of policy are adjusted in the right way. The lags in the effects on the other sectors appear to be considerably longer. Forecasting is also a difficult task, but there is no way to escape the need for it. Not the least of the difficulties of monetary policy, as has been demonstrated several times in the last three years or so, is the forecasting of fiscal policy.

While the ultimate goals of policy are high employment, price stability, the rate of growth of output, and so on, these cannot be used as immediate guides to policy, because it takes so long for policy measures to affect them. The authorities must choose as guides to policy some more immediate and more specifically monetary variables that appear to be related to the goals they are trying to achieve.

There are a number of monetary aggregates that the Federal Reserve can control with varying degrees of precision if it chooses to do so. It can obviously control its portfolio of securities exactly, and it can control unborrowed reserves plus currency outside member banks quite closely by employing defensive open-market operations to offset changes in uncontrollable factors affecting reserves, such as float, gold stock, Treasury deposits at Federal Reserve banks, etc. It can probably control total reserves plus currency (the monetary base) fairly accurately either by using open-market operations to offset changes in member bank borrowing or by changing the administration of discount policy to reduce the fluctuations in borrowing. The stock of demand deposits and currency would be more difficult to control, but I suspect that its average value over a quarter's time could be controlled fairly satisfactorily.

Alternatively, policy could be directed at regulating interest rates, although some interest rates would be easier to control than others. The Treasury bill rate could be controlled with any desired degree of accuracy under present operating procedures, because the Federal Reserve deals directly in the Treasury bill market. By a shift in its operating procedures, the Federal Reserve could control the yield on some other maturity of Federal debt. I believe it could, instead, maintain fairly close control of a variety of alternative interest rates on private debt—such as the Aaa corporate bond yield—although it would have to influence such rates indirectly unless it were to deal in private debt.

The basic issue of monetary policy is: Should the Federal Reserve focus primarily on controlling some monetary aggregate or should it focus on controlling interest rates? I believe there is a very strong *prima facie* case for a policy that is oriented toward interest rates. The reason is that the portfolio effects, wealth effects, and credit availability effects through which the impacts of monetary policy are transmitted to the economy are better measured by changes in interest rates than by changes in monetary aggregates. The vast bulk of the empirical evidence supports this view, indicating that it is through interest rates that monetary policy affects expenditures on goods and services. Indeed, I know of no evidence that any monetary aggregate that the Federal Reserve could control has an effect on expenditures.

Of course, if there were tight and well understood linkages between some monetary aggregate—say, the stock of demand deposits and currency —and interest rates, it would matter little which the Federal Reserve attempted to control, because a money target would imply an interest rate target. There are indeed linkages between monetary aggregates and interest rates—these linkages are, in my judgment, sufficient to prevent the Federal Reserve from controlling both monetary aggregates and interest rates except to a very limited extent. But the linkages are not well understood and are subject to change as a result of financial innovations and changes in patterns of financial behavior. Consequently, it does make a difference whether the Federal Reserve selects a monetary aggregate or an interest rate as a guide to policy.

ADVANTAGES OF TREASURY BILL RATE AS A GUIDE TO POLICY

My specific suggestion is that the Federal Reserve focus on the Treasury bill rate as its basic guide for monetary policy. There are several advantages in this approach. First, the Federal Reserve can, without any basic change in its operating procedures, control the Treasury bill rate with virtually any degree of accuracy it desires. Secondly, there are many occasions on which the bill rate must be a focus of attention anyway, because it is the key short-term rate affecting international capital flows. Thirdly, the bill rate is closely related to market interest rates on those forms of short- and intermediate-term debt that compete with fixed-value redeemable claims and are therefore of critical importance for the availability of mortgage funds. Fourthly, there is considerable evidence that the bill rate works through an expectational mechanism to affect those long-term rates that are important in determining the cost of capital to business firms, State and local governments, and home buyers. Moreover, the wealth effect of monetary policy works through capitalization rates that would be indirectly affected by a policy aimed in the first instance at the Treasury bill rate.

Of course, the bill rate target would have to be selected on the basis of a forecast of economic activity several quarters ahead, including a forecast of fiscal policy. One could, for example, use a model such as the FRB-MIT model to estimate a pattern of behavior of the bill rate that could be expected to achieve the desired performance of the economy over the next three or four quarters, given the anticipated fiscal policy. This target could then be adjusted on the basis of special factors or judgmental considerations. I would not propose to peg the bill rate exactly but to establish a range of, say, 20 basis points within which it would be permitted to fluctuate. The bill rate target would, of course, be reexamined at each meeting of the FOMC on the basis of the latest forecast of the economic outlook.

I would not, however, adhere dogmatically to such a "bills-only" policy. If long-term interest rates should fail to respond in the anticipated way to a change in the bill rate target, I would not hesitate to nudge them along by open-market operations in long-term Treasury securities. Nor would I entirely neglect monetary aggregates. I would want to supplement the bill rate target with some kind of quantitative guideline to prevent gross mistakes in policy. In the case of a non-growing economy, using the stock of demand deposits and currency as the quantitative guideline, the matter is relatively simple—one should be sure that this stock increases when the economy is below full employment and declines when it is above full employment. The problem here is one of distinguishing between automatic and discretionary elements of policy—similar to the problem in fiscal policy that gave rise to the full-employment surplus concept. When the economy is weak, for example, interest rates decline automatically even if the monetary authorities do nothing, and it is desirable to be sure that the authorities are reinforcing this tendency by discretionary measures rather than offsetting it as they sometimes appear to have done in the past.

The problem of developing a suitable monetary guideline is considerably more complicated in the case of a growing economy. My procedure would be to begin by estimating a "normal" rate of monetary growth. For example, if the target point on the Phillips Curve is 4 percent unemployment which is judged to be associated with 2 percent inflation, if the rate of growth of productive capacity under full employment conditions is estimated to be 4 percent per year, and if the income elasticity of demand for monetary assets is judged to be unity, the "normal" rate of monetary growth would be estimated at 6 percent per year. At any particular time, if the objective of policy was to restrain the economy, growth should be less than 6 percent; if the objective was to stimulate the economy, growth should be more than 6 percent.

There is a problem of deciding what aggregate to use as an index of monetary growth. Should it be the monetary base as calculated by the Federal Reserve Bank of St. Louis, the money supply, total bank credit, or some other aggregate? Unfortunately, the significance of a change in the rate of growth of any of the commonly used aggregates depends upon the public's preferences for different categories of financial assets, including currency, demand deposits, time deposits, and securities. Since these preferences appear to change for reasons that we do not yet fully understand, problems of interpretation are bound to arise. My quite tentative suggestion would be to use the monetary base as the index of monetary growth. But I would also monitor the behavior of the other aggregates closely. If the selected bill rate target resulted in growth of the base inconsistent with the guideline for several weeks and if the behavior of the other aggregates seemed to support the conclusion that monetary growth was too slow or too fast, the whole situation, including the bill rate target, should be carefully reexamined.

OTHER DIMENSIONS TO BE CONSIDERED

I think an approach along the lines developed above would make sense in providing an overall rationale for monetary policy. But there are important dimensions that are omitted in the above discussion. It has long been my contention that those responsible for the conduct of monetary policy must pay close attention to its impacts on particular sectors of the economy, especially when a restrictive policy is being followed. An example of this dimension of monetary policy is the variety of measures that have been taken by the Federal Reserve and a number of other Federal Government agencies during the past year to cushion the impact of high interest rates on homebuilding.

The Federal Reserve has attempted to shield the savings and loan associations from bank competition by maintaining low ceiling rates on savings deposits and those forms of time deposits that compete most directly with savings and loan shares. The Federal Home Loan Bank Board has acted to encourage continued mortgage lending by savings and loan associations by reducing the liquidity requirement applicable to the associations and by making advances available to them. In addition, the Home Loan Banks have attempted to manage their own borrowings in the capital market in such a way as to minimize the possible impact on deposit flows. The Federal National Mortgage Association increased its mortgage holdings by $1.6 billion in 1968, and increased the scope and flexibility of its stabilizing activities in the mortgage market by introducing a new program of weekly auctions of mortgage commitments, beginning in May 1968. The ceiling rate applicable to FHA and VA mortgages was raised from 6 percent to $6\frac{3}{4}$ percent in May and was raised further to $7\frac{1}{2}$ percent in January 1969. Finally, in its general conduct of monetary policy, the Federal Reserve has kept its eye on the flows of funds to savings and loan associations with a view to avoiding, if possible, a rise in short- and intermediate-term interest rates sufficient to set off a "disintermediation crises" of the type that occurred in 1966.

The impact of monetary policy on the economy would, I believe, have been substantially different in 1968, and thus far in 1969, in the absence of these precautionary actions by the Federal Reserve and by the various agencies with responsibilities in the housing field. In all probability, we would long since have experienced a sharp decline in housing starts and residential construction expenditures similar to that which occurred in 1966. There are a number of reforms which might be adopted to increase the efficiency and flexibility of the mortgage market and to reduce the excessive impact that monetary policy now tends to have on homebuilding. Unless and until such reforms are implemented, however, I believe it is appropriate for the monetary authorities to concern themselves specifically with the effects of their policies on the housing sector. Indeed, I believe structural measures of the kind employed in 1968–69 should be thought of as part of monetary policy and should be applied as the situation seems to warrant on the basis of close cooperation between the Federal Reserve and the other agencies involved.

No matter how skillfully monetary policy is conducted, things are bound to go wrong from time to time. The underlying strength of private demand will sometimes prove to be stronger or weaker than was anticipated; fiscal policy will depart from its expected path; and the timing and magnitude of the economy's response to monetary actions will seldom be exactly as anticipated. I do not count myself among the group of economists who believe the business cycle is dead. If we seriously attempt to keep the economy moving along a selected high-employment growth path, resisting departures from that path in either direction, I believe we can still expect some economic fluctuations. The hope is that we can keep these fluctuations mild. But our success in that respect is much more critically dependent on improving the performance of fiscal policy than it is on changing the techniques of monetary management. Improved fiscal policy would relieve the Federal Reserve of its recent impossible task of offsetting the effects of profoundly destabilizing movements of the Federal budget. Even operating within the framework established by a reasonably well-designed fiscal policy, the Federal Reserve is bound to make occasional mistakes, but it should be able to make an effective contribution to economic stabilization and do so without the sharp gyrations in monetary variables that we have witnessed recently.

RULES VERSUS AUTHORITIES

There is no reason, in principle, why one holding Keynesian views must necessarily favor discretion over a monetary rule. One could believe that our knowledge of the responses and the lags in the system is so poor that efforts to conduct a discretionary policy add to instability rather than subtract from it. I think discretion conducted on the basis of the best information available can do a better job than a rule, but I find the question a very complex one, and I do not see how anyone can be sure of the answer.

Before a rule involving steady growth of some aggregate such as the monetary base could be seriously considered, however, it seems to me there would have to be procedural or institutional changes in three areas.

First, there would have to be some assurance of better fiscal policy than we have had recently. Our problems of the last three years are primarily the result of inaction and inordinate delay in fiscal policy, and discretionary monetary policy has helped by either taking the place of needed fiscal restraint or supplementing it when it was too-long delayed.

Secondly, if monetary policy is to disregard interest rates entirely, I believe we need an overhaul of the arrangement for financing housing.

And, thirdly, interest rates cannot be disregarded until the international monetary system has been reformed in some way to remove the balance-of-payments constraint on domestic interest rates.

Having said all of this, let me add that I believe the discussion of monetary rules is largely academic anyway. Even assuming that a rule were adopted, I feel certain that there would be overwhelming pressure to abandon it the first time it appeared that discretion would enable us to achieve a better performance—and that, I believe, would occur quite soon after the rule was adopted.

6/ ALLAN H. MELTZER

Comments on the Role of Money in National Economic Policy

As I listen to this debate, and it seems to have gone on for a long time, I notice that people take various positions. One is that Milton Friedman is completely wrong; another is that Friedman is almost completely wrong. A third is that there is a grain of truth to what Friedman says, but it is not very important; and, therefore, fiscal policy matters far more than the so-called monetarists say. Always, there is subtle suggestion that some of us know a great deal more about the way in which the economic system operates than we have time to tell. If the argument and evidence could be presented, everyone could see that there is a considerable amount of evidence available showing the sizable effect of fiscal policy operations and supporting some very detailed econometric model of the economy.

Now, I haven't seen that evidence, and I would like to see it. I do know that last November, at the University of Michigan forecasting conference, the forecast of the Michigan econometric model for the first quarter of 1969 was that GNP would increase by $4.4 billion. At about the same time, the Wharton econometric forecasting unit predicted a $5.2 billion rise in first quarter GNP and a $7.4 billion rise in second quarter GNP. We now know that these predicted changes, made only six weeks before the start of the quarter, missed from $\frac{2}{3}$ to $\frac{3}{4}$ of the actual change. We will soon know that the second quarter GNP changes predicted by those mod-

The following comments were made by Professor Meltzer during a panel discussion on the role of money in national economic policy.

Reprinted from *Controlling Monetary Aggregates*: Proceedings of a Monetary Conference of the Federal Reserve Bank of Boston, June 1969, by permission of the author. Allan H. Meltzer is Maurice Falk Professor of Economics and Industrial Administration, Carnegie-Mellon University.

els are considerably less than 50 percent of the actual second quarter change. Moreover, the econometric models forecast larger changes in the second and third quarters than in the first quarter, contrary to the pattern that we can now expect.

You may also recall that a year ago Arthur Okun, the Chairman of Council of Economic Advisers, warned us of the dangers of "fiscal over-kill"; talked about the threat of a downturn in the third and fourth quarter of last year as if it were almost a certainty; and argued that the surtax and the prospective reduction in expenditures were likely to push the economy into a recession. These predictions, like the predictions of the Wharton and Michigan models, proved incorrect. The last few years have shown that it is very difficult to forecast GNP a year in advance until we know what the Federal Reserve is going to do about the quantity of money. In periods like 1961 to 1965 or 1964, when the quantity of money grows at a relatively steady rate, it is easier to make accurate GNP forecasts. In periods when there are large gyrations in the stock of money, it is difficult to forecast by using models that ignore changes in the stock of money or minimize their effects. And, I believe, that piece of evidence is buttressed by the demonstrated superior predictive performance of the Andersen-Jordan model. Small and unimportant as these two facts may seem in isolation, they are two of the more important facts we have obtained from recent experiences.

If these facts were isolated, we might dismiss them or leave to the model builders to search for the source of their errors. The determinants of GNP and its components are not so well known that large forecasting errors are remarkable; and GNP predictions are not so precise that occasional large errors are either unexpected, or noteworthy. Recent errors, however, are part of a continuing sequence and follow closely the sizable errors in fore-casting made in recent years by econometric models that minimize the effect of changes in money.

REASON FOR FORECASTING ERRORS

There is at least one important common element in the models that make for large forecasting errors. The Wharton and Michigan model builders share a common disdain for any possible influence that might be exercised by changes in the quantity of money. Professor Suits, a principal contributor to the Michigan model, has expressed his view that the neglect of changes in money has no important consequences for his model. Mr. Okun takes a similar position. He writes that the effect of monetary policy is given by the change in market interest rates. A rise in market interest rates is judged to be contractive, and a fall in interest rates is called expansive. The 1969 report of the Council of Economic Advisors, written when Okun was chairman, repeatedly takes that position and states it in terms that are too clear to be misinterpreted.

I believe that the position is incorrect, and that the cause of the error is that market interest rates are an unreliable indicator of monetary policy. That statement doesn't mean that changes in interest rates are independent of fiscal policy or real variables, and it doesn't deny that the demand for money depends on interest rates. Samuleson and Tobin raise the latter point repeatedly and force me to confess my ignorance publicly. How do you get from the fact on which we all agree—that the demand for money depends on interest rates—to the conclusion that interest rates are a reliable indicator of monetary policy?

In fact, we know very little about the determinants of short-term changes in market rates. By using interest rate changes to judge the content of current monetary policy, we are very likely to be misled. The closer the economy is to full employment, the more we are likely to be misled.

Of several different errors underlying the incorrect notion that levels or changes in the market interest rates are solely, or mainly, the result of monetary policy, two errors seem to me to be most important. One is the failure to distinguish between credit and money. Most of the changes in market interest rates that we observe are the result of activities taking place on the credit market, not on the theoretical "money market" of economic analysis. The second is the failure to distinguish between changes in interest rates that result from changes in productivity and thrift, and changes that result from inflation. The latter distinction, the distinction between nominal and real magnitudes, is one of the oldest in economics, but it has been neglected in policy discussions and in many econometric models. To understand the effect of change in money on economic activity, both distinctions have to be kept in mind: the distinction between credit and money, and the distinction between real and nominal values.

TWO OPPOSING VIEWS

An understanding of monetary policy, of the role of money as an indicator, and of the difference between the effects of changes in credit and money can be obtained by contrasting two frameworks. In one view, monetary and fiscal policies are seen as the means by which the public sector offsets instability in the economy resulting from changes that occur in the private sector. Fluctuations in prices and output are seen as the result primarily of real forces and changes mainly in attitude or outlook that raise or lower investment, thereby raising or lowering the nominal value of income, market interest rates, and the demand for money. The task of monetary policy, in this framework, is to offset undesired changes in interest rates caused by the unforeseen changes in investment. The task of fiscal policy is to offset the unforeseen changes in the private expenditure and maintain expenditures at the full employment level. Monetary policy is called "restrictive" if market rates are permitted to rise; "permissive" if market rates are prevented from rising; and "coordinated" if the balance of payments is in deficit, and market rates are permitted to rise so as to attract an inflow of short-term capital from abroad. With this framework, it appears reasonable to accept interest rates as the main indicator of monetary policy. If the framework were correct, the decision might be more tenable—although still not correct.

The alternative view—at least my view—does not deny that changes in market interest rates are partly the result of changes in attitude or changes in technology that shift private expenditures. The difference—and it is an important difference—is a difference of emphasis and interpretation. Not only are changes in private expenditure assigned a smaller role, but many of these so-called autonomous changes are viewed as a delayed response to past monetary and fiscal policies.

The effect of a monetary or fiscal policy is not limited to the initial change in interest rates. An expansive monetary policy raises the monetary base, stocks of money and bank credit, and initially lowers market interest rates. The expansion of money increases expenditure, increases the amount of borrowing, and reduces the amount of existing securities that individuals and bankers wish to hold at prevailing market interest rates. These changes in borrowing and in desired holdings of securities reverse the initial decline in interest rates; market rates rise until the stock of existing securities is reabsorbed into portfolios, and the banks offer the volume of loans that the public desires. If expansive operations continue, expenditures, borrowing, and interest rates rise to levels above those in the starting equilibrium. Later, prices rise under the impact of increases in the quantity of money, further reducing the desired holdings of bonds and other fixed coupon securities, and increasing desired borrowing. A rise in holdings of currency relative to demand deposits adds to the forces raising interest rates on the credit market.

In this interpretation, the effect of monetary (or fiscal policy) is not limited to the initial effect. The response to a maintained change in policy includes the effects on the credit market, the acceleration and deceleration of prices, and ultimately, if policy makers persist, the changes in attitudes and particularly in anticipations of inflation or deflation. These changes, however, are regarded as reliable consequences of maintaining an expansive or contractive monetary policy, just as much to be expected as the initial effect.

It is the temporary changes in the level of interest rates observed on the credit market that frequently mislead monetary policy makers into believing their policy is restrictive when it is expansive. Large changes in the growth rate of money become a main source of instability precisely because the credit market and price effects dominate the initial effect of monetary policy in an economy close to full employment. Misled by the change in market interest rates—or their interpretation of the change—the Federal Reserve permits or forces the stock of money to grow at too high or too low a rate for too long a time. Excessive expansion and contraction of money becomes the main cause of the fluctuations in output and of inflation or deflation. Inappropriate public policies, not changes in private expenditures, become the main cause of instability.

A portion of the second interpretation has now been accepted by the principal spokesman of the Federal Reserve System. In his March 25th statement to the Senate Banking Committee, Chairman Martin said:

> I do not mean to argue that the interest rate developments in recent years have had no relation to monetary policy. We know that, in the short run, expansive monetary policies tend to reduce interest rates and restrictive monetary policy to raise them. But in the long run, in a full employment economy, expansive monetary policies foster greater inflation and encourage borrowers to make even larger demands on the credit markets. Over the long run, therefore, expansive monetary policies may not lower interest rates; in fact, they may raise them appreciably. This is the clear lesson of history that has been reconfirmed by the experience of the past several years.*

With that statement, Chairman Martin abandoned the framework that has guided Federal Reserve policy through most of its history and has been responsible for major errors in policy. Recognition that interest rates generally rise fastest under the impact of monetary expansion—that the credit market effects dominate short-term changes in interest rates—is probably the single most important step toward an understanding of the role of money that has been taken in the entire history of the Federal Reserve System.

If we develop our analysis and concentrate on improving our understanding of money and of the differences between money and credit, rather than on the issue of whether Milton Friedman is wholly right or wholly wrong, we will have more progress to report next time we meet.

*This statement was made in 1969. William McChesney Martin was succeeded as Chairman of the Board of Governors of the Federal Reserve System by Arthur F. Burns in 1970.

7/ KARL BRUNNER

The Role of Money and Monetary Policy

The development of monetary analysis in the past decade has intensified the debate concerning the role of money and monetary policy. Extensive research fostered critical examinations of the Federal Reserve's traditional descriptions of policy and of the arrangements governing policymaking. Some academic economists and others attribute the cyclical fluctuations of monetary growth and the persistent problem concerning the proper interpretation of monetary policy to the established procedures of monetary policy and the conceptions traditionally guiding policymakers.

The critique of established policy procedures, which evolved from this research into questions concerning the monetary mechanism, is derived from a body of monetary theory referred to in this paper as the Monetarist position. Three major conclusions have emerged from the hypotheses put forth. First, monetary impulses are a major factor accounting for variations in output, employment and prices. Second, movements in the money stock are the most reliable measure of the thrust of monetary impulses. Third, the behavior of the monetary authorities dominates movements in the money stock over business cycles.

A response to the criticisms of existing monetary policy methods was naturally to be expected and is welcomed. Four articles which defend present policy procedures have appeared during the past few years in various Federal Reserve publications.[1] These articles comprise a counter-

Reprinted from the Federal Reserve Bank of St. Louis *Review*, Vol. 50 (July 1968), by permission of the author and publisher. Karl Brunner is professor of Economics at the University of Rochester.

This paper owes a heavy debt to my long and stimulating association with Allan H. Meltzer. I also wish to acknowledge the editorial assistance of Leonall C. Andersen, Keith M. Carlson, and Jerry L. Jordan of the Federal Reserve Bank of St. Louis.

[1]Lyle Gramley and Samuel Chase, "Time Deposits in Monetary Analysis," Federal Reserve *Bulletin*, October 1965. John H. Kareken, "Commercial Banks and the

critique which argues that monetary impulses are neither properly measured nor actually transmitted by the money stock. The authors reject the Monetarist thesis that monetary impulses are a chief factor determining variations in economic activity, and they contend that cyclical fluctuations of monetary growth cannot be attributed to the behavior of the Federal Reserve authorities. These fluctuations are claimed to result primarily from the behavior of commercial banks and the public.

The ideas and arguments put forth in these articles deserve close attention. The controversey defined by the critique of policy in professional studies and the countercritique appearing in Federal Reserve publications bears on issues of fundamental importance to public policy. Underlying all the fashionable words and phrases is the fundamental question: What is the role of monetary policy and what are the requirements of rational policymaking?

The following sections discuss the major aspects of the countercritique. These rejoinders may contribute to a better understanding of the issues, and the resulting clarification may remove some unnecessary disputes. Even though the central contentions of the controversy will remain, the continuous articulation of opposing points of view plays a vital role in the search for greater understanding of the monetary process.

A SUMMARY OF THE COUNTERCRITIQUE

The four articles relied on two radically different groups of arguments. Gramley-Chase, Kareken and Cacy exploit the juxtaposition "New View versus Traditional View" as the central idea guiding their countercritique. The analytical framework developed by the critique is naturally subsumed for this purpose under the "Traditional View" label. On the other hand, Davis uses the analytical framework developed by the critique in order to organize his arguments.

Gramley-Chase describe their general argument in the following words:

> (New) developments have reaffirmed the bankers' point of view that deposits are attracted, not created, as textbooks suggest. In this new environment, growth rates of deposits have become more suspect than ever as indicators of the conduct of monetary policy. . . . A framework of analysis [is required] from which the significance of time deposits and of changing time deposits can be deduced.

Supply of Money: A Market Determined Demand Deposit Rate," Federal Reserve *Bulletin*, October 1967. J. A. Cacy, "Alternative Approaches to the Analysis of the Financial Structure, *Monthly Review*, Federal Reserve Bank of Kansas City, March 1968. Richard G. Davis, "The Role of the Money Supply in Business Cycles," *Monthly Review*, Federal Reserve Bank of New York, April 1968.

Traditional methods of monetary analysis are not well suited to this task. The 'New View' in monetary economics provides a more useful analytical framework. In the new view, banks—like other financial institutions—are considered as suppliers of financial claims for the public to hold, and the public is given a significant role in determining the total amount of bank liabilities. . . . Traditional analysis . . . fails to recognize that substitution between time deposits and securities may be an important source of pro-cyclical variations in the stock of money even in the face of countercyclical central bank policy.[2]

This general argument guided the construction of an explicit model designed to emphasize the role of the public's and the banks' behavior in the determination of the money stock, bank credit and interest rates.

Kareken's paper supplements the Gramley-Chase arguments. He finds "the received money supply theory" quite inadequate. His paper is designed to improve monetary analysis by constructing a theory of an individual bank as a firm. This theory is offered as an explanation of a bank's desired balance sheet position. It also appears to form the basis of a model describing the interaction of the public's and the banks' behavior in the joint determination of the money stock, bank credit and interest rates. The whole development emphasizes somewhat suggestively the importance of the public's and banks' behavior in explanations of monetary growth. It is also designed to undermine the empirical hypotheses advanced by the Monetarist position. This is achieved by means of explicit references to specific and "obviously desirable" features of the model presented.

Cacy's article develops neither an explicit framework nor a direct critique of the basic propositions advanced by the Monetarist thesis. However, he provides a useful summary of the general position of the countercritique. The Monetarist analysis is conveniently subsumed by Cacy under a "Traditional View" which is juxtaposed to a "New View" of monetary mechanisms: "The new approach argues . . . that there is no essential difference between the manner in which the liabilities of banks and nonbank financial institutions are determined. Both types of institutions are subject in the same way to the portfolio decisions of the public."[3] The new approach is contrasted with the Traditional View, which "obscures the important role played by the public and overstates the role played by the central bank in the determination of the volume of money balances."[4] The general comparison developed by Cacy suggests quite

---

[2]Gramley-Chase, pp. 1380, 1381, 1393.

[3]Cacy, pp. 5 & 7.

[4]*Ibid.*, p. 7.

clearly to the reader that the Traditional View allegedly espoused by the Monetarist position cannot match the "realistic sense" of the New View advocated by the countercritique.

In the context of the framework developed by the critique, Davis questions some basic propositions of the Monetarist position:

> In the past five to ten years, however, there has come into increasing prominence a group of economists who would like to go considerably beyond the simple assertion that the behavior of money is a significant factor influencing the behavior of the economy. . . . In order to bring a few of the issues into sharper focus, this article will take a look at some evidence for the 'money supply' view. . . .
>
> It confines itself to examining the historical relationship between monetary cycles and cycles in general business. The article concludes that the relationship between these two kinds of cycles does not, in fact, provide any real support for the view that the behavior of money is the predominant determinant of fluctuations in business activity. Moreover, the historical relationship between cycles in money and in business cannot be used to demonstrate that monetary policy is, in its effects, so long delayed and so uncertain as to be an unsatisfactory countercyclical weapon.[5]

AN EXAMINATION OF THE ISSUES

A careful survey of the countercritique yielded the following results. The Gramley-Chase, Kareken, and Cacy papers parade the New View in order to question the status of empirical theories used by the Monetarist critique in its examination of monetary policy. The Davis paper questions quite directly, on the other hand, the existence and relevance of the evidence in support of the Monetarist position, and constitutes a direct assault on the Monetarist critique. The others constitute an indirect assault which attempts to devalue the critique's analysis, and thus to destroy its central propositions concerning the role of money and monetary policy.

The indirect assault on the Monetarist position by Gramley-Chase, Kareken and Cacy requires a clarification concerning the nature of the New View. A program of analysis must be clearly distinguished from a research strategy and an array of specific conjectures.[6] All three aspects

---

[5] Davis, pp. 63–64.

[6] These three aspects of the New View will subsequently be elaborated more fully. Their program of analysis refers to the application of relative price theory to analysis of financial markets and financial institutions. Their research strategy refers to a decision to initiate analysis in the context of a most general framework. Their specific conjectures refer to propositions concerning the causes of fluctuation of monetary growth and propositions about proper interpretation of policy.

are usually mixed together in a general description. It is important to understand, however, that neither research strategy nor specific empirical conjectures are logical implications of the general program. The explicit separation of the three aspects is crucial for a proper assessment of the New View.

Section A examines some general characteristics of the countercritique's reliance on the New View. It shows the New View to consist of a program acceptable to all economists, a research strategy rejected by the Monetarist position, and an array of specific conjectures advanced without analytical or empirical substantiation. Also, not a single paper of the countercritique developed a relevant assessment of the Monetarist's empirical theories or central propositions.

In sections B and C detailed examinations of specific conjectures centered on rival explanations of cyclical fluctuations of monetary growth are presented. The direct assault on the Monetarist position by Davis is discussed in some detail in Section D. This section also states the crucial propositions of the Monetarist thesis in order to clarify some aspects of this position. This reformulation reveals that the reservations assembled by Davis are quite innocuous. They provide no analytical or empirical case against the Monetarist thesis. Conjectures associated with the interpretation of monetary policy (the "indicator problem") are presented in Section E.

A. THE NEW VIEW

The countercritique has apparently been decisively influenced by programmatic elaborations originally published by Gurley-Shaw and James Tobin.[7] The program is most faithfully reproduced by Cacy, and it also shaped the arguments guiding the model construction by Kareken and Gramley-Chase. The New View, as a program, is a sensible response to a highly unsatisfactory state of monetary analysis inherited in the late 1950's. A money and banking syndrome perpetuated by textbooks obstructed the application of economic analysis to the financial sector. At most, this inherited literature contained only suggestive pieces of analysis. It lacked a meaningful theory capable of explaining the responses of the monetary system to policy actions or to influences emanating from the real sector. The New View proposed a systematic application of economic analysis, in particular an application of relative price theory, to the array of financial intermediaries, their assets and liabilities.

---

[7] John G. Gurley and Edward F. Shaw, *Money in a Theory of Finance*, (Washington: Brookings Institute, 1960). James Tobin, "Commercial Banks as Creators of Money," *Banking and Monetary Studies*, ed. Deane Carson (R. D. Irwin, 1963).

This program is most admirable and incontestable, but it cannot explain the conflict revealed by critique and countercritique. The Monetarist approach accepted the general principle of applying relative price theory to the analysis of monetary processes. In addition, this approach used the suggestions and analytical pieces inherited from past efforts in order to develop some specific hypotheses which do explain portions of our observable environment. The New Viewers' obvious failure to recognize the limited content of their programmatic statements only contributes to maintenance of the conflict.

A subtle difference appears, however, in the research strategy. The New View was introduced essentially as a generalized approach, including a quite formal exposition, but with little attempt at specific structuring and empirical content. The most impressive statements propagated by the New View were crucially influenced by the sheer formalism of its exposition. In the context of the New View's almost empty form, little remains to differentiate one object from another. For instance, in case one only admits the *occurrence* of marginal costs and marginal yields associated with the actions of every household, firm, and financial intermediary, one will necessarily conclude that banks and non-bank financial intermediaries are restricted in size by the same economic forces and circumstances. In such a context there is truly no essential difference between the determination of bank and non-bank intermediary liabilities, or between banks and non-bank intermediaries or between money and other financial assets.

The strong impressions conveyed by the New View thus result from the relative emptiness of the formulation which has been used to elaborate their position. In the context of the formal world of the New View, "almost everything is almost like everything else". This undifferentiated state of affairs is not, however, a property of our observable world. It is only a property of the highly formal discussion designed by the New View to overcome the unsatisfactory state of monetary analysis still prevailing in the late 1950's or early 1960's.[8]

---

[8] Adequate analysis of the medium of exchange function of money, or of the conditions under which inside money becomes a component of wealth, was obstructed by the programmatic state of the New View. The useful analysis of the medium-of-exchange function depends on a decisive rejection of the assertion that "everything is almost like everything else." This analysis requires proper recognition that the marginal cost of information concerning qualities and properties of assets differs substantially between assets, and that the marginal cost of readjusting asset positions depends on the assets involved. The analysis of the wealth position of inside money requires recognition of the marginal productivity of inside money to the holder. Adequate attention to the relevant differences between various cost or yield functions associated with different assets or positions is required by both problems. The blandness of the New View's standard program cannot cope with these issues. The reader may consult a preliminary approach to the analysis of the medium of exchange function in the paper by Karl Brunner and Allan H. Meltzer, in the *Journal of*

Two sources of the conflict have been recognized thus far. The Monetarists' research strategy was concerned quite directly with the construction of empirical theories about the monetary system, whereas the New View indulged, for a lengthy interval, in very general programmatic excursions. Moreover, the New Viewers apparently misconstrued their program as being a meaningful theory about our observable environment. This logical error contributed to a third source of the persistent conflict.

The latter source arises from the criticism addressed by the New Viewers to the Monetarists' theories of money supply processes. Three of the papers exploit the logically dubious but psychologically effective juxtaposition between a "New View" and a "Traditional View." In doing this they fail to distinguish between the inherited state of monetary system analysis typically reflected by the money and banking textbook syndrome and the research output of economists advocating the Monetarist thesis. This distinction is quite fundamental. Some formal analogies misled the New Viewers and they did not recognize the logical difference between detailed formulations of empirical theories on the one side and haphazard pieces of unfinished analysis on the other side.[9]

A related failure accompanies this logical error. There is not the slightest attempt to assess alternative hypotheses or theories by systematic exposure to observations from the real world. It follows, therefore, that the countercritique scarcely analyzed the empirical theories advanced by the Monetarist critique and consequently failed to understand the major implications of these theories.

Finance, 1964, listed in footnote 9. He should also consult for both issues the important book by Boris Pesek and Thomas Saving, *Money, Wealth and Economic Theory*, The Macmillan Company, New York, 1967, or the paper by Harry Johnson, "Inside Money, Outside Money, Income, Wealth and Welfare in Monetary Theory," to be published in *The Journal of Money, Credit and Banking*, December 1968.

[9] As examples of the empirical work performed by the Monetarists, the reader should consult the following works: Milton Friedman and Anna Jacobson Schwartz, *A Monetary History of the United States, 1867-1960*, (Princeton: Princeton University Press, 1963). Philip Cagan, *Determinants and Effects of Changes in the Stock of Money*, (Columbia: Columbia University Press, 1965). Karl Brunner and Allan H. Meltzer, "Some Further Investigations of Demand and Supply Functions for Money," *Journal of Finance*, Volume XIX, May 1964. Karl Brunner and Allan H. Meltzer, "A Credit-Market Theory of the Money Supply and an Explanation of Two Puzzles in U.S. Monetary Policy," *Essays in Honor of Marco Fanno*, 1966, Padova, Italy. Karl Brunner and Robert Crouch, "Money Supply Theory and British Monetary Experience, *Methods of Operations Research III—Essays in Honor of Wilhelm Krelle*, ed. Rudolf Henn (Published in Meisenheim, Germany, by Anton Hain, 1966). Karl Brunner, "A Schema for the Supply Theory of Money," *International Economic Review*, 1961. Karl Brunner and Allan H. Meltzer, "An Alternative Approach to the Monetary Mechanism," *Subcommittee on Domestic Finance, Committee on Banking and Currency, House of Representatives*, August 17, 1964.

For instance, they failed to recognize the role assigned by the Monetarist view to banks' behavior and the public's preferences in the monetary process. The objection raised by the New View that "the formula [expressing a basic framework used to formulate the hypothesis] obscures the important role played by the public" has neither analytical basis nor meaning. In fact, the place of the public's behavior was discussed in the Monetarist hypotheses in some detail. Moreover, the same analysis discussed the conditions under which the public's behavior dominates movements of the money stock and bank credit.[10] It also yielded information about the response of bank credit, money stock and time deposits to changes in ceiling rates, or to changes in the speed with which banks adjust their deposit-supply conditions to evolving market situations. Every single aspect of the banks' or the public's behavior emphasized by the countercritique has been analyzed by the Monetarist's hypotheses in terms which render the results empirically assessable. Little remains, consequently, of the suggestive countercritique assembled in the papers by Gramley-Chase, Kareken and Cacy.[11]

[10]The reader will find this analysis in the following papers: Karl Brunner and Allan H. Meltzer, "Liquidity Traps for Money, Bank Credit, and Interest Rates," *Journal of Political Economy*, April 1968. Karl Brunner and Allan H. Meltzer, "A Credit-Market Theory of the Money Supply and an Explanation of Two Puzzles in U.S. Monetary Policy," *Essays in Honor of Marco Fanno*, Padova, Italy, 1966.

[11]The reader is, of course, aware that these assertions require analytic substantiation. Such substantiation cannot be supplied within the confines of this article. But the reader could check for himself. If he finds, in the context of the countercritique, an analysis of the Monetarists' major hypotheses, an examination of implication, and exposure to observations, I would have to withdraw my statements. A detailed analysis of the banks' and the public's role in the money supply, based on two different hypotheses previously reported in our papers will be developed in our forthcoming books. This analysis, by its very existence, falsifies some major objections made by Cacy or Gramley-Chase. Much of their criticism is either innocuous or fatuous. Gramley-Chase indulge, for instance, in modality statements, i.e. statements obtained from other statements by prefixing a modality qualifier like "maybe" or "possibly." The result of qualifying an empirical statement always yields a statement which is necessarily ture, but also quite uninformative. The modality game thus yields logically pointless but psychologically effective sentences. Cacy manages, on the other hand, some astonishing assertions. The New View is credited with the discovery that excess reserves vary over time. He totally disregards the major contributions to the analysis of excess reserves emanating from the Monetarists' research. A detailed analysis of excess reserves was developed by Milton Friedman and Anna Schwartz in the book mentioned in footnote 9. The reader should also note the work by George Morrison, *Liquidity Preferences of Commercial Banks*, (Chicago: University of Chicago Press, 1966), and the study by Peter Frost, "Banks' Demand for Excess Reserves," an unpublished dissertation submitted to the University of California at Los Angeles, 1966. The classic example of an innocuous achievement was supplied by Cacy with the assertion: ". . . the actual volume of money balances determined by competitive market forces may or may not be equal to the upper

B. A MONETARIST EXAMINATION OF THE NEW VIEW'S MONEY SUPPLY THEORY

Three sources of the conflict have been discussed thus far. Two sources were revealed as logical misconstruals, involving inadequate construction and assessment of empirical theories. A third source pertains to legitimate differences in research strategy. These three sources do not explain all major aspects of the conflict. Beyond the differences in research strategy and logical misconceptions, genuinely substantive issues remain. Some comments of protagonists advocating the New View should probably be interpreted as conjectures about hypotheses to be expected from their research strategy. It should be clearly understood that such conjectures are not logical implications of the guiding framework. Instead, they are pragmatic responses to the general emphasis associated with this approach.

A first conjecture suggests that the money stock and bank credit are dominated by the public's and the banks' behavior. It is suggested, therefore, that cyclical fluctuations of monetary growth result primarily from the responses of banks and the public to changing business conditions. A second conjecture naturally supplements the above assertions. It is contended that the money stock is a thoroughly "untrustworthy guide to monetary policy."

Articles by Gramley-Chase and Kareken attempt to support these conjectures with the aid of more explicit analytical formulations allegedly expressing the general program of the New View. The paper contributed by Gramley-Chase has been critically examined in detail on another occasion,[12] and only some crucial aspects relevant for our present purposes will be considered at this point. Various aspects of the first conjecture are examined in this and the next section. The second conjecture is examined in sections D and E.

A detailed analysis of the Gramley-Chase model demonstrates that it implies the following reduced form equations explaining the money stock (M) and bank credit (E) in terms of the extended monetary

---

limit established by the central bank." (p. 8). Indeed, we knew this before the New View or Any View, just as we always knew that "it may or may not rain tomorrow." The reader should note that similar statements were produced by other authors with all the appearances of meaningful elaborations.

[12]The reader may consult my chapter "Federal Reserve Policy and Monetary Analysis" in *Indicators and Targets of Monetary Policy*, ed., by Karl Brunner, to be published by Chandler House Publishing Co., San Francisco. This book also contains the original article by Gramley-Chase. Further contributions by Patric H. Hendershott and Robert Weintraub survey critically the issues raised by the Gramley-Chase paper.

$$M = g(B^e, Y, c) \qquad g_1 > 0 < g_2,$$
$$E = h(B^e, Y, c) \qquad h_1 > 0 > h_2, \text{ and } h_1 > g_1 \text{ }^{13}$$

base (B^e), the level of economic activity expressed by national income at current prices (Y), and the ceiling rate on time deposits (c).[14]

The Gramley-Chase model implies that monetary policy does affect the money stock and bank credit. It also implies that the money stock responds *positively* and bank credit *negatively* to economic activity. This model thus differs from the Monetarist hypotheses which imply that both bank credit and the money stock respond *positively* to economic activity. The Gramley-Chase model also implies that the responses of both the money stock and bank credit to monetary actions are independent of the general scale of the public's and the banks' interest elasticities. Uniformly large or small interest elasticities yield the same response in the money stock or bank credit to a change in the monetary base.

A detailed discussion of the implications derivable from a meaningfully supplemented Gramley-Chase model is not necessary at this point. We are foremost interested in the relation between this model and the propositions mentioned in the previous paragraph. The first proposition can be interpreted in two different ways. According to one interpretation, it could mean that the marginal multipliers g_i and h_i ($i = 1,2$) are functions of the banks' and the public's response patterns expressing various types of substitution relations between different assets. This interpretation is, however, quite innocuous and yields no differentiation relative to the questioned hypotheses of the Monetarist position.

A second interpretation suggests that the growth rate of the money stock is dominated by the second component (changes in income) of the differential expression:

$$\Delta M = g_1 \ \Delta B^e + g_2 \ \Delta Y$$

This result is not actually implied by the Gramley-Chase model, but it is certainly consistent with the model. However, in order to derive the desired result, their model must be supplemented with special assumptions about the relative magnitude of g_1 and g_2, and also about the comparative cyclical variability of ΔB^e and ΔY. This information has not been provided by the authors.

Most interesting is another aspect of the model which was not clarified

---

[13]In the Gramley-Chase model, g_3 and h_3 are indeterminant.

[14]This implication was demonstrated in my paper listed in footnote 12. The monetary base is adjusted for the accumulated sum of reserves liberated from or impounded into required reserves by changes in requirement ratios.

by the authors. Their model implies that policymakers could easily avoid procyclical movements in ΔM. This model exemplifying the New View thus yields little justification for the conjectures of its proponents.

A central property of the Gramley-Chase model must be considered in the light of the programmatic statements characterizing the New View. Gramley-Chase do not differentiate between the public's asset supply to banks and the public's demand for money. This procedure violates the basic program of the New View, namely, to apply economic analysis to an array of financial assets and financial institutions. Economic analysis implies that the public's asset supply and money demand are distinct, and not identical behavior patterns. This difference in behavior patterns is clearly revealed by different responses of desired money balances and desired asset supply to specific stimuli in the environment. For instance, an increase in the expected real yield on real capital *raises* the public's asset supply but *lowers* the public's money demand. It follows thus that a central analytical feature of the Gramley-Chase model violates the basic and quite relevant program of the New View.

Kareken's construction shares this fundamental analytical flaw with the Gramley-Chase model, but this is not the only problem faced by his analysis. The Kareken analysis proceeds on two levels. First, he derives a representative bank's desired balance sheet position. For this purpose he postulates wealth maximization subject to the bank's balance sheet relation between assets and liabilities, and subject to reserve requirements on deposits. On closer examination, this analysis is only applicable to a monopoly bank with no conversion of deposits into currency or reserve flows to other banks. In order to render the analysis relevant for a representative bank in the world of reality, additional constraints would have to be introduced which modify the results quite substantially. It is also noteworthy that the structural properties assigned by Kareken to the system of market relations are logically inconsistent with the implications one can derive from the author's analysis of firm behavior developed on the first level of his investigation.

This disregard for the construction of an economic theory relevant for the real world is carried into the second level of analysis where the author formulates a system of relations describing the joint determination of interest rates, bank credit, and money stock. A remarkable feature of the Kareken model is that it yields no implications whatsoever about the response of the monetary system to actions of the Federal Reserve. It can say nothing, as it stands, about either open market operations or about discount rate and reserve requirement actions. This model literally implies, for instance, that the money stock and the banking system's deposit liabilities do not change as a result of any change in reserve requirement ratios.

None of the conjectures advanced by the countercritique concerning the behavior of the money stock and the role of monetary policy find analytical support in Kareken's analysis. To the extent that anything is implied, it would imply that monetary policy operating directly on bank reserves or a mysterious rate of return on reserves dominates the volume of deposits—a practially subversive position for a follower of the New View.[15]

C. ALTERNATIVE EXPLANATIONS OF CYCLICAL FLUCTUATIONS IN MONETARY GROWTH

The examination thus far in this article has shown that even the most explicit formulation (Gramley-Chase) of the countercritique, allegedly representing the New View with respect to monetary system analysis, does assign a significant role to monetary policy. This examination also argued that the general emphasis given by the New View to the public's and the banks' behavior in determination of the money stock and bank credit does not differentiate its product from analytical developments arising from the Monetarist approach. It was also shown that the only explicit formulation advanced by the New Viewers does not provide a sufficient basis for their central conjectures. It is impossible to derive the proposition from the Gramley-Chase model that the behavior of the public and banks, rather than Federal Reserve actions, dominated movements in the money supply. But the declaration of innocence by the countercritique on behalf of the monetary authorities with respect to cyclical fluctuations of monetary growth still requires further assessment.

The detailed arguments advanced to explain the observed cyclical fluctuations of monetary growth differ substantially among the contributors to the countercritique. Gramley-Chase maintain that changing business conditions modify relative interest rates, and thus induce countercyclical movements in the time deposit ratio. These movements in demand and time deposits generate cyclical fluctuations in monetary growth. On the other hand, Cacy develops an argument used many years ago by

[15] Two direct objections made to Brunner-Meltzer analysis by Kareken should be noted. He finds that the questioned hypotheses do not contain "a genuine supply function" of deposits. Accepting Kareken's terminology, this is true, but neither does the Gramley-Chase model contain such a supply function. But the objection has no evidential value anyway. If a hypothesis were judged unsatisfactory because some aspects are omitted, all hypotheses are "unsatisfactory." Moreover, the cognitive status of an empirical hypothesis does not improve simply because an "analytical underpinning" has been provided. Kareken also finds fault with our use of the term "money supply function." Whether or not one agrees with his terminological preferences surely does not affect the relation between observations and statements supplied by the hypothesis. And it should be clear that the status of a hypothesis depends only on this relation, and not on names attached to statements.

Wicksell and Keynes, but attributes it to the New View. He recognizes a pronounced sensitivity of the money stock to variations in the public's money demand or asset supply. These variations induce changes in credit market conditions. Banks, in turn, respond with suitable adjustments in the reserve and borrowing ratios. The money stock and bank credit consequently change in response to this mechanism.

Davis actually advances two radically different conjectures about causes of cyclical fluctuations of monetary growth. The first conjecture attributes fluctuations of monetary growth to the public's and banks' responses. Changing business conditions modify the currency ratio, the banks' borrowing ratio, and the reserve ratio. The resulting changes generate the observed movements in money. His other conjecture attributes fluctuations in monetary growth to Federal Reserve actions: "the state of business influences decisions by the monetary authorities to supply reserves and to take other actions likely to affect the money supply."[16]

The various conjectures advanced by Gramley-Chase, Cacy, and Davis in regard to causes of movements in money and bank credit can be classified into two groups. One set of conjectures traces the mechanism generating cyclical fluctuations of monetary growth to the responses of banks and the public; the behavior of monetary authorities is assigned a comparatively minor role. The other group of conjectures recognizes the predominant role of the behavior of monetary authorities.

In the following analysis the framework provided by the Monetarist view will be used to assess these conflicting conjectures. The emphasis concerning the nature of the causal mechanisms may differ between the various conjectures regarding sources of variations in money, but the following examination will be applied to an aspect common to all conjectures emphasizing the role of public and bank behavior.

In the context of the Monetarist framework, the money stock (M) is exhibited as a product of a multiplier (m) and the monetary base (B), (such that $M = mB$). This framework, without the supplementary set of hypotheses and theories bearing on the proximate determinants of money summarized by the multiplier and the base, is completely neutral with

---

[16]Davis, p. 66. One argument about monetary policy in the same paper requires clarification. Davis asserts on p. 68 that the money supply need not be the objective of policy, and "given this fact, the behavior of the rate of growth of the money supply during the period cannot be assumed to be simply and directly the result of monetary policy decisions alone". This quote asserts that the money supply is "simply and directly the result of policy alone" whenever policy uses the money supply as a target. This is in a sense correct. But the quote could easily be misinterpreted due to the ambiguity of the term "policy". This term is frequently used to designate a strategy guiding the adjustment of policy variables. It is also frequently used to refer to the behavior of the policy variables or directly to the variables as such. The quote is quite acceptable in the first sense of "policy", but thoroughly unacceptable in the second sense.

respect to the rival conjectures; it is compatible with any set of observations. This neutrality assures us that its use does not prejudge the issue under consideration. The Monetarist framework operates in the manner of a language system, able to express the implications of the completing conjectures in a uniform manner.

The first group of conjectures advanced by the countercritique (behavior of the public and banks dominates movements in money) implies that variations in monetary growth between upswings and downswings in business activity are dominated by the variations in the monetary multiplier. The second group (behavior of monetary authorities dominates movements in money) implies that, in periods with unchanged reserve requirement ratios and ceiling rates on time deposits, variations in the monetary base dominate cyclical changes in monetary growth. The movements of the monetary multiplier which are strictly attributable to the changing of requirement ratios can be separated from the total contribution of the multiplier and combined with the monetary base. With this adjustment, the second group of conjectures implies that the monetary base, supplemented by the contribution of reserve requirement changes to the multiplier, dominates variations in the money stock.

In this examination of contrasting explanations of monetary fluctuations, values of the money stock (M), the multiplier (m), and the monetary base adjusted for member bank borrowing (B) are measured at the initial and terminal month of each half business cycle (i.e., expansions and contractions) located by the National Bureau of Economic Research. We form the ratios of these values and write:

$$\frac{M_1}{M_0} = \frac{m_1}{m_0}\frac{B_1}{B_0} \; ; \; \text{ or } \; \mu = \alpha\beta$$

The subscript 1 refers to values of the terminal month and the subscript 0 to values of the initial month. These ratios were measured for each half cycle in the period March 1919 to December 1966. They were computed for two definitions of the money stock, inclusive and exclusive of time deposits, with corresponding monetary multipliers.

Kendall's rank correlation coefficients between the money stock ratios (μ) and the multiplier ratios (α), and between (μ) and the monetary base ratio (β) were computed. We denote these correlation coefficients with $\rho(\mu, \alpha)$ and $\rho(\mu, \beta)$. The implications of the two rival conjectures can now be restated in terms of the two coefficients. The first group of conjectures implies that $\rho(\mu, \alpha) > \rho(\mu, \beta)$; while the second group implies that in periods of unchanged reserve requirement ratios and ceiling rates on time deposits, the coefficient $\rho(\mu, \beta)$ exceeds the coefficient $\rho(\mu, \alpha)$. The second group implies nothing about the relation of the two coefficients in periods of changing reserve requirements and ceiling rates on time deposits. It follows, therefore, that observations yielding the inequality $\rho(\mu,\beta) > \rho(\mu,\alpha)$ disconfirm the first group and confirm the second group.

The correlations obtained are quite unambiguous. The value of $\rho(\mu,\beta)$ is .537 for the whole sample period, whereas $\rho(\mu,\alpha)$ is only .084. The half-cycle from 1929 to 1933 was omitted in the computations, because movements in the money stock and the multiplier were dominated by forces which do not discriminate between the rival conjectures under consideration. The sample period, including 1929 to 1933, still yields a substantially larger value for $\rho(\mu,\beta)$. The same pattern also holds for other subperiods. In particular, computations based on observations for 1949 to 1966 confirm the pattern observed for the whole sample period. The results thus support the second group of conjectures but not the first group. These results also suggest, however, that forces operating through the multiplier are not quite negligible. The surprisingly small correlation $\rho(\mu,\alpha)$ does not adequately reveal the operation of these forces. Their effective operation is revealed by the correlation $\rho(\mu,\beta)$, which is far from perfect, even in subperiods with constant reserve requirement ratios. This circumstance suggests that the behavior of the public and banks contributes to the cyclical movements of monetary growth. The main result at this stage is, however, the clear discrimination between the two groups of conjectures. The results are quite unambiguous on this score.

Additional information is supplied by Table 1. For each postwar cycle beginning with the downswing of 1948-49, the average annual growth rate of the money stock was computed. The expression $M = mB$ was then used to compute the contribution to the average growth rate of money from three distinct sources: (i) the behavior of monetary authorities (i.e., the monetary base and reserve requirement ratios), and the public's currency behavior, (ii) the time deposit substitution process, and, (iii) the variations in the excess reserve and borrowing ratios of commercial banks (Wicksell-Keynes mechanism).

TABLE 1

A Comparison of Alternative Contributions to the Average Annual Growth Rate of the Money Stock and Bank Credit

	Rank Correlations	
Contribution made by:	Money	Bank Credit
Public's currency and authorities' behavior	.905	.333
Time deposit substitution mechanism	.048	.381
Wicksell-Keynes mechanism	.143	−.333

Remarks: The figures listed state the rank correlation between the average growth rate of the money stock and bank credit with three different contributing sources.

The rank correlations between each contribution, and the average growth rate of the money stock over all postwar half-cycles clearly support the conclusion of the previous analysis that cyclical movements in the money stock are dominated by Federal Reserve actions.

Table 1 also presents the results of a similar examination bearing on causes of movements in bank credit. The reader should note the radical difference in the observed patterns of correlation coefficients. The behavior of monetary authorities, supplemented by the public's currency behavior, does not appear to dominate the behavior of bank credit. The three sources contributing to the growth rate of money all exerted influences of similar order on bank credit. It appears that bank credit is comparatively less exposed to the push of Federal Reserve actions than was the money stock. On the other hand, the money stock is less sensitive than bank credit to the time-deposit substitution mechanism emphasized by Gramley-Chase, and the Wicksell-Keynes mechanism suggested by Cacy. Most astonishing, however, is the *negative* association between the average growth rate of bank credit and the Wicksell-Keynes mechanism emphasized by Cacy.

It should also be noted that the average growth rate of money conforms very clearly to the business cycle. Such conformity does not hold for bank credit over the postwar half-cycles. This blurring occurred particularly in periods when the ceiling rate on time deposits was increased. These periods exhibit relatively large contributions to the growth rate of bank credit emanating from the time deposit substitution mechanism.

A regression analysis (Table 2) of the reduced form equations derived from the Gramley-Chase model confirms the central role of the monetary base in the money supply process. Estimates of the regression coefficient relating money to income are highly unstable among different sample periods, relative to the coefficient relating money to the monetary base. Furthermore, estimates of regression coefficients relating money to income occur in some periods with signs which contradict the proposition of Gramley-Chase and Cacy, or exhibit a very small statistical significance. These diverse patterns of coefficients do not occur for the estimates of coefficients relating money and the monetary base. It is also noteworthy that the average growth rate of the monetary base (adjusted for changes in reserve requirement ratios), over the upswings, exceeds without exception the average growth rate of adjacent downswings. This observation is not compatible with the contention made by Gramley-Chase that policy is countercyclical.

Additional information is supplied by Table 3, which presents some results of a spectral analysis bearing on the monetary base and its sources. Spectral analysis is a statistical procedure for decomposing a time series into seasonal, cyclical, and trend movements. After such an analysis was conducted on the monetary base and its sources, a form of correlation

TABLE 2

Regressions of the Money Supply
On the Monetary Base and Gross National Product*

	Regression Coefficients For:			
	Monetary Base		Gross National Product	
Cycle	First Differences	Log First Differences	First Differences	Log First Differences
IV/48	2.03	.77	.04	.11
to	(9.80)	(10.02)	(3.12)	(3.39)
II/53	.92	.93	.62	.65
II/53	1.75	.63	.02	.07
to	(1.89)	(1.96)	(1.02)	(1.23)
III/57	.44	.45	.26	.30
III/57	4.59	1.66	.06	.19
to	(11.76)	(11.81)	(5.10)	(5.34)
II/60	.97	.97	.86	.67
II/60	2.76	1.08	-.01	-.03
to	(7.56)	(8.54)	(-.33)	(-.27)
III/65	.87	.89	-.08	-.07

*The monetary base was adjusted for reserve requirement changes and shifts in deposits. All data are quarterly averages of seasonally adjusted figures. The first entry in a column for each cycle is the regression coefficient, t-statistics are in parentheses, and partial correlation coefficients are below the t-statistics.

analysis was run between movements in the monetary base and movements in its various sources. The results of this procedure (Table 3) indicate that movements in Federal Reserve credit dominate seasonal and cyclical movements in the monetary base.

In summary, preliminary investigations yield no support for the contention that the behavior of banks and the public dominates cyclical movements in the money stock. The conjectures advanced by Gramley-Chase or Cacy are thus disconfirmed, whereas Davis' second conjecture that fluctuations in monetary growth may be attributed to Federal Reserve actions seems substantially more appropriate. However, further investigations are certainly useful.

D. RELEVANCE OF MONEY AND MONETARY ACTIONS WITH RESPECT TO ECONOMIC ACTIVITY

At present, a broad consensus accepts the relevance of money and monetary policy with respect to economic activity. But this consensus concerning the relevance of money emerges from two substantially different views about the nature of the transmission mechanism. One

TABLE 3

*Spectral Correlation Between the Monetary Base,
Federal Reserve Credit and Other Sources of the Base*

| | **Spectral Correlation Between** | |
Period in Months	Monetary Base and Federal Reserve Credit	Monetary Base and Other Sources of the Base
∞	.65	.24
120	.69	.61
60	.74	.71
40	.74	.45
30	.73	.25
24	.71	.18
20	.60	.11
17.14	.43	.11
15	.51	.07
13.33	.82	.48
12	.94	.71
6	.91	.21
4	.92	—
3	.90	—

Remarks: The monetary base equals Federal Reserve Credit plus other sources of the base. The spectral analysis is based on first differences between adjacent months. The data used were not seasonally adjusted.

view is the Keynesian conception (not to be confused with Keynes' view), enshrined in standard formulations of the income-expenditure framework. In this view, the interest rate is the main link between money and economic activity. The other view rejects the traditional separation of economic theory into parts: national income analysis (macro economics) and price theory (micro economics). According to this other view, output and employment are explained by a suitable application of relative price theory. With regard to discussions of the impact of money and monetary actions on economic activity, this latter view has been termed the Monetarist position. This position may be divided into the weak Monetarist thesis and the strong Monetarist thesis. In a sense, both the New View and the Monetarist extension of the "traditional view" are represented in the weak Monetarist position.

The following discussions develop the weak and the strong Monetarist thesis. The weak thesis is compared with some aspects of the income-expenditure approach to the determination of national economic activity. The strong thesis supplements the weak thesis with special assumptions about our environment, in order to establish the role of monetary forces in the business cycle.

1. The Weak Monetarist Thesis. According to the weak Monetarist thesis, monetary impulses are transmitted to the economy by a relative price process which operates on money, financial assets (and liabilities), real assets, yields on assets and the production of new assets, liabilities and consumables. The general nature of this process has been described on numerous occasions and may be interpreted as evolving from ideas developed by Knut Wicksell, Irving Fisher, and John Maynard Keynes.[17]

The operation of relative prices between money, financial assets, and real assets may be equivalently interpreted as the working of an interest rate mechanism (prices and yields of assets are inversely related). Monetary impulses are thus transmitted by the play of interest rates over a vast array of assets. Variations in interest rates change relative prices of existing assets, relative to both yields and the supply prices of new production. Acceleration or deceleration of monetary impulses are thus converted by the variation of relative prices, or interest rates, into increased or reduced production, and subsequent revisions in the supply prices of current output.

This general conception of the transmission mechanism has important implications which conflict sharply with the Keynesian interpretation of monetary mechanisms expressed by standard income-expenditure formulations.[18] In the context of standard income-expenditure analysis, fiscal actions are considered to have a "direct effect" on economic activity, whereas monetary actions are considered to have only an "indirect effect." Furthermore, a constant budget deficit has no effect on interest rates in a Keynesian framework, in spite of substantial accumulation of outstanding government debt when a budget deficit continually occurs. And lastly, the operation of interest rates on investment decisions has usually been

[17]The reader may consult the following studies on this aspect: Milton Friedman and David Meiselman, "The Relative Stability of Monetary Velocity and the Investment Multiplier in the United States, 1897–1958," in *Stabilization Policies*, prepared by the Commission on Money and Credit, Englewood Cliffs, 1963. The paper listed in footnote 21 by James Tobin should also be consulted. Harry Johnson, "Monetary Theory and Policy," *American Economic Review*, June 1962. Karl Brunner, "The Report of the Commission on Money and Credit," *The Journal of Political Economy*, December 1961. Karl Brunner, "Some Major Problems of Monetary Theory," *Proceedings of the American Economic Association*, May 1961. Karl Brunner and Allan H. Meltzer, "The Role of Financial Institutions in the Transmission Mechanism," *Proceedings of the American Economic Association*, May 1963. Karl Brunner, "The Relative Price Theory of Money, Output, and Employment," unpublished manuscript based on a paper presented at the Midwestern Economic Association Meetings, April 1967.

[18]The paper on "The Effect of Monetary Policy on Expenditures in Specific Sectors of the Economy," presented by Dr. Sherman Maisel at the meetings organized by the American Bankers Association in September 1967, exemplifies very clearly the inherited Keynesian position. The paper will be published in a special issue of the *Journal of Political Economy*.

rationalized with the aid of considerations based on the effects of borrowing costs.

These aspects of the income-expenditure approach may be evaluated within the framework of the weak Monetarist thesis. The effects of fiscal actions are also transmitted by the relative price mechanism. Fiscal impulses, i.e., Government spending, taxing, and borrowing, operate just as "indirectly" as monetary impulses, and there is no *a priori* reason for believing that their speed of transmission is substantially greater than that of monetary impulses. The relative price conception of the transmission mechanism also implies that a constant budget deficit exerts a continuous influence on economic activity through persistent modifications in relative prices of financial and real assets. Lastly, the transmission of monetary impulses is not dominated by the relative importance of borrowing costs. In the process, marginal costs of liability extension interact with marginal returns from acquisitions of financial and real assets. But interest rates on financial assets not only affect the marginal cost of liability extension, but also influence the substitution between financial and real assets. This substitution modifies prices of real assets relative to their supply prices and forms a crucial linkage of the monetary mechanisms; this linkage is usually omitted in standard income-expenditure analysis.

The description of monetary mechanisms in Davis' article approaches quite closely the notion developed by the weak Monetarist thesis. This approximation permits a useful clarification of pending issues. However, the criticisms and objections advanced by Davis do not apply to the weak Monetarist position. They are addressed to another thesis, which might be usefully labeled the *strong Monetarist thesis*.

2. The Strong Monetarist Thesis. If the theoretical framework of the weak Monetarist thesis is supplemented with additional and special hypotheses, the *strong Monetarist thesis* is obtained. An outline of the strong thesis may be formulated in terms of three sets of forces operating simultaneously on the pace of economic activity. For convenience, they may be grouped into monetary forces, fiscal forces, and other forces. The latter include technological and organizational innovation, revisions in supply prices induced by accruing information and expectation adjustments, capital accumulation, population changes and other related factors or processes.

All three sets of forces are acknowledged by the strong thesis to affect the pace of economic activity via the relative price process previously outlined. Moreover, the strong Monetarist point of view advances the crucial thesis that the variability of monetary forces (properly weighted with respect to their effect on economic activity) exceeds the variability of fiscal forces and other forces (properly weighted). It is argued further that major variabilities occurring in a subset of the other forces (e.g., expectations and revisions of supply prices induced by information arrival) are conditioned by the observed variability of monetary forces. The conjecture thus involves a comparison of monetary variability with the variability of fiscal forces and independent "other forces." According to the thesis under consideration, the variability of monetary impulses is also large relative to the speed at which the economy absorbs the impact of environmental changes. This predominance of variability in monetary impulses implies that pronounced accelerations in monetary forces are followed subsequently by accelerations in the pace of economic activity, and that pronounced decelerations in monetary forces are followed later by retardations in economic activity.

The analysis of the monetary dynamics, using the relative price process, is accepted by both the weak and the strong Monetarist theses. This analysis implies that the regularity of the observed association between accelerations and decelerations of monetary forces and economic activity depends on the relative magnitude of monetary accelerations (or decelerations). The same analysis also reveals the crucial role of changes in the rate of change (second differences) of the money stock in explanations of fluctuations in output and employment. It implies that any pronounced deceleration, occurring at any rate of monetary growth, retards total spending. It is thus impossible to state whether any particular monetary growth, say a 10 per cent annual rate, is expansionary with respect to economic activity, until one knows the previous growth rate. The monetary dynamics of the Monetarist thesis also explains the simultaneous occurrence of permanent price-inflation and fluctuations in output and employment observable in some countries.

The nature and the variability of the "Friedman lag" may also be analyzed within the framework of the Monetarist thesis. This lag measures the interval between a change in sign of the *second* difference in the money stock and the subsequent turning point located by the National Bureau. In general, the lag at an upper turning point will be shorter, the greater the absorption speed of the economy, and the sharper the deceleration of monetary impulses relative to the movement of fiscal forces and other forces. Variability in the *relative acceleration* or deceleration of monetary forces necessarily generates the variability observed in the Friedman lag.

What evidence may be cited on behalf of the strong Monetarist thesis? Every major inflation provides support for the thesis, particularly in cases of substantial variations of monetary growth. The attempt at stabilization in the Confederacy during the Civil War forms an impressive piece of evidence in this respect. The association between monetary and economic accelerations or decelerations has also been observed by the Federal

Reserve Bank of St. Louis.[19]   Observations from periods with divergent movements of monetary and fiscal forces provide further evidence. For instance, such periods occurred immediately after termination of World War II, from the end of 1947 to the fall of 1948, and again in the second half of 1966.   In all three cases, monetary forces prevailed over fiscal forces.   The evidence adduced here and on other occasions does not "prove" the strong Monetarist thesis, but does establish its merit for serious consideration.

Davis' examination is therefore welcomed.   His objections are summarized by the following points: (a) observations of the persistent association between money and income do not permit an inference of causal direction from money to income; (b) the timing relation between money and economic activity expressed by the Friedman lag yields no evidence in support of the contention that variations in monetary growth cause fluctuations in economic activity; (c) the correlation found in cycles of moderate amplitude between magnitudes of monetary and economic changes was quite unimpressive; (d) the length of the Friedman lag does not measure the interval between emission of monetary impulse and its ultimate impact on economic activity. Furthermore, the variability of this lag is due to the simultaneous operation and interaction of monetary and non-monetary forces.

Davis' first comment (a) is of course quite true and well known in the logic of science.   It is impossible to derive (logically) causal statements or any general hypotheses from observations.   But we can use such observations to confirm or disconfirm such statements and hypotheses.   Davis particularly emphasizes that the persistent association between money and income could be attributed to a causal influence running from economic activity to money.

Indeed it could, but our present state of knowledge rejects the notion that the observed association is essentially due to a causal influence from income on money.   Evidence refuting such a notion was presented in Section C.   The existence of a mutual interaction over the shorter-run between money and economic activity, however, must be fully acknowledged.   Yet, this interaction results from the conception guiding policymakers which induces them to accelerate the monetary base whenever pressures on interest rates mount, and to decelerate the monetary base when these pressures wane.   Admission of a mutual interaction does not dispose of the strong Monetarist thesis.   This interaction, inherent in the weak thesis, is quite consistent with the strong position and has no disconfirming value.   To the contrary, it offers an explanation for the occurrence of the predominant variability of monetary forces.

[19] *U.S. Financial Data*, Federal Reserve Bank of St. Louis, week ending February 14, 1968.   Also see "Money Supply and Time Deposits, 1914–1964" in the September 1964 issue of this *Review*.

The same logical property applies to Davis' second argument (b). The timing relation expressed by the Friedman lag, in particular the chronological precedence of turning points in monetary growth over turning points in economic activity, can probably be explained by the influence of business conditions on the money supply. Studies in money supply theory strongly suggest this thesis and yield evidence on its behalf. The cyclical pattern of the currency ratio, and the strategy typically pursued by monetary policymakers explain this lead of monetary growth. And again, such explanation of the timing relation does not bear negatively on the strong conjecture.

The objection noted under Davis' point (c) is similarly irrelevant. His observations actually confirm the strong thesis. The latter implies that the correlation between amplitude of monetary and income changes is itself correlated with the magnitude of monetary accelerations or decelerations. A poor correlation in cycles of moderate amplitude, therefore, yields no discriminating evidence on the validity of the strong thesis. Moreover, observations describing occurrences are more appropriate relative to the formulated thesis than correlation measures. For instance, observations tending to disconfirm the strong Monetarist thesis would consist of occurrences of pronounced monetary accelerations or decelerations which are *not followed* by accelerated or retarded movements of economic activity.

Point (d) still remains to be considered. Once again, his observation does not bear on the strong Monetarist thesis. Davis properly cautions readers about the interpretation of the Friedman lag. The variability of this lag is probably due to the interaction of monetary and non-monetary forces, or to changes from cycle to cycle in the relative variability of monetary growth. But again, this does not affect the strong thesis. The proper interpretation of the Friedman lag, as the interval between reversals in the rate of monetary impulses and their prevalence over all other factors simultaneously operating on economic activity, usefully clarifies a concept introduced into our discussions. This clarification provides, however, no relevant evidence bearing on the questioned hypotheses.

In summary, the arguments developed by Davis do not yield any substantive evidence against the strong Monetarist thesis. Moreover, the discussion omits major portions of the evidence assembled in support of this position.[20]

[20]Milton Friedman's summary of the evidence in the *Forty-fourth Annual Report of the National Bureau of Economic Research* is important in this respect. Davis overlooks in particular the evidence accumulated in studies of the money supply mechanism which bears on the issue raised by point (a) in the text. A persistent and uniform association between money and economic activity, in spite of large changes in the structure of money supply processes, yields evidence in support of the Monetarist theses.

E. COUNTERCYCLICAL POLICY AND THE INTERPRETATION OF MONETARY POLICY

The usual assertion of the New View, attributing fluctuations of monetary growth to the public's and the banks' behavior, assumed a strategic role in the countercritique. The countercritique denied, furthermore, that monetary actions have a major impact on economic activity. With the crumbling of these two bastions, the monetary policymakers' interpretation of their own behavior becomes quite vulnerable. In a previous section, the substantial contribution of the monetary base to the fluctuations of monetary growth has been demonstrated. These facts, combined with repeated assertions that monetary policy has been largely countercyclical, suggest the existence of a pronounced discrepancy between actual behavior of the monetary authorities and their interpretation of this behavior.

A crucial question bearing on this issue pertains to the proper measure summarizing actual behavior of the monetary authorities. Two major facts should be clearly recognized. First, the monetary base consists of "money" directly issued by the authorities, and every issue of base money involves an action of the monetary authorities. This holds irrespective of their knowledge about it, or their motivation and aims. Second, variations in the base, extended by suitable adjustments to incorporate changing reserve requirement ratios, are the single most important factor influencing the behavior of the money stock. And this second point applies irrespective of whether Federal Reserve authorities are aware of it or wish it to be, or whatever their motivations or aims are. Their actual behavior, and not their motivations or aims, influences the monetary system and the pace of economic activity. Thus, actual changes in the monetary base are quite meaningful and appropriate measures of actual behavior of monetary authorities.[21]

The information presented in Table 4 supports the conjecture that

---

The reader should also consult chapter 13 of the book by Milton Friedman and Anna Schwartz listed in footnote 9; *Studies in the Quantity Theory of Money*, edited by Milton Friedman, University of Chicago Press, 1956; and a doctoral dissertation by Michael W. Keran, "Monetary Policy and the Business Cycle in Postwar Japan," Ph.D. thesis at the University of Minnesota, March 1966, to be published as a chapter of a book edited by David Meiselman.

[21] The reader may also be assured by the following statement: ". . . monetary policy refers particularly to determination of the supply of (the government's) demand debt . . ." This demand debt coincides with the monetary base. The quote is by James Tobin, a leading architect of the New View, on p. 148 of his contribution to the Commission on Money and Credit, "An Essay on Principles of Debt Management," in *Fiscal and Debt Management Policies*, Prentice-Hall, Englewood Cliffs, 1963.

monetary policymakers' interpretation of their own behavior has no systematic positive association with their actual behavior. Table 4 was constructed on the basis of the scores assigned to changes in policies, according to the interpretation of the Federal Open Market Committee.[22] Positive scores were associated with each session of the FOMC which decided to make policy easier, more expansionary, less restrictive, less tight, etc., and negative scores indicate decisions to follow a tighter, less expansionary, more restrictive course. The scores varied between plus and minus one, and expressed some broad ordering of the revealed magnitude of the changes.

TABLE 4

The Association between Policymakers' Interpretation of Policy, Changes in the Monetary Base and Changes in Free Reserves

Periods	Cumulative Scores of Policymakers' Interpretation over the Period	Changes in Free Reserves over the Period in $ Million	Changes in the Monetary Base over the Period in $ Million
11/49– 5/53	−4.75	−1030	+5216
6/53–11/54	+2.63	+ 286	+1321
12/54–10/55	−3.37	− 818	+ 345
11/55– 7/56	+1.12	+ 352	+ 399
8/56– 7/57	−1.00	− 44	+ 657
8/57– 7/58	+3.50	+1017	+1203
7/58– 6/59	−2.12	−1059	+ 531
7/59–12/60	+2.62	+1239	− 53
1/61–12/62	− .63	− 428	+3288

An examination of the sequence of scores easily shows that the period covered can be naturally partitioned into subperiods exhibiting an overwhelming occurrence of scores with a uniform sign. These subperiods are listed in the first column of Table 4. The second column cumulated the scores over the subperiods listed in order to yield a very rough ranking of the policymakers' posture according to their own interpretation.

Table 4 reveals that the FOMC interpreted the subperiods from August 1957 to July 1958, and from July 1959 to December 1960 as among the most expansionary policy periods. The period from November 1949 to May 1953 appears in this account as a phase of persistently tight or restrictive policy. The next two columns list the changes of two important variables during each subperiod. The third column describes changes in free reserves, and the fourth column notes changes in the monetary base.

[22]The scores were published as Appendix II to "An Alternative Approach to the Monetary Mechanism." See footnote 9.

A cursory examination of the columns immediately shows substantial differences in their broad association. The rank correlation between the various columns is most informative for our purposes.

These rank correlations are listed in Table 5. The results expose the absence of any positive association between the policymakers' own interpretation or judgement of their stance and their actual behavior, as indicated by movements in the monetary base. The correlation coefficient between the monetary base and cumulated scores has a *negative* value, suggesting that a systematic divergence between stated and actual policy (as measured by the monetary base) is probable. On the other hand, the correlation between the policymakers' descriptions of their posture,

TABLE 5

Rank Correlation Between Changes in the Monetary
Base, Changes in Free Reserves and the
Cumulated Scores of Policymakers' Interpretations

Cumulated scores and base	−.09
Cumulated scores and free reserves	+.70
Free reserves and base	−.26

and the movement of free reserves, is impressively close. This correlation confirms once again that the Federal Reserve authorities have traditionally used the volume of free reserves as an indicator to gauge and interpret prevailing monetary policies. Yet little evidence has been developed which establishes a causal chain leading from changes in free reserves to the pace of economic activity.

Another observation contained in Table 4 bears on the issue of policymakers' interpretation of their own behavior. Changes in the cumulated scores and free reserves between the periods listed always move together and are perfect in terms of direction. By comparison, the co-movement between cumulated scores and changes in the monetary base is quite haphazard; only three out of eight changes between periods move together. This degree of co-movement between cumulated scores and the monetary base could have occurred by pure chance with a probability greater than .2, whereas the probability of the perfect co-movement between cumulated scores and free reserves occurring as a matter of pure chance is less than .004. The traditional selection of free reserves or money market conditions as an indicator to interpret prevailing monetary policy and to gauge the relative thrust applied by policy, forms the major reason for the negative association (or at least random association) between stated and actual policy.

Attempts at rebuttal to the above analysis often emphasize that policymakers are neither interested in the monetary base, nor do they attach any significance to it. This argument is advanced to support the claim that the behavior of the monetary base is irrelevant for a proper examination of policymakers' intended behavior. This argument disregards, however, the facts stated earlier, namely, movements in the monetary base are under the direct control and are the sole responsibility of the monetary authorities. It also disregards the fact that actions may yield consequences which are independent of motivations shaping the actions.

These considerations are sufficient to acknowledge the relevance of the monetary base as a measure summarizing the actual behavior of monetary authorities. However, they alone are not sufficient to determine whether the base is the most reliable indicator of monetary policy. Other magnitudes such as interest rates, bank credit, and free reserves have been advanced with plausible arguments to serve as indicators. A rational procedure must be designed to determine which of the possible entities frequently used for scaling policy yields the most reliable results.

This indicator problem is still very poorly understood, mainly because of ambiguous use of economic language in most discussions of monetary policy. The term "indicator" occurs with a variety of meanings in discussions, and so do the terms "target" and "guide." The indicator problem, understood in its technical sense, is the determination of an optimal scale justifying interpretations of the authorities' actual behavior by means of comparative statements. A typical statement is that policy X is more expansionary than policy Y, or that current policy has become more (or less) expansionary. Whenever we use a comparative concept, we implicitly rely on an ordering scale.

The indicator problem has not been given adequate treatment in the literature, and the recognition of its logical structure is often obstructed by inadequate analysis. It is, for instance, not sufficient to emphasize the proposition that the money supply can be a "misleading guide to the proper interpretation of monetary policy." This proposition can be easily demonstrated for a wide variety of models and hypotheses. However, it establishes very little. The same theories usually demonstrate that the rate of interest, free reserves, or bank credit can also be very misleading guides to monetary policy. Thus, we can obtain a series of propositions about a vast array of entities, asserting that each one can be a very misleading guide to the interpretation of policy. We only reach a useless stalemate in this situation.

The usual solution to the indicator problem at the present time is a decision based on mystical insight supplemented by some impressionistic arguments. The most frequently advanced arguments emphasize that central banks operate directly on credit markets where interest rates are formed, or that the interest mechanism forms the centerpiece of the transmission process. Accordingly, in both cases market interest rates should "obviously" emerge as the relevant indicator of monetary policy.

These arguments on behalf of market interest rates are mostly supplied by economists. The monetary authorities' choice of money market conditions as an indicator evolved from a different background. But in recent years a subtle change has occurred. One frequently encounters arguments which essentially deny either the existence of the indicator problem or its rational solution. A favorite line asserts that "the world is very complex" and consequently it is impossible or inadmissible to use a single scale to interpret policy. According to this view, one has to consider and weigh many things in order to obtain a "realistic" assessment in a complicated world.

This position has little merit. The objection to a "single scale" misconstrues the very nature of the problem. Once we decide to discuss monetary policy in terms of comparative statements, an ordinal scale is required in order to provide a logical basis for such statements. A multiplicity of scales effectively eliminates the use of comparative statements. Of course, a single scale may be a function of multiple arguments, but such multiplicity of arguments should not be confused with a multiplicity of scales. Policymakers and economists should therefore realize that one either provides a rational procedure which justifies interpretations of monetary policy by means of comparative statements, or that one abandons any pretense of meaningful or intellectually honest discussion of such policy.

Solution of the indicator problem in the technical sense appears obstructed on occasion by a prevalent confusion with an entirely different problem confronting the central banker—the target problem. This problem results from the prevailing uncertainty concerning the nature of the transmission mechanism and the substantial lags in the dynamics of monetary processes.

In the context of perfect information, the indicator problem becomes trivial and the target problem vanishes. But perfect information is the privilege of economists' discourse on policy; central bankers cannot afford this luxury. The impact of their actions are both delayed and uncertain. Moreover, the ultimate goals of monetary policy (targets in the Tinbergen-Theil sense) appear remote to the manager executing general policy directives. Policymakers will be inclined under these circumstances to insert a more immediate target between their ultimate goals and their actions. These targets should be reliably observable with a minimal lag.

It is quite understandable that central bankers traditionally use various measures of money market conditions, with somewhat shifting weights, as a target guiding the continuous adjustment of their policy variables. This response to the uncertainties and lags in the dynamics of the monetary mechanism is very rational indeed. However, once we recognize the rationality of such behavior, we should also consider the rationality of using a particular target. The choice of a target still remains a problem, and the very nature of this problem is inadequately understood at this state.

This is not the place to examine the indicator and target problem in detail. A possible solution to both problems has been developed on another occasion.[23] The solutions apply decision theoretic procedures and concepts from control theory to the determination of an optimal choice of both indicator and target. Both problems are in principle solvable, in spite of the "complexity of the world." Consequently, there is little excuse for failing to develop rational monetary policy procedures.

CONCLUSION

A program for applying economic analysis to financial markets and financial institutions is certainly acceptable and worth pursuing. This program suggests that the public and banks interact in the determination of bank credit, interest rates, and the money stock, in response to the behavior of monetary authorities. But the recognition of such interaction implies nothing with respect to the relative importance of the causal forces generating cyclical fluctuations of monetary growth. Neither does it bear on the quality of alternative empirical hypotheses, or the relative usefulness of various magnitudes or conditions which might be proposed as an indicator to judge the actual thrust applied by monetary policy to the pace of economic activity.

The Monetarist thesis has been put forth in the form of well structured hypotheses which are supported by empirical evidence. This extensive research in the area of monetary policy has established that: (i) Federal Reserve actions dominate the movement of the monetary base over time; (ii) movements of the monetary base dominate movements of the money supply over the business cycle; and, (iii) accelerations or decelerations of the money supply are closely followed by accelerations or decelerations in economic activity. Therefore, the Monetarist thesis puts forth the proposition that actions of the Federal Reserve are transmitted to economic activity via the resulting movements in the monetary base and money supply, which initiate the adjustments in relative prices of assets, liabilities, and the production of new assets.

The New View, as put forth by the countercritique, has offered thus far neither analysis nor evidence pertaining relevantly to an explanation of variations in monetary growth. Moreover, the countercritique has not

---

[23]The reader may consult the chapter by Karl Brunner and Allan H. Meltzer on "Targets and Indicators of Monetary Policy," in the book of the same title, edited by Karl Brunner. The book will be published by Chandler House Publishing Co., Belmont, California.

developed, on acceptable logical grounds, a systematic justification for the abundant supply of statements characterizing policy in terms of its effects on the economy. Nor has it developed a systematic justification for the choice of money market conditions as an optimal target guiding the execution of open market operations.

But rational policy procedures require both a reliable interpretation and and adequate determination of the course of policy. The necessary conditions for rational policy are certainly not satisfied if policies actually retarding economic activity are viewed to be expansionary, as in the case of the 1960-61 recession, or, if inflationary actions are viewed as being restrictive, as in the first half of 1966.

The major questions addressed to our monetary policymakers, their advisors and consultants remain: How do you justify your interpretation of policy, and how do you actually explain the fluctuations of monetary growth? The major contentions of the academic critics of the past performance of monetary authorities could possibly be quite false, but this should be demonstrated by appropriate analysis and relevant evidence.

Index

3